The American College and University

D0169895

The
American College
and University

A History

BY FREDERICK RUDOLPH

Introductory Essay and

Supplemental Bibliography

BY JOHN R. THELIN

The University of Georgia Press

ATHENS AND LONDON

© 1962, 1990 by Frederick Rudolph
"Rudolph Rediscovered" and "Supplemental Bibliography"
© 1990 by The University of Georgia Press
This edition published in 1990 by The University of Georgia Press
Athens, Georgia 30602

All rights reserved

The paper in this book meets the guidelines for permanence and
durability of the Committee on Production Guidelines for Book
Longevity of the Council on Library Resources.

Printed in the United States of America

06 07 08 09 10 P 15 14 13 12 11

Library of Congress Cataloging-in-Publication Data

Rudolph, Frederick.
The American college and university : a history /
by Frederick Rudolph ; introductory essay and
supplemental bibliography by John R. Thelin.
xxvii, 563 p. ; 22 cm.
Reprint. Originally published: New York: A. Knopf, 1962.
Includes bibliographical references (p. [497]–525) and index.
ISBN 0-8203-1285-1 (alk. paper). — ISBN 0-8203-1284-3 (pbk. :
alk. paper)
1. Universities and colleges — United States — History.
I. Thelin, John R., 1947– . II. Title.
LA226 .R72 1990
378.73 — dc20   90-40967
CIP

Paperback ISBN-13: 978-0-8203-1284-2

British Library Cataloging-in-Publication Data available

FOR
Marta and Lisa

CONTENTS

Contents   viii

RUDOLPH
REDISCOVERED

Absence *does* make the heart grow fonder. Since Frederick Rudolph's *The American College and University: A History* went out of print in 1986, higher education historians have suffered withdrawal pains. For over twenty-five years Rudolph's book had been at the heart of courses that introduced the heritage of the American campus. "Out of print" has meant "out of luck" for most professors who teach seminars in the history of education as they experienced the immediate panic of what to do about textbook orders for the forthcoming semester. During this period of "life without Rudolph" I have spent each summer making pilgrimages to numerous university bookstores around the country to scrounge for secondhand copies of the book, which I could then place on library reserve as readings for a new

An abbreviated version of this essay was published as "Life after Rudolph," part of a retrospective forum in the *Review of Higher Education* 13, no. 3 (Spring 1990): 411–15. I wish to thank L. Jackson Newell, editor of the *Review of Higher Education*, for permission to draw from that forum on Frederick Rudolph's *The American College and University: A History*. David Webster has kindly allowed me to paraphrase and respond to points he presented in his own perceptive essay review. Frederick Rudolph generously provided copies of correspondence and took time to recall events associated with publication of his book. I am especially grateful for his cooperation without constraint.

generation of graduate students. That the University of Georgia Press is reprinting the classic work is grounds for celebration. It is also cause for thoughtful review of two matters: the genesis of the book that has become central to our study of higher education; and the scholarship in the history of higher education since *The American College and University: A History* was first published in 1962.

A danger of celebration is that contemporary readers assume post hoc that a famous book was destined to be so. My review of the correspondence and negotiations from three decades ago suggests a different story for *The American College and University.* Celebrating success, for example, might gloss over the point that one major research foundation rejected Rudolph's grant request to work on the project; or, that in 1960 Rudolph endured sharp criticism from colleagues who thought his attention to inter-collegiate sports was inappropriate for serious historical scholarship. Even though the book has enjoyed favorable reviews and sustained sales in both hardback and paperback editions, Rudolph is an unassuming academic hero who retains the same modesty today as he did about the writing project he undertook in 1958. This reserve hints at another peculiar dimension of historical scholarship that festschrift tends to obscure: we often know little about how historians go about their work. Apart from L. P. Curtis's 1970 anthology, *The Historian's Workshop*, there are few glimpses into the historian's craft.

CONTEXT: HIGHER EDUCATION
SCHOLARSHIP COMES OF AGE

Ironically, this successful book was almost not a book; and, it certainly was not originally intended to be a text. Editors at Yale University Press, which in 1956 had published Rudolph's historical study of the collegiate ideal at Williams College, *Mark Hopkins and the Log*, urged him to consider writing a book for general readers that would provide a broad context for the history of American colleges. Rudolph initially responded that he lacked the "macro" background for the proposed "general" history of higher education. After his research proposal dealing with the history of American higher education was turned down by one foundation, he eventually did gain the opportunity to acquire broad context for the study of colleges and universities in 1958 and 1959, when he was awarded a Guggenheim fellowship. While working in the Library of Congress on the research for the proposed book (in a study office made available by then Massachusetts senator John F. Kennedy), Rudolph received an invitation from Dean Francis Keppel of the Harvard Graduate School of Education to develop and teach a course in the history of American higher education. Thus, what had been background research for a proposed book turned into a series of notes for a lecture class intended primarily for graduate students in Harvard's master of arts in teaching program in 1960–61.

To risk a cliché, the rest *was* history. *The American College and University* was published by Alfred A. Knopf in 1962 and received favorable reviews in scholarly journals and in the national press, including the *New York Times* and such general literary magazines as *The Saturday Review, Harper's,* and the *Atlantic Monthly.* Over a quarter century, the book sold fifty-five thousand copies. The initial success of *The American College and University: A History* did make Rudolph a reluctant expert of sorts; leaders in higher education paid him tribute by following the course of logic that anyone who knew this much about the past of colleges and universities would, of course, be well suited to solve campus problems of the present. Hence, he received several inquiries and invitations to be a candidate for college and university administrative positions, and the influence of his book on education as a field of study led to discussions about faculty appointments in graduate schools of education at major research universities. Rudolph, however, did not see himself either as a campus administrator or as a professor in a graduate school of education. He declined both options to stay with his original calling: what he describes as "the life of the teacher scholar" that Williams College made possible as a history professor.

Publication of Rudolph's book coincided with a remarkable ground swell of research about higher education. Economist

Howard Bowen, psychologists Nevitt Sanford and C. Robert
Pace, sociologists David Riesman, Martin Trow, and Burton
Clark, and economist-administrator Clark Kerr represented a
galaxy of established scholars and influentials who wrote timely
and timeless works about various dimensions of American colleges and universities. It is no exaggeration to say that they
and their colleagues made higher education a bona fide area of
multidisciplinary and interdisciplinary scholarly study between
1960 and 1965. The early 1960s were also promising times for
both scholarship and scholars in the history of education, a
distinct yet related field. Hugh Hawkins at Amherst College,
Wilson Smith at Johns Hopkins, Richard Hofstadter and Lawrence Cremin at Columbia, and Merle Borrowman at Wisconsin indicated that first-rate "mainline" historians were giving
serious, sustained attention to colleges and universities as part of
American social history. All this led Rudolph and others to believe that those who fused history and education could look forward to a place in the university cosmos. Indeed, Wilson Smith's
1961 article in the *Harvard Educational Review*, "The New Historian of American Education: Some Notes for a Portrait," set
an exciting agenda. Within this atmosphere of scholarly excitement and rising expectations, Rudolph's work carried out the
agenda.

CONTRIBUTIONS AND CHARACTERISTICS

After having carefully reread *The American College and University*, I suggest four enduring contributions Rudolph has made to
our thinking about colleges and universities. First, in making the
bold decision to emphasize student life within the history of
higher education, he contributed an analytic model of the extracurriculum that transcends the particular episodes and cases
he described. Although he gave specific attention to the literary
societies, evangelical groups, debating teams, eating clubs, and
athletic teams of the nineteenth and early twentieth centuries,
the truly significant finding is the residual pattern: such activities tended to go through a life cycle of being founded by and for

students outside the formal course of study; successful activities then faced official sanctions or abolition, but, persistence as a "renegade" activity ultimately led to faculty and administrative acquiescence and, ultimately, official adoption. This is the kind of analysis that edged historical writing from description to become a powerful tool for subsequent inquiry by historians and by scholars from other social and behavioral disciplines.

A second related point associated with the study of the extracurriculum was Rudolph's decision to devote a chapter to intercollegiate athletics. Chapter 18, "The Rise of Football," endures as a model freestanding essay that connected a campus activity to American popular culture and to organizational behavior; a topic that others had dismissed as peripheral or frivolous was, thanks to Rudolph's insights and writing style, both serious business and lively reading.

Third, Rudolph provided scholars of higher education with intriguing prospects for pertinent issues of the 1960s. His Epilogue is an underappreciated essay that fuses historical writing with some of the immediate events, reports, and trends, circa 1960. He cited recent federal government documents, foundation studies, and commission reports concerned with the trade-offs of quality and quantity for higher education in a mass society. Indeed, his emphasis on undergraduate extracurriculum from 1650 to 1960 anticipated by several years the attention that campus administrators and the popular press would devote to student unrest in the late 1960s and early 1970s.

Finally, a feature that places Rudolph's history in a special category is the Bibliography. A more accurate depiction is its subtitle, "Historiography of Higher Education in the United States." Again, there are signs of underappreciated insight and scholarly courage. Rudolph dared to reject the convenient notion that the history of education was a field that had long been the turf of "old grads" and "professional educators." Rather, he brought renewed attention to a rich legacy of scholarship that a generation of historians had tended to overlook or ignore. In so doing, he gently chided scholars for this neglect and then provided a comprehensive, thoughtful guide through the higher education landscape that would promote the "return of the historians" to the study of the American college and university.

REVISING RUDOLPH: THE NINETEENTH-CENTURY CAMPUS

When a work is elevated to a classic we tend to lean toward extremes of praise and criticism. In reconstructing the events at the time of the book's writing and publication, it is important to remember that Rudolph was keenly aware of topics and themes he omitted or compressed. He was forthright in the Preface, noting that he had not attempted a definitive history of higher education, reserving primary attention to the question, "How and why and with what consequences have the American colleges and universities developed as they have?" Even with this focus, he warned readers that "the universities themselves have not yet created the body of historical literature from which a multivolume and definitive work might be written" (vii–viii).

If there is a single area where Rudolph's interpretation has been most subject to revision it is in the depiction of the nineteenth-century American campus. In the 1970s such historians as David Potts, Hugh Hawkins, James Axtell, Colin Burke, and David Allmendinger reworked the social and institutional history of the century, with data that questioned the caricature of the struggling small college: controlled by a religious denomination, hamstrung by a moribund "classical" curriculum, staffed by transient beleaguered instructors, and bound to a declining constituency of reluctant, ill-prepared adolescents. The new, additional scholarship on the topic points to institutional diversity, in which localism and "boosterism" coexist with denominationalism as sources of college support. Above all, on close inspection, a subsequent generation of historians found evidence that the dichotomy of the "stagnant college" versus the "robust, ascending university" confused more than clarified the subject of American higher education in the latter part of the nineteenth century. If by 1975 such revision fleshed out and complicated the profiles sketched by Rudolph, along with

Richard Hofstadter and Walter Metzger, it did so with a relative absence of the polemics and venom that characterized the so-called Great School Debate clashes among historians of education whose focus was on, for example, the continuity and change in American public school systems. One irony is that some of the higher education revisionists in the 1970s argued that Rudolph overestimated the elitism of undergraduates in the early nineteenth-century colleges, providing a refreshing twist on the usual direction of reinterpretation.

Celebration for *The American College and University* has not been without critical review. David Webster, writing in the Spring 1990 issue of the *Review of Higher Education*, provides a perceptive retrospective on Rudolph's book, including questions about the book's limitations: its emphasis on the traditional campus; inordinate attention to the nineteenth-century colleges; relative inattention to the period after World War II; attention to students and extracurriculum that deters the study of other serious issues; heavy reliance on institutional histories; and its neglect of demography and statistics. Finally, Rudolph's writing style is described as overly anecdotal and entertaining. These are intriguing questions and, in a spirit of scholarly point-counterpoint, warrant reply.

Rudolph's emphasis on the traditional campus: Rudolph's attraction to the idyllic, landscaped, residential American campus is in accord with most students' expectations—and with public sentiment. Henry Seidel Canby's *Alma Mater: The Gothic Age of the American College* (1936) notes that at the turn of the century, "the younger colleges, whether they were 'state' or 'privately endowed' institutions, modeled their life and aspirations upon the older colleges, which were usually in the East, and which drew heavily from the best schools and the wealthiest or most cultivated classes."[1] The newer urban institutions certainly faced an uphill battle in gaining acceptance as "the real thing" in both the popular and student image of "college." A good illustration of this comes from President William Rainey Harper of the new University of Chicago who, according to both Edwin Slosson in

1909 and Laurence Veysey in 1965, was obsessed with making the urban University of Chicago appear to "grow older" as it "became newer." Historian Allan Nevins's study, *The State Universities and Democracies*, reinforces this interpretation of the ways in which new public institutions sought to acquire campus identity and legitimacy: "One of the more difficult obligations of these new institutions has been the creation of an atmosphere, a tradition, a sense of the past which might play as important a part in the education of sensitive students as any other influence. This requires time, sustained attention to cultural values, and the special beauties of landscape and architecture. . . . This spiritual grace the state universities cannot quickly acquire, but they have been gaining it."[2]

Decades later the emulation continued, as illustrated by the campaign John H. Finley waged as president of the City College of New York from 1903 to 1910 to convince his students that their downtown commuter institution might someday "sparkle with true college life."[3] When Dwight Eisenhower visited Dartmouth in 1953 he exclaimed, "Why this is how I always thought a college should look!"—an interesting perspective from one who had served recently as president of urban Columbia University. His view was shared by immigrant parents of first-generation college students; for example, Philip Roth's family who lived in industrial New Jersey was charmed by the pastoral Bucknell campus in the late 1940s and insisted that going to the landscaped campus was important.[4] If Rudolph was "wrong" in his fascination with the liberal arts campus, he was in good company. An important historical aside is that about 70 percent of today's campus buildings have been constructed since 1965 and suggest a drastically altered campus design.[5] The danger is that we fault Rudolph after the fact for not having envisioned in 1962 what has been called "neo-Muskovite" institutional architecture, while we forget that the residential campus whose design was characterized by some variation of historic revivalism was the norm at the time Rudolph was writing his book.

Critics are correct in pointing out that Rudolph had little to say about engineering schools, community colleges, teachers colleges, Catholic colleges, and black colleges. That treatment is more a product of focus than oversight, as one recalls Henry Seidel Canby's earlier point that even these new special interest institutions shaped themselves in the image of established colleges—or attempted to graft themselves to a university model. Another question helps answer why Rudolph had little discussion of the community college: When Rudolph was writing his book, were there any first-rate generic histories of the American community college that he might have consulted as a secondary source? I do not believe so. The community college did not really blossom as a pervasive institution until the 1960s; in fact, the term "junior college" was still prevalent even in such large public systems as California. Is it fair to fault Rudolph for not tackling such a large, understudied topic at the end of his work?

Rudolph's inordinate attention to the nineteenth-century colleges: At the time Rudolph was writing, the emphasis on nineteenth-century colleges was relatively novel. His research on this topic was part of a larger effort to rescue American historical scholarship from preoccupation with the colonial period. This shift and balance in conceptualization may be taken for granted today but was not so in the late 1950s. Rudolph has also noted that the nineteenth century was especially important as a century of college building and college founding.

The more troubling and enduring problem is that long after Rudolph's book we still have relatively few historical studies of American higher education since World War II. Christopher Jencks and David Riesman's *The Academic Revolution* (1968) grasps the major themes of American higher education in the twentieth century, but the work stands more as historical sociology than social history. David O. Levine's *The American College and the Culture of Aspiration, 1915–1940* (1986) stands out not only as excellent scholarship but also as one of the rare attempts to write a comprehensive historical narrative that interprets broadly the issues and institutions following World War I.

Rudolph's relative inattention to the period after World War II: This charge stands more accurately as a limit of the book rather than as a fault, and the indictment might be overly harsh. Rudolph's

Epilogue gives clear (but admittedly concise) comment on such key themes as funding, mission, expansion, financial aid, and access that would be important in the 1960s. He provides a good summary of references to major commission reports and foundation studies published between 1947 and 1960 and underscores the balancing of "quantity and quality" as the crucial policy issue of the coming decades, with the comment: "For the problem of numbers was not a problem of numbers alone; it was also a matter of purpose" (485). A good way to view Rudolph's 1962 commentary on the post-World War II period is that the Epilogue anticipates Clark Kerr's 1963 book, *The Uses of the University*.

Rudolph's exclusive attention to students and the extracurriculum: This point does not square with Chapter 9, "Financing the Colleges." For the modern university, Rudolph's chapters 20 and 21, "Academic Man" and "The Organized Institution," respectively, deal expressly with the issues of academic freedom, the emergence of disciplines, departments, and an academic profession, along with developments in institutional structure and governance. Contrary to the charge, these two chapters are a useful prelude to Laurence Veysey's *The Emergence of the American University*, which was not published until 1965.

Rudolph's inordinate reliance on institutional histories: True, Rudolph relies heavily on the myriad institutional histories as secondary sources. But this is misleading because the charge fails to acknowledge the interesting and selective way in which he gleans these "house histories." He certainly warns of their limits and is wary of them as critical, interpretative "good history." I am impressed that he read dozens, even hundreds, of such works and carefully culled episodes and illustrations that he then blended into his own general interpretation. In sum, he is to be commended because he did not "buy into" the sanitized hagiography that dominated the tones of such works. I, for one, am grateful that he was able to find and extract numerous good cases from such unwieldy secondary sources—thus sparing me from having to read the house histories in toto.

I also find a puzzle, or perhaps an incongruence, in this critique. Rudolph is scolded for having tended to neglect campus
presidents and administrators while being faulted for reliance on
the official institutional histories. My senses of the house history
books is that they provide relatively little information on student life even though they are often written by old grads. The
genre tends to be dominated by an organizational and concep-
tual scheme that radiates from the president and board of trustees; institutional history written from the top down. Rudolph's
admirable contribution was that he used the house history genre
without succumbing to its temptation. For this he deserves
praise not criticism.

Rudolph's research neglects demographic and statistical analysis: Rudolph has been criticized for having neglected to connect campus
history with demographic trends and the statistical data that are
central to social history. Even though Rudolph does not stand as
a cliometrician, I offer a plea bargain of sorts: in some important
places he does ground his interpretation in statistics. A good example is in the Epilogue where he discusses the remarkable policy commitments of American higher education after World
War II:

> Where else was the generalization of educational op-
> portunity so dramatically portrayed as in the statistics of
> college and university enrollment? In 1870 American in-
> stitutions of higher learning enrolled somewhat over 50,000
> young men and women; a hundred years later the City Uni-
> versity of New York alone would be enrolling almost four
> times that number. In 1870 but 1.7 per cent of the young
> people aged 18–21 were enrolled in colleges and univer-
> sities; by 1970 half of the age group 18–21 would be at
> college. In 1960 approximately 3,500,000 young men and
> women attended institutions of higher learning; by 1970
> that figure would be doubled. In 1876 there were 311 col-
> leges and universities; in 1960 there were 2,026 (486–89).

Rudolph goes back in time with statistical context. In chapter
10, "Jacksonian Democracy and the Colleges," his analysis of

early nineteenth-century decline in college enrollment discusses the qualitative issue of the low appeal of the college curriculum in terms of a quantitative dimension: "Statistics showed that in New England the number of students in colleges was declining both actually and proportionately to the population." He continues:

> Over seven hundred colleges died in the United States before 1860. How could there have been so many? Between 1850 and 1866, for instance, fifty-five Catholic colleges were started, of which twenty-five were abandoned by 1866. And in the live colleges, matters were not much better. In 1846 in New York City with a population of half a million the two colleges enrolled a total of 247. In 1848 at Lafayette College, which had been chartered over twenty years before, the board of trustees was larger than the student body. In 1853 Denison College in Ohio had been in operation for twenty years and had graduated but sixty-five students. In 1859 in Ohio there were twenty-two colleges with an average college enrollment of eighty-five. In 1860 Harvard graduated its first class of a hundred (218–19).

One might argue that Rudolph's statistics have since been supplanted by "better" statistics. Indeed, contemporary research in the history of higher education gains much from such works as Seymour Harris's 1972 compendium for the Carnegie Commission, *A Statistical Portrait of Higher Education*, or from Colin Burke's monumental study in historical statistics, *American Collegiate Populations: A Test of the Traditional Review*. Burke's revised statistics make a sound case for rethinking estimates about nineteenth-century college fragility and mortality. But in 1962 Rudolph did not have the benefit of reference to either Harris's or Burke's books. The situation, then, is less a sign of neglect in Rudolph's work and more a tribute to the good product of subsequent research (and research methods) by later scholars.

Rudolph's writing style is anecdotal and entertaining: Yes, Rudolph must plead guilty to being a lively, entertaining writer. This is cause for thanks, not complaint because his prose is a writing model that endures as a refreshing antidote to what George Keller has called "Bibliospeak: the new language of higher education."[6] David Webster, in a 1990 *Review of Higher Education* essay observed, "While Rudolph's book is, in general, an exceptionally entertaining work of scholarship, he seems constitutionally incapable of resisting a charming anecdote, even (especially?) when the behavior it describes is strange and sheds little light on the topic he is discussing."[7] Webster builds his case by pointing out Rudolph's accounts of nineteenth-century college life that emphasized calamities and bizarre events, including colleges that burned down, incidents of student and faculty misbehavior, and student ridicule of tutors. All this is illustrated by Rudolph's anecdotes about a German scholar at the University of South Carolina who, after reprimanding misbehaving students, exclaimed, "Mein Gott! All dis for two tousand dollars!" (106).

This criticism may lead to a stalemate in which the adage (probably suspect as a vestige of the classical curriculum endorsed by an 1828 Yale Report) *de gustibus non est disputandum* prevails. However, good writing usually is marked by a distinctive author's tone; in this domain, Rudolph has opted for wit and irony. And, good historical writing usually is grounded in specifics. His anecdote about the German professor at the nineteenth-century University of South Carolina is indeed appropriate for illustrating the gap between advanced scholars and their host institutions and undergraduates. In this episode Rudolph shows remarkable restraint, as many of the universities showed a decidedly local organizational culture and provincial outlook that seldom included total understanding, let alone acceptance of the continental universities' style or substance. At the risk of being anecdotal in my own writing, I add the research finding that the early University of Virginia was intended to have a variety of ethnic cuisines associated with its proposed foreign language pavilions; the plan collapsed in deference to students' provincial taste for local home cooking.[8] The best litmus for Rudolph's anecdotes is whether they accurately illustrate general trends. My

estimate is that Rudolph's rationale was that items about burning buildings illustrated the fragile character and high mortality
rate of the young, undersubscribed colleges. The stabbings, kill-
ings, and rebellions that dotted accounts of undergraduate life
prompt us to analyze what happens when young students were
concentrated into an approximation of a residential campus.
And, in fairness to Rudolph, review of his accounts of student
life indicates attention to the remarkable organization and activities, whether in literary societies, debating clubs, varsity teams,
or Christian service organizations. Accounts of faculty disgust
or frustration in the nineteenth-century college suggest that the
role of "professor" had not been congealed, and, then as now,
led to substantially different expectations among faculties and
boards of trustees.

FROM REVIEW TO REVISION

There is agreement among Rudolph, revisionists, critics, and
admirers that it is time for a new history of American higher
education. First, we are participant observers to the history of
higher education in our own time, and we need a comprehensive
work that incorporates interpretation of the significant events of
the recent past, from 1960 to present. Second, there is need for
an overarching synthesis that respects and digests the excellent
yet scattered scholarship in the history of higher education.
This latter body of work includes not only "new" chronological
periods but also innovations in such areas as historical research
methods, revisionism of familiar themes, and conception of historical research questions from the seventeenth century to the
present. It includes research attention to issues of gender, race,
ethnicity, social class, and other aspects of diversity within American life and education. The dilemma is that these works published
as journal articles, special topic books, and monographs over the
past quarter century have yet to find a sage or troubadour to tell
this composite story of the recent past as part of our complete
higher education heritage.

These two voids are hardly Rudolph's fault. To the contrary, they illuminate the inordinate shelf life and appeal of his 1962 work. Hence, we are left with the puzzling questions: Why has the present generation of scholars not been able to write its own version? Where is a 1980s or 1990s sequel to Rudolph's *The American College and University: A History?* Whatever the limits Frederick Rudolph's 1962 book has, my view is that our situation today resembles the medieval scholar's relation to the ancient philosopher, "a dwarf standing on the shoulders of a giant"—a friendly, modest giant. I offer this interpretation less as a conclusion and more as an invitation for readers in the 1990s to rediscover Rudolph.

JOHN R. THELIN

The College of William and Mary
1990

NOTES

1. Henry Seidel Canby, *Alma Mater; The Gothic Age of the American College* (New York: Farrar and Rinehart, 1936), xi.
2. Allan Nevins, *The State Universities and Democracy* (Urbana: University of Illinois Press, 1962), 82.
3. Marvin E. Gettleman, "John H. Finley at CCNY, 1903 to 1913," *History of Education Quarterly* (Winter 1970), 427.
4. Philip Roth, "Joe College: Memories of a Fifties Education," *Atlantic Monthly* (December 1987), 41–61.
5. S. Williams, "The Architecture of the Academy," *Change* (March/April 1985), 14–30, 50–55.
6. George Keller, "Learning to Love Bibliospeak: The New Language of Higher Education," *Change* (January/February 1989), 19.
7. David S. Webster, "Rudolph's *American College and University: A History*: An Appraisal a Generation after Publication," *Review of Higher Education* 13, no. 3 (Spring 1990): 398–411.
8. John R. Thelin and David H. Charlton, "Food for Thought: Dining Halls and the Collegiate Ideal," *William and Mary Magazine* (Summer 1987), 28.

PREFACE

For some time now the general reader and the professional historian have had greater access to the history of almost any skirmish of the Civil War than they have had to the history of education in the United States. This book is intended in some way to redress the balance, as far as the American experience with higher education is concerned.

I have not attempted a definitive history of higher education, which might be loosely defined as education beyond the level of the high school or its equivalent. As worthwhile and as necessary as such a project may be, it would require scholarly explorations of a sort that no individual could make alone. The universities themselves have not yet created the body of historical literature from which a multivolume and definitive work might be written. I have therefore attempted only to give some sense of the historical understanding which is now possible.

I am aware of the shortcomings of any study that proposes to encompass in time, physical area, and numbers what is suggested by my subject. Conscious of the need for compression, even of omission, I have not made of this book a history of the life of the mind in the United States, nor have I in any fundamental way approached the large question of the role of formal agencies of higher education in creating and shaping

popular as well as esoteric taste, knowledge, and opinion. The
creative role of the American college and university in American society, a concern but not the major focus of the book,
raises an exciting set of questions for which the present condition of American scholarship can provide only partial or
unsatisfactory answers. I have, nevertheless, tried to create a
volume to which any American might turn for an informed
answer to the question, "How and why and with what consequences have the American colleges and universities developed
as they have?" This question is not, of course, the only one
answered, but it is the first question we need to have answered.

A fellowship from the John Simon Guggenheim Memorial
Foundation permitted me to launch this study with a year of
research at the Library of Congress, 1958-9. During the spring
terms, 1960 and 1961, the Fund for the Advancement of Education supported my appointment as visiting lecturer in history and education at Harvard University; this appointment
considerably advanced my researches and the preparation of
the manuscript. The President and Trustees of Williams College granted the leaves of absence which made these excursions from Williamstown possible and also provided grants
from the Class of 1900 Fund for secretarial assistance. My
colleagues in the Department of History at Williams deserve
my apologies for the adjustments and impositions which these
absences introduced into their teaching schedules. The researches on which this study is based would not have been
possible without the friendly assistance to scholarly inquiry
which inspires the staffs of the Library of Congress, Widener
Library at Harvard, and the Williams College Library. Colonel
Willard Webb and Mrs. Evelyn Lincoln took special interest
in providing study space during my year at the Library of
Congress. In one version or another, the manuscript has been
read with profit to me by Professor Bernard Bailyn of Harvard, Dr. Charles R. Keller of the John Hay Whitney Foundation, and Mrs. Sidney D. Ross of Williamstown. My wife
cheerfully listened or read her way through the first draft and
all those that followed; this book owes much to her. Miss

Elizabeth Kidder of Cambridge typed the first draft of the manuscript; Miss Bessie Wright of Williamstown, the final draft. Professor Luther S. Mansfield of Williams gave the proof a critical and beneficial reading. Miss Judith Hillery, for Alfred A. Knopf, has provided editorial guidance of high quality and considerateness. I am grateful to them all for their particular assistance in helping this book along the way.

FREDERICK RUDOLPH

Williamstown, Massachusetts
September 30, 1961

The
American College
and University

I

❦

The Colonial College

On the eve of the American Revolution, England's colonies in the New World were supporting, in one fashion or another, nine colleges, nine home-grown variations on a theme known in the mother country as Oxford and Cambridge. Whether the colonies needed the nine was another matter, just as it would always be a question of some controversy whether the United States needed all the colleges it would spawn in the centuries that followed.

This proliferation of colleges—Harvard, William and Mary, Yale, New Jersey, King's, Philadelphia, Rhode Island, Queen's, Dartmouth—all before 1770, this planting of temples of piety and intellect in the wilderness was no accident. Nor was it stubbornness, foolhardiness, even the booster spirit of a pioneering people which placed at the disposal of American youth so extraordinary a number of educational institutions. At the beginning, higher education in America would be governed less by accident than by certain purpose, less by impulse than by design.

Higher education in America began with Harvard. As the author of *New Englands First Fruits* told it in 1643, after erecting shelter, a house of worship, and the framework of government, "One of the next things we longed for, and looked after, was to advance *Learning* and perpetuate it to Posterity. . . ."[1] And then, it would seem, almost as a matter of course, there was Harvard.

But not without the active support of a nucleus of Cambridge and Oxford-trained gentlemen who "stoutheartedly refused to yield an inch to pioneer prejudices or frontier values."[2] Approximately a hundred Cambridge men and a third as many Oxford men emigrated to New England before 1646; among them were the founders of Harvard, the fathers of the first generation of Harvard students. Their purposes were complex, but among other things, they intended to re-create a little bit of old England in America. They did what people a long way from home often do, and certainly what Englishmen have often done. If it was the most natural thing in the world for an officer of the colonial service in the nineteenth century to dress for dinner in the jungle as if he were dining at his club in London, it was no less natural for the Englishmen of early Massachusetts to found themselves a college, an English college such as those they had known at Oxford but particularly at Cambridge where Puritan theology and Puritan aspiration had been especially nurtured.

And then there was Harvard? Not without the active support of the General Court, the colonial legislature which performed for Puritan Massachusetts in the tradition of intervention and responsibility that made of Elizabethan authority such a great instrument of statecraft. On the same day—October 28, 1636—that the Massachusetts General Court passed the legislative act which led to Harvard College, it put in a day of work which revealed much of the concept of state that motivated colonial Massachusetts: it granted £5 for loss of an eye to a certain George Munnings; it ordered the towns of the colony to fix wages; and it ceded an island to the town of Charlestown on condition that it be used for

[1] *New Englands First Fruits* (London, 1643), p. 12.
[2] Samuel Eliot Morison: *The Founding of Harvard College* (Cambridge, 1935), p. 5.

fishing.[3] A legislative body with so expansive a notion of its
authority and responsibility did not have to be prodded into
founding a college. Lucy Downing, on hearing of the plans
for the college—which the General Court decided to locate
at Newtowne, the name of which was soon quite naturally
changed to Cambridge—wrote to her brother John Winthrop: "I beleev a colledg would put noe small life into the
plantation. . . ."[4] And Increase Mather, the Puritan divine,
with the hindsight of fifty years, remarked in 1688: " 'Twas
therefore a brave and happy thought that first pitched upon
this Colledge. . . ."[5] Both were quite right.

If allowance is made for the existence of a body of college-
trained gentlemen in the colony, if recognition is taken of the
General Court as an instrument of far-flung purpose and responsibility, still the dynamic necessity which lay at the basis
of Harvard College is not understood. For the really important fact about Harvard College is that it was absolutely necessary. Puritan Massachusetts could not have done without it.
Unable to set the world straight as Englishmen in England,
the Puritan settlers of Massachusetts intended to set it straight
as Englishmen in the New World. This sense of mission
clearly required more than an ordinary share of self-confi-
dence. But it did not lack humility, and the sense of pride
which strengthened it was a pride that was rigorous in the
demands which it placed upon self. While they could count
on annual increments of recruits from the Old World, the
Puritans charged themselves with a mission which they recognized as requiring a full effort. Intending to lead lives no
less than the purest, aspiring to serve God and their fellow-
men in the fullest, they acknowledged a responsibility to the
future. They could not afford to leave its shaping to whim,

[3] Ibid., p. 168.
[4] Ibid., p. 171.
[5] Samuel Eliot Morison: *Harvard College in the Seventeenth Century* (Cambridge, 1936), II, 536.

fate, accident, indecision, incompetence, or carelessness. In the future the state would need competent rulers, the church would require a learned clergy, and society itself would need the adornment of cultured men.

Such men, the Puritans well knew, had to be created from the material at hand. A society that intends to live rigorously, moreover, cannot afford to train its rulers haphazardly. A world that finds the deepest expression of its purposes and its goals in the Scriptures cannot afford to ignore the training of its Biblical expositors. A people that expects to have its pretensions taken seriously must recognize its responsibility to the inherited wisdom of the ages, to literature, to science, to learning.

And so it was that "the two cardinal principles of English Puritanism which most profoundly affected the social development of New England and the United States were not religious tenets, but educational ideals: a learned clergy, and a lettered people."[6] Central to these ideals was the development of Harvard College, the college which would train the schoolmasters, the divines, the rulers, the cultured ornaments of society—the men who would spell the difference between civilization and barbarism.

The sense of obligation which Harvard took upon itself, the responsibility which society placed upon it, were apparent in the charge with which President Dunster presented new fellows to the board of overseers in the seventeenth century: "You shall take care to advance in all learning, divine and humane, each and every student who is or will be entrusted to your tutelage, according to their several abilities; and especially to take care that their conduct and manners be honorable and without blame."[7] The broad purposes which the college served were further clarified by a commencement orator in the 1670's: "The ruling class would have been subjected to mechanics, cobblers, and tailors; . . . the laws

[6] Morison: Harvard: *Founding*, p. 45. My understanding of early Harvard relies heavily on this study.
[7] Morison: Harvard: *Seventeenth Century*, I, 19.

would not have been made by *senatus consulta*, nor would we have rights, honors, or magisterial ordinance worthy of preservation, but plebiscites, appeals to base passions, and revolutionary rumblings, if these our fathers had not founded the University. . . ." [8] This was no statement of narrow religious purpose, as has so often been attributed to the founders of the colonial colleges. Of course a religious commonwealth required an educated clergy, but it also needed leaders disciplined by knowledge and learning, it needed followers disciplined by leaders, it needed order. For these purposes Harvard was absolutely essential.

In greater or lesser degree, the same purposes would find expression in the eight subsequent foundations which joined Harvard in becoming the colonial colleges. The same broad purposes, for instance, were revealed in the royal charter of 1693 which founded the College of William and Mary in Virginia. The new college was to provide a supply of clergymen (in this case, Anglican clergymen for a Crown colony), but it was also to ensure "that the youth . . . [were] piously educated in good letters and manners." [9] From such men it was expected that the colony would draw its public servants. In 1724 a friend of the college made the bold suggestion that William and Mary be officially recognized as a school of civil-service training and that from each graduating class there be appointed surveyors, clerks to the colonial government, and county clerks.[1] His formal proposal was not adopted, but Virginia learned to draw on the human resources and alumni of its college, not the least of whom was Thomas Jefferson.

Virginia had experienced unusual difficulties in achieving its seminary of learning, for which the Crown had appropriated 9,000 acres as early as 1619, only to have an Indian massacre in 1622 eliminate many friends of the proposed institution—as well as Mr. George Thorpe of His Majesty's Privy

[8] Morison: Harvard: *Founding*, p. 250.
[9] Albea Godbold: *The Church College of the Old South* (Durham, 1944), p. 5.
[1] Herbert Baxter Adams: *The College of William and Mary* (Washington, 1887), p. 21.

Council, who had been sent over to get the institution going. A 1660 vote of the Virginia Assembly to create a college did not, in fact, create one, for Virginia lacked both the concentration of population and the pervading sense of mission which were to facilitate the development of higher education in Massachusetts. Even when the Crown acceded to Virginia's request for a college charter in 1693, the atmosphere was clouded by their Majesties' attorney general, who was unimpressed by the suggestion that a college would be useful in saving souls. He exploded, perhaps because he had a war on his mind: "Souls! Damn your souls! Raise tobacco!" Virginia got its college, but it also complied with the attorney-general's demands.[2]

Yale and Princeton contributed a new purpose to the life of the colonial college—the carrying on of sectarian controversy, the pursuit of denominational survival in an environment of religious diversity.[3] The Collegiate School in Connecticut, which was to become Yale College, at first had some difficulty settling down, for it was troubled by the very serious question of whether, having been chartered in 1701, it should be located in Saybrook, Killingsworth, Hartford, Wethersfield, or New Haven. A comparable problem would often beset young American colleges, but probably none would move as many times as did the school which became Yale, nor would any other actually function in three places at the same time. The Collegiate School operated at both Killingsworth and at Saybrook before New Haven captured the institution for itself in 1716 and then, with the help of a disgruntled fellow of the Harvard corporation, proceeded to capture Elihu Yale, a Boston-born Englishman who was living

[2] Godbold: *The Church College of the Old South*, p. 4; Adams: *William and Mary*, pp. 11-15.
[3] See Edwin Oviatt: *The Beginnings of Yale (1701-1726)* (New Haven, 1916); and Thomas Jefferson Wertenbaker: *Princeton 1746-1896* (Princeton, 1946).

in London amid "the magnificent oriental plunder" of his days with the East India Company at Madras.[4] The trustees of the Collegiate School in New Haven, looking back over the sixteen years during which their institution had literally been wandering around the Connecticut countryside, assured the affluent Mr. Yale that things were indeed looking up. Having chosen to address themselves to Elihu Yale in the metaphor of pregnancy, the New Haven group pushed their thoughts where their metaphor perforce took them:

> The affair of our School hath been in a Condition of Pregnancy: Painfull with a witness have been the Throwes thereof in this General Assembly; But We just now hear, that after the Violent Pangs threatening the Very life of the Babe, Divine Providence as a kind Obstetrix hath mercifully brought the Babe into the World, & behold A Man-child is born, whereat We all Rejoice.[5]

In the meantime, Cotton Mather of the Harvard corporation, if not able to qualify as midwife, was at least prepared to act as godfather at the christening. Peeved at the liberal turn taken in religious affairs at Harvard, he wrote to Elihu Yale, reminding him that the time was at hand for him to give "his serious regard unto the account which we are to give of our stewardship," and suggesting—completely without authority from New Haven—that "what is forming at New Haven might wear the name of Yale College." And, as memorials go, Mather added, Yale College might "indeed be much better than an Egyptian pyramid." Mr. Yale, despite his great wealth, responded with a quantity of assorted dry goods which in the end realized over £550 in the American market and placed a new name on the American collegiate landscape.[6] But what of the curious role in this whole epi-

[4] Oviatt: *Yale*, p. 291.
[5] Ibid., p. 344.
[6] Ibid., pp. 347-8.

sode of Cotton Mather, who aspired to the presidency of Harvard but who in the end was offered the presidency of Yale? Mather's flirtation with Yale was a reflection of declining Puritan orthodoxy at Harvard, where honest disagreement among good Puritans led to a spirit of toleration; where, as the decades passed, economic prosperity introduced into the student body young men who would live, if not as saints, then as gentlemen; where the college was moving out from under the firm grasp of a monolithic theology into a world more receptive to theologic and philosophic diversity.[7]

Yale was not an offshoot of Harvard. Indeed, there would have been a college of sorts in Connecticut even if it had not been called Yale and even if a significant group of disaffected Harvard men had not come to its early support. Nonetheless, Yale proceeded to make a place for itself in the sun by being what it was said Harvard had promised to be—a safe, sound institution where the faith of the fathers was carefully protected. By adding a sense of rivalry, a spirit of controversy, to the catalogue of purposes which might animate an American college, Yale surely helped to open up remarkable possibilities for the future. For if one reason for Yale was Harvard, there was no telling where sectarian controversy and denominational rivalry might lead.

Actually where it next led was to the College of New Jersey at Princeton. The chartering of Princeton in 1746 announced the success of one faction of the widely split Presbyterians of the middle colonies in achieving a college of their own. Princeton, as the college came to be known, was a product of the great religious awakening of the eighteenth century, a quickening of religion that filled the American colonies with outbursts of emotion they had not before known. Emphasizing a religion of conversion, of individual experience, the new movement deplored the religion of faith and of form which had come to characterize the more settled churches, communities, colleges, and colonies. The Great

[7] Richard Hofstadter and Walter P. Metzger: *The Development of Academic Freedom in the United States* (New York, 1955), pp. 107 ff.

Awakening was a movement of popular dimensions: it spoke
not for the learned clergy, not even so much for learning,
as it did for a clergy and a people who had known the
sweet taste of soul-shattering religious experience. One consequence was to divide congregations and churches into conservatives and liberals, into Old Lights and New Lights, into
factions that followed the quieter religious behavior of the
past and factions that had the new enthusiasm of the present.
Princeton was a product of the new enthusiasm; through it
New Light Presbyterians hoped to achieve an element of respectability and refute the charge that they were hostile to
learning, and their ministers illiterate.[8]

Princeton was not alone in joining the ranks of American
colleges as a creature of the Great Awakening. The Congregationalists of New England were also bitten by the new enthusiasm; unable to make headway at Harvard or Yale, they
supported Eleazar Wheelock in the founding of Dartmouth.
The Baptists were not to be denied; they founded the College
of Rhode Island at Providence in 1765. The next year at New
Brunswick in New Jersey the Dutch Reformed troops entered the fray with a college called Queen's.[9]

Yet, the American colleges were not in the process of becoming simply religious outposts or religious training schools,
where the captains might be trained for the religious wars in
which the various branches of Calvinism, the Quakers, the
Baptists, and the Anglicans were now embroiled. For all of the
injection of denominationalism into the life of the colleges,
the old broad purposes also prevailed. The College of New
Jersey promised that there would be no religious tests for

---

[8] Wertenbaker: *Princeton, passim.*
[9] See Leon Burr Richardson: *History of Dartmouth College* (2 vols.,
Hanover, 1932); Walter C. Bronson: *The History of Brown University
1764-1914* (Providence, 1914); William H. S. Demarest: *A History of
Rutgers College 1766-1924* (New Brunswick, 1924); Beverly McAnear:
"College Founding in the American Colonies, 1745-1775," *Mississippi
Valley Historical Review*, XLII (1955), 24-44.

students, thus acknowledging the manner in which denominational rivalry and competition for students would underwrite freedom.[1] It promised as well that it would be not so much a seminary for Presbyterian divines as a school for statesmen. When the College of Rhode Island was chartered in 1764, its founders inserted in its charter a statement as broad and as noble in purpose as any that characterized the beginnings of Harvard over a hundred years before: "Institutions for liberal Education are highly beneficial to Society, by forming the rising Generation to Virtue[,] Knowledge & useful Literature & thus preserving in the Community a Succession of Men duly qualify'd for discharging the Offices of Life with usefulness & reputation. . . ."[2] Moreover, in the thriving urban coastal cities of Philadelphia and New York, institutions of learning were developing which were prepared to state their purposes in the broadest, most secular terms. Provost William Smith of the college at Philadelphia let it be known that "Thinking, Writing and Acting Well . . . is the grand aim of a liberal education."[3]

When George III appealed to English benefactors in behalf of the colleges in Philadelphia and New York in 1762, his catalogue of purposes suggested the variety of directions in which American higher education was developing: to combat the inconveniences of an uninstructed population drawn from "different Parts of the World . . . to guard against total Ignorance . . . to instil . . . just principles of Religion, Loyalty and a Love of Our Excellent Constitution"; to instruct in branches of useful knowledge; to train instructors to go among the people and among the Indians.[4] There they were—

[1] Hofstadter and Metzger: *Development of Academic Freedom*, p. 152.
[2] Bronson: *Brown*, p. 1.
[3] Edward Potts Cheyney: *History of the University of Pennsylvania 1740-1940* (Philadelphia, 1940), p. 83.
[4] John Howard Van Amringe, et al.: *A History of Columbia University 1754-1904* (New York, 1904), p. 32; see also Cheyney: *Pennsylvania*, pp. 61-6.

all the reasons that might be summoned for having a college. A college develops a sense of unity where, in a society created from many of the nations of Europe, there might otherwise be aimlessness and uncontrolled diversity. A college advances learning; it combats ignorance and barbarism. A college is a support of the state; it is an instructor in loyalty, in citizenship, in the dictates of conscience and faith. A college is useful: it helps men to learn the things they must know in order to manage the temporal affairs of the world; it trains a legion of teachers. All these things a college was. All these purposes a college served.

These many purposes, whether at the oldest of the colonial colleges or at the youngest, were carried out with varying degrees of success. Obviously several of the colleges were barely able to prove their existence before the American Revolution gave a new twist to their fortunes. Uniformity, whether of performance or of organization and spirit, never characterized the colonial colleges. Variety carried the day, as the relations between college and state and between college and church certainly made clear. Harvard, William and Mary, and Yale, for example, were creatures as much of the state as of the established churches they were intended to serve. And whether they should be thought of as state colleges or as church colleges is a problem in semantics that is perhaps best resolved by calling them state-church colleges.

As such, they were clearly recognized as being engaged in a relationship of mutual obligation and responsibility with the state. Harvard was supported by the General Court from the moment of its birth; it relied on such support long past the colonial period. In 1652 and 1653 the General Court donated 2,000 acres of land to the college, and the next year it ordered a tax levy of £100 in its support.[5] But the state's responsibility went beyond economic assistance. Under the ad-

[5] Morison: Harvard: *Seventeenth Century*, I, 30-1.

ministration of Nathaniel Eaton, Harvard fell into such straits that the General Court began an investigation and effectively closed the college for a year by dismissing Eaton from his post. Having done so, the General Court fulfilled its obligations to Harvard the next year by assigning the Charlestown Ferry rents to the college, a source of revenue that continued in one form or another for the next two hundred years.⁶ In 1725 when the corporation elected to the presidency a leading liberal Congregationalist, he declined the position after sounding out the General Court and finding himself extremely obnoxious to the conservatives there. In 1737 the General Court awarded to the church at Marblehead £140 as a bit of balm for losing its minister, Edward Holyoke, to the presidency of Harvard.⁷

At William and Mary a similar pattern of strong ties with the state prevailed. The main street of colonial Williamsburg, Duke of Gloucester Street, extended from the capitol building at one end to the college at the other; such an arrangement was both convenient and symbolic. For variety of financial support nothing compared with the generosity of Virginia to its college. The 1693 charter privileges of William and Mary put a tobacco tax at its disposal and "brought the entire land system of the colony into the hands of a collegiate land office." George Washington, for example, received his commission as county surveyor from the president of the college. In 1693 the college was awarded the returns from an export duty on skins and furs; in 1759 it enjoyed the fruits of a tax on peddlers.⁸

Yale, which for a long time was tossed around by a squabbling legislature, in the end built up a firm and useful relationship with the state. It early discovered that the state could be helpful in other than direct subsidies. In 1712 all students at the moribund Collegiate School were assured that enroll-

⁶ Morison: Harvard: *Founding*, pp. 228, 292 ff.
⁷ Samuel Eliot Morison: *Three Centuries of Harvard 1636-1936* (Cambridge, 1936), pp. 77, 82-3.
⁸ Adams: *William and Mary*, p. 15. See also Sadie Bell: *The Church, the State, and Education in Virginia* (Philadelphia, 1930).

ment relieved them of both taxes and military service.' As at
Harvard, Yale's success in recruiting presidents led to legislative appropriations to communities deprived of their ministers. In 1726 Newington and in 1739 Windham received from
the legislature what in a later century and for another purpose
would be called alimony. A unique financial support of Yale
during the eighteenth century was "the avails of a French
prize brought into New London by an armed vessel of the
State."¹ This close relationship was neither permanently secure nor always a certain blessing; in 1763 a group of citizens
hostile to the Yale administration called on the legislature to
fulfill its parental responsibility by standing as a court of last
appeal for Yale undergraduates who were displeased with the
college administration and its concept of discipline. The legislature, aghast at the democratic rumblings which sought to
assert popular control over the Yale corporation, recoiled, and
while the decision of the legislature had the effect of
strengthening the independence of Yale, the ties between
state and college were still strong.²

Yet, it would be misleading to speak of the colonial college
as a state institution in the sense in which the term was later
understood. State officials were given a degree of control over
Harvard by the charter provision that guaranteed representation on the board of overseers, but Yale was governed during
the colonial period by a board composed entirely of clergymen. When Princeton in 1748 added the governor of New
Jersey and four members of his council to its board of trustees, this action was taken as insurance against possible consequences of the religious controversies of the time rather than
as an avowal of significant ties with the state.³ Actually, neither the college at Princeton nor its later rival at New Brunswick ever received any financial support from the state,

⁹ Oviatt: *Yale*, p. 288.
¹ William Lathrop Kingsley, ed.: *Yale College: A Sketch of its History* (New York, 1879), I, 57, 65, 192.
² Ibid., 90-3.
³ Wertenbaker: *Princeton*, p. 27.

largely because a growing denominationalism and religious toleration made state support of the colleges both politically dangerous and philosophically unnecessary.

The colleges that were inspired by the Great Awakening might seek and accept favors from the state, but nothing so certain, nothing so regular, nothing so generous as the aid that flowed into Cambridge, Williamsburg, and New Haven, where what were generally thought of as state-church institutions had taken shape. The later colleges, "largely because of sectarian hostilities and inhibitions, could not safely call upon the state governments" with the same sense of right and the same prospect of success as the older institutions.[4]

The effect of the Great Awakening clearly was to shatter the pattern of state-church colleges which had developed in Massachusetts, Connecticut, and Virginia. The rivalry and diversity inspired by the Great Awakening created colleges in which the strength of religious ties varied, and by the end of the colonial period diversity and toleration had become values of such importance that colleges could be founded that claimed only an incidental interest in religion or only a loosely acknowledged denominational connection. In the case of the College of Philadelphia denominational affiliation was nonexistent, although it was widely known that the chief executive officer, the provost, was an Anglican. At King's College the official persuasion was also Anglican, but wisdom dictated that the college's charter provide for election of clergy from four rival Protestant denominations to the board of governors.[5] These arrangements were a far cry from the traditions at William and Mary, where professors were required to be Anglicans and where the president, as representative of the Bishop of London, was head of the church in Virginia.

At colonial Harvard rigid Puritan control gave way to a more liberal ecclesiastical polity and to a spirit of toleration

---

[4] Hofstadter and Metzger: *Development of Academic Freedom*, p. 145.
[5] Van Amringe: *Columbia*, pp. 16-17.

as secular interests increased. Indeed, there developed a sense
of live-and-let-live which contrasted sharply with the early
years of the Puritan commonwealth, when absolute religious
conformity was impossibly demanded. In the 1740's Harvard
took an interested, even for a time a sympathetic, look at the
Great Awakening, but it was already too fully committed to
the world, too aware of the excitements and wonders of
learning and of living to lose itself in sectarian controversy.
On a visit to New England in 1744 George Whitefield, the
great revivalist, received no invitation from Cambridge, a
gesture on the part of the Harvard authorities which helped
to launch, at so early a date, the reputation of "godless Harvard." [6] It is true that godlessness had been stalking the campus for some time, as testified by the clubs formed in self-
defense by pious students in the 1720's. But the very limits of
religious irresponsibility were not reached until 1760, when
the Harvard faculty granted permission to Anglican students
to attend Christ Church, Cambridge, instead of the Congregational meetinghouse.[7] The trouble with Harvard, obviously,
was that it was developing a dangerous liberality of spirit,
which might be useful in the sharpening of intellect, but
which was unquestionably damaging to true and holy character.

True character, however, could still count on Yale. At a
time when Harvard was spurning George Whitefield, Yale
was being thrown into considerable turmoil by the controversies which he inspired in New Haven. For a time official
Yale withstood the new revivalism, not with the almost studied indifference of Harvard, however, but with a tenacity that
led the Yale authorities in 1744 to go so far as to expel two
students for attending a revival with their parents during vacation time—in violation of the law of God, colony, and college, the Yale officials said.[8] (This phrase would achieve later

[6] Morison: Harvard: *Three Centuries*, pp. 84-9.
[7] Ibid., pp. 61-2, 88.
[8] Kingsley: *Yale*, I, 72; Ralph Henry Gabriel: *Religion and Learning
at Yale: The Church of Christ in the College and University, 1757-
1957* (New Haven, 1958), pp. 16-17.

currency as "For God, for country, and for Yale.") In 1748
Yale required all officers and students to subscribe to the
Westminster Confession of Faith, a decision which helped to
hold Yale in the conservative camp in the religious controversies of the time. But the winds of diversity and of toleration blew strong, and by 1765 even at Yale young Anglicans
were free to worship according to the dictates of their own
conscience.*

The orientation of the colonial college was religious, but
the relations between church and college were characterized
by diversity. Denominational rivalry encouraged toleration,
but rivalry was also a source of costly injury to the cause of
higher education in colonial America. Surely Yale was weakened by the founding of Princeton, nor could mid-eighteenth-
century New Jersey properly support two colleges—New
Jersey at Princeton and Queen's at New Brunswick. And
King's College in New York found that its Anglican orientation was a cause of so much sectarian opposition that it actually relinquished a sum of money which it had raised by lottery rather than risk the alienation of the community and the
hostility of prospective students. The board of governors of
the college turned over half the proceeds of the lottery to
the city government, which proceeded to build an apparently
much needed new jail and "a proper Pest-House for the Reception of such Persons as may be infected with any contagious Distempers." Higher education in New York was off to
a proper American start: befuddled by denominationalism, in
search of a public, short of money; but equally certain, as
George III was to make clear in 1762, that the future demanded its existence.[1]

The colleges were in no sense popular institutions. They
were shaped by aristocratic traditions and they served the
aristocratic elements of colonial society, a society which was

* Kingsley: *Yale*, II, 497.
[1] Van Amringe: *Columbia*, p. 10.

being subjected increasingly to the stresses of New World conditions. For in colonial America there was taking shape an environment that encouraged individual effort, that looked with jealousy and hostility at privilege, an environment that could not and would not hold a good man down. Order was giving way to the dynamics of mobility; labor was bringing rewards as nowhere else in the world.

It is no accident that of the two men most often referred to as characteristic Americans of the eighteenth century, one of them, Benjamin Franklin, had no more than a few years of elementary schooling, and the other, Jonathan Edwards, undertook the first great religious revival of modern times. Franklin was a symbol of the self-made man in social and economic terms, while Edwards was a symbol of the self-made man in religious terms, a symbol of that emphasis on conversion, on individual expression and experience which was characteristic of the Great Awakening.

While exerting a profound influence on such an environment through the civil and religious leaders it trained, the colonial college failed to establish itself as a popular institution intimately affecting the lives of the people. Said one of Anne Hutchinson's followers: "I had rather hear such a one that speakes from the meere motion of the spirit, without any study at all, than any of your learned Scollers, although they may be fuller of Scripture. . . ."[2] A perhaps self-pitying Harvard commencement orator in 1677 observed that "Mad nobodies, haranguers at street-corners, have more influence with the populace than reverent men, filled with singular gifts of the divine spirit."[3]

Not only did the college movement in the colonial era fail to become as popular as the religious awakening; it had also to compete with the early discovery that the American frontier was a potential and remarkably accessible source of material abundance. As he contemplated his fellow settlers busily pursuing material riches on the frontier or in new

[2] Morison: Harvard: *Founding*, p. 176.
[3] Morison: Harvard: *Seventeenth Century*, II, 433.

channels of commerce in the 1660's, President Chauncy of
Harvard complained: "They have 'waxed fat and kicked' at
supporting education."[4] And when in the 1720's the enrollment of the college began to reflect the results of some of this
materialism, the notion that Harvard was a rich man's college
was broadcast by sixteen-year-old Benjamin Franklin, who
charged in the family newspaper, *The New England Courant*,
that wealthy parents sent their sons to Harvard "where, for
want of a suitable Genius, they learn little more than to carry
themselves handsomely, and enter a Room genteely. . . ."[5]

Nothing about colonial America suggested that the college
was going to become a characteristic American institution
nor that in time it would be a popular American institution.
A South Carolina newspaper took the position in 1770 that
one of the worst things that could happen to South Carolina
would be a college, not because the newspaper was hostile to
education but because, as the editorial writer put it: "Learning would become cheap and too common, and every man
would be for giving his son an education."[6]
Every man, however, was far from wanting to give his
son an education. The institutions themselves helped to keep
the people away. The curriculum was not of the sort that appealed to men of practical inclination. The costs required
available cash, something which many people of middling
and lower class did not have. The distances were often excessive. When the College of New Jersey opened its doors in
1746, it was the only college between Williamsburg and New
Haven. Most American farmers—and most Americans *were*

---

[4] Ibid., I, 330.
[5] Morison: Harvard: *Three Centuries*, p. 61. The erroneous notion
that colonial Harvard and Yale ranked students by wealth and social
position is put to rest in Clifford K. Shipton: "Ye Mystery of Ye Ages
Solved, or, how Placing Worked at Colonial Harvard & Yale," *Harvard
Alumni Bulletin*, LVII (1954-5), 258-9, 262-3.
[6] James Harold Easterby: *A History of the College of Charleston
Founded 1770* (Charleston, 1935), p. 10.

farmers—could not afford to give up their sons, their sons'
labor, their sons' help at home. In 1704 in Westchester County,
New York, there were but six families that could spare their
children enough time to learn more than reading and writing.[7]

On the eve of the American Revolution, except in New England, there was no public provision for elementary education
in the American colonies.[8] Charity schools conducted by the
denominations were the common institutions of elementary
learning in New York, Philadelphia, and other eastern coastal
towns. The responsibility for education rested largely with
the parents who, if they could manage a little instruction in
reading, writing, and arithmetic, felt they had done well by
their children, as indeed they had. There were itinerant free-
lance teachers who accounted for some of the formal training
of the period, and in the South planters sometimes hired
northern college graduates or employed indentured servants
to tutor their children and run plantation schools. But as far
as most Americans were concerned, they were on their own
when it came to education during the colonial period. Only a
relatively few colonial Americans received any formal education beyond the elementary subjects. Secondary schools were
rare. Private tutors and the local clergyman carried the main
burden of college preparation. There were public secondary
schools in New England, probably the best being the Boston
Latin School, three graduates of which were to sign the
Declaration of Independence. There were a few secondary
schools in the middle colonies, and even fewer in the South.
    As for college, it has been estimated that as of 1775 "per-
haps one out of every thousand colonists . . . had been to

[7] James Truslow Adams: *Provincial Society 1690-1763* (New York,
1927), p. 131.
[8] For colonial education see Samuel Eliot Morison: *The Intellectual
Life of Colonial New England* (Ithaca, 1956), first published as *The
Puritan Pronaos* (New York, 1935); Bernard Bailyn: *Education in the
Forming of American Society* (Chapel Hill, 1960).

college at some time or other," and many of those who had gone to college had done so for less than a full course.[9] The largest graduating class at Harvard before the American Revolution was the Class of 1771, with sixty-three graduates, a number that would not again be approached for forty years.[1] In 1776 there were 3,000 living graduates of the American colleges.[2] The college had long been a necessity for society, but it had not become a necessity for the people. The college was clearly a source of political leaders, but not everyone aspired to be a leader. The college sustained a literate, indeed a learned, ministry, but many Americans could get along without any ministry at all. For most colonial Americans, college was something that could wait.

It is often pointed out that some middle- and lower-class families sent their sons to the colonial colleges, and unquestionably some of them did. But it should not be forgotten that the overwhelming majority of their sons stayed home, farmed, went West, or became—without benefit of a college education—Benjamin Franklin or Patrick Henry.

[9] Evarts Boutell Greene: *The Revolutionary Generation 1763-1790* (New York, 1943), p. 123.
[1] Morison: Harvard: *Three Centuries*, p. 102.
[2] Walter Crosby Eells: *Baccalaureate Degrees Conferred by American Colleges in the 17th and 18th Centuries* (Washington, 1958).

2

Legacy of the Revolution

While the purposes of the colonial colleges were not narrow, the charge was sometimes made against them that their curriculum was stultifying, unimaginative, inadequate to the times—a veritable baggage of subjects, methods, and attitudes almost certain to keep the student and his world at a standstill. No curriculum, whatever its merits, has been spared comparable complaints.

The curriculum of Harvard and the other colonial colleges was drawn from many sources. Had these colleges been only creatures of the Reformation, the emphasis would perhaps have been so overwhelmingly on the preparation of clergymen that the course of study would hardly have served any other purpose. The colonial colleges, however, were also creatures of the Renaissance and therefore cherished the humanistic ideal of classical scholarship. If Latin was the language of the Reformation, Greek and ancient Greece were the discovery of the Renaissance, and the curriculum of the colonial college necessarily made room for both. Beside the Reformation ideal of the learned clergyman was placed the Renaissance ideal of the gentleman and scholar. Of course the

Reformation and the Renaissance were not movements that deeply stirred the `American forest, except indirectly. The founders of Harvard attempted to re-create at Cambridge the college they had known at the old Cambridge in England. And old Cambridge, as they had known it, represented an amalgam of Reformation and Renaissance emphases, a consequence of the fact that simultaneously in early sixteenth-century England there had occurred the Protestant Reformation, the emergence of a gentleman class and a need for its training, and the first hints of humanistic learning. With an appropriate curriculum old Cambridge had been turning out clergymen, scholars, squires, public servants, men of contemplation and men of action, governors and governed.

Emmanuel at Cambridge, a Puritan foundation, was the model for Harvard; Queen's at Oxford was the model for William and Mary. With rare exception the American college for many years was significantly shaped by the English universities. Yet, if the immediate ancestor of the American colonial college was the English university, the lineage was ancient. The American college was also conceived as a descendant of the schools of Hebrew prophets. Not until the administration of President John Leverett, in the first quarter of the eighteenth century, did a narrowing view of the world dictate that graduates of Harvard be known as "the sons of Harvard." Until then the old antecedents had been stressed, and the Sons of Harvard had been known as the Sons of the Prophets.[1] And while there may in fact be no important distinction, the more provincial appellation did have the effect of beclouding the ancient heritage.

It was altogether impossible, however, to disguise or ignore the debt owed the English universities, for the colonial cur-

[1] Samuel Eliot Morison: *Three Centuries of Harvard 1636-1936* (Cambridge, 1936), p. 60. For curricular foundations see especially Samuel Eliot Morison: *The Founding of Harvard College* (Cambridge, 1935), pp. 50-7.

riculum was the proper amalgam of the medieval arts and
sciences and of Renaissance interest in the study of literature
and belles-lettres. The fundamental discipline was Latin—the
language of the law, of the church, of medicine; the language
through which translations of Aristotle from the Greek had
dominated the medieval course of study; the language in
which Aristotle's three philosophies—natural, moral, and
mental—entered the medieval universities. Taking its place
beside Latin was Greek, the language of the new humanism,
of Renaissance learning; it brought Homer and Hesiod, Greek
lyrics and idylls, into the experience of the educated man.

So fundamental were these two languages and two litera-
tures that until 1745 they were the only subjects in which applicants for admission to a colonial college were expected to
fulfill entrance requirements. And so fundamental was Latin
that most textbooks, including Greek and Hebrew grammars,
were written in that tongue. As the language of the prophets,
Hebrew was more widely read in the American college than
in England, and on occasion it was argued that Hebrew was
the language of the angels as well; yet at no time did Hebrew
challenge the dominance of Latin and Greek.

These ancient languages were put to work in the colonial
curriculum, often serving as the tools with which teacher and
student found their way through Aristotle's three philosophies and through the liberal arts of the medieval curriculum.
Thus, the languages were not studied for their own sake alone.
They were living languages, the languages in which explorations were made into logic, rhetoric, ethics, metaphysics,
astronomy, physics, and mathematics.[2]

In varying proportions these subjects were the basic course
of study not only of Harvard but of the colonial colleges in
general. During the first year Latin, Greek, logic, Hebrew,
and rhetoric were the staples of the curriculum. During the
second year logic, Greek, and Hebrew were continued, and a
beginning was made on natural philosophy, which some cen-

[2] Morison: Harvard: *Founding*, pp. 12-17, 26; Morison: *Harvard
College in the Seventeenth Century* (Cambridge, 1936), I, 147, 186.

turies later would be called physics. In the third year there
was added to natural philosophy mental philosophy or metaphysics and moral philosophy, a veritable grab bag of subject
matter out of which one day would come economics, ethics,
political science, and sociology. The fourth year provided
review in Latin, Greek, logic, and natural philosophy. A
modest beginning in mathematics was the only new departure
of the senior year. At Yale the order was different, the proportions were different, but the intent, the emphasis, and the
subject matter were the same.[3] The English university was
everywhere a fountain of inspiration and influence.

Not only was the curriculum brought from abroad. The concept of effective religious control was patterned on the kind
of control which made Emmanuel College at Cambridge a
Puritan see. The residential pattern which made every American college a home away from home was of English origin.
The idea of the college as essentially aristocratic in clientele
and purpose reflected English experience. The names of the
four college classes—freshman, sophomore, junior sophister,
senior sophister—came from England. The emphasis on teaching rather than on study; on students, rather than scholars; on
order and discipline, rather than learning—all this also derived
from patterns which had been emerging in the residential
colleges of the English universities.[4]

What else could Harvard have become but an English college on the American frontier of Western Europe? And because it was an English college, its officers included a steward,
a cook, a butler; and the regular order of servants by necessity included a brewer, a baker, a bedmaker or so. Because
it was an English college, provision was made for a kitchen
and for a president's wife to supervise it, even if, as was al-

[3] Edwin Oviatt: *The Beginnings of Yale (1701-1726)* (New Haven,
1916), p. 200; William Lathrop Kingsley, ed.: *Yale College: A Sketch
of its History* (New York, 1879), II, 496.
[4] W. H. Cowley: "European Influences upon American Higher Education," *Educational Record*, XX (1939), 168-71.

leged, she served bad fish, mackerel "with guts in them," and "goat's dung in the hasty pudding." Therefore, too, there was that minute regulation of conduct that was not peculiarly Puritan as much as it was peculiarly collegiate, breathing not the free spirit of adult scholarly inquiry but the atmosphere of a boarding school for small boys.[5] In some ways Harvard was so successful at being a small boys' school that some of the finest rakes in England were sent overseas to the reformatory on the banks of the Charles. Enough of them, at any rate, to send a friend of the college into sorrowful complaint in 1651:

> This hath been a place certainly more free from temp-tations to lewdness than ordinarily England hath been, yet if men shall presume upon this to send their most ex-orbitant children intending them more especially for God's service, the Justice of God doth sometimes meet with them. . . , for of late the godly Governors of this colledg have been forced to expell some, for fear of cor-rupting the Fountain. . . .[6]

Surely it can hardly be argued that the nurture of intellect required the standard means of discipline, which until 1718 was flogging. Flogging was displaced in that year by the per-haps somewhat more humane practice of boxing, in which a bad boy was made to kneel at the feet of his tutor, who pro-ceeded to smack him sharply on the ear. This custom was sus-pended in 1755 and omitted from college laws in 1767. The abandonment of these practices clearly recorded the hu-manitarian spirit that was loose in the Western world, but it may also have meant that the English college in Massachusetts was being Americanized. For there was something of the ring of the New World in the complaint of a father whose son was flogged in 1718: "I rather *have* my son abused as a man, [than as] . . . a beast."[7]

[5] Morison: Harvard: *Seventeenth Century*, I, 55; Morison: Harvard: *Founding*, pp. 37 ff, 232.
[6] Morison: Harvard: *Seventeenth Century*, I, 77-8.
[7] Morison: Harvard: *Three Centuries*, p. 113.

The curriculum would also respond to new conditions. It did not remain what it had been. Harvard, which was something of a fountain of light and inspiration in curricular matters in colonial America, was "founded after the new learning of the renaissance had been sifted into the old scholastic curriculum, but before the new scientific leaven had begun to work." [8] As a consequence a curriculum designed to make clergymen and statesmen, a curriculum in which ancient tongues were fundamental tools and in which truth was of ancient origin, was of course diluted by a rising empiricism, a scientific point of view that questioned old truths and established new ones.

By 1659 in astronomy the Ptolemaic system was dead at Harvard. The Copernican system was firmly established, and in 1672 with a new telescope Harvard students and scholars were scanning the skies. Under the tutelage of Charles Morton, late in the seventeenth century, natural philosophy at Harvard took on a Newtonian orientation. But it was with the founding of the Hollis Professorship of Mathematics and Natural Philosophy in 1727 and the appointment of John Winthrop as the incumbent in 1738 that science made significant inroads at Harvard. Winthrop was Harvard's first real scientist. He presided over the first laboratory of experimental physics in America. By proving that earthquakes were natural phenomena he annoyed a few clergymen, but he also advanced academic learning and freedom from ignorance. The quality of his leadership was revealed by the skill with which he persuaded the Massachusetts General Court to fit out the first astronomical expedition in American history—to Newfoundland in 1761 to observe the transit of Venus.[9]

These new departures would be a long time in developing

[8] Morison: Harvard: *Founding*, p. 58.
[9] Morison: Harvard: *Seventeenth Century*, I, 216 ff.; Morison: Harvard: *Three Centuries*, pp. 79, 92-3. See also Theodore Hornberger: *Scientific Thought in the American Colleges, 1638-1800* (Austin, 1945).

and adjusting to a new language. As late as 1880 most science in the American college was taught under the label of natural philosophy, scientific equipment was known as philosophical apparatus, and laboratories were called philosophical chambers.[1] But although Aristotelian terminology persisted almost until the end of the nineteenth century, it could not cloak the rising mastery of Newtonian science.

Yale's first two tutors, excited and awakened by a parcel of books sent from London, were soon opening the minds of their students to Locke, Newton, and Copernican theory.[2] In 1734 Yale imported from Europe a reflecting telescope, a microscope, and a barometer, but this was only a beginning. Five years later the old curriculum felt the impact of the new philosophical apparatus, and as the years passed the time allotted to logic and other staples of the old course of study was reduced, while increasing attention was paid to natural philosophy, mathematics, surveying, and navigation. All this enthusiasm for science inspired Benjamin Franklin, always a friend of practical and useful education, to send an electrical machine off to New Haven in 1749. With it Ezra Stiles, then tutor and later president, conducted the pioneer electrical experiments in New England.[3]

The intrusion of science on the old course of study was apparent in the career of mathematics in the Yale curriculum. In 1726 the only mathematics was a smattering in the fourth year. In 1745 Yale made arithmetic an entrance requirement, thus ending the exclusive reign of Latin and Greek. Three years later mathematics found a welcome in the second and third years; in 1766, in the first year as well.[4]

Mathematics was becoming a tool subject, a new and living language that acquainted "undergraduates with the idea of inquiry . . . [and encouraged] the feeling that it was the business of the mind to discover things hitherto unknown." The

[1] Morison: Harvard: *Founding*, p. 28.
[2] Oviatt: *Yale*, pp. 396-9.
[3] Kingsley: *Yale*, I, 62, 66-7; II, 497; I, 78.
[4] Ibid., II, 498.

old and dying language was the language of scholasticism, the language of the already known. Newtonian empiricism was challenging revealed Christianity. Induction was challenging deduction. By the eve of the Revolution everywhere more attention was being paid to natural science and mathematics. By 1766 six of the eight colonial colleges supported professorships of mathematics and natural philosophy. The early ferment of the Enlightenment, the examples of the English dissenting academies and of the Scottish universities, which were remarkably receptive to secular learning, were beginning to inspire effective inroads on old practices.[5]

The shift was revealed no more clearly than in what was happening to the syllogistic disputations which had been adornments of the medieval university and which had carried much of the burden of scholasticism in the colonial college. The disputation, while employed throughout the year as a means of conducting discussion, was a characteristic commencement exercise of the colonial college. Confronted with a thesis, a statement of some universal truth, two students, one serving as disputant and one serving as questioner, would apply their powers of deduction to establish the validity of the thesis. The method of thought was characteristically scholastic and served as an examination of what the students had learned during their four years. The commencement disputation put on display not only the senior class, but the truths they had been taught.[6]

How deeply did this scholasticism penetrate the colonial college? How completely did it dominate the curriculum?

[5] Richard Hofstadter and Walter P. Metzger: *The Development of Academic Freedom in the United States* (New York, 1955), p. 197. This book has an excellent account of the relationship between the rise of science in the colonial colleges and the development of a climate of freedom and inquiry, pp. 192-201.
[6] See Morison: Harvard: *Founding*, p. 24; Morison: Harvard: *Seventeenth Century*, I, 279; Mary Lovett Smallwood: *An Historical Study of Examinations and Grading Systems in Early American Universities* (Cambridge, 1935), pp. 12-13.

How thoroughly did it represent the prevailing mode of thinking? [7] That the methods of the scholastics were in vogue there can be no doubt. In 1693 Harvard students were considering such ethical theses as: "Prudence is the most difficult of virtues"; "Death is rather to be undergone than any sin perpetrated." And as late as 1769 deduction was asserting itself in such theses as: "Human reason alone does not suffice to explain how the true religion was introduced and built up so firmly in the world"; "There was need of divine revelation for Christianity." [8] The colonial college was overwhelmingly concerned with right conduct. And scholasticism contributed its share to that orientation, for, after all, scholasticism was *the* tradition.

Yet, scholasticism was not the vital tradition on the eve of the Revolution. By then it was but one ingredient in the philosophic outlook of the American college, and it was deeply in trouble. For while on occasion it could make room for new thought and new knowledge, its spirit was counter to the spirit which was identified with Descartes, Bacon, Newton, Locke, and Hume, a spirit which recognized the role of experiment and of experience as a source of knowledge. Scholasticism was the philosophy of thoughtfulness, of deduction, of "ought." A new spirit was arguing for a philosophy of experience, of experimental evidence, of "is."

Where the colleges were going was best revealed by new departures at New York and Philadelphia. In 1754 the friends of King's College announced in the New York press that its course of study would emphasize surveying, navigation, geography, history, and natural philosophy—or "the Knowledge . . . of every Thing *useful* for the Comfort, the Con-

---

[7] James J. Walsh: *Education of the Founding Fathers of the Republic; Scholasticism in the Colonial Colleges; a Neglected Chapter in the History of American Education* (New York, 1935) argues for extensive influence. Samuel Eliot Morison demurs in a review of the Walsh book in *New England Quarterly*, VIII (1935), 455-7.

[8] Walsh: *Education of the Founding Fathers*, pp. 81, 85.

venience and Elegance of Life . . . and everything that can contribute to . . . true Happiness." A serious but failing effort to encompass these rather large ambitions was attempted, but the failure was not nearly as important as the try.⁰

Before the Revolution the one college that made serious headway in the new directions was the College of Philadelphia, under the leadership of Scotch-born William Smith. In 1753 Smith had published a somewhat visionary proposal for a new college in New York. It failed to become a blueprint for King's, but in Philadelphia his awareness of American, as opposed to English, conditions recommended him to the board of local citizens and men of affairs who were developing a new college. In his earlier proposal Smith had argued that peace and economic abundance would require of Americans a special effort in "forming a succession of sober, virtuous, industrious citizens and checking the course of growing luxury." [1] Now, in 1756 in Philadelphia, with the blessings of Franklin and the support of his board, Smith set up a three-year course of study which put as much as one third of the time into science and practical studies. He was not permitted to establish a parallel "mechanic arts" college as a companion to the traditional classical college, but in the classical college he emphasized English, English literature, and other tool subjects that would be useful to a far wider range of men than had sought and found utility in the old curriculum. Provost Smith's program of studies was the first systematic course in America not deriving from the medieval tradition nor intending to serve a religious purpose.[2]

. . .

⁰ Louis Franklin Snow: *The College Curriculum in the United States* (New York, 1907), pp. 56-60.

[1] William Smith: "A GENERAL IDEA of the College of MIRANIA, and the Method of teaching Religion and Science therein; first published as a plan for a College in New-York in the Year 1753" in his *Discourses on Public Occasions in America* (2d. ed., London, 1762), pp. 41-2.

[2] Edward Potts Cheyney: *History of the University of Pennsylvania 1740-1940* (Philadelphia, 1940), pp. 71-81.

In a sense, the American Revolution had already begun. It
can hardly be argued that it waited for Paul Revere. The
Revolution was first made in the minds of men who became
accustomed to thinking of themselves as Americans, who at
first unconsciously and then openly spoke of the English as
"they" instead of as "we." The Revolution was made where-
ever Americans discovered and emphasized the differences
between colonial necessity, colonial aspiration, and colonial
purpose and what England expected them to be.This difference appeared most dramatically in the realm of politics and
economics, but it was not lacking where higher education was
concerned. The King's College prospectus of 1754 and the
College of Philadelphia's curriculum of 1756 may not have
been the first shots in an exchange heard around the world,
but they were nonetheless certain indications that the English colonies of North America were beginning to respond
not to English needs but to American aspirations.

The American colleges were caught up in the events of the
world by the Revolution, and they were never quite the same
again. Nassau Hall at Princeton, the largest building in North
America, became one of the most badly scarred buildings of
the war. Occupied by the British in December 1776, attacked
by the American troops in January 1777, occupied and van-
dalized by the continentals for the next five months, converted into a military hospital late in 1777, and finally serving
the Continental Congress in 1783 as a capitol for congressmen
in flight from disgruntled mutinous soldiers—Nassau Hall
symbolized the physical impact of the war on the American
college.[3]

At King's College the first casualty was not a building but
the president, Myles Cooper, a Tory—as was only proper at
a college so-named. One night in May 1775, with Alexander
Hamilton of the Class of 1774 holding an enraged mob at
bay, President Cooper escaped over his back fence in scanty
attire and found refuge on an English sloop of war headed

[3] Thomas Jefferson Wertenbaker: *Princeton 1746-1896* (Princeton,
1946), pp. 57-61, 64-5.

for home. Yale, unable to find adequate food for commons in the local markets, sent its students and tutors inland in 1777. William and Mary stayed open but shut down temporarily to house American and French troops during the siege of Yorktown. Friendly though these troops were, the college's magnificent Christopher Wren building was accidentally set on fire by the French. The Revolution also consumed the college's English endowment funds, the colonial tobacco tax which had been assigned to the college, and the western lands which had long been an important source of revenue. And along with all this, the capitol was moved from Williamsburg to Richmond.[4]

The Revolution damaged buildings, enrollments, endowments, and reputations, but far more fundamental was the damage done to the old purposes and to the old course of study. The war may have begun as an effort to define the limits of political authority or as an effort to redefine the economic relationships between mother country and colony. It may have become a movement for independence, but before it was over it was also a movement for democracy: a full-bodied statement to the effect that in America man counted for more, took less account of his superiors—indeed frequently denied their existence, achieved whatever distinction his own ability and the bounty of the land allowed him, looked any man in the eye and knew him as an equal before the law and before God.

The spirit of this rising democratic tide overtook the colleges, much to the despair of many for whom the old ways

[4] John Howard Van Amringe, et al.: A History of Columbia University 1754-1904 (New York, 1904), p. 48; Kingsley: Yale, I, 100-6; Herbert Baxter Adams: The College of William and Mary (Washington, 1887), pp. 29, 56-7. See also Morison: Harvard: Three Centuries, pp. 148-53; William H. S. Demarest: A History of Rutgers College 1766-1924 (New Brunswick, 1924), pp. 101-38; Cheyney: Pennsylvania, pp. 115-18.

were the best ways. President Charles Nisbet, Scotsman and president of the new Dickinson College in Pennsylvania, voiced a characteristic lament when he complained of the new United States: "Everything here is on a dead level. . . . Our gentlemen are all of the first edition; few of them live in their father's house. . . . In a republic the demagogue and rabble drivers are the only citizens that are represented or have any share in the government. . . . Americans seem much more desirous that their affairs be managed by themselves than that they should be well managed. . . ." [5] For evidence President Nisbet might have pointed to the absolutely preposterous phenomenon of almost a thousand northern New Yorkers in the year 1779 signing a petition which asked that a college be founded in the city of Schenectady. That was not the way colleges were founded in the old days, nor did their names have such a political sound as the one given the college in Schenectady—Union College it was called when it was chartered in 1795. Promptly that fine aristocrat, General Philip Schuyler, father-in-law to Alexander Hamilton, voiced his skepticism in a letter to a friend: "May indulgent Heaven protect and cherish an Institution calculated to promote virtue and the weal of the people!" [6] Heaven would have to be indulgent, for the people were unquestionably taking an interest in higher education in a way they never had before.

Sensitive to the new importance of the people, state legislatures everywhere established a new relationship to the existing institutions and to the many new ones which blossomed in the immediate postwar years. Between 1782 and 1802 nineteen colleges which are in existence today were chartered, more than twice as many colleges as had been founded dur-

[5] James Henry Morgan: *Dickinson College: The History of One Hundred and Fifty Years 1783-1933* (Carlisle, 1933), p. 66.
[6] Dixon Ryan Fox: *Union College: An Unfinished History* (Schenectady, 1945), p. 12.

ing the almost 150 previous years. Denominational rivalry, state loyalty, increasing wealth, and growing population all helped to stimulate this flowering, which would continue unchecked well into the nineteenth century.[7] The American college was also making a broader appeal to families of the middling sort. It was being recognized as a means of getting ahead, not just as a means of registering that one's father had.

During the war and postwar period the states moved into a more active role in the life of higher education. In the revolutionary constitution of North Carolina, adopted in 1776, there was an injunction to the effect that "all useful learning shall be duly encouraged and promoted in one or more universities."[8] Not only North Carolina, but Georgia, Tennessee, and Vermont also founded state-chartered, state-supported institutions before 1800. Columbia (formerly King's), the University of Pennsylvania at Philadelphia, and Dartmouth temporarily were taken over by state governments. Harvard, Yale, and William and Mary adjusted to increased state representation on their governing boards.[9]

One element in the new educational activity of the states was a public hostility to denominational education. The new Harvard overseers were intended to serve as watchdogs over an institution where liberal theology might go too far. The new members of the Yale corporation, on the other hand, were expected to see that Yale, in its orthodoxy, did not make life uncomfortable for young men of various denominational backgrounds.[1] Thomas Jefferson's efforts in 1779 to create a state university out of the College of William and Mary failed in part because his plan would have put an Epis-

[7] The standard study on the founding of colleges is Donald G. Tewksbury: *The Founding of American Colleges and Universities Before the Civil War: With Particular Reference to the Religious Influences Bearing Upon the College Movement* (New York, 1932).
[8] Kemp Plummer Battle: *History of the University of North Carolina* (Raleigh, 1907-12), I, 1-2.
[9] Tewksbury: *The Founding of American Colleges*, p. 64.
[1] Ibid., p. 143.

copal institution at the apex of the Virginia school system.[2] Benjamin Rush, seeking a charter from the Pennsylvania General Assembly for Dickinson College, understood the public mood perfectly: he proposed in 1783 that the college be Presbyterian, that its board include members of the German Reformed Church, and that it take the name of John Dickinson, a Quaker, who at the moment was president of the supreme executive council of Pennsylvania.[3]

Growing religious toleration and indifference were in part consequences of religious diversity and of religious competition; Americans could find no other way to accommodate such diversity except by acquiescing quietly in its existence. There was also, however, a vital stream of hostility to religion. To be free of England, of mercantilism, of royal governors, of agents of the Crown, of a powerful aristocracy, was a welcome situation, but it was not enough. The dawning Enlightenment promised to emancipate man a number of times and in a number of ways, one of which was to free him from religious institutions. Consequently there was a ready audience in the new United States for the philosophic positions that were popular in France at the time.

In the American college France was a discovery of the American Revolution. France had sealed the doom of the colonial relationship with England at Yorktown. And France, it was fondly believed, in 1789 had picked up the torch lit in America and had had a revolution of her own. Instruction in the French language appeared as early as 1779.[4] In 1784 the University of New York was patterned on the French model as a nonteaching and nondegree-granting supervisory institution.[5] In 1785 Hampden-Sidney announced a willing-

---

[2] Philip Alexander Bruce: *History of the University of Virginia, 1819-1919* (New York, 1920-2), I, 71.
[3] Morgan: *Dickinson*, pp. 12-14. See also Harry G. Good: *Benjamin Rush and his Services to American Education* (Berne, Indiana, 1918).
[4] Cowley: op. cit., 171-3.
[5] Frank C. Abbott: *Government Policy and Higher Education: A Study of the Regents of the University of the State of New York, 1784-1949* (Ithaca, 1958).

ness to substitute French for Greek in awarding the B.A. degree.[6] In 1793 William and Mary required French as an admissions credit. In 1795 Williams appointed its first professor, an itinerant instructor in French.[7] The same year Union College took as its motto no crusty wisdom from the Greeks or Romans but one in French which commemorated the brotherhood of war: *"Sous les lois de Minerve nous devenons tous frères."* [8]

These official responses to French influence were surpassed by undergraduate excursions into the world of French philosophy. Heady with the delights of independence, conscious of new dignity as free citizens, many Americans imbibed deism, flirted with atheism, adopted a firm indifference to religion.[9] In the 1790's the typical Harvard student was an atheist.[1] A few years later students at Williams College were conducting mock celebrations of the Lord's Supper. At Princeton the infidel leader of the undergraduate deists led his followers in burning the Bible of the local Presbyterian church.[2] And in 1802, looking on Nassau Hall in flames, President Samuel Stanhope Smith thundered: "This is the progress of vice and irreligion."[3] A trustee committee lent support to his suspicion that the fire was of incendiary origin, the work of undergraduate Jacobin infidels. As late as 1807, long after adulation of France had become unpopular in New England, which by then had been horrified by the excesses of the French Revolution, students at the University of South Carolina gathered one February night to read from the works of Tom Paine, sing French Revolutionary songs, and break into the night with their

[6] Alfred J. Morrison, ed.: *The College of Hampden-Sidney: Calendar of Board Minutes 1776-1876* (Richmond, 1912), pp. 33, 35.
[7] Charles Hart Handschin: *The Teaching of Modern Languages in the United States* (Washington, 1913), p. 19.
[8] Fox: *Union*, p. 13.
[9] See Howard Mumford Jones: *America and French Culture* (Chapel Hill, 1927), esp. pp. 350-487.
[1] Morison: Harvard: *Three Centuries*, p. 185.
[2] Wertenbaker: *Princeton*, pp. 134-7.
[3] Ibid., p. 127.

hoarse shouts: "Vive la Revolution." [4] In 1812 an imaginative Princeton student cut a cavity in the chapel Bible and neatly inserted a deck of cards. [5] The sputtering assessment of his times registered by President Nisbet of Dickinson revealed the mood with which the new tendencies were met by the substantial friends of the old order: ". . . Spirit of free inquiry . . . carried almost to madness . . . air-balloons, the Rights of Man, the Sovereignty of the People . . . Atheism, Socinianism. . . ." On the election of Jefferson to the presidency in 1800 Nisbet could but wail: "The Democrats of America have discovered that it is for the interest of Christianity to elect a president who is indifferent whether the people believe that there is one God or twenty gods, or no god at all." His advice: "God grant us patience to endure their tyranny." [6]

Jefferson's election was interpreted in a number of ways. John Adams saw it as a conspiracy of evil against good. What it suggested to many was that the political and social philosophy of Federalism, government by the rich, the well-born, the able, could not be made permanent in the United States. It meant that no political party could ignore the people and gain their support. The United States was not to be the friend of order nor of restraint nor of discipline. The future apparently belonged to the freewheeling democrats (democrats with a small *d*), to men of the nerve and self-assurance of the uninhibited Harvard students who petitioned President Samuel Langdon in 1780: "As a man of genius and knowledge we respect you; as a man of piety and virtue we venerate you, as a President we despise you." When the students demanded, President Langdon resigned his office. [7]

[4] Daniel Walker Hollis: *University of South Carolina* (Columbia, 1951-6), I, 53.
[5] Wertenbaker: *Princeton*, p. 156.
[6] Morgan: *Dickinson*, pp. 68-9.
[7] Morison: Harvard: *Three Centuries*, p. 162.

The legacy of the American Revolution to the American college was, then, a heady mixture of French deism, unruly students, state controls, and a widely held belief that the colleges were now serving a new responsibility to a new nation: the preparation of young men for responsible citizenship in a republic that must prove itself, the preparation for lives of usefulness of young men who also intended to prove themselves.

The curriculum responded accordingly. As the unsettling of the medieval course of study by the rise of science well demonstrated, the curriculum was in no sense an absolutely stationary instrument of the past; it had for a long time been in motion. In America the Enlightenment and the Revolution unsettled the curriculum still more. Captivated by the notion of man's perfectibility, the Enlightenment turned naturally to the institutions of education as instruments for doing the work that needed doing. A band of apostles stood ready to guide the Enlightenment spirit in the New World: James Otis, Benjamin Franklin, Thomas Jefferson, Thomas Cooper, Joseph Priestley, Benjamin Rush, Thomas Paine, and Richard Price among them. Natural law, the realm of reason, the realm of nature were in the ascendancy. The supernatural was in decline—still vigorous, still in charge, still respectable, but in decline.[8]

The first important challenge to the old rationale after the beginning of the Revolution occurred at William and Mary, where Thomas Jefferson, as governor of the state and as a member of the college's board of visitors, attempted to reorganize the entire course of study, hoping to bring it fully into line with the future. In a set of legislative proposals in

[8] See Agatho Zimmer: *Changing Concepts of Higher Education in America Since 1700* (Washington, 1938), pp. 7-17; and R. Freeman Butts: *The College Charts Its Course* (New York, 1939), pp. 58 ff.

1779 he called for the abolition of the professorships of
divinity and of oriental languages. The college, said Jefferson, must free men from superstition, not inoculate them
with it. He would establish a professorship of law and police,
which might better have been named a professorship of public administration, so clearly adapted was it to the preparation of public servants for positions of responsibility in a
democracy. He hoped to establish a professorship of anatomy, medicine, and chemistry, revealing as he did so the new
emphasis on utility which would characterize the American
college curriculum. Everywhere Jefferson proposed to bring
the curriculum within the range of the practical and the
public, adding a professorship of modern languages, introducing the law of nature and of nations into the work of the
professor of moral philosophy, adding natural history to the
responsibilities of the professor of natural philosophy. The
legislature did not enact Jefferson's program, but in his role
as visitor at the college Jefferson succeeded in having the
two divinity professorships abolished and in having many of
the new subjects added to the responsibilities of existing
professorships. The full development of Jefferson's scheme
was frustrated, but in time he would have a new university
with which to experiment.[9]

King's College not only changed its name to Columbia; it
also adopted a curriculum which would help young Americans fulfill the functions demanded of them in an aspiring
nation. Professorships of economics, natural history, and
French revealed in 1792 that Columbia had been bitten by
the Enlightenment. At Union a few years later French,
American history, and constitutional government broke into
the old course of study. At the University of North Carolina
plans were projected in 1795 for a course to consist of a
professorship of chemistry, agriculture, and the mechanic
arts, a professorship of belles-lettres, and a professorship of

---

[9] Adams: *William and Mary*, p. 39; Roy J. Honeywell: *The Educational Work of Thomas Jefferson* (Cambridge, 1931), pp. 54-6.

languages, including that most neglected and perhaps most useful of all languages, English.[1]

One consequence of the Revolution might have been the establishment of a national university. Certainly the idea received a hearing. It was discussed at the Constitutional Convention, it became the subject of college commencement addresses, and for George Washington it was a matter of deep and special concern, one to which he referred in his first annual message to Congress in 1790 and in his last address to Congress in 1796. It was a question which concerned and received the support of all of his successors until, with the coming of Andrew Jackson, a new era and a new mood overtook the land. Washington expected a national university to be a useful instrument in the shaping of patriotic citizens and of able civil servants; he hoped that a national university would enable the United States to develop a class of men free from the restricting prejudices of provincialism and sectionalism. The idea was premature: sectionalism and denominationalism would have been constant enemies of a national university. The idea of a national university was but a dream—a dream that would recur often in American history, each time to run afoul of some new combination of hostile interests and beliefs.[2]

The spirit of the Enlightenment, the liberating influence of the Revolution on American education, and the temper of the times were no place better illustrated than in the papers called forth in 1799 by the American Philosophical Society, which offered a prize for the best plan of an American system of education. The contest elicited papers from Benjamin Rush, the Philadelphia physician; from Noah Webster, who earlier had put together some spelling books and a dictionary—thereby doing more for the English tongue in the

[1] Snow: *The College Curriculum*, p. 93; Van Amringe: *Columbia*, p. 76; Fox: *Union*, p. 14; Battle: *North Carolina*, I, 93-5.
[2] Edgar Bruce Wesley: *Proposed: The University of the United States* (Minneapolis, 1936), pp. 4-10; Walter C. Bronson: *The History of Brown University 1764-1914* (Providence, 1914), p. 68; Adams: *William and Mary*, p. 43.

43 Legacy*Legacy of the Revolution*

United States than any grandiose plan could possibly do; from DuPont de Nemours, the Delaware powdermaker and physiocrat; and from many others.³ The plans spoke much of science, of preparation for democratic citizenship, of escaping from the past. Rush suggested setting up special schools "for teaching the art of forgetting." ⁴ He distrusted the ancient languages. "While Greek and Latin are the only avenues to science, education will always be confined to a few people," he argued, remarking that "it is only by rendering knowledge universal, that a Republican form of government can be preserved in our country." He warned that the ancient languages could stand in the way of the development of the country as well as in the way of its preservation. Said Rush: "To spend four or five years in learning two dead languages, is to turn our backs upon a gold mine, in order to amuse ourselves catching butterflies." ⁵ Whether Americans in the nineteenth century were going to spend their lives opening gold mines or chasing butterflies was a question that only the future could answer.

³ Allen Oscar Hansen: *Liberalism and American Education in the Eighteenth Century* (New York, 1926), p. 105.
⁴ Ibid., p. 61.
⁵ Ibid., pp. 52-3.

3

❦

The College Movement

On a cold drizzly day in January 1795, a two-story empty brick building that called itself the University of North Carolina was opened to the public. An unsightly landscape of tree stumps, rough lumber, scarred clay, and a bitter wind greeted the governor, who had wanted to be on hand for this important event. He was also met by the faculty which consisted of one professor doubling as president. A month later the first applicant for admission knocked at the door. In the same year, far to the north, the founders of a college that would be called Bowdoin were offering the entirety of a township in Maine to any contractor who would build them a four-story building. They could find no takers.[1]

In March 1802, Nassau Hall at Princeton was consumed by flames. The next year, at Dickinson College, Carlisle, Pennsylvania, its first building was burned down. At Burlington, Vermont, in 1806 President Daniel Clarke Sanders, who knew that the college had been in the process of creation since 1791, could not contain his enthusiasm for the way things now were going:

[1] Kemp Plummer Battle: *History of the University of North Carolina* (Raleigh, 1907-12), I, 63-5; Louis C. Hatch: *The History of Bowdoin College* (Portland, 1927), p. 9.

The college edifice [he reported] is nearly glazed. The
tower is finished and painted on the dome. The vane and
lightning rod are up. The bell proves a good one. The
masons are at work, and all the chimneys will probably
be finished before commencement.[2]

In 1811 the Reverend John W. Browne, who believed
deeply in the new Miami University in Ohio, set out on a
trip to raise funds and a library. His visit to James Madison
at the White House was unproductive, but he picked up a
five-volume history of Ireland from a senator from Kentucky; in the state of Delaware he collected $22.00, the good
president of Princeton gave him $5.00, and from old John
Adams at Quincy there were kind words, two books, and
$10.00. All in all, a wagonload of books and $700 for the
new college in Ohio. A few weeks later the Reverend
Browne, on a preaching mission, slipped as he crossed the
Little Miami River and was drowned.[3]

In 1818 at Ohio University in Athens the first college
building was struck by lightning; it was not yet completed,
and only torrential rains kept it from being totally destroyed
by fire. In 1822 there was a fire in Maine Hall, the first
building at Bowdoin, the college in Maine which had been
unable to give away a township in order to get it built. At
Burlington, Vermont, in 1824 the building that had so
pleased President Sanders in 1806 was lost in flames. The
college hovered on the edge of extinction; the president
went insane.[4]

In 1826 a group of citizens of the town of Easton, Pennsylvania, received a charter for a college that they would

[2] Thomas Jefferson Wertenbaker: *Princeton 1746-1896* (Princeton,
1946), p. 126; James Henry Morgan: *Dickinson College: The History
of One Hundred and Fifty Years 1783-1933* (Carlisle, 1933), p. 87; Julian
Ira Lindsay: *Tradition Looks Forward: The University of Vermont: A
History 1791-1904* (Burlington, 1954), pp. 63-4.
[3] Walter Havighurst: *The Miami Years 1809-1959* (New York, 1958),
pp. 11-20.
[4] Thomas N. Hoover: *The History of Ohio University* (Athens,
1954), p. 33; Hatch: *Bowdoin*, p. 403; Lindsay: *Vermont*, pp. 122-4.

call Lafayette. They went shopping for an academy in Philadelphia, hoping to move it to Easton and call it a college. They could not find one, and for the next four years they did not hold a meeting. Out on the prairies of Illinois a college called Illinois opened in 1829 with nine students, none of whom had ever studied English grammar. Seven years later three of them were graduated from the college. In 1830 half the plant of the University of Georgia was destroyed by fire.[5] At Bloomington, Indiana, also in 1830, the Reverend Andrew Wylie arrived to take up the presidency of Indiana College. He had written ahead to suggest that for the good of the college something should be made of his arrival, and so he was escorted into town by the leading citizens, where he was met by a double file of the citizenry. There were huzzas, fires in the president's house, and in the evening a grand illumination of the college building by man-size and boy-size candles. The building did not burn down.[6]

On the twenty-second of November 1832, five young Presbyterian ministers knelt down on the new-fallen snow in the woods near Crawfordsville, Indiana, and there asked God's blessing on the site of Wabash College. Six years later (the year that Wabash was destroyed by fire) Emory College in Georgia was opened on the strength of the unpaid interest on what were still unpaid pledges. One day in October 1841, half the dormitory space at Williams College in Massachusetts went up in flames. Eight French priests, brothers of the Congregation of the Holy Cross, few of them speaking tolerable English, rode and walked in company into northern Indiana in 1842 because their bishop had

[5] David Bishop Skillman: *The Biography of a College: Being the History of the First Century of the Life of Lafayette College* (Easton, 1932), I, 38-47; Charles Henry Rammelkamp: *Illinois College: A Centennial History 1829-1929* (New Haven, 1928), p. 40; E. Merton Coulter: *College Life in the Old South* (Athens, 1951), p. 99.

[6] James Albert Woodburn: *History of Indiana University: 1820-1902* (Bloomington, 1940), pp. 51-2.

given them permission to begin a college that would become
Notre Dame. On August 6, 1845, the University of Michigan held its first commencement exercises, awarding eleven
bachelor's degrees. Clearly the institution was in business,
and on the very same day the regents of the university
undertook measures to provide for a university burying
ground.[7]

Often when a college had a building, it had no students.
If it had students, frequently it had no building. If it had
either, then perhaps it had no money, perhaps no professors;
if professors, then no president, if a president, then no professors. Perhaps as many as seven hundred colleges tried and
failed before the Civil War.[8] Yet Absalom Peters, a friend
of the college movement, was unquestionably right when he
remarked in 1851: "Our country is to be a land of colleges."[9]
For against a record of discouragement, there must be placed
the remarkable staying powers which characterized the
founders of nineteenth-century American colleges. The
American people went into the American Revolution with
nine colleges. They went into the Civil War with approximately 250, of which 182 still survive.[1] Absalom Peters was
on safe ground in thinking of the United States as a land of
colleges. A few decades later it was being pointed out that
England was managing nicely with four universities for a

[7] James I. Osborne and Theodore G. Gronert: *Wabash College; the
first hundred years, 1832-1932* (Crawfordsville, 1932), pp. 1-2, 45-7;
Henry Morton Bullock: *A History of Emory University* (Nashville,
1936), p. 69; Leverett Wilson Spring: *A History of Williams College*
(Boston, 1917), p. 165; Arthur J. Hope: *Notre Dame: One Hundred
Years* (Notre Dame, 1943), p. 35; Elizabeth M. Farrand: *History of the
University of Michigan* (Ann Arbor, 1885), p. 59.
[8] In a study of institutional mortality in 16 states, Donald G. Tewksbury discovered 412 extinct colleges before the Civil War. In the same
states 104 colleges survived. In the remaining 18 states with 78 surviv-
ing colleges, a comparable ratio would give approximately 309 fatali-
ties. *The Founding of American Colleges and Universities Before the
Civil War* (New York, 1932), p. 28.
[9] Ibid., p. 1.
[1] Ibid., p. 15.

population of 23,000,000, while Ohio with a population of 3,000,000 boasted thirty-seven institutions of higher learning.[2]

One member of the governing board at Dickinson, General John Armstrong, should be remembered for having the "prophetic wisdom" to caution against the college mania. Said Armstrong: Why not erect modest academies in the back counties and thus prepare a certain number of students for entrance into the existing colleges, and as time passes, perhaps we will discover a place that actually needs a college, and then we might go ahead there.[3] But nothing could be further from the minds of most men who became involved in the college movement during the decades before the Civil War. One unwritten law of the early history of education in the United States would be: Where there are no elementary or secondary schools, there you will find a college. Another might go something like this: Offer a young man the principalship of an academy and he will try to make a college of it. For example, no sooner had Jasper Adams arrived in Charleston, South Carolina, than he set about changing the academy of which he was principal into a college. In no time at all he was passing out B.A. degrees, but things went too slowly for Jasper Adams, and in 1826 he went off to Geneva College in New York where he could be president of a really ambitious college. His action so stimulated the trustees in Charleston that Adams returned the very next year, convinced that Charleston was going to become a university before Geneva did.[4]

College-founding in the nineteenth century was undertaken in the same spirit as canal-building, cotton-ginning, farming, and gold-mining. In none of these activities did completely rational procedures prevail. All were touched by the American faith in tomorrow, in the unquestionable ca-

[2] Frederick A. P. Barnard: *Two Papers on Academic Degrees* (New York, 1880), p. 18.
[3] Morgan: *Dickinson*, pp. 21-2.
[4] James Harold Easterby: *A History of the College of Charleston Founded 1770* (Charleston, 1935), pp. 77-8.

pacity of Americans to achieve a better world. In the founding of colleges, reason could not combat the romantic belief
in endless progress.

President Philip Lindsley of the University of Nashville,
one of the really great figures in the history of American
education, addressed himself in 1837 to the very appropriate
question of whether the American people could sustain an
institution comparable to the English universities, where collegiate foundations clustered around a center and helped to
build up impressive monolithic institutions of great wealth
and influence. He concluded that "our busy, restless, specu-
lating, money-making people" required colleges as scattered
and mobile as the American people themselves.[5] Everything
about America conspired to enlarge the imagination—the
landscape, the geography, the distance from Europe, the
fertility of the soil, the endless bounty of nature, even
the necessity to be certain about the democratic experiment.
And if the American could not imagine an Oxford or a
Cambridge, he could imagine the beginnings of hundreds
of them and be certain that tomorrow would fulfill these
beginnings. It was no accident that the two state colleges of
Ohio were placed in towns named Oxford and Athens, for
from both the New World had taken the torch of learning.
America would be the democracy that ancient Greece had
promised, and the Greek revival in America would not only
dot the landscape with adaptations of classical architecture
but it would give almost every state its aspiring Athens.
There is even one in Arkansas. Appealing to the state legislature for aid in 1795, the trustees of Princeton declared: We
will make New Jersey the Athens of America.[6] At approximately the same time the trustees of Williams College, uncertain that Harvard could do the job by itself, proposed
to the General Court that state assistance to the little college
in the Berkshires would help Massachusetts become the

[5] Tewksbury: *The Founding of American Colleges and Universities
Before the Civil War*, p. 3.
[6] Wertenbaker: *Princeton*, p. 120.

Athens of the New World. From an enthusiastic supporter of the College of Charleston there burst forth in 1847 the plea: "Let us emulate the noble Bostonians. . . . [Let us make Charleston] the Athens of the South" (albeit the University of Georgia had already staked its claim at Athens, Georgia).[7]

In 1830 the Presbyterians of Indiana were called upon to give 25 cents a person toward a fund of $600 to provide Hanover College with a professor of theology. Only $100 was raised, but the college kept on. In fact, its president, in search of a charter, denied before the Indiana legislature that other state legislatures had placed limits on the number of colleges they were prepared to charter. The truth of the matter was that everywhere college-founding was out of control, and it would be unfair to Hanover to place it under control in Indiana. He got his charter.[8]

Every once in a while there would be something akin to the realistic appraisal of President John H. Lathrop of the University of Missouri, who in 1841 admitted that "the taste for a regular course of University instruction is in a good measure to be generated. . . . Let us," he argued, "not then be unwisely impatient of results, nor despise the day of small things. . . ." People who talked the way President Lathrop did were seldom listened to. The American way was much more in the vein of an enthusiastic delegate to the 1849 state constitutional convention in California. "Why should we send our sons to Europe to finish their education?" bragged this new son of California. "If we have the means here we can procure the necessary talent; we can bring the president of the Oxford University here by offering a sufficient salary." It was almost inevitable that later in the century when

[7] Easterby: *Charleston*, pp. 105-6.
[8] William Alfred Millis: *The History of Hanover College from 1827 to 1927* (Hanover, 1927), pp. 20, 31.

a college was founded in Los Angeles the college catalogue should carry on its cover the announcement:

UNIVERSITY HOMES IN OCCIDENTAL HEIGHTS TRACT

A beautiful site. Best water in the country piped to every lot. Rich soil. Pure air. An educational center. No better place in the State for a home. Prices $250, $300, $500. Terms to suit. Call on or write to the

President of the Occidental University[9]

Against such exhibitions as this, it is no wonder that seldom in the history of American higher education were college founders as modest, as reasonable, and as accurate as was Thomas Jefferson in the remarks with which he took notice of the University of Virginia toward the end of his life: "It is a bantling of forty years' birth and nursing, and if I can see it on its legs, I will sing, with serenity and pleasure, my *nunc dimittis.*"[1]

One reason for the founding of colleges was the federal system of states, with their provincial loyalties and rivalries. In 1784 young De Witt Clinton, on his way to enter Princeton, became the first student to enroll at the reconstructed Columbia College, solely because the mayor of New York appealed to his father's sense of loyalty to the state of New York. In 1819 the argument was made in behalf of the University of Virginia that during the previous twenty-eight years Virginia, in the absence of a state university, had lost fourteen million dollars to other states. In 1851 a Minnesota newspaper encouraged the development of a state university with the assertion that "not a single youth of either sex should be permitted to leave the territory to acquire an edu-

[9] Jonas Viles, *et al.*: *The University of Missouri: A Centennial History* (Columbia, 1939), p. 28; William Warren Ferrier: *Origin and Development of the University of California* (Berkeley, 1930), p. 8; Robert Glass Cleland: *The History of Occidental College, 1887-1937* (Los Angeles, 1937), p. 13.
[1] Philip Alexander Bruce: *History of the University of Virginia, 1819-1919* (New York, 1920-2), I, 5.

cation for want" of a suitable institution in Minnesota. This sentiment would echo throughout the century until in 1894 the president of Indiana University, pointing with horror at the 385 sons and daughters of Indiana studying outside the state, was begging the state legislature:

> Give us the money to make a great institution of learning and Indiana will not only save the greater part of the one-half million [dollars spent by Indianans elsewhere] but she will bring the sons and daughters of other states to spend a half million more.

Some state legislatures found arguments of this order convincing. The sheer continental dimensions of the United States and the difficulties of travel also tended to encourage localism and to augment the number of colleges. An important reason for the founding of Bowdoin was the unwillingness of people in the district of Maine to make the long trip to Cambridge.[2]

Another reason that the United States would become a land of colleges was the home missionary movement, which in the period after 1800 concentrated its attention on the West. Frequently Yale men were responsible for setting up Christian goals in the West, but they had a great deal of help from Princetonians.[3] Between the Congregationalists and the Presbyterians, many western communities had difficulty being as western as nature intended them to be. In Indiana the first four colleges—Vincennes, Hanover, Indiana, and Wabash, all established before 1832, did not develop in response to any expressed local desire or necessity. The necessity was discovered by a group of Presbyterian home missionaries who tossed in their beds sleeplessly when they thought of

[2] John Howard Van Amringe, et al.: *A History of Columbia University 1754-1904* (New York, 1904), p. 62; Bruce: *Virginia,* I, 232; James Gray: *The University of Minnesota 1851-1951* (Minneapolis, 1951), p. 17; Woodburn: *Indiana,* pp. 426-7; Hatch: *Bowdoin,* p. 1.

[3] William Lathrop Kingsley, ed.: *Yale College: A Sketch of its History* (New York, 1879), I, 412-4; Wertenbaker: *Princeton,* p. 114.

the benighted condition of life on the western frontier. Eastern Congregationalists and Presbyterians joined forces in sponsoring in 1843 the Society for the Promotion of Collegiate and Theological Education at the West, so successful an enterprise that Horace Mann, good Unitarian that he was, one day would lament that the great West had been conquered not only by Black Hawk but by John Calvin as well.[4]

If the colleges were not the work of missionaries, they were sometimes the work of people who might have been missionaries had they not decided to go west as permanent settlers. The process of re-creating a New England town in the West was often repeated. No urging from the outside was required to found such colleges as Oberlin, Carleton, Grinnell, Colorado, Whitman, and Pomona. These colleges were the natural outgrowth of New England-type towns that had been planted in the West by New Englanders; in the tradition of the Puritans, colleges dotted the countryside.[5] One of the last of the colleges in the Puritan tradition was Pomona, established in 1888 by the Congregationalists of southern California who had gone on record three years earlier as being in favor of developing what they called "a college of the New England type." With the help of a board of trustees composed of graduates of Williams, Colby, Dartmouth, Yale, and Oberlin, they could hardly fail.[6]

·   ·   ·

[4] Tewksbury: *The Founding of American Colleges and Universities Before the Civil War*, pp. 10-14, 69; Osborne and Gronert: *Wabash*, pp. 60-1; Arthur G. Beach: *A Pioneer College: The Story of Marietta* (Marietta, 1935), pp. 66-7; Rammelkamp: *Illinois College*, pp. 17-20 ff., 90.

[5] Robert Lincoln Kelly: *The American Colleges and the Social Order* (New York, 1940), p. 31; Robert Samuel Fletcher: *A History of Oberlin College from its Foundation through the Civil War* (Oberlin, 1943), I, 3 ff.; John Scholte Nollen: *Grinnel College* (Iowa City, 1953), pp. 3-40 ff.

[6] Charles Burt Sumner: *The Story of Pomona College* (Boston, 1914), pp. 4, 52-71.

Of course the busiest agents of all this college-founding were the religious denominations—some more so than others, some later than others, but few were not involved. They worked in an environment of national ambition, democratic aspiration, geographic isolation, and romantic imagination, and state by state they turned their own rivalries into sets of competing colleges. As the population moved westward, so did the denominations. Every state became a battlefield. Few were as productive as Ohio, where the rate of survival was apparently high: Franklin, Presbyterian; Western Reserve, Congregational; Kenyon, Episcopal; Denison, Baptist; Oberlin, Congregational; Marietta, Congregational; Muskingum, United Presbyterian; St. Xavier, Roman Catholic; Ohio Wesleyan, Methodist; Mount Union, Methodist; Baldwin, Methodist; Wittenberg, Lutheran; Otterbein, United Brethren; Heidelberg, Reformed; Urbana, Swedenborgian; Antioch, Christian; Hiram, Disciples. All were founded before 1850, and without the usual spate of Presbyterian colleges, which were not necessary in Ohio, since the Presbyterians had captured the two state colleges, Miami and Ohio.[7]

Inspired by the results of a second period of religious awakening and revivalism in the early decades of the nineteenth century, an awakening that turned back the forces of deism and atheism, the churches looked forward to a new day when Christianity would prevail in the lives of men. The successes of this counter movement of religious enthusiasm, however, whetted denominational appetites. The spirit of toleration that had characterized the colleges in the late colonial period and during the early years of the republic was now threatened by denominational ambition. The intellectual prospects of the American college were now jeopardized by a torrent of piety. The earliest and strongest friends of the new era of college-founding were the Congregationalists of New England and the Presbyterians of the middle and southern states. Both denominations were bitten by the

[7] Lucy Lilian Notestein: *Wooster of the Middle West* (New Haven, 1937), pp. 6, 277-8.

new enthusiasm and committed to the Calvinist belief in an educated clergy. Other Calvinist denominations—German Reformed, Dutch Reformed, and Unitarians—fell in with them in the college movement. Last of the denominations to found colleges, naturally, were those with a dedicated hostility to learned clergymen, but even they, particularly the Methodists and Baptists, surrendered. Before long even those sects claiming to be closest to the people and least in need of the fancy obscurantist learning of scholars—the Disciples, United Brethren, Christians, and Universalists—would abandon their hostility. The Quakers, who had no need at all for clergymen, made a relatively slight contribution to the college movement. Roman Catholics, whose needs and opportunities would grow as immigration from the Catholic countries of Europe increased, would make their great contribution in a later era.

Denominationalism, more than any other factor, accounted for the founding of eleven colleges in Kentucky before 1865, twenty-one in Illinois before 1868, thirteen in Iowa before 1869.[8] One Amherst graduate, explaining the founding of Amherst, remarked that in the commonwealth of the Puritans there was much need for "a college . . . not quite so far west as Williams, and not quite so far toward Plato as Cambridge."[9] Mindful of the Unitarian heresies emanating from Harvard, President Edward Dorr Griffin of Williams often asked his students in chapel to remember the people of Boston in their prayers; but that was hardly as effective as having a citadel of orthodoxy in the Connecticut Valley; there had to be Amherst. By 1861 denominational ambition had covered the country with colleges.

Among those responsible were the Methodists. At first they had been hostile to the college movement, largely because they felt more at ease with ministers who had found

[8] Jesse B. Sears: *Philanthropy in the History of American Higher Education* (Washington, 1922), p. 35.

[9] Thomas Le Duc: *Piety and Intellect at Amherst College 1865-1912* (New York, 1946), p. 5.

their way to the understanding of God not through books but through experience. The conditions which led to a change of heart among the Methodists were the subject of a report at the 1832 Indiana Conference of the church:

> When we examine the state of the literary institutions of our country, we find a majority of them are in the hands of other denominations, so that our people are unwilling (and we think properly so) to send their sons to those institutions. Therefore we think it very desirable to have an institution under our own control from which we can exclude all doctrines which we deem dangerous; though at the same time we do not wish to make it so sectarian as to exclude or in the smallest degree repel the sons of our fellow citizens from the same.[1]

This statement was pregnant with colleges. It advanced the competitive necessity of founding Methodist colleges. It established the obligation of the denomination to its own people, and it indulged in the magnificent conceit of claiming that other sects were more sectarian than the Methodists. This conceit was a powerful justification, perhaps even a stimulant, of the college movement. Surely every denomination practiced it. For fundamentally it was an assertion that the denomination's colleges would be strong enough to serve the church and wide enough to catch members of other denominations. Such colleges of course would therefore have so many students they could hardly avoid success.

Methodists and Baptists everywhere were coming to much the same conclusions as the Indiana Methodist Conference of 1832. The Methodists, more impressed by the successes of their rivals than by their failures, sometimes took advantage of those failures and moved into abandoned buildings. Wesleyan in Connecticut began in 1831 in the empty buildings of a defunct military academy. In 1833 two floundering

[1] William Warren Sweet: *Indiana Asbury-DePauw University, 1837-1937: A Hundred Years of Higher Education in the Middle West* (New York, 1937), p. 26.

Presbyterian colleges in Pennsylvania, Dickinson and Allegheny, were saved from extinction by the embrace of Methodism. Randolph-Macon appeared in the South, McKendree in Illinois, Indiana Asbury in Indiana. A committee on education at the general conference of the Methodist Church might lament in 1856: "We have, in many parts of the land, called into existence institutions that were not needed and could not be sustained." The same sentiment might be echoed at the general conference in 1860 and again in 1891. But the answer was the same as the answer of the president of Presbyterian Hanover when efforts were made to limit the number of colleges in Indiana in the early 1830's: Everybody's doing it.[2]

For the Methodists and Baptists, founding colleges became a part of that apparently endless American process of coming to terms with an essentially middle-class society. As churches of the meek and the disinherited, the Methodist and Baptist persuasions had at first been able to get along without educated clergymen and educated laymen. But opportunity in the United States being what it was, no church could establish itself as a permanent refuge for the permanently meek and disinherited. American life did not work that way, and Baptists and Methodists discovered that they were at the very least candidates for rank in the middle reaches of society. With that discovery went the necessity of erecting colleges, institutions which not only catered to some of the requirements of middle-class life, but which also helped to lend an aura of respectability to Methodists and Baptists as they worked their way from poverty to plenty.

The particular aptitude of Presbyterians for founding colleges enabled them to outdistance all their rivals. By the eve of the Civil War they were operating, through one form of control or another, over 25 per cent of the existing colleges that would survive into the twentieth century. Presbyterian

[2] Carl F. Price: *Wesleyan's First Century* (Middletown, 1932), pp. 19 ff.; Sylvanus M. Duvall: *The Methodist Episcopal Church and Education up to 1869* (New York, 1928), pp. 65-70, 72, 113-14.

success in founding colleges owed much to an evangelical revivalist fervor which provided great reservoirs of denominational enthusiasm. Equally important were the financial and bureaucratic support of a tightly organized church hierarchy and the fortuitous flow of Scotch-Irish Presbyterian immigrants into the advancing West. Sometimes co-operating with the Presbyterians were the Congregationalists, who had been founding colleges in America since 1636, but by 1860 they had fallen behind even the Baptists.[2]

The American college was conceived of as a social investment. Certainly, no college president in the early decades of the nineteenth century was guilty of issuing the invitation to self-indulgence which the president of one midwestern university issued in his greeting to freshmen in 1940: "I want you to have a good time. I want you to learn to know people. I want you to learn to be an American." Perhaps such purposes were in the process of development even earlier than 1800. To a degree perhaps they were nothing more than an Americanization of what the young Elizabethan gentleman looked for at Oxford or Cambridge. But they were a far cry from the sentiments expressed by President Joseph McKeen at Bowdoin in 1802:

> It ought always to be remembered, that literary institutions are founded and endowed for the common good, and not for the private advantage of those who resort to them for education. It is not that they may be able to pass through life in an easy or reputable manner, but that their mental powers may be cultivated and improved for the benefit of society. If it be true no man should live for himself alone, we may safely assert that every man who has been aided by a public institution to acquire an education and to qualify himself for useful-

[2] Tewksbury: *The Founding of American Colleges and Universities Before the Civil War*, pp. 62-129.

ness, is under peculiar obligations to exert his talents for
the public good.'

President McKeen spoke not only in the tradition of the
Puritan colleges of New England, but of the entire Western
world of the time, a tradition that recognized institutions of
education as social institutions and learned men as both masters and servants of society. The college which President
McKeen represented and all other colleges of early nineteenth-century America were committed to social needs
rather than to individual preference and self-indulgence.
When college presidents thought of their students they
were reminded not of society's obligation to young men
but of the obligation of young men to society. In describing
Bowdoin as a public institution, President McKeen acknowledged the public nature of the private educational corporation, as indeed any early nineteenth-century college president would have done, and he reminded the students that
they owed their benefactor, society, a return on its investment.

The notion that a college should serve society through
the lives of dedicated graduates was not new. As a collegiate
purpose it would never disappear. What would be new would
be the degree to which such purpose would be diluted as
the century progressed. It would know some moments of
high esteem before the century was over, but as the nature
of American society changed, so would the expectations
which society placed upon its colleges. As the public displaced the public servant in the conduct of civil affairs, the
college was denied some of its sense of purpose. As Americans lost their sense of society and substituted for it a reckless individualism, there was less demand on the colleges to
produce dedicated leaders such as President McKeen had in
mind. In time colleges would be more concerned about the

' James E. Pollard: *History of the Ohio State University: The Story
of its First Seventy-Five Years 1873-1948* (Columbus, 1952), p. 350;
Hatch: *Bowdoin*, p. 19.

expectations of their students than about the expectations of society. In time going to college would come very close to being an experience in indulgence rather than an experience in obligation. For many years, however, a fundamental purpose of the college movement in the United States was the one which President McKeen had expressed so well in 1802.

This broad social purpose took many forms. It might appear in the role of social control, as was the case in South Carolina, where a leading purpose in the founding of South Carolina College in 1801 was the desire to create an institution that would help to unite a state seriously torn by up-country and down-country rivalries, by the legacy of bitterness inherited from internal conflicts of the Revolutionary era, and by other divisive tendencies. South Carolina College was the design of low-country aristocrats. With it they intended to educate and thereby make more conservative the leadership of the great Piedmont majority which threatened aristocratic control of the state. In this tradition late in the century the president of the University of North Dakota addressed the sober, responsible interests of the state in a time of agrarian unrest and appealed to the legislature for increased appropriations with the challenge: "We must educate our young men of today so that they will not become the mad socialists of tomorrow." [5]

Or this social purpose might be nothing more than a recognition that on any college campus were to be found the responsible, creative political leaders of tomorrow. It was not for narrow reasons of self-advancement and success in business that the University of North Carolina in 1837 recommended Chapel Hill for the "formation of lasting friendships and associations . . . among those who are to consti-

[5] Daniel Walker Hollis: *University of South Carolina* (Columbia, 1951-6), I, 14 ff.; Louis G. Geiger: *University of the Northern Plains: A History of the University of North Dakota 1883-1958* (Grand Forks, 1958), p. 47.

tute no small portion of our future rulers." * A sense of this
purpose was conveyed by a president of the University of
North Carolina who was attempting to explain the meaning
of a degree from Chapel Hill in the years before the Civil
War:

> The University diploma, while it did not, unless accom-
> panied by an honor, prove scholarship, yet was of great
> value. Its possessor in this little world had learned much
> that gave him an advantage over his neighbors not
> blessed as he was. He had learned human nature and
> how to manage men. He had learned to a considerable
> extent polished manners. He could think and speak on
> his feet. In county meetings he knew rules of order
> and how to conduct business. He had confidence in him-
> self, and realized that he secures the fruit who has the
> boldness to seize it and to hold it with tenacious grasp.
> He saw that his neighbors expected much of him and his
> self-respect forced him not to disappoint them, on the
> principle 'noblesse oblige.' '

Here were the social advantages and social obligations of a
graduate of Oxford reduced to the requirements of rural
life and county government in North Carolina. There was a
world of difference, but the same great tradition prevailed.

Social purpose might also be defined as national purpose. A
commitment to the republic became a guiding obligation of
the American college. The American people were conducting an experiment in free government of a nature and scope
that the world had not yet known. The American college
intended to serve that mission. The act of incorporation of
Indiana College in 1828 matter-of-factly committed the institution to the education of youth in the "American" lan-

* Luther L. Gobbel: *Church-State Relationships in Education in
North Carolina Since 1776* (Durham, 1938), p. 42.
' Battle: *North Carolina*, I, 781-2.

guage. The country and the colleges would walk into the future together, as the Ohio Baptist Educational Society made clear in its report on its work at Denison in 1832:

> Our object has been, and is, to build up a useful Institution—suited to the wants, and calculated to promote the welfare of a rapidly growing and free country, where virtuous intelligence, industry, and enterprise are sure to meet a quick reward.

Danger to a firmly held social purpose lurked in this 1832 statement of the Baptists of Ohio, as it did in the 1835 charter of Oglethorpe University in Georgia, which declared that "the cultivation of piety and the diffusion of useful knowledge greatly tend to preserve the liberty and to advance the prosperity of a free people." For to the degree that the colleges and the country became captivated by the notion that "virtuous intelligence, industry, and enterprise are sure to meet a quick reward"; to the degree that they developed a commitment to "prosperity"—to that degree they were in danger of substituting for the old sense of society a concern for the success of individuals. By 1868 it would be difficult to know exactly what Andrew D. White meant when he declared to his students at Cornell: "You are here to begin a man's work in the greatest time and land the world has yet known." Whether these words were an invitation to personal success or public service there could be some question, as there never could have been in the words of President McKeen to his students at Bowdoin almost seventy years before.[8]

The American college was faced with one problem with which its aristocratic tradition of social purpose was never

[8] Woodburn: *Indiana*, p. 32; G. Wallace Chessman: *Denison: The Story of an Ohio College* (Granville, 1957), p. 58; Allen P. Tankersley: *College Life at Old Oglethorpe* (Athens, 1951), p. 147; White quoted in Orrin Leslie Elliott: *Stanford University: The First Twenty-Five Years* (Stanford University, 1937), p. 409.

intended to cope. The American college, for all of its European origins, was expected to be democratic. As Lyman Beecher, one of that tribe of self-appointed keepers of the public conscience, declared in 1836:

> Colleges and schools . . . break up and diffuse among the people that monopoly of knowledge and mental power which despotic governments accumulate for purposes of arbitrary rule, and bring to the children of the humblest families of the nation a full and fair opportunity . . . , giving thus to the nation the select talents and powers of her entire population.

By 1850 the man soon to be president of the University of Michigan was aghast at how closely the United States had adhered to the spirit of Beecher's comments. He wailed: "We have cheapened education so as to place it within the reach of everyone." [9] In another twenty-five years his complaint would run the risk of being misunderstood as a congratulatory report on democratic progress.

Because democratic growth in the United States was contemporaneous with the growth of the colleges, they experienced some difficulty in establishing rigorous learning as one of their fundamental interests. Americans were on the whole much impressed by the careers of self-taught, self-made men, men whose elevation to positions of responsibility, eminence, and wealth was accomplished without benefit of formal schooling. Against this record of success the colleges could with difficulty advance the necessity of close, rigorous intellectual exercise as a justification for attending college. In the end, the colleges to a certain extent incorporated a posture of anti-intellectualism in their behavior.

Collegiate anti-intellectualism, essentially democratic in origin, was bound to enter any institution founded by Methodists or Baptists, neither of which could fully commit themselves to the necessity of an educated clergy. In other

[9] Tewksbury: *The Founding of American Colleges and Universities Before the Civil War*, pp. 6, 8.

collegiate foundations, however, piety also held a higher place in the scale of values than intellect, and as a consequence intellectual purpose would necessarily have to struggle for recognition in the American college. As early as 1837 Philip Lindsley, president of the University of Nashville, concluded that "Massachusetts is perhaps the only State which continues to bestow spontaneous honours and unsought offices upon superior talent, learning and integrity." Surveying the world as he had come to know it in Tennessee, Lindsley contrasted the ritual devoted to learning that characterized a New England commencement with the horse races and cock fights of a commencement day in Nashville. He could not avoid the conclusion that the future of America was being determined not in Cambridge but in Nashville. In 1869 Charles William Eliot took the occasion of his inaugural address at Harvard to register his own suspicion that in America the self-made man had achieved a popular appreciation denied the Harvard-made man. "We are accustomed," complained President Eliot, "to seeing men leap from farm or shop to court-room or pulpit, and we half believe that common men can safely use the seven league boots of genius." [1]

In a society that embodied its suspicion of learning in the symbol of the self-made man, the college was bound to adopt either some shield of protective coloration or some sincere indifference to learning. By the end of the nineteenth century a combination of popular and pietistic influences had led the American college to a point at which it could be said that among the purposes of the American college was the purpose not to take learning very seriously. Of Yale at the end of the century it was remarked: "The life of the campus was so dynamic and vital that even professors . . . at heart half accepted the fact that ideas, the search for

---

[1] LeRoy J. Halsey, ed.: *The Works of Philip Lindsley, D.D.* (Philadelphia, 1866), I, 426; *Addresses at the Inauguration of Charles William Eliot as President of Harvard College, Tuesday, October 19, 1869* (Cambridge, 1869), p. 39.

truth, and scholarship must be among the lesser products of
their show." [2] Theodore Roosevelt could dedicate a new law
school building at the University of Chicago in 1903 with
the warning: "We need to produce, not genius, not brilliancy, but the homely, commonplace, elemental virtues.
. . . Brilliancy and genius? Yes, if we can have them in addition to the other virtues." In 1904 Dean Briggs of Harvard
announced his preference for "moderate intelligence," and
fifteen years later the dean of Yale was advising the Eli
freshmen: "A man should not put more than half of his time
into his studies." [3]

Inevitably the American college would face up to the self-
made man on his own terms and in the process discover a
new purpose. In the end, it became necessary to argue and
possible to prove, on the basis of selected individuals, that
going to college was a way of making more money than if
you did not. In the very early years such an idea had not
been an expressed purpose of the colleges. But the time came
when graduates discovered that a college education as social
investment was now of less importance than a college education as a personal investment. When did this time come?
Surely before 1878 when the College of Wooster held out to
the farm population of Ohio the assurance that: "It is better
to give a son a complete education than to give him a farm.
He will then be able to earn far more in a year than a farm
could produce, and he may besides wield a great influence
for good." Surely before 1871, when a Harvard student
said to Henry Adams: "The degree of Harvard College is
worth money to me in Chicago." Even before 1863, when
the University of Notre Dame catalogue admitted that "A

[2] George Wilson Pierson: *Yale: College and University 1871-1937*
(New Haven, 1952-5), I, 269-70.
[3] Thomas Wakefield Goodspeed: *A History of the University of
Chicago Founded by John D. Rockefeller: The First Quarter Century*
(Chicago, 1916), p. 351; Le Baron Russell Briggs: *Routine and Ideals*
(Boston, 1904), p. 5; Pierson: *Yale*, II, 193.

few years in college would be profitably employed, if nothing else were learned but to converse and behave with the dignity and propriety of gentlemen [sic]." [4]

There had, of course, always been some correlation between wealth and going to college, but the relationship had either been incidental or unavoidable in a world where wealth and college diplomas were the marks of a ruling aristocracy. As preprofessional institutions, colleges had always intended to serve those who were expected to make out best in this world. In nineteenth-century America, however, the nature of the ruling aristocracy was in the process of change; an atomistic, mobile society, as Alexis de Tocqueville had predicted, was creating an aristocracy of manufacturers—at first largely unacquainted with formal collegiate learning, but finally drawing freely from those for whom college-going was recognized as a social elevator.

At the ceremonies which launched Allegheny College in 1817 someone put into the cornerstone "a chip off Plymouth Rock, one from Dido's temple, and another from the tomb of Virgil." [5] These chips symbolized the broad and ancient commitment of the American college in the nineteenth century, a commitment fervently expressed in 1868 by the president of the board of trustees of the College of California:

> This, then, is our vocation—to make men more manly, and humanity more humane; to augment the discourse of reason, intelligence and faith, and to kindle the beacon fires of truth on all the summits of existence. [6]

[4] Morgan: *Dickinson*, p. 107; Notestein: *Wooster*, p. 290; Henry Adams: *The Education of Henry Adams* (Boston, 1918), pp. 305-6; Sebastian A. Erbacher: *Catholic Higher Education for Men in the United States 1850-1866* (Washington, 1931), p. 105.

[5] George P. Schmidt: *The Old Time College President* (New York, 1930), p. 97.

[6] Ferrier: *California*, p. 273.

This fundamental commitment was sometimes distorted. Denominational fervor on occasion might overwhelm it. The demands of a population grasping for economic and social satisfactions could warp it. But the variety, the vitality, the spontaneity of the American colleges cannot be denied simply because the records they compiled were often records of discouragement or because the purposes they chose to serve were often confused or self-contradicting.

The institutions of the college movement in America intended to be, to the best of their ability and knowledge, democratic institutions for a democratic society. Necessarily they reflected both the best and the worst of that society. In 1854 an English traveler, impressed by the high morale and effective discipline of the United States Military Academy, sought an explanation and was told by a cadet: "We must get up early, for we have a large territory; we have to cut down the forests, dig canals, and make railroads all over the country." [7] The English traveler would not have found the same discipline or the same morale in every American college, but everywhere he would have found the same dynamic belief that there was work to do. He would have found highly motivated students, young men—and later, young women—and institutions which knew what they intended to do with these young people during the few years at their disposal. With its denominational and religious orientation, the English traveler would have found the American college something of a Sunday school. He would have found it something of a success school, given the degree to which the United States was synonymous with opportunity. And perhaps most of all he would have found it a place where the Americans were eloquently putting to a test their unbounded faith in man, their unquestioning belief in progress.

[7] Sidney Forman: *West Point: A History of the United States Military Academy* (New York, 1950), p. 86.

4

❧❧

The Religious Life

Andrew D. White, the first president of Cornell, a man possessed by a dream of true university proportions, once referred to the pre-Cornell period in the history of American higher education as "the regime of petty sectarian colleges." [1] From his vantage point above Cayuga's waters, this was perhaps so.

In many places, however, religion could thrive without petty sectarianism. A less dramatic but a more accurate description of the pre-Cornell era would be "the regime of the religious-oriented college." This description allows for the variety that was fundamental to the American collegiate experience. It permits a variety that necessarily includes the petty sectarian institutions. Princeton was perhaps the best of these, but there were dozens of frighteningly narrow and inconsequential Presbyterian, Baptist, and Methodist colleges in the backwaters of the South and West. There must also be included colleges such as Amherst and Williams where religion was more important than sect, where the denominational ties were informal but the religious commitment strong. Allowance must also be made for the University of

[1] Walter P. Rogers: *Andrew D. White and the Modern University* (Ithaca, 1942), p. 82.

Virginia, where a Jeffersonian bias against institutional religion was combined with such gestures as were necessary to avoid giving the university a reputation as a center of infidelity and irreligion.[2] And what is to be done about Harvard, where as early as 1830 President Quincy made clear that he was not going to hold Harvard for Calvin? In that year President Quincy announced that all Harvard students could go to any church on Sunday which they or their parents chose. As for the religious influence of the Harvard faculty, critics could make what they would of the fact that in 1831 it consisted of six Unitarians, three Roman Catholics, one Calvinist, one Lutheran, one Episcopalian, one Quaker, and one Sandemanian.[3]

One reason that "religious-oriented" is more satisfactory than "petty sectarian" is that White's phrase did not accommodate the paradox that while most colleges of the period were founded by denominations, they were also forbidden either by charter or public opinion to indulge in religious tests for faculty or students. The nineteenth-century American college could not support itself on a regimen of petty sectarianism; there simply were not enough petty sectarians or, if there were, there was no way of getting them to the petty sectarian colleges in sufficient numbers. The high mortality rate of colleges in the first half of the nineteenth century was proof that petty sectarianism did not pay off.

Denominationalism *did* spawn the colleges of the college era; it often helped to keep the colleges provincial and poor. The organized church surely had a blighting effect on the careers of such diverse institutions as Princeton, Vanderbilt, and Miami University during the second half of the nineteenth century. Yet, was not Orestes Brownson very close to the mark when he described the religious affiliation of most Americans of the time as "nothingarian"? Did not great

[2] Philip Alexander Bruce: *History of the University of Virginia, 1819-1919* (New York, 1920-2), III, 134-47.
[3] Samuel Eliot Morison: *Three Centuries of Harvard 1636-1936* (Cambridge, 1936), p. 257.

popular distaste develop whenever a state institution fell under the sway of denominational influence? The least organized and the least narrowly sectarian of all the major college-founding denominations, the Congregationalists, supported the most successful institutions and sent into the twentieth century a remarkable group of healthy, respected colleges, institutions that had outgrown the image of narrow sectarianism: Yale, Dartmouth, Williams, Amherst, Oberlin, and Western Reserve among them. Sectarians thrived on the issues which many of the college leaders of the period refused to take seriously. Mark Hopkins of Williams once remarked, in reference to a dispute over proper modes of baptism, that "it has always seemed to me so far secondary that I have found it difficult to understand the importance attached to it." In "the renewing of the Holy Ghost," he said, "the quantity of water is not important." [4]

Of course the dynamics of denominationalism gave strength and purpose to the religious life of many of the colleges. These dynamic purposes—consisting so often of fighting one another, fighting Rome, fighting the idea of public education —could be terribly narrow and they could be petty. But they could also find expression in more attractive motives, perhaps in the rather expansive and essentially humanitarian desire to Christianize the world or in a persistent effort to remind young college students of their obligations beyond self, to God and to society.

In fighting one another, the denominational colleges were probably at their ugliest and most foolish. Even President McKeen in his 1802 inaugural address at Bowdoin, an address in other respects so noble and inspiring, had the pettiness to suggest that Congregationalist Bowdoin could do a great deal for the Methodists and Baptists of Maine, whose clergymen were "illiterate vagrants who understand neither

[4] Frederick Rudolph: *Mark Hopkins and the Log: Williams College, 1836-1872* (New Haven, 1956), p. 94.

what they say, nor whereof they affirm." In Indiana in the
1830's the Methodists, unhappy with Presbyterian control of
Indiana College, insisted on equal privileges, and for fifty
years the battle continued. On one occasion a Presbyterian
in the Indiana legislature rose from his chair long enough to
announce, in effect: "There is not a Methodist in America
with sufficient learning to fill a professor's chair if it were
tendered him." Denominational competition led one Georgia
Baptist in 1836 to raise the embarrassing question: "Shall it
be said that six thousand Presbyterians built a college at Midway [Georgia] and that forty thousand Baptists were unable
to build [a college here] at Washington, [Georgia]?" Presbyterians, however, were also subject to embarrassment. In
1847 the Presbyterian clergymen on the Princeton board of
trustees sent the college into turmoil when they discovered
that the new chapel, the walls of which were two-thirds constructed, was cruciform. Princeton was too impoverished to
tear the building down, but this Popish architecture was a
source both of embarrassment and deep irritation. In the
1840's Miami University became an object of desire for two
competing groups of Presbyterians; when they were finished,
Miami was no longer the leading college in Ohio.[5]

The internal health, the endowment, and the enrollment
of many of the institutions that fell into contention hardly
made them worth the struggle, but the most rugged denom-
inationalists certainly thought so. In the 1850's the Methodists wrested control of Ohio University from the Presbyterians, and within three years every member of the Ohio
faculty was a Methodist minister. In Illinois Congregationalists and Presbyterians fought over Illinois College and Knox
College. When the Congregationalists lost, there was but one
thing to do: they founded Wheaton College. In Kentucky

[5] Louis C. Hatch: *The History of Bowdoin College* (Portland, 1927),
p. 19; James Albert Woodburn: *History of Indiana University: 1820-
1902* (Bloomington, 1940), pp. 111-24; Albea Godbold: *The Church
College of the Old South* (Durham, 1944), p. 67; Thomas Jefferson
Wertenbaker: *Princeton 1746-1896* (Princeton, 1946), p. 239; Walter
Havighurst: *The Miami Years 1809-1959* (New York, 1958), p. 59.

the Presbyterians surrendered Transylvania (which once had known the fresh breath of Unitarianism) to the Disciples, returned to the fray by founding Centre College, only to be outflanked by the Disciples who put another college into the breach.[6]

A new motive, and therefore a compelling new force, for denominational college activity appeared early in the century in the form of the foreign missionary movement, which received its earliest inspiration at Williams College. One summer day in 1806 five Williams undergraduates sought refuge from a thunderstorm under a haystack and there decided to dedicate their lives to winning the heathen for Christ. For two years they held informal meetings, finally taking the name of "Society of Brethren." Enough of them moved on to the Andover Theological Seminary to justify taking the society with them. By 1810 they were influential in creating the American Board of Commissioners for Foreign Missions, the mission agency of the Congregational churches.[7]

The need for missionaries created a new need for colleges. The developing Baptist interest in higher education derived in part from the new enthusiasm for foreign missions. Luther Rice, a Williams graduate of the Class of 1807, was converted to the Baptist persuasion while en route to India on a mission of conversion for the Congregationalists. On returning to the United States in 1813, he stimulated sufficient missionary enthusiasm in a number of trips through the South that five colleges grew up in the wake of his travels, one of them the present-day George Washington University in Washington.[8] In the colleges, interest in foreign missions

[6] Thomas N. Hoover: *The History of Ohio University* (Athens, 1954), pp. 101 ff.; Donald G. Tewksbury: *The Founding of American Colleges and Universities Before the Civil War* (New York, 1932), pp. 76-7. For early Transylvania see N. H. Sonne: *Liberal Kentucky, 1780-1828* (New York, 1939), pp. 46-77.
[7] Clarence P. Shedd: *Two Centuries of Student Christian Movements: Their Origin and Intercollegiate Life* (New York, 1934), pp. 48-60.
[8] Godbold: *The Church College of the Old South*, pp. 18-19.

was sustained by a chain of student organizations, of which
the parent was the "Society of Inquiry on the Subject of
Missions," founded by the Brethren at Andover in 1811. By
mid-century, especially in the Presbyterian, Congregational,
and Baptist colleges, approximately one hundred student missionary societies were in operation, imparting new strength
to the religious life of the American college.[9]

The outstanding example of an institution which owed little
to the spirit of denominationalism and sectarian controversy
was Harvard, which fell away from orthodox Calvinism very
early in the century, with the election of a Unitarian to the
Hollis Professorship of Divinity in 1805 and with the election of a Unitarian to the presidency of the college the next
year. These elections made orthodox Calvinists the enemies
of Harvard; they led to the founding of the Andover Theological Seminary as a bastion of orthodoxy; and they helped
to create at Harvard an environment congenial to science, to
learning, and to religion—if not to sectarian wrangling. The
Calvinist attacks on Harvard during these years were effective enough to reduce enrollment and income for a time. In
1843 the Democrats won in the state elections and unleashed
a violent attack on Harvard for being a hotbed of infidelity.
President Quincy was not to be intimidated. He fought back,
pointing out that the Calvinists already had Yale, Williams,
Amherst, Bowdoin, Dartmouth, Middlebury, the University of Vermont, and Andover Theological Seminary. In the
era of the colleges, however, denominational appetite was
strong, and it must have been particularly annoying to watch
Harvard moving into a virtual intellectual awakening *without* benefit of the great moving force behind all but a handful of American institutions of higher learning.[1]

·   ·   ·

[9] Shedd: *Two Centuries of Student Christian Movements*, pp. 61-102.
[1] Morison: Harvard: *Three Centuries*, pp. 187-91, 220-1, 258-9.

The colleges, whatever the intensity of their denominationalism or the sincerityof their nonsectarianism, developed suitable agencies of religious life, relationships and organizations
and customs, that would help to define the American college
in this era as a religiously oriented institution. Some colleges
strengthened and formalized denominational ties. All adhered to some form of compulsory religious services and encouraged the formation of undergraduate religious societies.
Many subscribed to the evangelical annual season of prayer
for the colleges, and most relied heavily on those quickenings
of spirit and religious enthusiasm known as revivals. In
combination with the clerical background of the faculty and
the religious leadership of the college president, these agencies of religious life helped to make certain that no one
would confuse the American college with Harvard during
the first half century or so after 1800.

In Maine denominational warfare was so rife that Bowdoin
in 1841 decided to certify itself as a Congregational college
in order to make a more effective appeal for funds to the
Congregationalists of the state. With the help of the certificate, one professor collected $70,000 in subscriptions. In Penn-
sylvania, the trustees of Lafayette College decided to turn
the institution over to the control of the Presbyterians of
Philadelphia in exchange for an annual appropriation of
$1,000. Later in the century Cyrus McCormick said that he
would be glad to give $7,000 to little Tusculum College in
Tennessee if Tusculum would assure him that its president,
two professors, and two thirds of its board of trustees were
Presbyterians. For Tusculum such an agreement was worth
$7,000.[*]

Most institutions, however, tried to maintain an aura of

[*]Hatch: *Bowdoin*, p. 112; David Bishop Skillman: *The Biography
of a College: Being the History of the First Century of the Life of
Lafayette College* (Easton, 1932), I, 192, 206-7; Allen E. Ragan: *A History of Tusculum College, 1794-1944* (Bristol, 1945), p. 87.

nonsectarianism which firm denominational ties would not permit. The colleges could not really afford to make themselves any more unattractive than they frequently were, and for most Americans there was something unattractive about the bickering controversies which denominations sometimes got themselves into, much to the damage of their own reputation and to the good name of religion itself. The strengthening of denominational ties, therefore, did perhaps least to encourage religion in the life of the colleges.

Probably as unsuccessful was the much-maligned regimen of compulsory prayers and church services. At one time compulsory morning and evening prayers and Sunday church services were fundamental to the American collegiate experience, and of all the early characteristics of American higher education they have in many places been the most enduring. They were, however, more a symbol of collegiate respectability, more a certificate of religious purpose, than a real or effective instrument of religious conviction.

In many colleges, late into the century, a student's compulsory religious exercises equaled his literary exercises, and in the little would-be colleges in the woods, those academy-level, earnestly sectarian institutions whose reputations remained purely local, the tradition would last even longer. Whatever the degree of compulsion, however, the devout never thought of looking at the blinking, dreary faces of the young men and young women at morning prayers to discover whether there had been any new religious experiences on campus. Morning and evening prayers were a routine— for most students, a routine nuisance, and everywhere they made clear their views.

At Illinois College in 1842 Thomas Beecher of the junior class, who happened to be the brother of the president of the college, was suspended for "repeated disorders tending to disturb the worship of God in chapel." At the University of Georgia in 1857 a student showed his disgust by dancing in the chapel aisle during prayers. At Williams in the 1850's and 1860's (a time when its reputation for religious soundness was strong), the hours of compulsory prayer were characterized by deliberate absenteeism, indifference, disrespect; by ogling female visitors, the writing of obscene doggerel on the flyleaves of hymnals, by expectorating in the chapel aisle.[3]

The gradual abandonment of compulsion during the second half of the nineteenth century was clearly a response to the widespread recognition during the first half of the century that compulsion did not work. In search of an explanation, one college professor noticed the impatience which Americans showed for all kinds of religious forms and their preference for spontaneous religious experience.[4] How could they, therefore, sincerely subscribe to compulsory religion?

A friend of prayer suggested a number of remedies in the 1850's and most of his suggestions were incorporated in the religious life of one college or another: the singing of hymns and the use of responsive readings, so that the students would have something to do; brevity, carpets, and choirs; a less unseasonable time for morning prayers, removing from them the stigma of being an alarm clock or bugle; the elimination of evening prayers, in recognition of the discovery of outdoor sports and the development of collegiate athletics; perhaps even the attendance at chapel by members of the faculty.[5] In the 1850's evening prayers began to give way and morning prayers were moved to more seasonable hours.[6] In the 1870's at the private denominational

[3] Charles Henry Rammelkamp: *Illinois College: A Centennial History 1829-1929* (New Haven, 1928), p. 80; E. Merton Coulter: *College Life in the Old South* (Athens, 1951), pp. 82-3; Rudolph: *Williams,* p. 126.
[4] F. D. Huntington: "Public Prayers in Colleges," *American Journal of Education,* IV (1857), 23-36.
[5] Ibid.
[6] Morison: Harvard: *Three Centuries,* p. 296; William Lathrop Kingsley, ed.: *Yale College: A Sketch of its History* (New York, 1879), II, 506-7; Walter C. Bronson: *The History of Brown University 1764-*

colleges such as Yale, Brown, and Dartmouth, the second Sunday church service was abandoned.⁷ Most of the old institutions had given up evening prayers by 1890; a way out was found in the playing field, the spirit of which, it was argued, should not be asked to mingle with the spirit of the chapel. And here and there voluntary chapel services were instituted—at the new Johns Hopkins in 1876, at Chicago and Stanford in the 1890's, and increasingly in the state universities.⁸ Wisconsin abolished compulsory chapel in 1868, Harvard put all religious exercises on a voluntary basis in 1886, as did Columbia five years later.⁹

The really effective agency of religion in the life of the colleges was the revival, that almost unexplainable combination of confession, profession, joy, and tears which brought many young college men into the church and into the ministry. Most college presidents and college faculties of this era felt that they—or God—had failed a collegiate genera-

1914 (Providence, 1914), p. 231; Arthur G. Beach: *A Pioneer College: The Story of Marietta* (Marietta, 1935), p. 187; Carl F. Price: *Wesleyan's First Century* (Middletown, 1932), p. 113.

⁷ Kingsley: *Yale*, II, 506-7; Bronson: *Brown*, p. 414; Leon Burr Richardson: *History of Dartmouth College* (Hanover, 1932), II, 637.

⁸ John C. French: *A History of the University Founded by Johns Hopkins* (Baltimore, 1946), p. 324; Thomas Wakefield Goodspeed: *A History of the University of Chicago Founded by John D. Rockefeller: The First Quarter Century* (Chicago, 1916), pp. 194, 449-50; Orrin Leslie Elliott: *Stanford University: The First Twenty-Five Years* (Stanford University, 1937), p. 106; Elizabeth M. Farrand: *History of the University of Michigan* (Ann Arbor, 1885), p. 280; Allan Nevins: *Illinois* (New York, 1917), p. 205.

⁹ Merle Curti and Vernon Carstensen: *The University of Wisconsin: A History, 1848-1925* (Madison, 1949), I, 409; Morison: *Harvard: Three Centuries*, pp. 366-7; Samuel Eliot Morison, ed.: *The Development of Harvard University since the Inauguration of President Eliot 1869-1929* (Cambridge, 1930), li-lviii; Richard Hofstadter and C. Dewitt Hardy: *The Development and Scope of Higher Education in the United States* (New York, 1952), p. 35. For Yale's later decision (1926) see George Wilson Pierson: *Yale: College and University 1871-1937* (New Haven, 1952-5), II, 84-103.

tion if once during its four years in college there did not occur a rousing revival.

Student interest was also directed toward religion by a network of religious societies, theological or devotional or missionary in orientation. The earliest theological society at Harvard set the pattern for those that would follow elsewhere. In the eighteenth century its meetings were often devoted to the consideration of such diverse theological questions as:

Whether the happiness of Heaven will be progressive.

Whether it be Fornication to lye with ones Sweetheart (after Contraction) before marriage.

Whether any Sin is Unpardonable.

Whether there be any Standard of Truth.

At Williams the nineteenth-century descendants of these Harvard theologians built their meetings around disputes on such matters as whether Episcopalians could be pious and whether Christians should take one another into courts of law.[1]

From 1797 to 1861 the Moral Society of Yale College required its members to live according to the Bible, to "suppress vice and promote the interests of morality," and to refrain from profanity, playing games for money or gain, playing cards, and consuming spirituous liquor. Meetings were given over to such interesting activities as the confessions and expulsion of erring members. In 1814 the society forced a group of gambling students to give up their pleasures on threat of being reported to the Yale authorities. If the code of the fine gentleman frowned on informers, it may be said in defense of the young moralists in New Haven that they were *Christian* gentlemen prepared to recognize depravity where they found it. The same may be said of their contemporaries at Dartmouth. In 1813 the Dartmouth The-

[1] Shedd: *Two Centuries of Student Christian Movements*, p. 13; Rudolph: *Williams*, p. 126.

ological Society dismissed a member, the record shows, for being "disguised with liquor," the expulsion being required, the record further states, "from an imperious sense of duty."[2]

The religious societies carried on an extensive intercollegiate correspondence. In 1815 the theologians at Bowdoin reported to their colleagues elsewhere: "We assure you this is a most wretched place." In this tradition, at Oberlin a few years later one young man who had written indiscreetly to a young woman student was treated to twenty-five lashes on the back by a band of his Christian fellow students.[3] And Brown reported to Yale, speaking of Harvard: "We have occasion to rejoice that the Lord Jesus has, even there, a remnant who worship him in spirit and in truth." As Americans gave up their belief in human depravity, however, the religious societies that had flourished during the first half of the nineteenth century disappeared; or, later in the century, they were absorbed by that more worldly and ebullient manifestation of religion in America, the Young Men's Christian Association.

Another agency of the religious life was the annual day of prayer for colleges, which may have originated at Yale in 1750 when a January day of prayer was set aside for college students. Known to the cynical, early in the next century, as "the Day of Whist for colleges," prayer day was usually in February when classes did not meet and when the attention of the young men was deliberately directed toward the salvation of their souls.[4] By 1815 the day of prayer was a

[2] Shedd: *Two Centuries of Student Christian Movements*, pp. 25-31, 40.
[3] Ibid., pp. 76-7; Robert Samuel Fletcher: *A History of Oberlin College from its Foundations through the Civil War* (Oberlin, 1943), I, 444-7.
[4] Cornelius Howard Patton and Walter Taylor Field: *Eight O'Clock Chapel: A Study of New England College Life* (Boston, 1927), pp. 211-212.

fixture at Yale, Williams, Brown, and Middlebury. It seems to have worked its way into the customs of a number of southern denominational colleges in the 1820's. It moved westward with the Presbyterian and Congregational colleges, and it received a new lease on life when it fell under the care of the Y.M.C.A. later in the century.[5]

The annual day of prayer for colleges was a moment fraught with expectation and drama for the already converted, for the religious leaders on the faculties, and for the exceptional young men of the theological societies. In 1840, on the eve of prayer day at Williams, a member of the faculty preached a sermon in which he melodramatically stopped midway and then broke out: "Where are the men to whom I am preaching? They are in yonder rooms; they are not here. But they will hear my sermon tonight." They heard, and by morning the college was in the throes of a revival.[6]

No college could sustain a revival every year. A revival might be sparked by the day of prayer, or by a dramatic and especially effective sermon, or by the tragic sudden death of a popular undergraduate. Whatever the inspiration, its manifestations would be much the same, whatever the decade, whatever the college. In the religion of experience, the fundamental individual response was the confession of sin and the profession of profound religious experience and conviction. One day a Princeton sophomore spoke up in chapel:

I do, O Lord, in hopes of thy assisting Grace, solemnly make an entire and perpetual surrender of all that I am

[5] Shedd: *Two Centuries of Student Christian Movements*, pp. 82, 164-5; Godbold: *The Church College of the Old South*, p. 70; Fletcher: *Oberlin*, I, 211-12, and II, 757 ff.; Price: *Wesleyan*, p. 79; Rammelkamp: *Illinois College*, p. 289; Frank P. Brackett: *Granite and Sagebrush: Reminiscences of the First Fifty Years of Pomona College* (Los Angeles, 1944), p. 74.
[6] Rudolph: *Williams*, p. 98.

and have unto thee. . . . To thy direction I resign myself and all that I have, trusting all future contingencies
in thy hands, and may thy will in all things, and not
mine, be done. Use me, O Lord, as an instrument of thy
service. I beseech thee, number me among thy people. . . .[7]

At Dickinson in 1823 a young student was carried off by a
typhus epidemic. At his simple funeral, as the Dickinson students lifted the casket, the boy's father cried out: "Young
men, tread lightly, ye bear a temple of the Holy Ghost."
And he turned to a clergyman friend, imploring, "Dear Mac,
say something which God may bless to his friends." The
clergyman responded and a revival was on the way.[8]

At Marietta in Ohio in 1834 a revival was inspired by a
student's fervent objections to the reading of the infidel
works of Virgil and Caesar in the classroom. At Denison in
1840 a student reported:

We had gone to chapel simply because it was duty, when
in the dull routine, "Little Kerr" . . . , who was sitting
back by the chimney, rose and asked us to pray for
him! . . . In a little while seven or eight of as wild boys
as were in the college, broke down, and sobbing, begged
us to pray for them . . . [For several days this season of
religion continued, and then one night] Albert Baldwin
struck up in his beautiful tenor voice, "Go to Dark
Gethsemane," and that was too much. The student at
my right side fell helpless to his seat before we got
through the first verse, the one on my left hand held on
till we were in the second verse, then he, too, gave it
up, and went down. . . .[9]

[7] Quoted in Andrew Van Vranken Raymond, ed.: *Union University:
Its History, Influence, Characteristics and Equipment* (New York,
1907), I, 74.
[8] James Henry Morgan: *Dickinson College: The History of One
Hundred and Fifty Years 1783-1933* (Carlisle, 1933), p. 213.
[9] Beach: *Marietta,* p. 106; G. Wallace Chessman: *Denison: The Story
of an Ohio College* (Granville, 1957), pp. 81-2.

In March 1840, public confession of guilt and sinfulness
was so great at Williams that Mark Hopkins wrote to his
mother that "we have the greatest reason to bless God that
he has visited a place so dreadfully wicked. . . . Young men
of irreproachable character and high standing in the community came out with disclosures that no one could have
expected." In 1848 James T. Ford of the freshman class
underwent a profound experience and called upon the president of Williams in order to tell him about it.

> He said [Hopkins wrote to his mother] he had long
> been trying to make his heart better so that God could
> accept him, but all at once he saw that he could never
> succeed in that, but that if God could accept him in
> Christ just as he was, then indeed he should be saved,
> and God would have all the glory, and he thought he
> was able to go just as he was and cast himself upon
> the Savior, and he believed that he was accepted. Then
> he had peace.[1]

At Amherst in the 1850's a student told in his diary how
a classmate, moved by a revival, banished from his room all
the servants of sin—playing cards, a cane for hazing freshmen, the brandy bottle. "Instead of the curse," he wrote,
"from almost every room may now be heard the voice of
prayer." At Randolph-Macon in 1852 a student confided to
his diary: " Tonight I. H. Spud received the pardoning grace
of God and is now sitting by me with a countenance expressing peace and glory." In 1853 David Coit Scudder walked
into his Williams College room, "threw himself on the floor,
and began to weep and moan and roll about, seemingly in
great agony. It was that night," his roommate supposed,
"that the struggle was over." As with many other young
men, the struggle was not over, and the next year, in a letter to his family, young Scudder wrote: "Circumstances con-
spire to render me perfectly miserable; a very agreeable con-

[1] Rudolph: *Williams,* pp. 99-100.

dition, I assure you. . . . Today I have almost wished to die."[2]

Revivalism spent itself in such ways wherever it appeared, and it was a regular visitor at most American colleges before the Civil War. Of few colleges could it be said, as has been said of Harvard, that it was "a college where hot-gospelling was poor form, hell was not mentioned, and venerable preachers treated the students not as the limbs of Satan, but as younger brothers of their Lord and Saviour."[3]

The last great revival year was 1858—a time of economic depression and of deep uncertainty as to where the slavery controversy was leading, a year when revivalism found inspiration in the unsteadiness of the American economy and the spectre of Romanism with which immigrant followers of the Pope were filling the land. Revivals occurred in 1858 at Williams, Wofford, Amherst, the University of North Carolina, Wake Forest, Trinity, Wabash, the University of Georgia, and Emory. Unquestionably the revivalism of that year, which had Wall Street bankers slipping into churches at noon, touched dozens of other colleges as well.[4]

Before the Civil War most of the evangelical denominations were successful in creating an atmosphere conducive to revivalism and to the professions of faith, seasons of ex-

[2] Thomas Le Duc: *Piety and Intellect at Amherst College 1865-1912* (New York, 1946), p. 33; Godbold, *The Church College of the Old South*, p. 131; Rudolph: *Williams*, p. 100.
[3] Morison: Harvard: *Three Centuries*, pp. 244-5.
[4] Rudolph: *Williams*, p. 124; David Duncan Wallace: *History of Wofford College* (Nashville, 1951), pp. 61-2; George R. Cutting: *Student Life at Amherst College* (Amherst, 1871), p. 200; Kemp Plummer Battle: *History of the University of North Carolina* (Raleigh, 1907-12), I, 691; Godbold: *The Church College of the Old South*, p. 142; Nora Campbell Chaffin: *Trinity College, 1839-1892: The Beginnings of Duke University* (Durham, 1950), p. 204; James I. Osborne and Theodore G. Gronert: *Wabash College; the first hundred years, 1832-1932* (Crawfordsville, 1932), p. 80; Coulter: *Georgia*, pp. 162-5; Henry Morton Bullock: *A History of Emory University* (Nashville, 1936), p. 98.

emplary student conduct, and ministerial recruitment for which they had been working. Between 1823 and 1870 at Amherst there was a revival at least every four years. A similar victory was achieved elsewhere. But evangelical religion—with its emphasis on a great outpouring of spirit, of individual professions of experience, with its goal of total victory always waiting to be achieved—would never have as good a year again as it had in 1858.

From some points of view, perhaps it never had a good year. It talked about a better world to come to a people who found the world as it was remarkably generous and bountiful. In the end, evangelical religion had remarkably little to say to nineteenth-century America. It was perhaps inevitable that it would run dry finally and that one day in 1914 Billy Sunday would stand up before a collegiate audience and bring a revival to conclusion with the words: "Oh, Jesus isn't this a fine bunch? Did you ever look down on a finer crowd?" [5] The crowd was at the University of Pennsylvania, and the questions were addressed to divine authority. Whatever the correct answers may have been, the questions themselves suggested what had happened to evangelicalism and to revivalism in America. No revivalist in the era of the colleges would have indulged in such blatant optimism, such flattery, such certainty as to the essential goodness of a collegiate audience. Anyone who knew the wellsprings of evangelicalism, anyone who knew what stirred the colleges with tears and joy, with confession and profession, during the first half of the nineteenth century, knew that in the old days the questions would have been: "Oh, Lord, isn't this a depraved gathering? Did you ever look down on a more miserable crowd?" Yet, of course, the old questions did not carry the day.

Nineteenth-century America was too full of excitement,

[5] John E. Kirkpatrick: *Academic Organization and Control* (Yellow Springs, 1931), p. 106.

too full of the yet untransacted for otherworldliness to dig its roots deeply. Nineteenth-century America was no place to ask young men and women to reject the delights of this world. The most dramatic evidence existed in the biography of almost every young college student. Here he was—in college, as his father had not been; preparing to assume a position of leadership in society, as his brother back on the farm would not. Here he was—acquainted with the great humanist tradition, watching it find new outlets in a country that would prove an example to the world, not yet in books, but now in actions—here he was about to justify man's faith in man. Who could talk to him about eternal damnation? About depravity? About the sins of his fellow men? Gathered with his classmates, he would not have been able to avoid the most unorthodox thought of all. He might even have expressed it in these words: "Oh, Jesus isn't this a fine bunch? Did you ever look down on a finer crowd?"

5

The Collegiate Way

William Tecumseh Sherman, who would be remembered for marching through Georgia, began his career in the South as president of a military college that became Louisiana State University. Reporting on the opening of the institution in 1860 he remarked: "The dullest boys have the most affectionate mothers and the most vicious boys here come recommended with all the virtues of saints. . . . Of course I promised to be a father to them all." A Princeton alumnus, searching in 1914 for some way to define the Princeton spirit, decided that he could best convey his meaning by describing Princeton as a place "where each man . . . may enter dozens of rooms whose doors are never locked nor their tobacco jars empty." In despair, the personnel counselors of a large urban university reported to their administrative superiors in 1938:

> Our students are markedly lacking in social skills, the ability to meet people and to get along with them. They frequently feel ill at ease in a social group and cannot engage in conversation in other than argumentative fashion.
>
> Our students are constantly being frustrated by financial difficulties, by their immaturity, by their social awk-

wardness and by their lack of practical and social experience. . . .

All these remarks have in common one of the oldest traditions of the American college, a tradition so fundamental, so all-encompassing, that to call it merely a tradition is to undervalue it. For what is involved here is nothing less than a way of life, the collegiate way.[1]

The collegiate way is the notion that a curriculum, a library, a faculty, and students are not enough to make a college. It is an adherence to the residential scheme of things. It is respectful of quiet rural settings, dependent on dormitories, committed to dining halls, permeated by paternalism. It is what every American college has had or consciously rejected or lost or sought to recapture. It is William Tecumseh Sherman promising to be a father to an entire student body; it is comfort and full tobacco jars in a Princeton dormitory; in an urban university it is counselors helping the socially inept to overcome their weaknesses.

Imported with so much of everything else from England, the collegiate way in America was from the beginning the effort to follow in the New World the pattern of life which had developed at the English colleges. Had the first American colleges been the work of Scotchmen or of continental Europeans, perhaps a curriculum, a library, faculty, and students would have been enough. But, then, Americans would have had to wait longer for their colleges. For the development of the English pattern in the New World was not simply a conscious effort to adapt the collegiate system to American circumstances. It was at first the only solution to the absence of large concentrations of population. Not to have the collegiate way would have required cities—cities that could offer up sufficient numbers of students and that could find rooms in their attics and in their basements for students attracted to the

[1] Walter L. Fleming: *Louisiana State University 1860-1896* (Baton Rouge, 1936), p. 47; Varnum Lansing Collins: *Princeton* (New York, 1914), p. 368; S. Willis Rudy: *The College of the City of New York: A History, 1847-1947* (New York, 1949), p. 398.

college from the surrounding countryside. In the absence of
cities and knowing the English pattern, the founders of Harvard and other colonial colleges naturally subscribed to the
collegiate way. By the time that the colleges in Philadelphia
and New York were under way, the collegiate pattern was
not a necessity, for there were cities. But by then what had
been a necessity had become a tradition, and from then on
the founders of American colleges either adhered to the tradition or clumsily sought a new rationale.

For the adherents of that tradition, the college was "a large
family, sleeping, eating, studying, and worshiping together
under one roof." The claims made for it were often extrav-
agant, but they became so much of the language of the colleges that in time it was difficult to separate the real thing
from the myth which collegians and college officials created
out of the collegiate way. Who would challenge President
Eliot in 1869 when he would claim: "In spite of the familiar
picture of the moral dangers which environ the student,
there is no place so safe as a good college during the critical
passage from boyhood to manhood"? Who could deny that
association with one's peers in the close communal life of the
college gave to students a new standard of self-measurement,
one which eased the liberation from home and facilitated the
assumption of manhood? Surely the kindly paternalism, the
rationale of discipline and guidance, was what made a college.
As President Smith of Dartmouth wrote to President McCosh
of Princeton in 1873, he even had proof:

Earnest young men crave real guidance [he wrote].
They welcome, too, a proper system of compulsion and
restraint. One of our students was led a year or two since
by a certain blare of trumpets to exchange Dartmouth
for Cornell. After a time he returned to us. "What has
brought you back?" I said, as he applied for readmis-

sion. "Oh," said he, "I would rather be where there is more discipline." [2]

Adherents of the collegiate way became ecstatic over the beneficial influence which classmates exerted on one another, over the superiority of the college community as an agency of education over mere studies. They pointed with satisfaction to the extracurriculum, to the whole range of social life and development, to the benefits of religious influence and orientation. Until, finally, what had been a rationale for a seventeenth-century English college became in the nineteenth-century American college a prop for low academic standards and a rationale for a de-emphasis on intellectual values. After all, a college could not be everything.

President Noah Porter of Yale, which had always conceived of itself as peculiarly responsible for the health and perpetuation of the collegiate tradition, stated the case in 1870:

> The effects [of the collegiate way] are so powerful and salutary that it may well be questioned whether the education which they impart does not of itself more than repay the time and money which it costs, even to those idlers at college who derive from their residence little or nothing more than these accidental or incidental advantages. . . . Such idlers sometimes awake to manliness and to duty when they leave college. . . . To many who persistently neglect the college studies, the college life is anything rather than a total loss. Even those who sink downward with no recovery, find their descent retarded.

He was joined a few years later by Alice Freeman Palmer of Wellesley who announced what many already knew:

[2] Walter C. Bronson: *The History of Brown University 1764-1914* (Providence, 1914), p. 111; *Addresses at the Inauguration of Charles William Eliot as President of Harvard College, Tuesday, October 19, 1869* (Cambridge, 1869), p. 44; Leon Burr Richardson: *History of Dartmouth College* (Hanover, 1932), II, 546.

"Merely for good times, for romance, for society, college life offers unequaled opportunities." [3]

The collegiate way did have its critics, both general and specific. When Benjamin Rush was preparing his plans for Dickinson College he rejected dormitories as being a bit of "monkish ignorance" and proposed that students live with local families. President Philip Lindsley at the University of Nashville in 1848 had the wisdom to affirm: "This is certain: that parents need never look to a college for any miraculous moral regeneration or transformation of character." Francis Wayland, the imaginative and influential president of Brown, pointed out that the American friends of the English pattern had not even carried out their intentions with proper care. For in the English colleges instructors usually ate with their students and the collegiate architecture provided complete quadrangles with single exits, which could be effectively guarded by a porter.[4] Neither of these safeguards of the collegiate way made much headway in the American college. An enclosed quadrangle was more of a building than most colleges either needed or could afford. A successful commons or dining room, let alone one at which faculty could or would eat, was something that no college achieved in the nineteenth century.

Wayland, who was anxious that Americans develop institutions that would serve American purposes, rejected the Oxford-Cambridge tradition as being "utterly unsuited," inasmuch as it had been intended for "the education of the medieval clergy, and modified by the pressure of an all-powerful

[3] Noah Porter: *The American Colleges and the American Public* (New Haven, 1870), pp. 177-8; Waitman Barbe: *Going to College. With the Opinions of Fifty Leading College Presidents and Educators* (Cincinnati, 1899), p. 51.

[4] James Henry Morgan: *Dickinson College: The History of One Hundred and Fifty Years 1783-1933* (Carlisle, 1933), p. 11; LeRoy J. Halsey, ed.: *The Works of Philip Lindsley, D.D.* (Philadelphia, 1866), I, 567-8; Francis Wayland: *Thoughts on the Present Collegiate System in the United States* (Boston, 1842), pp. 28-31.

aristocracy." President Frederick A. P. Barnard of Columbia
echoed Wayland's sentiments in an 1870 pamphlet in which
he insisted that "there is no situation in the world in which an
individual is more completely removed from all effectual
[re]straint, whether the restraint of direct authority or that
of public opinion, than within the walls of an American college." [5] If Barnard was right, there were critics who were sure
that the collegiate way did cultivate another kind of restraint
which was less than healthy. Said one French observer of the
American scene, echoing the sentiments of generations of
visitors: "The American student is not left to himself enough.
Instead of being encouraged to reflect, he is constantly
guided." [6]

Even so, the collegiate way had its attractions, its charm.
George Santayana, the Harvard philosopher, was forced to
report on returning to Cambridge from a visit to New Haven
in 1892: "[The students] are like passengers in a ship or fellow countrymen abroad; their sense of common interests and
common emotions overwhelms all latent antipathies. They
live in a sort of primitive brotherhood, with a ready enthusiasm for every good or bad project, and a contagious good-
humor." [7]

The first requirement for the full development of the collegiate way was a proper setting. Paris, Bologna, Prague, Vienna, Padua, Cologne—the great medieval universities were
urban, but the founding of the English universities in the
country shaped the American predilection for country col-

[5] Francis Wayland: *The Education Demanded by the People of the U. States* (Boston, 1855), p. 28; Frederick A. P. Barnard: *Analysis of Some Statistics of Collegiate Education* (New York, 1870), p. 28. Wayland's struggles with the collegiate way at Brown are the subject of Theodore R. Crane: "Francis Wayland and the Residential College," *Rhode Island History*, XIX (1960), 65-78, 118-28.

[6] W. J. Osborn: *Foreign Criticism of American Education* (Washington, 1922), p. 136.

[7] George Wilson Pierson: *Yale: College and University 1871-1937* (New Haven, 1952-5), I, 7.

leges. An argument of 1770 against locating the College of Rhode Island in Providence, which then had four hundred houses, was the insistence that "a Considerable Degree of Retirement is very Requisite in Order to acquire any Great Proficiency in literary Pursuits." The founders of the college were ready to take the chance with Providence, although it may be claimed that at the time they were not taking a terribly large one. When eight Maine towns were contending for the location of Bowdoin, North Yarmouth argued in its own behalf that it was "not so much exposed to many Temptations to Dissipation, Extravagance, Vanity and Various Vices as great seaport towns frequently are." [8]

The antipathy to towns as college sites was so strong in North Carolina that the charter for the University of North Carolina in 1789 provided that it could not be located within five miles of any seat of government or any place where law or equity courts met. In Georgia the trustees succeeded in getting as deep into the woods and as far away from civilization as possible; in 1801 they selected a hilltop in northwest Georgia, acquired a tract of forest, and called it Athens. Oglethorpe College, also in Georgia, was placed at Midway, two miles from the contaminating influences of the village of Milledgeville. The 1835 act chartering Oglethorpe forbade the establishment and operation of any shop for selling anything within a mile and a half of the college. The catalogue of Tusculum College, Tennessee, carried the reassuring notice in 1847 that "Its distance from Greeneville and Rheatown is such as gives it all the advantages of a location in a town, and also guards it from all the ensnarling and demoralizing influence of a town. . . ." [9] At Williams College, Mark Hopkins told an audience in 1836 that "fine scenery" was an important

[8] Bronson: Brown, pp. 47, 50; Louis C. Hatch: The History of Bowdoin College (Portland, 1927), p. 2.

[9] Kemp Plummer Battle: History of the University of North Carolina (Raleigh, 1907-12), I, 7; E. Merton Coulter: College Life in the Old South (Athens, 1951), p. 7; Allen P. Tankersley: College Life at Old Oglethorpe (Athens, 1951), p. 6; Allen E. Ragan: A History of Tusculum College, 1794-1944 (Bristol, 1945), p. 49.

agency in the formation of character. Forty years later a popular guide to American colleges would agree: "If Yale were located at Williamstown, Harvard at Hanover, Columbia at Ithaca, the moral character of their students would be elevated in as great a degree as the natural scenery of their localities would be increased in beauty." Henry Ward Beecher was to say of the scenery of Amherst that it was a liberal education merely to be in its presence for four years.[1]

Institutions which by design or accident were located in cities did not always lament their fate. The city institution had its warm friends. William and Mary was not planted in the country. It was put at the other end of the street from the capitol building of a bustling colonial center of trade and government. As one historian has remarked, "The early Virginians had no idea that professors and students should be turned out to pasture like superannuated horses and untrained colts, and expected to feed on grass like Nebuchadnezzar." [2]

A number of American colleges chose to follow the William and Mary precedent, while not necessarily surrendering other agencies of the collegiate way such as dormitories and professors solicitous for student welfare. Friends of the college which became New York University stated their case in 1830: "Seclusion may be the nurse of poetry and the parent of romance, but not so of literature and true philosophy." In the same tradition, Frederick Barnard argued in 1855: "If study were a pursuit to be prosecuted in the open streets, the argument [for the country college] might have . . . weight. . . ." By 1865 the argument was being advanced for San Francisco as a college site that "country towns are less

[1] Frederick Rudolph: *Mark Hopkins and the Log: Williams College, 1836-1872* (New Haven, 1956), p. 17; Charles F. Thwing: *American Colleges: Their Students and Work* (New York, 1878), p. 48; Cornelius Howard Patton and Walter Taylor Field: *Eight O'Clock Chapel: A Study of New England College Life* (Boston, 1927), p. 26.
[2] Herbert Baxter Adams: *The College of William and Mary* (Washington, 1887), p. 23.

religious . . . and are steeped in a coarser, baser depravity." While admitting that a disadvantage of the city was the possibility that "the young men will sometimes get their ship launched before the keel is laid," spokesmen for the College of the Pacific contended that the disadvantages of a country college were even greater: "There is a certain vulgarity . . . in provincial vices, which makes them more brutalizing." [3]

Looking back on his undergraduate days at Dartmouth and his graduate days at Yale, the president of Trinity College in North Carolina agreed. He remarked in 1889 that there were "three times as much licentiousness and hypocrisy" in Hanover as in New Haven, and with that conviction he helped to move Trinity from a village to Durham and from poverty to affluence and a new name under the aegis of Washington Duke. [4]

As the nineteenth century wore on, as the United States became more urbanized, spokesmen for city colleges became bolder and they swelled almost to a chorus. One busy new agency of college-founding, the Roman Catholic Church, needed no prodding to follow the counsel of St. Ignatius to place colleges in the cities. For that was where great concentrations of the faithful were expressing a need for higher learning. The Catholic Church responded to that desire with a legion of new colleges. [5]

In the shadows of the oldest American college, Henry Wadsworth Longfellow asked, "Where should the scholar live? In solitude, or in society, in the green stillness of the country, where he can hear the heart of Nature beat, or in the dark gray town, where he can hear and feel the throbbing

[3] Theodore F. Jones, ed.: *New York University 1832:1932* (New York, 1933), p. 13; Frederick A. P. Barnard: *Letters on College Government, and the Evils Inseparable From the American College System in its Present Form* (New York, 1855), p. 99; William Warren Ferrier: *Origin and Development of the University of California* (Berkeley, 1930), pp. 163-5.

[4] Nora Campbell Chaffin: *Trinity College, 1839-1892: The Beginnings of Duke University* (Durham, 1950), p. 482.

[5] David R. Dunigan: *A History of Boston College* (Milwaukee, 1947), p. viii.

heart of man?" And from Brattle Street in Cambridge he replied, "I make answer for him, and say, in the dark gray
town." [6] Charles Francis Adams, Jr., looking out on the remains of Harvard's long-lost remoteness, accepted the loss
and asked in 1906, "If the young man is to live in the city, is
it quite wise to bring him up in the country's sweet seclusion?" [7] The state legislature of Nevada had found an answer
to that question by placing its university among the gambling
dens and sporting palaces of Reno.

But everywhere there lingered the belief that life was
sounder, more moral, more character-building where the college was nestled among the hills or planted on the prairie.
Supporting this belief was the attachment of the American
people to an agrarian myth, to a view of the world that saw
the land as the source of virtue and as the great moving force
in history. Elevated by Thomas Jefferson to the level of
fundamental American democratic political theory, the agrarian myth would take many forms. One historian of American
culture has described the Homestead Act of 1862 as the
agrarian myth at work in politics, the frontier hypothesis of
Frederick Jackson Turner as the agrarian myth in American
historiography, and the nineteenth-century notion that rain
followed the plow as the same myth applied to meteorology.[8]
The country-college tradition—either in the country colleges
themselves or in the romantic efforts to simulate the country
colleges in the city—reinforced the agrarian myth. It became
one more instrument with which a modern, urbanized, industrial people helped to convince themselves that their farm
problem was bigger than their urban problem, their highway
problem more important than their railroad problem. The
country-college tradition, feeding on a longing for what used

---

[6] Quoted in Frederick Paul Keppel: *Columbia* (New York, 1914),
p. ix.
[7] Charles Francis Adams: *Three Phi Beta Kappa Addresses* (Boston,
1907), p. 112.
[8] Henry Nash Smith: *Virgin Land* (Cambridge, 1950).

to be, has both enabled and required college administrators to expend their energies and resources on matters of living rather than on matters of learning. But whatever else it has done, the country-college tradition has testified to the tremendous strength, the remarkable persistence, of the collegiate way in the history of American higher education.

The first requirement of the country college was the dormitory. It was one instrument often employed by the urban college as well, and it was the one agency which a one-time country college would hold onto long after it had been engulfed by the city. The often crude rooming arrangements, lacking in privacy or comfort, which these dormitories provided were the setting in which the collegiate way took form.

For the dormitory held young men to a common experience. It took them from the bosom of a sheltering home and placed them under the same roof, where they might share the experiences which made men of boys. The dormitory made possible—so the argument went—the supervision and parental concern of the faculty for the well-being of their young charges. The dormitory brought to bear the sense of common decency and the sense of self-respect which taught responsibility. In the dormitory young men talked deep into the night deeply about deep matters. A revival might be sparked in the dormitory, where under the influence of a wiser chum a young man might move from indifference to belief, from idleness to profound inspiration. So the argument went, and everywhere the dormitories went up—because it was the tradition, because students had to be housed, and finally because people actually believed the dormitory rationale.

They believed it regardless of what the evidence showed. For the dormitory also brought into close proximity, under the harshest of conditions, young men on whose time the intellectual purposes of the colleges placed too few demands. It also became a place where tempers tightened until they snapped, where in quiet desperation plots were hatched, and where what may have begun in innocence often ended in tragedy and misfortune. The dormitory helped to create an atmosphere that invited frustration, argument, and crime. In the commons room of a dormitory at South Carolina College in 1833 two students at the same moment grabbed for a plate of trout: only one of them survived the duel that ensued. Among the victims of the collegiate way were the boy who died in a duel at Dickinson, the students who were shot at Miami in Ohio, the professor who was killed at the University of Virginia, the president of Oakland College in Mississippi who was stabbed to death by a student, the president and professor who were stoned at the University of Georgia, the student who was stabbed at Illinois College, the students who were stabbed and killed at the University of Missouri and the University of North Carolina.[9] For their misfortune these victims of college life could thank the dormitory, the sometime house of incarceration and infamy that sustained the collegiate way.

The dormitory concentrated into groups eager, active, healthy, young men who were as capable of being whipped into an explosive rebellion as into a religious revival. Not every college underwent a rebellion, and the rebellions were inspired by a variety of conditions. Generally, however, they took the form of a concerted strike of a majority of the undergraduates, protesting against some real or imagined wrong, threatening to withdraw from the college and to abandon it to the uncertainties of enrollment and finance that were bound to follow.

The colleges were usually successful in holding out against

[9] Daniel Walker Hollis: *University of South Carolina* (Columbia, 1951-6), I, 92-3; Morgan: *Dickinson*, p. 297; Walter Havighurst: *The Miami Years 1809-1959* (New York, 1958), p. 53; Philip Alexander Bruce: *History of the University of Virginia, 1819-1919* (New York, 1920-2), II, 302-11; W. Storrs Lee: *God Bless Our Queer Old Dean* (New York, 1959), p. 62; Charles Henry Rammelkamp: *Illinois College: A Centennial History 1829-1929* (New Haven, 1928), p. 81; Jonas Viles, *et al.*: *The University of Missouri: A Centennial History* (Columbia, 1939), pp. 76-8; Battle: *North Carolina*, I, 690-2.

the students, but every rebellion left a public impression that something was seriously amiss. President Ashbel Green remarked of one of Princeton's six rebellions between 1800 and 1830 that "the true causes of all these enormities are to be found nowhere else but in the fixed, irreconcilable and deadly hostility . . . to the whole system established in this college . . .[,] a system of diligent study, of guarded moral conduct and of reasonable attention to religious duty. . . ."[1] The collegiate way, President Green all but admitted, sometimes was too much for vigorous young men to bear.

Princeton was not alone. Between 1800 and 1875 students were in rebellion on at least one occasion at Miami University, Amherst, Brown, University of South Carolina, Williams, Georgetown, University of North Carolina, Harvard, Yale, Dartmouth, Lafayette, Bowdoin, City College of New York, Dickinson, and DePauw.[2] The rebellions documented the failure of the colleges to provide altogether suitable "rites of adolescence," satisfactory outlets for quite normal animal energy and human imagination. They also emphasized the difficulty, even the impossibility, of following aristocratic traditions in a dynamic democratic society. And for certain they proved that in the United States, at least, the dormitory was in a sense a tactical error. For the dormitory, by concentrat-

[1] Thomas Jefferson Wertenbaker: *Princeton 1746-1896* (Princeton, 1946), p. 169.

[2] Havighurst: *Miami*, pp. 93-6; George R. Cutting: *Student Life at Amherst College* (Amherst, 1871), pp. 95-6; Bronson: *Brown*, p. 153; Hollis: *South Carolina*, I, 62-3, 136-69, *passim;* Rudolph: *Williams*, pp. 217-21; Edward J. Power: *A History of Catholic Higher Education in the United States* (Milwaukee, 1958), p. 133; Battle: *North Carolina*, I, 201-15; Samuel Eliot Morison: *Three Centuries of Harvard 1636-1936* (Cambridge, 1936), p. 211; William Lathrop Kingsley, ed.: *Yale College: A Sketch of its History* (New York, 1879), I, 136-8; Richardson: *Dartmouth*, II, 489; David Bishop Skillman: *The Biography of a College: Being the History of the First Century of the Life of Lafayette College* (Easton, 1932), I, 344-6; Hatch: *Bowdoin*, pp. 132-48; Rudy: *C.C.N.Y.*, p. 106; Morgan: *Dickinson*, pp. 298-300; William Warren Sweet: *Indiana Asbury-DePauw University, 1837-1937: A Hundred Years of Higher Education in the Middle West* (New York, 1937), pp. 76-83.

ing students in barrackslike structures, actually facilitated rebellion.

Not everyone was unimpressed by the arguments against the dormitory as a way of life. In 1701 Cotton and Increase Mather firmly suggested to the founders of the Collegiate School in New Haven that they ought to avoid the expense and trouble of the collegiate way. The Mathers were listened to because the people of New Haven did not have enough money to do anything else, but when the money was available, a dormitory was erected. Manasseh Cutler, a good New Englander who helped to settle Ohio and to found the Ohio University as well, registered his opposition to a dormitory plan in 1800 and sounded very much as if he were in the Mather tradition: "Chambers in colleges are too often made the nurseries of every vice and cages of unclean birds." [3]

The two most outspoken critics of dormitories were Francis Wayland of Brown and Frederick Barnard of Columbia. In 1842 Wayland described dormitory life as unnatural. Indeed, in Wayland's estimation most of the evils of college life could be attributed to dormitories: the inappropriateness of the same rules and regulations for students of all ages, the spread of disease by epidemics, the tendency of students to exercise too little, the exposure of many young men to the vice and habits of evil leaders, the isolation of the college from the life of the community and of the world, the expenditure of money needed for libraries on living facilities, the imposition on the college of responsibilities it was unable and unprepared to carry out effectively. His sentiments were echoed by Barnard in 1855. During the 1850's at the University of Michigan they inspired the abandonment of dormitories under the leadership of Henry Tappan, who in other

[3] Edwin Oviatt: *The Beginnings of Yale (1701-1726)* (New Haven, 1916), pp. 306-8; Thomas N. Hoover: *The History of Ohio University* (Athens, 1954), pp. 15-16.

respects was unsuccessful in his attempts to transform Michigan from an English college into a German university.[4]

President Eliot unsuccessfully tried to kill off dormitories at Harvard; Yale never weakened. Yale influence, in the person of a graduate, William Rainey Harper, the first president of the University of Chicago, had instituted dormitories at Chicago, and the Chicago example tremendously encouraged a wave of dormitory construction at the large urban universities. Between 1896 and 1915 Columbia, the University of Minnesota, Cornell, the University of Illinois, and the University of Michigan for the first time subscribed fully to the dormitory rationale.[5]

The movement was irresistible. At Princeton Dean West created a residence hall for graduate students and thus established collegiate values on the graduate level. There was no way to meet the 1870 argument of the student newspaper at the University of Rochester except by building dormitories:

> It sems to us [said the paper] that the greatest need of our university is that of dormitories, since without them we can never enjoy a decent supply of that delightful article, vaguely called *college spirit*. . . . The absence of dormitories . . . deprives us of all those delightful associations and those lifelong friendships which add so much to the glory of college days, and which, after all, are the only things to which students love to revert in after years.[6]

Tradition and sentiment worked against the enemies of dormitories, but so did economics and social changes as well.

[4] Wayland: *Thoughts on the Present Collegiate System*, pp. 112-31; Barnard: *Letters on College Government*, pp. 72-84; Elizabeth M. Farrand: *History of the University of Michigan* (Ann Arbor, 1885), pp. 130, 143.

[5] W. H. Cowley: "European Influences upon American Higher Education," *Educational Record*, XX (1939), 186-8.

[6] Jesse Leonard Rosenberger: *Rochester, the Making of a University* (Rochester, 1927), pp. 188-9.

The "better people," the good families, on whom critics of dormitories such as Wayland and Barnard counted to provide housing, were no longer willing to do so. In a more affluent America they neither needed the money nor welcomed the stigma attached to earning it by caring for roomers and boarders. Sharp-minded real-estate men and investors were increasingly aware of the financial possibilities of catering to the housing and boarding needs of university students. In the university and college communities where facilities were inadequate, the institutions often found themselves unwillingly in the dormitory business.[7] Willing or unwilling, however, they had chalked up another victory for the collegiate way.

The experience of the colleges with that other related agency of the collegiate way—commons—was more unsuccessful than was their experience with dormitories. The decisions to worship scenery, to be residential, and to cherish isolation obligated the colleges to provide board for their students. In 1771 Eleazar Wheelock asked a Boston friend to secure "a skillful, faithful, prudent, virtuous and able-bodied cook" for Dartmouth.[8] Wheelock did not get one, and the history of college commons in the nineteenth century would suggest that perhaps no other college did either.

The steward at South Carolina College was outsmarted by his student patrons in 1811 when an old bull he had bought for slaughter was driven into the river and drowned. But most students, while quite able to anticipate the wormy salt pork or the breakfast slum made of yesterday's boiled beef and potatoes now hashed and fried, were unable to do very much about it. The best they might do perhaps was to accept their fate with the grace and good humor of Augustus Torrey, a young Harvard student, who recorded in his diary in 1822:

[7] See Viles: *Missouri*, p. 136, for the experience of one university.
[8] Richardson: *Dartmouth*, I, 108.

"Goose for dinner. Said to have migrated to this country with our ancestors." [9]

The rebellions inspired by commons filled the early nineteenth century colleges with bitterness and rancor, and they seldom had any lasting effect on the quality of food. President Cooper of South Carolina complained: "The College is in yearly jeopardy of being destroyed by the disputes about eating." [1] With the support of presidents and professors, the collegiate way carried out its paternal responsibilities. But the problem of providing a substitute for mother's home cooking proved in most cases to be insurmountable. Many colleges simply gave up, either surrendering their students to local eating houses or leasing the college dining hall to some courageous entrepreneur.

The college-commons movement, however, was not dead. It received a new lease on life in the decades after the Civil War, when higher costs and enrollment ambitions placed a new responsibility for board costs on the shoulders of the colleges. In the 1860's, for instance, Yale, Harvard, and Williams —all of which had in previous years given up dining halls —opened up college commons especially for poor students. [2] The intrusion of class and economic distinctions which were thereby emphasized may not have been in the best tradition of the collegiate way, but the new dining halls themselves surely were. Probably the most notable achievement of the college dining hall in the history of American higher education occurred at Lafayette College in 1847, where the assistant steward, Harrison Woodhull Crosby, faced with an excess of tomatoes, first experimented with hermetically sealed canning. [3]

[9] Hollis: South Carolina, I, 64-8, 90-1; Clarence P. Shedd: Two Centuries of Student Christian Movements: Their Origin and Intercollegiate Life (New York, 1934), p. 35.
[1] Quoted in Alfred J. Morrison, ed.: The College of Hampden-Sidney: Calendar of Board Minutes 1776-1876 (Richardson, 1912), p. 25n.
[2] Kingsley: Yale, I, 297-306; Pierson: Yale, I, 29; Morison: Harvard: Three Centuries, pp. 313, 332; Rudolph: Williams, p. 230.
[3] Skillman: Lafayette, I, 179-80.

·   ·   ·

The agency that perhaps best served the purposes of the collegiate way was paternalism, whether in the conscious ordering of the college regimen or in the informal relationships that grew up between faculty and student in the smaller colleges. Few institutions organized the paternal scheme to the degree that Union College did during the early days of Eliphalet Nott. President Nott pushed the collegiate way to an extreme, settling faculty families in the college dormitories. One result was a high level of student decorum, so high that for awhile Union was something of a showcase.[4]

In a letter to the parents of one of his charges President Nisbet of Dickinson in 1792 explained the function of collegiate paternalism:

> A Parent cannot but be anxious when his Child is at a Distance from him, & exposed to Dangers of different kinds, but as in Education a certain Risk must be run, in order to gain a certain Advantage, every good Parent, as well as every good Teacher ought to be satisfied when he is taking the best means for preserving the Morals of his Child, as well as for improving his Understanding. Your son is well, tho' some few of our students have been troubled with Colds and Sore Throats.

In this tradition, President Asa Messer of Brown wrote to one mother in 1812, "Though I have examined the case, I cannot find that Henry is addicted to gambling . . . ," and to a father, "I have requested your son not to contract any other debts without my knowledge; for I find that the value of Money has not yet engaged his attention." [5]

President Green of Princeton tried the custom of inviting eight undergraduates at a time to his home for dinner, but

---

[4] Andrew Van Vranken Raymond, ed.: *Union University: Its History, Influence, Characteristics and Equipment* (New York, 1907), I, 144-6.

[5] Morgan: *Dickinson*, p. 116; Bronson: *Brown*, pp. 197-9.

his conclusion was that the collegiate way could not really compete effectively with natural depravity. "I found that it had but little effect in reclaiming the vicious" was the verdict that he delivered on his dinner experiment. Paternalism *could* have a beneficial effect on the students, however. As one young man at Dartmouth revealed: "I like to hear Dr. Lord pray. . . . I like to hear him say: 'The Lord bless these young men, every one of them,' for then I feel safe for the day." One would only have had to see the student Sidney Lanier tramping in the woods about Oglethorpe in Georgia, playing his flute and conversing at length with Professor James Woodrow, to know that faculty-student relations could be one of the strongest agencies of collegiate life.*

The system of discipline used in many colleges, however, thoroughly failed to achieve either its purpose or the larger purposes it intended to serve. For while discipline was an aspect of paternalism, the strict, authoritarian, patriarchal family was making no headway in American life, and for the colleges to insist upon it was for them to fight the course of history. When unmarried professors and tutors lived in dormitories and functioned as spies, policemen, and judges, they may have helped in their way to sustain a rigid, minute, and often trivial code of laws, but they did not endear themselves as parents to the undergraduates.

Unquestionably there was exaggeration in the series of letters carried by a Portland newspaper in the 1820's accusing the Bowdoin College faculty of "driving fourteen-year-old boys almost insane with anxiety and fear," but the "moral depravity" school of discipline clearly was not succeeding anywhere. Eleazar Wheelock once said of one of his Indian students: "I have taken much Pains to purge all the Indian out of him, but after all a little of it will sometimes appear." In their discipline policies most of the early colleges

* Wertenbaker: *Princeton*, p. 155; Richardson: *Dartmouth*, II, 440-1; Tankersley: *Oglethorpe*, p. 44.

simply substituted "boy" for Indian. The problem for the colleges was bound to be a large one, regardless of the policy, particularly in the kind of society which the United States was developing. The problem was well stated by a professor at Davidson College in 1855:

> Indulged, petted, and uncontrolled at home, allowed to trample upon all laws, human and divine, at the preparatory school, . . . [the American student] comes to college, but too often with an undisciplined mind, and an uncultivated heart, yet with exalted ideas of personal dignity, and a scowling contempt for lawful authority, and wholesome restraint. How is he to be controlled? . . .

That indeed was the question: how was the student to be controlled? [7]

President Moses Waddel at Georgia would sweep the horizon of Athens with a spyglass in search of students leaving town contrary to college laws. President Bishop of Miami would pray in chapel with one eye open, the better to be prepared for any disciplinary emergency. President MacLean of Princeton was believed by the students to sleep with his clothes on, so that he might rush from his official residence, lantern in hand, at every instance or suspicion of trouble. President Lord at Dartmouth would take his place in the chapel, recite memorized chapters from the Bible, and from behind dark green glasses his eyes would roam throughout the room in search of misbehavior. [8]

In the South the problem was complicated by the fact that the strict New England code of college laws—which almost everywhere in the United States seems to have derived from the 1745 codification at Yale—in effect sought to repeal the southern way of life and to apply or threaten punishments

[7] Hatch: *Bowdoin*, p. 73; Richardson: *Dartmouth*, I, 31; Albea Godbold: *The Church College of the Old South* (Durham, 1944), p. 117.
[8] Coulter: *Georgia*, p. 86; George P. Schmidt: *The Old Time College President* (New York, 1930), p. 92; Wertenbaker: *Princeton*, p. 244; Richardson: *Dartmouth*, II, 472.

that southern students knew were reserved for slaves.[9] Everywhere the laws were difficult to administer, particularly since they amounted almost to a wholesale prohibition against the enjoyment of life.

There was a limit to how many times a faculty could meet on disciplinary problems—although the Dartmouth faculty did meet 68 times in 1832-3, and in 1851 at the University of North Carolina 282 cases of delinquency came before the faculty from a student body of 230. It was all very well for President George Junkin to take the view in his inaugural address at Miami in 1841 that "every good school is a monarchy," but this policy when undertaken did not work.[1]

In the absence of any organized approach to recreation and in an increasingly democratic society, the efforts of the strict disciplinarians to protect college students from all the innocent pleasures of life, as well as the less innocent, were doomed to failure. The result was frustration. President Thomas Cooper at South Carolina College wrestled unsuccessfully with his own Jeffersonianism and a Puritan code of college laws and concluded: "Republicanism is good: but the 'rights of boys and girls' are the offspring of Democracy gone mad." One of his professors, the immigrant political economist Francis Lieber, did not permit his distaste for discipline to keep him from being conscientious; yet frustration was his lot. On one occasion, in pursuit of a student with a stolen turkey, he stumbled and fell on a pile of bricks, got up, rubbed his shins, and was heard to exclaim, "Mein Gott!! All dis for two tousand dollars."[2]

A more relaxed view had been developing, however, and before the nineteenth century was half over, many of the leading institutions had abandoned the strict discipline and the extended code of laws which had characterized so many

---

[9] Hollis: *South Carolina*, I, 52-62; Coulter: *Georgia*, p. 65.
[1] Richardson: *Dartmouth*, II, 461; Battle: *North Carolina*, I, 627; Havighurst: *Miami*, p. 83.
[2] Hollis: *South Carolina*, I, 89, 189.

of the colleges. President Jared Sparks of Harvard summed up
the new mood when facing his faculty colleagues, he gave
vent to an exasperated, "Oh, gentlemen, let the boys alone!"
Clearly what was happening was a rejection of the Puritan
view of man, an unwillingness to accept depravity as a
natural condition, an unreadiness to make of a college
nothing but a reformatory or penal institution. Timothy
Dwight apparently led the way at Yale, where the extreme
code of 1745 was replaced during his administration late in
the century by what might be called the treat-them-like-
gentlemen school—or, more simply, treat them like men
instead of like minions of the devil.[3]

That such a development should have taken place in early
nineteenth-century America was not surprising, nor that it
became the policy of so many of the effective and beloved
college teachers and college presidents—James Marsh at Vermont, Eliphalet Nott at Union, Simeon North at Hamilton,
Francis Wayland at Brown, Mark Hopkins at Williams. All of
these men introduced the more democratic, permissive system of discipline. All of them withheld from the faculty as
much authority as possible in order to frustrate lingering
attachment to the old "depravity" school. And all were
remarkably more effective than their predecessors.[4]

The psychology of the new approach was effectively
stated by President Nott of Union in 1854:

> Little reliance has been placed on appeals to the principle
> of fear. Emulation has been appealed to. . . . Moral and
> religious instruction, the sense of honor, and the love
> of knowledge have been principally relied on; whilst
> the chief concern has been to teach the young men to

[3] Morison: Harvard: *Three Centuries*, p. 281; Kingsley: *Yale*, I, 119,
125-6.
[4] [James Marsh]: *Exposition of the System of Instruction and Discipline Pursued in the University of Vermont* (Burlington[?], 1829),
pp. 25-8; Raymond: *Union*, I, 157-65; Charles Elmer Allison: *A Historical Sketch of Hamilton College, Clinton, New York* (Yonkers,
1889), pp. 32-3; Bronson: *Brown*, p. 247; Rudolph: *Williams*, pp. 57-60.

bring themselves under the rule of inward principle rather than of outward fear and restraint.[5]

Student conscience was now being developed in an atmosphere of freedom rather than of authority. At one time convinced of the natural depravity of man, Americans had now come to believe in his inherent goodness.

The collegiate way helped to establish the philosophic and historical foundations for many of the nonintellectual purposes of the American college. The values that it cherished helped to restrain the intellectual (and therefore university) potential of many of the older foundations. Yale in particular would have difficulty launching itself as a university because of its attachment to the collegiate way. It often led to an excessive paternalism, a handholding, spoon-feeding that would prolong adolescence unnecessarily. The collegiate way lent itself to the idea that a college could be a reformatory, a school of moral regeneration. Its residential orientation would be responsible for the failure of American colleges to develop or encourage a tradition of transfer students or itinerant students. It would account for the fact that no American institution of higher learning can be an institution of learning alone.

But, at its best, the collegiate way justified the claims of President Porter of Yale, who was fond of saying:

Let any reflecting man think for a moment of . . . the trickery of business, the jobbing of politicians, the slang of newspapers, the vulgarity of fashion, the sensationalism of popular books, the shallowness and cant that dishonor pulpit and defile worship, and he may reasonably rejoice that there is one community which for a considerable period takes into its keeping many of the most susceptible and most promising of our youth, to impart to them better tastes, higher aims, and, above all, to

[5] Raymond: *Union*, I, 159.

teach them to despise all sorts of intellectual and moral shams.[6]

These claims the collegiate way at its best could honestly sustain.

[6] Noah Porter: *The American Colleges and the American Public,* p. 182.

6

❧❧❧

Reform and Reaction

What is an American college? War, declining enrollments, the sudden instability of whole areas of knowledge, dynamic social and economic changes—these and a multitude of other developments have often thrown the American college back upon itself and forced upon it a moment, perhaps even an era, of critical self-assessment and redefinition.

Fundamental to this phenomenon of changing definition has been the dynamic quality of American life. The likelihood was remote that the American college would enjoy stability while everything else experienced growth, flux, and ferment. The United States in the early decades of the nineteenth century was exchanging Republicans and Federalists for Democrats and Whigs. It was building canals where turnpikes had sufficed, and before long it would be giving up canals in favor of railroads. Everywhere the states were throwing away old constitutions, writing new ones more acceptable to the age. A country that was hurrying into the future required colleges that would hurry along with it. The American colleges would therefore experience the same challenge as political parties, state constitutions, and economic institutions. They would be asked to pass a test of utility. They would have to answer to the question of whether they were serving the needs of a people whose interest in yester-

day hardly existed, and whose interest in today was remarkably limited to its usefulness for getting to tomorrow.
The Americans were also participating in two movements
of such depth and importance that ferment and flux were
certain to be characteristic for many years to come. The
achievement of American nationality, a goal which kept the
American eagle screaming well into the twentieth century,
became a consuming interest. Americans, it has been said,
won their independence in the Revolution but did not
certify it until the War of 1812, an excursion into military
and naval adventures that was a tremendous boon to the
development of a national spirit. In the years after 1815 Americans assumed a pose of flamboyant self-assurance which
may well have rested on a sense of insecurity; but behind
the pose burned a sincere desire for some sense of identity,
for some understanding of the meaning of being an American.
In the early 1820's when James Fenimore Cooper was delineating the American character in his studies of frontier
life, John Quincy Adams was laying the foundations of an
American foreign policy and Henry Clay was patching together a domestic policy which took the grandiose name
of the "American System." In these circumstances, it is no
wonder that there were abroad in the land critics of the
colleges intent on finding out what the American college
should be and would be, intent on discovering how, in
matters educational, the new nation would throw off the
habits and systems of the Old World.

The other movement that directed new attention to the
role of the American college was the movement toward
democracy which everywhere was leaving its mark. Gentlemen and scholars might be turned out by the neat packaging
of a renovated medieval curriculum, an officially encouraged
religious atmosphere, and a carefully nurtured collegiate way.
Conceivably the saturation of a number of such men in the
learning of ancient Greece and Rome had provided the infant United States with a legion of good men who served
well as founding fathers. But the question was now being

raised of whether gentlemen-scholars could create cities out of the wilderness, explore the unknown regions of the West, and cope with the raw necessities which the exploitation of a vast and immensely rich continent demanded. Nothing was as important to an American in these years as was his labor, for with it he might transform a continent— or, at any rate, a sizable portion of it—and, in doing so, transform his own station in life. Whether ancient Greece and Rome could guide that labor effectively, whether antiquity could speak to the problems that opening a new continent created—these were the questions which critics of the colleges were asking. How American was the American college to be? How democratic? How prepared to enter into the exciting conquest of nature, how prepared to enjoy the spiritual fulfillment which this conquest offered? How willing to enlist in the great American adventure? How ready to diffuse learning, how ready to advance it?

The reform impulse dealt both with the diffusion of learning and with the advancement of learning. It proposed on the one hand that the colleges be more popular, and on the other that they be more intellectual. Critics of the colleges found them unprepared to serve the people and lacking in the will to achieve higher standards of excellence and of learning. A foursome of dedicated reformers appeared in the 1820's at Harvard, Amherst, and the University of Vermont in the North and at the University of Nashville in the South. At the University of Virginia under the careful guidance of Thomas Jefferson and at the University of the City of New York new institutions promised to establish an American definition of higher education, in much the way that national purpose and identity were being established by John Quincy Adams in diplomacy, Henry Clay in economics, and James Fenimore Cooper in letters.

Stirrings of dissatisfaction and reform, however, were not limited to these few leaders and few institutions. The modest reforms of the Revolutionary period were now greatly multiplied. Between 1796 and 1806 Princeton admitted special scientific students, and although they did not receive a bachelor's degree, they were awarded certificates of proficiency in a course of study which was shorn of great quantities of Latin and Greek. At Princeton this experiment was abandoned but it was taken up at Union College in 1802 with considerable zeal. A partial course program, permitting students to study what they wished, even encouraging the substitution of French for Greek, became one of the distinguishing features of the new college at Schenectady. At the University of Pennsylvania in 1816 the trustees organized a four-man "Faculty of Physical Science and Rural Economy." [1]

In the 1820's dissatisfaction became a movement. When the founders of Lafayette College cast around for support in 1824 they promised to include modern languages in the course of study. They well understood the popular mood: within two years their failure to jettison the classics was being described as adding "no more to scientific knowledge than the croaking of frogs." In Ohio during the 1820's and 1830's Ohio University fell increasingly under great popular pressure to shift emphasis from the traditional course of study to something more meaningful and useful for contemporary life.

Its rival state institution, Miami University, responded more readily to public criticism. In 1825 Miami offered a course called "English Scientific," in which modern languages, applied mathematics, and political economy were substituted for the ancient subjects. As was generally customary wherever a similar course was adopted, the new program at Miami led to a certificate of proficiency but not to a bachelor's degree. At first, curricular reform was not an attack

[1] Thomas Jefferson Wertenbaker: *Princeton 1746-1896* (Princeton, 1946), p. 123; Andrew Van Vranken Raymond, ed.: *Union University: Its History, Influence, Characteristics and Equipment* (New York, 1907), I, 85; Edward Potts Cheyney: *History of the University of Pennsylvania 1740-1940* (Philadelphia, 1940), p. 205.

on the integrity of the B.A. degree, but it was an assertion that there should be a place at the colleges for young men who were not degree candidates. The public announcement of the Miami program asserted: "Literary and scientific knowledge is no longer to be the exclusive property of a few professional men. . . . It is to become the common property of the mass of the human family." Miami intended to make both its curriculum and its clientele more democratic. It proposed to offer a course of study that would be generally useful and to bring into the college curriculum subjects that heretofore had generally been confined to the academy. At the same time Miami would bring within the society of educated men young farm boys who, attracted by the new subjects, would experience a literary and scientific training of an order long associated with a limited professional class.[2]

A similar program launched Hobart College at Geneva, New York, in 1825, and by 1828 at Union College Eliphalet Nott had perfected the college's popular and now long-established parallel course of study, which had imparted collegiate dignity to modern languages, mathematics, and science. The effective treat-them-as-gentlemen disciplinary policy of President Nott and the perfected parallel course of study helped to make Union a leading American institution. By 1829 it stood third in enrollment among American colleges, and by 1839 it was second only to Yale. Its success in attracting students, a success which most American colleges were being denied, must have contributed to the gradual adoption of the parallel-course idea elsewhere.[3]

[2] David Bishop Skillman: *The Biography of a College: Being the History of the First Century of the Life of Lafayette College* (Easton, 1932), I, 25, 29, 35-6; Thomas N. Hoover: *The History of Ohio University* (Athens, 1954), p. 43; Walter Havighurst: *The Miami Years 1809-1959* (New York, 1958), pp. 44-5.

[3] Raymond: *Union*, I, 156. The standard histories of the American college curriculum are R. Freeman Butts: *The College Charts Its Course* (New York, 1939); and Louis Franklin Snow: *The College Curriculum in the United States* (New York, 1907).

•   •   •

The development of a parallel course of study, one that
would compete on equal or almost equal terms with the
classical course, would take time. A program without the
classics could not achieve equality overnight, and it certainly
did nothing of the sort during the 1820's and 1830's. James
Marsh of the University of Vermont, one of the most outspoken critics of the ancient curriculum, was nonetheless a
strong defender of the value of the classics for "all men of
cultivated minds" and of "the *absolute necessity* of its
possession by all whose labors and studies regard the highest
interests of man." But when Hampden-Sidney in Virginia in
1828, Columbia in New York in 1830, and Wesleyan in
Connecticut in 1831 introduced a literary-scientific course,
it was apparent that the search for some alternative to the
classics was not to be limited to western colleges such as
Miami or experimental colleges such as Union.[4]

Most institutions, however, did not develop a parallel
course of study. There were two ways in which the classical program could be weakened: one was to offer a popular
parallel course which ignored the classics altogether, the
other was to dilute the classical program by reducing the
time allotted to the ancient subjects and substituting small
prescribed doses of the new subjects. The more adventuresome—and perhaps more desperate—institutions were experimenting with the parallel program, but most of the rest
were bending to the winds of reform only to the extent
of now prescribing (and therefore certifying as legitimate college subjects) some study in the modern languages,
as well as increased attention to new branches of mathe-

[4] [James Marsh]: *Exposition of the System of Instruction and Discipline Pursued in the University of Vermont* (Burlington[?], 1829), p.
5; Alfred J. Morrison: *The College of Hampden-Sidney: Calendar of
Board Minutes 1776-1876* (Richmond, 1912), p. 98; Edwin C. Broome:
*A Historical and Critical Discussion of College Admission Require-
ments* (New York, 1903), pp. 75 ff.; Snow: *The College Curriculum*,
p. 108; Butts: *The College Charts Its Course*, pp. 134-40.

matics and science. In either case, the colleges were being adapted to new goals and to new social and economic facts.

The four reformers who left a significant mark on the academic history of the 1820's were Philip Lindsley of the University of Nashville, George Ticknor of Harvard, James Marsh of the University of Vermont, and Jacob Abbott of Amherst. Lindsley, who was thirty-eight when he began his career in Nashville in 1824, was the oldest; Jacob Abbott, the youngest, was twenty-two when he was made professor of mathematics and natural philosophy at Amherst in 1824. All four were graduates of traditional colleges—one of Princeton, one of Bowdoin, and two of Dartmouth. Of the four, only George Ticknor of Harvard was not a clergyman; he was both a lawyer and the first professionally trained professor of modern languages in an American college. Other than relative youth and graduation from a traditional college, what these four had in common was a readiness to undertake fundamental reform in the course of study. Their success would never equal their readiness, but all four were willing pioneers in the effort to bring higher education in the United States closer to the people and closer to some level of intellectual excellence. To undertake both these designs simultaneously was the perilous ambition of all four, but it was perhaps typically American that it should have been Philip Lindsley on the frontier of Tennessee whose ambitions soared most freely.

Lindsley was an 1804 graduate of Princeton, where he became professor of ancient languages in 1816. A forward-looking liberal Presbyterian, he was a frustrated potential reformer in the Princeton atmosphere. In 1824 he accepted the challenge presented by the University of Nashville, serving a vast region of the American interior. In Nashville he attempted with some success to develop a program that would fulfill the injunction of his inaugural address of 1825:

"The farmer, the mechanic, the manufacturer, the merchant, the sailor, the soldier . . . must be educated." [5]

Not content with doing something for the farmer and the mechanic, he envisioned a great university at Nashville, one that would be modeled on the German rather than the English plan, a university of faculties rather than dormitories, a university that would breathe the spirit of change and of learning: "We may commence the enterprise, and leave posterity to carry it onward toward completion. For *complete*, in the nature of things, it never can be. It must be growing, advancing, enlarging, accumulating, till the end of time. No university in Europe is *complete*—not even in one department." [6]

Lindsley possessed one of the most exciting imaginations of any American college president. His idea of what an American college or university was and could be, his commitment to intellectual excellence, his rejection of denominationalism as a secure basis for a great institution, his recognition of a need for broadly practical education, yet his devotion to the humanist tradition—all this set him apart. His unremitting, even heroic, struggle to develop a great university in Tennessee was probably impossible from the start. In the end, it fell afoul of the ambitions of the sectarian colleges and, ironically, of the uninformed opposition of the democracy he sought to serve. When Lindsley went to Nashville in 1824 there was no college within two hundred miles; by 1848 there were thirty, nine of them within fifty miles of Nashville. Against this array of embattled sectarians, Lindsley was helpless. His greatness did not lie in his achievements so much as it did in his dreams and in the visions which he transferred to graduates of the college at Nashville who carried on in the Lindsley tradition throughout the Southwest. The demand for his services from other colleges was

[5] LeRoy J. Halsey, ed.: *The Works of Philip Lindsley, D.D.* (Philadelphia, 1866), I, 81. See also Wertenbaker: *Princeton*, pp. 162-4, 175.
[6] Halsey, ed.: *The Works of Philip Lindsley, D.D.*, I, 406.

eloquent evidence not only of widespread stirrings against the old course of study but of the reputation which Lindsley himself had achieved as a critic of the old order.

The self-appointed instrument of reform at Harvard was George Ticknor, an 1807 graduate of Dartmouth whose desire to make a thorough study of the classics led him in 1815 to become (with one other, Edward Everett) the first American to attend a German university for the purpose of doing advanced scholarly work. During his studies at Göttingen he was offered the newly founded Smith Professorship of French and Spanish and belles-lettres at Harvard, and after two more years of study, he returned to Harvard and took up the professorship in 1819. Ticknor and Everett were responsible for introducing Harvard to the world and manner of German scholarship, but a mere introduction did not mean that Harvard would therefore seek to change its identity. Ticknor could not wait to see Harvard pattern itself on the German model, so impressed was he by the standards of German scholarship, the freedom of the teacher-scholar, and the consuming interest in learning which characterized the reviving German universities. But to make a German university out of an English college in Massachusetts would be no small undertaking, and at first Ticknor could find no enthusiasm for his plans except among certain visionary souls on the corporation.[7]

An occasion for reform, however, was created by a particularly disastrous undergraduate rebellion in 1823, one of such exceptional disorder that forty-three of the seventy members of the Class of 1823 were expelled almost on the eve of commencement. Obviously something was wrong at

[7] Samuel Eliot Morison: *Three Centuries of Harvard 1636-1936* (Cambridge, 1936), pp. 230-1; Butts: *The College Charts Its Course*, pp. 100-2; Richard J. Storr: *The Beginnings of Graduate Education in America* (Chicago, 1953), pp. 16-22.

Harvard, and while the faculty and corporation were unwilling to go as far as Ticknor, yet when the reformers and the
conservatives were finished, it was for the first time possible
for a Harvard department that so desired to section students
according to ability and to offer elective courses.

In time, only Ticknor's department adhered strictly to the
spirit of the new regulations, regulations intended to encourage learning and a temper of scholarship at Harvard.
Ticknor's was a prophetic voice, however, and if he could
not single-handedly engineer a program of great reform, he
pointed the way, unsettling Cambridge with his searching
commentary on the Harvard course of study. His outlook,
if widely adopted, would have enabled Harvard to diffuse
learning as well as to advance it. As it turned out, the potential contained in even the few reforms which were
adopted was never realized.

Ticknor's catalogue of complaints, which he published,
ranged broadly across the Harvard way of doing things, a
way of doing things which had become traditional and deeply
embedded in the life of the American college. Why must
there be over twenty weeks of vacation and holidays a
year, he wanted to know. Why should students not be
classified according to talent and the level of their learning,
rather than according to their date of entrance to Harvard or
according to the alphabet, "as if," Ticknor added, "a young
man's talent and character depended on the letter with which
his name happens to begin." Why should Harvard in its
course offerings ignore the fact that the United States was
heading for a future in which manufacturing and finance
would open great careers to men who ought to have the
benefit of a Harvard education? Why should the college adhere to an antiquated and obviously unworkable system of
discipline, fines, and punishments? Why should the United
States Military Academy be superior to Harvard in the seri-
ousness and effectiveness of examinations, in the scheduling
of vacations, and in attention to the business at hand—

education? Why should an instructor's time be fully occupied in discovering through dull recitations whether the
young men assembled in his presence had read the day's
assignment?[8]

Ticknor's questions reached to the heart of American
academic customs. And wherever he looked he found reason
to be alarmed at the superficiality which was encouraged by
the American system of vacations, discipline, recitations, and
undifferentiated classes. "Who in this country," he asked,
"by means here offered him, has been enabled to make himself a good Greek scholar? Who has been taught thoroughly to
read, write, and speak Latin? Nay, who has been taught anything at our colleges with the thoroughness that will enable
him to go safely and directly onward to distinction in the
department he has thus entered . . . ?"[9] The spirit of the
German university ran through Ticknor's penetrating questions, but Harvard was not yet ready to undertake the great
changes which would have to wait for President Eliot almost a half century later.

When Josiah Quincy assumed the presidency of Harvard in
1829 he tendered a cautious but certain invitation to a consideration of change in the curriculum; his conservative
but sympathetic outlook enabled two Harvard professors in
1831 to establish an advanced seminary in classics for the
preparation of American teachers of classics. This new program called for more advanced work than did the bachelor's
degree and for at least a fifth year of study. Lacking fellowship funds, it soon withered and disappeared. Here were seeds
of a university, of an institution with the capacity and the
desire to advance and to diffuse learning. But the time was not
yet ripe. Ticknor held to an elective program and to
dividing the language courses of his own department into
sections according to ability, and his successor, Henry Wadsworth Longfellow, adhered to the changes. But elsewhere

[8] George Ticknor: *Remarks on Changes Lately Proposed or Adopted,
in Harvard College* (Boston, 1825), *passim.*
[9] Ibid., p. 45.

at Harvard, with few exceptions, fundamental change would have to wait.[1]

James Marsh was graduated from Dartmouth in 1817, ten years after George Ticknor. In 1826 he became the president of the University of Vermont, where he inaugurated an era of curricular reform and performed the scholarly service of introducing the writings of Samuel Taylor Coleridge to a growing American audience. Marsh must have been the only college president in the country who was a transcendentalist.[2] In a paper that he read to the Vermont faculty soon after he became president, he proposed that the studies of the college be divided into four departments and that students not seeking degrees be permitted to pursue the studies of a single department if they desired. In defense of his proposal, he argued, "It is certainly best for one to get a *part well* rather than attempt all with the certainty of universal *failure*."[3] Let us, said Marsh, help those who want to be helped and not deny our help to those who cannot take the bachelor's program. Let us free students who will not be taking Greek and Latin from the admission requirements in Greek and Latin. Let us abolish the division of students into four classes through which they progress year by year. Let us simply have students, subjects of study, and standards of excellence, and move students toward their bachelor's degrees or certificates according to their talents and their application. Let us abandon the stultifying adherence to textbooks and recitations; let us turn the classroom into an arena of wide-ranging discussion and inquiry.

[1] Snow: *The College Curriculum*, p. 163; Storr: *The Beginnings of Graduate Education*, pp. 24-8.

[2] James Torrey: *The Remains of the Rev. James Marsh, D.D., Late President and Professor of Moral and Intellectual Philosophy, in the University of Vermont; with a Memoir of His Life* (Boston, 1843), pp. 77-85.

[3] [James Marsh]: *Exposition of the System of Instruction and Discipline Pursued in the University of Vermont*, p. 3.

How long Vermont was able to sustain so clear a departure from normal practice is unknown. Marsh himself finally resigned, discouraged by religious and philosophic wrangling as well as by the multitude of problems that beset a college president in the exercise of his duties. But unquestionably even before then Marsh had learned that his design for Vermont called for students and teachers with a scholarly ambition rare on the American scene, and for libraries and scientific equipment that were costly. Yet, his proposals and their trial at Vermont identified Marsh as a college president of vision. It is not surprising that he and George Ticknor should have consulted when pioneering as curriculum reformers, nor that Francis Wayland, a later day reformer at Brown, should have acknowledged an indebtedness to Marsh.[4]

At Amherst leadership in the reform movement fell to a committee of the faculty under young Jacob Abbott, the professor of mathematics and natural philosophy, a Bowdoin graduate of the Class of 1820. Abbott would become better known as the founder in 1828 of the Mount Vernon School in Boston, a pioneer academy for women, and as the author of the Rollo books, a popular series of didactic children's stories.

In 1827 the Amherst faculty issued two reports, the first being an inquiry into the inadequacies of the prevailing course of study, the second being a set of proposals for improvement. The first report, echoing a sentiment expressed in Ticknor's 1825 pamphlet on the Harvard reforms, addressed itself immediately to the public dissatisfaction with the American college: "The complaint is . . . that while every thing else is on the advance, our Colleges are stationary; or, if not quite stationary, that they are in danger of being left far behind, in the rapid march of improvement." The Amherst faculty was, in a sense, documenting the way in

[4] Julian Ira Lindsay: *Tradition Looks Forward: The University of Vermont: A History 1791-1904* (Burlington, 1954), pp. 129, 139-40.

which the idea of progress, the cult of improvement and change, would invalidate the classical course of study, and it agreed with the complaint that the cult inspired. It went on to consider the usefulness of such neglected studies as United States history and government for citizenship, and French and Spanish languages for businessmen. It admitted that the traditional curriculum was one from which a student derived "no material advantage." Indeed, as for the classics, the Amherst faculty was prepared to state that "in an age of universal improvements, and in a young, free, and prosperous country like ours, it is absurd to cling so tenaciously to the prescriptive forms of other centuries." And it deplored the failure of the American colleges to provide instruction in the science of education.[5]

The second report which Abbott and his committee presented to the Amherst corporation made concrete proposals. The Amherst faculty asked permission to establish a parallel program, one in which an Amherst student might study—as he could not in the prescribed classical program of 1826: French, Spanish, German, and Italian; English literature; agricultural chemistry, engineering, architecture, experimental and practical physics; American political and religious history, with an emphasis on the Puritan age; the American Constitution; and new fields of scientific knowledge. These subjects were to enter the parallel course of study only at the expense of Latin and Greek, which would be completely omitted, but not at the expense of such equally traditional subjects as moral and intellectual philosophy, rhetoric, and oratory.[6]

Apparently the Amherst trustees were somewhat overwhelmed at the breadth of the proposals, but they were willing to have them printed and they promised that when the funds were available they would be glad to try the

[5] *The Substance of Two Reports of the Faculty of Amherst College, to the Board of Trustees, With the Doings of the Board Thereon* (Amherst, 1827), pp. 5-6, 7 ff.
[6] Ibid., pp. 9-21.

parallel course of study and even to set up a department of education for the proper training of teachers. The funds never were available to launch the full program, but steps in that direction were taken in 1827, only to be abandoned in 1829. The early collapse of Jacob Abbott's pioneer dream at Amherst must be attributed to the tentative and partial nature of the experiment, to the inability of the French professor to maintain discipline in his classes, to an undercurrent of faculty skepticism, and to insufficient election of courses in the modern languages and sciences by students who knew what the prestigious subjects still were.[7]

Lindsley, Ticknor, Marsh, and Abbott, noble dreamers all—every one of them in the end was a prophet without honor. For while they were responsible for modest reforms, the fulfillment of their larger plans awaited another generation. The country was moving faster than the colleges. Centuries of academic tradition had been poured into the making of the American college, with its tightly prescribed course of study, with its classical orientation, with its indebtedness to the English collegiate way of life. To accommodate the American college to the needs and the desires of the great majority beyond its reach would not be the accomplishment of the 1820's and the 1830's. But what this generation would do, what Lindsley, Ticknor, Marsh, and Abbott would do, would be to state the problems and to point the way toward solutions.

Dealing as they were with institutions whose habits and purposes were deeply rooted in the past, the collegiate reformers were not as fortunate as the founders of the University of Virginia and the founders of the University

[7] Claude M. Fuess: *Amherst: The Story of a New England College* (Boston, 1935), pp. 98-101.

of the City of New York. For, charged with the responsibility of creating new colleges, the founders of these two institutions were less beholden to the past and under stronger obligation to the mood of the present.

In Virginia a Board of Commissioners was appointed by the government to prepare plans for a state university in 1818, and final curricular decisions were made by the university's board of visitors in 1824. But fundamentally, while the development of a university is of necessity a joint endeavor, the founder of the University of Virginia was Thomas Jefferson, that apostle of the Enlightenment who was to make of the university one of his enduring monuments. His genius guided the commission of 1818; his plans were adopted by the board of visitors in 1824. The University of Virginia, as conceived by Thomas Jefferson, combined an attention to the popular and practical new subjects with an intellectual orientation of university dimensions. Jefferson would have his university diffuse knowledge and advance knowledge, and with the ingenuity of a man who could make of Monticello a veritable delight of gadgets and contraptions, he designed a scheme of instruction that was unique.[8]

The university was divided into eight schools: ancient languages, modern languages, mathematics, natural philosophy, natural history, anatomy and medicine, moral philosophy, and law. Each school was an independent operation, beginning with a single professor but capable of developing a staff and differentiating itself into departments. Each school was assigned to a particular location in the architectural scheme which Jefferson provided for the university. Each school had the capacity to expand indefinitely, as the growth of knowledge in its area of learning demanded and as funds were made available.[9]

[8] See Philip Alexander Bruce: *History of the University of Virginia, 1819-1919* (New York, 1920-2), I; and Roy J. Honeywell: *The Educational Work of Thomas Jefferson* (Cambridge, 1931).

[9] Bruce: *Virginia*, I, 322 ff.

Every student was free to elect work in whichever schools he chose. One of the most liberating regulations in the history of American higher education—indeed, in the history of liberty in America—was the one adopted by the University of Virginia board of visitors in 1824: "Every student shall be free to attend the schools of his choice, and no other than he chooses." At the University of Virginia every student was a free agent. He was not a freshman, sophomore, junior, or senior; he was a student, free to study where his inclinations took him, free to choose work in the schools of his particular interest.

The university awarded no degrees; each school gave its own diploma which recognized completion of a certain body of work, and this diploma made a student no less a graduate of the university than if he had received eight diplomas. Only lack of funds kept Jefferson from opening the university with schools of commerce, manufacturing, and diplomacy, for this man of wide-ranging intellectual curiosity and practicality recognized the national need for training in applied subjects.[1]

The university was unable to hold to this scheme of things for long. By 1831 it was abandoning its no-degree system and offering an M.A. to students who received diplomas in the five schools that covered what was everywhere becoming the standard classical course of study: ancient languages, mathematics, natural philosophy, chemistry, and moral philosophy. Two years later the school of modern languages, where work in two languages was required, was added to the group necessary for the award of an M.A. degree. Whether the work at Virginia was actually of M.A. rather than B.A. quality is doubtful, but the intentions of the university were clearly honorable, if somewhat ambitious. For Jefferson had believed that Virginia would do work on the very highest level, and when, after his death, it was decided to award a degree for such work, it is understand-

[1] Ibid., 324-30.

able why the university officials thought in terms of an M.A. rather than a B.A.[2]

The Virginia experience was a remarkable deviation from the normal American pattern. An institution which would not give a B.A., at which commencement was called Public Day, which opened in over a quarter of a million dollars' worth of buildings designed by Thomas Jefferson, which offered a wide-ranging elective curriculum, and which thought of itself as a graduate institution—such an institution was a remarkable feat of the Jeffersonian imagination. The great virtue of the University of Virginia system of schools was its avoidance of superficiality and compulsion, the two evils which finally undermined the classical course of study and let loose an elective system of significant proportions. The influence of Jefferson's experiments at Virginia was not widespread. Perhaps there was too much novelty in the scheme, and it was terribly expensive. There was interest in the Virginia program, however; Ticknor of Harvard and Wayland of Brown both visited Charlottesville, and the public addresses of Philip Lindsley were full of allusions to the Virginia program and to Jefferson. All the northern reformers were unquestionably aware of what was going on at Charlottesville. The elective principle would eventually establish itself in the United States, but it would be the function and destructive influence of the rise of science on the old course of study that would make election prevail. The elective principle in the United States in the twentieth century owes little to the Jeffersonian philosophy which established it as a cardinal principle of the University of Virginia. In the 1860's and 1870's, when founding universities and transforming colleges into universities developed some of the characteristics of a fad in the United States, the University of Virginia was rediscovered. Particularly in the South and West, but also at Cornell and at M.I.T., the Jeffersonian scheme was recognized as a means

[2] Ibid., II, 140; III, 28-41, 61-4.

of facilitating the degree of election that the rising importance of science demanded. In its own day and in its own
way, however, the early University of Virginia was in part
an inspiration and in part an answer to the questions which
Lindsley, Ticknor, Marsh, and Abbott propounded.[3]

Another answer was attempted at the University of the City
of New York which opened in 1832, after the most thorough
public consideration of the American collegiate situation
that the country had yet known. In the fall of 1830 a group
of leading intellectuals met in New York in an effort to lay
the foundations of a new type of American institution of
higher learning.[4]

Aware of the successful launching of the University of
London in 1828 as a utilitarian institution, friends of a practical collegiate course saw the new university as an answer
to the need for training in subjects more likely to be used
in a country that was undergoing such dynamic expansion.
The election of Andrew Jackson in 1828 so disturbed
many leading citizens that they were prompted to propose
that the university meet the inevitable rise of the people with
a broad program of education. The friends of the future
university were also interested in the advancement of learning. They felt a need for professional schools with more
rigid standards. They were aware of the distinction between
the scholarly foundations in Germany and the more leisurely,

[3] Ibid., III, 244-55; Honeywell: *The Educational Work of Thomas
Jefferson*, pp. 130-3; Halsey, ed.: *The Works of Philip Lindsley, D.D.*,
I, 135-6, 142, 216-17, 297, 387, 417; Daniel Walker Hollis: *University of
South Carolina* (Columbia, 1951-6), II, 16, 27; Clarence Ray Aurner:
History of Education in Iowa (Iowa City, 1916), IV, 28; James F.
Hopkins: *The University of Kentucky: Origins and Early Years* (Lex-
ington, 1951), pp. 78-9; Walter P. Rogers: *Andrew D. White and the
Modern University* (Ithaca, 1942), pp. 14, 51.
[4] *Journal of the Proceedings of a Convention of Literary and Scien-
tific Gentlemen, Held in the Common Council Chamber of the City
of New York, October 1830* (New York, 1831). See also Storr: *The
Beginnings of Graduate Education*, pp. 33-43; Theodore F. Jones, ed.:
New York University 1832:1932 (New York, 1933), pp. 6-35.

collegiate order of things in England, and they favored the German orientation.[5]

An unprecedented gathering of eminent men at New York City Hall in October 1830 projected an institution that would satisfy these varied ambitions. Those gathered included Albert Gallatin, Benjamin Silliman, Theodore Dwight Woolsey, Francis Lieber, James Marsh, and Jared Sparks. From their deliberations and efforts there developed the University of the City of New York which opened in 1832 with parallel courses of study, one in the classical tradition and one on the new English-scientific pattern. In addition, a program of graduate instruction leading to an earned M.A. degree was established in 1835.

These efforts were largely premature, destined for failure. A spokesman at the opening ceremonies of the university unintentionally revealed one of the difficulties when he referred to the classical course of study as being for those young men "whose inclinations might lead to a . . . more exalted measure of attainments" than would be achieved by those taking the course of practical studies. This official announcement that the practical course of study was inferior to the classical course did not thereby make the practical course more attractive, and it unquestionably inhibited the growth of the university itself. As long as the sponsors of the practical programs were unready to embrace them fully, it is no wonder that many young men would either not go to college or, if they did so, would follow the worn path of classical learning.

The founders of the university gathered an eminent faculty, but it would take more than a desire on their part to make a university dedicated to the advancement of learning in the United States in the 1830's. The president of the institution preferred to assign available funds to a building program, and students did not flock to the institution in sufficient numbers to encourage the university's scholarly pretensions. Among other things, there was not a job in the

[5] Jones: *New York University*, p. 35.

United States for which an M.A. was required or desired. The financial panic of 1837 did not finish off the university, but it did lead to the dismissal in 1838 of seven professors. With that action, the university became just another American college.

The day was not carried by any of the reforming colleges, by any of the pioneers, by either the University of Virginia or the University of the City of New York. The threat to the old order was recognized and squarely met, and the reformers were so successfully routed that for almost fifty years the American college was necessarily put beyond the sympathy and understanding of the American people. Stagnation rather than dynamism became the order of the day. Self-satisfaction overtook the American college. Of course there was a change, but it was reluctant, almost imperceptible, the kind of change which added an hour of botany here or a term of German there, always making the new course required or only narrowly optional, maintaining the dominance of the old subjects. The college year was not lengthened nor was the range of subjects narrowed. Instead, everything became more and more superficial, more and more a matter of daily recitations on elementary material, more and more deadly and deadening.

Basil Hall, an accomplished English traveler in North America, reported with enthusiasm of what he had found in New Haven in the years 1827 and 1828. What he found there, of course, was Yale, but what impressed him so much, he said, was "to see so many good old usages and orthodox notions kept up as vigorously . . . as possible." [*] There can be no question about the vigor of Yale under the direction of President Jeremiah Day, whose report in behalf of the Yale faculty in the year 1828 became a classic statement in defense of the old order. The report of the faculty to the corporation and the answering report of the corporation to the faculty

[*] Quoted in Storr: *The Beginnings of Graduate Education*, pp. 29-30.

in that year stated the case for the classical curriculum in America with such finality that not until the next generation would another band of reformers assail the old course of study. The Yale Report of 1828 put the weight of a great American college behind things as they were. Ready to join Yale in perpetuating the old course of study, in combating the subversive tendency of the new subjects, and in fighting off the principles of option and election was Princeton. These two institutions, far more influential than provincial Harvard where Unitarianism and the absence of a missionary impulse were encouraging a climate of self-satisfied isolation, were in the process of becoming national colleges. By sending out enthusiastic young graduates to found colleges in the barbaric West and South and by training clergymen to become college presidents, Yale and Princeton, in a way that the University of Virginia was not, were in a position to define what the American college would be. The report of 1828 gave them their rationale. The first catalogue of Beloit College in 1849 carried the assurance that its course of study was "drawn up exactly on the Yale plan."

Although there was not an original idea in it, the report was published in 1829 in Benjamin Silliman's *American Journal of Science and Arts* as "Original Papers in relation to a Course of Liberal Education," and thereby received widespread circulation.[7] The ideas that it purveyed were as old as the classical course of study itself. The psychology of learning to which it adhered was Aristotelian. The scale of values that it promoted appeared in hundreds of inaugural addresses and commencement addresses published long before Jeremiah Day became president of Yale. A trustee committee of Columbia College in 1810 issued a report that advanced the

---

[7] "Original Papers in relation to a Course of Liberal Education," *The American Journal of Science and Arts*, XV (1829), 297-351. Also published separately as *Reports on the Course of Instruction in Yale College; by a Committee of the Corporation, and the Academical Faculty* (New Haven, 1828). *The Journal of Science* text has been used in the present study.

same theories of learning, the same collegiate purposes. What was important about the Yale Report was the strength that it gave to the forces of reaction; it served as a gospel, and before long it was being quoted or misquoted or paraphrased by college presidents, faculties, and governing boards everywhere.

The Yale faculty met the reformers head on. It was obvious that they and the corporation had been moved into action by the mumblings of discontent at Harvard and elsewhere and by the dramatic new departure at Charlottesville. Initiated in September 1827 as an inquiry into whether Yale should substitute "other studies" for the *dead languages*," the deliberations in New Haven led to a full-scale inquiry into the nature of higher education in America. The Yale faculty rejected the suggestion that they had been hearing "from different quarters . . . that our colleges must be *new-modelled;* that they are not adapted to the spirit and wants of the age; that they will soon be deserted, unless they are better accommodated to the business character of the nation." [8] And then, after defining the object of a college as the laying of foundations for a superior education, the Yale professors explained exactly how that object might best be achieved.

Fundamental, of course, was knowing what one was up to, and therefore the professors restated the ancient psychology of learning which saw the mind as a receptacle and as a muscle with various potentialities waiting to be trained. "The two great points to be gained in intellectual culture, are the *discipline* and the *furniture* of the mind; expanding its powers, and storing it with knowledge." [9] These points might be best gained by adherence to the ancient subjects, for these were the subjects most certain to discipline and most worthy to furnish a balanced mind. Mathematics shaped the mind as an instrument of reasoning. The classics helped to achieve balance by bending the mind toward

[8] Ibid., 300.
[9] Ibid.

taste. In answer to the question of why each student should not "be allowed to select those branches of study which are most to his taste, which are best adapted to his peculiar talents, and which are most nearly connected with his intended profession," the Yale people had a ready answer. To those critics seduced by the meddling with ancient custom that was going on in Virginia and Vermont they warned: "Our prescribed course contains those subjects only which ought to be understood . . . by everyone who aims at a thorough education." [1]

To the Ticknors and Lindsleys and others who had been bitten by the bug of university aspiration, they directed the assurance: "We hope at least, that this college may be spared the mortification of a ludicrous attempt to imitate . . . [the German universities], while it is unprovided with the resources necessary to execute the purpose." [2] Friends of the modern languages were reminded that French and German "are studied, and will continue to be studied, as an accomplishment rather than as a necessary acquisition." [3] As for all of the worry and fuss about the need for practical collegiate education for "those who are destined to be merchants or manufacturers, or agriculturists," Yale held firm. Indeed, recognizing the social and political elevation of the uneducated in the life of the nation, Yale argued that such men needed a classical course far more than they needed a practical course. "Is it not desirable," the professors asked, that the new men of wealth and influence being created by American abundance "should be men of superior education, of large and liberal views, of those solid and elegant attainments, which will raise them to a higher distinction, than the mere possession of property; which will not allow them to hoard their treasures, or waste them in senseless extravagance; which will enable them to adorn society by their learning, to move in the more intelligent circles with dignity, and to make such an application of their wealth, as will be

[1] Ibid., 312.
[2] Ibid., 315.
[3] Ibid., 333.

most honorable to themselves, and most beneficial to their country?"⁴ Some advocates of the free elementary public school movement argued that schools would tame the masses. Yale now proposed to use the classical curriculum and the colleges for taming the millionaires.

Although prefaced by the assurance "that changes may, from time to time be made with advantage," obviously the Yale Report was no invitation to the future.⁵ Even the use of textbooks and recitations was defended as being superior to an arrangement that would send students into libraries, there to read the sources and conflicting authorities: "The diversity of statement in these, will furnish the student with an apology for want of exactness in his answers."⁶ For the Yale faculty the American college would continue to serve its essentially aristocratic purpose. "The young merchant must be trained in the counting room, the mechanic in the workshop, the farmer, in the field." On the other hand "the laboring classes" would be introduced to what they needed to know by "men of superior education," by college men, the trained, balanced leaders whose minds had been furnished and disciplined, tested and proven by a course of study that had not only stood the test of time but had as well been remarkably practical and receptive to change.⁷ It was not true that the curriculum of 1828 was the same as the Harvard curriculum of 1636. And one subject after another had demonstrated its utility in the lives of countless college men who had adorned the learned professions. Indeed, "the changes in the country during the last century, have not been greater than the changes in the college."⁸

The Yale Report was a magnificent assertion of the humanist tradition and therefore eventually of unquestionable importance in liberating the American college from an excessive religous orientation. In the meantime, however, the

⁴ Ibid., 323-4.
⁵ Ibid., 299.
⁶ Ibid., 304.
⁷ Ibid., 310.
⁸ Ibid., 340.

report gave a convincing defensive weapon to people who wanted the colleges to stay as they were.[9] The inertia of social institutions, the simple ordinary laziness of men, would of course support the Yale professors and their disciples. They were joined by men of profound religious conviction who were disturbed by the suggestions of the reformers that colleges should prepare men to meet the needs of this world, rather than the needs of the next world. They received encouragement from the pious, for whom an excessive concern with matters of intellect had always seemed a threat to the true faith. The privileged orders were pleased that Yale chose to withstand the demands for a more popular and practical education, demands that threatened to unleash the multitudes. And these—the religious, the very pious, the privileged—were the people who ran the colleges, people who also knew that the American college was running on a shoestring and that the old course of study, while the best, was also the cheapest.

The report echoed everywhere. Behind it the American college curriculum remained almost immovable until after the Civil War. Behind it President Lord of Dartmouth was able to declare that a college education was not meant for people who planned to "engage in mercantile, mechanical or agricultural operations."[1] Behind it, thousands of teachers would send thousands of students through thousands of days of boredom. Behind it, the catalogue of Tusculum College in Tennessee would sound as if the only difference between Tusculum and Yale was a matter of geography.

[9] For the argument that the Yale Report created a climate in which intellectual purpose might develop, see Ralph Henry Gabriel: *Religion and Learning at Yale: The Church of Christ in the College and University, 1757-1957* (New Haven, 1958), pp. 98-108.

[1] Leon Burr Richardson: *History of Dartmouth College* (Hanover, 1932), I, 389.

7

◆◆◆

The Extracurriculum

The American college, for all of the pervasiveness of the Yale Report of 1828, was unable to stand still. To an increasingly disenchanted public, the American college continued to present itself as little more than a body of established doctrine, an ancient course of study, and a respectable combination of piety and discipline. Within the college, however, there was taking place what might readily be called the unseen revolution. For the American college, if it could not be reformed from the top, could be redefined from the bottom. If it was not seriously reshaped by the Jeffersons, Lindsleys, Ticknors, and Marshes, it was nonetheless significantly changed by now unknown and forgotten hosts of undergraduates.

The college as construed by the officials might neglect intellect in the interest of piety. It might adhere to a regimen of discipline so constraining that the joys of this world were neglected in the interest of preparing for life in the next. It might ignore the body but be captivated by the career of the soul. It might do all these things, and did, but the American college became something more, much more than this. In the end it became a battlefield where piety and intellect fought for the right to dominate; it became an arena in which undergraduates erected monuments not to the soul of man but to man as a social and physical being. When the students were finished they had planted beside the curriculum an extracurriculum of such dimensions that in time there would develop generations of college students who would not see the curriculum for the extracurriculum; who would not believe that the American college had any purpose other than those that could best be served by the vast array of machinery, organizations, and institutions known as student activities. To what had been a curriculum in the 1820's was added a vital extracurriculum by the 1870's.

The students were perhaps more effective in intruding manners and muscles into the life of the American college than they were in establishing the priority of the mind, but there is no question about whether student agencies were friendlier to intellect than they were to piety. The first effective agency of intellect to make itself felt in the American college was the debating club or literary society, as it was generally called. Children of the Enlightenment, these societies first appeared at Yale, beginning in 1753, and soon thereafter at Princeton and Harvard. Yale undergraduates established the tradition of two competing societies which, in New Haven, took the names of Linonian and Brothers in Unity. At Princeton, the debating clubs were called American Whig and Cliosophic. Harvard's clubs were finally absorbed into the American Institute of 1770. Nurturing its passion for difference, Harvard did not adapt its extracurricular debating and literary interests to two rival clubs.[1] Elsewhere there was hardly a college that did not have a pair of debating clubs, usually with names that invoked memories of Greece: De-

[1] Henry Davidson Sheldon: *The History and Pedagogy of American Student Societies* (New York, 1901), p. 93; William Lathrop Kingsley, ed.: *Yale College: A Sketch of its History* (New York, 1879), I, 78, 95, 307-23; Thomas Jefferson Wertenbaker: *Princeton 1746-1896* (Princeton, 1946), pp. 201, 206; Samuel Eliot Morison: *Three Centuries of Harvard 1636-1936* (Cambridge, 1936), pp. 138-41.

mosthenian, Philanthropic, Diognothian, Atheneum, Alexandrian, Philolexian, Philomathean, Philologian, Philotechnian, Philodemic, Philonomosian.[2]

The first debating clubs probably owed something of their origin to the general atmosphere of colonial political debate that surrounded their birth and something to the continued lively political interest of the times. In debating clubs students could face squarely the exciting political issues of the day, issues that occupied the attention of their elders in the partisan press, at the village tavern, or around the cracker barrel of the country store. The tradition of the medieval disputation which had been declining as a commencement activity also found new lodgment in the debating societies, and the oratorical and declamatory exercises of the curriculum received new encouragement. But it was the Enlightenment faith in intellect, the commitment to reason, that most accounted for the development of the literary societies as a characteristic expression of undergraduate life.

Nowhere else was reason so fully enthroned in the college as in the activities of the literary societies. The classroom, while officially dedicated to disciplining and furnishing the mind, was in reality far better at molding character and at denying intellect rather than refining it. The literary societies, on the other hand, owed their allegiance to reason, and in their debates, disputations, and literary exercises, they imparted a tremendous vitality to the intellectual life of the colleges, creating a remarkable contrast to the ordinary classroom where the recitation of memorized portions of text was regarded as the ultimate intellectual exercise.

[2] For accounts of literary-society activities see especially George R. Cutting: *Student Life at Amherst College* (Amherst, 1871), pp. 13-37; James I. Osborne and Theodore G. Gronert: *Wabash College; the first hundred years, 1832-1932* (Crawfordsville, 1932), pp. 102-16; E. Merton Coulter: *College Life in the Old South* (Athens, 1951), pp. 103-33; Walter Havighurst: *The Miami Years 1809-1959* (New York, 1958), pp. 73-89; Frederick Clayton Waite: *Western Reserve University: The Hudson Era* (Cleveland, 1943), pp. 228-50.

Intellectual activity that was not strongly protected from arrogance and worldliness by Christian nurture received little encouragement in the American college. President Lord of Dartmouth expressed a characteristic outlook in 1828: "The very cultivation of the mind has frequently a tendency to impair the moral sensibilities, to induce that pride of conscious ability and variety of attainments which . . . are . . . affectations offensive to God." Ten years later the president of Davidson College would warn: "Remove the restraints and sanctions of religion, and talents and intellectual attainments can't stay the demons of human depravity." At Amherst President Heman Humphrey was capable of the phrase, "irreligious men . . . mere philosophers and scholars," and a member of his faculty insisted that "to have prayed well is to have studied well." [3]

Hostility to intellect appeared at a cornerstone ceremony in 1852 at Wofford College in South Carolina, when its first president remarked: "We have no faith in the capabilities of mere intellectual training." In the same year to the north Mark Hopkins of Williams observed: "It is pleasant to see young men study well, but that is nothing to seeing them inquiring earnestly & practically what God placed them in the world for, & giving themselves up to do his will." At Trinity College in North Carolina in 1868 the president wrote in his diary: "Without religion a college is a curse to society." Four years later at Amherst President Stearns stated the case succinctly: "Character . . . is of more consequence than intellect," and at Denison President Talbot warned: "At college we tend to exaggerate the importance of the intellectual." [4]

[3] Leon Burr Richardson: *History of Dartmouth College* (Hanover, 1932), I, 390; Albea Godbold: *The Church College of the Old South* (Durham, 1944), p. 52; Thomas Le Duc: *Piety and Intellect at Amherst College 1865-1912* (New York, 1946), p. 22.
[4] David Duncan Wallace: *History of Wofford College* (Nashville, 1951), p. 45; Frederick Rudolph: *Mark Hopkins and the Log: Williams College, 1836-1872* (New Haven, 1956), p. 57; Nora Campbell Chaffin: *Trinity College, 1839-1892: The Beginnings of Duke University* (Durham, 1950), p. 297; Le Duc: *Amherst*, p. 26; G. Wallace Chessman: *Denison: The Story of an Ohio College* (Granville, 1957), p. 137.

Of course the truth of the matter was that any exaggeration of the intellectual life at an American college was not likely to originate in the faculty or governing board, nor was it likely to arise in the curriculum. Not only did the collegiate way and the religious orientation of the colleges undercut any possibility of a pervading intellectual purpose, but the course of study itself, with its capstone senior year in moral and intellectual philosophy, usually taught by the president, led students along the path to piety not to intellect.[5]

The American college had developed an impressive arsenal of weapons for making men out of boys. Unrelenting revivals, unheated dormitories, and underpaid professors made their own small contribution toward helping the colleges to fulfill their major objective. But the heaviest burden for accomplishing the college's purpose rested upon the shoulders of the president. In his course for seniors, known almost everywhere as moral and intellectual philosophy, the full force of a mature mind and personality was turned upon a variety of subjects considered essential to the formation of true character. Transplanted from the universities of eighteenth-century England and Scotland, the course in moral and intellectual philosophy embraced the tough problem of how to reconcile man's newly emancipated reason and natural law with the old theology and Christian law.

The tortuous methods by which this problem was solved, in an age innocent of psychology and scarcely acquainted with the complexities of the human constitution, cannot be made readily understandable. Not surprisingly, however, the efforts of these self-proclaimed collegiate philosophers led to the discovery that human reason, when applied to nature and man's consciousness, simply reaffirmed the old truths. It

[5] The sections of this chapter dealing with the course on moral philosophy, literary-society activities, fraternities, and early collegiate athletics draw heavily on my *Mark Hopkins and the Log* (New Haven, 1956). I am grateful to the Yale University Press for permission to include portions of that book in this chapter.

was discovered that religious conviction and Christian ethics
rested not only upon the word of God but upon the verification which man's reason found in nature. This comforting Christian message, masquerading as philosophy, dominated the senior year of study in the American college.[6]
Preconceived theological views and evangelistic purposes
combined to deprive the course of anything resembling
earnest philosophical investigation. One student described
the course as embracing "man in his unity, and God in his
sovereignty," and he was not exaggerating. Mark Hopkins at
Williams, whose reputation rested in part on his conduct of
the senior year, once described the course to a gathering of
alumni. "We take up first the physical man, and endeavor to
give . . . an idea of every organ and tissue of the body,"
he explained and went on to describe the systematic route
which led the Williams senior through the byways of mental
faculties, grounds of belief, logic, and emotion, to the ultimate destination, the moral government of God.[7] Although
the course was everywhere accepted as philosophy, it was
both in purpose and practice a mixture of religious orthodoxy and personal opinion. Mark Hopkins, Eliphalet Nott of
Union, and Francis Wayland of Brown were some of the
many college presidents who earned a reputation for being
undogmatic by teaching a course that was dedicated to the
propagation of Christian dogma.

On the other hand the propagation of dogma was not the
purpose of the literary societies. They, instead, respected
reason, nurtured intellect, and subjected much that was
established to scrutiny and debate. At Princeton they debated
such questions as: "Ought freedom of thought to be granted
to all men? . . . Is the theater prejudicial to public morals?
. . . Which tends more to relieve a female of celibacy, wealth

[6] See George P. Schmidt: *The Old Time College President* (New
York, 1930); and Wilson Smith: *Professors and Public Ethics: Studies
of Northern Moral Philosophers before the Civil War* (Ithaca, 1956).
   [7] Mark Hopkins: *An Address, Delivered before the Society of
Alumni of Williams College, at the Celebration of the Semicentennial
Anniversary* (Boston, 1843), p. 31.

or a beautiful face? . . . Do the talents of man deteriorate in the Western Hemisphere?"[8] And everywhere the current affairs of the day, the destiny of the American people, the nature of American institutions provided young men with the subjects of debate.

At commencement they put on their own exhibitions of talent and in addition in most colleges they brought an eminent, even a controversial, speaker to the campus to deliver an address. During the 1850's, favorite literary-society commencement speakers were Rufus Choate, Ralph Waldo Emerson, Henry Ward Beecher, Edwin P. Whipple, and Wendell Phillips—not one of them a man that a contro-versy-fearing college would choose to honor. Most of these men appeared at numerous literary-society exhibitions at many American colleges, catering to the desire of the under-graduates to face the world head on and to face it with benefit of thought. George William Curtis's famous oration of 1856, "The Duty of the American Scholar to Politics and the Times," was a commencement offering of the literary societies at Wesleyan.[9] Ralph Waldo Emerson spoke on three occasions at Williams College, all three times under the auspices of students, who were denied the use of college buildings for the display of the subversive, if distinguished, philosopher from Concord.

The literary societies were often responsible for founding college literary magazines, which were another agency of intellect in the colleges. Frequently they published the ad-dresses that were delivered before them by prominent Amer-icans. The rivalry between the two literary societies at Miami University led one of them in 1830 to commission a bust of the college's president by a talented but obscure artist who had recently created a set of wax figures for a museum in Cincinnati. As a consequence Hiram Powers, who would later produce the most famous statuary of the time, was

[8] Wertenbaker: *Princeton*, p. 205.
[9] Carl F. Price: *Wesleyan's First Century* (Middletown, 1932), p. 182.

provided by a college literary society with his first commission for a bust.[1]

In their libraries the literary societies made most clear the degree to which the purposes they served were alien to those of the college. Not only did the literary societies often outstrip the college libraries in numbers of volumes, but the wide range of subject matter allowed far greater opportunity for the play of intellect than did the narrow religious fare of the usual college library. In 1835 the literary societies at the University of North Carolina contained 6,000 volumes, the best collection in the state. By 1840 the literary societies at Bowdoin boasted between 5,000 and 6,000 volumes; at Brown 3,000; and at Williams 10,000. In every case, these libraries were superior to the college libraries.[2] Works of fiction, history, politics, and science were available to students because their literary societies purchased them. English literature and American fiction were first welcomed in the American college by the literary societies, their libraries, and the student magazines. The young man at Marietta who wrote a study of current political problems for the student quarterly, the would-be Addison or Steele who indulged in polite letters for the *Yale Lit*, the young man at Williams who in 1845 shot and stuffed forty native birds for the student natural-history museum, the young men everywhere who turned to their literary-society libraries for Dickens, Thackeray, Scott, Hawthorne, Melville, and Emerson—they knew that there was more than one way to reform an American college.

[1] Havighurst: *Miami*, pp. 76-8.
[2] Kemp Plummer Battle: *History of the University of North Carolina* (Raleigh, 1902-12), I, 410; Sheldon: *The History . . . of American Student Societies*, p. 131. See also Daniel Walker Hollis: *University of South Carolina* (Columbia, 1951-6), I, 230-54; Coulter: *Georgia*, p. 132; Kingsley: *Yale*, I, 188-9; David Bishop Skillman: *The Biography of a College: Being the History of the First Century of the Life of Lafayette College* (Easton, 1932), I, 68-9; Jonas Viles, et al.: *The University of Missouri: A Centennial History* (Columbia, 1939), p. 44; Louis Shores: *Origins of the American College Library 1638-1800* (Nashville, 1934), pp. 224 ff.

In a sense, the literary societies and their libraries, the clubs, journals, and organizations which compensated for the neglect of science, English literature, history, music, and art in the curriculum—this vast developing extracurriculum was the student response to the classical course of study.[2] It brought prestige to the life of the mind. It helped to liberate the intellect on the American campus. It was one answer to the Yale Report of 1828, an answer so effective that by the end of the century at Yale itself there would be real concern over which was really more fundamental, which more important, the curriculum or the extracurriculum.

On another front the undergraduates determined to redefine the American college. Their purpose was to change the focus from the next world to this. Their instrument was the Greek-letter fraternity movement. From parent chapters founded at Union and Hamilton in the late 1820's and 1830's, the Greek-letter fraternity was introduced into most of the colleges of New England and New York by 1840. Between the founding at Union of Kappa Alpha in 1825 and Theta Delta Chi in 1847, four other national fraternities were born there: Sigma Phi, Delta Phi, Chi Psi, and Psi Upsilon. Founded in the country, they moved into the cities, where frequently the demand for new chapters came from graduate members in attendance at law or medical schools.

Alpha Delta Phi, founded at Hamilton in 1832, sponsored within a decade the first fraternity chapters at Amherst, Bowdoin, Brown, Columbia, Harvard, Yale, Western Reserve, and Miami. Beta Theta Pi, founded at Miami in 1839, introduced the Greek-letter society into Michigan, Princeton, Wabash, Washington and Jefferson, and Centre College of Kentucky before 1850. Local fraternities appeared at the University of Vermont, Wesleyan, and Dartmouth between 1837

[2] See Sheldon: *The History . . . of American Student Societies;* James Bruce and J. Vincent Forrestal: *College Journalism* (Princeton, 1914), p. 3; Kingsley: *Yale,* I, 338-60.

and 1842.[4] Few American colleges were left untouched by this movement which so ably characterized the enterprise and initiative of the nineteenth-century college undergraduate.[5] Before they quite knew what had happened, most college presidents found that their undergraduates had ushered into the American college community a social system that they had neither invited nor encouraged.

In 1845 the president of Amherst was asking the president of Williams, "Would it be desirable to have these societies cease in our colleges?" During the decade the same question was being asked at the University of North Carolina, Lafayette, Bowdoin, University of Michigan, Princeton, Brown, Dartmouth, Miami, and Dickinson. The question was often asked, but the fraternities grew apace.

Everywhere the literary societies declined in the decades after the introduction of fraternities. In the East by 1870 the literary societies were remnants of their former selves. By then many had given up altogether. Where fraternities were later in being introduced, literary societies were later in declining. But the pattern almost everywhere was the same. The literary societies declined not so much because the fraternities robbed them of their purpose but because the fraternities created a higher level of loyalty and intruded new political complications into literary-society elections. They also declined as the colleges themselves took over some of their old purposes: built up broader collections of books, opened the libraries more than once a week, intro-

[4] For fraternity statistics see *Baird's Manual: American College Fraternities* (Menasha, Wisconsin; 1940).

[5] See Morison: Harvard: *Three Centuries*, pp. 203, 310; Havighurst: *Miami*, pp. 90-101; Farrand: *Michigan*, pp. 74-82; Morgan: *Dickinson*, pp. 419-26; Woodburn: *Indiana*, pp. 155-9; Van Amringe: *Columbia*, p. 121; Bullock: *Emory*, pp. 130 ff.; Wertenbaker: *Princeton*, pp. 280-2, 323-4; Bronson: *Brown*, pp. 241-2, 348; Fuess: *Amherst*, pp. 118 ff.; Hatch: *Bowdoin*, pp. 311, 314 ff.; Skillman: *Lafayette*, I, 226, 294-9; Battle: *North Carolina*, I, 476, 621; Nevins: *Illinois*, pp. 128-31; Bruce: *Virginia*, III, 166-70; Chessman: *Denison*, pp. 172-7; Rudy: *C.C.N.Y.*, p. 77; Demarest: *Rutgers*, pp. 342 ff.; Price: *Wesleyan*, pp. 244-57; Waite: *Western Reserve*, pp. 251-79.

duced respectable study in English literature, discovered history as a field of study, expanded the sciences.[6]

Fraternities began at a time when it was natural that they should have aped the literary societies and developed literary exercises as one of their functions, but that was not the reason they were founded. Literary exercises amounted to no more than something to do, once a fraternity was founded. The Greek-letter fraternity and its counterpart, the social club, were intended to fill an emotional and social rather than a curricular vacuum. A Kappa Alpha historian concluded: "The atmosphere of Phi Beta Kappa, strictly academic, stimulated in the imagination the dream of new and more intimate relationships. . . . The yearning of the unsatisfied was for fellowship of kindred souls." Another of the early fraternities, in setting forth the criteria for membership, received the help of a young man in 1836 who suggested that the simplest approach was to ask the question: "Would you want your sister to marry him?" The spirit, and therefore the purpose, of the fraternity and social-club movement may merely be implicit in these fragmentary statements, but it is obvious: among the barbarians, we are the Greeks.[7]

Greek-letter fraternities were intended to bring together the most urbane young men on the campus into small groups that would fill the vacuum left by removal from the family and the home community, but they served a further purpose, too. The fraternities offered an escape from the monotony, dreariness, and unpleasantness of the collegiate regimen which began with prayers before dawn and ended with prayers after dark; escape from the long winters and ingrown college world, from the dormitory with its lack of

[6] Kingsley: *Yale*, I, 320-3; Wertenbaker: *Princeton*, p. 329; Woodburn: *Indiana*, p. 316; George Franklin Smythe: *Kenyon College: Its First Century* (New Haven, 1924), p. 245; Richardson: *Dartmouth*, II, 495; Chessman: *Denison*, p. 155; Bronson: *Brown*, p. 349; Cutting: *Amherst*, p. 29; Price: *Wesleyan*, p. 42; Joseph D. Ibbotson and S. N. D. North: *Documentary History of Hamilton College* (Clinton, 1922), p. 249; Sheldon: *The History . . . of American Student Societies*, pp. 133 ff.
[7] Rudolph: *Williams*, p. 103.

privacy. Fraternities institutionalized various escapes—drinking, smoking, card playing, singing, and seducing—but they did not introduce these diversions, which long antedated their founding. By introducing traditional means of escape into a brotherhood of devoted men, the fraternity gave new meaning to a cigar, a drink, a girl, a song, and in time it was not really possible to distinguish purpose from manifestation.

To the trappings of Greece were added those of Freemasonry. Aided by the disclosure of the practices and terminology of Freemasonry (a disclosure produced by the anti-Masonic movement which captured eastern politics in the years after 1826), the fraternities incorporated much of the Masonic spirit into their movement. The ritual of Beta Theta Pi was patterned on Freemasonry; a Kappa Alpha or Chi Psi chapter house and a Masonic chapter house are still known as lodges.

As instructive as any events in the history of the American fraternity movement were two that took place at Williams College, one in 1834 with the launching of an anti-secret society movement, and the second at the time of a religious revival in 1840. The evangelical revivalist ritual of confession proved unequal to fraternal loyalties. Forced to choose between the evangelical injunction to reveal the nature of their new brotherhoods and the fraternal injunction to bare no secrets, the young Greeks made a fateful choice. Their decision to tell nothing succeeded in frustrating a revival that had promised to be a great success.

Evangelical religion could not cope with the fraternity movement, nor in the end could the spirit of political liberalism which animated the anti-secret-society men, who in November 1834 took a determined stand against exclusiveness and secrecy. The constitution of the Social Fraternity which they formed declared its hostility to "all combinations and societies not founded upon liberal principles," and a revised constitution in 1838 announced, in a spirit which revealed its indebtedness to the Enlightenment: "We would invest no class of our fellow students with factitious advantages, but would place all upon an equal footing in running the race of honorable distinction." These sentiments appealed to students elsewhere, and by 1847 similar organizations from Union, Amherst, Hamilton, and Williams joined forces; in 1858 an even larger group decided to call themselves Delta Upsilon. Known variously during its history as the Social Fraternity, the Anti-Secret Society, the Equitable Fraternity, Oudens, and finally Delta Upsilon, the anti-secret movement in its early days fought valiantly for democratic values. But it was as unequal as the evangelically religious to the task of coping with the very situation that had inspired the Greek-letter fraternities.[8]

For it did not matter that Mark Hopkins could agree with President Humphrey of Amherst that college authorities should band together and abolish the fraternities. "The influences have been evil," Hopkins declared. "They create class and factions, and put men socially in regard to each other into an artificial and false position. . . . The alienation of feeling and want of cordiality thus created are not favorable to a right moral and religious state." It did not matter that the anti-secret society for a while developed strength. Opposition to fraternities was clearly unproductive.[9] For the critics did not altogether understand what the fraternity movement actually involved. Who could expect them to see that it proposed the substitution of worldly prowess for spiritual grace as a measure of prestige; the substitution of social status for Christian status; the substitution of attitudes and skills necessary for success in this world, for those considered appropriate for success in the next? In essence, the fraternity movement was institutionalizing new prestige values, the attributes of a successful man of the world, *this* world, at the expense of those various signs of Christian

[8] Ibid., p. 108. Wiliam F. Galpin: *Delta Upsilon: One Hundred Years, 1834-1934* (New York, 1934) is a model fraternity history.
[9] Rudolph: *Williams*, p. 110.

grace—humility, equality, and morality—which had long been the purpose of the colleges to foster.[1]

Contrary to what the friends of religion had thought when their prospects for revival collapsed in 1840, neither secrecy nor mysticism made the fraternity movement so powerfully antireligious. The fall from grace was facilitated by the recognition that the fraternity movement gave to secular values, to good friendship, good looks, good clothes, good family, and good income. Mark Hopkins was unhappy about fraternities but he did confess, in their behalf, that "one object of some of the Societies here is the cultivation of manners, and so far they have improved." One object! This concern with manners was at the very basis of the movement. For in the end polished manners were necessary for success in *this* world, not the next.[2]

As long as the American college remained under the influence of evangelical orthodoxy, as long as a religious orientation was both persistent and sincere, the colleges continued their preference for a brotherhood of professing Christians rather than a multiplicity of Greek brotherhoods. But in no case, regardless of its intentions, could the American college argue very persuasively against the attributes and values of worldly success. The fraternity was one more response of the American college undergraduate to the officials who would keep the college as it was. The mother chapter of Delta Phi at Union was less than three years old when the Yale faculty issued its report in behalf of things as they were in 1828. It had become perfectly clear to the young men of the United States that there were great things stirring, and as they had watched the world about them, it had not seemed to them that pious Christians were chalking up any significant victories over polished gentlemen.

Probably the students would have preferred not to have had to make a choice between Christianity and success.

[1] Ibid., p. 113; Le Duc: *Amherst*, p. 123.
[2] Rudolph: *Williams*, p. 115.

Many college presidents in their courses in moral and intellectual philosophy in any case tried very hard to make material success the result of Christian living. Mark Hopkins at Williams was an early exponent of such a gospel; Russell Conwell at Temple picked up the theme in the early decades of the twentieth century. What was becoming apparent was the degree to which a success-oriented society would no longer accommodate itself to undiluted Christian ethics, could no longer take a full dose of undiluted piety, could no longer in fact sustain colleges that failed to prepare young men for success in this world. The fraternities, then, were schools of success, institutions that prepared young men to take their place among men, not among the angels.

The American college student was not content with liberating the mind, giving it free range in organizations that served the intellect. He was not content with enthroning manners, enshrining the ways of success in this world in a far-flung system of fraternities and social clubs. He also discovered muscle, created organizations for it; his physical appearance and condition had taken on new importance. Man the image of God became competitive, boisterous, muscular, and physically attractive. Man the image of God became the fine gentleman—jolly, charming, pleasant, well-developed, good-looking. He became an obvious candidate for fraternity membership.

There was nothing sudden about the development of organized athletics. At first a combination of hostility and indifference kept the movement from developing at all. At Princeton, for example, in 1787 the faculty forbade Princeton students to play strenuous games of shinny, a kind of hockey, on the grounds that it "is in itself low and unbecoming gentlemen and scholars, and is attended with great danger to the health." At R.P.I. early in the 1820's an official announcement declared: "Such exercise as running, jumping, climbing, scuffling, and the like are calculated to detract from that dignity of deportment which becomes a man of science." [3]

No official answer to the problem of the physical condition of the American college undergraduate was forthcoming until the outdoor gymnasium movement arrived from Europe in the baggage of a trio of German refugees. In 1826 Charles T. Follen inaugurated collegiate gymnastic exercises in a Harvard dining hall and soon thereafter erected outdoor gymnastic apparatus and led the entire college on a cross-country dogtrot. The United States had seen nothing like this before. Between 1826 and 1828 outdoor gymnasiums appeared at Yale, Amherst, Williams, Brown, Bowdoin, and Dartmouth. In Providence, Francis Wayland, the newly elected president of Brown, joined his students on the swings and parallel bars of the new Brown gymnasium. Nonetheless, this early gymnastic movement was premature. The swings and the bars and the rings were soon in disrepair.[4]

The Puritan ethic objected to the kind of frivolity and play suggested by an outdoor gymnasium. William Paley, the eighteenth-century English theologian whose works were read in connection with the moral philosophy course in many colleges, argued that if young men had an itch to do something, they should plant a garden. This was exactly what was done at Bowdoin, Kenyon, Hamilton, Marietta, Williams, and at many of the Catholic colleges, and with a great deal more success than met the gymnastic movement of the 1820's.[5]

[3] Wertenbaker: *Princeton*, p. 138; Sheldon: *The History . . . of American Student Societies*, p. 147; Palmer Chamberlain Ricketts: *History of Rensselaer Polytechnic Institute 1824-1914* (3d. ed.; New York, 1934), pp. 44-5.
[4] See Fred E. Leonard: *Pioneers of Modern Physical Training* (New York, 1915), and *A Guide to the History of Physical Education* (3d. ed.; Philadelphia, 1947).
[5] Hatch: *Bowdoin*, p. 342; Smythe: *Kenyon*, p. 83; Ibbotson and North: *Hamilton*, p. 214; Arthur G. Beach: *A Pioneer College: The Story of Marietta*, p. 112; Rudolph: *Williams*, pp. 168-70; Sebastian A.

In an America full of dreams yet to be fulfilled, unproductive physical exercise of the sort suggested by an outdoor gymnasium also appeared to be unnecessarily trivial. Most college students in the early nineteenth century were drawn from farms where they had been trained to work but not to play. Young men did not need to be reminded that Americans judged their neighbors by their industry, not by their capacity for enjoyment. How many fathers must have written their sons as did Alvan Hyde to his son at Williams in 1831: "I hope you will not be seen with the ball-club in your hand this summer." [6]

Until another wave of German immigrants brought the gymnasium movement to the United States once again (in 1848), the American college undergraduate would channel his energies into physical activities appropriate to his surroundings: bowling, boxing, marbles, shinny, dancing, hunting, swimming, walking, skating, fishing, wrestling, fox and geese, foot races, and early free-for-all versions of football and baseball. And he would devote himself to all the worldly pleasures frowned on by the college and encouraged by the fraternity.

When the new German immigrants of the late 1840's and 1850's brought with them the *turnvereine*, however, they found the American college student prepared to emulate them. By 1853 there were at least sixty German gymnastic clubs in American cities, and by the end of the decade the American college was deeply committed to the new gymnastic movement. Students often built the gymnasiums themselves, wheedled partial financial support from the authorities, or broadcast their desires among willing alumni. At Princeton the students provided half the cost of a gymnasium. At Miami in Ohio the student Gymnastic Association

Erbacher: *Catholic Higher Education for Men in the United States 1850-1866* (Washington, 1931), p. 110.
    [6] Rudolph: *Williams*, p. 158.

rented a barn and hired a German tumbler from Cincinnati to give them gymnastic instructions. By 1860 new gymnasiums were in operation at the University of Virginia, Harvard, Yale, Amherst, Williams, Bowdoin, and Oberlin.[7]

By the 1860's the colleges themselves were assuming responsibility for gymnastics. To this position they were led by Amherst, where in 1860 there was established a Department of Hygiene and Physical Education, charged with responsibility for the health of the undergraduates. So that there should be no misunderstanding about what led the Amherst authorities to this departure, the new gymnasium prominently displayed the motto: "Keep thyself pure: the body is the temple of the Holy Ghost." It was not untypical of the American college that it would attempt to graft an old utility on a new student enthusiasm. The readiness of the Amherst authorities, and following them almost every other American college, to accept the new gymnastic movement did not mean that the colleges acquiesced in new student values. What it did mean was that they hoped that all this enthusiasm for muscles could be channelled to good purpose.[8] In the meantime, the students were once more leaving the college authorities way behind. At the University of Virginia a student observed: "A gymnasium has in it something so mechanical, so business-like, that exercise ceases to be a pleasure and becomes a labor. Where are the sports that become a great university, and the vigorous youth of a great State? Where are our cricket matches? . . . [Where is our] boat club?"[9]

Since 1843 at Yale, since 1844 at Harvard, an attempt had been made to find an answer to these student complaints in

[7] Fred E. Leonard: *Pioneers of Modern Physical Training*, pp. 268 ff.; Wertenbaker: *Princeton*, pp. 277-8; Havighurst: *Miami*, p. 111; Bruce: *Virginia*, III, 150-3; Fuess: *Amherst*, p. 158; Rudolph: *Williams*, pp. 159-161; Robert Samuel Fletcher: *A History of Oberlin College from its Foundation through the Civil War* (Oberlin, 1943), II, 824-6.

[8] See Leonard: *Pioneers of Modern Physical Training*, pp. 89 ff.; Le Duc: *Amherst*, pp. 128-34; Edward Hitchcock: *The Results of Anthropometry: As Derived from the Measurements of the Students in Amherst College* (Amherst, 1892), pp. 3-5.

[9] Bruce: *Virginia*, III, 154.

boating. In 1852 at Lake Winnepesaukee the first intercollegiate contest of any sort was a boat race between Harvard and Yale. The game, however, that answered the needs of the American undergraduate for thrills, for competition, for physical development was baseball. On July 1, 1859, at Pittsfield, Massachusetts, Amherst and Williams played the first game of intercollegiate baseball. Within ten years baseball moved into every section of the country and made demands on the colleges that suggested that a new era was on its way.[1]

At Dartmouth, before long, the father of one student would withdraw his son in protest over the growth of athletics. At the Massachusetts Agricultural College in 1870 an athletic victory over Harvard was met with special joy because, as was pointed out at the time, it gave the "agricultural college standing as a real college," and in due time the state legislature increased its appropriations accordingly. And at Syracuse the new dispensation was greeted in 1875 by a snort from Chancellor Erastus O. Haven: "As well might the Methodist, Presbyterian, and Baptist ministers of New York City select a crew to exhibit their prowess in a boat race on the Hudson."[2]

Chancellor Haven did not quite understand. Undergraduate values and ministerial values were not the same. Nor were undergraduate values and those to which the colleges had so long subscribed the same. For the American college student the gymnasium, the boat club, the baseball team (and before long the track team, the football team, the cricket team) were necessary for the fullest enjoyment of life. They were institutions in which the student embedded his values, the

[1] Sheldon: *The History . . . of American Student Societies*, pp. 192-231; Morison: Harvard: *Three Centuries*, p. 314; Kingsley: *Yale*, II, 274-364; Fuess: *Amherst*, pp. 197-8; Rudolph: *Williams*, p. 164.
[2] Richardson: *Dartmouth*, II, 566; Alfred C. True: *A History of Agricultural Education in the United States, 1785-1925* (Washington, 1929), p. 149; Walter P. Rogers: *Andrew D. White and the Modern University* (Ithaca, 1942), p. 190.

values of worldly success; institutions in which he clarified the nature of the distance that stretched between his view of life and the view that the college purveyed.

In the extracurriculum the college student stated his case for the human mind, the human personality, and the human body, for all aspects of man that the colleges tended to ignore in their single-minded interest in the salvation of souls. In the institutions of the extracurriculum college students everywhere suggested that they preferred the perhaps equally challenging task of saving minds, saving personalities, saving bodies. When they were finished the college that the reformers of the 1820's had attempted to reshape would be unrecognizable. On the whole the curriculum would still be intact, and compulsory chapel was only beginning to give way. But in the extracurriculum the students erected within the gates a monster. Taming it would now become as necessary a project as the long-delayed reform of the curriculum itself.

8

❧❧❧

Academic Balance
of Power

The vigor of the extracurriculum was proof that the undergraduates had succeeded in assuming significant authority over college life and that as a result they had become a remarkably important element in the power structure of the American college. That they were able to do so was in part a function of the American tendency to favor the young, whatever their endeavors, but also operative was a conscious policy of laissez faire, an administrative acquiescence in, if not approval of, these student excursions into the world of the extracurriculum. Faternities and organized athletics especially disturbed many college authorities, but with few exceptions they learned not to interfere.

Although the authorities did not intend to create the power vacuum that gave the students their opportunities, yet in adhering to the prescribed classical course of study, this was very much what they did do. For the classical course and all that went with it and that constituted the official collegiate scheme inspired vigorous young men to seek some better means of expressing their goals, their values, and their interests than the authorities were willing or able to provide.

The extracurriculum which these young men developed—
the agencies of intellect, the deeply embedded social system,
the network of organized athletics—would become the repositories of their power. Through the extracurriculum the
student arrived at a position of commanding importance in
the American college. By opposing the literary societies,
journals, and other clubs to the curriculum, by opposing the
fraternities to the collegiate way, and by setting up in the
athletic hero a more appealing symbol than the pious Christian, the students succeeded, although not really intentionally, in robbing the college professor of a certain element
of prestige and of a sizable area of authority.

Yet, the era of the colleges was in many ways the era of
the professor, as it was the era of other simple and somewhat romantic figures—the steamboat captain, the Yankee
peddler, the southern senator. The era of the colleges was
the era of Professor George Blaetterman, the German-born
professor of modern languages at the University of Virginia,
who in the past had been subjected to stonings by his students and who in 1840 was dismissed from the Virginia faculty after having twice during the previous week beaten his
wife, once on the public road. It was also the era of his per-
plexed successor, a Hungarian wanderer, Charles Kraitser,
who also was dismissed. Said Kraitser, whose overpowering
wife often turned him out of the house at night: "The
Board of Visitors . . . were gentlemen whom it was hard to
please. They had kicked Dr. Blaetterman out because he had
whipped his wife, and they have kicked me out because I
have been whipped by my wife. What did they really
want?" [1]
    What the American college really wanted and needed was
someone like Alpheus Spring Packard, who taught for sixty-
five happy years at Bowdoin and there earned a reputation

[1] Philip Alexander Bruce: *History of the University of Virginia,
1819-1919* (New York, 1920-2), II, 159-62.

as the students' "beau ideal of a Christian gentleman"; someone like Julian Sturtevant, who was appointed the first member of the faculty of Illinois College in 1829 and who enjoyed a tenure of fifty-six years before his retirement in
1885.[2] The American college wanted and revered men like
Professor Fletcher O. Marsh, who in 1866 hauled manure all
one day that the grounds of Denison College might in some
way be made more beautiful; men of all work like John
Smith of Dartmouth, whose appointment made him "Professor of English, Latin, Greek, Chaldee, etc., and such
other languages as he shall have time for." What the American college wanted or needed was a man like Father William
Stack Murphy of Fordham who in the 1840's would, while
shaving and gesticulating with his razor, listen to his students
practice orations and then go off to conduct classes which
were a wonder of charm, interest, and successful teaching.[3]

In the professors, and only in the outstanding professors at
that, the colleges located that effective Christian impulse,
that kindly paternalism, that moral rectitude on which their
best intentions rested. For one thing, only rarely were the
professors scholars. When Thomas Jefferson in 1824 recruited a faculty, including four Englishmen and a German,
on the basis of intellectual promise and learning rather than
piety, he invited the hostility of the press, which was much
more interested that a faculty be American than that it be
learned. One scandalized Connecticut newspaper remarked:
"Mr. Jefferson might as well have said that his taverns and
dormitories should not be built with American brick." A
Philadelphia newspaper charged: "[One of the] greatest in-

[2] Louis C. Hatch: *The History of Bowdoin College* (Portland, 1927),
p. 50; Charles Henry Rammelkamp: *Illinois College: A Centennial History 1829-1929* (New Haven, 1928), *passim*.
    [3] G. Wallace Chessman: *Denison: The Story of an Ohio College*
(Granville, 1957), p. 111; Leon Burr Richardson: *History of Dartmouth
College* (Hanover, 1932), I, 175-6; Thomas Gaffney Taaffe: *A History
of St. John's College, Fordham, N.Y.* (New York, 1891), pp. 76-8.

sults which the American people had ever received."[4]

Mark Hopkins, who in many ways has come to symbolize the old-time professor, won a place in the history of American education, not because he was learned but in part because he considered himself and his task as beyond the realm of learning—in that nobler area where the souls of men, especially young men, were touched with moral truth. Hopkins once said to one of his colleagues: "You read books. I don't read books, in fact I never did read any books." His great contemporary, Eliphalet Nott at Union, once said to a member of *his* faculty, a professor of Greek: "I care less for Greek than you do, and less for books, generally, as a means of educational discipline." Even so, both Hopkins and Nott were more than adequately equipped to be two of the great representative professors and college presidents of the era. What they needed was a reservoir of faith, an abiding conviction, a capacity for transferring their confidence in God's rule to others, and these they had in abundance.[5]

The professors in the era of the colleges were recruited from men who believed "that in serving the cause of knowledge and truth by promoting liberal education," they were serving the cause of religion.[6] Many had hoped to be active clergymen but for reasons of health had turned to what was considered the less demanding profession of teaching. Edward Wigglesworth, the first Hollis Professor of Divinity at Harvard, was prevented by deafness from earlier obtaining a parish. Albert Micajah Shipp was elected to a professorship at Wofford College when his voice became too weak to command a parish.[7] If a college professorship was never a sinecure, it was sometimes intended to be a rest cure.

[4] Bruce: *Virginia*, II, 1-2, 35.

[5] Frederick Rudolph: *Mark Hopkins and the Log: Williams College, 1836-1872* (New Haven, 1956), p. 77; Andrew Van Vranken Raymond, ed.: *Union University: Its History, Influence, Characteristics and Equipment* (New York, 1907), I, 176.

[6] Andrew Fleming West: *The Changing Conception of "The Faculty" in American Universities* (San Francisco, 1906[?]), p. 3.

[7] Samuel Eliot Morison: *Three Centuries of Harvard 1636-1936*

THE AMERICAN COLLEGE AND UNIVERSITY 160

The old-time college professor was often a clergyman or had at least some theological training. Of 130 members of the Union College faculty between 1795 and 1884, 55 were clergymen. Two thirds of the professors at Dartmouth between 1828 and 1862 had had theological training. The first faculty of the College of Charleston was unusual in its variety but not in its clerical flavor: an Episcopal bishop, a Huguenot pastor, and a Catholic priest. The faculty at Lafayette was composed entirely of clergymen in 1841, and in 1868 at Princeton on a faculty of ten, there were seven Presbyterian ministers.[8]

The professors were also recruited from men who were prepared to indulge in a kind of psychological, if not physical, expatriation. As long as the clergy were the most esteemed figures in the community, the clergyman-teacher and the teacher were not isolated from the main currents of American life. But even in the era of the colleges the clergyman was being surpassed in public estimation by the squire, the successful lawyer-politician, the man of affairs. The professor necessarily became someone who was not fully participating in American life, someone who stood aside while red-blooded Americans sought the main chance.

This divorce from the world—which was nothing less than a rejection of the enterprising, exploiting, self-seeking qualities of American life—would not recommend the professors to their students or, increasingly, to their students' fathers and to the governing boards as well. Not yet had things come to the state at which they would be in 1888, when President Francis L. Patton would unabashedly declare in

(Cambridge, 1936), p. 67; David Duncan Wallace: *History of Wofford College* (Nashville, 1951), p. 66.

[8] Raymond: *Union*, I, 398; Richardson: *Dartmouth*, II, 457; James Harold Easterby: *A History of the College of Charleston Founded 1770* (Charleston, 1935), p. 19; David Bishop Skillman: *The Biography of a College: Being the History of the First Century of the Life of Lafayette College* (Easton, 1932), I, 147; Thomas Jefferson Wertenbaker: *Princeton 1746-1896* (Princeton, 1946), p. 287.

his inaugural address at Princeton: "College administration
is a business in which trustees are partners, professors the
salesmen and students the customers."[9] The professors in the
era of the colleges, however, were already on the road
there, on the way from being teaching fellows charged with
ultimate responsibility to being hirelings of those men of
the world who increasingly dominated collegiate governing
boards. This development was hastened after midcentury
by the tendency of governing boards to become a locus of
alumni affection and authority at a time when the faculty itself, once almost exclusively drawn from alumni, was becoming less parochial in its recruitment. In time this change
would encourage the governing boards to think of themselves as the preservers of collegiate virtue and to look upon
the professors as a band of invaders. They would suffer the
professors to attend to those matters of curriculum and college management for which they, as busy men of affairs,
had no time, but they would not permit the professors to
forget that the definition and public image of the institution
itself were peculiarly matters for trustee decision.

That other adornment of college faculties, the tutor, was
often the subject of ill will, but not from governing boards.
The tutor was a young man just out of college, perhaps
with nothing else to do, unlikely to make a career of teaching but conceivably so, probably interested merely in earning a few dollars shortly before going on to theological
school or before definitely committing himself to a career.
The tutor was a cheap labor device. Although barely any
older than the students, he was not only called upon to instruct them in class but was also expected "to maintain discipline without being harsh, to be friendly without sacri-
ficing dignity, to distinguish between harmless pranks and
real defiance of authority."[1]

[9] Wertenbaker: *Princeton*, p. 9.
[1] Ibid., pp. 190-1.

A major functional difference between a professor and a tutor existed in their teaching assignments. In most institutions the professor taught a subject—Latin, Greek, natural philosophy, or mathematics, while a tutor taught a class— the Class of 1826 or 1827 or 1828 or 1829, for example. He was perhaps assigned to a class on its entrance to college and if he stayed that long he would still be with it at the time of its graduation. In the meantime he would have taught it both in subjects for which the college had no professors and in elementary studies in subjects for which the college did have professors. The saving to the college was considerable. So was the effect on undergraduate discipline, morale, and respect for the course of study.

Tutors seldom lasted long enough to become experienced at anything but dodging stones thrown through their windows or bottles thrown at their dormitory doors by unappreciative students. Even experience of this sort was not always sufficient protection. At the University of North Carolina in the 1820's wisdom required that one tutor's room be fortified with wooden shutters. It was no wonder that tutors should on occasion have otherwise fortified themselves, as did two disillusioned tutors at South Carolina in 1827 who were dismissed for insobriety.[2] One shining exception to the record of student abuse and of tutorial inexperience was Henry Flynt, Harvard A.B., Class of 1693, who served Harvard as a tutor without promotion for fifty-five years. The custom of giving tutors pieces of silver plate as a token of appreciation at graduation time was especially challenging in the case of one who stayed so long. One year his students gave Henry Flynt a suitably engraved silver chamber pot.

When a tutor revealed endearing qualities the results could be as surprising as a letter which was read to a departing University of North Carolina tutor in 1833:

[2] Kemp Plummer Battle: *History of the University of North Carolina* (Raleigh, 1902-12), I, 275; Daniel Walker Hollis: *University of South Carolina* (Columbia, 1951-6), I, 79.

We are about to bid adieu to him that has so honorably
conducted us through the Sophomore year, to him that
has laid the foundations of our future eminence, to him
that has connected the beauties of the scholar and the
refinements of the gentleman. . . . Now, in all the emotion which the word naturally suggests, we bid you an
affectionate "farewell." In the name of the whole class,
"farewell." [3]

The institution of the tutor itself would in time be given a
fond farewell, only to revive in the twentieth century as an
aspect of the psychological return to England and to the
country, which was made possible by the Harkness house
system at Harvard.

In 1767 Harvard dignified the job considerably by giving
tutors a subject instead of a class to teach. Yale followed in
1830. This change, as it was more widely accepted, had the
effect of transforming tutors into scholars or instructors with
professional ambitions. In any widespread sense such a development would not occur until the last quarter of the
nineteenth century when "the old dichotomy [of professors
and tutors was] . . . converted into a hierarchy" of instructors, assistant professors, associate professors, and professors. In such ways was the tutor transformed and made to
serve the needs of a society where everywhere the organization man was emerging.[4] The old tutor was in no sense an
organization man—he was merely passing through. When he
was changed into an instructor, however, and invited to join
in a competitive race for rank, he found that the college had
become a bureaucracy, and like his classmates at Bethlehem
Steel or National City or Standard Oil, he was working his
way up a ladder. One day he might be a professor.

[3] Samuel Eliot Morison: *Harvard College in the Seventeenth Century*
(Cambridge, 1936), II, 525; Battle: *North Carolina*, I, 349-50.
[4] Samuel Eliot Morison: *The Founding of Harvard College* (Cambridge, 1935), pp. 137 ff.; George Wilson Pierson: *Yale: College and
University 1871-1937* (New Haven, 1952-5), I, 142-3.

But in the era of the colleges there was no ladder, and while many tutors did become professors, their tutorial years were not looked upon as years of apprenticeship. In the power structure of the American college there was no one lower than a tutor—a young man who had given up his rights as a student to become a lackey, a spy. Generally despised by students, exploited or ignored by professors, he was perhaps one answer to inadequate collegiate financial resources. But even so, always allowing for those cherished exceptions, he was one reason that the American college presented such a dreary picture to its critics.

If the picture was not dreary, the president of the college was often thought to be responsible for the difference. His office was the creation of conditions peculiar to the American experience with higher education, and he conducted it in a manner to lead one historian, albeit with considerable exaggeration, to conclude that "the president was by all odds the greatest single educative force encountered by the students. . . . The president . . . was in most institutions the dominating influence . . . the greatest single force in college life." The prerogatives and functions of the chief executive officer of the American college certainly developed from crude beginnings, but even at the beginning, in his relationship to faculty and governing board, the president was on his way to that day in the twentieth century when it would be said of him: "He has become a mere administrator, the business manager of a great plant, a lobbyist often at the general assembly of the state, a peripatetic raiser of funds, an applauded lecturer before women's clubs and rotary clubs and boards of trade, a dignitary in gorgeous robes at intercollegiate functions, resplendent at commencement, an absentee for long periods from the college campus." [5] As such, of

[5] George P. Schmidt: *The Old Time College President* (New York, 1930), pp. 11, 42; Fred Lewis Pattee: *Tradition and Jazz* (New York, 1925), p. 132.

course, he would no longer be, from the point of view of students, much of an educative force or influence at all.

It is certain that the president's job had always been demanding and exhausting. Eleazar Wheelock in November 1771 cast a longing look at approaching winter in Hanover and expressed the hope that it would provide him with sufficient relief from work to permit him "to have leisure to swallow down . . . [his] spittle." But the great difference between the old-time president and the one who replaced him toward the end of the nineteenth century was that the old-time president lived at the college, was not absent for long periods of time, probably taught every member of the senior class, knew most of the students by name, indeed probably made a practice of calling on them in their rooms. For these reasons he was an influence and asserted an authority in the life of the undergraduates that his successor never could.[6]

If the president was losing authority in one area, however, he was gaining in his power over the faculty, a gain which began almost as soon as the office appeared in the person of President Dunster at early Harvard. In the colonial college the power of the president derived in part from the considerable distance which often stretched between him and the rest of his faculty, which might consist entirely of tutors. "Harvard had been established for more than eighty-five years, Yale for more than fifty, and Princeton for more than twenty before each had its first professor, and it was to be many years more before regular professors outnumbered transient tutors." In the early colleges only the president could stand before the governing body as a mature man of learning. By the time that a complement of professors was recruited to assist him in teaching, the president had become the locus of "the prestige and pride [and power] that elsewhere were vested in the faculties." A president might lead or dominate such a faculty. He might even share his authority with it, but increasingly the president was becoming not

[6] Richardson: *Dartmouth*, I, 109.

the leader of a college faculty but the spokesman and representative of an absentee board of governors.[7]
It was not always so. In fact, it had been the clear intention of the founders of Harvard to carry on the English
tradition of resident-faculty control. The first compromise
with English practice was necessitated by the fact that a
company of scholars could not assemble in the woods of
Massachusetts without being called together by someone.
Harvard had to be founded; it could not simply develop;
there were insufficient resources and scholars for English
precedent to prevail. At Harvard these official founders were
institutionalized into a board of overseers; at William and
Mary, into a board of visitors. Thus there developed at both
institutions two bodies: the faculty corporation which was in
the tradition of English practice, and the external lay body
which represented the founders.

Until 1697 no teacher at Harvard failed of appointment as
a fellow of the corporation; before 1697 only three non-
teachers had been made fellows. But by 1716 nonresident
control of the corporation was clearly indicated; in 1778 it
was established and has ever since been maintained. The appearance of fellows on the corporation not drawn from the
faculty derived in part from the fact that a Harvard fellowship had become a position of influence and prestige, a step-
ping stone to the Harvard presidency, much sought after by
outside clergymen. By 1778 men of affairs other than clergymen were being elected to the Harvard corporation.[8]

At William and Mary by the charter of 1693 the president
was first among equals on a faculty of resident masters, who
comprised the corporation. In a dispute between the masters
and visitors in 1755 the president sided not with his faculty

[7] Richard Hofstadter and Walter P. Metzger: *The Development of
Academic Freedom in the United States* (New York, 1955), pp. 124-5.
[8] Ibid., pp. 126-30; John E. Kirkpatrick: *The Rise of Non-Resident
Government in Harvard University and How Harvard is Governed*
(Ann Arbor, 1925), pp. 12-27 ff.; John E. Kirkpatrick: *Academic Or-
ganization and Control* (Yellow Springs, 1931), pp. xiv-xix; Morison:
Harvard: *Three Centuries*, pp. 160-1, 212-13, 233, 359.

but with the board of visitors. When the consequences of this action were finally recorded in statutes and practice, the president of William and Mary had become representative of the board of visitors and faculty control and authority had been severely limited.[9]

Yale inaugurated a type of governing board which would become standard American practice—the single absentee body. Yale raised "an expedient to the rank of principle" when in 1701 its charter simply made the ten organizing clergymen the corporation. Henceforth the normal American procedure would be to follow the Yale precedent. The development of nonresident control helped to change the president from being either first among equals or spokesman or leader of the faculty into something far different—representative of the governing board and a significant power in his own right.[1]

By 1848 Samuel Eliot, a historian of Harvard, was writing, in reference to an unsuccessful effort of the Harvard faculty in 1824 to regain their long-lost authority as fellows: "Gentlemen almost exclusively engaged in the instruction and discipline of youth are not, usually, in the best condition to acquire that experience in affairs, and acquaintance with men, which, to say the least, are extremely desirable in the management of the exterior concerns of a large literary institution. Arrangements for instruction must be adapted to the state of the times, and to that of the world around, as well as of that within, the college walls; and of this state men engaged in the active business of life are likely to be better judges than the literary man."[2]

Eliot's remarks were not only a classic statement of the

[9] Kirkpatrick: *Academic Organization and Control*, pp. 52–8; Hofstadter and Metzger: *The Development of Academic Freedom*, pp. 130–4.

[1] Kirkpatrick: *American Organization and Control*, p. xvii; Hofstadter and Metzger: *The Development of Academic Freedom*, pp. 135–9.

[2] Samuel A. Eliot: *A Sketch of the History of Harvard College and of its Present State* (Boston, 1848), p. 49.

rationale for absentee control. They were also an epitaph for faculty government, the English tradition of a corporation of resident teaching fellows. They drew a picture of the college as an ivory tower, a retreat for educators in whose hands busy practical men could not altogether afford to leave questions of education. And they described the environment from which the American college president emerged as a figure of tremendous power, power that he did not always use well, but power that was nonetheless his by virtue of its not belonging to anyone else. For if the busy trustees did not have complete confidence in the professors, neither did they always have the time or the interest to assume all responsibilities themselves. In these circumstances, with trustee approval, power quite naturally flowed to the president. The old-time college president, however, was not yet fully the busy man-of-affairs, almost as total a stranger to his faculty as to his students. The old-time college president was busy, but the pace was slower. He was a fund-raiser, but he also had time to fulfill his paternal responsibilities to the collegiate way.

With characteristic bluntness Upton Sinclair remarked in 1923 that "the college president spends his time running back and forth between Mammon and God."[3] Sinclair may actually have achieved a more accurate description of the old-time president than of the twentieth-century model, whose running may perhaps better have been described in terms of Mammon alone. The experience of John Finley Crowe, president of Hanover College, Indiana, was typical of hundreds of nineteenth-century college presidents, for whom fund-raising rather than educational leadership became an absorbing but hardly rewarding necessity.

President Crowe went East from Indiana in the winter of 1830–31 and began his campaign in Philadelphia, where although his reception was cordial he was told that it was a bad time of the year, the philanthropic merchants were not

[3] Upton Sinclair: *The Goose-Step, a Study of American Education* (Pasadena, 1923), p. 386.

doing much business, and perhaps he should return in the spring. In the meantime, why not try Princeton? At Princeton his welcome was cordial—as, indeed, it would be everywhere—and he was there given letters of introduction to men of good will in New York. In New York he met the same story as in Philadelphia, but he was advised to try Albany, where the merchants were not engaged in the western trade and not, therefore, limited in their benevolence by the seasons of the year. By then he had to borrow money in order to get to Albany, where he found the legislature just convening and was advised that under the circumstances it was not an auspicious time for raising money in Albany. Perhaps he should try Troy and Lansingburgh and return to Albany later. At Troy he found himself in the midst of a religious revival—no time, the pastor pointed out, for diverting the attention of his flock to another object. Too discouraged at this point to care, John Finley Crowe campaigned quietly and subversively among the congregation and began to meet some success in Troy, then in Hudson where a snowstorm confined him for a week, in other Hudson valley towns, and finally even in New York and Philadelphia. He returned to Hanover with three thousand dollars and a hundred books.[4]

The president's paternal responsibilities were burdensome and time-consuming, yet as rewarding as any of the demands placed upon him. President Martin Brewer Anderson of the University of Rochester described his responsibilities in 1868: "No class passes through my hands which does not contain more or less young men who are on the eve of ruin from wayward natures, bad habits, or hereditary tendencies to evil. These men must be watched, borne with, and if possible saved to the world and to their families. . . . This work must mainly be done by the president. . . .

[4] William Alfred Millis: *The History of Hanover College from 1827 to 1927* (Hanover, 1927), pp. 21-8.

Those private and confidential reproofs, suggestions, and admonitions which, when judiciously made, do so much to form manners and character, must be attended to by the president." [5] These obligations to the collegiate way were taken up by presidents who overwhelmingly were clergymen, men who would have exercised such responsibilities toward parishioners, had they had a parish. Before the Civil War eleven out of twelve college presidents were clergymen. One student has been able to discover no more than twenty-six who were not. The first was John Leverett at Harvard, 1708-24, who, although trained for the ministry, gave up divinity for the law. The second was John Wheelock at Dartmouth in 1779; the next at Harvard was Josiah Quincy in 1829. [6]

Columbia, William and Mary, and the University of South Carolina were more receptive to the nonclergyman president than most other colleges, but almost everywhere the clergyman president prevailed. Brown, Hamilton, and Princeton all went into the twentieth century without yet having experienced a nonclerical administration. The University of Georgia elected a clergyman to the presidency in 1811 and maintained that tradition for the next hundred years. James B. Angell, dynamic and effective president of the University of Michigan in a later era, remarked of the age of the colleges in 1895: "Almost any clergyman who could make a good appearance in the pulpit of his denomination and teach from text-books the elements of intellectual and moral philosophy could fill the presidency acceptably." [7]

[5] Jesse Leonard Rosenberger: *Rochester, the Making of a University* (Rochester, 1927), p. 196.

[6] Schmidt: *The Old Time College President*, p. 184.

[7] John Howard Van Amringe, *et al.*: *A History of Columbia University 1754-1904* (New York, 1904), pp. 21, 25, 82, 97, 123; Herbert Baxter Adams: *The College of William and Mary* (Washington, 1887), p. 18; Hollis: *South Carolina*, I, 77-88, 143, 148; Walter C. Bronson: *The History of Brown University 1764-1914* (Providence, 1914), p. 469; Charles Elmer Allison: *A Historical Sketch of Hamilton College,*

President Angell underestimated the sense of responsibility and the motivation of the old-time college presidents. They may not have had to deal with the kind of problems that made a famous man of James B. Angell, but they were capable of the intense sincerity and dedication which Julian M. Sturtevant revealed in 1844 when he was wrestling with the question of whether he should accept the presidency of Illinois College. "May the Lord give me wisdom," he wrote to a friend. "If I am to be placed at the head of this College, may he pour out upon [me] his spirit till I am fully qualified for the holy and responsible work—to be wise, to be firm, to be humble, to shed over this College the holy influence of piety and to lead the successive generations of students to Christ. How can *I* ever be sufficient for these things? . . . *Pray for me.* . . ." [8]

Obviously not all the old-time college presidents were thoroughly effective. They were subject to the usual human failings. The Reverend Samuel Locke wisely resigned the presidency of Harvard College after confessing to the corporation in 1773 that he was responsible for the interesting condition of a maid in the president's house. Some presidents did not know when to resign: Eliphalet Nott extended his reign at Union to sixty-two years and the college later suffered because of it. Some presidents were remarkably petty. The Reverend William M. Blackburn, early president of the University of North Dakota, appeared before the Board of Regents and complained that Mrs. E. S. Mott, preceptress and instructor in English, regularly and deliberately began to eat before he asked the blessing. Mrs. Mott retorted that the

Clinton, New York (Yonkers, 1889), p. 425; Thomas Jefferson Wertenbaker: *Princeton 1746-1896* (Princeton, 1946), p. 389; E. Merton Coulter: *College Life in the Old South* (Athens, 1951), p. 20; James Burrill Angell: *Selected Addresses* (New York, 1912), p. 118.
[8] Rammelkamp: *Illinois College*, p. 139.

food was equally poor before and after the blessing. The board of regents wisely dismissed them both.[9]

On the whole, however, a thankless task was performed reasonably well by scores of now forgotten clergymen who tirelessly went about their work with the determination and the humility of President Ashbel Green of Princeton, whose diary for May 5, 1814, recorded: "This morning the Faculty admonished four students and dismissed two. . . . I took the examination of the senior class on belles lettres and wrote letters to the parents of the two dismissed students. The Faculty met in the evening and a pistol was fired at the door of one of the tutors. I ought to be very thankful to God for his support this day."[1] More than one president subscribed to the sentiments of Francis Wayland who, after retiring from the presidency of Brown, heard the college bell summoning faculty and students to the opening of a new college year and then remarked: "No one can conceive the unspeakable relief and freedom which I feel at this moment to hear that bell rung, and to know, for the first time in nearly twenty-nine years, that it calls me to no duty."[2]

Unquestionably one source of Wayland's relief was his knowledge that no longer would he, a president of exceptional vision and reforming zeal, have to deal with a governing board which had once led him to ask: "How can colleges prosper directed by men[,] very good men to be sure[,] but who know about every other thing except about education. The man who first devised the present mode of governing colleges in this country has done us more injury than Benedict Arnold."[3]

[9] Morison: Harvard: *Three Centuries*, p. 100; Raymond: *Union*, I, 314 ff.; Louis G. Geiger: *University of the Northern Plains: A History of the University of North Dakota (1883-1958)* (Grand Forks, 1958), p. 45.

[1] Wertenbaker: *Princeton*, p. 157.

[2] Bronson: *Brown*, p. 302.

[3] To James Marsh, 1829, quoted in Julian Ira Lindsay: *Tradition*

The American mode of governing colleges was, as the Harvard and Yale experiences indicated, a child of necessity. Nothing traitorous was intended when the government of the American college to an important degree was taken out of the hands of educators and put, as Wayland suggested, in the hands of men of affairs, men whose outlook on education would often be shaped by a nostalgic recollection of what college had been in the days long since gone when they were in residence.

If members of college governing boards were unfit by training or inclination to deal with matters of education, what were they doing on the boards of trustees, or regents, or curators, or governors that managed the affairs of the American college? Some trustees were, as Wayland on another occasion suggested, window dressing: men who commanded some respect for their professional or political achievements and whose presence on the governing board was to be construed by society at large as an endorsement of the institution. Wealthy men were expected to give the college a reputation for financial soundness, either by contributing money or advice or assistance in raising funds from other wealthy men.[4]

On the whole, the sound, conservative men of wealth who came to dominate the college governing boards were pillars of the better classes, and while their duties permitted them to perform a social responsibility, their authority also enabled them to keep the colleges true to the interests and prejudices of the classes from which they were drawn. Although clergymen at first prevailed on the collegiate corporations, their usefulness in an increasingly secular United States was seriously questioned. The first college governing board to include no ministers at all must have been the founding board of the College of Philadelphia. The first

Looks Forward: The University of Vermont: A History 1791-1904 (Burlington, 1954), p. 140.
    [4] Francis Wayland: *Thoughts on the Present Collegiate System in the United States* (Boston, 1842), pp. 53-5.

board of regents at the University of Michigan in 1837 included no clergymen, and for the first fifteen years no more than a quarter of the board were clergymen. Even a place like Williams never had a majority of clergymen on its board. Of its original board of twelve, only four were ministers, and between 1836 and 1872 a comparable proportion was maintained. At Harvard the charter provision requiring some clergymen on the corporation was repealed in 1851.[5]

Probably the financial insecurity of the colleges and an unfavorable public image initiated the growing preference for mercantile and professional men over clergymen, and since (except in the case of state universities) most college governing boards were self-perpetuating, once a preference for businessmen was expressed, then only charter provisions or sentiment could maintain a sizable clerical representation on the board. After the Civil War, when college alumni asserted themselves and gained official representation on governing boards, the first victims of their new-won power were the clergymen. The movement away from the clergy was so certain that when Johns Hopkins chose twelve citizens of Baltimore to set up his university in 1867 he selected seven businessmen, four lawyers, and a doctor.[6]

Because most college governing boards were self-perpetuating, the proportion of old men serving the colleges in this capacity was likely to be very large. In 1883 when he was still busily engaged in reforming Harvard, President Eliot, while prepared to admit that "such elderly men may be distinguished representatives of the alumni," was also

[5] See Theodore F. Jones, ed.: *New York University 1832: 1932* (New York, 1933), p. 5; Schmidt: *The Old Time College President*, p. 35; Elizabeth M. Farrand: *History of the University of Michigan* (Ann Arbor, 1885), pp. 60-2; Rudolph: *Williams*, pp. 91, 131; Morison: Harvard: *Three Centuries*, pp. 289, 293.

[6] Richardson: *Dartmouth*, II, 69; John C. French: *A History of the University Founded by John Hopkins* (Baltimore, 1946), p. 21.

convinced that "their personal recollections of college life
are less serviceable to them as university legislators than the
recollections of much younger men would be." [7]
The kind of man who was becoming a trustee in the era
of the colleges and who would clearly dominate by the end
of the century, except in the state universities, was the man
whom President Eliot described to a state university audience twenty-five years later. In selecting trustees, the endowed colleges, he said, were "free . . . from the political,
commercial, or class influences which" sometimes controlled
choices in public institutions. They were free, he continued,
from "class influences such as that exerted by farmers as
a class, or trade-unionists as a class." What did the endowed
institution substitute for these dangerous influences? "The
highly educated, public-spirited, business or professional man
—, a man who has been successful in his own calling. . . ."
Such men were perhaps also capable of exerting class influences, but for President Eliot such influences would
not be dangerous. For these men represented the classes
whose point of view was increasingly welcome and increasingly dominant in that instrument of power—the college corporation. [8]

Trustee power was not unlimited. Much of its authority was
necessarily delegated to the president. Much of it was actually appropriated by the students. And at all times college
governing boards were aware of such shifting influences as
those exerted by alumni, by potential clientele, by prospective donors. Many fundamentally educational matters were
actually left to the faculty, but by retaining control over

[7] Quoted in Walter Schultz Stover: *Alumni Stimulation by the
American College President* (New York, 1930), pp. 20-1.
[8] Charles W. Eliot: *University Administration* (Boston, 1908), pp.
2-3. An informative study of a later generation of university trustees is
Hubert P. Beck: *Men Who Control Our Universities* (New York,
1947).

budget, priorities, and planning, college governing boards also maintained effective control of the collegiate power structure.

In the era of the colleges influences were clearly at work that would enable a twentieth-century college professor to assert without fear of contradiction: "The faculty are employees; the trustees are employers; the president is the superintendent of the plant." [9] Within such a developing framework the American college in the nineteenth century was achieving a balance of power, an equation in which one other element, of course, should be included—the customers. The students, unlike customers, were not always right, and the nature of the power that they achieved did not require that they be. Yet, trustees, presidents, professors, and students were formalizing a host of relationships that defined responsibility, prestige, and power on the American campus. Out of the ingredients of potential war they were laying the foundations of peace.

[9] Kirtley Mather quoted in Chessman: *Denison,* p. 283.

9

❧§❧

Financing the Colleges

During the War of 1812 military forces of the United States
commandeered the only building of the University of Vermont for use as a barracks. The university necessarily called
off classes and waited for peace. For its troubles it received a
government check in the amount of $5,600.[1] Few American
colleges would not have benefited from a similar misfortune. The American college, when open, was often on the
verge of bankruptcy. Vermont had discovered, when closed,
how to experience prosperity. But the War of 1812 did not
solve the financial problems of the American college. War
and misfortune and Uncle Sam did not pay the bills. Who
did?

The students did not. From the beginning the American
college was cloaked with a public purpose, with a responsibility to the past and the present and the future. The college was expected to give more than it received—not more
than it received from the society which it served, but more
than it necessarily received from the particular young men

[1] An earlier version of this chapter appeared as "Who Paid the Bills?
An Inquiry into the Nature of Nineteenth-Century College Finance"
in *Harvard Educational Review*, XXXI (1961), 144-57. Julian Ira Lindsay: *Tradition Looks Forward: The University of Vermont: A History
1791-1904* (Burlington, 1954), p. 109.

who were being prepared to do society's work. The college was not to be an institution of narrow privilege. Society required the use of all its best talents, and while it would, of course, always be easier for a rich boy than a poor boy to go to college, persistence and ambition and talent were not to be denied.

The American college, therefore, was an expression of Christian charity, both in the assistance that it gave to needy young men and in the assistance that it received from affluent old men. While the colonial economy could not support philanthropy of the dimension that founded the colleges at Oxford and Cambridge, individual benevolence was nonetheless in the English tradition, and the colonial colleges therefore naturally looked to it for sustenance. At first England itself was the only reliable source of significant philanthropy. The Englishmen John Harvard and Elihu Yale, while not the founders of the colleges that took their names, were the first substantial private benefactors of collegiate education in New England. The first scholarship fund given to an American college was an act of Christian benevolence on the part of Lady Anne Mowlson, whose maiden name had been Radcliffe.

But, although colonial life was poor, the tradition which supported the English colleges in England was not abandoned in the New World. It was necessarily supplemented by other means, but it was also encouraged by the vital sense of stewardship nurtured by the Christian denominations. From this concept of stewardship would flow many of the benefactions that sustained the American college, until in combination with the great fortunes which opportunity in America underwrote, there would emerge in the second half of the nineteenth century full-blown institutions, each (as had often been the case at Oxford and Cambridge) the creation of a single originating donor: Vassar, Smith, Johns Hopkins, Stanford, Chicago, and Wellesley.[2]

[2] Samuel Eliot Morison: *The Founding of Harvard College* (Cambridge, 1935), pp. 89, 210 ff., and *Three Centuries of Harvard 1636-1936*

Samuel Johnson, the eighteenth-century English lexicographer, defined a patron as "Commonly a wretch who supports with insolence, and is paid with flattery." The world surely has had its share of such wretches, but they did not predominate in the era of the colleges. The early patrons were of the sort who established a model for Eliam E. Barney, a post-Civil War benefactor at Denison who enforced upon himself and his family "the strictest kind of personal economy" in order to multiply his good works.[3]

A model ante bellum benefactor was Amos Lawrence, a Boston merchant, who carried around in his wallet a piece of paper on which he had scribbled, "What shall it profit a man, if he gain the whole world, and lose his own Soul?" Into his account book Lawrence wrote in January 1828: "My property imposes upon me many duties, which can only be known to my Maker. May a sense of these duties be constantly impressed upon my mind." A sense of these duties made Amos Lawrence the leading individual benefactor of Williams College before 1875, made his brother Abbott Lawrence the donor of a scientific school to Harvard, and his son Amos Adams a founder of Lawrence College at Appleton, Wisconsin. At Amherst, Samuel Williston, a Connecticut Valley button manufacturer, was the good steward; at Wesleyan in Connecticut, Isaac Rich, a Boston fish merchant; at Lafayette in Pennsylvania, Ario Pardee, an anthracite mine operator.[4]

(Cambridge, 1936), p. 12; Walter C. Bronson: *The History of Brown University 1764-1914* (Providence, 1914), pp. 38-9; Edward Potts Cheyney: *History of the University of Pennsylvania 1740-1940* (Philadelphia, 1940), pp. 61 ff.; Jesse B. Sears: *Philanthropy in the History of American Higher Education* (Washington, 1922), pp. 1-9, 67-72. See also Beverly McAnear: "The Raising of Funds by the Colonial Colleges," *Mississippi Valley Historical Review*, XXXVIII (1952), 591-612.

[3] G. Wallace Chessman: *Denison: The Story of an Ohio College* (Granville, 1957), p. 97.

[4] Frederick Rudolph: *Mark Hopkins and the Log: Williams College, 1836-1872* (New Haven, 1956), pp. 175-88; Claude M. Fuess: *Amherst: The Story of a New England College* (Boston, 1935), p. 130; Carl F. Price: *Wesleyan's First Century* (Middletown, 1932), p. 56; David Bishop Skillman: *The Biography of a College: Being the History of*

Not every college was fortunate enough to find a single sustaining benefactor, for fortunes of great size were just emerging, and many of them were being put to more popular purpose than higher education. John Lowell's $250,000 founded Lowell Institute in 1836; John Jacob Astor gave $400,000 to establish a library for the City of New York in 1848; and in 1857 Peter Cooper contributed $300,000 toward the creation of the Cooper Institute. The benefactions which founded these institutions revealed a concern for educating the masses in practical matters. The popular Lowell lectures, the great public library, the practical education emphasized at the Cooper Institute were intelligent investments in social control.

Men of property, sensing the economic and social unrest that was manifest in the infant labor movement and in the growth of popular democracy, were desirous of creating a climate fully favorable to American individual enterprise. A dollar spent in giving a mechanic a sense of self-improvement and self-importance was, from this point of view, a better and more immediately rewarding investment than was a dollar spent on the classics. The consequence was that all benefactions of the period did not flow to colleges; many of them went instead to the more popular academies or to more practical educational enterprises.

The colleges that did receive benefactions could rely on the knowledge that stewardship might be combined with a yearning for self-monumentation. Certainly on more than one occasion the image of pure Christian charity was blurred by flattery and conceit. President Manning of Rhode Island College, for instance, was led to remark in 1783, for the benefit of the descendants of a wealthy man: "Cambridge College was so fortunate to attract the attention of an Hollis; New Haven of a Yale & New Hampshire of a Dartmouth. . . . We should think ourselves no less happy in the Patron-

the First Century of the Life of Lafayette College (Easton, 1932), I, 265 ff.

age of a *Llewelin. Llewelin College* appears well when written & sounds no less agreeably when spoken." Twelve years
later another president of Rhode Island College was writing
to a friend in the South: "The corporation at their last meeting past [sic] a resolution that if any person would previous
to the next Commencement, give to the College $6,000, he
should have the right to name it. Have you no eminent
rich man among you, who might be disposed?" Within a
decade the price was down to $5,000, and a year later Nich-
olas Brown took up the offer—one which cost him $160,000
before his benefactions ended. Similar arrangements were
worked out elsewhere for James Bowdoin, William Denison,
Henry Rutgers, and William Carleton.[5]

A college, however, could sell or give its name only once.
And it could not, either through flattery or simply through
fervent Christian appeal, create affluent benefactors where
they would not grow. On at least two occasions the name of
Amherst College was apparently available, but there were no
bidders.[6] Much time would pass before benefactors would be
standing in line to build monuments to themselves: that moment would wait until later in the nineteenth century, at a
particularly low moment in the history of American architecture.

Only six professorships were endowed in American colleges before the American Revolution, four of them at Harvard.[7] Endowments of sizable proportions were a contribution to the American college of the Industrial Revolution,
of the remarkable rewards which it brought on the emin-
ently exploitable American continent, and of the sense of
stewardship which invigorated the possession of private
wealth with a sense of public responsibility. In the absence

[5] Bronson: *Brown*, pp. 78, 144, 155-7; Louis C. Hatch: *The History
of Bowdoin College* (Portland, 1927), p. 4; Chessman: *Denison*, p. 55;
William H. S. Demarest: *A History of Rutgers College 1766-1924*
(New Brunswick, 1924), p. 274; Delavan L. Leonard: *The History of
Carleton College* (Chicago, 1904), p. 178.
[6] Fuess: *Amherst*, pp. 50, 78-9.
[7] Sears: *Philanthropy*, p. 30.

of significant endowment and of great numbers of men of wealth, the colleges at first found it necessary to turn to other sources of financial support.

One obvious device was simply to turn to the people and solicit modest subscriptions, a solution that had the added advantage of emphasizing the public nature and popular intentions of the college. In colonial America, where there was more corn than cash, the subscription method of pledging aid to a college might bring in more produce than pounds. Agents of the College of New Jersey in 1769 rounded up approximately £1,000 in contributions in Georgia, most of it in produce, and the college promptly chartered a vessel and sent for it. The subscription method was generally resorted to when a college was being founded or when it was in more peril than usual: it permitted an appeal to local pride or to some special interest—perhaps sectarian—and it had the rather important effect of suggesting that the support of higher education was a popular responsibility, regardless of one's wealth.[8]

The names that appeared on the subscription lists of colleges in New England, Ohio, Illinois, and Kentucky were seldom the names of the wealthy. Most of them belonged to God-fearing farmers for whom a college was of perhaps no immediate value, but for whom the *idea* of a college was of transcending importance. Often these subscribers were never able to pay their pledges: a cold spring, a frost in July, a visitation of grasshoppers could make the difference.

Subscriptions, sometimes of labor, erected many of the first college buildings, an adaptation of Nassau Hall at Princeton, for example, or of the Bulfinch building at the Andover Theological Seminary. Or they justified a board of trustees in going ahead with the task of assembling a faculty and a student body. But subscriptions seldom meant much more than that a college was now—or still—in business and apparently with some element of local support. Public sub-

[8] Ibid., pp. 15-16; Thomas Jefferson Wertenbaker: *Princeton 1746-1896* (Princeton, 1946), p. 53.

scriptions did not mean that the college would necessarily be in business next year.

The imagination and resourcefulness and necessity which made many an American a jack-of-all-trades and a master of none also characterized collegiate financing. One college might turn to an annuity arrangement such as Azariah Williams of Concord, Vermont, entered into with the University of Vermont in 1839, when he deeded the university land to the value of $25,000 in return for an annual income until death. In New England in the 1820's there were numerous "Kenyon Circles of Industry," local sewing circles that did what they could for Kenyon College in Ohio.[*]

Assistance to many colleges came from the American Education Society, founded in 1815 to deal with "the deplorable condition of the inhabitants of these United States, the greater part of whom are either destitute of competent religious instruction or exposed to the errors and enthusiasm of unlearned men." The American Education Society's solution was to raise funds in the Congregational churches and to help send promising ministerial candidates to the appropriate colleges. By 1830 approximately a quarter of the promising future ministers then in college were beneficiaries of the American Education Society or of similar organizations founded by the Baptists, Presbyterians, or Dutch Reformed. Between 1845 and 1854 the number of beneficiaries at Amherst ranged between 17 and 31 per cent of the student body.[1]

The employment of paid agents was often resorted to, and while they were in no sense professional fund-raisers such as the twentieth century developed, they were the best substitute that the era offered—dedicated clergymen who were willing to take a percentage of the proceeds for their canvassing efforts.

Roman Catholic institutions, so lacking in endowments

[*] Lindsay: *Vermont*, p. 169; George Franklin Smythe: *Kenyon College: Its First Century* (New Haven, 1924), p. 65.
[1] Sears: *Philanthropy*, pp. 47-9, 74.

that by 1866 only St. Mary's College in Texas was endowed, did have one source of support not available to other American colleges, namely, missionary societies in such European cities as Vienna, Munich, and Lyons; these societies were prepared to cater to the educational needs of the faithful in Protestant America. Unable yet to draw upon the resources of wealthy laymen, the Catholic colleges also devised methods that tapped more humble resources. In the early days of Boston College, its friends operated a four-week fair in Boston Music Hall, where tables of homemade items, games, and Gilmore's Band helped to net over $30,000 in October 1866.[2]

Few colleges were as fortunate as Union, to which its President, Eliphalet Nott, turned over a fortune of $600,000 in 1854, the result of Nott's invention of a particularly successful stove and of wise investments. Other college presidents were seldom able to translate their imagination and desperation into collegiate endowment; Union was the most richly endowed college in the United States before the Civil War. Both Lafayette and Marietta, under the influence of a get-rich-quick craze in the 1830's, made unsuccessful efforts to coax endowments out of mulberries and silkworms. In this tradition late in the century at Pomona College, President Cyrus Grandison Baldwin, hoping to solve the financial problems of his college for all time, tried unsuccessfully to harness a mountain torrent to provide light and power for Claremont and profits for Pomona to eternity.[3]

Recognizing the degree to which domestic philanthropy by itself would be unequal to the needs of higher education, the

[2] Sebastian A. Erbacher: *Catholic Higher Education for Men in the United States 1850-1866* (Washington, 1931), p. 74; David R. Dunigan: *A History of Boston College* (Milwaukee, 1947), pp. 91-5; Arthur J. Hope: *Notre Dame: One Hundred Years* (Notre Dame, 1943), p. 108.
[3] Andrew Van Vranken Raymond, ed.: *Union University: Its History, Influence, Characteristics and Equipment* (New York, 1907), I, 221-44; Arthur G. Beach: *A Pioneer College: The Story of Marietta* (Marietta, 1935), p. 64; Skillman: *Lafayette*, I, 128-9; Charles Burt Sumner: *The Story of Pomona College* (Boston, 1914), pp. 138-9.

state stepped into the breach. The crucial support by the state has often been clouded by the highly romantic regard held by Americans for unaided effort and by the confusion introduced by the use of such terms as "public" and "private" to describe institutions in a world that was itself in the process of defining the meaning of such terms. One great barrier to determining who paid the bills of the American college is the myth of the privately endowed independent college, a myth that was not encouraged until the colleges discovered that they could no longer feed at the public trough and had, in one sense, indeed become private.

Speaking in 1873 against the creation of a tax-supported national university, President Eliot of Harvard advanced the argument that "our ancestors well understood the principle that to make a people free and self-reliant, it is necessary to let them take care of themselves, even if they do not take quite as good care of themselves as some superior power might." Had this principle actually been well understood by Mr. Eliot's ancestors there would have been no Harvard and no presidential office there for him to use against the principle of government-financed higher education. On over one hundred occasions before 1789 the General Court of Massachusetts appropriated funds for Harvard College, which clearly was not capable of taking care of itself.[4] Indeed, Harvard, Yale, and Columbia could not have survived the colonial period without support of the state.[5] How important to Harvard was the $100,000 which the Commonwealth gave in annual installments of $10,000 between 1814 and 1823? In the case of Bowdoin and Williams, each of which received $30,000 as a result of the same legislative act, state aid underwrote whatever solvency the two institutions attained during the period.[6]

Permission to operate lotteries and the granting of lands

[4] Eliot's remarks were reported in the *Boston Daily Advertiser* for August 9, 1873.

[5] Sears: *Philanthropy*, pp. 25-6.

[6] Morison: Harvard: *Three Centuries*, pp. 213-4; Rudolph: *Williams*, p. 193.

were the favorite forms of state assistance in colonial times and in the early national period. State-authorized lotteries supported all of the colonial colleges in New England. Princeton was given permission to operate lotteries in three states—New Jersey, Pennsylvania, and Connecticut. Colleges in New York, Pennsylvania, Virginia, and South Carolina also resorted to lotteries in their early days. Without any significant sources of revenue, states could seldom give much more than permission to operate lotteries. But land was often at their disposal; Massachusetts was generous with townships in Maine; and in 1785 Vermont gave a half township in northwestern Vermont to Dartmouth, a college in neighboring New Hampshire.[7]

Not every college was saved by state aid; but how important to the survival of Columbia was the $140,000 which it received, how important to the University of Pennsylvania was the $287,000[8] poured into its resources before the end of the nineteenth century by the Commonwealth of Pennsylvania? Loans from the state governments apparently enabled many of the new denominational colleges of the South to survive in the 1840's and 1850's.[9] Probably state grants had a similar effect on the fortunes of such institutions in New York as the University of the City of New York, Hamilton,

[7] Morison: Harvard: *Three Centuries,* p. 173; William Lathrop Kingsley, ed.: *Yale College: A Sketch of its History* (New York, 1879), I, 77, 192; Bronson: *Brown,* pp. 37, 144; Leon Burr Richardson: *History of Dartmouth College* (Hanover, 1932), I, 216-17, 227-8; Wertenbaker: *Princeton,* pp. 32-4; Demarest: *Rutgers,* pp. 263 ff.; John Howard Van Amringe, et al.: *A History of Columbia University 1754-1904* (New York, 1879), pp. 3-7; Joseph D. Ibbotson and S. N. D. North: *Documentary History of Hamilton College* (Clinton, 1922), pp. 17-18, 163-6; Raymond: *Union,* I, 140, 148; Cheyney: *Pennsylvania,* pp. 60-1; Alfred J. Morrison, ed.: *The College of Hampden-Sidney: Calendar of Board Minutes 1776-1876* (Richmond, 1912), p. 23; James Harold Easterby: *A History of the College of Charleston Founded 1770* (Charleston, 1935), p. 19.

[8] For statistics on government support of specific institutions see Frank W. Blackmar: *The History of Federal and State Aid to Higher Education in the United States* (Washington, 1890).

[9] Luther L. Gobbel: *Church-State Relationships in Education in North Carolina Since 1776* (Durham, 1938), pp. 32-4.

and Geneva. Certainly the $385,000 in state grants and pro-
ceeds from state-authorized lotteries underwrote Union College while Nott experimented with his inventions and in-
vestments.[1] At Dickinson College support provided by the
Pennsylvania legislature between 1783 and 1832 often took the
form of emergency grants that were essential to the preservation of the college.[2]

At Williams College state aid was an indispensable support
during its first ninety years. The college would probably not
have survived its first fifty years without the $50,000 which
the General Court injected into the struggling institution
between 1793 and 1823, a sum exactly equal to the resources
which the college itself had been able to raise in subscriptions, bequests, and state-authorized lotteries during the
same years. Of later state aid, a total of $100,000 between
1859 and 1868, Mark Hopkins himself referred to the $75,000
appropriation of 1868 with profound gratefulness: "But for
an unexpected gift by the state . . . I do not see how the
College could have got on." [3]

Gifts from the state, expected or unexpected, would not
continue forever. They had, after all, been given in recognition of the public nature of the collegiate corporation. But
with the unleashing of hundreds of little colleges, the state
governments were financially and emotionally in no position
to support them all. Sectarianism, even before the end of the
colonial period, had cut off some state support. In the years
after 1820 the sectarian spawning of colleges and the tendency of many institutions to draw students from beyond
state boundaries had the effect of diminishing the partnership of state and college, thus emphasizing the private rather
than the public nature of the colleges. "The establishment of
a College is also imposing upon the Government the necessity of bestowing upon it a very liberal and expensive Pa-

[1] Blackmar: *The History of Federal and State Aid*, pp. 140-1.
[2] James Henry Morgan: *Dickinson College: The History of One
Hundred and Fifty Years 1783-1933* (Carlisle, 1933), pp. 125-30.
[3] Rudolph: *Williams*, pp. 190-200.

tronage" was the way in which the New York Board of
Regents viewed state responsibility toward the support of
higher education in 1811.[4] By 1825, however, in the neighboring Commonwealth of Massachusetts, where first had
been established the tradition of state support, a charter
would be granted to the new college at Amherst that would
declare: "The granting of this charter shall never be considered as any pledge on the part of the Government, that
pecuniary aid shall hereafter be granted to the College."[5]
Institutions more readily identified with a religious denomination than with the state increasingly lost popularity as
objects of public support. Every tendency toward the recruitment of students on a national basis further undermined
the old partnership that, for example, had existed when the
president of Harvard was paid by an annual appropriation
of the Massachusetts General Court.

After the Civil War, moreover, the states discovered more
popular educational outlets for their generosity, namely, the
state universities and the federally endowed agricultural and
mechanical colleges. Massachusetts, which last supported
Harvard in 1823, poured $200,000 into M.I.T. before 1890
and provided $600,000 for the development of the Massa-
chusetts State College between 1865 and 1890.[6] In discovering or strengthening their obligations to such institutions,
the state legislatures were supporting higher education of a
more popular nature than the old-time college with its religious orientation and adherence to the classical course of
study.

Most states abandoned public assistance to the so-called
private colleges, but the change was uneven and uncertain,
waiting for a general recognition and understanding of the
American college as, finally, a private institution.[7] The col-

[4] Ibbotson and North: *Hamilton*, p. 105.
[5] Fuess: *Amherst*, p. 73.
[6] Blackmar: *The History of Federal and State Aid*, pp. 98-100.
[7] For further evidence of colleges that were successful in receiving
aid in the period before the Civil War see Price: *Wesleyan*, p. 56;
Kingsley: *Yale*, I, 192; Fuess: *Amherst*, p. 132; Easterby: *Charleston*,

leges themselves, while jealous of the rights of corporate
independence, did not construe their private nature as forbidding endless petitions to state governments for financial
relief.[8] Sometimes, but with increasing irregularity, they
were successful. New Hampshire between 1893 and 1921
added $200,000 to the resources of Dartmouth (which had
once won a famous law suit confirming its independence of
the state), and as late as 1926 state legislatures were still
supporting "private" colleges in Vermont, New York, New
Jersey, Pennsylvania, and Maryland.[9]

After the Civil War the colleges found new means of
support among their alumni and among a crop of especially
affluent millionaire benefactors; only then were they prepared to recognize what their unavailing petitions to the
state legislatures had made clear to many others: the day of
public support had ended, the private college had emerged.
With this recognition developed a remarkable lapse of memory and the beginnings of a myth. Before long college presidents would be talking like President Eliot, as spokesmen for
rugged individualism, for the virtues of independence and
freedom from state support. A partnership in public service,
which had once been essential to the colleges and inherent
in the responsibilities of government, now became insidious,
or it was forgotten altogether.

p. 116; Elsie Garland Hobson: *Educational Legislation and Administration in the State of New York 1777-1850* (Chicago, 1918), pp. 151-2
(for Fordham); Jesse Leonard Rosenberger: *Rochester: the Making of
a University* (Rochester, 1927), p. 128; Skillman: *Lafayette*, I, 88; Sylvanus N. Duvall: *The Methodist Episcopal Church and Education up
to 1869* (New York, 1928), p. 87 (for Dickinson, Allegheny, Baltimore
Female College, Iowa City College); Theodore F. Jones, ed.: *New
York University 1832-1932* (New York, 1933), pp. 47, 63; Alfred Williams Anthony: *Bates College and its Background* (Philadelphia, 1936),
p. 106.
    [8] William Storrs Lee: *Father Went to College: The Story of Middle-
bury* (New York, 1936), p. 117; Demarest: *Rutgers*, pp. 324 ff.; Morrison: *Hampden-Sidney*, pp. 108 ff., 136.
    [9] Richardson: *Dartmouth*, II, 686-8; Lester William Bartlett: *State
Control of Private Incorporated Institutions of Higher Education* (New
York, 1926), p. 3.

In time the friends of the American college would be asked to increase their benefactions in order to avoid that awful day when the privately endowed independent college would have to turn to government for support. In time the myth of the private college would bury its honest, respectable past as a creature sustained in its most trying days by the responsible assistance of the state. Of course hundreds of colleges had, in the way of state support, nothing more substantial than their tax exemptions, an indirect subsidy of incalculable and uncalculated value. Certainly any "exception in favor of property invested in educational institutions . . . necessarily increase[d] the taxes on other property, which . . . [was] equivalent to voting a tax for the support of education."[1] Direct support was not universal—it was not even as universal as private benefactions—but in numerous instances it clearly was one of the agencies that essentially made the difference whether a college survived or not.

The failure of state governments to respond generously to the proliferation of denominational colleges and to institutions with national ambitions led the colleges into financial projects even more harebrained than raising silkworms or harnessing mountain streams. No scheme could compare with the widespread and desperate device of selling what were called perpetual scholarships, a device that would not have been necessary had private philanthropy or public support been able and prepared to sustain an apparently unending number of competing little colleges. In an effort to collect funds to erect buildings or to augment endowments, many colleges authorized their agents to sell at a set price—generally in the neighborhood of five hundred dollars—a perpetual scholarship to the college, entitling the owner to free tuition for one person in perpetuity.

An early, perhaps the first, college to resort to this device was North Carolina in 1789, but the heyday was in the years 1835-60, when the perpetual scholarship became the last re-

[1] Blackmar: *The History of Federal and State Aid*, p. 25.

sort for many of the sectarian institutions. In these years
the scholarship scheme commended itself to the governing
boards of Cumberland, Lafayette, Wesleyan, New York University, Dickinson, Antioch, Hampden-Sidney, Wofford, Kenyon, DePauw, Ohio University, Ohio Wesleyan, Oglethorpe,
Oberlin, Columbia, Vermont, Emory, Denison, Genesee,
Hanover, Indiana University, and unquestionably also dozens of other small struggling colleges. The perpetual scholarship scheme was a particularly attractive idea to the colleges
because it promised to solve their basic problems: it would
give the colleges the funds that they badly needed in order
to stay open, and it would provide them with an immediate
supply of students who would justify their being open at all.[2]

Of course, like so many other get-rich-quick schemes
to which Americans turned in the nineteenth century, the
perpetual scholarship did not work. McKendree College
seems to have done about as well as any: it lost only $1.02
for each $1.00 it raised by selling scholarships. Dickinson
College adopted the plan in 1851 and by 1855 the college
was running at a deficit of $3,000: the funds raised by sell-

[2] Kemp Plummer Battle: *History of the University of North Carolina* (Raleigh, 1907-12), I, 7; Winstead Paine Bone: *A History of Cumberland University 1842-1935* (Lebanon, Tennessee, 1935), p. 88; Skillman: *Lafayette*, I, 215; Duvall: *The Methodist Episcopal Church and
Education*, p. 88; Jones: *New York University*, p. 17; Morgan: *Dickinson*, pp. 300-10; Morrison: *Hampden-Sidney*, pp. 133, 135, 146, 156;
David Duncan Wallace: *History of Wofford College* (Nashville, 1951),
p. 50; Smythe: *Kenyon*, p. 152; William Warren Sweet: *Indiana Asbury-
DePauw University, 1837-1937: A Hundred Years of Higher Education
in the Middle West* (New York, 1937), pp. 55, 111; Thomas N. Hoover:
The History of Ohio University (Athens, 1954), pp. 97-8; Allen P.
Tankersley: *College Life at Old Oglethorpe* (Athens, 1951), p. 28;
Robert Samuel Fletcher: *A History of Oberlin College from its Founda-
tion through the Civil War* (Oberlin, 1943), I, 498; Van Amringe:
Columbia, pp. 100 ff.; Lindsay: *Vermont*, p. 174; Henry Morton Bul-
lock: *A History of Emory University* (Nashville, 1936), p. 69; Chessman: *Denison*, p. 92; William Freeman Galpin: *Syracuse University:
The Pioneer Days* (Syracuse, 1952), p. 9; William Alfred Millis: *The
History of Hanover College from 1827 to 1927* (Hanover, 1927), pp.
60-1; James Albert Woodburn: *History of Indiana University: 1820-
1902* (Bloomington, 1940), pp. 244-5.

ing scholarships were gone and the college was full of students who did not have to pay tuition.[3]

The experience of Lafayette College with the scholarship idea proved the madness of the scheme. The theory behind Lafayette's campaign of 1850-4 was that the funds raised would be used to endow faculty salaries. Students would be expected to pay for heat, room, and similar services, but there would be no need to charge for tuition. The beauty of this hope was perfectly clear: it promised a way of paying the faculty and of procuring students. In one great campaign Lafayette could provide itself with faculty salaries and tuition-free students forever. The Lafayette campaign netted $101,000 in pledges, of which at least $67,000 never went into the proposed endowment of faculty salaries. Thirty-one thousand dollars was never collected; fourteen thousand went toward the payment of old debts; three thousand went to the agents; two thousand dollars was absorbed by vital repairs on college buildings, six thousand went into new buildings; five thousand dollars was consumed immediately for current salaries, six thousand for other current expenses. Slightly less than a third of the sum pledged remained for endowment investment.[4]

The experience of other institutions was similarly dismal. Not only were the collected funds frittered away, but great numbers of tuition-free students now knocked at college doors and became one more drain on limited resources. The situation at DePauw became so unwieldy that in 1873, in order to invalidate the perpetual scholarships sold in earlier days, the college simply adopted a universal policy of free tuition and substituted a schedule of miscellaneous fees. At Denison in 1907, there were still eighty-eight tuition scholarships outstanding; in 1910 the college started buying them back.[5]

[3] Duvall: *The Methodist Episcopal Church and Education,* p. 114; Morgan: *Dickinson,* pp. 300-10.
[4] Skillman: *Lafayette,* I, 200-14.
[5] Sweet: *DePauw,* pp. 127-8; Chessman: *Denison,* p. 213.

•   •   •

The one agency that was not only fully available to every
college but also fully exploited was the faculty. More reliable
than the state, less subject to the fundamental laws of economics than the perpetual scholarship scheme, the professors
became philanthropists.

Essentially what was happening on the American college
campus was the creation of a profession that was not expected, and finally not permitted, to enjoy or to aspire to
the material pleasures and living standards that elsewhere defined American goals. An occasional institution revealed what
a living salary might be: $1,500 at South Carolina in the
1800's and at Virginia in the 1820's; $2,000 at Harvard in the
1830's and $4,000 in the 1860's. But the overwhelming ma-
jority of American college professors knew such salaries as
these: $600 at Dartmouth in 1805, $600 at the University of
Georgia in 1815, $700 at Bowdoin in 1825, $700 at Williams
in 1835, $600 at Wabash in 1845, $775 at Emory in 1855,
$600 at Denison in 1865.[*]

As if it were not enough to underpay the professors, there
developed a half dozen or so methods of not paying them at
all or of paying them far less than their appointments warranted. One method was to keep salary payments in arrears
while continuing to promise full payment. This policy was
resorted to at Oglethorpe and Hamilton in the 1830's, Illinois
College and DePauw in the 1840's, and Wofford in the

[*]Daniel Walker Hollis: *University of South Carolina* (Columbia,
1951-6), I, 30; Philip Alexander Bruce: *History of the University of
Virginia, 1819-1919* (New York, 1920-2), II, 182-3; Morison: Harvard:
Three Centuries, p. 460; Richardson: *Dartmouth,* II, 236; E. Merton
Coulter: *College Life in the Old South* (Athens, 1951), p. 21; Hatch:
Bowdoin, pp. 212-16; Rudolph: *Williams,* p. 11; James I. Osborne and
Theodore G. Gronert: *Wabash College; the first hundred years, 1832-
1932* (Crawfordsville, 1932), p. 69; Bullock: *Emory,* pp. 84, 91; Chessman: *Denison,* pp. 96, 99. At the few Catholic colleges of the period,
of course, the nonpaid priests and members of religious communities
endowed the colleges heavily with their services.

1850's.[7] Obviously this was not a preferred policy. It was transparent, even ugly. At Illinois College in 1845 the president and his family, in the absence of salary payments, were eating breadcrumbs and water, sweetened with molasses.[8]

A favorite way of keeping a college from bankruptcy was to allow a professor to resign or die and then to apportion his teaching responsibilities among those who remained. Such a situation developed at Lafayette in 1860 and helped temporarily to erase the annual deficit of a thousand dollars. Profit-sharing was another method, although no one had the honesty to call it deficit-sharing—which is what it was. Often, under this scheme of things, the faculty simply shared on an equal basis whatever funds were left after all other obligations were met. Such a policy at least was honest, and it was given a try at Trinity, Tusculum, Dickinson, and Illinois.[9]

Straightforward salary-cutting was often resorted to. In 1855 the professors at Hanover College in Indiana were told that although their contracts called for salaries of $800, they would have to get along that year on $335. Kenyon College one year sought to balance its budget by denying the faculty its customary privilege of "pasturage for one cow." A variety of other devices was perfected. Allegheny College in Pennsylvania closed down for a year in 1844 so that the professors could go out and raise money. McKendree College in Illinois closed the same year and opened in 1846, occasionally paying its professors with produce begged from neighboring farmers.[1]

[7] Tankersley: *Oglethorpe*, p. 22; Ibbotson and North: *Hamilton*, pp. 234-5; Charles Henry Rammelkamp: *Illinois College: A Centennial History 1829-1929* (New Haven, 1928), p. 141; Sweet: *DePauw*, p. 56; Wallace: *Wofford*, p. 63.
[8] Rammelkamp: *Illinois College*, p. 141.
[9] Skillman: *Lafayette*, I, 238; Nora Campbell Chaffin: *Trinity College, 1839-1892: The Beginnings of Duke University* (Durham, 1950), p. 182; Allen E. Ragan: *A History of Tusculum College, 1794-1944* (Bristol, 1945), pp. 64, 81; Morgan: *Dickinson*, pp. 319 ff.; Rammelkamp: *Illinois College*, p. 261.
[1] Millis: *Hanover*, p. 66; Smythe: *Kenyon*, p. 215; Duvall: *The Methodist Episcopal Church and Education*, p. 110.

In 1838 and again in 1858 appointments to the Williams faculty were made with the certainty that the partial, inadequate salaries paid by the college would be supplemented by the charity of the appointees' friends. From 1835 to 1852 chemistry at Williams was taught by a man of independent wealth who spent his token salary on laboratory equipment. The appointment of Henry D. Rogers as the first professor of geology and mineralogy at the University of Pennsylvania in 1835 was a response to his offer to serve without salary. Amasa Walker joined the Oberlin faculty as professor of political economy on the same terms. At Dartmouth in 1853 a professorship in natural philosophy went to a wealthy man in part because he would have to be paid little or no salary. The extent to which the colleges depended on professors with outside income would perhaps be impossible to determine, but independent means clearly became an aspect of academic life at Harvard and Yale, and probably in very many colleges the governing boards counted on the durability of the professor or professors who did not depend upon salary to keep body and soul together.[2]

The exploitation of college professors by governing boards developed a rationale of its own. Clearly there was among the professors a certain willingness to be exploited, a certain sense of Christian sacrifice which invited martyrdom on the altar of Christian learning. They often accepted their inadequate salaries as evidence of the ways of a society that had mixed its values or they accepted them as being adequate enough in the fleeting life of this world. No other explanation can account for the action of the already underpaid professors at Indiana University who in 1848 happily divided the responsibilities of a vacant chair in mathematics and petitioned the governing board to appropriate for books and scientific equipment the funds thereby saved.[3]

President Eliot turned the low pay of professors into a

[2] Rudolph: *Williams,* p. 53; Cheyney: *Pennsylvania,* p. 225; Fletcher: *Oberlin,* I, 489-90; Richardson: *Dartmouth,* II, 506.
[3] Woodburn: *Indiana,* p. 175.

national virtue. In his inaugural address of 1869 there were
these comforting sentences:

> The poverty of scholars is of inestimable worth in this
> money-getting nation. It maintains the true standards of
> virtue and honor. The poor friars, not the bishops, saved
> the Church. The poor scholars and preachers of duty
> defend the modern community against its own material
> prosperity. Luxury and learning are ill bed-fellows.[4]

There are all kinds of psychic incomes, but it is doubtful
whether many college professors thought that salving the
conscience of a materialistic society was really a justification
for their inadequate salaries.

In time all kinds of people would have a stake in professorial poverty. The theory that for the good of everyone
concerned professors ought to be poor became the basis of
a committee report of the Iowa legislature which in 1874
recommended severe salary reductions: "Those who labor in
the work of education, to be successful, *must* be endowed
with such love of their profession as will make them content
with less remuneration than can be obtained in ordinary
business." A university president who knew that his chances
of getting salary increases from the state legislatures were
slim might reassure his faculty, as one did in 1876: "Teachers' salaries are small, and always will be small, as compared
with corresponding positions in other callings." [5]

"No professor worth his salt," glowed *The New York
Times* in 1883, "ever devoted himself to learning for any
other reason than that he loved learning." The corollary to
this academic truth was added by President Eliot in 1908:
"The profession can never be properly recruited by holding
out pecuniary inducements." *The Nation* and *The New Republic*, in a later day—the third decade of the twentieth cen-

[4] *Addresses at the Inauguration of Charles William Eliot as President
of Harvard College* (Cambridge, 1869), p. 48.
[5] Clarence Ray Aurner: *History of Education in Iowa* (Iowa City,
1914-16), IV, 48; Woodburn: *Indiana*, p. 322.

tury, proved apparently that every segment of society, now including the left, held some stake in professors' low salaries. Said *The Nation:* "Boost the professors as a group into the high salaried class . . . and you create a strongly intrenched university vested interest in the status quo. . . . Rich professors are all too often social bourbons." Low salaries, said *The New Republic,* free professors from "the pecuniary criterion of value," and we are glad.[6]

Even so, everyone knew that faculty salaries were distressingly low and even the acquiescing Christian professors on occasion were forced to grumble. The history of American higher education is full of petitions from complaining professors asking for modest raises; in the literature of the country public sympathy is frequently expressed for the plight of the professor; and the annals of the colleges contain many biographies of professors who flowed from one college to another seeking some element of financial security. One professor of mathematics at Marietta College in 1864 asked for a year's leave of absence in the simple hope, as he put it, that he might "do . . . better by my family than I would be able to do in teaching." The Marietta board, which clearly had a stake in his poverty, denied the request; he resigned, went into the oil business, and made a considerable fortune which later permitted him to accept a professorship at Cornell.[7]

Was this pattern of underpayment and exploitation necessary? If the colleges were to stay in business, yes; they would have to be sustained by their faculties. The choice was a simple one: the colleges could either pay their professors to teach or they could pay their students to enroll. They chose the latter course because it was the only way they

[6] Walter P. Rogers: *Andrew D. White and the Modern University* (Ithaca, 1942), p. 147; Charles W. Eliot: *University Administration* (Boston, 1908), p. 98. The 1930 *Nation* and 1929 *New Republic* comments are quoted in Claude Charleton Bowman: *The College Professor in America: An Analysis of Articles Published in the General Magazines, 1890-1938* (Philadelphia, 1938), p. 54.

[7] Arthur G. Beach: *A Pioneer College: The Story of Marietta* (Marietta, 1935), p. 170.

could achieve the enrollment that justified their existence.
Francis Wayland, the reforming president of Brown, in 1842
described the colleges as making such a choice:

> I doubt whether anyone could attract a respectable num-
> ber of pupils . . . did it charge for tuition the fees
> which would be requisite to remunerate its officers at
> the rate ordinarily received by other professional men.
> . . . We cannot induce men to pursue a collegiate course
> unless we offer it vastly below its cost, if we do not give
> it away altogether. . . . If the number of students in
> college increases, the additional receipts are devoted to
> the erection of buildings, the employment of other pro-
> fessors, or the reduction of the price of tuition and not
> to the augmentation of the salaries of present instructors.

In desperation he asked, "Can [a liberal education] not be
made to recommend itself; so that he who wishes to obtain
it shall also be willing to pay for it?" [8]
Wayland himself knew that the answer to his question was
necessarily a resounding "no" as long as the American college insisted on holding rigidly to the prescribed classical
course of study. Until the curriculum changed, the colleges,
if they were to have students, would have to buy them.
Cumberland College in Tennessee, for instance, enrolled
eight hundred preministerial candidates between 1842 and
1876, and not one of them paid tuition. Who paid the forty
to fifty thousand dollars which the students did not pay?
Members of the Cumberland faculty, their wives, their children. At Hanover in Indiana a constant effort was made to
reduce the percentage of costs paid by the student in order
to increase the enrollment. At Brown in 1821 the treasurer's
records showed almost six thousand dollars in uncollected
tuition bills and steward's bills, owed by alumni and students.
At early Dartmouth Eleazar Wheelock "encountered no difficulty in securing sufficient numbers of students, so long as

[8] Francis Wayland: *Thoughts on the Present Collegiate System in
the United States* (Boston, 1842), pp. 15-17, 26.

he charged them nothing for the services of the college."
His successors adopted a similar policy.[*]

The colleges were impelled to this decision to pay the
students instead of the professors by two considerations:
one, the desire to project a more democratic image in a society that had interpreted the strength of the classical curriculum as a sign of aristocratic attachments; the other, the
necessity of competing among an almost unlimited number
of colleges for the rather limited number of students who
could afford and who wished to avail themselves of the
classical course of study. Thus Princeton in 1827, in order
to attract students and dispel its reputation as a rich man's
college, simultaneously reduced tuition and faculty salaries.
At Yale, President Jeremiah Day, worried about the moral
and religious tone of a student body drawn too largely from
the privileged orders, began in about 1830 to encourage the
growth of charity or scholarship funds. To combat its reputation for wealth and snobbishness, Harvard, too, in 1852
launched a campaign for scholarship funds. Few colleges
were spared the rich man's reputation. They sought to overcome it by finding poor boys and persuading them to accept
free tuition.[1]

The remission of tuition and the growth of scholarship
funds were also required by the endless multiplication of
colleges without regard to the nature of the collegiate market. As the number of colleges increased, they found themselves bidding even more highly for students. Tuition fees
remained low while the cost of education went up; the hidden difference was paid by the faculty. All these tendencies
would be accelerated or even exaggerated after the Civil
War, when state universities, land-grant colleges, technical
institutes, and the old-time colleges would all be competing
in the student market.

[*]Bone: *Cumberland*, p. 264; Millis: *Hanover*, p. 120; Bronson:
Brown, p. 176; Richardson: *Dartmouth*, I, 118.
[1]Wertenbaker: *Princeton*, p. 178; Kingsley: *Yale*, I, 142; Morison:
Harvard: *Three Centuries*, p. 295.

.   .   .

The meaning for the American college and for American life in general of this pattern of faculty exploitation was profound. It permitted the wealthy benefactor to neglect the endowment of faculty salaries while at the same time he indulged his desire for self-monumentation in buildings and bestowed scholarships to indulge his romantic fondness for poor promising boys. Underpayment robbed a developing profession of dignity and helped to reinforce the hired-help bias of governing boards. It permitted the executive committee of the Cornell board of trustees to complain of high salaries at a time when room and board for an unmarried professor practically consumed his annual salary. It encouraged governing boards composed of men for whom $100,000 incomes were not unusual to exaggerate their own competence in educational matters, rather than to yield their opinions to men willing to put an annual value of $2,500 on their skills. It helped to alienate a large body of American intellectuals from the mainstream of American life.

The exploitation of the faculties may even have robbed the professors in some degree of that will to excel, that desire to achieve, which became so central to the American experience. Was it possible for a course of study that every student had to take and a confirmed policy of low salaries to encourage a professor to individual exertion? "The system," said Francis Wayland, "has . . . removed all the ordinary stimulants to professional effort." [2] The system, it must be admitted, also saved the colleges, at a time when their adherence to the rationale of the Yale Report meant that they could be saved in no other way.

[2] Wayland: *Thoughts on the Present Collegiate System*, p. 27.

10

❧❦❧

Jacksonian Democracy and the Colleges

The Yale Report of 1828 gave expression to one of the most durable positions on the nature of the American college, but another event of the same year was of more lasting consequence. In 1828 Andrew Jackson was elected to the presidency of the United States. Jackson did not tangle with the professors of New Haven nor, probably, did that unschooled orphaned soldier so much as express himself on the subject of American higher education. Jackson, nonetheless, symbolized and furthered tendencies in American life that would in the end spell defeat either for the Yale Report or for the American college itself.

When Harvard chose to award an honorary degree to Jackson in 1833, John Quincy Adams erupted to President Quincy that he, for one, "would not be present to witness [Harvard's] . . . digrace in conferring her highest literary honors upon a barbarian." [1] Many others thought so, too, and

---

[1] Charles Francis Adams, ed.: *Memoirs of John Quincy Adams, Comprising Portions of His Diary From 1795 to 1848* (Philadelphia, 1874-77), VIII, 546.

Harvard was so stunned by the reaction that it did not honor another American president for almost forty years. As the first man of the people to achieve the American presidency, Jackson came to symbolize the fundamental changes that were taking place in American society during the years when the American college, as defined by the Yale Report, was wrestling with the problem of being an institution cradled in privilege in an age that insisted upon being democratic.

The Jacksonian movement was both a protest of labor groups against the prevailing order and a significant moment in the unleashing of American capitalism. In both these moods Jacksonianism harbored a fundamental hostility to privilege. The eastern workingman who sought a larger share of the results of his own labor, who asked for a shorter working week that he might enjoy the benefits of freedom, was not in essential disagreement with the New York or Kentucky banker who suffered from the monopolistic privileges of the United States Bank in Philadelphia. If it was nothing else, Jacksonian democracy was a war on privilege, on artificial or accidental advantage. Of course it was more than that. It went beyond the agrarianism of Jefferson and recognized the development of manufacturing as an American interest; it saw beyond Jefferson's yeoman farmer to the creation of a more complex class structure, one that encompassed men of property and men of labor as well. It committed itself so fully to the Jeffersonian faith in the people that all of Jefferson's fine distinctions, all of his careful reliance on an aristocracy of talent, all of his wise reservations on human capacities were abandoned in a heady embrace of the people.

In an atmosphere of expanding universal manhood suffrage, of unlimited belief in the inevitability of material and moral progress, the Jacksonians were overwhelmingly persuasive. When they were finished, almost everyone either was a Jacksonian or sounded like one. Everyone was for the people; everyone was against monopoly; everyone recognized in the common man the finest expression of the American experience—or said they did. Equal before God, equal before one another, Americans under Jacksonianism chose to put their house in order. Equality, the concept that placed Andrew Jackson in the White House and on a Harvard commencement platform, was the rule of the day.

The colleges were sensitive to the Jacksonian temper, but they were hard-pressed to accommodate it to their traditions and their purposes. Regardless of their preference for piety over intellect, regardless of the priority which they accorded character over learning, the colleges had never befriended ignorance nor esteemed it a quality to be recommended in public servants. On the other hand, if the Jacksonians did not say as much, their insistence that public office be uncomplicated enough to survive the talents of almost anybody came close to eradicating ignorance as a handicap. The belief of the colleges that they existed to provide American democracy with educated leaders received a number of rude shocks during the Jacksonian period, and when the opposition to Jackson allowed itself to be symbolized by a backwoods congressman named Davy Crockett, there was no reason for the colleges to be encouraged. The whole history of uncollected tuition fees, expanding scholarships, and unpaid or underpaid professors was in part a response of the colleges to the growing American belief that unless an institution served all men equally, it served America poorly.

In the colleges the pious had not succeeded in maintaining their own peculiar climate of equality against the onslaught of the Greek-letter fraternities and the social clubs. Spokesmen for an open community of Christian believers had made no headway against the exclusiveness and the privilege which were finding institutional support in the fraternities. The students in the colleges had perhaps had too much of equality—the same class program, the same subjects, the same cubicles called rooms, the same prayers, the same professors, the same everything. In any case at the very time when the Jacksonian spirit was manifesting itself almost everywhere, it was being very clearly rejected by the young men in the colleges who preferred the privileges of club life and secrecy to equality before God, and who found inspiration in the very exclusiveness which the Jacksonian temper rejected.

The pious, conservative leaders of the colleges found themselves enveloped by conditions with which they could hardly cope. When they spoke for equality, it was not the Jacksonian kind. When they defended inequality, it was not the Greek-fraternity kind. In a sermon before the General Court of Massachusetts in 1839 (by which time the main tendencies of Jacksonianism had become the permanent facts of American life), Mark Hopkins of Williams revealed the dilemma that events had posed. Said Hopkins: "Men are upon an equality only as they are equally upon trial in the sight of God, and nothing will ever reconcile . . . [men] to the unavoidable inequalities of the present state, but the consciousness that their circumstances were allotted to them by Him who best knew what trials they would need." [2] Here was no comfort for the Jacksonians, for whom men were equal in the very presence of one another. Here was no comfort for the young Greek-fraternity men for whom inequality was not so much an unavoidable condition of life as it was an absolute necessity for mental health. Nor was there any comfort for the young men who looked on the fraternities from the outside; it was difficult, indeed it was impossible, to believe that their circumstances had been allotted to them by God instead of by the Greeks. Hopkins was representative of a collegiate leadership that found itself increasingly alienated from the people. Perhaps in one sense it was no more alienated than in an earlier day, but the

[2] Frederick Rudolph: *Mark Hopkins and the Log: Williams College, 1836-1872* (New Haven, 1956), p. 184.

difference now was that the people mattered more. The colleges were committed to a religious orientation that necessarily engaged them in quarrel with the man-centered Jacksonians. The colleges were tied, by a tradition of training leaders of quality and excellence, to values that did not rank high in the Jacksonian scale.

Moreover, the colleges proved themselves exceptionally clumsy in dealing with the problem that the costly collegiate way presented. In a more orderly pre-Jacksonian day, the colleges might set aside funds for what they honestly called "charity students." But the mood of Jacksonianism would brook no charity with its implication of inferiority. It is not likely that adherence to the term "charity funds" helped to close the distance between the colleges and the people. One index of the victory of the Jacksonian spirit was the eventual abandonment of the term "charity students" and the substitution for it of the term "scholarship students," a substitution that took place without any change in actual meaning, for scholarship meant "needy" long before it also meant "qualified by scholarly excellence." This substitution of terms seldom took place before the Civil War, when the colleges were still feeling their way toward some kind of accommodation with the rising tide of democracy.

The problem presented by costly commons was met at Yale in 1827 by the operation of two dining halls, one at 20 per cent less than the regular commons as a convenience and inducement to poor students. The same solution—an upper-class commons and a lower-class commons, a rich-boy commons and a poor-boy commons—was seized upon at Princeton in 1831 and at Brown in 1832. It did not work: it failed to bring running to the colleges any great upswelling of the people. There were probably a number of steps that the colleges might have taken in order to attract the enrollment they badly needed and in order to dispel their reputations as rich-men's institutions, but there was something singularly inept about a scheme that proposed to make the collegiate way attractive to poor boys by offering it to them in a second-rate version.[3]

That the colleges were peculiarly vulnerable to the "rich-man's college" epithet there can be no doubt. At Princeton the way of life was being shaped by wealthy young sons of the southern plantation aristocracy; at Harvard, by the proper young men from Boston. Out in Indiana in 1829 the popular press proved the aristocratic orientation of Indiana College by pointing an accusing finger at the professors, who were tempting students from the English to the Latin course of study. At the University of the City of New York, which opened in 1832, the first enrollment included the following names, every one of them recognizable as belonging to a prominent New York family of the period: Crosby, Van Alen, Ward, Coit, MacLay, Hyde, Suydam, Acheson, Dodge, Belknap, Wainwright, Livingston, and Pell. That fine old Jeffersonian Albert Gallatin, who hoped that the new university in New York would "tame" the people, found no encouragement in this list of young aristocrats.[4]

In Georgia the University at Athens inspired one citizen to ask: "How are the people to be benefited in a pecuniary point of view, by giving the people's money to support a set of lazy professors?" In Kentucky the governor in 1825 denounced the tradition of state support that had helped to make Transylvania an ornament of culture in the West: "The State has lavished her money for the benefit of the rich, to the exclusion of the poor; . . . the only result is to add to the aristocracy of wealth, the advantage of superior knowledge." In South Carolina, too, and in Missouri the people did not allow to go unnoticed the fact that the university stu-

[3] William Lathrop Kingsley, ed.: *Yale College: A Sketch of its History* (New York, 1879), I, 302; Thomas Jefferson Wertenbaker: *Princeton 1746-1896* (Princeton, 1946), p. 193; Walter C. Bronson: *The History of Brown University 1764-1914* (Providence, 1914), p. 249.

[4] James Albert Woodburn: *History of Indiana University, 1820-1902* (Bloomington, 1940), pp. 73-4; Henry M. MacCracken, *et al.*: *New York University* (Boston, 1901), pp. 76-8.

dents were overwhelmingly drawn from the wealthy counties.[5]

The colleges were not yet really as sympathetic to poor boys as they said they were. How interested were they in an education that would help a poor boy to do a better job in the places where opportunity was developing in the United States—engineering, merchandising, manufacturing, the merchant marine, canals, railroads? How interested were they in the poor boy who knew that he did not want to be a lawyer or a preacher or a doctor, and who had too much ambition to want to be a teacher? Indeed, widespread among the colleges themselves were sputterings of hostility toward the desire of the poor to be educated. The proposed founding in 1847 of the college that became the City College of New York was opposed for its "unerring indications of the spread of that Agrarianism which preceded the decline and fall of the Roman republic. . . . The determination . . . of the pauper class . . . to levy upon the active, industrious (and, if you please, affluent) portion of the community, the expense of furnishing to the sons of the former, a college education. . . ."[6] After all, not yet had pauper *or* prince decided that what every American needed was a college education. In the colleges, therefore, the barriers were up; and on the outside rejection or jealous hostility to privilege would for a time prevail.

In the Jacksonian climate, however, the colleges were required to find some manner of accommodation. They were encouraged in part to do so by the Dartmouth College case of 1819, a landmark in the history of the Supreme Court and

[5] E. Merton Coulter: *College Life in the Old South* (Athens, 1951), p. 175; James F. Hopkins: *The University of Kentucky: Origins and Early Years* (Lexington, 1951), p. 33; Jonas Viles, *et al.: The University of Missouri: A Centennial History* (Columbia, 1939), pp. 20, 39 ff.; Daniel Walker Hollis: *University of South Carolina* (Columbia, 1951-6), I, 263.

[6] S. Willis Rudy: *The College of the City of New York: A History, 1847-1947* (New York, 1949), pp. 19-20.

in the history of the American college. While political, theological, and finally constitutional issues arose, the question that lay at the basis of the Dartmouth College case was whether the Wheelock dynasty as represented by President John Wheelock (son of Dartmouth's founder, Eleazar Wheelock) was to run the institution or whether effective control was to be located in the absentee board of trustees.[7]

By 1815 Wheelock was prepared to make a public issue of the locus of authority at Dartmouth College and therefore, on his invitation, the legislature of New Hampshire, which had originally chartered the institution, voted to investigate the affairs of the college. An infuriated board of trustees thereupon promptly removed Wheelock from his three connections with the college, from his positions as president, professor, and trustee. His dismissal won him popular sympathy with the less privileged orders in society, and before long the Republican party in the state rushed to Wheelock's side not apparently from any deep conviction on matters of collegiate government but out of sheer political opportunism. It was on the college issue that the Republicans won the election of 1816.

In his inaugural address the new Republican governor raised the question of Dartmouth College, charging it with harboring in its small self-perpetuating governing board aristocratic rather than democratic principles. In June the legislature passed and the governor approved a law that changed the name of the institution from Dartmouth College to Dartmouth University and brought the institution in a number of ways under more effective state control. In the contest which then ensued between Wheelock and the trustees it became clear that neither side to the controversy was concerned by or about state control. Clearly, on the other hand, this was an issue that did interest the governor, for it had won the election for the Republicans.

[7] Leon Burr Richardson: *History of Dartmouth College* (Hanover, 1932), I, 287-346, has a detailed account of the case.

At their commencement meeting in 1816 the Dartmouth trustees, in order to preserve their control, decided to go to the courts. The next year while the trustees and the state prepared their cases for delivery before the Superior Court of New Hampshire, two institutions were operating in Hanover—the trustees' Dartmouth College and Wheelock's Dartmouth University. When the case was presented before the court, it became clear that at contention was the question of whether Dartmouth College was a public or private corporation. On November 6, 1817, the court decided that Dartmouth was indeed a public corporation, that its trustees were public officers responsible to the people and therefore subject to legislative control. The court rejected the notion that a corporation charter was a contract; it could find no precedent and, moreover, such a notion put a public institution beyond public control.

On March 10, 1818, the case was carried before the Supreme Court in Washington. For five hours an unknown lawyer, a Dartmouth graduate of the Class of 1801, argued the position of the trustees and, as he drew to a close, legend has it that Daniel Webster broke into tears. The Chief Justice, Mr. Marshall, bending over to catch every word, was himself in tears as Daniel Webster closed his plea:

> This, sir, is my case. It is the case, not merely of that humble institution, it is the case of every college in the land. It is more. It is the case of every eleemosynary institution throughout our country . . . the case of every man who has property of which he may be stripped— for the question is simply this: Shall our state legislature be allowed to take that which is not their own, to turn it from its original use, and apply it to such ends or purposes as they, in their discretion shall see fit? Sir, you may destroy this little institution . . . , but if you do . . . you must extinguish, one after another, all those great lights of science, which, for more than a century,

have thrown their radiance over the land! It is, sir, as I have said, a small college, and yet there are those that love it. . . .[8]

On February 2, 1819, the Court handed down its decision, Chief Justice John Marshall speaking for a Court that was divided 5-1, with one not participating. The Supreme Court reversed the decision of the New Hampshire Superior Court. The Chief Justice remarked that Dartmouth College was not a civil or public institution, nor was its property public property. Dartmouth College was indeed a private eleemosynary institution with an object to benefit the public, but it was not a public institution under public control. Therefore, the charter of Dartmouth College was a contract, a contract which the New Hampshire law of 1816 violated by substituting the will of the state for the will of the trustees.

The Dartmouth College decision is a landmark in America jurisprudence because it became a "bulwark of private property" by safeguarding private institutions from legislative interference. It gave expression to a changing definition and understanding of the American corporation. It became a part of that judicial fabric with which Chief Justice Marshall and his successors protected property from popular passion.

For higher education in America, the Dartmouth College decision put on the way toward clarification the distinction between private and public institutions, a distinction that had not been made nor required a half century before.[9] Although serving a public purpose, Dartmouth, said the Court, was essentially an expression of private philanthropy. It was therefore a private agency subject not to the control of the state but to the control of a board of trustees into whose care had been committed the money and the benevolent intentions of many good men.

[8] Ibid., 337.
[9] John Maynard Hoffman in a History 172 course paper at Harvard, 1960, "The Background of the Dartmouth College Case: An Essay in American Educational History," contributed to my understanding of the emerging concept of the "private" college.

The decision also gave to the Court the incidental opportunity of endorsing the American principle of academic organization whereby control resides not in the hands of the faculty but in an external board.[1] The decision unleashed an era of denominational college-founding by making clear that no exclusive or monopolistic relationship necessarily existed between a college corporation and the state that had chartered it, and that once chartered a college was beyond the control of the state.[2] Each new college was now assured of its right to exist, if not of its right to survive the competition that the decision helped to unleash. By encouraging an era of college-founding, the Dartmouth College case allowed the American college to participate in the competitive enterprising spirit of the Jacksonian period.

The decision discouraged the friends of strong state-supported and state-controlled institutions. For state universities now could not be reshaped from existing institutions, as had been tried in New Hampshire and as would be tried without success in Maine. Nor could they expect much in the way of public support now that a horde of small struggling colleges, each with its own band of adherents, was casting a hungry eye at the public treasury. The Dartmouth College decision, by encouraging college-founding and by discouraging public support for higher education, probably helped to check the development of state universities for half a century.[3]

And, perhaps most important, the decision put the American college beyond the control of popular prejudice and passion; it assured the further alienation of the people from the colleges, but on the eve of the Jacksonian movement it also put the colleges beyond the control of people who understood neither the colleges nor their problems. The decision left the colleges free to work out their own future

[1] John E. Kirkpatrick: *Academic Organization and Control* (Yellow Springs, 1931), p. xix.
[2] Donald G. Tewksbury: *The Founding of American Colleges and Universities Before the Civil War* (New York, 1932), pp. 64 ff.
[3] Ibid., p. 151.

without orders from the state or political pressures from the people. It allowed all of the incompetence, variety, and final achievement which are associated with competitive American enterprise, and in that respect it allowed the colleges to suffer the results and to reap the benefits of their own decisions. It set up a barrier against Jacksonian extremists while permitting the colleges to indulge in the Jacksonian mood of enterprise, competition, and opportunity, in the Jacksonian mood which substituted competition for monopoly and opportunity for privilege.

If the decision spared the colleges the likelihood of popular meddling, the temper and the interests of Jacksonian democracy also spared them much in the way of direct financial assistance. The height of the Jacksonian movement was probably a historical low point in legislative generosity to the colleges. The Jacksonians were not hostile to vigorous state governments, but they did object to using the people's money for institutions of privilege. This objection was strengthened by the practical difficulty of supporting what appeared to be an endless number of such institutions. When Lafayette College was chartered in 1826 a provision in the charter for ex officio membership on the board of trustees by four state officials was struck out by the Pennsylvania Senate in order to protect the Commonwealth from even the suspicion that state funds might flow toward the college. During the long period when New York politics were enlivened by the common-school controversy, no state aid was given to the colleges. In 1834 both houses of the Missouri legislature memorialized Congress to allow the state to direct university funds to the support of the common schools.[4]

After 1842 the Georgia legislature stopped supporting the

[4] David Bishop Skillman: *The Biography of a College: Being the History of the First Century of the Life of Lafayette College* (Easton, 1932), I, 30; Frank W. Blackmar: *The History of Federal and State Aid to Higher Education in the United States* (Washington, 1890), pp. 131-48; Viles: *Missouri*, p. 15.

state university. In 1845 a newspaper in Virginia took issue with the policy of state appropriations for the university
at Charlottesville and asked: "Cannot the annual appropriation of fifteen thousand dollars to the University be more
profitably expended for the great cause of education than in
instructing from one hundred to one hundred and fifty
youths, all of whom have the means of finishing their
course through their own resources?" It was suggestive of
the Jacksonian emphasis that when the states distributed or
appropriated their share of the United States Treasury surplus in 1837 they overwhelmingly ignored the colleges and
employed the funds in such popular projects as common
schools, new roads, and bad banks.[5]

Colleges chartered during the period, an era of expanding
democratic purpose and national confidence, were subjected
to appropriate Jacksonian limitations. Fear of the potential
power and the privileged position of the colleges was registered in the 1830's by legislatures which carefully limited
the amount of property that might be held by the colleges.
The use of this limitation was not new, but it was vigorously employed during this period when popular suspicion
of corporate literary institutions was widespread. The property limitation placed in the charter of Davidson College in
1838 was to deprive it of a $50,000 legacy fifteen years
later.[6]

As a result of the Dartmouth College case, many states in
chartering colleges decided to reserve for themselves the
right to alter, repeal, or renew charters. Such a provision

[5] Coulter: *Georgia*, pp. 187-90; Philip Alexander Bruce: *History of
the University of Virginia, 1819-1919* (New York, 1920-2), III, 9-10;
Edward G. Bourne: *The History of the Surplus Revenue of 1837* (New
York, 1885), pp. 122-3.
[6] Luther L. Gobbel: *Church-State Relationships in Education in
North Carolina Since 1776* (Durham, 1938), p. 35; Charles Henry Ram-
melkamp: *Illinois College: A Centennial History 1829-1929* (New
Haven, 1928), p. 67; Albea Godbold: *The Church College of the Old
South* (Durham, 1944), pp. 12-13.

appeared in the charters of Western Reserve, Lafayette, De-
Pauw, the University of the City of New York, Tufts, and
Northwestern. But nothing in the way of college chartering
was quite so revealing of Jacksonian democracy as the provision inserted into the charter of Wabash College in 1834
entitling every contributor of ten dollars to vote for the
board of trustees. The provision stood for ten years, but the
Hoosier Democrats were throughly frustrated by eastern
affluence and generosity, which were able consistently to
outvote the people of Indiana.[7]

Popular suspicion—indeed popular misunderstanding—of
colleges helped to frustrate the dreams and the efforts of
President Philip Lindsley at the University of Nashville.
Lindsley was a good Jeffersonian, and the distinction between
a Jeffersonian and a Jacksonian was well-demonstrated by
the gulf that yawned between Lindsley and the people of
Tennessee on the subject of higher education. In his inaugural address of 1825 Lindsley had declared: "I affirm
. . . that every individual, who wishes to rise above the level
of a mere labourer at task-work, ought to endeavour to obtain a liberal education." [8] By 1829, however, he was fully
aware that, in urging education for all to the level of excellence that they were capable of achieving, he was not really
speaking to the people of Tennessee. Looking out on the
educational wasteland that was Tennessee, he pointedly remarked: "The levelling system, which is so popular and
captivating with the multitude, may be made to operate in
two ways, with equal success. . . . Colleges and universities,
as implying odious pre-eminence, may be prevented from
growing up among us: or every petty village school may be

[7] Lester William Bartlett: *State Control of Private Incorporated Institutions of Higher Education* (New York, 1926), pp. 27-8; Skillman:
Lafayette, I, 35; William Warren Sweet: *Indiana Asbury-DePauw
University, 1837-1937: A Hundred Years of Higher Education in the
Middle West* (New York, 1937), p. 37; James I. Osborne and Theodore
G. Gronert: *Wabash College; the first hundred years, 1832-1932* (Crawfordsville, 1932), p. 26.
[8] LeRoy J. Halsey, ed.: *The Works of Philip Lindsley, D.D.* (Philadelphia, 1866), I, 81.

dignified with the name and legal attribute of a college."⁹ As Lindsley suggested, the implications of popular democracy for American higher education would be profound, for democracy had the habit of confusing excellence with privilege and of mistaking quantity for quality.

Lindsley's 1829 baccalaureate address was full of the heartbreak and the discouragement, but not the despair, of a confirmed Jeffersonian who believed in popular government and education but who also knew that the people who most needed the education he favored did not want it. What, he must often have wondered, can I do to dissuade the people from the notion that education is an aristocratic prerogative? His attempt in the 1829 baccalaureate was an interpretation of the promise of America, in which he rejected European ideas of class and privilege, ideas that he accused the opponents of higher education of harboring. Let us not talk of the rich and the poor in the manner of Europeans, he argued. Let us recognize the American experience for what it is—an invitation to achievement in an open mobile society.¹

That Lindsley found it advisable to instruct the people of Tennessee in the differences between classbound Europe and the United States suggested that class consciousness imported from Europe might have explained the average American's hostility to the colleges. The Jacksonians, of course, with their support of common schools and general laws of incorporation, were intent on making American society even more fluid, more mobile than it was. Yet Lindsley's experiences were instructive. Until the American people were fully convinced that their society was as fluid as Lindsley argued, until they were adequately assured that their customs and their institutions supported a high level of mobility, they would continue to view the colleges with suspicion and contempt.

The hope of the colleges that they would serve the people as social, economic, and political elevators was not yet shared

⁹ Ibid., 213-14.
¹ Ibid., 209-77.

in a substantial way by the people themselves. George Ticknor expressed an American truism in 1825 when he observed: "There is, at this moment, hardly a father in our country, who does not count among his chief anxieties, and most earnest hopes, the desire to give his children a better education than he has been able to obtain for himself." [2] But this observation could not be translated into growing college enrollments, for the common elementary school ably provided the children of a vast majority of Americans with better education than their fathers. And beyond the common schools were the private academies which, while serving in one capacity as college preparatory schools, also provided a terminal education in many useful and popular subjects that the colleges neglected.

In Ohio in 1830 Philander Chase was prepared to turn what became Kenyon College into a "People's College": "to teach the children of the poor to become school-masters, . . . to teach the children of the poor to rise by their wisdom and merit into stations hitherto occupied by the rich; to fill our pulpits, to sit in our senate chambers, and on our seats of justice; and to secure in the best possible way the liberties of our country." [3] Chase was dreaming. First the children of the poor would have to acquire the habit of going to the common schools, and after that a democratic institution would have to be developed that would prepare them for college. Andrew Jackson himself shared the mood of Bishop Chase and in 1837 said of the United States Military Academy: "It was for the descendants of those revolutionary parents who died poor that the military academy was established." [4] Jackson's remarks were a perversion of history, but they were one with Lindsley, Ticknor, Chase, and even the Yale Report of 1828 in the belief that educa-

---

[2] George Ticknor: *Remarks on Changes Lately Proposed or Adopted in Harvard College* (Boston, 1825), p. 3.

[3] George Franklin Smythe: *Kenyon College: Its First Century* (New Haven, 1924), pp. 42-3.

[4] Sidney Forman: *West Point: A History of the United States Military Academy* (New York, 1950), p. 50.

tion in America was to be a remarkable means of social and economic mobility. As yet, however, higher education was not called upon to perform this function in any large-scale way.

The adjustment of the colleges to the Jacksonian mood was reflected in their tendency to give up the custom of ranking students publicly at commencement. It was revealed in the willingness of Ohio University to accept partial-course, non-degree students in 1831 for the purpose of preparing teachers for the new common schools, and in the intention of Lafayette College to establish in 1838 a Model, or Laboratory, School to train teachers for the new public-school system. At Wabash the college laws of 1834 gave students a right of appeal from the president of the college to the board of trustees. At Illinois College in 1835 a faculty plan to encourage scholarship by publicly reading marks in chapel was abandoned when the students objected.[5]

These scattered, fleeting adjustments of curriculum and rules of discipline did not really come close to the fundamental problems of the colleges. The one typically Jacksonian adventure that developed into a movement among the colleges was the manual-labor system, which theoretically made going to college self-financing, gave students experience in practical skills, and even paid some attention to their physical condition. The notion that young men could pay their own way through college by working at some useful trade was inspired by the work of Fellenburg and Pestalozzi in Europe. It was introduced in dozens of colleges, and much to almost everyone's satisfaction it was generally killed off by the Panic of 1837.[6] The farms operated by the col-

---

[5] Thomas N. Hoover: *The History of Ohio University* (Athens, 1954), pp. 64-5; Skillman: *Lafayette*, I, 118; Osborne and Gronert: *Wabash*, p. 34; Rammelkamp: *Illinois College*, p. 80.

[6] See Godbold: *The Church College of the Old South*, pp. 13-15, 23-5, 38-9, 56, 59; William Alfred Millis: *The History of Hanover College from 1827 to 1927* (Hanover, 1927), pp. 145-7; G. Wallace Chess-

leges usually lost money; the students malingered; the mechanical shops were underequipped; at Marietta and Ohio University the students made so many wooden barrels that they glutted the market. According to the president of Lafayette, surveying the wreckage of the system at his college, even the social and economic classes to whom the scheme was supposed to appeal found it objectionable. "I am constrained to believe," he said, "that all classes of men who live by manual labor, are hostile to its introduction into a College. It operates, even with them, to make the Institution unpopular." Workingmen were simply not taken in by this rather uncharacteristic fumbling effort of the colleges to lend the weight of their traditions to dignifying the labor of the workingman. Moreover, it was questionable whether the students at Centre College, Kentucky, who labeled the two college farms "Do Little" and "Do Less," really dignified labor.[7]

The truth of the matter was that very little which the colleges did helped to bridge the gap between them and the people. The choice, said Francis Wayland in 1850, was between adopting a course of study that appealed to all classes or adhering to a course that appealed to one class. The colleges took the second choice, but by the 1850's they were becoming aware of the consequences. Statistics showed that in New England the number of students in colleges was declining both actually and proportionately to the population, and if such a thing was happening in New England, God save the United States from what was happening elsewhere![8]

man: Denison: The Story of an Ohio College (Granville, 1957), p. 61; Woodburn: Indiana, pp. 107-8; Rammelkamp: Illinois College, pp. 61-3; Skillman: Lafayette, I, 3, 55; William Storrs Lee: Father Went to College: The Story of Middlebury (New York, 1936), pp. 115-16; Robert Samuel Fletcher: A History of Oberlin College from its Foundation through the Civil War (Oberlin, 1943), I, 117 ff., II, 634-64; Hoover: Ohio University, p. 53; Arthur G. Beach: A Pioneer College: The Story of Marietta (Marietta, 1935), p. 50.
[7] Skillman: Lafayette, I, 127-8; Osborne and Gronert: Wabash, p. 33.
[8] Francis Wayland: Report to the Corporation of Brown University, on Changes in the System of Collegiate Education, Read March 28,

Over seven hundred colleges died in the United States before 1860. How could there have been so many? Between 1850 and 1866, for instance, fifty-five Catholic colleges were started, of which twenty-five were abandoned by 1866. And in the live colleges, matters were not much better. In 1846 in New York City with a population of half a million the two colleges enrolled a total of 247. In 1848 at Lafayette College, which had been chartered over twenty years before, the board of trustees was larger than the student body. In 1853 Denison College in Ohio had been in operation for twenty years and had graduated but sixty-five students. In 1859 in Ohio there were twenty-two colleges with an average college enrollment of eighty-five. In 1860 Harvard graduated its first class of a hundred.[9]

The problem before the colleges was complex. Not only did they have to combat the voice of the people as it was expressed in such places as the legislature of Illinois, where in 1835 one opponent of chartering a new college won a round of applause with the observation: "[I was] born in a briar thicket, rocked in a hog trough, and . . . never had . . . [my] genius cramped by the pestilential air of a college." The colleges also had to face the perhaps far more threatening developments to which Henry Tappan, soon to be president of the University of Michigan, drew their attention in 1851. Said Tappan: "The commercial spirit of our country, and the many avenues of wealth which are opened before enterprise, create a distaste for study deeply

---

1850 (Providence, 1850), pp. 21-34; Frederick A. P. Barnard: *Analysis of Some Statistics of Collegiate Education; A Paper Read Before the Trustees of Columbia College, New York, January 3, 1870, by the President of the College* (New York, 1870).

[9] Tewksbury: *The Founding of American Colleges and Universities Before the Civil War*, p. 28; Sebastian A. Erbacher: *Catholic Higher Education for Men in the United States 1850-1886* (Washington, 1931), p. 116; Rudy: *C.C.N.Y.*, p. 11; Skillman: *Lafayette*, I, 190-1; Chessman: *Denison*, pp. 32-6; James E. Pollard: *History of the Ohio State University: The Story of its First Seventy-Five Years 1873-1948* (Columbus, 1952), p. 1; Samuel Eliot Morison: *Three Centuries of Harvard 1636-1936* (Cambridge, 1936), pp. 415-16.

inimical to education. The manufacturer, the merchant, the gold-digger, will not pause in their career to gain intellectual accomplishments. While gaining knowledge, they are losing the opportunities to gain money." [1]

By 1850 the rising tide of democracy had expressed its attitude toward the colleges either in the hostility of the Illinois demagogue or in the indifference of the great numbers who were achieving material success without a college education. Surveying the collegiate scene in 1850, Francis Wayland of Brown summed up a half century of American collegiate history and then asked the question that the next half century would answer: "We have produced an article for which the demand is diminishing. We sell it at less than cost, and the deficiency is made up by charity. We give it away, and still the demand diminishes. Is it not time to inquire whether we cannot furnish an article for which the demand will be, at least, somewhat more remunerative?" [2]

[1] Rammelkamp: *Illinois College,* p. 65; Henry P. Tappan: *University Education* (New York, 1851), p. 64.
[2] Wayland: op. cit., p. 34.

II

❦

Crisis of the 1850's

The American college did not find the answers to the questions raised by the rising tide of democracy until after the Civil War. Nor did it, until then, begin effectively to grapple with the question of quality, of standards, of excellence. Whether higher education in the United States was going to serve the people was one question; whether it was going to serve learning was another.

The old-time college had been willing to serve both, but on *its* terms, which meant that the people must take from the colleges what the colleges had decided was good for the people and that learning must not interfere with the colleges' commitment to character. Both the people and learning would find new allies in postwar America. As an expanding dynamic industrial society set about making itself into a colossus of power, new institutions would be developed that would better meet the requirements of such a society. The college of the first half of the nineteenth century was the creature of a relatively simple, agrarian community, a community of settled ways and of ancient certainties. It would survive, partly as an instrument of class or religious purposes. In the next hundred years, however, the old-time college would change significantly and it would find itself increasingly surrounded by new institutions that were addressing themselves effectively to the questions of intellectual and popular purpose to which the first two hundred and twenty-five years of American higher education had given but faltering, uncertain answers. The likelihood that such questions would soon be answered became apparent in the 1850's when the voices of complaint were more insistent, when the always expanding domain of science registered new and significant victories, and when under the leadership of Francis Wayland, Brown took steps that provided a new rallying point for critics of the Yale Report of 1828.

The maturing of the natural and physical sciences profoundly influenced the colleges; and while the role of science as the great disrupter of the classical course of study would have to wait until after the war, the first half of the nineteenth century suggested that if anything were going to shake the colleges loose from many of their old convictions, it would be science.

The very first inroads on the classical curriculum had been made in 1727 with the appointment of a professor of mathematics and natural philosophy at Harvard. By 1792 botany had entered the course of study at Columbia, and three years later John MacLean, at Princeton, became the first professor of chemistry in an American college. By mid-nineteenth century the so-called new subjects—mathematics, natural philosophy, botany, and chemistry, to which were added zoology, geology, and mineralogy—had insinuated themselves into the course of study in most colleges. Accompanied as they were by French, German, history, and English literature, they were not given more than passing attention. Sometimes they were packaged in such a way as to offer a degree of election. At Dartmouth they were placed in the winter term when most students were absent, teaching in New England district schools.[1]

[1] Palmer Chamberlain Ricketts: *History of Rensselaer Polytechnic*

The new scientific subjects had not yet achieved anything like ultimate respectability, but thanks to a band of curious, inquiring pioneers, science was popularized in the United States and before long was recognized as offering that broadly utilitarian orientation which the ancient studies lacked. The work of the pioneers, both in advancing science and in popularizing it, combined with the richness of the American continent in making science an instrument for exploiting the great natural wealth of inland America. Not even the most hidebound of the college conservatives were able to deny to the sciences limited entry.

Instrumental in developing American interest in science was Benjamin Silliman, a Yale graduate of the Class of 1796 who was appointed professor of chemistry and natural history at Yale in 1802, even before he had ever seen a chemical experiment performed, let alone performed one himself. Preparatory to taking up his professorship, Silliman studied for two years at the University of Pennsylvania in Philadelphia, among other places, and at the laboratory of John MacLean at Princeton, where he saw his first chemical experiment. Silliman gave his first course of lectures at Yale in 1804 and followed it by a trip to Europe, where in addition to purchasing scientific equipment and books, he undertook further study in Edinburgh and London. In 1813 he acquired for Yale a celebrated American collection of minerals which enabled him to give the first illustrated course in mineralogy and geology in an American college. In 1818 he founded the *American Journal of Science and Arts*, a learned journal where aspiring American scientists found an audience for their researches and a hearing for their speculations.[2]

Silliman became a magnet for young men with scientific

Institute 1824-1914 (3d. ed.; New York, 1934), p. 1; Thomas Jefferson Wertenbaker: *Princeton 1746-1896* (Princeton, 1946), p. 124; Leon Burr Richardson: *History of Dartmouth College* (Hanover, 1932), II, 434.
[2] William Lathrop Kingsley, ed.: *Yale College: A Sketch of its History* (New York, 1879), I, 115-18; Russell H. Chittenden: *History of*

aspirations, and outside the university he won fame as a popularizer of the scientific outlook. He was selected to inaugurate the lecture series of the Lowell Institute in the winter of 1839-40, when he made Boston and Cambridge for the first time acutely aware of science. Silliman taught at Yale from 1802 to 1853, assisted by his son Benjamin, an eminent chemist in his own right, and by his son-in-law James Dwight Dana, a pioneer mineralogist. The Sillimans made Yale a fountainhead of scientific study in America, and the fact that their work could take place within the temple of the report of 1828 unquestionably helped to lend an aura of respectability to their activities. Soon after Silliman's course of lectures in 1804, young men began arriving in New Haven to study chemistry and then to go out and become pioneer professors elsewhere. Still later the publication of James Dwight Dana's textbook in mineralogy in 1837 would open the way for mineralogical instruction in the American college.

Similarly, a band of pioneer botanists led by Amos Eaton, who studied under Silliman, went about the task of collecting, describing, classifying, and popularizing the study of botany. Eaton published a pioneering botany manual in 1817 and as an itinerant lecturer helped to awaken an interest in science in countless young Americans. One of these was Edward Hitchcock, who became professor of chemistry and natural history at Amherst, and who in 1833 completed for the Commonwealth of Massachusetts the first state geological survey in the United States; another was Ebenezer Emmons, who became professor of natural history at Williams and the pioneer state geologist of New York and North Carolina. John Torrey, a celebrated southern botanist, whose father was a jailkeeper in Greenwich Village, is supposed to have come under the influence of Eaton while Eaton was serving a sentence for nonpayment of debts. Asa Gray, the most eminent

---

the Sheffield Scientific School of Yale University 1846-1922 (New Haven, 1928), I, 26-30.

botanist of the period, was led to science by the writings
of Eaton. In 1842 Gray was appointed Fisher Professor of
Natural History at Harvard, and in 1859 his ranking as a
scientist was certified when he became one of three scientists to receive from Charles Darwin an advance copy of
Origin of Species.[3]

Here and there in the old colleges equally dedicated men
were pioneering in the discovery of science. At Princeton,
Joseph Henry explored the world of physics, experimented
with electricity, and in 1846 resigned in order to become the
first secretary and director of the Smithsonian Institution in
Washington, an agency of education which he shaped into a
foundation for the diffusion of scientific knowledge. At William and Mary and then at Virginia, William Barton Rogers
established an international reputation in geology and physics.[4]

Interest in science during these years fed on the natural
enthusiasm and ambition of American youth. It also was unquestionably strengthened by the deepening mood of nationalism which by the 1840's was speaking the language of
manifest destiny. Also becoming interested in science were
men of strong religious conviction, who were prepared to
turn this scientific enthusiasm to their own benefit. Albert
Hopkins, who assisted his brother Mark in guiding the religious life at Williams, while in Europe in 1834 purchased
instruments which went into the completion under his direction in 1838 of the first permanent astronomical observatory in the United States. This observatory served science,
but that had not altogether been the purpose—as Albert
Hopkins revealed at the exercises of dedication in 1838. In
their worship of the practical, he declared, men were losing
sight of the moral. Education itself was being subverted by a
prevailing notion that it was intended to whet the intellect,
sharpen mental powers, and prepare for "action, action, ac-

[3] See Ethel M. McAllister: *Amos Eaton: Scientist and Educator*
(Philadelphia, 1941).
[4] Wertenbaker: *Princeton*, p. 220: Philip Alexander Bruce: *History
of the University of Virginia, 1819-1919* (New York, 1920-2), II, 166-7.

tion." To counteract these influences, he confessed, he had decided that what Williams College needed most was an astronomical observatory where the students could elevate their thoughts "toward that fathomless fountain and author of being, who has constituted matter and all its accidents as lively emblems of the immaterial kingdom." [5]

The religious orientation of the American colleges provided a climate in which pioneer science could be effectively nurtured, for it was not really necessary for the orthodox to capture or constrain science. The early scientists on the whole were men of religious conviction who could pursue their studies of the natural world without involving their deeply held belief in the supernatural. The evangelical saw science as a useful tool in demonstrating the wondrous ways of God. Science, therefore, gained entry into the American college not as a course of vocational study but as the handmaiden of religion. As early as 1788, at Princeton, Professor Walter Minto recognized the intrusion of science into the curriculum and welcomed it: "Natural philosophy . . . by leading us in a satisfactory manner to the knowledge of one almighty all-wise and all-good Being, who created, preserves and governs the universe, is the very handmaid of religion. Indeed I consider a student of that branch of science as engaged in a continued act of devotion. . . ." [6] Throughout the era of the colleges this sentiment would be echoed by college presidents, by the pioneer scientists themselves, as they built the structure of American collegiate science.

During these years the colleges developed their natural science museums and their mineralogical cabinets. Sometimes it seemed as if a stage of intercollegiate rivalry was being carried on by the rock, butterfly, and plant collectors. Princeton in 1805 was able to summon as much enthusiasm as was later reserved for a football game with Yale when a

[5] Frederick Rudolph: *Mark Hopkins and the Log: Williams College, 1836-1872* (New Haven, 1956), p. 137.
[6] Wertenbaker: *Princeton*, p. 95.

superior natural-history collection was purchased from a
French collector in New York. The very first purchase authorized by the board of regents of the University of Michigan in 1838 was a collection of 4,000 minerals. The stuffed
zebras, bears, and assorted animals which from time to time
made their way into chapel pulpits or bell towers reflected
the collecting passion which was one aspect of the early
scientific movement.[7]

The extracurriculum of course also developed a scientific
branch. A short-lived mineralogical society appeared at Williams in 1817, apparently in response to a series of lectures
given by Amos Eaton. From 1818 to 1827 an undergraduate
scientific society existed at Brown. Others developed at
Amherst, Lafayette, Wesleyan, Gettysburg College, Union,
the University of Nashville, and Miami. Unquestionably
there were many others, but probably few that compared
with the Lyceum of Natural History at Williams, founded in
1835, which sent out to Nova Scotia the first American college scientific expedition in the same year, erected its own
museum building in the 1850's, and in 1851 (thanks to the
thoughtfulness of a Williams missionary) became the first
American museum to own examples of Assyrian bas-reliefs.[8]

If the experience of the Williams lyceum was any indication of the nature of undergraduate interest in science elsewhere, then college students everywhere were finding purposes other than the purely pietistic in science. The lyceum
made up for the official neglect of science by undertaking,
between 1835 and 1871, expeditions to Nova Scotia, Florida,
Greenland, South America, and Honduras; by building a remarkable natural-history collection; and by devoting their

[7] Ibid., p. 125; Elizabeth M. Farrand: *History of the University of
Michigan* (Ann Arbor, 1885), p. 30.
[8] Rudolph: *Williams,* pp. 144-55; Claude M. Fuess: *Amherst: The
Story of a New England College* (Boston, 1935), p. 113; David Bishop
Skillman: *The Biography of a College: Being the History of the First
Century of the Life of Lafayette College* (Easton, 1932), II, 177; Carl
F. Price: *Wesleyan's First Century* (Middletown, 1932), p. 43; Walter
C. Bronson: *The History of Brown University 1764-1914* (Providence,
1914), p. 181.

meetings to the consideration of such matters as flying machines, dyestuffs, the manufacture of silk, the culture and
manufacture of cotton, and the principle of artesian wells.
Students reported at society meetings on coal beds, whale
fisheries, oil wells, and iron ores. Over the front doors of
their museum building these young Williams scientists
perched a great bronze cast of an American eagle, a symbol
of the adventuresome spirit with which they applied their
sense of the practical to the discovery of science. The lyceum was a manifestation of a national spirit in which the
young men of Williams freely joined, a spirit that recognized
the vast American continent as a limitless expanse in which
to roam, dig, and shape careers around the life that applied
science made possible.

The success of the two educational foundations that most
clearly expressed that spirit did not escape the attention of
critics and observers of the American collegiate scene. At
both the United States Military Academy at West Point and
the Rensselaer Polytechnic Institute at Troy, the commitment to applied science was paramount.

When the Congress of the United States established the
Military Academy in 1802 it created what was to become
the first technical institute in the United States. Under the
influence of its first superintendent, Jonathan Williams, there
grew up at West Point between 1802 and 1812 an intramural
"Military and Philosophical Society" which nurtured military
science in ways that the official plans did not permit. This
extracurricular organization created the "richest collection of
technical books in the United States." It published works on
military subjects and succeeded in transforming West Point
into a national center of scientific study. Under its auspices
all sciences became pertinent to military purposes, the study
of analytical trigonometry was introduced into the United
States, and a significant number of cadets fell under the sway
of a scientific approach to military problems.

The curriculum that took shape at West Point included moral philosophy in the last year, but in many other particulars it was a marvel of innovation. From the beginning, for instance, French was a required subject because of its usefulness in scientific study. Advanced mathematical instruction, chemistry, drawing, and civil engineering were central in the course of study. Cadets were divided for instruction into sections based on ability; their textbooks were the most advanced European works on the subject, often translated from the French by their instructors.[9]

Not every cadet flourished under this regimen. One who did not was Edgar Allan Poe, who during his year there, in 1830-31, wrote in a sonnet:

> *Science! meet daughter of old Time thou art*
> *Who alterest all things with thy peering eyes!*
> *Why prey'st thou thus upon the poet's heart,*
> *Vulture! whose wings are dull realities!*

And another was the artist James McNeill Whistler whose comment on his Military Academy days was the terse observation: "Had silicon been a gas, I would have been a major general." [1]

Farther up the Hudson at Troy the benefactions of Stephen Van Rensselaer, last of the great patroons, founded a technical school in 1824 which under the leadership first of Amos Eaton and then of B. Franklin Greene would become the center of applied science in the United States. After the Civil War the Rensselaer Polytechnic Institute would suffer from the development of wealthier foundations elsewhere, but during the era of the colleges it was something of a constant reminder that the United States needed railroad-builders, bridge-builders, builders of all kinds, and that the institute in Troy was prepared to create them even if the old institutions were not. In a remarkable letter in 1824, so

---

[9] Sidney Forman: *West Point: A History of the United States Military Academy* (New York, 1950), pp. 23–60, 85.

[1] Ibid., pp. 74, 86.

alien to the spirit and purpose of the Yale Report four years later, Van Rensselaer described his purpose as being to train teachers who could go out into the district schools and there instruct "the sons and daughters of farmers and mechanics . . . in the application of experimental chemistry, philosophy, and natural history, to agriculture, domestic economy, the arts, and manufactures." Van Rensselaer had clearly anticipated the rationale of the American land-grant college. For in his letter of 1824 he expressly stated that what he had in mind was "the diffusion of a very useful kind of knowledge, with its application to the business of living." [2]

Under the direction of Amos Eaton as senior professor (1824-42) the Rensselaer Institute, as it was first known, successfully incorporated new methods and new subjects into an American course of study. Students at the institute in Troy learned by teaching, by lecturing, by demonstrating experiments. For them instruction began with the practical application of the subject at hand. They were introduced to the scientific principles involved as progress in their studies required. Thus, a visit to a bleaching factory, tannery, or to a millstone-maker always preceded the appropriate laboratory experiments.

The great out-of-doors became an important classroom at Rensselaer, where surveying, engineering, collecting specimens, touring workshops, and gardening were an integral part of the course of study. Under the direction of Eaton the Rensselaer Institute provided the first systematic field work in an American institution of learning; established in 1824 the first laboratories in chemistry and physics for the instruction of students; and set up the first engineering curriculum, awarding the first engineering degree in 1835. In 1830 the institute offered its students a group of optional field trips: New York to Lake Erie by steamboat and canal, for botanical and geological purposes; the Connecticut River Valley; or the Carbondale, Pennsylvania, coal fields. These

[2] Ricketts: *R.P.I.*, pp. 9-12, 27, 43-5, 58-9.

field excursions were the forerunners of similar expeditions in the traditional colleges.

Under B. Franklin Greene the school was reorganized in 1849 and 1850. The progress in technical education achieved by French scientific schools was incorporated in the new programs. The course was expanded from one to three or more years. Well-developed courses in natural science and civil engineering were added. The institution began to place a new emphasis on fundamental research in chemistry and physics. The new program in civil engineering was widely copied in the 1850's at institutions that were otherwise traditional, thereby helping to point the way toward fundamental change in the American college in the half century that lay ahead.[3]

In the meantime, at Harvard and at Yale science had established important new beachheads. At Yale, in response to the arguments of Benjamin Silliman and with faculty concurrence, the corporation in 1846 authorized the creation of two new professorships, a professorship of "agricultural chemistry and animal and vegetable physiology" and a professorship of "chemistry and the kindred sciences as applied to the arts." The same year at Harvard plans were undertaken to establish a graduate school of arts and sciences. Eventually these stirrings became the Sheffield and Lawrence Scientific Schools.[4]

In Cambridge in 1847 the plans of the Harvard faculty ran into a $50,000 benefaction for scientific education from Abbott Lawrence, and what had been intended as a graduate school in arts and sciences became an undergraduate program in science leading to a Bachelor of Science degree. Even Lawrence's expectation that the school would emphasize engineering was frustrated by the commanding pres-

[3] Ibid., pp. 92-109.
[4] Kingsley: *Yale*, I, 150-2; Chittenden: *Yale*, I, 38-71.

ence and authority of Louis Agassiz, an eminent Swiss scientist who had come to the United States in 1845. His tremendous energy and knowledge stimulated science at Harvard in a way that Silliman's presence had earlier at Yale, and under his direction the Lawrence School fostered the natural sciences—particularly Agassiz's special interest, comparative zoology—rather than engineering.[5]

In New Haven in 1847 Benjamin Silliman, Jr., and John P. Norton developed a School of Applied Chemistry as a section of a newly authorized Department of Philosophy and the Arts. In 1852 they added instruction in civil engineering; in 1854 this department was reorganized as the Yale Scientific School, and with a $100,000 benefaction of Joseph Sheffield in 1860 became the Sheffield Scientific School.

Harvard solved the problem of what degree to offer its scientific students by giving its first Bachelor of Science degree in 1851; Yale solved the problem by creating the degree of Bachelor of Philosophy in 1852. The two old foundations kept the B.A. degree inviolate and protected it from dilution. At both Yale and Harvard admission standards for candidates for these degrees were lower than for the B.A. degree; the length of the course of study was three years rather than the normal four; and in both institutions the scientific students were considered second-class citizens, too benighted to aspire to the only worthy degree and therefore to be treated with condescension. At Yale, for instance, Sheffield students were not permitted to sit with regular academic students in chapel.

The scientific school idea was contagious. In 1851 Dartmouth received a bequest of $50,000 with which to support a separate scientific department. During the 1850's variations of the scientific department idea, offering the B.S. or Ph.B. degree, were introduced at the University of Rochester, Denison, the University of Michigan, Illinois College, the University of North Carolina, New York University, the State

[5] Samuel Eliot Morison: *Three Centuries of Harvard 1636-1936* (Cambridge, 1936), p. 279.

233   *Crisis of the 1850's*

University of Iowa, and the University of Missouri.⁶ Between
1860 and 1870 at least another twenty-five institutions would
open scientific departments. Significant, too, was the fact that
two men who perhaps would do most to shape the future of
American higher education began their teaching careers in
the new scientific schools in the 1850's: Charles William Eliot,
the president who remade Harvard, at the Lawrence Scientific School in 1854; and Daniel Coit Gilman, who would be
the first president of Johns Hopkins, at the Scientific School
at Yale in 1857.⁷

The era of science still lay ahead, but the emergence of the
B.S. and Ph.B. degrees and the creation of scientific departments, first at Harvard and Yale and then at other institutions,
suggested that the American college was perhaps in the
neighborhood of discovering some way of making a vital connection with American society.

The 1850's in many ways compiled a record of frustrated
beginnings in graduate education. At the University of Michigan Henry Philip Tappan in 1852 began to show an amazed
board of regents what could happen when a university president was ambitious to create a great American university.
Impressed by the scholarly ideal of the German universities,
Tappan proposed to make the University of Michigan central
in the life of the state. It would hold high the ideal of a true
university of advanced scholarship, but it would also respond

⁶ Richardson: *Dartmouth*, I, 422-7; Jesse Leonard Rosenberger:
Rochester, the Making of a University (Rochester, 1927), pp. 44-5, 79-
80; G. Wallace Chessman: *Denison: The Story of an Ohio College*
(Granville, 1957), p. 56; Burke A. Hinsdale: *History of the University
of Michigan* (Ann Arbor, 1906), p. 44; Charles Henry Rammelkamp:
Illinois College: A Centennial History 1829-1929 (New Haven, 1928),
pp. 168-9; Kemp Plummer Battle: *History of the University of North
Carolina* (Raleigh, 1907-12), I, 642-4; Theodore F. Jones, ed.: *New
York University 1832:1932* (New York, 1933), p. 81; Clarence Ray
Aurner: *History of Education in Iowa* (Iowa City, 1914-16), IV, 11-12,
22; Jonas Viles, *et al.: The University of Missouri: A Centennial History* (Columbia, 1939), pp. 91, 97.
⁷ Walter P. Rogers: *Andrew D. White and the Modern University*
(Ithaca, 1942), pp. 11, 113.

to popular needs. It would send its graduates into the public schools of the state and thus perfect the whole system of education in Michigan. No friend of pure vocationalism, Tappan had made clear before he went to Michigan that the true university would be "a powerful counter influence against the excessive commercial spirit, and against the chicanery and selfishness of demagogueism" which prevailed in American society. An American university, he said, would demonstrate to a skeptical public what real scholarship was: "We shall have no more acute distinctions drawn between scholastic and practical education; for, it will be seen that all true education is practical, and that practice without education is little worth; and then there will be dignity, grace, and a resistless charm about scholarship and the scholar." [8]

Tappan, however, had difficulty in advancing his university ideal in Michigan which, after all, in the 1850's was a somewhat crude setting for a German university. He hired some scholars, Andrew D. White and Charles Kendall Adams among them, and with the support of the regents the University of Michigan in 1858 offered courses of study leading to earned M.A. and M.S. degrees. The response was slight, however, and increasingly Tappan was subjected to popular abuse. His Germanic pretensions rubbed Michigan the wrong way; his habit of drinking wine with dinner was greeted with ridicule; one newspaper described him as "the most completely foreignized specimen of an abnormal Yankee, we have ever seen." In 1863 Henry Tappan was dismissed from the presidency of the University of Michigan, victim of anti-intellectualism and a popular prejudice in favor of the practical, victim also of his own premature dreams of an American university. [9]

If Michigan could not support a true university in the

[8] Richard J. Storr: *The Beginnings of Graduate Education in America* (Chicago, 1953), pp. 64-81; Farrand: *Michigan*, pp. 90-5; Henry P. Tappan: *University Education* (New York, 1851), pp. 65-6, 69.
[9] R. Freeman Butts: *The College Charts Its Course* (New York, 1939), pp. 150-5; Storr: *The Beginnings of Graduate Education*, pp. 112-17.

1850's, the city of New York could not create a new one or make over an old college. Beginning in 1852 the faculty at Columbia wrestled with the question of how it might translate its own awareness of the need for advanced study in the American colleges into some workable program. The decision was to offer, beginning in 1857, a program leading to an earned M.A., but the response was not encouraging. For while the professors sensed a national need for the encouragement of pure scholarship, not yet could it be demonstrated that any American professor needed an M.A. degree. The Columbia offerings, moreover, were not yet rich enough. Columbia would have to wait.[1]

Between 1855 and 1857 an effort to create a great new university in New York called into action the unhappy Henry Tappan of Michigan, the frustrated men of science and scholarship in the colleges, the mayor of New York, and such potential benefactors as William Astor and Peter Cooper. During the deliberations that decided the fate of the projected university in New York, Henry Tappan found himself writing to William Astor: "Now amid all my thinking on this subject—do you deem it possible that I should not have said to myself—'What a noble destiny is possible to this family!' . . ." But it was impossible to get all the interested groups to focus on the same project, on the same needs, on the same future; and as the final shape of William Astor's and Peter Cooper's benefactions revealed, the philanthropists in particular were not yet prepared to accept a true university as a worthy project. Failure to achieve a successful reformation of the traditional colleges or to achieve a new American university helped to swell the insistent voices of hostility into a growing chorus of protest.[2]

One young Princetonian complained that he and his friends were being provided with an education "about as fit for the

[1] Ibid., pp. 94-111.
[2] Ibid., pp. 82-93.

station they . . . [were] to occupy through life as the military tactics of the Baron de Steuben for fighting the Blackfoot Indians among the passes and glens of the Rocky Mountains." The New York City Board of Education asked in 1847 that the city be provided with a college that was not so fully committed to the needs of the ancient professions. In 1850 a committee of the Massachusetts General Court called on Harvard to reform its curriculum in order to prepare "better farmers, mechanics, or merchants." [3]

At New York University Professor John William Draper confronted the old order with a forceful and telling challenge. Explaining the failure of N.Y.U. to become a popular institution, he argued: "To use language which this mercantile community can understand, . . . we have been trying to sell goods for which there is no market. . . . In this practical community of men, hastening to be rich, we found no sympathy. . . . But few American youth . . . care to saunter to the fountains of knowledge through the pleasant winding of their flowery path. The practical branches must take the lead and bear the weight, and the ornamental must follow." And then Draper warned: "Mere literary acumen is becoming utterly powerless against profound scientific attainment. To what are the great advances of civilization for the last fifty years due—to literature or science? Which of the two is it that is shaping the thought of the world?" [4]

Up in Concord, Massachusetts, Henry David Thoreau was prepared to turn in his verdict on Harvard College. His complaint was with the method and psychology of learning that held the traditional college in its grip. The students, he observed, "should not *play* life, or *study* it merely, while the community supports them at this expensive game, but ear-

[3] Wertenbaker: *Princeton*, pp. 235-6; S. Willis Rudy: *The College of the City of New York: A History, 1847-1947* (New York, 1949), p. 13; Morison: Harvard: *Three Centuries*, p. 287.

[4] John William Draper: *The Indebtedness of the City of New York to Its University: An Address to the Alumni of the University of the City of New York at their Twenty-First Anniversary, 28th June, 1855* (New York, 1853), pp. 20-4.

nestly *live* it from beginning to end. How could youths better
learn to live than by at once trying the experiment of living?
Methinks this would exercise their minds as much as mathematics." He asked: "Which would have advanced the most
at the end of a month,—the boy who had made his own jack-
knife from the ore which he had dug and smelted, reading as
much as would be necessary for this,—or the boy who had
attended the lecture on metallurgy at the Institute in the
meanwhile, and had received a . . . penknife from his father?
Which would be most likely to cut his fingers?" As for his
own experiences at Harvard, Thoreau could only relate: 'To
my astonishment I was informed on leaving college that I had
studied navigation!—why, if I had taken one turn down the
Harbour I should have known more about it." [5] In Georgia,
a newspaper in 1857 announced: "We are now living in a different age, an age of practical utility, one in which the State
University does not, and cannot supply the demands of the
State. The times require practical men, civil engineers, to
take charge of public roads, railroads, mines, scientific agriculture, etc." In California, the superintendent of public instruction in 1858 asked: "For what useful occupation are the
graduates of most of our old colleges fit?" [6]

These voices had found a rallying point and a spokesman in
Francis Wayland at Brown. As astute a critic of the old college as the century was to develop, Wayland had already, in
the 1840's, reminded the colleges that there was something
ridiculous about their preference for buying students rather
than offering a curriculum that students would buy. Discouraged by his inability to make much headway with the
Brown governing board, he resigned the presidency in 1849
and then agreed to reconsider, on the promise that the corpo-

[5] Henry D. Thoreau: *Walden: or, Life in the Woods* (Boston, 1854),
pp. 56-7.
[6] E. Merton Coulter: *College Life in the Old South* (Athens, 1951),
p. 201; William Warren Ferrier: *Origin and Development of the University of California* (Berkeley, 1930), p. 34.

ration would face up to the pressing problems that thus far
Brown and most other American colleges had succeeded in
ignoring, partly by taking refuge in the Yale Report of 1828.[7]

In 1850 Wayland came forth with a report of equal influence.[8] It shattered the calm in many of the traditional foundations. It encouraged such reformers as Henry Tappan and
John W. Draper. And it hauled the American college before
the public and there gave it a vigorous beating. The colleges
were becoming more and more superficial, he noted. As
efforts were made to accommodate new subjects within the
old framework, all subjects were offered in diluted quantities, and one consequence was that the colleges were turning
out men who were not expert at anything. "The single academy at West Point," he charged, "has done more toward the
construction of railroads than all our . . . colleges united." [9]
Wayland argued that the old course of study made no sense
in an environment defined by the exploitive possibilities of an
abundant continent, the development of new scientific tech-
niques, and the existence of a self-reliant, ambitious, and democratic people bent on achieving economic and social independence. "What," he asked, "could Virgil and Horace and
Homer and Demosthenes, with a little mathematics and natural philosophy, do towards developing the untold resources
of this continent?" [1]

Appealing for a course of study that would be "for the
benefit of all classes," but especially for the rising middle
class, he called for "a radical change . . . [in] the system of
collegiate instruction," proposing such reforms as: an end to
the fixed four-year course, thereby offering the students freedom, within limits, to carry whatever load they wished; a new
system of course-accounting that would allot time to a course
according to its utility; a system of completely free course

[7] Bronson: *Brown,* pp. 259-62.
[8] Francis Wayland: *Report to the Corporation of Brown University
on Changes in the System of Collegiate Education, Read March 28,
1850* (Providence, 1850).
[9] Ibid., p. 18.
[1] Ibid., pp. 12-13.

election; a system that would enable a student to begin a subject and carry study in it to completion without interruption.[2] In this framework Wayland proposed to the Brown corporation that it offer a new program of courses in applied science, agriculture, law, and teaching. The report, as a whole, was direct, soberly argued, temperate, nondoctrinaire, and its proposals were remarkably flexible. At one point, in considering the possibility of programs of study ranging from two to six years, it anticipated a university way of looking at things. The main concern of Wayland's report, however, was to bring the American college into line with the main economic and social developments of the age.

Wayland's plans met with the immediate approval of the reform element in the colleges and also, significantly, of the Rhode Island General Assembly and the Providence Association of Mechanics and Manufacturers. The Brown corporation indicated its readiness to put the proposals into effect when it had raised $125,000.[3] In 1851 the great experiment was begun. Because Wayland was motivated both by a deeply held democratic faith and by an acute awareness of Brown's pecuniary needs, he chose to offer an M.A. for four years' work and a B.A. for something less than that, and he also included a Ph.B. degree for three-years' work in the practical subjects.

Enrollment increased, but not enough to support Wayland's expectations. The university was unable to offer enough courses to permit any real specialization. The faculty had difficulty adjusting the old rigid system of discipline to the new flexible curriculum. The new order attracted to Brown essentially a group of students of lower academic quality.[4] By 1856 the faculty and corporation were in revolt, and Wayland was replaced that year by President Barnas Sears who made clear that he was prepared to return Brown to the safe ways of the past. "We are in danger," he com-

---

[2] Ibid., pp. 50-2.
[3] Bronson: *Brown*, pp. 275 ff.
[4] Ibid., pp. 282-300.

plained, "of becoming an institution rather for conferring degrees upon the unfortunate than for educating a sterling class of men." He had friends elsewhere, many of them. At South Carolina College President James H. Thornwell proudly proclaimed: "While others are veering to the popular pressure . . . let it be our aim to make Scholars and not sappers or miners—apothecaries—doctors or farmers." At Marietta in Ohio President Israel Ward Andrews heaped scorn and sarcasm on the reformers: "Let us then give up our Algebra and Astronomy and Rhetoric, and inquire into the proper proportions of a piece of meat which can be swallowed without our incurring the hazard of being choked to death. Substitute Physiology for Grammar, Physiology for Arithmetic, Physiology for everything. . . ." The day for Francis Wayland had not yet arrived, but although they did not know it, the days of James H. Thornwell and of Israel Ward Andrews were already numbered.[5]

[5] Ibid., p. 322; Daniel Walker Hollis: *University of South Carolina* (Columbia, 1951-6), I, iv; Arthur B. Beach: *A Pioneer College: The Story of Marietta* (Marietta, 1935), p. 86.

12

◄◦♦◦►

Dawning of a New Era

One day in 1867 Ralph Waldo Emerson wrote into his journal an observation that anticipated how thoroughly higher education in the years after the Civil War would differ from the era of the colleges. "The treatises that are written on University reform may be acute or not," suggested Emerson, "but their chief value to the observer is the showing that a cleavage is occurring in the hitherto granite of the past and a new era is nearly arrived." [1] The new era, which was about to dawn, would pass the old-time college by or perhaps convert it into a precious preserve of gentility or into a defiant outpost of denominationalism. In any case, it would never be the same again.

The opportunities for redefinition that lay before the American college in the years after the Civil War were large. Not only did the long record of frustrated reform continue to make its challenge, but new institutions and new approaches now seemed to announce in the clearest of voices that the time had come when the old-time colleges would have to de-

---

[1] Quoted in Walter P. Rogers: *Andrew D. White and the Modern University* (Ithaca, 1942), p. 4.

cide whether they would be instruments of the past or of the future, and how they would meet the now imperative needs of an expanding industrial nation and of a developing national power.

For the Civil War in many ways clarified the dimensions and the prospects of the American experiment. It swept away the pretensions of the southern plantation aristocracy and all the dreams that had sustained it. And if the Civil War destroyed the southern version of an agrarian way, it likewise hastened the day when the sway of the independent yeoman farmer would come to an end. The Civil War cemented the East and the great Middle West into a formidable alliance of resources—natural, human, industrial, financial. The shape of things to come was etched in the war-built factory towns of New England, in an ever expanding network of railroads, in the new fortunes and the gingerbread houses built on the hills overlooking the towns. The Civil War conquered space. It freed thousands of Americans from a village orientation. It suggested remarkable opportunities in markets created by railroads, in needs created by an expanding population.

The Civil War, also, as Lincoln had intended, proved the flexibility and the durability of popular government: it proved that in the severest kind of testing democratic government could summon the will, the intelligence, and the power to prevail. It put an end to any effective efforts to deny the supremacy of the people. In the person of Lincoln it found the ultimate answer to the questions that had separated Hamilton and Jefferson and agitated the enemies of Andrew Jackson: Would popular government work? Could it be trusted?

And the Civil War likewise put an end to any doubts as to whether the United States would survive; it finished off any suspicions or lingering hopes on the part of hostile Europeans that the United States would eventually be broken into pieces, a patchwork of weak and servile republics. The prospect of American national power which the Civil War projected was acknowledged in the diplomatic victories that the American minister, Charles Francis Adams, achieved over the British Foreign Office during the war. It was forecast in the oil refineries of Cleveland, the iron furnaces of Pittsburgh, in the great rail center and stockyards of Chicago. It was underwritten by the most remarkable combination of human ambition and natural resources that the world had ever known.

In a world remade by the Civil War the American college found that it could not avoid the questions that it had for so long evaded. In his inaugural address at the University of Michigan in 1871 James B. Angell noted: "The public mind is now in a plastic, impressionable state, and every vigorous college, nay, every capable worker, may help to shape its decisions upon education." [2] The extent of this plastic, impressionable state—largely supported by a sense that in every way a new era was upon the United States—was responsible for inspiring what became probably the most widely known aphorism in the history of American education.

To a professor's complaint at an alumni banquet in 1871 that Williams College was falling behind the times, James A. Garfield, then a relatively obscure Republican politician, rose to the defense of the college as he had known it and uttered the words that evolved into: "The ideal college is Mark Hopkins on one end of a log and a student on the other." [3] Garfield's remarks were a defense of the old-time college, the small unpretentious institution at which inspired teaching molded young men of good character rather than of accomplished scholarship. Garfield had not intended to create an epitaph, but in a sense he did, for henceforth the ideal that he evoked would compete at an ever-increasing disadvantage with a host of new ideals, ideals more compatible with the America that the Civil War both created and uncovered. These were the decades when American educators, bene-

[2] James Burrill Angell: *Selected Addresses* (New York, 1912), p. 7.
[3] Frederick Rudolph: *Mark Hopkins and the Log: Williams College, 1836-1872* (New Haven, 1956), pp. 225-31.

factors, and governments repudiated the Yale Report of 1828.

The movement for technological and scientific education, which had been underway before the war, spawned new and more popular colleges and institutes. Between 1861 and 1865 Matthew Vassar and John Howard Raymond created at Poughkeepsie not the first college for women nor the first college that women might attend, but the first college to make the world take notice of the neglect which had long characterized the higher education of women. Vassar College established the collegiate rights of American women, at the time the largest and most underprivileged of American minority groups. On yet another level, the Morrill Act of 1862 put federal largess at the disposal of every state government, and thereby helped to develop a whole new network of institutions with a popular and practical orientation, the land-grant colleges, which by 1955 would be enrolling more than 20 per cent of all American college students. The state universities, so long neglected, now showed promise of increasing popularity and usefulness. In 1867 Johns Hopkins pledged his fortune in Baltimore and Ohio Railway stock to the creation of what would become the first substantial American effort to support pure scholarship. Two years later Harvard would elect to its presidency Charles William Eliot, under whose leadership the prescribed classical curriculum in the American college would come tumbling down with such force that a later generation at Harvard would turn to General Education as a remedy for his success.

Only in the desolated, abandoned Southland was there an absence of these dynamic movements. Laid waste by war, impoverished, robbed by death and poverty of the college-going generation, the southern colleges, like the South itself, could but hold on, hold on to romantic dreams of an Old South that never was or hold on until the day when the Union might become one again.

In other parts of America, however, the postwar years bred new institutions and leaders: Andrew D. White of Cornell, John Howard Raymond of Vassar, William Bartram Rogers of M.I.T., Daniel Coit Gilman of Hopkins. These men and Eliot and Angell seized the initiative in American higher education after the war in the way that John D. Rockefeller seized it in oil, Andrew Carnegie in steel, Washington Duke in tobacco. In different ways they responded to the needs and the demands of a society that was experiencing an increase in material wealth, in the standard of living, in industrialization and urbanization. They responded to the unleashing of new impulses to social and economic mobility, to the emergence of a more democratic psychology which stressed individual differences and needs, and to a more democratic philosophy which recognized the right to learning and character-training of women, farmers, mechanics, and the great, aspiring middle class. They recognized that a new society needed new agencies of instruction, cohesion, and control.

For the new leaders and the new institutions that rode the wave of reform, the old ways and the old curriculum were too narrow, elementary, or superficial. There was insufficient attention to the German-university ideals of free teaching, study, and research. There was insufficient attention to the technical and practical. The colleges were too sectarian, too undemocratic. Their psychology was faulty; their philosophy, wanting.

No one reformer, no one college, knew, or indeed cared to know, what to do about all of these complaints. What would happen as the years passed was a multiple effort to reform the American college and to substitute for the old definition perhaps a half-dozen new ones. By the dawn of the twentieth century, under the aegis of necessity and, later, of the richly endowed educational foundations, there would be an almost frantic effort to put some order into the collegiate and university scene. For the old unity, the old sameness, were by then utterly destroyed, and the paramount problem was to determine what had taken their place.

·   ·   ·

The fundamental movement that destroyed the old unity was unquestionably the persistent rise of science, which had already before the war—at Harvard, Yale, Dartmouth, and elsewhere—begun to make inroads on the old dispensation. The institution that would soon be setting standards in engineering and other fields of applied science was chartered by the General Court of Massachusetts in 1861, given a grant of land in the Back Bay by the Commonwealth, and opened as the Massachusetts Institute of Technology in 1865. By 1897 its enrollment of 1,200 was ample testimony to the proposition that the United States could sustain a separate independent institute of applied and pure science, where young men and women were free to pursue science without the inhibiting, and perhaps one should add the refining and inspirational, study of the humanities.[4]

In 1874 Princeton was on its way to accommodating a department of engineering within the shadow of Nassau Hall. At Bethlehem in Pennsylvania Asa Packer provided the resources that created Lehigh University as a scientific and technical college in the heart of the complex of factories, mines, and foundries of eastern Pennsylvania. When Ario Pardee provided $100,000 in 1866, nearby Lafayette, which had known nothing but misery in its search for purpose and stability, was able to pioneer in the establishment of large-scale scientific programs in small colleges. The growth inspired by the college's scientific orientation revealed a freshman class of 115 in 1872 where an entire college with the same enrollment had existed seven years before. Even at Harvard and Yale there was a sense of falling behind. "These colleges mainly make lawyers and dilettanti" was the remark of Andrew D. White of Cornell who needed neither: what he wanted in 1870 was a botanist, and neither the mighty Harvard nor the great Yale was able to recommend one of its students.[5]

[4] Samuel C. Prescott: *When M.I.T. was "Boston Tech": 1861-1916* (Cambridge, 1954), pp. 29-166.
[5] Thomas Jefferson Wertenbaker: *Princeton 1746-1896* (Princeton,

Before long, however, in one way or another the spirit of scientific inquiry would be overtaking all the old foundations. At Amherst in 1877 one of the old guard was horrified to discover that Professor Benjamin K. Emerson, a German-trained doctor of philosophy in biology and geology, was keeping "his juniors 4 or 5 weeks on the dissection & study of the clam & then . . . [requiring] a thesis on the subject from every student." Amherst had not known such nonsense before, and soon Professor Emerson was deprived of biology, which was turned over to the safekeeping of a professor who agreed to the president's injunction that he teach biology "as an absolutely dependent product of an absolutely independent and spiritual Creator." By 1885 Clarence L. Herrick was editing the significant *Bulletin of the Scientific Laboratories of Denison University*, and in 1890 in a most symbolic gesture Professor Herman C. Bumpus, professor of zoology at Brown, literally threw aside "the stuffed walrus and the stuffed giraffe of the old natural history tradition . . . and set the students down at the dissecting table." •

If science was everywhere the instrument of reform, the institution that did probably the most to change the outlook of the American people toward college-going was the land-grant college, creation of the Morrill Federal Land Grant Act of 1862. In the background of the Morrill Act was over a half century of stumbling efforts and promises to establish something in the way of agricultural education. Before 1800 Columbia had promised work in agricultural chemistry, and here and there for the next fifty years an occasional college

---

1946), pp. 307-8; Catherine Drinker Bowen: *A History of Lehigh University* (Bethlehem, 1924), *passim;* David Bishop Skillman: *The Biography of a College: Being the History of the First Century of Lafayette College* (Easton, 1932), I, 280 ff., 350; Rogers: *Cornell,* p. 159.
    • Thomas Le Duc: *Piety and Intellect at Amherst College 1865-1912* (New York, 1946), pp. 83-6; Donald Fleming: *Science and Technology in Providence 1760-1914: An Essay in the History of Brown University in the Metropolitan Community* (Providence, 1952), p. 48.

made what were generally unsuccessful efforts to achieve some vital relationship with the practical needs of an agrarian society.[7]

By the 1850's the industrial potential of the United States was as apparent as its agrarian past, and there emerged a growing awareness that a new age required new training and new preparation. What were lacking, however, were any certain institutional foundations upon which to erect programs of agricultural and mechanical training as well as any deeply held respect for expertness. The ordinary farmer and the ordinary mechanic neither sensed the changing nature of their world nor felt any need for training beyond the job itself, but there did exist among local and regional agricultural societies and among educational reformers a belief that changing times required a new look at the competence of the American farmer and the American mechanic. The Sillimans at Yale and Agassiz at Harvard had done something to develop a concept of scientific agriculture, and actually until the land-grant college movement was well launched, the most substantial work in the field was done at Yale under the Sillimans. But the Harvard and Yale accomplishments were in no sense popular.

A much-discussed venture, the People's College at Havana, New York, was chartered in 1853 and opened in 1858, and while it really did not get off the ground before the Civil War, it was widely publicized in the press and was responsible for widespread consideration of the proper orientation for a popular technical education. In the meantime the activities of agricultural societies and educational reformers led in the 1850's to the chartering and opening of a number of very low-grade institutions that foreshadowed the land-grant college movement. The New York State Agricultural College was incorporated in 1853 and opened in 1860. In Pennsyl-

[7] See Edward Danforth Eddy, Jr.: *Colleges for Our Land and Time: The Land-Grant Idea in American Education* (New York, 1957), pp. 1-22; Alfred C. True: *A History of Agricultural Education in the United States, 1785-1925* (Washington, 1929), pp. 9-43; Whitney Shepardson: *Agricultural Education in the United States* (New York, 1929).

vania in 1854 the Farmer's High School was chartered; by
1861 it was giving the degree of Bachelor of Scientific Agriculture; the next year it changed its name to the Agricultural
College of Pennsylvania; and in 1862 it received state support
to the extent of $100,000. Comparable, although not always
equally effective, stirrings were apparent in Maryland, Massachusetts, Georgia, Kentucky, and Virginia. In the West, in
the great agrarian center of the country, there was insufficient
interest in the idea of scientific agriculture to launch more
than one institution—the Michigan State College of Agriculture at East Lansing in 1857.[8]

All these activities owed little if anything to the views of
dirt farmers and workingmen's associations. They were the
work of middle-class reformers who were prepared to advance some theoretical and ideological notions of what popular technical education ought to be. Comparable impulses
were registered in the Land Grant College Act of 1862,
which was the legislative, if not the theoretical and ideological, achievement of Congressman Justin Smith Morrill of
Vermont.

Morrill as early as 1848 had suggested that American colleges might well "lop off a portion of the studies established
centuries ago as the mark of European scholarship and replace
the vacancy—if it is a vacancy—by those of a less antique
and more practical value." By 1857, the year that Morrill first
introduced his bill, it had become apparent to him that the old
foundations were not likely to change in any significant way.
He thus incorporated in his bill the leading reform notions on
technical education, stating explicitly that its purpose was "to
promote the liberal and practical education of the industrial
classes in the several pursuits and professions of life." [9]

---

[8] See Earle D. Ross: *Democracy's College: The Land-Grant Move-
ment in the Formative Stage* (Ames, 1942), pp. 14-45; Wayland Fuller
Dunaway: *History of the Pennsylvania State College* (Pennsylvania
State College, 1946), pp. 1-30; Madison Kuhn: *Michigan State: The
First Hundred Years* (East Lansing, 1955), pp. 1-70.

[9] Eddy: *Colleges for Our Land and Time*, p. 27; Ross: *Democracy's
College*, p. 47.

His bill, however, clearly also served other purposes. It provided a presumably popular and wise method of disposing of the public lands. It promised to help in the development of a scientific agriculture that might deal effectively with the growing problem of soil exhaustion and waste. In some way it might succeed in exposing humble folk to the refining influences of higher education. Some hoped that the bill would help the states less blessed by nature to achieve better use of their resources. Others hoped that the United States would be enabled to compete with the efficiency of European agriculture, where a scientific approach was well advanced. And here and there, certainly, a Republican politician was prepared to admit that in any case the bill would not hurt the Republican cause among the farmers.[1]

The bill did not become law until Morrill resubmitted it in 1862, after the South had withdrawn from the Union and after Buchanan, who had vetoed the earlier version, had been succeeded by Lincoln. Southerners had raised questions of a constitutional nature, one senator from Virginia charging that what Morrill proposed was "an unconstitutional robbing of the Treasury for the purpose of bribing the States." Others were unwilling to strengthen the artisan and laboring classes of the North, and their own sense of *noblesse oblige* to the vast majority of hard-working white southern farmers did not extend to education. Popular northern and western hostility to any kind of higher education also had to be overcome. There was a deeply American ring to the insistence of the senator from Minnesota that "we want no fancy farmers; we want no fancy mechanics."[2]

The bill passed in July 1862, two months after Lincoln approved a bill creating an office of agriculture. In conjunction with the Homestead Act of the same year, this parcel of legislation gave political recognition to the yeoman farmer on the eve of his displacement as the characteristic American. In the debates over the bill, which seldom touched upon its educa-

[1] Eddy: *Colleges for Our Land and Time*, pp. 27-30.
[2] Ibid., pp. 31-2.

tional features, Morrill at one point advanced the argument that the land-grant colleges would serve to "induce the farm‌er's sons and daughters to settle and cluster around the old homesteads." In Iowa, where (independent of the movement in Congress) efforts were being made to establish a state agri‌cultural college, the legislature heard advocates of the college argue that agricultural education would keep able young men on the farm and give them an opportunity to achieve a truly respected occupation in farming. One spokesman for the Iowa college urged: "We want . . . [our young men] to be able to stand on this floor, and in our national councils on terms of equality with the best legal men of the times . . . to urge there our claims, advocate our principles, and defend our interests." [3]

In these arguments in Washington, Iowa, and elsewhere, there was the suggestion that the land-grant college move‌ment owed something both to those forces that were destroy‌ing the agrarian orientation of American society and to those sentiments that would seek to perpetuate the past as an agrar‌ian myth. To the extent that the Land-Grant College Act was an effort to save the farm or the farmer or to keep him down on the farm even after he had seen Kansas City, to that ex‌tent Morrill's legislation was an aspect of that romantic effort of the American people to remain philosophically agrarian while on the road not only to Kansas City but to New York, Cleveland, Chicago, St. Louis, and San Francisco. [4]

By 1872 the dean of the college of agriculture at the Uni‌versity of Missouri openly revealed the degree to which the land-grant college movement was caught up in the events that were forcing fundamental readjustments in American

<hr />

[3] Rogers: *Cornell*, p. 122; Earle D. Ross: *A History of the Iowa State College of Agriculture and Mechanic Arts* (Ames, 1942), pp. 19-20.

[4] See Kuhn: *Michigan State*, p. 2; W. H. Glover: *The College of Agriculture of the University of Wisconsin: A History* (Madison, 1952), p. 28; Andrew D. White: *Address on Agricultural Education, Delivered before the N. Y. State Agricultural Society, at Albany, Febru‌ary 10, 1869* (Albany, 1869), p. 47.

life. "We will teach the science of high production," he said. "Our college shall be a living and ever multiplying power to make the farms prosperous and happy and enable them to compete with the cities for the best talent of the land." But the debates in Congress in 1862 were more extensively concerned with whether the bill damaged states' rights, whether it favored some sections over others, whether the western states would suffer from the use of their lands to endow eastern colleges. Although the bill passed with comfortable margins in both houses, it met with no public enthusiasm of importance, and there were rumblings of dissatisfaction in the West. The *New York Tribune* in summarizing the legislative achievements of the Congress omitted the Morrill Act from any consideration at all.[5]

The act itself provided for the support in every state of at least one college "where the leading object shall be, without excluding other scientific or classical studies, to teach such branches of learning as are related to agriculture and the mechanic arts." Each state was given public lands or land script equal to 30,000 acres for each senator and representative under the apportionment of 1860. The consequence of this particular provision was to turn the proceeds of the sale of 17,430,000 acres of public lands over to the new colleges. The average return per acre was $1.65; the lowest was achieved by Rhode Island at $.41, and the highest by New York at $6.73. This range in yield per acre had less to do with the quality of the land than with the financial and administrative qualities of the men who handled the arrangements of the states. Although 10 per cent of the fund to be set up by the sale of land could be used for the purchase of a college site or of experimental farm land, all the rest of the fund had to be maintained as a perpetual endowment, invested at a return of 5 per cent.[6]

[5] Jonas Viles, *et al.*: *The University of Missouri: A Centennial History* (Columbia, 1939), p. 298; Ross: *Democracy's College*, pp. 46-47.
[6] Ross: *Democracy's College*, pp. 46-7; True: *A History of Agricultural Education*, pp. 95-119.

By 1961 sixty-nine American colleges were being supported by this legislation and by subsequent legislation of a related nature. Because the act provided nothing in the way of supervision and because the concept of agricultural and mechanical education had not yet received any precise definition, the founding of the new colleges revealed an amazing variety of arrangements. Four states—Michigan, Pennsylvania, Maryland, and Iowa—created A & M colleges (as they came to be known) out of previously chartered agricultural colleges. A large number of states—including Wisconsin, Minnesota, North Carolina, and Missouri—turned over to existing state universities both the land-grant endowment and the responsibility of discovering how to serve the agricultural and mechanic interests. Many states—including Oklahoma, Texas, South Dakota, and Washington—set up entirely new colleges which would henceforth compete with existing state universities for the favor of the public purse.

Endless possibilities presented themselves. Four states— Ohio, California, Arkansas, and West Virginia—founded new state universities and added A & M components. Six other states arranged for existing private colleges to provide the new popular education. In Connecticut the Sheffield Scientific School of Yale became the land-grant college; in Rhode Island, Brown; in New Hampshire, Dartmouth; in New Jersey, Rutgers; in Kentucky, the sectarian Transylvania College; in Oregon, the Methodist College of Corvallis. Delaware revived the moribund Delaware College with its land grant and further developed it into a state university. Massachusetts founded a new agricultural college with part of its endowment and donated a share of it to the Massachusetts Institute of Technology. Both Indiana and New York combined a new college with an independent benefaction: in the case of Indiana, the $100,000 of John Purdue; in the case of New York, the $500,000 of Ezra Cornell.

In time every state would have its land-grant foundation, and seventeen of them would have two. When a second Morrill Act was passed in 1890 providing for regular annual appropriations for the land-grant colleges, the act stipulated that no appropriations would go to states that denied admission to the colleges on the basis of race unless they also set up separate but equal facilities. Seventeen states were so moved.[7]

Almost everywhere the scrambling of the old-time colleges for the federal largess was an indication of economic instability and of an ideological willingness to accept federal support.[8] It soon became clear, however, that the claims of the old foundations would be ignored. And by 1872, when Congress was debating whether to increase the federal endowment of the land-grant colleges, President McCosh of Princeton would be lobbying against such proposals as a representative of the sectarian interest and President Eliot of Harvard would be speaking out against federal endowments as a representative of high principle.[9]

In opposing supplemental federal aid for the land-grant institutions in 1872 and subsequent years, the older colleges gave expression to a laissez-faire philosophy on federal aid to education. The state governments had already lost interest in the welfare of the old colleges, and now the federal bounty was increasingly being turned to the support of the new foundations. Everywhere spurned by government, the old colleges discovered the principle of the independent, self-reliant, private college. That their discovery occurred at the same time as the revelation of scandals in the use of the public lands by the railroads gave strength to a developing philosophic distrust of federal activity. Men of the caliber of McCosh and Eliot indulged in one of the shabbiest episodes in American academic history, not only because they were

[7] Ross: *Democracy's College*, pp. 73-76.
[8] Ibid., pp. 68-85; Edward Potts Cheyney: *History of the University of Pennsylvania 1740-1940* (Philadelphia, 1940), p. 254; William Murray Hepburn and Louis Martin Sears: *Purdue University: Fifty Years of Progress* (Indianapolis, 1925), p. 27; Dunaway: *Pennsylvania State*, p. 48; Glover: *Wisconsin*, p. 28; James E. Pollard: *History of the Ohio State University: The Story of its First Seventy-Five Years 1873-1948* (Columbus, 1952), pp. 4-11.
[9] Ross: *Democracy's College*, pp. 173-4.

prepared to deny, on principle, to the new colleges the kind
of support that so many of the older colleges had in the past
found vital for survival, but also because they often combined their opposition to the new popular colleges with an
unconcealed condescension. That "excellent college at New
Brunswick, managed by a few Dutchmen" was the President
of Princeton's not altogether friendly way of referring to the
land-grant foundation at Rutgers.[1]

The difficulty of channeling the land-grant funds into operative institutions was met in a variety of ways. So was the
difficulty of discovering what a college that catered to the
needs of the farmer and the mechanic ought to be. There was
an absence, for instance, of secondary schools available to
farm children; a shortage of trained natural science teachers;
no trained teachers of agriculture; not even, really, a science
of agriculture. Moreover, the United States was still full of
land requiring no skill to be exploited and producing well beyond demand. Who needed to go to college to learn how to
be a farmer? And the same question was asked of the practical
mechanic.[2]

The search for a rationale for the land-grant colleges led to
a controversy between the classicists, who would find room
for the new subjects, and the "popularists" who would provide only practical technical education.[3] Were the new colleges to turn out trained scientists or improved mechanics
and laborers? No one knew for sure. Jonathan Baldwin Turner, an early agricultural reformer in Illinois, had said in
1853: "The industrial classes . . . want, and they ought to
have, the same facilities for understanding the true philosophy, the science, and the art of *their* several pursuits . . .
and of efficiently applying existing knowledge thereto and
widening its domain, which the professional classes have long
enjoyed in *their* pursuits." [4]

[1] Ibid.
[2] True: *A History of Agricultural Education*, pp. 110-11.
[3] Ross: *Democracy's College*, pp. 88 ff.
[4] Quoted in Norman Foerster: *The American State University*
(Chapel Hill, 1937), pp. 24-5.

Ten years later, when only the first of the land-grant foundations was in operation, Isaac Newton, the United States Commissioner of Agriculture, suggested that the new colleges perhaps were really not going to be different after all. "These colleges are not to be agricultural only," he said. "The sons of our farmers are not less ambitious of distinction than others, and an education that regards them as farmers only cannot meet their approbation. The purpose of an education is to teach men to observe and to think. . . . All pursuits . . . may have a common course of instruction." On the other hand a Philadelphia agricultural paper commented the next year: "Instead of introducing the student of agriculture to a laboratory and chemical and philosophical apparatus, we would introduce him to a pair of heavy neat's leather boots and corduroy pants, and learn him how to load manure." [5]

In 1870 Rutherford B. Hayes, then governor of Ohio, saw the proposed A & M college in Ohio as a venture in equipping the industrial classes with technical competence. Four years later, however, the first president of Ohio State, Edward Orton, pledged in his inaugural address that the university would adhere to "the education of a man as man, rather than that which equips him for a particular post of duty." At the University of Missouri the next year a comparable outlook was advanced by a trustee who warned that "too much in practical education should not be expected, as the main purpose is to develop the social and mental nature of the students." "That is good," retorted a member of the state board of agriculture, "but what are they going to do about hog cholera?" [6]

[5] Quoted in William Warren Ferrier: *Origin and Development of the University of California* (Berkeley, 1930), pp. 62-3; Ross: *Democracy's College,* pp. 90-1.

[6] Pollard: *Ohio State,* pp. 16-35; Viles: *Missouri,* p. 300. See also Julius Terrass Willard: *History of the Kansas State College of Agriculture and Applied Science* (New York, 1940), pp. 56 ff.; Hepburn and Sears: *Purdue,* pp. 61-2 ff.; James Gray: *The University of Minnesota 1851-1951* (Minneapolis, 1951), p. 44; James F. Hopkins: *The University of Kentucky: Origins and Early Years* (Lexington, 1951), p. 76; Dunaway: *Pennsylvania State,* pp. 60, 118; Ross: *Iowa State,* p. 117;

The dilemma suggested by this diversity of opinion would never be altogether resolved, and each institution found its own solution. Ohio State, for instance, tended to support the solid scientific and classical studies with sufficient effectiveness to challenge successfully the many old-line colleges in Ohio. In Illinois in 1870, of 200 students at the university only 20 were taking some Latin. Now so flexible had become the definition of a college education that no one was studying Greek. Yet, fifteen years later when the institution changed its name from Illinois Industrial University to the University of Illinois, all the old suspicions were aroused. One rural newspaper observed that apparently it was time for the university to change its motto from "Learning and Labor" to "Lavender and Lily White." Another sneered: "Dude factory."[7] On the whole, the tendency of the land-grant institutions was to enthrone the practical and ignore the traditional. The so-called cultural and classical studies were neglected, and in time Iowa State almost struck from its curriculum a course of study that was too purely scientific and not sufficiently vocational in orientation.

Even when technical studies were given the greater emphasis, it was difficult to convince farmers and their sons that an agricultural education made sense. Engineering had at least been in the process of developing a body of principles and concepts, and once the new colleges decided that their mechanical purposes fell within the definition of engineering, the M of A & M was on relatively solid ground. But the A—for agriculture—caused some trouble.[8] Up to 1873 at the University of Vermont no student had applied for entrance in the agricultural course. In New Hampshire one Yankee was not impressed: "All the agricultural colleges between here

William H. Powers, ed.: *A History of South Dakota State College* (Brookings, 1931), pp. 23-34.

[7] Pollard: *Ohio State*, p. 94; Allan Nevins: *Illinois* (New York, 1917), pp. 64, 121.

[8] See Walter L. Fleming: *Louisiana State University 1860-1896* (Baton Rouge, 1936), pp. 472-3 ff.; Ross: *Iowa State*, pp. 282-7.

and the setting sun will not convert the rocky hills of New Hampshire into gardens of Eden." At the University of Illinois there were but twenty-two agricultural students in 1879. The University of Wisconsin graduated one agricultural student before 1880. When Ohio State offered a winter course for farmers in 1878 seven students appeared. In 1884 at the University of South Carolina, of 122 students pursuing degrees seven were registered in the department of agriculture.*

These statistics reflected the farmer's distrust of experts, his reliance on experience as the best teacher, as well as the obvious fact that an abundance of land still yielded crops without the need of intensive scientific cultivation. Moreover, farm children who went to college were more likely motivated by normal American ambition. An especially acute perception was not required for the farm son to realize that in the popular American estimation Jefferson's "chosen people of God" had become "hicks" and "hayseeds." Why should anyone want to be a better hick? The farm boy who went to college was probably headed for the city, for which the engineering course might make sense but certainly not a course in agriculture. The threshold of opportunity in America had shifted from the land to the factory; in combining the agricultural with the mechanical, the land-grant colleges were uniting the past and the future, two schemes of life. A devouring passion for success, a search for ever higher material standards, militated against the farm and therefore against agricultural education.

This very tendency of farm children to use the colleges as a means of escape from the farm instilled a deep bitterness in their fathers, a bitterness that was costly to the colleges in their early years and that found organized expression in the Grange. The regents of the University of Wisconsin thought

* Ross: *Democracy's College*, p. 155; Philip M. Marston, ed.: *History of the University of New Hampshire 1866-1941* (Durham, 1941), p. 92; Julian Ira Lindsay: *Tradition Looks Forward: The University of Vermont: A History 1791-1904* (Burlington, 1954), p. 236; Rogers: *Cornell*, p. 120; Pollard: *Ohio State*, pp. 41-2; Daniel Walker Hollis: *University of South Carolina* (Columbia, 1951-6), II, 115.

that they saw a silver lining in 1883: "Neither New York nor
Boston could maintain its ascendancy in commercial or professional strength but for the continual accession of hard
muscles and untainted brain from rural life." But the farmers
of Wisconsin were not so easily reassured. One critic flatly
asserted that "absence from home, the fascination and allure-
ments of professional and business life" weaned the children
of the farm "from the old love and enthusiasm for calves and
colts and lambs and growing crops, harvesting, haying, . . .
hard toil, horny hands. . . ." [1]

As if all this were not enough, the land-grant colleges
moved into agricultural instruction without direction, without the knowledge of European precedents and developments.
The early teachers of applied agriculture were likely to be
natural scientists without any practical experience at all. At
Dartmouth the agricultural professor allowed his two acres
of potatoes and twenty bushels of beets to freeze in the
ground. The first professor of agriculture at the University
of Missouri was George C. Swallow, a botanist whose spe-
cialty was grapes and whose passion was landscape gardening.
His mission, as he saw it, was to beautify the farms of Missouri. In the Missouri catalogue he introduced the epigram:
"He can work better and sleep better, who has well kept
lawns and beautiful perspectives." If this was what was passing as agricultural education in the colleges, no wonder that
the farmers were skeptical. No wonder that a major problem
was convincing them that scientific was not synonymous

[1] Rogers: *Cornell*, pp. 122-3; Merle Curti and Vernon Carstensen:
The University of Wisconsin: A History, 1848-1925 (Madison, 1949),
I, 464; Glover: *Wisconsin*, pp. 49-100. See also Kuhn: *Michigan State*,
p. 119; Hepburn and Sears: *Purdue*, p. 90; Lindsay: *Vermont*, p. 254;
John Hugh Reynolds and David Yancey Thomas: *History of the Uni-
versity of Arkansas* (Fayetteville, 1910), p. 137; Walter Stemmons:
Connecticut Agricultural College—A History (Storrs, 1931), p. 56;
Ross: *Iowa State*, pp. 93 ff.; Ferrier: *California*, pp. 355-8; Dunaway:
Pennsylvania State, pp. 95 ff.; Marston: *New Hampshire*, pp. 74-5 ff.;
Hopkins: *Kentucky*, p. 112; Philip R. V. Curoe: *Educational Attitudes
and Policies of Organized Labor in the United States* (New York,
1926), pp. 94-5.

with impractical. The judgment of one legislator in South Carolina in 1879 was surely typical: "[I've never] seen a man who could write a nice essay or make a good agricultural speech who could make corn enough to feed himself and a bob-tailed mule until the first day of March."[2]

Some efforts of the colleges to increase enrollment were more availing than others, but one that did not work was the offer of the University of Arkansas in 1892 to pay $25.00 to the agricultural student who made the best five pounds of butter. More effective was the almost complete abandonment of admissions standards. In the absence of rural high schools, the colleges merely said: "Come, and we will do what we can." At Ohio State in 1877, for example, by dropping algebra from the entrance requirements the college immediately picked up twenty new students. In 1885 the state legislature of Arkansas ordered its land-grant college to lower already incredibly low admissions standards. In 1888 candidates for admission to South Dakota State College were required to offer one year of preparatory work beyond the eighth grade. Not until 1914 did the Connecticut Agricultural College at Storrs limit its course to high-school graduates. Of course these standards improved as time passed, but ingrained in the land-grant idea was the concept of collegiate education for everyone at public expense. Against this popular democratic ideal, standards of excellence quite obviously would be at a disadvantage.[3]

In the end, what sold agricultural education to the American farmer and overcame the hostility of the Grange was evi-

[2] Rogers: *Cornell*, p. 116; Ross: *Democracy's College*, pp. 96 ff.; Marston: *New Hampshire*, pp. 45-6; Viles: *Missouri*, pp. 159-60; Ferrier: *California*, pp. 369-72; Hollis: *South Carolina*, II, 91.

[3] Reynolds and Thomas: *Arkansas*, p. 273; Ross: *Democracy's College*, p. 114; Pollard: *Ohio State*, p. 39; Reynolds and Thomas: *Arkansas*, p. 131; Powers: *South Dakota State*, p. 18; Stemmons: *Connecticut*, pp. 141-3. See also William H. S. Demarest: *A History of Rutgers College 1776-1924* (New Brunswick, 1924), p. 412; Enoch Albert Bryan: *Historical Sketch of the State College of Washington 1890-1925* (Spokane, 1928), pp. 138 ff.; Roy Gittinger: *The University of Oklahoma 1892-1942* (Norman, 1942), p. 11.

dence that scientific agriculture paid in larger crops, higher income, and a better chance to enjoy higher living standards —in other words, an opportunity to make frequent use of the Montgomery Ward or Sears Roebuck catalogue. Of primary importance were the pioneer efforts of natural scientists experimenting with seeds, livestock, and chemicals, who began to have something worth showing and saying to the farmers. Essential, too, was the Hatch Act of 1887 which provided federal funds for the creation of agricultural experiment stations which soon became extremely popular and effective instruments in winning farm support for the colleges. For the stations combined science and the solution of specific farm problems and helped to demonstrate to skeptical farmers that science could be a friend. Professor Liberty Hyde Bailey of Cornell investigated and cured black rot in the vineyards of a member of the state legislature who one day, as speaker of the assembly, would be of crucial help in gaining permanent state support for agricultural education at Cornell. At Michigan State Professor Robert C. Kedzie proved the usefulness of the state college by exposing a company that sold wallpaper tinted with arsenic, by campaigning against a particularly hazardous quality of kerosene, and by battling effectively for the regrading of a variety of wheat on which Michigan agriculture depended. In Texas questions of cotton agriculture and fertilizer found their solution at the state college; in Washington, professors turned to the study of salmon and salmon propagation. When the federal government in 1890 began to provide annual appropriations for the land-grant colleges, the sky in a sense cleared; soon state legislatures were fully doing their part.[4]

In the end, the growth of a body of applied agricultural science, the experiment stations, farmer approval, and federal and state financial assistance all fed upon one another,

[4] Ross: *Democracy's College*, pp. 136-51; Malcolm Carron: *The Contract Colleges of Cornell University: A Co-operative Educational Enterprise* (Ithaca, 1958), pp. 52-3; Kuhn: *Michigan State*, pp. 107 ff.; George Sessions Perry: *The Story of Texas A and M* (New York, 1951), pp. 146, 222; Bryan: *Washington State*, p. 332.

helping to develop the land-grant colleges into a significant educational movement. By 1890 the colleges were so certain that they had something to say to the farmer and the farmer was so ready to listen that in twenty-six states off-campus farmer institutes were literally taking the colleges to the farmers. In the meantime back in the laboratories, experimental farms, and model dairies, specialization in scientific agriculture was creating courses in animal husbandry, veterinary medicine, agronomy, horticulture, plant pathology, agricultural botany, agricultural chemistry, and farm management. A far cry, indeed, from the curriculum that had inspired the classic statement of Jeremiah Day and the faculty of Yale College in 1828.[5]

There were other differences too. In 1874, for instance, the legislature of Iowa accused President Adonijah S. Welch of aristocratic snobbishness for excluding the college janitor from the presidential dining table. In Oregon there was a teacher whose combined professorship included elocution, common law, physiology, and mechanical drawing. In South Dakota the professor of German, bookkeeping, penmanship, orthography, political economy, United States constitution, and history of civilization also gave farm-institute lectures on farm accounts, managed the men's dormitory, and was steward of an undergraduate boarding club. And when a land-grant college looked abroad for help it might turn, as did Mary B. Welch of Iowa State, to the London School of Maids where, mistaken for a servant in training, she learned enough to lay the foundations of home economics and domestic science in the college.[6]

At the Connecticut Agricultural College in 1884 the commencement exercises were graced by student addresses on "Irrigation and Drainage" and "The Feet of the Horse and

[5] Ross: *Democracy's College*, pp. 164-6; Willard: *Kansas State*, p. 32; Powers: *South Dakota State*, pp. 83-99; Hepburn and Sears: *Purdue*, p. 90; Glover: *Wisconsin*, pp. 89, 149-59; Kuhn: *Michigan State*, pp. 138 ff.

[6] Ross: *Iowa State*, pp. 97, 152; Ross: *Democracy's College*, p. 109.

Ox, and their Diseases." ⁷ None of this was like the old-time
classical college. Francis Wayland at last was being answered.
Vocational and technical education had become a legitimate
function of American higher education, and everywhere the
idea of going to college was being liberated from the classbound, classical-bound traditions which for so long had defined the American collegiate experience.

⁷ Stemmons: *Connecticut,* p. 48.

13

❦

The Emerging University

Higher education in the United States after the Civil War was transformed by more than one agency of innovation, but surely none came closer to representing fundamental developments in American social and intellectual life than did the land-grant college movement. "State College" would come to have as homely and honest a ring about it as any of the numerous institutions identified with agrarian America. State Fair. Fourth of July picnic. Church social. Saturday night in town. None of these came any closer than "State College" in evoking an appreciation of wholesome rural values—clean, hard-working, honest young men and women, determined to live good lives in a good world, gone down or up to the state college, there to broaden their horizons and to perfect their ingrained common sense.

In the state colleges Americans would create institutions intended, in part, to sustain an agrarian past. Obviously as scientific agriculture was perfected, the colleges spoke more and more to the big farmers, to the factories in the field, but on the level of the imagination "State College" continued to represent the independent American farmer—the personification of Crèvecœur's and Jefferson's self-reliant yeoman—

and his equally God-fearing, hard-working wife. "State College" also became synonymous with opportunity, which was a synonym for America itself. It was an invitation to leave the farm, to join the ever-growing movement to the cities, to achieve the technical competence to build bridges, to mine the earth, to win some final mastery over nature. For the land-grant college contained within itself not only a romantic regard for the farm but a hardheaded regard for the factory, for the city. And it therefore achieved, as perhaps no other institution, a symbolic value for a democratic society. "I am a farmer's boy," a young man wrote to the college at East Lansing, Michigan. "As soon as the wheat is sown, I am at liberty to go to school." [1]

The yeoman farmer and the self-made man are two versions of the same fundamental American myth: the myth of self-reliant free men achieving self-respect and security among equals. The land-grant college served both: it sustained the yeoman, it liberated the farm boy who would make his way in the city. And in doing so it kept its focus on the practical and allowed others to concern themselves with the theoretical. It made little effort to achieve a happy union between theory and practice; it became in America the temple of applied science, essentially institutionalizing the American's traditional respect for the immediately useful. In the end, the land-grant college incorporated in its rationale the Jacksonian temper; it became the common school on a higher level; it became one of the great forces of economic and social mobility in American society; it brought the government, both federal and state, firmly into the support of higher education. In the land-grant institutions the American people achieved popular higher education for the first time.

The institution that helped to achieve respectability for the land-grant idea, Cornell, was only partly a land-grant col-

[1] Madison Kuhn: *Michigan State: The First Hundred Years* (East Lansing, 1955), p. 23.

lege. Cornell contained in its outlook not only the practical vocationalism of the land-grant idea but also the science, technology, and spirit of scholarship of the new university movement. These two lines of influence at Cornell were represented by Ezra Cornell, its great benefactor, and by Andrew D. White, its first president. Cornell imparted to the new institution the spirit of his famous statement: "I would found an institution where any person can find instruction in any study." And White contributed the ambition and imagination which enabled him to write, two years before he met Cornell, that "my main aim has been to fit myself to help in founding and building a worthy American University. . . . [My decision] is not the result of a sudden whim; it is the result of years of thought and yearning for better things in our beloved country." [2]

Cornell and White met in 1864 in the New York Senate, where White was the youngest senator and chairman of the committee on education and where Cornell, a self-made man who had become the largest stockholder of Western Union, was chairman of the committee on agriculture. In 1865 the New York legislature chartered Cornell University, turning over to it New York's share of the federal land grants of 1862 and applauding the $500,000 benefaction of Ezra Cornell which justified its name and the controlling role which he would play in shaping the new institution. [3]

In selecting White to develop and preside over the new institution, Cornell perhaps unwittingly added a dimension to the university that had been no part of his own thinking on the subject. Ezra Cornell had essentially thought of his university as a trade school, but White convinced him that instead it should train what White later referred to as "captains in the army of industry." Cornell University was therefore designed to join in the new spirit of scholarship as well

[2] Walter P. Rogers: *Andrew D. White and the Modern University* (Ithaca, 1942), pp. 47, 51-2, 54.
[3] Ibid., pp. 46-9, 62, 112.

as to foster the vocational subjects and the courses in applied science which were implicit in the land-grant idea.[4]

When the new university opened in 1869 White and Cornell had obviously created something that appealed to the college-age market. Before long alarums and fright would overtake many of the old institutions, for which Cornell became a reincarnation of the devil itself. On the other hand, both land-grant colleges and new or reviving state universities would discover in Cornell a full-blown experiment in the new education, and as the decades passed, Cornell became a pacesetter, a spokesman, and a kind of experimental laboratory for the new dispensation. On opening day in 1869 only one building was completed, but White had corralled seventeen resident and six nonresident professors. Moreover, in addition to accepting four hundred students, he had experienced that incredible luxury for an American institution of higher learning of actually rejecting fifty applicants for admission—young men who, on being tested, revealed that "London is in the west of England, Havre in the south of France, Portugal the capital of Spain, Borneo the capital of Prussia, India a part of Africa, Egypt a province of Russia. . . ."[5]

The spirit of innovation which animated the new Cornell ran through the statement of principles that White read at the opening exercises. At Cornell, he said, practical and liberal learning would be united; the control would be nonsectarian; the university would try to conduct itself in such a way as to be the apex of the New York State system of education; all courses of study would be equal, there would be no second-class students at Cornell; scientific studies would receive appropriate encouragement. And while these clear departures from traditional collegiate practice as much as said that Cornell was at war with the old-time American college, White

[4] See *Report of the Committee on Organization, Presented to the Trustees of the Cornell University, October 21st, 1866* (Albany, 1867), pp. 3-4, 18-24.
[5] Rogers: *Cornell,* p. 65; *Account of the Proceedings at the Inauguration October 7th 1868* (Ithaca, 1869), p. 17.

returned to the oldest collegiate purpose of all for his final principle: the development of the individual in the fullest sense and the preparation of that individual for a useful role in society.[6]

That these principles met with approval there could be no doubt. The third freshman class at Cornell, in 1871, was over 250 in number, the largest freshman class in the history of American higher education. The total enrollment was greater than that of any three other colleges in New York. "My whole soul is wrapped up in this enterprise," White admitted, and when he found Ezra Cornell developing a time-consuming interest in railroads he became so chagrined and annoyed that he wrote to him, warning against frittering away his time on railroad enterprises when a great university was in the making.[7]

Of course there were doubters and detractors, and it was to be expected that in 1873 Cornell simultaneously would be attacked for debasing classical studies and be investigated for neglecting agricultural and mechanical studies. But the public vindication of the new university had not long to wait. In 1875 and 1876 Cornell achieved widely advertised victories in the intercollegiate academic contests held in New York and the intercollegiate regattas held on the Hudson.[8] The new university had paid off.

At Cornell the equality of studies, the decline of the classics, and the free election of courses were clearly a function of the vocationalism of the land-grant idea, but the same developments were necessary to promote a shift from the controlled, prescribed atmosphere of the old foundations to "a spirit of free and universal inquiry" appropriate to a university that would serve scholarship.[9]

. . .

[6] *Account of the Proceedings* . . . , pp. 6-9, 15.
[7] Rogers: *Cornell*, pp. 94, 168-71.
[8] Ibid., pp. 173-4, 235.
[9] Ibid., p. 101. See also Waterman Thomas Hewett: *Cornell University: A History* (New York, 1905), I.

Another new institution, Johns Hopkins in Baltimore, proposed to make its commitment to the scholarly ideal paramount. Just how to meet that commitment was in no sense a
matter that could be easily determined. The Johns Hopkins
University was incorporated in 1867 and Hopkins's will was
probated in 1874. Between 1874 and 1876, when the university opened, the trustees planned and created a new American institution, but they could find no agreement on what a
great American university ought to be.[1] Yale, which had
awarded the first Ph.D. from an American university in 1861,
was moving slowly toward university status by keeping graduate and undergraduate education distinct; Harvard, also
moving slowly, chose to tie graduate and undergraduate instruction into a scheme of studies that emphasized the unity of
learning; Cornell and Michigan were attempting to marry the
practical and the theoretical, attempting to attract farm boys
to their classrooms and scholars to their faculties. The visits
of the Hopkins trustees to other universities, their reading,
their consultations led them to the conclusion that the time
was ripe for the development of a great graduate university
on the German model. In their decision they were perhaps
helped by President Angell of Michigan, who argued that
whatever they did ought to be something new and different.[2]

As was often the case in pioneering institutions, much of
the success of the new undertaking depended upon the first
president. In April 1874, Daniel Coit Gilman, a Yale graduate then involved in an unhappy attempt to make a respectable and responsible institution of the University of California, wrote to his fellow Yale man and fellow college president,
Andrew D. White of Cornell, that sometimes he thought

[1] See Hugh Hawkins: *Pioneer: A History of the Johns Hopkins
University, 1874-1889* (Ithaca, 1960), pp. 3-13; John C. French: *A History of the University Founded by Johns Hopkins* (Baltimore, 1946),
p. 1.
[2] Richard J. Storr: *The Beginnings of Graduate Education in America*
(Chicago, 1953), pp. 129-34; French: *Johns Hopkins*, pp. 23-5; Hawkins:
Johns Hopkins, pp. 14-20.

that he would like to be the president of the new institution being planned at Baltimore. One trouble, however, was that he had no connections there. He did not need connections, for when the trustees asked Eliot, Porter, Angell, and White for recommendations, every one of them recommended Gilman.[3]

Gilman, who had been instrumental in reorganizing the Sheffield Scientific School after the war, was ready to take the assignment, and by 1876 when the new institution opened he had assembled a faculty by enticing an eminent Greek scholar from the University of Virginia and a promising chemist from Williams, both of them holders of German doctorates. At the Rensselaer Polytechnic Institute he found a highly regarded young physicist and from England he imported an eminent retired mathematician and a promising biologist, a student of Huxley's.

To this faculty there was added an instructor in Latin and Greek to work with undergraduates only, for, regardless of its graduate orientation, Johns Hopkins had an undergraduate department from the beginning. It was necessary as a feeder of graduate students, and it was necessary as a public-relations gesture to the people of Baltimore, who would surely have been unhappy if all that money made by the Baltimore & Ohio Railroad were put to turning out rarefied scholars. The new institution had problems enough without adding to them all the local hostility which the absence of an undergraduate course would have inspired. Already the idea was being advanced that what the war-ravished states of the Old Confederacy needed was a college that would make an immediate practical attack on the problems of the region. Moreover, it was asked, what can all that emphasis on natural science mean but a rejection of God? [4]

Unquestionably the Johns Hopkins University at Baltimore

[3] Hawkins: *Johns Hopkins,* pp. 14-15; and MS. copy of doctoral dissertation, same title (1958), at Johns Hopkins, p. 145.

[4] Hawkins: *Johns Hopkins* (MS. copy), pp. 38-62; French: *Johns Hopkins,* pp. 34-9, 64 ff., 82.

was different, speaking a language, breathing a spirit that had long been anticipated but never before achieved in the United States. The difference was revealed in the experience of Ira Remsen, the young chemist with the German Ph.D., who had asked on his appointment to the Williams College faculty if a small room might be made available for a private laboratory and who had been told, "You will please keep in mind that this is a college and not a technical school." No wonder that Remsen applied for the opening in chemistry at Baltimore, where the spirit of inquiry and a sense of professionalism encouraged him to achieve a notable career in chemistry. [5]

Everyone expected the students to be different, too; they proved their difference by disregarding the tradition of two literary societies and founding but one, which in 1884 was converted into what was called the Hopkins House of Commons by a graduate student named Woodrow Wilson. Even the trustees were different. One was so opposed to the idea of incorporating any formal athletic program into the university that he proposed to deliver a lecture on "Physical Strength as a Cause of Premature Decay." [6]

A most striking difference was the way in which Johns Hopkins developed as a faculty-centered institution. The University of Virginia had revealed a more than ordinary attention to faculty in its planning and recruitment, but central to the Virginia experience was a democratic philosophy as expressed by Thomas Jefferson. The institution in Baltimore, however, saw the faculty, its needs, its work, as so central to its purpose that Gilman insisted that the faculty be given only students who were sufficiently well prepared to provide the faculty with challenging and rewarding stimulation. Nothing could have been more remote from the spirit of the old-time college, where the teachers were theoretically busily engaged in stimulating the students. As a consequence there

[5] Hawkins: *Johns Hopkins* (MS. copy), p. 274.
[6] French: *Johns Hopkins*, p. 265; Hawkins: *Johns Hopkins* (MS. copy), p. 28.

developed at Johns Hopkins the apparatus and the spirit, as well as the salaries, necessary to the creation of a respected profession of university teachers. Perhaps no other American university would ever go as far as Johns Hopkins in this direction, but the spirit that it revealed would necessarily become a part of any college that found itself participating in the developing discovery of scholarship.[7]

The collegiate tradition in the United States could not find new inspiration in the spirit of the German university without some loss to the collegiate way. Voluminous as was the correspondence between Gilman and President Eliot of Harvard, not once did they address themselves to such questions as the methodology of teaching on the college level, not once did they concern themselves with "the management of student affairs, including educational and personal guidance." These were irrelevant to the new orientation, to the university spirit, to the Germanism which was erecting German-style beer parlors on the edge of the campus, which led Syracuse University to designate a select list of preparatory academies as gymnasia, and which in 1886 found Harvard indulging in voluntary class attendance until a father discovered that his son was in Havana and the university had no knowledge of it.[8]

Gilman and Johns Hopkins became leaders in the cultivation of the new spirit. Gilman was a kind of ambassador from the developing society of scholars to the world at large. "The university," he once said, ". . . renders services to the community which no demon of statistics can ever estimate. . . ." These services, he pointed out, were "the acquisition, conservation, refinement and distribution of knowledge." The new university, in other words, found its purpose in knowledge, in the world of the intellect. And it made no apologies,

[7] French: *Johns Hopkins*, p. 32.
[8] Willis Rudy: "Eliot and Gilman: The History of an Academic Friendship," *Teachers College Record*, LIV (1953), 312; William Freeman Galpin: *Syracuse University: The Pioneer Days* (Syracuse, 1952), pp. 40-1; Samuel Eliot Morison: *Three Centuries of Harvard 1636-1936* (Cambridge, 1936), pp. 368-9.

for its touchstone was truth.[9] "No truth which has once been discovered is allowed to perish," Gilman continued, ". . . but the incrustations which cover it are removed. It is the universities which edit, interpret, translate and reiterate the acquisitions of former generations both of literature and science. Their revelation of error is sometimes welcomed but it is generally opposed; nevertheless the process goes on, indifferent alike to plaudits or reproaches." [1]

Gilman was equally prepared to explain to a skeptical audience the utility of pure scientific research. "If you persist," he said, "in taking the utilitarian view and ask me what is the good of Mr. Glaisher's determination of the least factors of the missing three out of the first nine million numbers . . . , I shall be forced to say I do not know; and if you press me harder I shall be obliged to express my conviction that nobody knows; but I know, and you know, and everybody may know, who will take the pains to inquire, that the progress of mathematics underlies and sustains all progress in exact knowledge." For those who were still dubious of his claims Gilman rattled off a number of contemporary wonders that were the result of applied mathematics: steam locomotion, telegraph, telephone, photography, and electric lighting. "These wonderful inventions," he asserted, "are the direct fruit of university studies." [2]

Noting the vast application of chemical knowledge that had been developed since the announcement of Dalton's law of atomic theory in 1804 and the pioneer experimental laboratory of Liebig in Germany, Gilman pointed out that the fundamental research on which so much material progress rested was done in laboratories that "were the creation not of industrial fabrics, not of mercantile corporations, not even of private enterprise, but of universities and that the motive which inspired their founders and directors was not the ac-

[9] Daniel Coit Gilman: *The Benefits Which Society Derives from Universities* (Baltimore, 1885), pp. 15-16.
[1] Ibid., pp. 18-19.
[2] Ibid., pp. 31, 33.

quisition of wealth, but the ascertainment of fundamental law." [3]

Johns Hopkins was committed to a never-ending search for truth. In reality, the old-time college had all the truth it needed in revealed religion and in the humanist tradition, and for that reason alone the philosophy of research and inquiry that Gilman advanced was calculated to force a major adjustment in the purposes of American higher education. It would have been impossible, for instance, for any old-time college professor to have remarked as one Johns Hopkins professor did in 1885: "As the region of the unknown is infinitely greater than the known,—there is no fear of there not being work for the whole world for centuries to come. . . . The telephone, the telegraph, and electric lighting, are but as child's play to what the world will see." [4]

This open embrace of the scientific point of view, this almost wide-eyed admiration for the unfolding of layer after layer of the unknown and for the application of the known to the benefit of man, all this was a far cry from the old-time professor who in 1858 warned: "Tell me what is to be done with the leisure that . . . machinery . . . is beginning to give, and will yet give more fully to the race, and I will tell you what the destiny of the race will be"; a far cry from the professor of natural philosophy in a New England college who in 1838 observed: "I have no doubt that science is useful, but still the time is so near when knowledge shall vanish away, that I become sometimes almost discouraged at the idea of tasking my energies and occupying my time about it." [5]

For the acceptance of revealed religious truth the new university in Baltimore substituted a search for scientific truth. For preparation for life in the next world it substituted a search for an understanding of this world. Johns Hopkins

[3] Ibid., p. 37.
[4] Ibid., p. 36.
[5] Frederick Rudolph: *Mark Hopkins and the Log: Williams College, 1836-1872*, pp. 35, 95.

elevated man's reason to a position it had not before attained in the United States. It released the energies of scholarship, combined them with the national impulse to human betterment and material progress. The task it set for itself was immense and unending, and in time the spirit of Johns Hopkins would penetrate everywhere.

One place where the Hopkins spirit caught on was in the state universities. They did not catch the Hopkins spirit undilute; eventually, however, the state universities became the repositories of the spirit of science and scholarly inquiry across the land.

The state universities in the United States are the product of at least three movements. The earliest, beginning with the University of Georgia, chartered in 1785, were inspired by the success of the war for independence and by an effort to find institutional expression for the Age of Reason and for a developing nationalism. The great flowering of state universities, however, was in consequence of the westward movement after the adoption of the Constitution and in consequence of the accepted government practice of giving two townships of federal lands to each new state as support for a "seminary of learning." Not until after the Civil War, on the other hand, did many states choose to turn their university endowments over to the support of universities, nor was it until then that the states themselves began to recognize in such foundations the bases of potentially popular and useful institutions.

The group of state universities founded relatively soon after the adoption of the Constitution was concentrated in the South, in states where colonial colleges had not taken root; in the North the older foundations with their ambiguous public-private nature inhibited the growth of the state-university idea. Another group developed out of the pattern of federal land grants that first appeared in a 1787 contract between the government and the Ohio Company, a group of New England speculators and settlers.°

A provision in the contract awarding the company two townships of land for the development of a university was the result of the lobbying activity of a Massachusetts clergyman by the name of Manasseh Cutler, who considered the existence of such a university endowment necessary to induce emigration from New England. This first government land grant for higher education was not essentially the result of a conscious policy of federal support for collegiate foundations. The land-grant provision was intended, after all, not to further education but to further the sale of land. From this initial venture in the encouragement of land sales, however, came the Ohio University at Athens. A second large sale of land in Ohio, with a comparable provision for collegiate endowment, led to the chartering of Miami University at Oxford in 1809. Ohio University and Miami University, therefore, were the prototypes of the land-grant-supported state universities. These early grants set the precedents that provided each state thereafter admitted to the Union with two townships of slightly more than 46,000 acres of public lands to support a "seminary of learning." ⁷ Three states were denied this federal largess—Texas, Maine, and West Virginia— because the federal government never owned the public lands of these states and therefore was in no position to give them away. By the eve of the Civil War perhaps a dozen universities had been created by these grants but as institutions of learning they were almost indistinguishable from the denominational colleges which made so much trouble for them.

After the war, under the leadership of the University of

°Richard G. Axt: *The Federal Government and Financing Higher Education* (New York, 1952), pp. 24-8; Andrew Ten Brook: *American State Universities, their Origin and Progress* (Cincinnati, 1875), pp. 58-74; Merle Curti and Vernon Carstensen: *The University of Wisconsin: A History, 1848-1925* (Madison, 1949), I, 3-34.

⁷ Thomas N. Hoover: *The History of Ohio University* (Athens, 1954), pp. 1-11; Walter Havighurst: *The Miami Years 1809-1959* (New York, 1958), pp. 13-14.

Michigan, and later of the University of Minnesota and the University of Wisconsin, the state universities achieved an identity of their own.[8] To an extent they had already done this in the ante bellum South, where, according to one historian, "In each of the states of the Old South the state university did more to mold and influence the character of the people than any other one institution."[9] Unquestionably everywhere in the South more fundamental than the state university was the pervasive institution of slavery, but in the ante bellum South the state universities did set what standards there were in intellectual and cultural matters, turned out the political leadership, and put the sons of the plantation aristocracy through a course of social preparation. To some extent they functioned in ways comparable to the northern colonial colleges during the first half of the nineteenth century: as standard bearers of traditional knowledge, as centers of cultural adornment, and as finishing schools for political and social leaders drawn from a very small segment of the population.

In the post-Civil War period, however, it became apparent that the American state university would be defined neither in the South, the first home of the state university movement, nor in the Northeast, where the old colonial institutions precluded its growth. The American state university would be defined in the great Midwest and West, where frontier democracy and frontier materialism would help to support a practical-oriented popular institution. The emergence of western leadership in the movement stemmed in part from the remarkable rapidity with which western states were populated and from the accelerated speed with which their population grew. Michigan, Minnesota, and Wisconsin, among others, found that the small denominational colleges with their feeble endowments and backward-glancing curricula

---

[8] See Elizabeth M. Farrand: *History of the University of Michigan* (Ann Arbor, 1885); James Gray: *The University of Minnesota 1851-1951* (Minneapolis, 1951); Curti and Carstensen: *Wisconsin*, I.

[9] Albea Godbold: *The Church College of the Old South* (Durham, 1944), pp. 169-70.

could meet neither the needs of a growing population nor its preferences. These states established the concept of a unified system of free state education, on the European pattern, with the state university at the head of the system.[1]

Designed to cope with numbers, the midwestern and western universities were also prepared to cope with the practical demands and the intellectual ferment which were seeking expression in postwar higher education. "The University," said a member of the California board of regents in 1872, "is founded primarily on that essential principle of free Republican government which affirms that the state is bound to furnish the citizen the means of discharging the duties it imposes on him: if the state imposes duties that require intelligence, it is the office of the state to furnish the means of intelligence." [2] This rationale of course was completely Jeffersonian; indeed, the state universities were reviving the old Jeffersonian position, a position which had suffered earlier in the century from denominational colleges, from the Dartmouth College case, and from the tremendous influence of such older private institutions as Harvard, Yale, and Columbia.

The effectiveness of the state universities in giving expression and a new dynamism to the Jeffersonian position certainly accounted in part for the defensive posture taken by President Eliot at a meeting of the National Education Association in 1873, when he took a not-so-subtle poke at the idea of state-supported higher education: "There is a skepticism of the masses in Massachusetts as to the justice of everybody paying for the advanced education of somebody's child. The mechanic, the blacksmith, the weaver says: 'Why should I pay for the professional education of the lawyer's son, the minister's son? The community does not provide *my* son his

[1] Vernon Rosco Carstensen: "The History of the State University of Iowa: The Collegiate Department from the Beginning to 1878," *University of Iowa Studies in the Social Sciences, Abstracts in History III*, X (1938), 95.
[2] William Warren Ferrier: *Origin and Development of the University of California* (Berkeley, 1930), p. 322.

279 *The Emerging University*

forge or loom.' " [3] This spectacle of a Harvard president indulging in Jacksonian demagoguery in order to subvert the Jeffersonian concept of state education was not particularly attractive. But it was inspired by the knowledge that the state university idea had at last caught on in the United States and by an awareness that the old colleges no longer had within their power the exclusive right to speak for American higher education, to guide its destiny, to set its standards, or to monopolize the resources available for its support.

President Eliot's great antagonist, in a sense, was President James B. Angell of the University of Michigan, who gladly served as an agent of the state universities before the American public. For Angell higher education was not a luxury but a necessity that should be made available to all. It would not have occurred to him to make the assumption that came so naturally to President Eliot that the blacksmith's son was destined to be a blacksmith. President Angell argued that all human beings should be given opportunities to develop talent and character to the fullest. "We need all the intelligence, all the trained minds we can have," he insisted in an address delivered in 1879. The state university was a bulwark against an aristocracy of wealth: it was the inevitable and necessary expression of a democratic society; it was Christian equality in action. [4]

These were formidable arguments, arguments that the aspiring middle classes of the West found convincing. And if an Eliot of Harvard could turn the village blacksmith against state higher education, Angell was not unprepared to turn the village storekeeper against Harvard. He could not conceive, he said, "anything more hateful, more repugnant to our natural instincts, more calamitous at once to learning and to the people, more unrepublican, more undemocratic,

[3] Quoted in Philip R. V. Curoe: *Educational Attitudes and Policies of Organized Labor in the United States* (New York, 1926), p. 81.
[4] James Burrill Angell: *Selected Addresses* (New York, 1912), pp. 42-56.

more unchristian than a system which should confine the priceless boon of higher education to the rich." [5]

The rise of the state universities to eminence was a perilous process. In the South, where the universities had been the strongest before the Civil War, most now lay prostrate, victims of war, poverty, or politics. Others struggled against the loss of endowment incurred through mismanagement in the disposal of the original land grants. Their dependence on legislative support exposed them to all the vicissitudes of politics. The denominations regarded them as godless or as friendly to some *other* denomination. The head of the Louisiana State University remarked in 1873: "[We are] required by public opinion to have religion—in a general way, somehow, yet forbidden to have it in any particular way." [6]

The popular distrust of the old colleges was so intense that the intention of the state universities to carry on in the old academy tradition and offer both classical and scientific courses of study was often interpreted as a capitulation to aristocratic influences. When the University of Illinois included a classical course in its offerings, one newspaper asked, "Why did not these astute committeemen include crocheting, embroidery, and lessons on the harp?" [7] Yet, the state universities survived both the condescension and the

[5] Ibid., p. 49.

[6] Walter L. Fleming: *Louisiana State University 1860-1896* (Baton Rouge, 1936), p. 245; Godbold: *The Church College of the Old South*, p. 148; Louis G. Geiger: *University of the Northern Plains: A History of the University of North Dakota 1883-1958* (Grand Forks, 1958), p. 51; Henry D. Sheldon: *History of University of Oregon* (Portland, 1940), p. 63; E. Merton Coulter: *College Life in the Old South* (Athens, 1951), pp. 152-8; Philip Alexander Bruce: *History of the University of Virginia, 1819-1919* (New York, 1920-2), I, 289; Farrand: *Michigan*, p. 140; Henry Morton Bullock: *A History of Emory University* (Nashville, 1936), pp. 219-20; Daniel Walker Hollis: *University of South Carolina* (Columbia, 1951-6), II, 85; Curti and Carstensen: *Wisconsin*, I, 88 ff.

[7] Allan Nevins: *Illinois* (New York, 1917), p. 50.

outright attacks of the older colleges. They survived the suspicions of the people themselves, and in time, as they would clearly demonstrate toward the end of the century and at the beginning of the next, they would combine in a typically American institution that Jeffersonian emphasis on excellence and learning which had become the special commitment of Johns Hopkins and the Jacksonian emphasis on numbers and on the practical which had become the special commitment of the land-grant colleges.

In the meantime, the first task before the state universities was to discover a bridge between the free public elementary school and the public university. For before the Civil War, except in the large urban centers of the Northeast, free secondary education had not yet taken hold. The privately incorporated academy was the most generally available school, and while in one of its functions it served as a college-preparatory school, it was nonetheless not a publicly supported, publicly controlled institution. Therefore, in the postwar period the aspiring state universities set about achieving some way of moving ambitious young men and women from the common schools to the public universities.

A traditional instrument for funneling students into collegiate programs was an attached or integral preparatory department, which caught students at a tender age and insulated them from the blandishment of rival institutions. In 1870 there were only five states in the country where none of the colleges was doing preparatory work: all five were in the Northeast, four of them in New England where the academy movement was strong; and all five were states where the idea of private higher education was so strong that the land-grant foundations of 1862 were added to existing private institutions. The states where the colleges were *not* in the preparatory business were New Hampshire, Massachusetts, Rhode Island, Connecticut, and New Jersey. Everywhere else in the country the pattern of integral college preparation was well established. Indeed, outside of these five states there were but twelve colleges that did not operate preparatory departments, and some of these had only recently abandoned the practice.[8]

Some colleges had of necessity found themselves in the preparatory business at the very beginning. Insisting upon erecting colleges that neither need nor intelligence justified, college governing boards often had the choice of giving up or of taking any student who came along and starting with him at whatever point his ignorance required. The result was that a college might not get around to a graduating class until it had been in operation for as long as eight years; in the meantime it had become the classical academy as well as the college for the district that it served.[9]

In any case, all of the state universities except Michigan at first accepted the pattern established for them by the private colleges. Michigan, as a consequence, needed some system of admitting students. It needed a preparatory department, or a system of entrance examinations that was customary at New England and Middle Atlantic colleges without preparatory departments, or it needed to develop something entirely new. The solution that was adopted by Acting President Henry S. Frieze in September 1870 was in the direction of state educational leadership to which the university in the past had made halting, partial overtures.[1]

In the interest of the university's role as educational leader in the state and in the interest of some formal, effective articulation between the schools and the university, Michigan began in 1870 to admit to the university students from certain Michigan public schools that the university certified

[8] Joseph Lindsey Henderson: *Admission to College by Certificate* (New York, 1912), pp. 24-8.
[9] John Howard Van Amringe, et al.: *A History of Columbia University 1754-1904* (New York, 1904), p. 39; Charles Henry Rammelkamp: *Illinois College: A Centennial History 1829-1929* (New Haven, 1928), pp. 56-7; James Albert Woodburn: *History of Indiana University: 1820-1902* (Bloomington, 1940); Charles Burt Sumner: *The Story of Pomona College* (Boston, 1914), p. 99; Kemp Plummer Battle: *History of the University of North Carolina* (Raleigh, 1907-12), I, 65.
[1] Henderson: *Admission to College by Certificate*, pp. 42-4, 49.

as offering respectable collegiate preparation. This device was charged with tremendous power, for not only did it promise to leave the university free of preparatory commitments and therefore free to develop in the direction of a true university; it also invited the schools of the state to extend their responsibilities and to achieve full programs of collegiate preparation. It was a device that unleashed the high-school movement in the Middle West and that enabled the state universities to cultivate scholarly aspirations.[2] It was a device, therefore, that was popular and democratic, in the impetus it gave to the development of an effective system of public education from the common school through the university; and it was friendly to the elevation of American university standards and scholarship, in the role it gave to the university in setting its own goals and in leading the schools to the achievement of higher standards.

In the Middle West it was not necessary for the common schools to turn into high schools, for by 1870 most students were spending some part of sixteen years in the public schools. The public-school system was apparently prepared to deliver college-age, if not college-prepared, students to the university. Essentially what the University of Michigan and other state universities that followed in its footsteps needed to do was to reshape loosely organized, extended, combined public primary-secondary schools into clearly differentiated elementary schools and high schools. This they succeeded in doing, always conscious of the aim to raise the state university to the standards of scholarship and learning demanded of a true university and to lead the high schools to a higher level.

The degree to which university ambition on the German model helped to inspire the certification movement and the subsequent growth of high schools was revealed in an overly ambitious announcement of the University of Minnesota in 1871 that it intended as soon as possible to shift the work of its preparatory *and* collegiate departments to the high schools

[2] Ibid., p. 51.

and eventually to limit the work of the university to professional study and graduate study in science, literature, and the arts.

By 1872 the state universities in Michigan, Minnesota, Iowa, and Wisconsin were working out certificate systems with the high schools. The next year Indiana and Illinois began to move toward certification; Ohio followed in 1874. Before 1890 firm, well-developed systems of certification had been adopted in all these states, as well as in Texas, Missouri, and California. Before 1900, 42 state universities and land-grant colleges and at least 150 of the private institutions had adopted some form of certification or accrediting, as the system was also known. The system was, of course, of remarkable assistance in establishing the public high school as a college-preparatory institution. And it was so successful that many Catholic colleges adhering to Jesuit tradition, in order to meet the competition of the high school-state university pattern, abandoned the old seven-year college course and took on a more American coloration.[3]

The leading state universities of the Midwest had come to depend almost entirely on the high schools by 1890. In the East the high-school movement was making comparable headway, greatly influenced by the urbanization taking place and by the existence of such institutions as Harvard, M.I.T., Columbia, and Cornell where students were relatively, or absolutely, free from the stranglehold of the old classical curriculum. In 1895, of students admitted to American colleges and universities 40 per cent were graduates of college-preparatory departments, which were a dying institution; 17 per cent were graduates of private preparatory schools; and already 41 per cent were graduates of the public high school, the agency which would make the American college a democratic institution.[4]

[3] Ibid., pp. 52-82; Edwin C. Broome: *A Historical and Critical Discussion of College Admission Requirements* (New York, 1903), pp. 116 ff.; Raphael N. Hamilton: *The Story of Marquette University: An Object Lesson in the Development of Catholic Higher Education* (Milwaukee, 1953), pp. 53 ff.

[4] Curti and Carstensen: *Wisconsin*, I, 476-98, II, 233-66; George Wil-

For not only did the public high school make college-going a possibility for a greater number of young Americans and provide great reservoirs of students for both the developing state universities and the older foundations which learned how to tap this new source of students. The high school, which was closer to the people than any other comparable institution and which therefore necessarily had to serve them, also was friendlier to the so-called new subjects, the modern languages and the sciences, and before long the universities and colleges were accepting for admission credit subjects that went beyond the traditional lethal doses of Latin, Greek, and arithmetic.[5]

Part of this extension of subjects necessary for admission was a function of pushing former college-level work down into the preparatory schools, and in this movement Harvard was the leader. But part of it was also a matter of gaining college-entrance credit for such popular subjects as American history, physical geography, natural philosophy, physiology, English, and the modern languages, and in this movement the high schools and the state universities were the leaders. By 1910, for instance, the University of California was accepting thirty different subjects for admission; at the other end of the scale were tried-and-true Princeton and Yale, which had relaxed so far as to recognize thirteen subjects suitable for admission credit. Somewhere in between was Harvard with twenty-two. The relationship between these admission subjects and the high schools was implicit in the percentage of high-school students attending a number of American universities in 1909: Princeton, 22 per cent; Yale, 35 per cent; Harvard, 53 per cent; M.I.T., 71 per cent; University of Wisconsin, 92 per cent; the University of Minnesota, 95 per cent.[6]

---

son Pierson: *Yale: College and University 1871-1937* (New Haven, 1952-5), I, 403 ff., II, 475-504; Henderson: *Admission to College by Certificate*, pp. 139, 147; Henry M. MacCracken, *et al.: New York University* (Boston, 1901), p. 5.
    [5] Henderson: *Admission to College by Certificate*, pp. 89-90.
    [6] Ibid., p. 147; Pierson: *Yale*, I, 392, 662.

In the decades after the Civil War, therefore, the American people turned to the state universities—and their subsidiaries, the public high schools—as institutions that were attempting to generalize what had once been the proper education for an English gentleman, attempting to democratize it, to transfer it from the exclusive domain of a particular religious-social purpose and group to the people at large. To this purpose were added a deep sense of public service and a commitment, however difficult to support, to the ideals that were embedded in the Johns Hopkins University at Baltimore. The state universities had their enemies but only the most foolish failed to recognize the meaning for the United States and for American higher education in the fact that in the year 1898 the Secretary of State of the United States, the Assistant Secretary of War in Charge of Mobilization, and the Chairman of the Senate Foreign Relations Committee were all graduates of one institution—the University of Michigan.[7]

[7] Kent Sagendorph: *Michigan: The Story of the University* (New York, 1948), p. 187.

14

The Elective Principle

A few days after the Battle of Bunker Hill a Harvard undergraduate wrote in his diary: "Amid all the terrors of battle
I was so busily engaged in Harvard Library that I never even
heard of . . . [it] until it was completed." [1] A hundred and
fifty years later professors who complained of apathetic students were advised by Knute Rockne, the great coach at
Notre Dame: "Make your classes as interesting as football." [2]
Obviously some time between the Battle of Bunker Hill and
the titanic football struggles of the 1920's at South Bend
there had developed in the American college what may
probably best be called "the motivation problem."

Before the Civil War a young man in college was quite
likely to be highly motivated by an ambition to excel in one
of the traditional professions. He found, however, on enrolling, that he was not seriously pressed by prevailing academic standards. Francis Leiber at South Carolina thought
that prompt dismissal was the only way to deal with the student who answered that the religion of the Jews was Moham-

[1] Quoted in Louis Shores: *Origins of the American College Library
1638-1800* (Nashville, 1934), p. 215.
[2] Quoted in James Wechsler: *Revolt on the Campus* (New York,
1935), p. 43.

medanism, and from one point of view of course Leiber was right.[3] But nowhere were students being dismissed for academic reasons and nowhere were really challenging intellectual demands being placed upon them. A student's well-defined career intentions, in combination with the college's relative indifference to scholarship, therefore helped to maintain a climate of sufficiently steady application to duty. And the extracurriculum absorbed a good share of excess undergraduate intellectual energy.

In the years after the Civil War, on the other hand, the colleges seemed to be running out of young men whose attention to study might lead them to miss the Battle of Bunker Hill. One evidence of apathy surely was the resort to artificial stimulation represented by the great attention to prizes, medals, and awards in the 1860's and 1870's. Bowdoin, which had last introduced an academic prize in 1795, indulged in a whole spate of prizes beginning in 1868. Brown, which had been unable to interest students in prizes in the 1840's, adopted a large-scale prize program in the 1870's. In 1871 at Williams one alumnus provided a prize for the student who won the most prizes. At Emory in Georgia an "Age of Medals" was inaugurated in 1876. At Harvard the faculty in 1871 was discussing the advantage of unannounced examinations as a means of inducing students to achieve a constant level of high performance. Everywhere more attention was being paid to various sectioning, grading, and marking schemes as instruments of scholarly stimulation.[4]

The existence of college students who found insufficient stimulation within themselves was certainly not a new phe-

[3] Daniel Walker Hollis: University of South Carolina (Columbia, 1951-6), I, 189.

[4] Louis C. Hatch: The History of Bowdoin College (Portland, 1927), pp. 238-40; Walter C. Bronson: The History of Brown University 1764-1914 (Providence, 1914), pp. 218-19, 402-3; Frederick Rudolph: Mark Hopkins and the Log: Williams College, 1836-1872 (New Haven, 1956), p. 233; Henry Morton Bullock: A History of Emory University (Nashville, 1936), p. 197; Mary Lovett Smallwood: An Historical Study of Examinations and Grading Systems in Early American Universities (Cambridge, 1935), p. 28.

nomenon on the American campus, but the presence of large numbers of them was. The country was wealthier than it had ever been before, and the colleges were in a sense getting their first large crop of students who could afford to waste their own time and their fathers' money. Moreover, their career orientation was less certain than that of earlier generations. Perhaps a job was waiting in the family business, or at least somewhere in business, for which the course of study itself was not a particularly pointed preparation, as indeed it still was for the ministry, law, and medicine.

Now what mattered for so many young men was not the course of study but the environment of friendships, social development, fraternity houses, good sportsmanship, athletic teams. The world of business was a world of dealing with people. What better preparation could there be than the collegiate life outside the classroom—the club room, the playing field, where the qualities that showed what stuff a fellow really was made of were bound to be encouraged. As the decades passed, college-going became for many a social habit, a habit which was sustained by an ever increasing standard of living and which was encouraged by the clear evidence that college men made more money than noncollege men and that money almost everywhere was the instrument of social elevation. In all of this the classroom was not terribly important.

Nor was the problem limited to the prestigious older foundations on the eastern seaboard. By the turn of the century at Yale the valedictorian could count on *not* being elected to a senior society, and at Harvard a study showed that the average undergraduate studied thirteen hours a week, an average considerably dependent on freshmen who had not yet learned how not to study. But even at the midwestern state universities a motivation problem developed. A member of the faculty at the University of Michigan in 1906 confessed, "The relative number of students who do not know just why they are at the University is increasing." The next year President Van Hise at the University of Wisconsin lamented the presence of a large number of men and women students "of no very serious purpose."[5] The students did not create a motivation problem unaided. The colleges and universities made a fundamental contribution. Their efforts to make scholarship more central to student life ran counter not only to vital anti-intellectual strains in the national culture but to some of the strongest of collegiate traditions as well. Their decision to find room for the new subjects within the framework of the prescribed curriculum not only robbed the extracurriculum of some of its vitality but also attached the stigma of compulsion to the new as well as to the old. In this environment a motivation problem was bound to develop as a significant percentage of the college population shifted from purposeful, professionally oriented, ambitious young men to somewhat aimless (to an extent, indulged) young men with a vague notion of taking up some career for which the real preparation occurred outside the classroom.

One of the most creative, and also one of the most destructive, educational developments of the post-Civil War years, the elective curriculum, played the paradoxical role of both contributing to the motivation problem and keeping it from being worse than it was.

The academic spokesman for election as an instrument of collegiate reform was Charles William Eliot, the first president of Harvard to achieve a national reputation. A Harvard graduate of the Class of 1853, Eliot served his teaching apprenticeship as a tutor and then as an assistant professor of mathematics and chemistry in the Lawrence Scientific

[5] George Wilson Pierson: *Yale: College and University 1871-1937* (New Haven, 1952-5), I, 240-1; Clarence F. Birdseye: *Individual Training in Our Colleges* (New York, 1907), p. 175; Burke A. Hinsdale: *History of the University of Michigan* (Ann Arbor, 1906), p. 156; Thomas Woody: *A History of Women's Education in the United States* (New York, 1929), II, 297.

School. Failing of reappointment in 1863, he accepted a
position at M.I.T., from where Harvard called him to the
presidency in 1869, but only after a determined corporation forced a hostile board of overseers to reconsider its
initial vote of disapproval. Eliot, in two articles in the *Atlantic
Monthly* on what he called "The New Education," had made
clear that he was on the side of collegiate reform. Indeed,
that was why the corporation wanted him and why the overseers did not.[6]

His forty years in the president's chair at Harvard produced a remarkable transformation in the institution. An exchange that occurred at a meeting of the medical faculty
soon after he took office indicated what Harvard was going
to be like under Eliot. "How is it," a doctor asked, "that
this faculty has gone for eighty years managing its own affairs and doing it well—and now within three or four months
it is proposed to change all our modes of carrying on the
school?" Eliot immediately spoke up. "I can answer . . .
[the doctor's] question very easily. There is a new president."[7] Under Eliot's leadership Harvard became a university, in the end surpassing even Johns Hopkins in the
strength of its graduate work in the arts and sciences. With
the help of Langdell and Ames in the Law School he pioneered in establishing new standards in the teaching of law.
In medicine he set examples that would profoundly improve
medical education in the United States. He made Harvard a
national rather than a provincial institution. He took advantage of his position to assert leadership in raising the
standards of secondary education. But the movement with
which he was most identified was the movement that substituted a broadly elective course of study for the old prescribed classical curriculum.

[6] Samuel Eliot Morison: *Three Centuries of Harvard 1636-1936*
(Cambridge, 1936), pp. 324-6.
[7] Quoted in Cornelius Howard Patton and Walter Taylor Field:
Eight O'Clock Chapel: A Study of New England College Life (Boston,
1927), p. 72.

Eliot had already made his allegiance to election clear in the *Atlantic* articles, but on the occasion of his inauguration apparently the overseers were not yet ready to face up to the fact that the man they had not wanted was about to treat Harvard to an era of reform.[8] John H. Clifford, president of the board of overseers, in charging Eliot during the ceremonies with the responsibilities of office, was either indulging in a gratuitous warning to Eliot or making the cloudiest prophesy in the history of American higher education when he referred to "the long procession of those who are to enter these halls, to pass through the prescribed curriculum of study." Eliot was not easily scared, and within minutes he was launched upon an address that would establish anew his allegiance to the elective principle. At the outset of his remarks he proposed a bold and full acceptance of the idea that "this University recognizes no real antagonism between literature and science, and consents to no such narrow alternatives as mathematics or classics, science or metaphysics. We would," he said, "have them all, and at their best." For those who feared for the classics he provided the assurance that "it will be generations before the best of American institutions of education will get growth enough to bear pruning." While the elective principle would add to the curriculum, it would take nothing away.[9]

He then made a frontal attack on the old faculty psychology which had been one of the strongest foundations of the prescribed course of study. "In education," he said, "the individual traits of different minds have not been sufficiently attended to." "[Moreover]," he continued, "the young man of nineteen or twenty ought to know what he likes best and is most fit for. . . . When the revelation of his own peculiar taste and capacity comes to a young man, let him reverently give it welcome, thank God, and take courage.

[8] Charles W. Eliot: "The New Education. Its Organization," *Atlantic Monthly*, XXIII (1869), 203-20, 358-67.

[9] *Addresses at the Inauguration of Charles William Eliot as President of Harvard College, Tuesday, October 19, 1869* (Cambridge, 1869), pp. 19-20, 29-30.

Thereafter, he knows his way to happy, enthusiastic work, and, God willing, to usefulness and success." [1]

Eliot's adherence to a psychology of individual differences then led him to suggest how the elective principle might meet the problem of student motivation. "The elective system," he said, "fosters scholarship, because it gives free play to natural preferences and inborn aptitudes, makes possible enthusiasm for a chosen work, relieves the professor and the ardent . . . [student] of the presence of a body of students who are compelled to an unwelcome task, and enlarges instruction by substituting many and various lessons given to small lively classes, for a few lessons many times repeated to different sections of a numerous class." And then as if to stretch even further the distance between himself and the old guard on the board of overseers, as if to make absolutely clear to John H. Clifford that Harvard had a new president, he made the calm, repeated observation: "The college therefore proposes to persevere in its efforts to establish, improve, and extend the elective system." [2]

The rationale that Eliot offered for the elective system rested on a combination of desire, necessity, principle, and preference. While Eliot's rejection of faculty psychology was finding some support in the work of pioneer experimental psychologists, his commitment to self-reliance and self-expression needed no academic credentials in order to appeal to American habits of thought. For the psychology of individual differences recognized the fundamental importance of the individual and in doing so merely stated in psychological terms what Americans had already come to believe through experience. Jefferson, Jackson, and Lincoln had already expressed on the level of democratic belief what Eliot was now saying should be an operative principle in higher education.

Eliot needed such a principle in order to achieve at Harvard a substantial lease on life for the natural and physical

[1] Ibid., pp. 39-40.
[2] Ibid., pp. 41-2.

sciences. And he needed it in order to move Harvard from its essentially narrow, New England orientation to a position in which it could become not only national in its clientele but national in its contributions. Harvard could become neither until it was free to develop departments of study in depth, until it was free to encourage scholarship and learning. All these purposes were served by the elective principle; and while it might be sold in one place as a natural application of the American belief in the free individual and in another as an expression of the new psychology, what Eliot really fashioned at Harvard was a device for bringing science and the other new disciplines into equality with the old subjects, a device for bringing a new spirit of inquiry and scholarship into the life of the university and for bringing Harvard itself once again into a position of commanding leadership in American life.

Step by step under Eliot's leadership Harvard abandoned prescription and expanded the domain of election. In 1872 all subject requirements for seniors were abolished. In 1879 all subject requirements for juniors were abolished. In 1884 the sophomores were liberated, and in 1885 subject requirements were materially reduced for freshmen. By 1894 a Harvard freshman's only required courses were rhetoric and a modern language. By 1897 the prescribed course of study at Harvard had been reduced to a year of freshman rhetoric.[3] During the forty years in which the elective principle was insinuating its way into every aspect of Harvard life, the faculty was growing from sixty to six hundred and the endowment from two to twenty million dollars.

These statistics recorded how well the elective principle served Eliot's larger purposes, but Harvard and Eliot could not abandon the past without a considerable battle. Once more Harvard became the bad boy of American higher education. For many it must have seemed in 1805 that Harvard could know no darker day than the one when the Hol-

[3] R. Freeman Butts: *The College Charts Its Course* (New York, 1939), pp. 175 ff., 231-50.

lis Professorship of Divinity fell into the hands of the Unitarians. The consequences of that victory were now at hand, and a new Unitarian president almost seemed intent on tearing to shreds whatever was left of the old fabric. "If at any time before 1886, perhaps before 1890, . . . [President Eliot's] policies had been referred to a plebiscite of Harvard alumni, they would surely have been reversed." His job was in jeopardy in 1885-6; the overseers were seeking his removal; eight New England college presidents were all but down on their knees, imploring, begging the corporation not to allow Eliot to drop Greek as an entrance requirement. The president of Harvard won, however, and in time an unfriendly voice at a later Harvard would conclude: "Mr. Eliot, more than any other man, is responsible for the greatest educational crime of the century against American youth —depriving him of his classical heritage." [4]

American youth for better or worse had long since broken loose from his classical heritage; as Francis Wayland kept pointing out, he was about to break loose not only from the classics but from the idea of college altogether. Mr. Eliot did not have sufficient control over American life either to destroy or to save the classics, but in the elective principle he did fashion an instrument that gave vitality to the American college at a time when its remoteness from society threatened the whole structure of American higher education with disaster.

The battle into which President Eliot led Harvard was in no sense a local affair. Elsewhere it had long since been joined. Wayland himself had given expression to one support of the elective principle in 1854 when he had asked: "Did God manifest himself in the flesh, in the form of a carpenter's son, to create an intellectual aristocracy, and consign the remaining millions of our race to daily toil, excluded from every opportunity for spiritual improvements?" But the

[4] Morison: Harvard: *Three Centuries*, pp. 358-61, 389-90.

friends of the old-time colleges who would not be convinced lingered on. Looking at the elective curriculum in 1885 a trustee of Bowdoin erupted: "Not symmetry but monstrosity." In 1892, with enrollment down to less than thirty, President Henry E. Shepherd of the College of Charleston proudly reported to his board of trustees: "The College of Charleston is one of the few institutions in the country which retains the time honored collegiate curriculum in full vigor . . . [,] the ancient curriculum, so admirable in its equipments for the symmetrical, harmonious development of every faculty." Five years later the College of Charleston surrendered to the elective principle, and two years after that had to build a new dormitory in order to handle the increase in enrollment.[5]

One institution with other means of increasing its enrollment was Boston College, for which low academic standards seemed a more appropriate policy than the abandonment of four centuries of curricular certainty. Harvard took these low standards into consideration in refusing to accept Boston College graduates for candidacy in the Harvard graduate and professional schools. Boston and Harvard had been at odds before, but in this instance the controversy was fought in the public press, and before it was over Eliot had become sufficiently exasperated to indict the whole tradition of Jesuit education in an article in the *Atlantic* with the judgment: "Nothing but an unhesitating belief in the Divine Wisdom of . . . [a four-hundred-year-old curriculum] can justify . . . [it], for no human wisdom is equal to contriving a prescribed course of study equally good for even two children of the same family, between the ages of eight and eighteen. Direct revelation from on high would be the only satisfactory basis for a uniform prescribed curriculum." While the Catholic colleges were more rigid in curricular matters than

[5] Francis Wayland: *The Education Demanded by the People of the U. States* (Boston, 1855), p. 6; Hatch: *Bowdoin*, p. 185; James Harold Easterby: *A History of the College of Charleston Founded 1770* (Charleston, 1935), pp. 164, 168-77.

any other group of institutions, nevertheless after 1887, under the leadership of St. Louis University, most of them moved increasingly toward the pattern of parallel courses and judicious election which was being established elsewhere. Father Thomas Walsh, president of Notre Dame, presented the case most simply: "Until the conductors of colleges . . . concede that students and their parents possess a certain right in the matter of determining the course of studies to be followed, they will be looked upon as men who have no sympathy with the world of beneficent actualities." [6]

Battles over the elective curriculum could be fought without Eliot. When Wabash College fell into a remarkably bitter struggle over the elective principle in 1900, Eliot after all was not there. Nor was he at Bryn Mawr when President Carey Thomas turned her sarcasm on some of the extremes to which the elective principle might lead. Said Miss Thomas: "In many colleges everything that is desirable for a human being to learn counts towards the bachelor's degree— . . . [including] ladder work in the gymnasium (why not going upstairs?) . . . [and] swimming in the tank (why not one's morning bath?)" [7] When the elective battles assumed major importance, however, Eliot *was* there. One such instance was a celebrated controversy with President James McCosh, the Scottish divine who was doing what he could to breathe new life into Nassau Hall.

McCosh, who had been made the president of Princeton in 1868, became a spokesman against the tendencies that were

[6] David R. Dunigan: *A History of Boston College* (Milwaukee, 1947), pp. 168-77; Edward J. Power: *A History of Catholic Higher Education in the United States* (Milwaukee, 1958), pp. 47, 55, 82, 84; Arthur J. Hope: *Notre Dame: One Hundred Years* (Notre Dame, 1943), p. 198; Thomas Gaffney Taaffe: *A History of St. John's College, Fordham, N. Y.* (New York, 1891), pp. 105-12 ff.
[7] James I. Osborne and Theodore G. Gronert: *Wabash College; the first hundred years, 1832-1932* (Crawfordsville, 1932), pp. 232 ff.; Woody: *A History of Women's Education*, II, 220.

being encouraged by the reforms at Harvard.[8] In February 1885 at the residence of Courtlandt Palmer in New York, the Nineteenth Century Club arranged to have McCosh and Eliot debate the merits of their respective positions. Mc-Cosh's argument was an instructive commentary on the stakes involved in the controversy over the elective principle. Surveying the Harvard curriculum, he refuted the notion that election would strengthen learning by observing: "There are twenty . . . dilettanti courses which may be taken in Harvard. I cannot allow that this is an advance in scholarship." Moreover, McCosh asked: "Has there been of late any great poem, any great scientific discovery, any great history, any great philosophic work, by the young men of Cambridge? I observe," he answered, "that the literary journals . . . have now fixed their seat in New York rather than Boston." As for all this business about election being animated by a typical American spirit of freedom, McCosh was not impressed: "Freedom is the catch-word of this new departure. . . . It is a bid for popularity." And with that, McCosh placed himself on the side of an essentially pre-scribed curriculum, compulsory class attendance, compulsory religious instruction, strict supervision and discipline, and limited specialization.[9]

McCosh rested his case on the old faculty psychology, and it was as if Jeremiah Day himself had walked into the room when McCosh proceeded to read: "Education is essentially the training of the mind. . . . The powers of mind are numerous and varied, the senses, the memory, the fancy, judgment, reasoning, conscience, the feelings, the will; the mathematical, the metaphysical, the mechanical, the poetical, the prosaic . . . ; and all these should be cultivated." To this fundamental attachment to faculty psychology McCosh added a basic distrust of students, a distrust which Eliot did

[8] Thomas Jefferson Wertenbaker: *Princeton 1746-1896* (Princeton, 1946), pp. 293, 304-7.
[9] James McCosh: *The New Departure in College Education: Being a Reply to President Eliot's Defence of it in New York, Feb. 24, 1885* (New York, 1885), pp. 4, 12, 22.

not share. McCosh fully expected students to take the easy way if given the opportunity, to go duck-shooting rather than to class, to carouse rather than to think deeply on matters of ethics, and consequently he was certain that they would benefit more from control than from freedom.[1]

He was a respecter neither of men nor of institutions: Harvard and Eliot were treated without deference. For at stake were some beliefs to which not only McCosh, but also the comfortable classes, which had been reared upon such beliefs, strongly adhered. Implicit in McCosh's point of view was an undying belief in the unity of knowledge, a belief both that such a unity was still possible and that a college could purvey the essence of that unity in a select body of courses. Explicit was a commitment to faculty psychology, to the certainty that what made for competence and excellence in this world was the rigorous training of a set of mental faculties that lay waiting to be called into development. Clearly, too, McCosh, good Calvinist that he was, was suspicious of unbridled freedom, not certain that man could be trusted to know what was good for him, disposed to the belief that some men more than others deserve to be given the authority and the responsibility of deciding what is best for the rest. His commitment to science was at best reluctant; he was not sure that the world was necessarily better because it could go faster, farther. Power, unless it was divine power, did not impress him. He liked the paternal atmosphere, the familial climate of the collegiate way, the sense of a community of teachers and young men engaged to good Christian purpose in studying the ancient God-given truths.

Here was a bundle of beliefs, of fundamental commitments, that would have difficulty in accommodating Eliot's touchstones: his strong commitment to science; his adherence to freedom, which made the elective principle the academic application of nineteenth-century liberalism; and his faith that an atmosphere of learning would accomplish what

[1] Ibid., pp. 8-9.

McCosh would achieve through discipline and a carefully cultivated religious atmosphere. The tendencies of the age clearly supported Eliot, but both positions were honestly held and ably argued.

Hardly an institution was spared the necessity of considering its own course of study in relation to the reforms that Eliot was carrying out at Harvard and Andrew D. White, with less opposition, at Cornell. Many of the old colleges held to the old rationale because they believed in it, but at many colleges, such as Denison, "the question was as much a financial matter as an intellectual concern." [2] For the elective program, in order to be effective, required an immediate and expensive expansion in faculty staff, laboratories, and libraries, and while many of the smaller institutions, forced now to compete with the more popular expanding state institutions, indulged in university pretensions, they seldom succeeded in doing more than confusing themselves as to what their assigned role should be. The intellectual anarchy fostered by the elective curriculum found some compensation in the depth of study and in the spirit of scholarship which it encouraged in the universities, but in the little colleges a combination of secularism and election often meant a loss of old purpose without the discovery of new purpose.[3]

The colleges that could afford to defy the public by resisting the elective principle on ideological grounds and the colleges that could not afford to indulge in the expansion which election required were at least comfortable in knowing what they believed. Of course, they were also consciously

[2] G. Wallace Chessman: *Denison: The Story of an Ohio College* (Granville, 1957), p. 135.
[3] Thomas Le Duc: *Piety and Intellect at Amherst College 1865-1912* (New York, 1946), pp. 89 ff.; Chessman: *Denison*, pp. 120-4; George Matthew Dutcher: *An Historical and Critical Survey of the Curriculum of Wesleyan University and Related Subjects* (Middletown, 1948), *passim*.

301   *The Elective Principle*

setting themselves apart from a movement which was helping to generalize the collegiate experience in the United States. Many of these small institutions, such as Hamilton and Williams, became for awhile the private preserves of the conservative, respectable classes or, in the case of Wooster and Hobart, of a narrow sectarian interest.

The elective principle commended itself to colleges that had been starved for students and that had resources enough to afford the necessary curricular growth, but it also benefited from the accelerating assault that experimental psychology was making on the old faculty psychology. In England Sir Francis Galton and in the United States James McKeen Cattell were undertaking significant work on human differences and were adding their weight in freeing American education from a curriculum that rested on the assumption of essential human similarity. The new psychology, which as early as 1887 had found a voice in a journal published at Johns Hopkins, was providing scientific evidence to support the suspicions that Francis Wayland had expressed as early as 1854 when he had asked, "Are mathematicians better reasoners than other men in matters not mathematical? . . . Are philologists or classical students more likely to become poets, or artists, than other men . . . ?" Without providing any theory of psychology to support his suspicions Wayland had anticipated a cardinal position of later educational practice when he concluded, "We generally find that wherever a distinct love for any pursuit exists, it is accompanied by those mental endowments which ultimately lead to success." [4]

What experience had taught Wayland and what John Dewey was learning in a laboratory at Johns Hopkins were now becoming a truism, and by the 1890's it would be possible to locate on the campuses of small midwestern sectarian institutions forthright expressions of the new psychology.

[4] Agatho Zimmer: *Changing Concepts of Higher Education in America Since 1700* (Washington, 1938), pp. 43-4; Wayland: *The Education Demanded by the People*, pp. 8-9, 11.

"The Old Education," said the president of DePauw in 1890, "ascribed the virtue to the subject, the New Education ascribes it to the process. If the virtue be chiefly in the process rather than in the subject, then, within proper limits, and under proper advice, the choice of that subject should depend largely on the tastes and probable future vocation of the student." Three years later the president of Illinois College remarked that to *his* mind, "the object of elective studies is not so much to permit a student to choose those branches which bear upon his future work as to enable him to select such as will interest him and thus lead his mind to act with greatest vigor." [5]

The classical course obviously could not withstand the psychology on which such statements rested, particularly when, as so often was the case, the elective principle was seen as a function of freedom. As one college president admiringly put it, "freedom for the pupil, freedom for the teacher, freedom in the subject." The movement toward election was gradual but irresistible. An 1895 survey showed that Harvard with its year of required rhetoric and Cornell with its year of required physical training and hygiene were the most elective. Rutgers with twenty-four required courses in its B.A. program was the least elective, and in close running were Williams, Hamilton, and Union. The defenders of the old curriculum looked to Yale and Princeton and the smaller colleges of New England and New York for leadership. Few institutions ever went as far as Cornell and Harvard, although close behind them were Columbia, Stanford, William and Mary, and several of the state institutions. A 1901 survey of 97 representative colleges found that 34 institutions offered courses of study that were 70 per cent elective, that 12 institutions offered courses of study that were between 50 per cent and 70 per cent elective, and that

[5] William Warren Sweet: *Indiana Asbury-DePauw University, 1837-1937: A Hundred Years of Higher Education in the Middle West* (New York, 1937), pp. 153-4; Charles Henry Rammelkamp: *Illinois College: A Centennial History 1829-1929* (New Haven, 1928), pp. 383-4.

51 or over half offered courses that were less than 50 per cent elective.[6]

Unquestionably the large state universities of the Midwest and West, with their commitment to public service and to learning, were more friendly than any other group of institutions to the elective principle. Next were the large, privately endowed universities, which were both wealthy enough and sufficiently oriented to larger national purposes to recognize election as essential to the spirit of a dynamic institution of learning. The women's colleges were perhaps marginal; they tended to combine the tradition of prescription with a degree of election necessary to accommodate subjects that were appropriately feminine. The least elective institutions of all were the state universities of the South, which were in the grasp of poverty, and the small colleges of New England and their counterparts elsewhere, which were in the grasp of the past and of social, economic, and religious interests for whom the past was useful.[7]

Everywhere the elective principle appeared in varying guises and in varying strengths, sometimes depending on the condition of the institution's treasury or on its distance, ideologically, from Ithaca or Cambridge. In the tradition of their colonial past, Harvard, not Yale or Princeton, led in this movement to unshackle the old institutions and to build within them a contagious respect for learning. But in the end Yale and Princeton found a way of supporting both the old and the new, of taking the middle road and achieving some level of moderation.

Yale agonized in the face of the movement and in some ways would have preferred to keep the new tendencies neatly locked in a closet called the Sheffield Scientific School, but the elective principle and the new developments that it supported were not skeletons. They were flesh and blood,

---

[6] Sweet: *DePauw*, p. 154; Albert Perry Brigham: *Present Status of the Elective System in American Colleges* (New York, 1897), p. 361; Butts: *The College Charts Its Course*, pp. 231-42.

[7] Butts: *The College Charts Its Course*, p. 242.

and they were imparting a new vitality to the onetime anemic, almost lifeless, American college. At Yale a slight relaxation in prescription took place in 1876, and in 1883, with President Noah Porter in dissent, the Yale faculty voted to free most of the junior and senior years from prescription. One thing led to another. In 1893 election was extended to the sophomore year, and in 1901 Yale freed upperclassmen entirely from course requirements. At Yale, however, there was a significant difference, for freedom from course requirements did not mean the freedom of choice that prevailed at Harvard. At Yale freedom was disciplined by sequence or graded courses, by grouping, and by requirements in concentration and distribution. Yale, in adopting a middle position, attempted to give responsible direction to the search for some accommodation between the old values and new opportunities.[8]

In time at Yale and elsewhere the elective principle would lead to a multiplicity of innovations—extensions of election itself or remedies intended to cure some of its less lovely consequences. Many of the characteristic curricular developments of the twentieth century would in one way or another go back to the elective principle for their inspiration: concentration and distribution, majors and minors, groups, tutorials and preceptorials, honors and independent study, reading periods, seminars, field studies, general education, and comprehensive examinations. But the significance for American education of the extension of the elective principle was more profound than any list of related curricular developments.[9] In 1908 President Eliot, who surely had a right to consider its consequences, said, "The largest effect of the elective system is that it makes scholarship possible, not only among undergraduates, but among graduate students and college teachers." His claim was certainly justified. The old prescribed course of study was a course in elementary subjects, and it not only held the student and teacher to the

[8] Pierson: *Yale*, I, 72, 80-5, 185, 258-66.
[9] Butts: *The College Charts Its Course*, pp. 408-26.

most superficial kind of knowledge, but also sustained colleges that got along quite well on a level of alarming superficiality. Election permitted the professor to indulge his interests and the students to follow theirs; it encouraged the accumulation of knowledge and welcomed into the world of learning subjects that had been forbidden through an ill-considered belief that the ancients knew everything worth knowing.[1]

The elective principle saw the rise of science and the remarkably expanding areas of knowledge for what they were: clear indications that no longer could any one person really know everything worth knowing. The elective principle moved the individual to the center of the educational universe and boldly asserted that all educated men need not know the same things. The elective system, by giving free play to the great motive power of interest, freed the curriculum from the deadening influence of latent or open disinterest and hostility, and perhaps thereby contributed to two subsidiary developments: the tendency of standards of academic performance to be set no longer by the slow students, but now by the most interested and more able students; and the tendency noted by a professor at the University of Michigan in 1880 who said: "The Professor and students are no longer enemies, but friends."[2]

The elective principle was the instrument by which departments of knowledge were built, by which areas of scholarly interest were enlarged, and therefore it was the instrument that enabled colleges to become universities. In the end, it was the instrument, secular and democratic, that permitted the American university to enter into a vital partnership with the society of which it was a part. It transformed the English college in America by grafting upon it German ideals and in the process created the American university.[3]

[1] Charles W. Eliot: *University Administration* (Boston, 1908), p. 150; Morison: Harvard: *Three Centuries*, pp. 341-8.
[2] Quoted in Walter P. Rogers: *Andrew D. White and the Modern University* (Ithaca, 1942), p. 102.
[3] Butts: *The College Charts Its Course*, pp. 172, 193.

Of course the ledger had its debits. The elective principle, enemy of one kind of superficiality though it was, could spawn a limitless number of short courses that might not add up to anything very substantial. On occasion it could make for a system that was "haphazard, illogical, postulated on too high an expectation of a young man's will to learn and too low an estimate of the many attractive side-shows outside the main tent." [4] It surely underwrote a good deal of the motivation problem in the American college and university by encouraging the notion that one subject was no more important than another and by making it possible for the nonserious student to find an easy berth. Too, it became the instrument but not the cause for ushering out of American experience the acquaintance with the classics which for centuries had been the mark of an educated man. It became the device with which the philosophic descendants of Bacon and Rousseau, now in the vast majority and in control, almost obliterated the humanist content of higher education and substituted for it an often excessive concern with practical power and the equality of men. But when all this is said, the conclusion is inescapable that the elective principle—whether at Harvard or Cornell, Amherst or De-Pauw, Vanderbilt or California—moved the American college and university into the mainstream of American life, where it had long been sorely needed and where it for long had sorely needed to be.

[4] Morison: Harvard: *Three Centuries,* p. 387.

15

The Education of
Women

Given the conditions of American life, it was inevitable that
the college classroom should one day be blessed with the
charms of femininity and graced by the presence of aspiring
American womanhood. But it would take time. Yale, in
1783, examined Lucinda Foote, age twelve, and found her
"fully qualified, except in regard to sex, to be received as a
pupil of the Freshman class of Yale University." [1] But the
doors were barred, and even the giving of an examination
was something of a cruel joke. Imagine a twelve-year-old
girl, on the edge of adolescence, examined by the illustrious
divines of New Haven, found equal to the brightest young
men of Connecticut in intelligence and learning, and then
abandoned to fate, denied the encouragement, the protection, the guidance of the Yale faculty; refused the stimulation, the inspiration, the challenge of a life of inquiry and
piety among her peers. The colonial view of woman was
simply that she was intellectually inferior—incapable, merely

[1] Thomas Woody: *A History of Women's Education in the United
States* (New York, 1929), II, 137.

by reason of being a woman, of great thoughts. Her faculties were not worth training. Her place was in the home, where man had assigned her a number of useful functions.[2]

Times would change. After the Revolution, Enlightenment and reason on the one hand and sheer necessity on the other liberated the American people from many traditional beliefs and practices. Indeed, as far as her status was concerned, a process of liberation had long been underway, for in America the woman benefited not only from participating equally with the man in the hard work that the frontier demanded of her, but also from her scarcity in proportion to man, who naturally was in more abundance in a pioneering society.

In the years after the American Revolution no one was busier than Benjamin Rush, the Philadelphia physician, in prescribing what ought to be done to achieve an American nationality. The national culture was as yet too plastic for anyone to speak either with certainty or authority on what it might mean to be un-American. But Rush was prepared to hasten that day by encouraging the development of institutions that would foster what he took to be tendencies in the national character. He had befriended the idea of a national university as an encouragement to the shaping of a definable national culture; he had befriended Dickinson College as a means of Americanizing the Pennsylvania Germans. Rush also had something to say not so much about Americanizing woman as about the necessity of dealing with the fact that woman had in some ways already been Americanized.

In 1787 he pointed out that the American woman was indeed different and that therefore Americans should not make the mistake of thinking of her in European terms. For instance, American women married earlier: perhaps because they were scarce, or because material plenty permitted it, or because so much work needed to be done in America that an unknown law insisted that children be born at the earliest

[2] Ibid., I, 88-123.

possible minute. In any case, American women married early; therefore, the time available for their education was not extensive. Another factor was the central role of opportunity in American experience: there was so much opportunity for material advancement that the men could not take advantage of it all by themselves, they needed the assistance of wives who knew how to help their husbands to make their fortunes, fortunes that were simply waiting to be created out of a decent amount of applied intelligence.

The European wife knew no such necessity, for opportunity did not there wait to be grasped; the uninformed European wife who could neither read nor write nor keep accounts was a suitable companion for a husband who in all likelihood was not going any farther than to the village church on Sunday. But this was America, the land of opportunity. And one consequence would be the extended absence of the father from the home, either for long periods of time or from early in the morning until late in the day. Whether the pursuit of wealth would take the father to the town, to sea, to the woods, or to the farthest reaches of tilled farmland, in his absence the mother herself had to be prepared to educate their children.

Moreover, the American woman possessed a responsibility which belonged to no other women in the world: her sons were free to partake actively in the affairs of government, and it was her obligation therefore to help prepare the manhood of tomorrow for responsible citizenship. One other factor, said Rush, conditioned the requirements of female education in America: there was no large permanent servant class, nor in an open mobile society was there ever likely to be one. Therefore the education of the American woman demanded an emphasis on domestic studies. "It is incumbent upon us," said Rush, "to make ornamental accomplishments yield to principles and knowledge, in the education of our women." [3]

In the common schools and in the academies, and in a

[3] Ibid., 302-3.

number of schools founded especially for girls, the American female was recognized as capable of being educated—up to a point. College was the point at which most Americans resisted, for before the Civil War the college was not considered a very appropriate place even for most American young men. Under those circumstances, there did not seem to be any compelling reasons why young women needed any more Greek, Latin, and mathematics than they learned in the academy, for after all God had intended them for marriage and motherhood.

All American women, however, did not agree, and enough of them, perhaps heady with a tradition of frontier equality and inspired by a climate of democracy, were prepared to establish what to many men very much seemed like woman's right to be a man. In 1847 Antoinette Brown claimed and obtained the right to be a pastor in South Butler, New York. Four years later Mrs. Amelia Bloomer emerged in the emancipating costume that proposed to free women from hobbling skirts and thus enable them to keep up with men. In 1855 Lucy Stone wed Dr. Henry P. Blackwell and succeeded in having the word "obey" omitted from the marriage ceremony. In 1860 Elizabeth Cady Stanton and Lucretia Mott were busily engaged in the movement to liberalize the divorce laws, thus making it easier for women to free themselves of cads, drunks, and other assorted husbands. In this climate the movement for the higher education of women was irresistible.

The movement toward the higher education of women drew on a tradition of educational emancipation which went back at least to the effective and respectable schools of the Moravians at Bethlehem, Pennsylvania, in 1749, and to other early schools in such places as Boston, Philadelphia, and Ipswich, New Hampshire. Female seminaries such as those founded by Emma Willard at Troy in 1821, by Catherine Beecher at Hartford in 1828, and by Mary Lyon in South Hadley in

1836 set precedents for the education of women; the woman's college movement was an extension upward of the female-seminary idea. Many of the academies, recognizing the conditions that had impressed themselves on the mind of Benjamin Rush, had turned to coeducation or had been founded as coeducational institutions; the coeducational-college movement was an extension upward of the coeducational-academy idea.[4]

The agitation for collegiate education for women shared the same inspiration as many of the humanitarian movements of the first half of the nineteenth century. In a world where everything and everyone was progressing, where the sacredness of the human personality and inherent rights of the individual in society were advanced as fundamental truths, in such a world higher education for women received the attention of mankind along with such causes as prison reform, education for the blind, the care of the insane, the rights of children, and the emancipation of slaves.

In 1837 Oberlin College in Ohio enrolled four female freshmen and thus inaugurated coeducational higher education for women, offering its young women not only the traditional B.A. course but also a special Ladies Course the completion of which was recognized by a diploma.[5] "Women are to be educated because we choose civilization rather than barbarism," one young man at Oberlin asserted.[6] Before the Civil War, however, fewer than a half dozen other American colleges adopted coeducation. Separate but theoretically equal institutions were somewhat more popular, although even the movement for separate women's colleges was a halting unimpressive affair. The first experiment in women's collegiate education was the Georgia Female College at Macon, chartered in 1836 and opened in 1839.[7]

Although these beginnings were not widely imitated, by

[4] Ibid., 301.
[5] Robert Samuel Fletcher: *A History of Oberlin College From its Foundation through the Civil War* (Oberlin, 1943), I, 290-315, 373-85.
[6] Ibid., 383.
[7] Woody: *A History of Women's Education*, II, 161.

1851 Catherine Beecher, a friend of collegiate education for women, sent up an alarm: "Those female institutions in our land which are assuming the ambitious name of colleges, have, not one of them, as yet, secured the real features which constitute the chief advantage of such institutions. They are merely high schools." Under Miss Beecher's prodding in 1852 the American Women's Education Association was formed for the purpose of putting some direction and some standards into the women's college movement. Perhaps a dozen would-be colleges for women were launched in the 1850's, the one most closely resembling a good man's college being Elmira Female College which gave its first degrees in 1859. These colleges of the 1850's remained largely local in reputation, and while they were the pathfinders, leadership (as would also be the case with coeducation) would actually be provided by a later group of institutions.[8]

The failure of coeducation and of separate women's colleges to make much headway before 1860 should be viewed in the context of those other educational reforms which also remained essentially blocked until after the war: the elective principle, technological education, graduate education, popular practical learning. Certainly some peculiar circumstances and factors would militate against the movement for higher education of women; but in company with other lagging reforms, the movement would suffer from the mental rigidity of college governing boards, from the inability of those who controlled American higher education to think beyond the classical course of study. It would suffer from the essential poverty of the collegiate foundations and from the widespread suspicion of the class- and sectarian-conscious colleges. In addition, higher education for women would have its own particular set of problems with which to deal. And until these problems were overcome, the idea of sending women off to college would continue to be looked upon as

[8] Ibid., II, 144-8; W. Charles Barber: *Elmira College: The First Hundred Years* (New York, 1955), pp. 52 ff.

one of those notions, subversive of the American home and family, that were likely to be entertained only by the more reckless members of the community.

Indeed, people often found themselves hard pressed to explain why good families, pillars of the church, not known for any particular foolishness in the past, were sending their daughters off to the female colleges. Maybe it was simply that a particular young daughter was a very bright girl, who had done better in Latin than any of the boys at the local academy, where the principal was prepared to vouch for the Christian atmosphere of one of the new female colleges. Maybe a young girl had been bitten by some of the reform bugs—although *one* would have been enough—and there was therefore no way to keep her from wanting to be a teacher in one of the new city high schools. That being the case, she might just as well take advantage of the normal department at the female college. In the case of a rich family, if the young women were going to be ornaments for the rest of their lives, probably it was just as well that they brushed up on piano and voice culture. An occasional father who had sent his girls off to college would say that he missed them very much, but because they were the very vessels of God's great goodness he felt obliged to see that they received the very finest of Christian nurture. An occasional girl was of the sort who had always had boy-notions, not that she cared for boys much, but whether it was foot races or tree-climbing, she usually outdid the boys; she might even have been heard to say she thought women ought to vote.

And so the female colleges and the struggling coeducational colleges gathered together a handful of pioneers, young women who for one reason or another found themselves where women never before had been. Their numbers would be appreciably swelled after the war, become a torrent in the twentieth century, and by 1960 a state supreme court would order a divorced father to provide, in the support of a daughter living with her mother, for her college education. Within a hundred years, downright foolishness would have become a legal necessity.

The extension of women's education was the function of two agencies: the land-grant colleges and state universities where coeducation took hold; and a trio of new women's colleges which contributed heavily toward elevating the standards and the reputation of collegiate education for women. First the University of Iowa in 1855 and then the University of Wisconsin in 1863 opened their doors to women, followed by Indiana, Missouri, Michigan, and California.[9] The readiness of the western institutions to adopt coeducation unquestionably derived in part from the facts of western life, where an equality of the sexes was achieved in the ordinary work of the farm. Western woman was not a thing apart. Neither pampered nor fragile, perhaps she was not even as feminine as she might be; but she was a person in her own right who had commanded the respect of her menfolk by assuming responsibility and working hard.

When the state universities, therefore, moved from the narrow class basis of the prewar years toward the development of large popular institutions, it was to be expected that women would be included. For the state universities owed their expansion in large measure to the success with which they articulated the common schools, the high schools, and the universities. In helping the extended combined elementary-secondary schools to achieve effective high-school status, the universities strengthened a public-school system that had long been coeducational. As the final rung in the ladder of state-provided education, the state universities of

[9] Merle Curti and Vernon Carstensen: *The University of Wisconsin: A History, 1848-1925* (Madison, 1949), I, 193-4; James Albert Woodburn: *History of Indiana University: 1820-1902* (Bloomington, 1940), p. 287; Jonas Viles, et al.: *The University of Missouri: A Centennial History* (Columbia, 1939), p. 131; Elizabeth M. Farrand: *History of the University of Michigan* (Ann Arbor, 1885), p. 201; William Warren Ferrier: *Origin and Development of the University of California* (Berkeley, 1930), p. 332.

the West were neither in a position nor in a mood to deny the fruits of higher education to its young women.[1]

In the East the situation was somewhat different. There the private schools and the private colleges had long set the patterns. Separate boys' academies funneled students into men's colleges, and as yet the private colleges and universities were assuming no leadership in developing effective state systems of public education. The wealthy, influential New England and Middle Atlantic states lacked state universities, and thus in the East there was an absence of that impulse to a co-ordinated state system of education which in the West meant so much for the high school and so much for coeducation. The land-grant colleges everywhere at first had some difficulty in rationalizing coeducation in view of the difficulty they were having in finding out what was meant by agricultural and mechanic. In New England, moreover, the land-grant foundations were overwhelmingly attached to the long-established men's colleges. All these institutional factors militated against any rapid success for the idea of higher education for women in the East. In addition, the reluctance of the better female seminaries such as Mount Holyoke and Emma Willard's school at Troy to take on work of collegiate level closed off one natural source of strength for the women's college idea.

To these barriers must be added those various social and intellectual considerations which argued that woman's place was in the home and that the home required at the most nothing more than an academy or seminary training. Eastern society had arrived at a point at which it could afford to regard woman as something both less than man and vastly superior. The eastern economy could underwrite a certain amount of chivalry, could afford to pamper women, provide them with Irish servant girls, indulge their not unusual fascination with clothes and jewelry, in other words provide them with a kind of women's world apart, where they were

[1] See Curti and Carstensen: *Wisconsin*, I, 369-87; Burke A. Hinsdale: *History of the University of Michigan* (Ann Arbor, 1906), pp. 130-8.

certainly not equal to men but at whose feet men could come to worship a kind of luxury. In the South, where a romantically cultivated concept of chivalry had transformed southern womanhood into a symbol of a sectional culture, the female college or seminary of finishing-school quality had recommended itself to some elements of southern society before the war. But now, as was the case with almost everything else, poverty put a stop to educational advance, and the South either stood still or retrogressed.

The West would not, however, be alone in recognizing the obviously increasing interest in female education. The war itself had done a great deal to draw forth the American woman from the home, placing her in situations demanding skills, temperament, and responsibilities normally reserved for men. Her success in meeting the wartime challenge not only silenced or at least deflated many of her critics but it also inspired the American woman herself, suggesting horizons of good works, useful and interesting lives so long denied her by the "man's world" tradition.

The massive skepticism, even hostility to higher education for women in the East, crumbled under the impact of a successful demonstration of coeducation at Cornell (the first coeducation on a higher level in an eastern institution) and of the opening in close succession of high-grade women's colleges at Vassar, Smith, and Wellesley.[2] The logic of Ezra Cornell's commitment to a scheme of education that would allow anyone to study anything certainly demanded that women be admitted to the new university. When a benefactor offered Cornell a women's dormitory, the die was cast; and in 1872 women were voted equal rights at Cornell. Even so, when the dormitory was begun the next year, Ezra Cornell was cautious enough to slip into the cornerstone a memorandum to the future explaining, if coeducation failed, why it did so. And before the favorable decision was made, Andrew D. White toured the country, studying one experiment in

[2] Waterman Thomas Hewett: *Cornell University: A History* (New York, 1905), I, 255-66.

coeducation after another, asking always whether coeducation nurtured "strong-minded" women and "unmanly" men.[3] In the meantime the cause of higher education for women had already been aided by the announcement in 1860 of Matthew Vassar, a Poughkeepsie brewer, that he intended to found a woman's college.[4] The announcement itself caused considerable discussion of the entire question of higher education for women and led to a benefaction on Vassar's part in the neighborhood of a million dollars. To John Howard Raymond went the task of giving to the new college in Poughkeepsie its ultimate shape as a college for women patterned on the traditional college for men.

The world at large needed proof that women deserved a collegiate education, proof that would never be supplied if college girls were served up a set of courses catering only to female needs: the management of domestics, for instance, or the science of the home; homemaking as a career; challenging problems in needlework; the home a thing of beauty, horticulture and interior decorating as ways to a man's heart. Courses of this sort might have recommended themselves to common-sense American males, and indeed before long home economics and domestic science would constitute special women's programs at the land-grant colleges and state universities; but the decision of the early planners at Vassar, Smith, and Wellesley to give the young ladies largely what had become the standard fare at the men's colleges was dictated by the necessity to prove that women could undertake a serious course of study. All of the institutions incorporated some studies, some emphases, that were clearly feminine in inspiration, but the main lines of curricular development in the new eastern women's colleges derived

[3] Andrew D. White: *Report Submitted to the Trustees of Cornell University in Behalf of a majority of the committee on Mr. Sage's Proposal to Endow a College for Women* (Ithaca, 1872).
[4] James Monroe Taylor: *Before Vassar Opened: A Contribution to the History of the Higher Education of Women in America* (Boston, 1914); James Monroe Taylor and Elizabeth Hazelton Haight: *Vassar* (New York, 1915).

from the old prewar classical course of study as it had been perfected at such places as Yale, Princeton, Amherst, and Williams.

If Vassar's earliest program was somewhat ambiguous, allowing for some subject unlikely ever to appear in the curriculum of a man's college, there was no doubt about the degree to which Smith and Wellesley provided a course of study "almost identical with that of the best men's colleges." Both these new institutions, which opened in 1875, found the way paved by Vassar's victory in achieving public support for the idea of women's collegiate education. Indeed, while Matthew Vassar's announcement in 1860 that he proposed to set up a women's college just like a man's occasioned widespread comment, by 1870 when Sophia Smith's will became known, the novelty was gone and higher education for women had clearly come to stay.[5] Sophia Smith's decision to provide approximately a half-million dollars for a woman's college at Northampton was nurtured by John Morton Greene, an Amherst man and the pastor of Sophia Smith's church at Hatfield, Massachusetts. A thrifty, deaf spinster in her middle sixties, Sophia Smith turned to Greene for comfort and guidance in 1861 on inheriting the estate of a parsimonious bachelor brother who was a successful speculator. Greene, who unsuccessfully attempted to interest Miss Smith both in his own college at Amherst and in the female seminary at South Hadley, saw her through five wills. The last, prepared in 1870, the year of her death, provided for the woman's college at Northampton. Mount Holyoke was to be twice denied during these years, on the second occasion by Henry Fowle Durant, one of the seminary's trustees, who decided, upon the death of a daughter in 1870, to devote his estate and the rest of his life to perfecting a woman's college at Wellesley.[6]

[5] Woody: *A History of Women's Education*, II, 148, 182.
[6] Florence Converse: *Wellesley College: A Chronicle of the Years 1875-1938* (Wellesley, 1939); Alice Payne Hackett: *Wellesley: Part of the American Story* (New York, 1949).

Under the impact of these developments the movement for the higher education of women became irresistible; and although in no sense did it become popular in the nineteenth century nor, in public estimation, as necessary to the cultivation of young women as college was to the cultivation of young men, nonetheless the battle had been won on many fronts. As the board of visitors of the University of Wisconsin proclaimed as early as 1872: "It is too late, amid the noontide splendours of the nineteenth century, to ignore the claims of woman to higher education. . . . Whatever shall make her wiser and better, that she may learn; whatever knowledge she may be able to use, either in adding to her own happiness, or in promoting the happiness of others— that knowledge she may rightfully acquire."[7] More and more institutions agreed. In the suburbs of Philadelphia in 1888 an institution patterned in spirit on the Johns Hopkins University was opened, and before long Bryn Mawr College was giving advanced degrees.[8] In 1888 the seminary at South Hadley decided to become a college.[9]

Toward the end of the century a number of Catholic girls' schools, including the Academy of the Sacred Heart at Manhattanville, began to move toward collegiate status, and in 1900 in Washington Trinity College opened as the first Catholic college for women not to grow out of an academy.[1]

There also developed that compromise between coeducation and a separate women's college called a co-ordinate college. As early as 1874 Harvard had revealed a willingness to give its examinations to women, awarding them certificates for study done elsewhere. These symbolic pats-on-the-back

[7] Woody: *A History of Women's Education*, II, 242.

[8] Cornelia Lynde Meigs: *What Makes a College? A History of Bryn Mawr* (New York, 1956); Edith Finch: *Carey Thomas of Bryn Mawr* (New York, 1947).

[9] Arthur C. Cole: *A Hundred Years of Mount Holyoke College: The Evolution of An Educational Ideal* (New Haven, 1940), pp. 180-204 ff.

[1] Sister Mary Mariella Bowler: *A History of Catholic Colleges for Women in the United States of America* (Washington, 1933), pp. 18-21, 28, 101-14.

did not admit women to a Harvard classroom, but they did say, in effect, "Nice going. We must admit that even though you are women you can pass our exams." In 1879, with the guidance and leadership of Elizabeth Cary Agassiz, a group of Harvard professors began to give courses for women outside the university. Offered under the auspices of "The Society for the Collegiate Instruction of Women," these courses constituted what was popularly known as the Harvard Annex. In 1893 the Annex achieved the full dignity of Radcliffe College, which was on its way toward establishing that strange complex of customs, traditions, phobias, and confusions which by the middle of the next century would have the outside world still thinking that Harvard was a man's college.[2]

Similar developments had been taking place in New York, where Columbia gave birth to Barnard.[3] If it is metaphorically confusing to think of these men's colleges as giving birth to women's colleges, Adam after all did precede Eve, and on these terms, Radcliffe may well be recognized as Harvard's rib, Barnard as Columbia's—and so Sophie Newcomb to Tulane, Pembroke to Brown, Jackson to Tufts, Flora Stone Mather to Western Reserve.

But neither co-ordinate education nor separate education would be the rule, for while both these movements would establish the right of women to higher education, and even prove in numerous ways that women could be educated to levels of understanding and brilliance equal to men, yet the characteristic institution for the higher education of women in the United States would be the coeducational college or the coeducational university. Indeed, except in New England and to a degree in some of the Middle Atlantic states, the characteristic institution for the higher education of *men* in

[2] Samuel Eliot Morison: *Three Centuries of Harvard 1636-1936* (Cambridge, 1936), pp. 391-3; Woody: *A History of Women's Education,* II, 304-20.

[3] Marian Churchill White: *A History of Barnard College* (New York, 1954).

321 The Education of Women

the United States was also in the process of becoming the coeducational college or university. As it did in so many other areas, Cornell played an important role in establishing coeducation in the United States. Its status as a developing model for land-grant colleges and state universities gave everything it did an aura of importance. A combination of superb executive management and of adequate financial resources permitted Cornell to show other institutions how to achieve that perhaps strangely mixed but characteristically American institution of higher learning where the advancement of knowledge and the diffusion of knowledge were precariously balanced, where theory and practice were brought into the service of the community at large, and where both human aspirations and material resources were unleashed in behalf of the American dream. Cornell's decision to adopt coeducation in the East surely must have sent another shiver of fear through the same old institutions that had not expressed delight when Cornell had achieved the largest entering class in the history of American higher education even without women.[4]

At Amherst in 1871, anticipating the possibility of coeducation, the students manfully went on record to the effect that they would accept women if the trustees so decided, but that they would miss the intimacy and the friendships of an all-man's college. Amherst did not succumb to the arguments for coeducation, and although in 1883 a scholarship was founded at Amherst for the exclusive use of women students when the walls would finally crumble, the scholarship has remained as untouched as Amherst's tradition of manly intimacy and friendships. At Williams for a number of years beginning in 1872 the alumni agitated the question of coeducation, but even with the help of John Bascom, soon to be the president of the University of Wisconsin, and of David Dudley Field, the eminent legal reformer, the coeducationists were unable to carry the day; the old order

[4] Walter P. Rogers: *Andrew D. White and the Modern University* (Ithaca, 1942), pp. 84-9.

prevailed. At Lafayette the subject also received a hearing in 1872, and reform likewise failed, although there was indeed something terribly persuasive about the argument that women students would not be able to enter on the old perpetual scholarships.[5]

Of New England institutions, few surrendered their right to maintain tradition, whatever the cost in immediate enrollment gains. Wesleyan, however, in the spirit of the Methodist seminary tradition of coeducation, introduced coeducation in 1872 and maintained it until 1909, when a decision to abandon sectarian affiliation also meant a return to the New England tradition of separate colleges for men and women. Middlebury adopted coeducation in 1883, when it could no longer resist the argument that it owed the daughters of Vermont an education close to home.[6]

But the strength of coeducation was clearly in the West: in 1872 there were ninety-seven major coeducational colleges and universities in the United States—major in the sense that they had revealed a tendency to survive and that they enrolled a majority of coeducational students in the United States. Of these ninety-seven colleges, sixty-seven were in the West, seventeen in the South, eight in the Middle Atlantic states, five in New England. By 1880 over 30 per cent of all American colleges admitted women and in another twenty years 71 per cent of all American colleges were coeducational. The way in which coeducation overtook the long-established men's colleges of the central states was dramatic. In 1894 in all the great Midwest beyond Ohio only three men's colleges remained: Beloit in Wisconsin, Wabash

[5] Woody: *A History of Women's Education*, II, 267; Frederick Rudolph: *Mark Hopkins and the Log: Williams College, 1836-1872* (New Haven, 1956), p. 231; David Bishop Skillman: *The Biography of a College: Being the History of the First Century of the Life of Lafayette College* (Easton, 1932), I, 353.

[6] Carl F. Price: *Wesleyan's First Century* (Middletown, 1932), pp. 50-1, 172; William Storrs Lee: *Father Went to College: The Story of Middlebury* (New York, 1936), p. 165.

in Indiana, and Illinois College. Beloit made the now almost inevitable shift in 1895 and Illinois in 1903, leaving Wabash that almost unique phenomenon—a midwestern men's college.[7]

Coeducation helped to save many one-time men's colleges of the small denominational type from being put out of business by the state institutions in the Midwest and West. The recovery of many of the old institutions from the doldrums of the 1850's was recorded in higher enrollments, but the degree to which those enrollments especially after 1870 reflected the shift to coeducation was significant. Wabash, which resisted the coeducation movement, enrolled a hundred fewer students in 1899 than in 1872, at a time when coeducational institutions were experiencing modest growth. Refusing to adopt coeducation, Wabash had to postpone its recovery into the next century, when the available pool of high-school graduates was enlarged.[8]

The meaning of coeducation for the liberal arts college was hidden in enrollment statistics of the college department of the University of Michigan where in 1870 there was one woman student to 429 men; in 1898 these figures had become 588 women and 745 men. Indeed, the acceleration of female enrollment meant that in 1898 53 per cent of the B.A. and Ph.B. degrees awarded that year by Michigan went to women. For all coeducational colleges, the increase in men students from 1875 to 1900 was threefold and of women students sixfold. At Northwestern the enrollment of women students so threatened the coeducational nature of the institution that an engineering course was added to bolster the dwindling male forces. At Stanford, the proportion of women

---

[7] Woody: *A History of Women's Education*, II, 252; Rogers: *Cornell*, p. 89; James I. Osborne and Theodore G. Gronert: *Wabash College; the first hundred years, 1832-1932* (Crawfordsville, 1932), p. 424.
[8] Osborne and Gronert: *Wabash*, pp. 211, 221-4 ff.

students was 25 per cent in 1892, 33 per cent in 1895, and 40 per cent in 1899. Finally a limit was adopted to preserve the college from an unwanted change in character.[9]

The growing proportion of women in the coeducational colleges was unquestionably due to a number of factors. More women than men were graduating from the high schools, and while clearly more men than women were going to college, the proportion of women was simply approaching some level of equality. On the other hand, technical schools were essentially all-male institutions.

One tendency of these developments therefore was the growth of the idea that the liberal arts programs and courses were essentially feminine. Coeducation helped to divide the subjects of the curriculum and the courses of study into those which were useful, full-blooded, and manly, and those which were ornamental, dilettantish, and feminine. Into the latter category, in the atmosphere provided by coeducation, went all the older liberal studies which were, and are, man's noblest inheritance.

While coeducation saved many of the one-time men's colleges, therefore, it may also be true that the men's liberal arts colleges like Yale and Princeton and Amherst and the co-ordinate institutions like Harvard and Columbia preserved the liberal inheritance of Western civilization in the United States by protecting it from the debilitating, feminizing, corrupting influences which shaped its career where coeducation prevailed. Women students were of course capable of doing well by Western tradition, but the nurture of that tradition in the United States was in danger of being monopolized by women. Even in the men's colleges the study of the languages, the humanities, the study of history were subjected to the insulting epithet "culture course," but how

[9] Hinsdale: *Michigan*, pp. 134-6; Rogers: *Cornell*, p. 89; Woody: *A History of Women's Education*, II, 317-18; Orrin Leslie Elliott: *Stanford University: The First Twenty-Five Years* (Stanford, 1937), pp. 132-6.

The Education of Women

much easier it was to defend, to nurture, to advance these studies where they were not being monopolized by women.[1]

Colleges catering to women experienced many of the same difficulties, many of the same movements, as colleges catering exclusively to men. They had difficulty with finances: the name of Mary Sharp College in Alabama cost one benefactor $5,000. In the early post-Civil War years they indulged in an overexpansion of facilities for women comparable to that in the early years of the men's college movement. They relied until the end of the century on preparatory departments for prospective students or on special arrangements with feeder schools. They became deeply committed to the collegiate way, a body of traditions and practices capable of insulating young women from the dangers and temptations of life. They readily indulged in the new scientific orientation of higher education in America and in the developing elective course of study.[2]

Yet, of course, there were differences. What did one call a first-year female student? Certainly not freshman! Elmira decided on protomathian and Rutgers on novian, but freshman in the end prevailed. The question of whether the separate women's colleges should be distinguished by the use of "Female" in their names was determined by the professional feminists. "What female do you mean? . . . A female donkey?" demanded Sarah Hale of Matthew Vassar, and before long "Female" was stricken from the name of the college in Poughkeepsie. The omission could not hide some of the differences. Sensitive to public expectation that college women would waste away under the stress of the intellectual

[1] For an early view of the "culture course" problem see Clarence F. Birdseye: *Individual Training in Our Colleges* (New York, 1907), pp. 193-5, 405. See also Elliott: *Stanford*, p. 476; Rogers: *Cornell*, pp. 215-16.
[2] Mabel Newcomer: *A Century of Higher Education for American Women* (New York, 1959), pp. 21-3, 25, 81.

life, colleges for women from the very beginning placed extraordinary stress on health, hygiene, and physiology. They and the coeducational colleges both recognized teaching as a likely career for the emancipated American woman and consequently paid much attention to teacher-training programs. Cornell, Bryn Mawr, and Vassar pioneered in developing courses in social work.[3] The tendency toward coeducation as the characteristic pattern of American higher education would in time, of course, obliterate many of the differences that at first seemed so important.

Be this as it may, either in separate institutions, or in coordinate institutions, or in coeducational institutions women achieved their right to collegiate education. In doing so they disposed of the fears of men like the Reverend John Todd who had objected: "Must we crowd education on our daughters, and for the sake of having them 'intellectual,' make them puny, nervous, and their whole earthly existence a struggle between life and death?" They faced head on an early critic of Oberlin who insisted: "This Amalgamation of sexes won't do. If you live in a Powder House you blow up once in a while." They overcame, but perhaps never completely, the criticisms implicit in the conversation attributed to a college girl and her father, in which the proud daughter reported, "I have made 100 in algebra, 96 in Latin, 90 in Greek, 88½ in mental philosophy and 95 in history; are you not satisfied with my record?" and her father responded, "Yes, indeed, and if your husband happens to know anything about housekeeping, sewing and cooking, I am sure your married life will be very happy."[4]

Of course not everywhere did the idea of higher education for women achieve victories. As late as 1895 the faculty of the University of Virginia announced its considered opinion that women students were often physically unsexed by the

[3] Ibid., pp. 20, 28, 53, 99.
[4] Woody: *A History of Women's Education*, II, 52, 155; Robert Samuel Fletcher: *A History of Oberlin College from its Foundation through the Civil War* (Oberlin, 1943), I, 377.

strain of study, and at Vanderbilt a student noted that "No man wants to come home at night and find his wife testing some new process for manufacturing oleomargarine, or in the observatory sweeping the heavens for a comet." The answer to a question asked by an early foreign visitor to Wellesley remained somewhat ambiguous: "This is all very fine," he said, "but . . . how does it affect their chances [of marriage]?" [5] Andrew D. White had reported of coeducation in Ohio that "from no Colleges did a more hardy, manly, brave body of young men go into our armies than from Oberlin and Antioch," but the suspicion would long linger that coeducation deprived women of some of their infinite charm and gentleness and robbed men of some of the sternness and ruggedness on which society depended for its protection.[6]

And could the problem to which the *San Francisco Examiner* alluded in 1892 ever be altogether solved? "When the little winged god comes in the window," said the *Examiner*, "study flies out." Of course *that* wasn't the half of it. As William C. Russell, the vice president of Cornell, confessed in 1879: "When I have heard of a lady student calling one young man into the room, shutting the door, kissing him, it has produced distress which has embittered months of existence." At Stanford in the 1890's the loss of athletic contests to the University of California was attributed to what was called too much "queening," too little hard athletic practice. The girls had their troubles, too, and a story is told of a young Radcliffe student at the turn of the century whose education had become a passport to teach at a local school "in which she was obliged to flog boys so large that nothing but

[5] Philip Alexander Bruce: *History of the University of Virginia, 1819-1919* (New York, 1920-2), IV, 63-9; Edwin Mims: *History of Vanderbilt University* (Nashville, 1946), pp. 130-1; Woody: *A History of Women's Education*, II, 152.
[6] White: *Report . . . on Mr. Sage's Proposal to Endow a College for Women*, p. 22. For examples see Daniel Walker Hollis: *University of South Carolina* (Columbia, 1951-6), II, 170; and Woody: *A History of Women's Education*, II, 274-77, 301.

gallantry on their part enabled her to do it." And at Barnard at least one young girl stood helpless before the great oaken doors of the Columbia library until chivalry swung them open.[7]

But when all the returns were in, the higher education of women was termed a success. Oberlin found that coeducation elevated table manners and dinner conversation. Kansas reported not a "whimper of scandal." Iowa described coeducation as an "incitement to every virtue." Antioch was convinced that its young men were more manly; Michigan was prepared to correlate coeducation and marriage. The president of Ohio State concluded in 1897 that "this inter-training and equal training takes the simper out of the young women and the roughness out of the young men." [8]

It is probably true, as Dean Briggs of Harvard suggested in a Wellesley commencement address in 1904, that the movement for collegiate education for women created the serious "danger of intellectual unrest, of chafing, in the daily duties of later life, at the meagreness of intellectual opportunity" in the life that matrimony and motherhood would cut out for her. But who, on the other hand, would deny that higher learning for women had fulfilled the aspirations that the trustees of Randolph-Macon set before themselves in 1891: "To establish . . . a college . . . where the dignity and strength of fully-developed faculties and the charm of the highest literary culture may be acquired by our daughters without loss to woman's crowning glory—her gentleness and grace." [9]

[7] Woody: *A History of Women's Education*, II, 272; Rogers: *Cornell*, p. 228; Elliott: *Stanford*, pp. 132-6, 178-9; LeBaron Russell Briggs: *Routine and Ideals* (Boston, 1904), p. 139; Annie Nathan Meyer: *Barnard Beginnings* (Boston, 1935), p. 21.

[8] Woody: *A History of Women's Education*, II, 296-303; James E. Pollard: *History of the Ohio State University: The Story of its First Seventy-Five Years 1873-1948* (Columbus, 1952), p. 149.

[9] Briggs: *Routine and Ideals*, p. 101; Woody: *A History of Women's Education*, II, 150.

16

❧❦❧

Flowering of the
University Movement

In a spirit of optimism appropriate to the age President James B. Angell of the University of Michigan looked out upon the collegiate world in 1871 and concluded, "In this day of unparalleled activity in college life, the institution which is not steadily advancing is certainly falling behind."[1] The little sleepy colleges, the reluctant universities, the friends of the status quo—if they did not hear this call to action from one of the important new spokesmen for American higher education, they could not avoid the growing evidence that indeed there had never before been an age of such stirrings, such changes, perhaps, as President Angell said, such advance.

James McCosh was prodding a reluctant board at Princeton, Charles William Eliot was conquering a reluctant board at Cambridge. At Ithaca and Baltimore new departures in American higher education were being plotted. The land-grant colleges were sprouting, and the state universities were assuming new roles. So dynamic were the changes, so remarkably accelerated the influence of the new institutions and the

[1] James Burrill Angell: *Selected Addresses* (New York, 1912), p. 27.

new movements, so rapid the tendency of one institution to emulate the advances of a rival that a short thirteen years later John W. Burgess, an astute and perceptive professor at Columbia College in New York, was led to the observation: "I confess that I am unable to divine what is to be ultimately the position of Colleges which cannot become Universities and which will not be Gymnasia. I cannot see what reason they will have to exist. It will be largely a waste of capital to maintain them, and largely a waste of time to attend them. It is so now."[2]

It was well enough for the Columbia professor to dispose of two hundred and fifty years of American collegiate history and now to proclaim that the colleges had either to become universities or to remain advanced high schools. Every institution knew that it had to do *something*, even, if necessary, defend its right to stand still. What no institution could be certain of, however, was exactly what was meant by a university. President Eliot might proclaim that "a university cannot be built upon a sect"—which was unquestionably true in Germany and Cambridge, but was it not worth trying in the United States, where all things were possible?[3] What was one to say to the warnings of Professor Henry Vethake of the college in Philadelphia that called itself the University of Pennsylvania? Professor Vethake had pointed out that the German universities were largely supported by students preparing for three professional careers that did not even exist in the United States—teaching, the civil service, and diplomacy. The answer to the professor unquestionably was that the day had come when the United States *needed* professional teachers, professional public servants, and professional diplomats, and that the needs could not be served by the colleges. Very well, then, a university was a place that turned out pro-

[2] John W. Burgess: *The American University: When Shall it Be? Where Shall it Be? What Shall it Be?* (Boston, 1884), p. 5.
[3] Quoted in George Wilson Pierson: *Yale: College and University 1871-1937* (New Haven, 1952-5), I, 61.

fessional career men for opportunities that did not exist but
ought to. Was that a way to command public support? ⁴

As the years passed, confusion was piled on confusion, not
only because colleges changed their letterheads to read "university," but because the road to university purpose, function,
or status was in no sense clearly defined. At Virginia the university concept rested on a broad base of courses and departments in which a student could study in depth and with a
freedom unknown in the traditional institutions. At Johns
Hopkins, on the other hand, the position was developed that
a true university was postcollegiate in its orientation, that its
essence was located in the graduate faculty of arts and sciences whose life revolved around the advancement of learning. In Cambridge President Eliot was moving Harvard toward university status by purposefully obliterating or at least
diffusing the lines between undergraduate and graduate, between collegiate and scholarly. For Eliot the idea of a university was essentially a matter of spirit, and if an institution had
that spirit, there was no place within it where the university
spirit was out-of-bounds. In New Haven, however, where
there was a certain vested interest in the collegiate way, the
university idea, while clearly in the ascendancy, was as yet
still caged, and the Yale faculty was reluctant to contaminate
Yale College with the spirit that President Eliot was employ-
ing to reshape the whole outlook of Harvard College. At
Ithaca it seemed as though a university was being defined as
a place where anything could be studied, as a place where
physical chemistry, Greek, bridge-building, the diseases of
the cow, and military drill were equal.⁵

Variations on these many themes would give to the United
States a remarkable flowering of the university idea in the late
nineteenth and early twentieth centuries, but they would not

⁴ Richard J. Storr: *The Beginnings of Graduate Education in America*
(Chicago, 1953), p. 79.
⁵ See Pierson: *Yale*, I, 44-5; Daniel Walker Hollis: *University of
South Carolina* (Columbia, 1951-6), II, 10-11; Samuel Eliot Morison:
Three Centuries of Harvard 1636-1936 (Cambridge, 1936), p. 326.

give any one answer to the question: What is an American university? For as in its people, its geography, its churches, its economic institutions, the United States in its universities was to reveal a remarkable diversity, an unwillingness to be categorized, a variety that would encompass differences in wealth, leadership, public influence, regional needs.

But if there was to be no American university, as there was to be no American system of education, there would one day be scores of institutions of university status and distinction. At Worcester, in Massachusetts, G. Stanley Hall would endeavor to pattern Clark University after Johns Hopkins. In the West the state universities substituted for the traditional B.A. curriculum a whole collection of undergraduate departments and courses specializing in vocational subjects. Everywhere little colleges, taking their cue from Harvard, introduced an elective curriculum and waited to become universities. New York University adopted three traditional collegiate practices that won it much-needed support: it forged an alliance with the Presbyterian community in New York; it abandoned its practice of not charging tuition (which among New York's better families had given the institution a reputation as a pauper's college); and it moved to an uptown site where a campus and other collegiate delights would be possible. And then, having assured itself of a nonuniversity base, New York University successfully inaugurated a vigorous program of postgraduate professional work and in time became a university.[6]

Probably for most Americans, however, the image of an American university would most closely approximate that which was being hammered out in the state universities of the West. John Hiram Lathrop, president of the University of Missouri, said in 1864: "The idea of an American University

[6] W. Carson Ryan: *Studies in Early Graduate Education: The Johns Hopkins, Clark University, The University of Chicago* (New York, 1939), pp. 47-90; Wallace W. Atwood: *The First Fifty Years: An Administrative Report* (Worcester, 1937), pp. 1-10; Theodore F. Jones, ed.: *New York University 1832-1932* (New York, 1933), pp. 137-50.

is a central school of Philosophy . . . , surrounded by the
Professional Schools, embracing not only the Departments of
Law, Medicine, and Divinity, but the Normal School for the
education of teachers, and Schools of Agriculture and the
Useful Arts." [7]

By 1872 this idea of a university as a collection of disparate
agencies was well-developed in the United States, and in his
inaugural address as president of the University of California, Daniel Coit Gilman gave expression to a university concept that was just about large enough to cover anything that
might henceforth occur under the roof of an American university: "It is a university, and not a high school, nor a college,
nor an academy of sciences, nor an industrial school which
we are charged to build [here]. Some of these features may
be included in or developed with the University, but the University means more than any or all of them. The university
is the most comprehensive term that can be employed to indicate a foundation for the promotion and diffusion of knowledge—a group of agencies organized to advance the arts and
sciences of every sort, and train young men as scholars for all
the intellectual callings of life." [8] Within Gilman's definition
were the seeds of growth which enabled the head of one of
the great philanthropic foundations to observe one day in the
next century: "From the exposition of esoteric Buddhism to
the management of chain grocery stores, . . . [the American
university] offers its services to the inquiring young American." [9] Perhaps no one will ever come closer to defining the
American university.

The university movement in the United States owed more
to the German than to English or French examples, with the
consequence that university did *not* mean—as it did in Eng-

[7] Jonas Viles, *et al.*: *The University of Missouri: A Centennial History* (Columbia, 1939), p. 108.
[8] Daniel C. Gilman: *The Building of the University: An Inaugural
Address Delivered at Oakland, Nov. 7th, 1872* (San Francisco, 1872),
p. 6.
[9] Henry S. Pritchett of the Carnegie Foundation in Howard J.
Savage, *et al.*: *American College Athletics* (New York, 1929), p. x.

land—purely an examining body for the products of the teaching bodies or colleges, nor did it mean—as it did in France—an administrative organization for supervising and regulating instruction at large. On the other hand the American university was no simple reflection of the German university, which was a group of faculties that prepared young men for the learned professions. As President Arthur Twining Hadley of Yale was fond of pointing out, the American university was everything and none of these things: a teaching body; an examining body; a supervisory and regulating body, in the case of the state institutions; and just as ready to prepare young men for the unlearned as for the learned professions.[1] Yet, because the German example was paramount, almost everywhere in the creation of an American university there was a fundamental attachment to the graduate faculty of arts and sciences, to the idea of a body of scholars and students pushing forward the frontiers of pure knowledge.

The distance between the era of the colleges and the era of the universities was everywhere apparent. And perhaps no more so than in the 1893 remarks of Professor Basil Gildersleeve, bearer of the tradition of scholarship at Johns Hopkins. Sensing the meaning for America of the young scholars flowing in accelerating numbers from the graduate schools in Baltimore, New York, Worcester, Chicago, New Haven, Cambridge, Ann Arbor, and Madison, he recalled how as a youth he had fled to Germany to prepare himself for a professorship, for to have prepared himself in the United States would have been impossible and to have argued for the necessity of professional preparation would have opened himself to ridicule and charges of absurdity.[2]

---

[1] Walton C. John: *Graduate Study in Universities and Colleges in the United States* (Washington, 1935), p. 35.

[2] John C. French: *A History of the University Founded by Johns Hopkins* (Baltimore, 1946), p. 275.

Now, all that was changed. It had begun at Yale in 1856 when James Dwight Dana had asked, "Why not have here, The American University?" The answer he wanted may not have been forthcoming, but in 1860 Yale decided to offer the Ph.D. for high attainments in its graduate Department of Philosophy and the Arts. In 1861 Yale awarded three doctoral degrees, the first earned Ph.D.'s in American history. By 1876, the year that Johns Hopkins dedicated itself to the development of the Ph.D., the precedent set by Yale was being followed in twenty-five institutions which that year awarded a total of forty-four Ph.D. degrees. The work represented by these degrees was of uneven quality; some of them were probably awarded to faculty members of the institution as a means of gilding the college catalogue. But the degrees meant that the notion of serious study beyond the B.A. was being widely established, and with the founding of Johns Hopkins impetus was given to the organization of graduate study into separate schools.[3]

Columbia created an advanced school of political and social science in 1880, and Michigan achieved something comparable the next year; Yale put its graduate studies into formal order in 1882. In 1889 Clark in Worcester and Catholic University in Washington were created in the image of Johns Hopkins. In 1890 a great old university, Harvard, and a great new university, Chicago, established graduate schools of arts and sciences. In the 1890's such state universities as Michigan, Wisconsin, Nebraska, and Kansas found the funds and the will to follow suit, and in the South, Vanderbilt led in the revival of southern intellectual life.[4]

[3] Storr: *The Beginnings of Graduate Education*, pp. 57-8; John: *Graduate Study*, p. 19.
[4] John Howard Van Amringe, et al.: *A History of Columbia University 1754-1904* (New York, 1904), pp. 220-60; Byrne Joseph Horton: *The Graduate School (its Origin and Administrative Development)* (New York, 1940), pp. 73-7; Elizabeth M. Farrand: *History of the University of Michigan* (Ann Arbor, 1885), p. 270; Burke A. Hinsdale: *History of the University of Michigan* (Ann Arbor, 1906), p. 85; Samuel Eliot Morison: *The Development of Harvard University Since the Inauguration of President Eliot 1869-1929* (Cambridge, 1930), pp.

Reviewing these remarkable indications of university development, President Eliot noted in 1902: "The graduate school of Harvard University . . . did not thrive, until the example of Johns Hopkins forced our Faculty to put their strength into the development of our institution for graduates. And what was true of Harvard was true of every other university in the land which aspired to create an advanced school of arts and sciences." By 1900 Hopkins had probably lost its eminence as "the premier American Ph.D. mill" to Harvard, but in 1926, just fifty years after its founding, Johns Hopkins could locate 1,000 of its 1,400 graduates on American college and university faculties. In twenty-four institutions ten or more Hopkins graduates testified to the role of the institution in Baltimore in establishing and in diffusing the university idea.[5] But the day had already passed when so major a control or so major an achievement could be continued in one institution. For Johns Hopkins had taught well: both its spirit and its instrument of recruitment, the graduate fellowship, were contagious.

The use of fellowships as an inducement for graduate students was known in the United States before Johns Hopkins demonstrated how important they would be to the flowering of the university movement. Indeed, in 1731 the Reverend Dean of Derry, Ireland, the later Bishop George Berkeley, had deeded to Yale College his farm in Newport, Rhode Island, with the stipulation that it be used to support fellowships in Greek and Latin for the period between the B.A. and the awarding of the M.A., a degree which customarily went to all college men who three years after graduation were not in jail. In 1822, also at Yale, funds were provided

451-62; Merle Curti and Vernon Carstensen: *The University of Wisconsin: A History, 1848-1925* (Madison, 1949), I, 630 ff.; Edwin Mims: *History of Vanderbilt University* (Nashville, 1946), p. 150.

[5] French: *Johns Hopkins*, pp. 86, 204-5; Morison: *Harvard: Three Centuries*, p. 336.

which were to accumulate until 1848 and then be used to
provide graduate fellowships.[6]

The idea of using fellowships as a means of stimulating advanced study in American institutions received encouragement in the 1850's from a rather popular book of the period, *Five Years in an English University*, the autobiographical account of a young American at Cambridge who had been impressed by the role of fellowships as inducements to advanced study in the English universities. In the 1850's, however, the university movement did not catch on, and although the faculty of the University of Pennsylvania gave thought to the idea of founding fellowships, they were more impressed by their colleague who asked where the money was going to come from and who then added, "The *Yankee* graduates, at any rate, will inquire before they start, whether the cash has been paid in."[7]

In the early 1870's a number of institutions—among them Princeton, Columbia, and Harvard—adopted the custom of subsidizing foreign study for especially promising graduates of their own colleges, but it fell to Johns Hopkins to establish and systematize the practice of populating graduate schools with subsidized students of promise from everywhere.[8] The Hopkins decision to offer $500 fellowships reflected the uncertainty which the board of trustees must have felt for the immediate success of their venture into graduate education, but it also revealed their determination to provide the Hopkins faculty with students capable of keeping the faculty "constantly stimulated." Their determination was rewarded, and unquestionably "the first twenty-one fellows at Johns

[6] William Lathrop Kingsley, ed.: *Yale College: A Sketch of its History* (New York, 1879), I, 57-62; Storr: *The Beginnings of Graduate Education*, pp. 32-3.

[7] Storr: *The Beginnings of Graduate Education*, pp. 60-1, 65-6, 172; Charles Astor Bristed: *Five Years in an English University* (New York, 1852); Storr: op. cit., p. 80.

[8] Thomas Jefferson Wertenbaker: *Princeton 1746-1896* (Princeton, 1946), pp. 301-2; Van Amringe: *Columbia*, pp. 142, 221; French: *Johns Hopkins*, pp. 39-41; Hugh Hawkins: *Pioneer: A History of the Johns Hopkins University, 1874-1889* (Ithaca, 1960), pp. 79-90, 120-2.

Hopkins were . . . a more remarkable group of college graduates than had ever before gathered for study anywhere in America." Among them were: Herbert Baxter Adams, who pioneered in the establishment of advanced historical studies in the United States; Henry C. Adams, who carried the new learning and the new history to the University of Michigan; Walter Hines Page, who became Woodrow Wilson's wartime ambassador to England; and Josiah Royce, who was headed for a career as an eminent Harvard philosopher. The early success of Johns Hopkins rested in part on its program of fellowships, a device which would become a characteristic element in the creation of every major American university.[9]

If the graduate school of arts and sciences with its auxiliary program of fellowships was central to the achievement of university status, another emphasis was provided by a spirit of vocationalism and by the incorporation of professional schools in the university structure. Frederick A. P. Barnard in an 1855 report which he prepared as president of the University of Alabama wrote with the blindest of certainty that a craft society and its characteristic apprentice system were so permanent a feature of American life that vocationalism would never intrude itself upon institutions of formal learning. "While time lasts," he then wrote, "the farmer will be made in the field, the manufacturer in the shop, the merchant in the counting room, the civil engineer in the midst of the actual operation of his science."[1]

The emergence, after the Civil War, of land-grant colleges and institutes of technology; the rapidly accumulating knowledge of a technical nature which required some orderly synthesis; the requirements of a now complex, industrial society with its need for experts of the most specialized sort—all this

[9] Hawkins: *Johns Hopkins*, p. 83.
[1] Walter P. Rogers: *Andrew D. White and the Modern University* (Ithaca, 1942), p. 108.

helped to unleash a spirit of vocationalism which many of the growing universities not only found impossible to resist but sought to encourage. And in a bid for survival, many small colleges which had no chance of becoming universities were led to introduce into their undergraduate programs such courses as pharmaceutical chemistry, engineering English, mechanical drawing, library science, and the history and philosophy of education. In the state universities whole undergraduate programs could be built around what might be only a course in one of the smaller institutions. Coeducation served this tendency to vocationalism by helping to turn most American colleges into teacher-training institutions; by the end of the nineteenth century, American colleges and universities were producing more teachers than anything else.[2] The strength of this vocational emphasis was demonstrated by the degree to which it became embedded even in a place like Yale. In 1899 Yale permitted B.A. candidates to include law and medical courses in their programs, and this movement continued until Yale found itself offering undergraduate majors in law, medicine, theology, art, and music.[3]

It became one function of the university movement in America to blur the distinction that had long existed between the connotation of profession and that of vocation. The tendency had been to reserve the word profession for those occupations that required some formal study and instruction. As a consequence, there were but three professions: divinity, law, and medicine, with perhaps a fourth, the military. All other occupations were of a lesser nature, of the sort that could be learned "on the job." Farmers, merchants, and manufacturers pursued vocations. The graduates of the theological seminaries, the law schools, and the medical schools pursued professions. College professors had long been in a kind of ambiguous no-man's land, in which specific preparation was not necessary but in which many practitioners had stud-

[2] Bailey B. Burritt: *Professional Distribution of College and University Graduates* (Washington, 1912), p. 77.
[3] Pierson: *Yale*, I, 213, 222-9.

ied and been certified as professional clergymen. The university movement, however, contained a respect for the changing world beyond the campus which recognized the need for rigorous professional training in engineering and many other phases of applied science; in its pursuit of scholarship and learning the movement created a profession of college and university teachers; it accepted the democratic argument that what had been the unlearned vocations could and should be learned professions.

In assuming responsibility for providing formal professional education, the universities revealed the degree to which American higher education had now broadly entered into the life of the people. The early collegiate reformers had failed in their efforts to bring the colleges into any vital connection with the economic life of the nation. Now, the tendencies of an equalitarian and expanding industrial society made no distinction between what might be learned on the job or in the university: in the United States all careers were honorable, and therefore the university would offer itself as an appropriate agency of instruction and preparation for all careers for which some formal body of knowledge existed. Increasingly, therefore, the universities supplanted the system of apprenticeship in the old professions and brought into equality with them a whole range of vocations on their way to professional status.

The blurring of the distinction between professional and vocational was paralleled by a blurring of the equally ancient distinction between the college, which had been considered preprofessional, and the separate or attached divinity, law, and medical schools, which had been considered professional.[4] The elective principle brought within the range of

[4] See Roland H. Bainton: *Yale and the Ministry* (New York, 1957); Henry K. Rowe: *History of Andover Theological Seminary* (Newton, 1933); George H. Williams, ed.: *The Harvard Divinity School* (Cambridge, 1954); Frederick C. Hicks: *Yale Law School: from the founders to Dutton, 1845-1869* (New Haven, 1936); Alfred Zantzinger Reed: *Training for the Public Profession of the Law* (New York, 1915); Willard Hurst: *The Growth of American Law* (Boston, 1950); Henry

undergraduates all kinds of courses and programs of concentration for which the most compelling argument was their usefulness in preparing for a career. A Harvard student who studied hardly anything but Greek and Latin was probably going to be a teacher of the classics, and certainly the young men who concentrated in physics and chemistry expected to put their learning to use in some practical way.

In one sense, this spirit of career preparation was not something new, for in the old-time colleges the student body was composed largely of young men headed for the three learned professions. The practical relationship between the ancient course of study and those professions had been one of the arguments of the Yale faculty in 1828. What was now happening, however, was an incredible expansion in the number of careers for which formal study and instruction was possible, useful, and demanded. The implications of the Jacksonian emphasis were quite clear: all careers were equal, and all careers demanded an equal hearing and an equal opportunity within the university. The colleges were now, in their university phase, required to welcome and to serve potential merchants, journalists, manufacturers, chemists, teachers, inventors, artists, musicians, dieticians, pharmacists, scientific farmers, and engineers on an equal basis with students of law, theology, and medicine.[5]

B. Shafer: *The American Medical Profession, 1783 to 1850* (New York, 1936); William Frederick Norwood: *Medical Education in the United States before the Civil War* (Philadelphia, 1944); Abraham Flexner: *Medical Education in the United States and Canada* (New York, 1910); Francis R. Packard: *History of Medicine in the United States* (2 vols., New York, 1931).

[5] Arthur C. Weatherhead: *The History of Collegiate Education in Architecture in the United States* (Los Angeles, 1941); Thomas Thornton Read: *The Development of Mineral Industry Education in the United States* (New York, 1941); Charles Riborg Mann: *A Study of Engineering Education* (New York, 1918); De Forest O'Dell: *The History of Journalism Education in the United States* (New York, 1935); Jessie M. Pangburn: *The Evolution of the American Teachers College* (New York, 1932); Robert A. Gordon and James E. Howell: *Higher Education for Business* (New York, 1959); Frank C. Pierson, et al.: *The Education of American Businessmen* (New York, 1959);

The university movement did not intrude the spirit of professionalism into the life of American higher education. The old college was, after all, preprofessional, regardless of its contention that the ancient course of study was a universally appropriate basic education. Moreover, many of the colleges, particularly in the cities, had spawned or entered into alliances with theological schools, law schools, or medical schools. Professorships in theology had been the first to appear, at both Harvard and Yale before 1750. Thomas Jefferson introduced the first law professorship at William and Mary, and in 1765 the first professorship in medicine appeared at the College of Philadelphia. Although professional schools of high standards would be one result of the university movement, during the collegiate era affiliated or integral schools of theology, medicine, and law were beginning to replace the more ancient practice of apprenticeship and to bring professional training to the campus. Yet, if the university movement did not introduce an element of professional concern to higher education in the United States, it was nonetheless largely responsible for recognizing and nurturing new professional interests that did not draw their inspiration from the ancient learning.[6]

The new professions, therefore, were not as respectable as the old professions. The old professionalism was characterized by a serious regard for the liberal studies and by the degree to which the central subject of every liberal study was man himself. The new professionalism, on the other hand, studied things, raised questions not so much about man's ultimate role and his ultimate responsibility as it did about whether this or that was a good way to go about achieving some immediate and limited object. There was, therefore, a difference, a *real* difference in kind between the old and the

Melvin T. Copeland: *And Mark an Era: The Story of the Harvard Business School* (Boston, 1958).

[6] Robert L. Kelly: *Theological Education in America* (New York, 1924). Useful short histories of early professional education may be found in Nicholas Murray Butler, ed.: *Monographs on Education in the United States* (2 vols., Albany, 1900).

new professions, a difference that had once been clarified by the distinction between profession and vocation. The flowering American university took what were vocations and turned them into professions; the old distinction would be lost in the process.

The American university, in one of its characteristic manifestations, thus became a collection of postgraduate professional schools, schools which replaced the apprentice system in law, put responsibility into the study of medicine, tended to relegate theology into a separate corner, created education as an advanced field of study, and responded—in one institution or another—to the felt necessities of the time or the region, thus spawning appropriate schools at appropriate times, whether they were schools of business administration, forestry, journalism, veterinary medicine, social work, or Russian studies.[7]

The developing universities revealed an appetite for expansion, a gluttony for work, a passion for growth which constituted one of their most fundamental characteristics. Because there was no agreed-upon idea of what an American university was or might be, there were no theoretical or philosophical limits which the university developers might place upon themselves. Only the lack of funds might keep them in harness, but even that could not be counted on in an era of building and rivalry which could draw on the resources of a remarkable number of millionaires.

If a university could not procure the faculty it wanted, it was not thereby frustrated: it borrowed a faculty. Andrew D. White of Cornell instituted the practice, and for a term each he was able to offer in Ithaca: James Russell Lowell, Louis

[7] For typical experiences see Curti and Carstensen: *Wisconsin*, II; Morison: *Harvard University Since the Inauguration of President Eliot;* Waterman Thomas Hewitt: *Cornell University: A History* (New York, 1905), II. Under the general editorship of Dwight C. Miner, Columbia University published a series of monographs on the schools of the University: *The Bicentennial History of Columbia University* (1954-7).

Agassiz, George William Curtis, and others. To Johns Hopkins, Daniel Coit Gilman brought for short periods Simon Newcomb, William James, Sidney Lanier, and Lord Bryce. At Stanford, David Starr Jordan put into service the talents of a former president of the United States, Benjamin Harrison.[8]

Another instrument of growth was the concept of federation which enabled semi-autonomous institutions to cluster around a core institution, which was probably an old college become a new university. The Rhode Island School of Design allied itself with Brown, the Institute of Paper Chemistry with Lawrence College, the California College of Pharmacy with the University of California, and most of the theological seminaries in New York with Columbia. The summer session and the extension course were likewise agencies devoted to the enlargement of university purpose. It took an institution in New York, City College, to discover a means for putting to full use whatever time the normal university program now left in the year: in 1909 it inaugurated the first night-school course of study leading to a bachelor's degree.[9]

But the spirit of the new American universities was far from adequately revealed in these devices. A more startling revelation was in the inaugural address with which Andrew Lipscomb in 1875 opened Vanderbilt University, the new capstone of Methodist education in the South. How remote from the narrow sectarianism, how different from the suspicion of intellect, how hostile to all the tendencies that held the little Methodist colleges in the grips of pettiness and ignorance, how remote from all this were the words that Methodism sponsored at Vanderbilt in 1875: "The University is

[8] Rogers: *Cornell*, pp. 71, 155-6; French: *Johns Hopkins*, pp. 88-92; Orrin Leslie Elliott: *Stanford University: The First Twenty-Five Years* (Stanford University, 1937), p. 114.

[9] Daniel Sammis Sanford, Jr.: *Inter-Institutional Agreements in Higher Education* (New York, 1934), pp. 18-19; Watson Dickerman: *The Historical Development of the Summer Session in the United States* (Chicago, 1948); Louis E. Reber: *University Extension in the United States* (Washington, 1914); S. Willis Rudy: *The College of the City of New York: A History, 1847-1947* (New York, 1949), p. 315.

bound to recognize every department of true thought, every branch of human knowledge, every mode of thorough culture. . . . What is best in the University is the catholicity of its views. . . . It must have an open-minded hospitality to all truth and must draw men together in the unity of a scholarly temper." [1]

In social arrangements as well, the university movement created its own spirit; and while the collegiate tradition was persuasive enough and strong enough to sustain and to expand the fraternity movement, there now appeared in the environs of the American university such an institution as the renowned rooming and boarding house of Mrs. DuBois Egerton at 132 West Madison Street in Baltimore. There elegant style in the grand southern manner, old silver, fine furniture, excellent food, and twenty paying guests—Johns Hopkins faculty and students—in the 1870's and 1880's created a salon of high distinction, where such men as G. Stanley Hall, Sidney Lanier, James Russell Lowell, and William James were not unknown. [2]

The new university spirit was likely to appear almost anywhere, and although in 1884 the president of the University of Arkansas actually rejected it, he publicly charged that some subversive university-minded faculty members had imported from the University of Virginia the two habits that were doing Arkansas the most harm: high standards of scholarship and faculty neglect of student conduct outside the classroom. At Indiana University in 1892 a professor with the true spirit suggested that the faculty should sit once a year to award diplomas to students who were ready and to deny diplomas to those who were not ready, "irrespective of how long . . . [they] may have been in residence." Let the college degree, he said, be a "certificate of proficiency" instead of a "certificate of residence." [3]

[1] Mims: *Vanderbilt,* pp. 63-4.
[2] French: *Hopkins,* pp. 77-8.
[3] John Hugh Reynolds and David Yancey Thomas: *History of the University of Arkansas* (Fayetteville, 1910), p. 125; James Albert

Where the universities most revealed their spirit was in the manner in which they accommodated science and secularism, freed themselves, for better or worse, from the religious orientation which had been so fundamental in the old colleges, embraced curiosity as a value, and enshrined intellect as the moving force of the university. This spirit would in turn be taken into the colleges themselves by the graduates of the universities, but in the universities it would achieve its most perfect expression.

Although it is probably true that throughout the nineteenth century piety outranked intellect as a consideration in the recruitment of faculty in most American colleges and universities, nowhere in the universities was there a prolonged or successful readiness to harness science to an outworn theology. The presidents of the new universities were more likely to take the direction of President Gilman. In his remarks one day to a group of Johns Hopkins students, Gilman said that it was all right with him if they purchased a bust of Charles Darwin, but it might be prudent to surround it with the busts of a few less controversial scientists. Princeton could harbor President James McCosh, one of the men in America most receptive to the theory of evolution, and then his successor, President Patton, a Presbyterian minister who said he was prepared "to fight the whole Presbyterian Church" in order to establish Princeton's right to put a beer and wine bar in the Princeton Inn.⁴ The forces of reaction had their day at Vanderbilt, but the atmosphere of the universities was increasingly secular, increasingly intellectual, increasingly charged with the excitement of a whole world of truth and exploration opened up by the concept of evolution.

The great academic leaders of the period—Eliot, White, and Gilman—were themselves evolutionists; the scientists,

Woodburn: *History of Indiana University: 1820-1902* (Bloomington, 1940), p. 410.
⁴ Mims: *Vanderbilt*, pp. 27-8, 64, 102; Varnum Lansing Collins: *Princeton* (New York, 1914), p. 223; Wertenbaker: *Princeton*, pp. 311-13, 374-5.

young and old, accepted Darwinism with remarkable readiness; and all the energies that had been undermining priestly influence and aristocratic tradition in America were friendly to the new orientation. In 1881 at Michigan State twenty-six of thirty-three seniors admitted to a belief in evolution.[5]

While Darwin and the implications of his theory for the whole fabric of moral certainty and divine authority would unsettle many campuses, there was also a significant effort to reconcile science and religion, either by ignoring the incompatibilities that scientific study and higher criticism now suggested or by discovering ways in which the two interests might be kept distinct. Conflict might be avoided by somehow holding religion apart or by refusing to recognize any conflict at all, but the determination to achieve reconciliation was so generally widespread that it is said that a visitor once found posted on Noah Porter's office door in New Haven the notice: "At 11:30 on Tuesday Professor Porter will reconcile science and religion." [6] The conflict over Darwinism in the colleges was less a matter of whether evolution was true than a matter of whether the old regime or the new regime would prevail, whether piety or intellect, whether authority resting on received truth or on scientific evidence.

[5] Madison Kuhn: *Michigan State: The First Hundred Years* (East Lansing, 1955), p. 91.

[6] Charles Elmer Allison: *A Historical Sketch of Hamilton College, Clinton, New York* (Yonkers, 1889), pp. 35-8; Hawkins: *Johns Hopkins*, p. 72; Pierson: *Yale*, I, 57; Richard Hofstadter and Walter P. Metzger: *The Development of Academic Freedom in the United States* (New York, 1955), pp. 320-66. See also David Duncan Wallace: *History of Wofford College* (Nashville, 1951), p. 57; Allen P. Tankersley: *College Life at Old Oglethorpe* (Athens, 1951), pp. 67-82; Henry Morton Bullock: *A History of Emory University* (Nashville, 1936), p. 142; G. Wallace Chessman: *Denison: The Story of an Ohio College* (Granville, 1957), pp. 144-6; Louis G. Geiger: *University of the Northern Plains: A History of the University of North Dakota 1883-1958* (Grand Forks, 1958), p. 72; Lucy Lilian Notestein: *Wooster of the Middle West* (New Haven, 1937), pp. 184-6; Charles Henry Rammelkamp: *Illinois College: A Centennial History 1829-1929* (New Haven, 1928), p. 386; Ralph Henry Gabriel: *Religion and Learning at Yale: The Church of Christ in the College and University, 1757-1957* (New Haven, 1958), pp. 152-86.

Another index of the new spirit was the decision to distinguish between academic grades and delinquency demerits in the ranking of students. In 1869 Harvard made a sharp distinction between scholarship and conduct, ranking students henceforth on the basis of academic grades alone. As for character, that no longer would count in the ranking of students. They would be equal in the ranks where clearly what now mattered was intellectual performance in the classroom, not model behavior in the dormitory or the village tavern.[7] A commitment to the needs of scholarship meant that the universities expressed their purposes no longer in chapel, no longer in the senior year with the president on moral and intellectual philosophy. That course was now a half-dozen subjects spread throughout the curriculum, and beginning to overshadow the chapel itself were the science laboratories and the libraries, as necessary to the new dispensation as the chapel had been to the old.

In the meantime, the American university, in all of its varieties, flowered. One by one the state universities arrived at a point at which they were taken in hand by a dynamic and university-minded president and sent on their way to becoming true universities. At Michigan the job was done by James B. Angell, at Minnesota by William Watts Folwell and Cyrus Northrup, at Wisconsin by Charles R. Van Hise, at California by Benjamin Ide Wheeler, at Georgia by Walter B. Hill. Ohio State moved into university territory in the late 1890's under President James H. Canfield, and in the South beginning in 1893 Chancellor James H. Kirkland at Vanderbilt provided university leadership for a developing southern movement that included Tulane, Duke, and Emory. In 1885 President McCosh began his successful campaign to achieve university status for Princeton, and at Columbia the impetus

[7] Mary Lovett Smallwood: *An Historical Study of Examinations and Grading Systems in Early American Universities* (Cambridge, 1935), p. 74.

to university growth provided by Frederick A. P. Barnard and Seth Low culminated by 1904 in a collection of eleven distinct faculties conducting fourteen federated colleges and schools. William Pepper and Charles C. Harrison led the way at the University of Pennsylvania.[8]

But no episode was more important in shaping the outlook and the expectations of American higher education during these years than the founding of the University of Chicago, one of those events in American history that brought into focus the spirit of an age. The cast of characters itself was remarkable: John D. Rockefeller, now busily engaged in good works, in 1888 having come to the conclusion that he would like to found a new college in Chicago, but waiting for the voice of his Baptist denomination to call upon him to do so; Thomas W. Goodspeed, secretary of the Baptist Union Theological Seminary in Chicago, using his influence to shape a decision for Chicago; Augustus H. Strong of the Rochester Theological Seminary, using his influence to shape a decision for New York; the Reverend Frederick T. Gates, secretary of the American Baptist Education Society, holding off the small and hungry Baptist colleges throughout the land; and William Rainey Harper, young Baptist layman and Hebrew scholar, in 1888 in his thirty-second year the holder of three professorships at Yale, one of the most incredible men to move across the university scene.[9]

In the two years between 1890 and 1892 while the univer-

[8] Farrand: *Michigan*, pp. 217 ff.; James Gray: *The University of Minnesota 1851-1951* (Minneapolis, 1951), pp. 39, 83 ff., 122-36; Curti and Carstensen: *Wisconsin*, II, pp. 87-8 ff.; Robert Sibley: *The Romance of the University of California* (San Francisco, 1928), pp. 39 ff.; Robert Preston Brooks: *The University of Georgia Under Sixteen Administrations 1785-1955* (Athens, 1956), p. 111; James E. Pollard: *History of the Ohio State University: The Story of its First Seventy-Five Years 1873-1948* (Columbus, 1952), pp. 140-3; Mims: *Vanderbilt*, pp. 13-98; Wertenbaker: *Princeton*, pp. 339-73; Van Amringe: *Columbia*, pp. 199-306; Edward Potts Cheyney: *History of the University of Pennsylvania 1740-1940* (Philadelphia, 1940), pp. 257-332 ff.

[9] Thomas Wakefield Goodspeed: *A History of the University of Chicago Founded by John D. Rockefeller: The First Quarter Century* (Chicago, 1916), pp. 1-44.

sity was taking shape, the American people were exposed to the kind of activity they were accustomed to associating with the great captains of industry. Harper enlisted the millionaires of Chicago in a friendly rivalry with Rockefeller, the outsider, and although all of them put together could not outgive John D. Rockefeller, an informal working agreement developed which by 1916 would have Chicago providing eight million dollars' worth of land and buildings and Rockefeller thirty-five million dollars' worth of endowment. Of course anything of this dimension had not occurred to Rockefeller, but as Harper's plans developed, as his vision began to chew up block after block of Chicago real estate, as he got around in late 1891 to recruiting his first faculty, he simply needed more money, and he put Gates, who by now was Rockefeller's chief philanthropic guide in Chicago, in pursuit of another two million dollars. To a telegram from Gates, Rockefeller replied: "It is of course a surprise," but soon he was adding a second million to the initial $600,000 which he had intended to be the limit of his Chicago venture; in ninety days the men of Chicago responded with a million of their own.[1]

All these new millions cramped the style of eastern skeptics who had charged that with insufficient funds the University of Chicago would never get beyond the planning stage, and unquestionably they furthered Harper's cause when he went East to recruit a faculty. They also characteristically made Harper want more—more millions, more professors, more buildings, and the word spread across the land that great things were taking place in Chicago.

Applications for professorships came from everywhere, and Harper was in an optimistic mood when he undertook the greatest mass raid on American college faculties in history. When he was finished he had collected eight former college or seminary presidents, including Alice Freeman Palmer of Wellesley; he had relieved Yale of five professors; he had swooped down on Clark University, torn by dissension, and flown off with a majority of the academic staff, including

[1] Ibid., pp. 178-88, 273-96.

fellows, instructors, and fifteen professors. The day that
Harper arrived in Worcester sixteen faculty and student biologists were engaged in study; twelve of them followed him
to Chicago. The president of the University of Wisconsin
was happy to accept the chairmanship of the department of
geology. Harper did so well that with a budget for a faculty
of eighty, he hired for the first year a faculty of a hundred
and twenty. No wonder that Gates could write to Rockefeller: "It has grown on our wondering eyes month by month.
. . . I stand in awe of this thing. God is in it in a most wonderful way. It is a miracle." [2]

The miracle was opened to the public on October 1, 1892.
The night before, Harper had said to a colleague: "I wonder
if there will be a single student there tomorrow!" He need
not have wondered. They came from 33 states and 15 foreign
countries and provinces: 328 undergraduates, 210 graduates,
204 divinity students. What they found was a new model
American university, one which divided the twelve months
of the year into four academic quarters and invited its students to take a minimum three or an accelerated four; a university which divided the traditional four collegiate years
into two equal parts—the first to be known as the junior college or academic college, where the spirit would be collegiate
and preparatory, and the second to be known as the senior
college or the university college, where the spirit would be
advanced and scholarly; a university where a system of major
and minor studies permitted a student to pursue one subject
in depth while devoting less time to another. [3]

These were heady days at the University of Chicago. In
one of the residence houses an imaginative student suggested
that "any person desiring to establish a tradition should
present the same in writing, and, after lying on the table for
two weeks it could be established by a two thirds vote."

[2] Ibid., pp. 195-217; Ryan: *Studies in Early Graduate Education*, pp.
62-3; Goodspeed: *Chicago*, pp. 180-1.
[3] Ibid., pp. 190-4, 242, 264; *University of Chicago: Official Bulletin
No. 1* (Chicago, 1891), pp. 7-8, 11-12, 15-16.

Harper himself contemplated with satisfaction the disappearance of "the whole custom of the annual graduation" under the impact of continuous sessions. He greeted undergraduate complaints about conditions in commons by simply transferring its management to the student body.[4] In 1866 at Cornell, Andrew D. White had been close enough to the collegiate tradition to announce as a matter of policy that "in an institution of learning, facility and power in imparting truth are even more necessary than in discovering it." Now, not quite thirty years later, the university idea was so strong that Harper could announce: "It is proposed in this institution to make the work of investigation primary, the work of giving instruction secondary." At Chicago promotion would depend upon publication. No one was allowed to forget that what was being built at Chicago was not a college but a model American university.[5]

By 1906 Rockefeller would be saying: "It is the best investment I ever made in my life," notwithstanding the voracious appetite of William Rainey Harper for endowment and growth, notwithstanding Rockefeller's reluctant willingness to cover the eventual large deficits. With Harper's connivance Rockefeller had actually been beaten, overcome by one of his own enterprises. And a great new monument to the university idea now spoke of America's coming of age.[6]

By contrast, on the West Coast a new institution that had held out promise of high hope was proving to be a miserable disappointment. No contrast could be greater than that between the early years at Stanford and the beginnings of the University of Chicago. Rockefeller as a benefactor was a model of noninterference; Leland Stanford referred to "my university," and after his death Mrs. Stanford thought of herself as its owner, as in fact she was until she was ready to re-

[4] Goodspeed: *Chicago*, pp. 144-5, 255, 266.
[5] *Report of the Committee on Organization, Presented to the Trustees of the Cornell University. October 21st, 1886*, p. 18; Ryan: *Studies in Early Graduate Education*, p. 126.
[6] Goodspeed: *Chicago*, pp. 273-96, 397-8.

linquish her proprietary control. The financial arrangements for Stanford were sloppy, and they were confounded by Stanford's death, the panic of 1893, his custom of living on money borrowed from one of the subsidiaries of the Southern Pacific Railroad, and a government suit against his estate for fifteen million dollars.[7]

The inspiration for the undertaking (the early death of an only son) was sentimental, and this meant that after the government lost its suit Mrs. Stanford turned to the erection of building after building, to the exclusion of every other need, even refusing to allow anyone to raise funds elsewhere, for this was *her* monument to *her* son. The first president, David Starr Jordan, unlike Harper, approached his job with obsequiousness and a sense of fatalism; he was anything but a free agent. By 1911 he was advising members of the faculty to accept jobs elsewhere.[8] One member of the faculty had said a few years earlier on looking out upon the haggard, strained faces of his colleagues and the latest of Mrs. Stanford's monuments: "A new twenty-five thousand dollar stone entrance to the grounds is replacing the old sphinxes. . . . It is too bad that the men can't feed their families buff sandstone; it seems to be the one plentiful thing." [9]

These contrasting experiences in Chicago and California were proof that the United States was now wealthy enough to support one man's achievement and another man's folly. But they were much more than that. They were reminders of how much difference it made who the benefactor was, who his advisers were, who the president was; reminders that for all of the university spirit that was loose in the land, it was still possible, as Stanford made clear, to found a college when what one had in mind was a university. The experience in Chicago was a reminder that the material promise of America which in the days of the colleges had militated against college-going was now underwriting whole new ventures in

[7] Elliott: *Stanford*, pp. 3-154, *passim.*
[8] Ibid., pp. 251-308.
[9] Ibid., p. 298.

higher education; a reminder that the American people were in the process of harnessing untold material and human resources and creating in the American university, as Chicago proved, an institution of remarkable power and influence.

17

◆§§◆

Progressivism
and the Universities

During the decades when the friends of the university idea in the United States were fed only by dreams, anticipation, and frustration, they indulged their fancy by answering the question, "What should the American university be?" Their answers revealed a variety that was surpassed only by the variety which history itself provided. For the university idea was a configuration far more complex than the college idea; it took root when financial resources were available for the support of a remarkable assortment of schemes; and it came to fruition in the United States under the auspices of a wide range of agencies, secular and denominational, public and private.

The college—a far simpler thing, after all—lent itself more readily to precise or picturesque definition. A college was professor and student, man and boy, on opposite ends of a log. A college was that which was small, although there were those who loved it. A college was the lengthened shadow of its president. "College is back!" undergraduates would shout after the winter recess, thus defining the word as themselves.

Essentially these definitions were all the same: they were the inspiration of the experience of the English college in America.

The university idea, on the other hand, was far more elusive. One of the more successful efforts at grasping the sense of the idea was made in 1906 by Lyman Abbott, an eminent liberal clergyman and editor of *Outlook,* an influential religious periodical of the era. Abbott decided that the best way to understand the American university was to contrast it with its English and German prototypes. The English university, he concluded, revolved around culture, the production of gentleman aristocrats. The German university found its life not so much in culture as such but in scholarship, in erudition, in the production of scholars. The American university, the symbol of which Abbott located in the new University of Chicago, he saw as a place where the emphasis was placed neither on culture nor scholarship but on service, on the preparation of young Americans for active lives of service.

Ready to admit that the differences were relative, a matter of emphasis only, Abbott argued that the scholarship which an English university "regarded as a means and measure of self-development" and which a German university regarded "as an end in itself," the American university "has regarded as an equipment for service," for active men of affairs. Conceivably Abbott was not defining the American university so much as he was delineating characteristic differences among various national cultures, and it may well be that the time when he wrote had more to do with his discovery of the service ideal than did any intrinsic outlook of the American university.[1]

Unquestionably the service ideal of the American university derived in part from the timing of its flowering, for the universities in the United States achieved significant popular status during the years between the Spanish-American War and World War I when the spirit of what was called Progres-

[1] Lyman Abbott: "William Rainey Harper," *Outlook,* LXXXII (1906), 110-11.

sivism filled the land, a spirit which in one important manifestation revealed itself as a kind of middle-class sense of
obligation, a readiness to bring American society to some
new sense of its problems and its promises. The simultane-
ous spread of the Progressive spirit and of the university idea
would of course tend to reinforce the service element of
both. Both movements would in a sense argue for stability in
society, for an equality of opportunity now challenged by
labor unionism and socialism from below and by vast concentrations of wealth and power from above; both would
serve the idea of inevitable material and moral progress and
see the future as a place that would not only be bigger but
also better.

Progressivism was Theodore Roosevelt as police commissioner of New York, setting forth in a black cloak at mid-
night, in search of crime and delinquent police officers; it was
Lincoln Steffens discovering the collapse of democracy in
municipal government and describing it as "The Shame of
the Cities"; it was Robert La Follette fighting the lumber interests of Wisconsin, as elsewhere good Progressives fought
other interests of privilege: the railroads, the utility gang,
the sugar trust, the farm-machinery trust, even the bicycle
trust. Progressivism was a gigantic effort to deal with the discovery that the United States was a land of small farms and
country stores no longer; an effort to deal with the discovery of the slum, the political machine, the immigrant, the
monopoly, and the decline in ethical standards which was
registered in poisoned toys, dishonest advertising, tainted
meat, and toxic drugs. Progressivism was an expression of
conscience—middle class conscience, if you will—in the presence of conditions that derived from the urbanization and
industrialization of an essentially simple agrarian republic.

The Progressive cure for the failures of democracy was
more democracy: the preferential party primary, the Austral-
ian ballot, the secret ballot, the initiative and referendum, the
city manager, and finally, the vote for women. The cure for
progress was more progress: the taming and regulation of the

trusts, the disciplining and regulation of the railroads, the beginnings at legislative control over conditions of work. The cure was neither labor unionism nor state socialism, both of which were solutions of disillusionment and despair. Progressivism responded to its discovery with a characteristic American sense of optimism and hope, which rested on several centuries of material and moral achievement; it avoided extremes and called on American men and women of good will to serve the cause of progress with a renewed sense of good citizenship, with a new sense of responsibility in a democratic society.

After the long decades of free-wheeling, atomistic individualism which characterized nineteenth-century America, the appearance of a movement for which service was a touchstone was of considerable importance to higher education. Before Progressivism called them to their ancient obligation to service, the American colleges were lacking the vitality, the close connection with society, that had characterized the relationship between Harvard and the Puritans or, indeed, the relationship between any of the colonial colleges and the colonial society that sponsored them. In the nineteenth-century college, service was an ideal that fought for attention with the self-seeking which the American experience encouraged. The colleges implored their young men to give themselves to God, but fewer and fewer of them did so. The colleges, in the end, could not argue persuasively or successfully against success which, unless chastened by some sense of philanthropy or modified by some rare sense of proportion, was likely to be quite the opposite of service.

The American university in the Progressive period drew not only upon its ancient purpose of service, but also on the degree to which that purpose had not been allowed to wither even during the nineteenth century. As late as 1825 George Ticknor referred to Harvard College as "the oldest of our greater public schools," thus recognizing the obligations of Harvard as an instrument of the public will. President Eliot in his inaugural address, in which the psychology of individual

differences and the elective principle combined to create a
charter of curricular rights for the American college student,
did not go so far as to define the American university as a
success school where young men might indulge their interests on the way to some useful career. The university, he
said, would promise the community "a rich return of learning, poetry, and piety. . . . It [would] foster the sense of
public duty." Harvard, in other words, would not forget to
serve.[2]

On the eve of the Progressive period President Angell of
Michigan commented on how isolated the college of the
1850's had been from the people at large, on the degree to
which the popular image of the college had been of a "home
of useless and harmless recluses," on how little the colleges
had done to interest themselves in the elementary or secondary schools and how uninfluential they had been in the life of
the state. All this, said Angell, was in remarkable contrast to
the ideal of public service which now enlivened the great universities and brought them into the mainstream of American
experience.[3]

As a matter of emphasis and as a matter of widespread effectiveness, Angell was unquestionably right, but in at least
three respects he credited too little in the way of public service to the old colleges. After all, to a very significant degree
they provided society, whether it wanted them or not, with a
good share of its clergymen, lawyers, and doctors. The colleges served as trustworthy fountains of religious revivalism,
and they were not so remote from society as to fail to become deeply involved in the temperance movement in New
England and in the antislavery movement in the Middle West.

[2] George Ticknor: *Remarks on Changes Lately Proposed or Adopted
in Harvard College* (Boston, 1825), pp. 3-4; *Addresses at the Inauguration of Charles William Eliot as President of Harvard College, Tuesday,
October 19, 1869* (Cambridge, 1869), pp. 64-5.
[3] James Burrill Angell: "The Old College and the New University"
(1899) in *Selected Addresses* (New York, 1912), p. 150.

And in the ante bellum South the state university "occupied the position of greatest strategy in the making of Southern leadership. It was basic and fundamental—not in the people it reached directly, but in the influence it exerted through its students." At the University of North Carolina between 1798 and 1868 a record was compiled that would deny to President Angell any exclusive claim for public service as an ideal of the newer universities. The University of North Carolina provided the state during those years with thirteen governors and five senators, and other states of the South with seven governors and three senators. It sent forty-one graduates to the United States House of Representatives, and for more than two thirds of the time after 1815 the speakers of both houses of the North Carolina legislature were graduates of the university. At the College of Charleston in the 1850's members of the faculty were instrumental in founding the Society of Natural History, the South Carolina Historical Society, and the Carolina Art Association.[4]

Yet, Angell was entitled to his emphasis. In taking responsibility for shaping coherent systems of public elementary and secondary education, in abandoning the classical curriculum and substituting for it a curriculum of wider usefulness and popularity, the postwar western state universities assumed a central role in the life of the state. As for the land-grant institutions the legislation that created them clearly ordered them to serve, although they had some difficulty in learning exactly how. Moreover, the complex industrial society in which the new universities were establishing their ties with the people gave the universities opportunities for service that a simpler, agrarian environment had not permitted.

Time itself was on the side of the new universities, which took charge of the past and almost everywhere were instrumental in founding state historical societies and journals;

361 Progressivism and the Universities

young Ph.D.'s from Johns Hopkins, trained in the seminars of Herbert Baxter Adams, worked their way into the history of Illinois, North Dakota, and Oregon as if they had at their disposal the history of a thousand years of some ancient dukedom. In Iowa a professor exposed a lightning rod fake; in Kansas a professor developed a prairie-dog eradication program; at Cornell, Andrew D. White hired an experienced foreign-service officer to deliver a course of lectures on "The Diplomatic and Consular System of the United States"; Johns Hopkins, although a private university, created strong bonds between itself and the state with a marine laboratory, soil and weather surveys, and the services of its school of medicine in the solution of problems of public health. The University of Virginia added a department of forestry to its other state services.[5]

Almost everywhere the state universities became the major teacher-training agencies, setting standards for the public schools. The agricultural services of the agricultural colleges made effective bids for public support: at the University of Illinois before World War I over 100,000 letters a year sought agricultural information and advice. The engineering departments of the large institutions found themselves making useful commercial and mechanical devices, solving industrial problems. In 1894 at their annual meeting the National Brick Manufacturers Association went on record as deploring the absence in any university or college in the United States of courses or special facilities for the study of ceramics; before

[5] Allan Nevins: *Illinois* (New York, 1917), pp. 323-46; Louis G. Geiger: *University of the Northern Plains: A History of the University of North Dakota 1883-1958* (Grand Forks, 1958), p. 222; Henry D. Sheldon: *History of University of Oregon* (Portland, 1940), p. 103; Earle D. Ross: *A History of the Iowa State College of Agriculture and Mechanic Arts* (Ames, 1942), p. 165; Julius Terrass Willard: *History of the Kansas State College of Agriculture and Applied Science* (New York, 1940), p. 163; Walter P. Rogers: *Andrew D. White and the Modern University* (Ithaca, 1942), p. 130; John C. French: *A History of the University Founded by Johns Hopkins* (Baltimore, 1946), pp. 227-33; Philip Alexander Bruce: *History of the University of Virginia, 1819-1919* (New York, 1920-2), V, 61.

long Ohio State was developing a program in ceramics. Departments of history and political economy, patterned after Johns Hopkins and often staffed by its graduates, assumed the responsibility of advancing the idea of good government.[6]

Not all of these services became permeated with the spirit of Progressivism, but even those that seemed to be of the most mundane money-making sort could be construed by the Progressive imagination as serving the purposes of a better world. The campus chapters of the Y.M.C.A. were in many ways an undergraduate expression of the mood of Progressivism and of the developing service rationale of the colleges and universities. Bruce Barton, undergraduate president of the Amherst Y.M.C.A. chapter, revealed the Progressive temper in 1907. "Any man," said Barton, "who believes that God is always on the side of right, that Amherst is the greatest college in the world and who is trying to do the square thing by his fellows is welcomed into membership." Trying to do the square thing by one's fellows was, of course, in the same mood as Theodore Roosevelt's Square Deal. It was also in the mood that found the University of Chicago in 1902 preparing young men for careers in public service and Woodrow Wilson in the same year delivering an inaugural address at Princeton with the title, "Princeton for the Nation's Service." It was the spirit that under President Charles R. Van Hise made the University of Wisconsin a showcase of Progressivism, for at Wisconsin the alliance between the university and the state was so strong that officers of the university framed and administered legislation for the regulation of corporations, staffed many of the new regulatory commissions, and directed their researches toward the solution of state problems.[7]

[6] Nevins: *Illinois,* pp. 323-46; Rogers: *Cornell,* p. 12; Hugh Hawkins: *Pioneer: A History of the Johns Hopkins University, 1874-1889* (Ithaca, 1960), pp. 55-6, 169-86.
[7] Thomas Le Duc: *Piety and Intellect at Amherst College 1865-1912* (New York, 1946), p. 141; Thomas Wakefield Goodspeed: *A History of the University of Chicago Founded by John D. Rockefeller: The First Quarter Century* (Chicago, 1916), pp. 323-4; Varnum Lansing

The Wisconsin Idea, as this program of university service was called, rested on the conviction that informed intelligence when applied to the problems of modern society could make democracy work more effectively. Hostile to pecuniary values, charged with more than a touch of moral righteousness, the Wisconsin Idea placed the people's university at the service of the people, sought to protect them from the greed, privilege, and corrupting power of great wealth, and made of the university a kind of teacher-counselor-companion to the people at large. In varying degrees other state universities revealed the same spirit, but none came as close as the University of Wisconsin in epitomizing the spirit of Progressivism and the service ideal.[8]

By 1908 President Eliot was describing Wisconsin as the leading state university, a position to which it was entitled by the success with which it incorporated in its rationale two curiously conflicting currents of Progressivism: the resort to an *expertise* in the affairs of state, and the development of popular nontechnical lectures which carried the university to the people. This latter development, which took the name of extension courses, was not peculiar to the University of Wisconsin nor to the Progressive temper, but it had an exceptionally vigorous life at Wisconsin during the Progressive period and set a pattern for other institutions. In time technical courses were also added, and the extension curriculum was considerably expanded. Beginning in the 1890's at such places as Columbia, Wisconsin, Chicago, Brown, Indiana, and Illinois, the extension movement had in part been a public-relations gesture, an effort to extend the influence and the popularity of the university into communities beyond the immediate vicinity of the institution.

This search for greater usefulness took the form of short courses of lectures, somewhat watered in content and re-

---

Collins: *Princeton* (New York, 1914), p. 270; Merle Curti and Vernon Carstensen: *The University of Wisconsin: A History, 1848-1925* (Madison, 1949), II, 3-122.

[8] Ibid.; Charles McCarthy: *The Wisconsin Idea* (New York, 1912).

duced in intellectual sophistication, delivered by leading members of the university faculty in the larger population centers of the state. By the first decade of the twentieth century the extension movement had been recognized as an instrument of influence in achieving a greater measure of legislative financial support for the state institutions, and it was a matter of no difficulty to adapt the extension movement to the uses and goals of Progressivism. At the University of Wisconsin the experts themselves, the men who knew how railroads should be regulated, how the banks should be reorganized, how the forests and the rivers and the ore beds should be protected from avarice and gluttony, went to the people and gave lecture courses that amply reflected the Progressive temper. [9]

In addition, there was an acceleration of how-to courses, courses which, if they did not show how to make American democracy more democratic, did show many an American who otherwise would have been beyond the effective range of the university how to make himself a more effective farmer or worker. One friend of the University of Wisconsin was bold enough to claim: "The cow is one of the many by-products of higher education in Wisconsin. For the university saved the dairy industry and brought it to a high state of efficiency." [1] The success of the extension idea and the degree to which it served the Progressive emphasis was revealed in the Smith-Lever Act passed by Congress in 1914, which put the federal government on a permanent sustaining relationship to the extension services of the land-grant colleges.

At the other end of the pole from these excursions into popular education was the opportunity that Progressivism provided for trained experts, men whose very existence denied the Jacksonian contention that government could and should be simple enough for its duties to be discharged by

[9] See Curti and Carstensen: *Wisconsin*, I, 711-39, II, 549-94; Alfred C. True: *A History of Agricultural Extension Work in the United States* (Washington, 1928).
[1] Frederic C. Howe: *Wisconsin: An Experiment in Democracy* (New York, 1912), p. 175.

any citizen of modest abilities. Progressivism established the administrative and regulatory agency as an aspect of government and insinuated the idea of an *expertise* into what had been a rather uncomplicated concept of the role of government. In doing so, Progressives naturally turned to the universities, where on the faculties the experts could be found and where, with time, new courses and new departments could be created to turn out the necessary experts. The universities, which in the decades after the Civil War had found themselves performing unaccustomed services for the American farm and the American factory, now found themselves catering to the needs of government for trained men and women knowledgeable in such fields as political economy, sociology, and public administration.[2]

In their extension and *expertise* manifestations, Progressivism and the universities themselves revealed a closer kinship to Thomas Jefferson than to Andrew Jackson. By 1915 President Hadley of Yale was saying that one test of a legitimate liberal arts subject was that "a public motive rather than a private . . . [motive] must constitute the dominant note in its appeal."[3] In the same year Professor Charles Homer Haskins of Harvard explained the rationale behind the social studies and social sciences which had been experiencing such remarkable curricular growth. "They are . . . practical," said Professor Haskins, "not in the narrower sense as leading to a livelihood, but in the larger sense of preparing for life."[4]

As his statement made clear, the social studies served the political Progressives and the educational progressives, both of whom had become acutely aware of man's relationship to society. What Theodore Roosevelt and Woodrow Wilson would achieve for the older generations by regulation, ex-

[2] Ibid., pp. 25-50, 133-91.
[3] George Wilson Pierson: *Yale: College and University 1871-1937* (New Haven, 1952-5), I, 250.
[4] *The American College; a Series of Papers Setting forth the Program, Achievements, Present Status, and Probable Future of the American College* with introduction by *William H. Crawford* (New York, 1915), p. 45.

hortation, and expertness, John Dewey and his followers would achieve for the children in the schoolroom. In either case, both placed their trust in the contention that there was little wrong with American democracy that could not be solved by more democracy. By some curious fate, as a vital political belief this notion did not survive the First World War, but as an educational faith it was headed for a most vigorous life in the decades ahead.[5]

Expressive of the Progressive spirit at Harvard were certain clubs that grew up between 1905 and 1915: the Harvard Men's League for Women's Suffrage, the Single Tax Club, the Social Politics Club, the Diplomatic Club. Elsewhere this was the period of the Good Government Clubs, Civics Clubs, and Sociology Clubs. An intercollegiate civics league fostered the cause of good government in the colleges, courses in municipal government appeared in college catalogues, and at the University of Virginia undergraduates in 1911 directed the attention of the Civic Club to the spiritual and moral life of the back-mountain people of Virginia.[6]

A characteristic collegiate expression of Progressivism, especially in urban institutions, was the college settlement house, an institution which enabled young men and women to combine the old Christian purposes of the colleges with the new efforts to cope with the breakdown of American promise in the cities.[7] The impulse to settlement work, to this sharing of the life of the poor by university and college people, began in England in the 1860's and encompassed young men at both Oxford and Cambridge. In the United States the first effective discussion leading to college settlement work took

[5] See Lawrence A. Cremin: *The Transformation of the School: Progressivism in American Education, 1876-1957* (New York, 1961).

[6] Samuel Eliot Morison: *Three Centuries of Harvard College 1636-1936* (Cambridge, 1936), pp. 435-7; Burke A. Hinsdale: *History of the University of Michigan* (Ann Arbor, 1906), p. 129; George Franklin Smythe: *Kenyon College: Its First Century* (New Haven, 1924), p. 279; Geiger: *North Dakota*, p. 138; Le Duc: *Amherst*, p. 143; Bruce: *Virginia*, V, 279-80.

[7] Caroline Williamson Montgomery: *Bibliography of College, Social[,] University and Church Settlements* (Chicago, 1905), pp. 18-102.

place among a group of Smith undergraduates in 1887 and led to the opening of what was known as the College Settlement at 95 Rivington Street in New York in 1889.

There a small group of women residents—graduates of Vassar, Smith, and Wellesley—lived and worked among the poor Jews and Catholics of the neighborhood, bringing to bear subtle Protestant influences.[8] The young ladies themselves observed in 1890, "We hope . . . that the rising generation in Rivington St. may be not only wealthier and wiser but also nobler than their fathers." As for the impulses that brought them there, the young graduates explained: "The object of the College Settlement is to bring into close relations this class [of college women], who having received much, are ready and eager to give of their best, and the other class, who in poverty, ignorance and degradation have yet a singular readiness to receive."[9] On Rivington Street the young women graduates offered public baths at ten cents each, put on effective demonstrations of neighborliness, and founded such clubs as the Penny Provident Fund which encouraged banking and the Good Seed Society which encouraged hymn-singing on Sundays.[1]

The College Settlement in New York was among the earliest expressions of the settlement movement; soon college women in Philadelphia and Boston and men and women undergraduates everywhere followed its example. In Chicago three settlements were operated by students from the University of Michigan, Northwestern University, and the University of Chicago. Butler College students coped with slum problems in Indianapolis; University of Wisconsin students introduced a neighborhood in Milwaukee to social action; in Cambridge Harvard faculty and students taught the philosophy of the co-operative idea to men from the tenements.[2] By 1895 the collegiate settlements were indulging in a whole

[8] Ibid., pp. 5-10.
[9] *The College Settlements Association* (New York, 1890), pp. 4-5.
[1] Ibid., pp. 2-5.
[2] Montgomery: *Bibliography of College . . . Settlements*, pp. 18-102.

parcel of activities that revealed the Progressive spirit: lectures on scientific subjects by university professors, dispensaries, diet counseling, libraries, English classes, co-operative coal clubs, studies in American history, and citizenship clubs.[3]

The affinity between the college settlements and the broader programs of social action being undertaken by state and municipal Progressive reformers was implicit in the creed of the settlement that University of Chicago students founded in the stockyards district, with the counsel of a professor of political economy from the university and of Jane Addams of Hull House. "[We believe,]" said the creed, "[in] self-sacrifice for the good of all the people. . . . We want to be good citizens. . . . [We want to make Chicago a place where] government may be pure, her officers honest, and every corner of her territory a place fit to grow the best men and women, who shall rule over her."[4]

The appeal to love and brotherhood which ran through Progressive literature; the decision of Tom Johnson, a Cleveland industrialist, to give away his fortune and turn to a life of good works; the efforts of Samuel M. Jones of Toledo to run his city on a platform based on the Golden Rule; the belief that the city political machine was a cause of democratic decline rather than a result of democracy; the confusion in the public mind, as well as in the minds of the great exponents of Progressivism—La Follette, Roosevelt, and Wilson—on the distinction between a good trust and a bad trust; the assumption that the problems of railroad rates, tenement conditions, sweat shops, and political graft resolved themselves essentially into conflicts between good and evil—all of this moralism so characteristic of Progressivism, while in so many ways attractive, was also in many ways no more effective in dealing with the problems of the modern city than were the ten-

[3] College Settlement News, I (1895), passim.
[4] Montgomery: Bibliography of College . . . Settlements, p. 37. See also Ralph Henry Gabriel: Religion and Learning at Yale: The Church of Christ in the College and University, 1757-1957 (New Haven, 1958).

cent baths which the young ladies from Vassar and Smith operated on Rivington Street.

On the campus, the Progressive movement left its mark in three aspects of undergraduate life which came to be characteristic of many American institutions of higher learning: student government, the honor system, and senior honorary societies. Student government in various manifestations had long been an aspect of the American college. Before the Civil War college classes were well-organized units of college government. Classes organized mountain-naming expeditions, petitioned college authorities for shorter reading assignments, took responsibility for the maintenance of college classrooms, and often indulged in a sincere, if sometimes misguided, interest in the welfare and reputation of the college. An 1828 attempt at Amherst to turn over to a student court of justice petty disciplinary cases was exceptional and unsuccessful; a somewhat similar system failed at the University of Virginia.

After the Civil War, however, here and there beginnings were made in shifting some of the disciplinary and regulatory burden from the faculty and administration to the students. This movement toward greater formal recognition of student responsibility was probably a response to the sudden massive growth of athletics, the tendency of many institutions to assume a posture of treating their students as if they were grown up, and a disinclination on the part of the new professors with their Ph.D. degrees and scholarly orientation to have anything to do with such trivial matters as discipline and the extracurriculum. Under the influence of the climate created by Progressivism, however, student councils, interfraternity councils, and other variations on the theme of student government became widespread during the first decade of the twentieth century. Fostering self-government in the colleges was a typical agency of Progressivism, the National Self-Government Committee, an organization which advocated student self-government on the campus as a means of encouraging responsible democratic citizenship. Student government thus lodged itself in the colleges, along with courses in municipal government and urban sociology, as evidence of the sensitivity of American higher education to the changing currents of American life.[5]

While the honor system was not a creation of the Progressive period, this appeal to the gentleman's code experienced its most dynamic growth between 1900 and 1915, when Progressivism was at its height.[6] In the colleges of the ante bellum south an informal code of honor placed violators in jeopardy of expulsion by decision of their fellows, although in 1842 at the University of Virginia the tradition was formalized and students were required to sign pledges on examination papers certifying that they had received no assistance.[7]

The operation of some kind of gentleman's code in the southern colleges was not inappropriate to a society that nurtured aristocratic pretensions, but the system did not make any significant headway elsewhere until the 1890's, when seventeen colleges adopted an honor code, nor any really significant break-through until the Progressive period when

[5] Frances E. Falvey: *Student Participation in College Administration* (New York, 1952), pp. 41-4; Henry Davidson Sheldon: *The History and Pedagogy of American Student Societies* (New York, 1901), pp. 148-51, 257-65; George R. Cutting: *Student Life at Amherst College* (Amherst, 1871), p. 73; Claude M. Fuess: *Amherst: The Story of a New England College* (Boston, 1935), pp. 220-2; Robert Sibley: *The Romance of the University of California* (San Francisco, 1928), p. 39; Louis R. Wilson: *The University of North Carolina, 1900-1930: The Making of a Modern University* (Chapel Hill, 1957), p. 153; William Warren Ferrier: *Origin and Development of the University of California* (Berkeley, 1930), pp. 452-6; G. Wallace Chessman: *Denison: The Story of an Ohio College* (Granville, 1957), p. 330.
[6] Bird T. Baldwin: *Present Status of the Honor System in Colleges and Universities* (Washington, 1915).
[7] Daniel Walker Hollis: *University of South Carolina* (Columbia, 1951-6), I, 89-90, II, 123-4; Battle: *North Carolina*, I, 563, 568-9; David Duncan Wallace: *History of Wofford College* (Nashville, 1951), p. 63; Bruce: *Virginia*, III, 52-61.

seventy-six colleges joined the movement. While it is clear
that the concept of honor was consonant with the moral emphasis of the age, outside of the South the movement made
headway largely in small, homogeneous institutions like Beloit, Haverford, Wesleyan, Williams, Princeton, and Hobart,
where the clientele could be addressed in terms of the gentle-
manly tradition and be expected to know what was meant.
On the other hand, in their efforts to become national institutions serving all classes, such places as Harvard, N.Y.U., Yale,
Chicago, and Wisconsin had denied themselves this particular
opportunity to enjoy the Progressive propensity to indulge
in self-righteousness and manly honor.[8]

*

But if most institutions could not rely upon a universal understanding of the gentleman's code, they were ready to support efforts to single out each year the young men or the
young women who best epitomized the spirit of selflessness,
service, and honor which denoted a gentleman or lady. From
this readiness derived the senior honorary-society movement
which established itself in the American college and university in the 1890's and in the first decade of the twentieth century.[9]

To a degree the senior honor societies were an attempt to
deal with large-scale campus problems which were perhaps
related to sudden enrollment gains and to the injurious effect
of the elective principle on college unity, but what they did

[8] Baldwin: *Present Status of the Honor System,* pp. 8, 24-6.
[9] Henry Morton Bullock: *A History of Emory University* (Nashville, 1936), p. 372; John Howard Van Amringe, *et al.: A History of
Columbia University 1754-1904* (New York, 1904), pp. 182-3; Edwin
Mims: *History of Vanderbilt University* (Nashville, 1946), p. 267; Nevins: *Illinois,* p. 252; James Henry Morgan: *Dickinson College: The History of One Hundred and Fifty Years 1783-1933* (Carlisle, 1933), p. 426;
Leon Burr Richardson: *History of Dartmouth College* (Hanover,
1932), II, 644, 732; Walter C. Bronson: *The History of Brown
University 1764-1914* (Providence, 1914), p. 484; David Bishop Skillman: *The Biography of a College: Being the History of the First Century of the Life of Lafayette College* (Easton, 1932), II, 142; Ross: *Iowa
State,* p. 248; Pierson: *Yale,* I, 236.

most effectively was to channel off into a small pool young men and women who best represented the values for which the Progressive temper stood: honor, character, a certain wholesomeness bordering on utter innocence, a tendency toward activity rather than reflection, an outlook that at a later day would make a good Boy Scout or Girl Scout and, at the time, a good member of the campus Christian Association. As Bruce Barton had said in 1907, "Any man who believes that God is always on the side of right, that Amherst is the greatest college in the world and who is trying to do the square thing by his fellows is welcomed into membership."

18

◆⧏⧐◆

The Rise of Football

Football of sorts was played in tenth-century England, where it was largely a matter of kicking a skull or a cow's bladder between towns. The Princeton-Rutgers game of 1869, which inaugurated American football, was in this tradition. During the next decade, initially at Harvard and at Yale, a shift occurred from the soccer or kicking style of play to the Rugby or running style of play. American football, therefore, was a cultural adaptation of the English game of Rugby.[1]

It took a few years for the game to catch on, but its growth was extraordinary. In 1873 football seemed sufficiently ridiculous to prompt a classic remark of President Andrew D. White of Cornell. In response to a challenge from thirty players of the University of Michigan who wanted to arrange a game in Cleveland, President White telegraphed: "I will not permit thirty men to travel four hundred miles

[1] David Riesman and Reuel Denney: "Football in America: A Study in Culture Diffusion," *American Quarterly*, III (1951), 309-25; Thomas Jefferson Wertenbaker: *Princeton 1746-1896* (Princeton, 1946), pp. 325-6; William H. S. Demarest: *A History of Rutgers College 1766-1924* (New Brunswick, 1924), pp. 428-30; Parke H. Davis: *Football: The American Intercollegiate Game* (New York, 1911), pp. 44-50; Morris Allison Bealle: *The History of Football at Harvard, 1874-1948* (Washington, 1948), pp. 17, 26-8. See also Allison Danzig: *The History of American Football* (Englewood Cliffs, 1956).

merely to agitate a bag of wind." [2] In time Cornell fell fully
in line, as indeed did almost everyone else. But no one should
have been surprised when within less than twenty years one
season's football *coach* at Syracuse turned out to be next
season's *captain* at Cornell.[3]

Few movements so captured the colleges and universities.
In 1881 Michigan—spurned by Cornell less than ten years
earlier—went East and played Harvard, Yale, and Princeton
in a period of less than a week. A few years later a young
bachelor president at Miami University in Ohio all but required his faculty to go out for the team: in those days there
were no problems of eligibility. In 1889 the University of
the South at Sewanee sent out *its* team for six successive days
of play away from home. At a common-sense hard-headed
institution like the Connecticut Agricultural College at Storrs
the official program for physical training had at first assigned
the young men to three sessions a week of picking up stones
from the college farm; in the 1890's they picked up footballs.[4]

Indeed, the game became so widely adopted that for the
first time since the founding of Harvard College in 1636 colleges began to recognize the existence of intercollegiate relations. Institutions that had never found it advisable to consult
on matters of curriculum now sought means of regulating
their athletic relations: from this impulse came the agreement
among a number of midwestern colleges in the early 1890's
to employ no more than two professionals per game.[5] The
need for regulation was generally admitted, for the game intruded a spirit of athletic professionalism into an atmosphere
where many believed that it did not belong. One year in the
1890's the University of Oregon football team in three suc-

[2] Kent Sagendorph: *Michigan: The Story of the University* (New
York, 1948), p. 150.
[3] William Freeman Galpin: *Syracuse University: The Pioneer Days*
(Syracuse, 1952), p. 170.
[4] Amos Alonzo Stagg: *Touchdown!* (New York, 1927), p. 70;
Walter Havighurst: *The Miami Years 1809-1959* (New York, 1958),
pp. 148-51; Walter Stemmons: *Connecticut Agricultural College—A
History* (Storrs, 1931), p. 83.
[5] Allan Nevins: *Illinois* (New York, 1917), p. 202.

cessive contests with three different colleges found themselves playing against the same young man.

The game, however, encouraged such a will to win that undergraduate and graduate imagination found its way around any traditional sense of ethics. A senior might invite the fullback on the freshman team to room with him and forget to ask him to share the charges. A student might make a preposterous wager with a star athlete and, of course, lose. Instead, the money might go directly to a father or brother. One college ball player so learned the price of his usefulness that without fear of failure he presented his laundry bill to the team manager just before game time with the words: "I cannot pay it. You pay it or I do not play." Efforts to regulate the sport had difficulty keeping up with its growth.[6]

The game prospered. In 1893 New York was thrown into a virtual frenzy by the annual Thanksgiving game between Yale and Princeton. Hotels were jammed. On Fifth Avenue blue and white Yale banners hung from the Vanderbilt and Whitney mansions. The Sloanes, the Alexanders, and the Scribners displayed the colors of Old Nassau. Clergymen cut short their Thanksgiving Day services in order to get off to the game in time. Clearly, football had arrived.[7]

The movement would continue to accelerate until 1905 when the growing brutality and professionalism of the game created an episode typical of the Progressive period. That year the American public, which was in the process of being aroused by other impurities in the national life, including tainted pork, political machines, and trusts, turned its righteousness on football. Eighteen Americans died playing football in 1905. At Harvard the season provided only two games without concussions. In Philadelphia during the Penn-Swarthmore game Bob Maxwell, an outstanding Swarthmore player, was subjected to a beating so systematic and thor-

[6] See Galpin: *Syracuse*, p. 169; Charles Henry Rammelkamp: *Illinois College: A Centennial History 1829-1929* (New Haven, 1928), p. 391; Clarence F. Birdseye: *Individual Training in Our Colleges* (New York, 1907), pp. 160-2.
[7] Stagg: *Touchdown!*, pp. 150-3; Wertenbaker: *Princeton*, p. 357.

ough that a photograph, showing him tottering off the field, his face a bloody mess, became a news sensation. That photograph called into action the President of the United States. From the White House Theodore Roosevelt thundered that if the colleges did not clean up football he would abolish it by executive order. And in a bit of moralism which revealed much of the temper of the age, he added: "Brutality and foul play should receive the same summary punishment given to a man who cheats at cards." [8]

On October 9, 1905, coaches and physical directors of Harvard, Yale, and Princeton met with T.R. for lunch at the White House, where he charged them with the responsibility of getting "the game played on a thoroughly clean basis." [9] This was much the same injunction that he, as captain of the Progressive movement, was accustomed to delivering to the managers of great American industrial corporations. The football people responded in appropriate fashion. They undertook a campaign of purification and control. In 1906 the forward pass was introduced, taking some of the advantage away from brute weight. Some colleges—notably Columbia, the University of California, and Stanford—gave up football for a decade; others—Northwestern and Union, among them—suspended it for a year.[1] But football was not dead.

As the first contact sport to make any headway among young gentlemen in America, it satisfied a whole set of values

[8] Wertenbaker: *Princeton*, pp. 253-4; Riesman and Denney: "Football in America," p. 319; Calvin M. Woodward: *Opinions of Educators on the Value and Total Influence of Inter-Collegiate and Inter-Scholastic American Football as Played in 1903-1909* (St. Louis, 1910), p. 17.

[9] Elting E. Morison, ed.: *The Letters of Theodore Roosevelt* (Cambridge, 1952), V, 46.

[1] Dwight C. Miner, ed.: *A History of Columbia College on Morningside* (New York, 1954), p. 207; Orrin Leslie Elliott: *Stanford University: The First Twenty-Five Years* (Stanford, 1937), pp. 232-3; Dixon Ryan Fox: *Union College: An Unfinished History* (Schenectady, 1945), pp. 35-6; Howard J. Savage, *et al.*: *American College Athletics* (New York, 1929), p. 25.

that under T. R.'s auspices took the name of "the strenuous
life." When President Eliot attempted to abolish football at
Harvard, Roosevelt erupted with proper vigor: "I think Harvard will be doing the baby act if she takes any such foolish
course." [2] And in a 1907 speech before a Harvard audience
the same man who had carried the Big Stick into the Ivy
League just two years before now said: "As I emphatically
disbelieve in seeing Harvard, or any other college, turn out
mollycoddles instead of vigorous men I may add I do not in
the least object to a sport because it is rough." [3] Theodore
Roosevelt and most of his contemporaries did not object to
anything because it was rough. They were not interested in
keeping life from being vigorous, even dangerous. They did
want it to be fair. And this was all that they demanded of football—a square deal for every player.

Football also well served the traditional purpose of the American college and the aspirations of the American people. A
1901 observer of the collegiate scene discovered in football
not only an antidote to physical softness created by material
plenty but also an antidote to the increasing complexity,
mechanization, and standardization in American life. [4] Football—early football, in any case—glorified the individual; it
put on display not the wonders of machines but the robust-
ness, ingenuity, and imagination of man. One has only to be
reminded of the imaginative young player from Wabash who
in 1891 created one of the greatest defensive plays of all time.
In the middle of the second half the score stood Purdue 44,
Wabash 0, when, without so much as a signal from the bench,
the young player from Wabash grabbed the ball and sped off
the field. Neither he nor another ball could be found, and to

[2] Morison, ed.: *The Letters of Theodore Roosevelt*, V, 172.
[3] Bealle: *The History of Football at Harvard*, p. 9.
[4] Henry Davidson Sheldon: *The History and Pedagogy of American
Student Societies* (New York, 1901), pp. 251-2.

this day the official score is 44-0, a tribute to rugged individualism. [5]

The rise of football in the colleges was also one democratic solution to the increasing number of rich men's sons on the American campus. President Hadley of Yale in 1906 reported that football had taken "hold of the emotions of the student body in such a way as to make class distinctions relatively unimportant" and had made "the students get together in the old-fashioned democratic way." [6] In the meantime, while the Harvard football captain was more often than not named Cushing, Cabot, Appleton, or Brooks, it unquestionably was true that there was room for Murphy of Yale on Walter Camp's 1895 All-American team and in 1900 Daly was elected captain of the team at Harvard. In 1904 Pierkarski of Penn made All-American. In the colleges football kept the social elevator running. [7] Eventually football would enable a whole generation of young men in the coal fields of Pennsylvania to turn their backs on the mines that had employed their fathers.

Football, moreover, did not find itself out of line with many other collegiate values. President Harry Garfield of Williams in 1908 might confess: "Here, as generally in American colleges, there is grave danger of departure from the essential idea of a college as distinguished from an institute of physical culture." [8] But friends of football everywhere were always quick to point out how much the essential ideals of the old colleges were actually being served. Coach Amos Alonzo Stagg insisted that until intercollegiate athletics came along the major college sport in America had been convivial drinking. [9] He might have also added that football appeared to be

[5] James I. Osborne and Theodore G. Gronert: *Wabash College; the first hundred years, 1832-1932* (Crawfordsville, 1932), p. 262.
[6] Arthur Twining Hadley: "Wealth and Democracy in American Colleges," *Harper's*, CXIII (1906), 452.
[7] Riesman and Denney: "Football in America," pp. 309, 322-5.
[8] Quoted in W. Carson Ryan, Jr.: *The Literature of American School and College Athletics* (New York, 1929), p. 130.
[9] Stagg: *Touchdown!*, p. 20.

responsible for cutting down the incidence of rebellions, riot-
ing, and hazing. One college president, a football enthusiast,
insisted that there was nothing like a "thorough fatiguing" of
the body to promote pure living and pure thinking.[1] Football
was in many ways clearly more effective than a faculty discipline committee or compulsory morning chapel.

It was also helping to restore the old collegiate unity which
had been broken by enrollment increases and the development of the elective curriculum: if every man did not take
the same courses at least he had an opportunity to cheer for
the same team. At Yale a faculty committee in 1902 pointed
out that football had captured the old evangelical ideal of
selflessness. Said the committee: "An impression is very
strong and very prevalent that the athlete is working for
Yale, the student for himself." A similar view was expressed
at Wisconsin. Even the old Puritan respect for work found
lodgment in football. The Dean of Columbia College observed: "Very few men play football for pleasure." At Stanford a turn-of-the-century coach commented: "You fellows
want to understand that this game is not fun; it is hard work."
In such ways, the new game of football became an instrument of the past. [2]

If football served the past, however, in even better ways it
served the present. The rise of football was contemporaneous with the development of a martial spirit which mani-
fested itself in two forms: in those warlike developments that
led to such victories as those of the Standard Oil Company,
and in that series of imperial and bellicose adventures that

[1] Louis G. Geiger: *University of the Northern Plains: A History of
the University of North Dakota 1883-1958* (Grand Forks, 1958), pp.
238-9.
[2] George Wilson Pierson: *Yale: College and University 1871-1937*
(New Haven, 1952-5), I, 240; Merle Curti and Vernon Carstensen: *The
University of Wisconsin: A History, 1848-1925* (Madison, 1949), II,
534; Frederick Paul Keppel: *Columbia* (New York, 1914), p. 163; Elliott: *Stanford*, p. 226.

planted the American flag in the Caribbean and the Pacific
and paraded the American navy around the world. One
would have had difficulty in deciding whether the following
list of qualities referred to John D. Rockefeller about to ab-
sorb a rival oil company or to Admiral Dewey at Manila
Bay: "courage, coolness, steadiness of nerve, quickness of
apprehension, resourcefulness, self-knowledge and self-
reliance." [3] Actually, these were the words of a college president in the 1890's describing an ideal football player.

There was a widespread recognition of the relationship between football and these larger national interests. Some saw
the football field as a battleground. Others, as a training program for careers in business. President Eliot of Harvard saw
it both ways. In 1904 he complained that the Harvard football
field had become a place where young men were being in-
structed in "driving a trade or winning a fight, no matter
how." And he expressed the hope that Harvard men would
shun the "reckless, unmotivated courage" of football and instead admire the courage that espoused "the cause of the
weak." [4] At California President Benjamin Ide Wheeler was
carried away by a military metaphor: "Two rigid, rampart-
like lines of human flesh have been created, one of defense,
the other of offense, and behind the latter is established a
catapult to fire through a porthole opened in the offensive
rampart a missile composed of four or five human bodies
globulated about a carried football with a maximum of initial
velocity against the presumably weakest point in the opposing
rampart." [5] At Stanford President Jordan boasted in 1910 of
the game of Rugby which had been substituted for football
at Stanford: "It is played, not in armor, but in cotton knee
breeches." [6] This happened to be a bad period in American
history for both weaklings and knee breeches. The application of the Darwinian analysis to social questions left

[3] Sheldon: *The History . . . of American Student Societies,* p. 250.
[4] Woodward: *Opinions of Educators on . . . Football,* pp. 12-13.
[5] Benjamin Ide Wheeler: *The Abundant Life* (Berkeley, 1926), pp. 113-15.
[6] Woodward: *Opinions on Educators on . . . Football,* p. 27.

little sympathy for the weak, and whether Americans preferred games played in cotton or in armor was answered by Stanford itself when it returned to football four years later.

In a celebrated essay entitled "The Moral Equivalent of War," the Harvard philosopher William James in 1910 did *not* locate his equivalent in football. He proposed, instead, a vast scheme of national peacetime conscription where the martial virtues—valor, "contempt of softness, surrender of private interest, obedience to command"—could be nurtured without recourse to war. How far the American game of football had gone in institutionalizing the martial virtues apparently escaped the Harvard philosopher.[7]

But then he probably was not in Philadelphia in the fall of 1896 where there was enacted a scene reminiscent of the Crusades: a hospital room, a few minutes before game time, the great captain of the Lafayette College football team, bedridden, stricken suddenly by appendicitis; surrounded by his uniformed teammates, he gives them last minute instructions and words of encouragement, and like Knights Templars they move on to Franklin Field and there vanquish the foe (in this case, the University of Pennsylvania), 6-4. The battle is over; they return to the bedside of their noble leader; and there they join in singing the doxology. If football was not everywhere the moral equivalent of war, surely it was that day in Philadelphia.[8]

Once the game had enlisted the support of alumni and administration, there was no stopping its growth. For, once the *sport* had been accepted, the *games* had to be won. Americans lacked a psychology for failure. They had developed a very workable ethic for success. In football, this ethic was revealed in "the almost invisible line between clever tactics

[7] William James: *Memories and Studies* (New York, 1917), pp. 267-96.
[8] David Bishop Skillman: *The Biography of a College: Being the History of the First Century of the Life of Lafayette College* (Easton, 1932), II, 115.

and foul play" and in all those excesses of enthusiasm, recruitment, and training which were aspects of total mobilization for victory.[9]

The invisible line was of course not peculiar to football. It was paralleled in American life by an equally almost invisible line between the Christian and fine gentleman, between the moral and immoral business man, between what the Progressives called a good trust and a bad trust; the almost invisible line between the compulsion to succeed and the injunction to be moral. In 1905, after all, the annual convention of Congregational churches could not reach agreement on whether the money of John D. Rockefeller was tainted. Football (and soon, indeed, intercollegiate debating as well) merely provided the American college and university with a fascinating new agency for teaching young Americans what they might have learned from their fathers had they been Yankee peddlers. One critic looked out upon the playing fields and concluded: "Men trained in such methods through all the years of school and college life may become future leaders, but they will be leaders in the art of evading taxes, manipulating courts, and outwitting the law of the land." [1]

Organized athletics in the American colleges and universities developed a pattern of student-alumni management because the faculty would have nothing to do with athletics. Old-time college professors contributed a tradition of helplessness in the presence of the extracurriculum, to which the new professors with their Ph.D. degrees now added a large dose of studied indifference. Therefore, when the apparatus of athletics grew too large and complex for student management; when the expenditure of much time and much money was required in the recruiting, coaching, feeding, and care of athletic heroes; when, indeed, all these things demanded a more efficient and perhaps also a more subtle touch, the alumni jumped to the opportunity which student ineffec-

[9] Samuel Eliot Morison: *Three Centuries of Harvard 1636-1936* (Cambridge, 1936), p. 406.
[1] Birdseye: *Individual Training*, p. 162.

tiveness and faculty indifference gave them. Later, when many faculties recognized what had happened it was too late.[2]

While intercollegiate football would have taken hold without alumni and administration support, certainly its growth would have been less dynamic and less rapid. If something was going to happen anyway, it always happened sooner on an American campus when it had the blessings of the administration and the support of the alumni. The older alumni, nurtured on a tradition of collegiate rivalry rooted in a now-waning denominational fervor or often in nothing more substantial than a competition for enrollment, found in football a new outlet for their loyalty. The younger alumni who had known the game as undergraduates were thoroughly captivated. As one young college graduate said in a national magazine in 1890: "You do not remember whether Thorpwright was valedictorian or not, but you can never forget that glorious run of his in the football game."[3] How many times there echoed on the American campus variations on the lament of a Bowdoin alumnus in 1903 when confronted by a 16-0 defeat by the University of Maine: "In my day the University of Maine was a standing joke. . . . We got licked to-day because we hadn't the stock—the stock, sir. . . . Old Bowdoin must fling wide open her gates and get some—some stock, sir."[4]

In the 1890's the alumni achieved their domination of college and university athletics. Perhaps not many alumni groups were as bold as that at Dartmouth which agreed to raise funds for a football field if they were given athletic control. Of course they were given it, for everywhere the same power vacuum needed filling, and only the alumni

[2] Stagg: *Touchdown!*, pp. 36-7; Savage: *American College Athletics*, pp. 23-4; Sheldon: *The History . . . of American Student Societies*, pp. 245-9.
[3] Sanborn Gove Tenney: "Athletics at Williams," *Outing*, XVII (1890), 142-9.
[4] Louis C. Hatch: *The History of Bowdoin College* (Portland, 1927), p. 242.

seemed eager and able to fill it.[5] At first, as at Harvard, faculty stirrings led to joint faculty-student and then joint faculty-student-alumni boards of control or supervision. The faculties were usually stirred into action by some gross excess—in the case of Harvard, a twenty-eight-game schedule in 1882, in which nineteen games were played away. By 1890 at Harvard each of the various sports had its own graduate advisory committee, which theoretically represented the conscience of Harvard in athletic matters but which also could not avoid representing the alumni will to win. In 1893 a salaried graduate manager of athletics was put in charge of the entire athletic program; this widely copied university office institutionalized alumni voice in athletic affairs and added an important new dimension, and problem, to college and university administration.[6]

The role of the press in the growth of football was unquestionably profound, for the rise of football and the development of the sports pages in the daily press were contemporaneous.[7] For the first time the American college was a source of popular news, and this fact significantly increased administrative encouragement of football. Athletics of all sorts in fact served the public-relations purpose of colleges and universities. In 1879 students at Illinois College, seeking faculty approval of an extended baseball trip, emphasized the publicity dividends such a trip would earn for the college. On orders of Andrew D. White an 1882 note held by the university against what was quaintly called the Cornell Navy was cancelled and "charged to advertising." An 1895 trip to the East by the University of California track team developed into a series of great victories and was widely rec-

[5] Leon Burr Richardson: History of Dartmouth College (Hanover, 1932), II, 724.
[6] Morison: Harvard: Three Centuries, pp. 410-11.
[7] Frank Luther Mott: American Journalism: A History of Newspapers in the United States through 250 Years 1690 to 1940 (New York, 1941), pp. 443, 578.

ognized as a major public-relations achievement. Intercollegiate athletics at Notre Dame were consciously developed
in the 1890's as an agency of student recruitment. Land-grant
colleges and state universities discovered that athletic victories often were more important than anything else in convincing reluctant legislators to open the public purse.[8]

Of all the various sports, however, football became the
major instrument of publicity because both on and off the
campus it was the sport that inspired the most enthusiasm, enlisted the most interest, and brought into the camp of college and university supporters people for whom the idea of
going to college was out of the question but for whom the
idea of supporting the team was a matter of course. If football served democracy on the campus by being an instrument of social elevation, it served off-campus democracy by
creating an important agency of popular entertainment. As
early as 1878 President McCosh of Princeton was writing to
an alumnus in Kentucky: "You will confer a great favor on
us if you will get . . . the college noticed in the Louisville
papers. . . . We must persevere in our efforts to get students
from your region. . . . Mr. Brand Ballard has won us great
reputation as captain of the football team which has beaten
both Harvard and Yale."[9] By 1900 the relationship between
football and public relations had been firmly established
and almost everywhere acknowledged as one of the sport's
major justifications.[1]

[8] Rammelkamp: *Illinois College*, p. 281; Walter P. Rogers: *Andrew
White and the Modern University* (Ithaca, 1942), p. 192; William War-
ren Ferrier: *Origin and Development of the University of California*
(Berkeley, 1930), p. 624; Arthur J. Hope: *Notre Dame: One Hundred
Years* (Notre Dame, 1943), pp. 279, 300; James Albert Woodburn:
History of Indiana University: 1820-1902 (Bloomington, 1940), p. 448;
Daniel Walker Hollis: *University of South Carolina* (Columbia, 1951-
6), II, 229-30; Earle D. Ross: *A History of the Iowa State College of
Agriculture and Mechanic Arts* (Ames, 1942), p. 217.
    [9] Wertenbaker: *Princeton*, p. 315.
    [1] See Woodward: *Opinions of Educators on . . . Football*, p. 25;
Elliott: *Stanford*, p. 192; Nora Campbell Chaffin: *Trinity College, 1839-
1892: The Beginnings of Duke University* (Durham, 1950), pp. 443-4;
Allen E. Ragan: *A History of Tusculum College, 1794-1944* (Bristol,

．　　．　　．

From football as public relations to football as business would not, at some institutions, be much of a distance. Obviously what enhanced both the publicity and business dimensions of football was the degree to which it became a game not for the players but for the spectators. Any chance of the game ever again being played for fun by college undergraduates was perhaps lost in 1915 when the University of Pittsburgh, in order to spur the sale of programs at football games, introduced the soon widely copied custom of plastering large numerals on the players' backs.[2] There was something tragically symbolic about that 1915 gesture at the University of Pittsburgh, for it suggested the degree to which the game had fallen beyond the control of those who played it, the degree to which it now belonged to the paying customers and to the treasurer of the athletic association. No one had ever had to number the players in Greek class, but then no one very much had cared what was going on there.

At last the American college and university had discovered something that all sorts of people cared about passionately. Now no self-respecting institution could get along without a color or two to unfurl in the breezes, with which to bedeck the spectators, and to encase the brawn of the players themselves. Princeton settled on orange, and both Williams and Amherst on purple. A tremendous effort of the imagination is required in order fully to appreciate the pose of the young editors at Dartmouth who in 1867 announced to an unsuspecting world: "Dartmouth claims green," or the chagrin of the students at C.C.N.Y. who, noting that all the colors were beginning to be used up, settled on lavender—only to have their choice protested by Wesleyan, which insisted upon the rights of a prior claim.[3]

1945), pp. 94-5; Birdseye: *Individual Training*, pp. 159-60; Skillman: *Lafayette*, II, 69, 147; Savage: *American College Athletics*, pp. 265-90.
  [2] Riesman and Denney: "Football in America," p. 231.
  [3] Richardson: *Dartmouth*, II, 562; S. Willis Rudy: *The College of*

Most college colors were selected in the early days of intercollegiate baseball, but intercollegiate football brought forth the banners, the songs, the posters, and such other carnival-like manifestations as led to the public identification of great institutions of learning with a particular color. From identifying an institution with a color to identifying it with a football team was a very short step, and before long very many Americans would be acting as if *the* purpose of an American college or university were to field a football team.

Of course this development and some of its consequences did not go unnoticed. For all of the enthusiasm and excitement probably fewer undergraduates were actually getting wholesome exercise than were in the days when at country colleges students sometimes walked a mile between their boarding houses and classrooms. One student at the University of California complained in 1904: "Athletics as conducted now in our larger universities is but for the few picked teams while the very students who most need physical development become stoop-shouldered rooting from backless bleachers. . . ." Perhaps all this could not be avoided, in view of the fact that in 1897 the department of health at Harvard was prepared to certify only 21 per cent of Harvard undergraduates as being in condition to participate in the intercollegiate blood bath known as football. By 1902 alumni were expressing concern over the tendency of spectator football to make Princeton men "athletes by proxy." [4]

Some friends of brawn sought an answer in the gymnasium, but nothing could arrest the decline of gymnastics as an interest of American college undergraduates who, like their elders, were discovering fresh air and sun and who

---

the City of New York: A History, *1847-1947* (New York, 1949), pp. 104-5.
    [4] Ferrier: *California,* p. 457; Sheldon: *The History . . . of American Student Societies,* pp. 253-4; Wertenbaker: *Princeton,* p. 357.

found gymnasiums dirty, smelly, and the proper place only for young men who needed physical correction or who lacked a healthy regard for competition. Track and field events, handball, and tennis offered modest opportunity for exercise that was not akin to armed warfare, but the most effective answer to the problem was an undergraduate movement of intramural sports which was soon supported by college and university athletic departments and directors.

The motives of the students were clear: they wanted some exercise, and they wanted some fun. As for the athletic departments, in many places they began to think of intramural leagues as recruiting and training teams for the varsity.[5] The intramural movement unquestionably enlarged the percentage of students participating in athletics, but it also introduced a strange and troublesome double standard in collegiate athletics: a standard of amateur fun for the mass of students; and for the expert a standard of near-professionalism and sheer hard work, in exchange for which he was elevated to a status surpassing that of any previous undergraduate type, including the student orator in the colleges of the Old South.

To accommodate football as a spectacle the colleges and universities indulged in an era of stadium- and field-house-building that reached its apex in the 1920's. The University of Michigan in 1923 completed a field house big enough to handle a football game, and in Los Angeles and Pasadena private business interests erected a "Coliseum" and a "Rose Bowl" capable of handling mammoth crowds. It had not taken many years to cover the ground from the first Tournament of Roses Game of 1902 to the great spectacles of the 1920's. The 1902 game between Stanford and Michigan at Pasadena was remembered as one of the stars in the crown of Fielding "Hurry Up" Yost, then in his second year of coaching at Michigan. In 1896 Yost had played for the Allegheny Athletic Club of Pittsburgh, Lafayette College, and his home

[5] Savage: *American College Athletics*, pp. 29-32.

team at the University of Virginia; and before going to
Michigan in 1900 he had coached at Ohio Wesleyan, the
University of Nebraska, and Stanford. During the 1901 season Michigan compiled 550 points to its opponents' zero,
and on New Year's Day, 1902, at Pasadena played with such
convincing ferociousness that in the middle of the second
half with Michigan leading 49-0, the Stanford coach waved
his exhausted team off the field. No wonder that at Michigan
football became a mania and that each year a major university
problem was the enlargement of spectator space at the games.
By 1927 at Ann Arbor 87,000 people could watch a football
game in comfort; by 1948 the university had a $4,000,000
athletic plant, all paid for out of football receipts.[6]

The extent to which intercollegiate football had created
the fan and then proceeded to feed upon him was revealed
almost everywhere in the 1920's. At Chicago in 1926 a record
110,000 people watched an Army-Navy game; at Yale in
1928 the athletic association reported a gross revenue of
$1,119,000, with a net profit of $348,500.[7] The meaning of
these and comparable figures for the history of American
higher education was to some extent incalculable, but what
they did establish was the emotional and financial investment
that the American public was prepared to make in collegiate
football. "Football had become a public possession" in a way,
fortunately, that the classroom never had.[8]

Football also elevated two new performers to star billing in
the cast of campus characters: the football hero and the
football coach. Baseball and boating had not been able to
achieve for the athletic hero and the athletic coach the
eminence and universal prestige that football earned for
young men whose heads were often permanently turned, and

[6] Sagendorph: *Michigan*, pp. 206-14, 292.
[7] Christian Gauss: "Will the Football Bubble Burst?," *Saturday Evening Post*, CCVIII (1935), No. 11, 12-13, 45-8; Stagg: *Touchdown!*,
opp. p. 342; Savage: *American College Athletics*, p. 87.
[8] Pierson: *Yale*, II, 128.

for coaches whose heads were often permanently at stake. The football hero was created by values manifest in the game itself, but he also was unquestionably fostered by non-intellectual or anti-intellectual emphases in the national culture, and by the degree to which he could be construed as the perfect symbol of the conflicts that lay at the basis of many of the national neuroses: the conflict between the need to win and the dictates of conscience; the conflict between the tradition of freedom and inner-direction, and the demands of organization, society, and responsibility; the conflict between thought and action.

President Eliot may have spoken nothing but the truth in his report for 1892-93:

> There is something exquisitely inappropriate in the extravagant expenditure on athletic sports at such institutions as Harvard and Yale, institutions which have been painfully built up by the self-denial, frugality, and public spirit of generations that certainly did not lack physical and moral courage, yet always put the things of spirit above the things of sense. At these universities there must be constant economy and inadequacy in expenditure for intellectual objects; how repulsive, then, must be foolish and pernicious expenditures on sports! [9]

But if President Eliot spoke the truth, so did Theodore Roosevelt, Jr., in a letter to his father after playing for the Harvard freshmen one Saturday in 1905: "I feel so large in my black sweater with the numerals on. Saturday's game was a hard one, as I knew it was bound to be. I was not seriously hurt at all. Just shaken up and bruised. I broke my nose." [1]

Was there not truth also in the inspiration of Coach Alonzo Stagg that led in 1908 to the installation in a tower on the University of Chicago campus of a set of chimes that were rung at 10:05 every night for the athletes of the University of Chicago. "Why not have a good night chime for our own

[9] Sheldon: *The History . . . of American Student Societies*, p. 238.
[1] Morison, ed.: *The Letters of Theodore Roosevelt*, V, 94.

athletes," Coach Stagg had asked, "to let its sweet cadence have a last word with them before they sleep; to speak to them of love and loyalty and sacrifice for their University and of hope and inspiration and endeavor for the morrow?" [2] Of such truths the football hero was made.

The early football coaches were inevitably young recent graduates who had played the game well. Harvard, Yale, and Princeton early set the pattern of calling upon the previous year's captain to put in an expenses-only appearance as coach during the football season, and in this custom they persisted long after other institutions had taken advantage of the inevitable development of football coaches, generally former professional trainers or men whose undergraduate football experiences could hardly be described as amateur. The decision for permanent, professional coaching was unquestionably hurried by Harvard's experience of 1903 when "no fewer than 39 graduates were invited, at various times through the season, to assist in the coaching. On the Tuesday before the Yale game, ten coaches were on the field." [3]

If the professional coach was a product of necessity, however, he also became much more than a mere instrument of victory: he was the agency by which departments of physical culture and athletics achieved parity status in the American university. This development was initiated at Amherst in the prefootball era with the appointment of Edward Hitchcock and given a significant boost at the University of Chicago in 1892 when Coach Stagg received professorial rank and tenure. [4] The coach became that strange phenomenon on an American campus—a person who could successfully lay claim to a share of the receipts attributable to his labors. Football, often the only money-making activity of an institution, supported coaches' salaries that were out of

[2] Thomas Wakefield Goodspeed: *A History of the University of Chicago Founded by John D. Rockefeller: The First Quarter Century* (Chicago, 1916), p. 346.
[3] Bealle: *The History of Football at Harvard*, pp. 380-404.
[4] Ibid., p. 384; Stagg: *Touchdown!*, p. 147; Goodspeed: *Chicago*, p. 378.

proportion to those of the professors. Of course the coaches were also assuming an old-time professorial function, one that the new doctors of philosophy had so little time for: in their coaches students often found advocates of clean-living and high-thinking, a substitute for the moral guidance once supplied by the professors.

But professional coaching also led coaches to have a tremendous personal stake in victory, a stake so important and so meeting with the mood of the alumni that in time the game was taken away from the students and became a contest between rival coaches for job security.

This tendency to subordinate the player and individual decision as well as the enjoyment of sport to the need for victory was not altogether of the coaches' making. The alumni also wanted and expected victory, a public whipped into a kind of enthusiasm appropriate to some barbaric bloodletting was naturally vindictive, and faculties which might have protected the coaches from the alumni and the public were now almost powerless in the supervision of athletics and were also hostile to helping coaches achieve tenure status. It was inevitable that at Washington State a coach would appear with a two-inch-thick rope which he used for speeding the young men from his football stable into the game, and it was appropriate that when Coach Andy Smith of California died in the 1920's his ashes were scattered on the field of Memorial Stadium.[5]

Women, for whom attendance at sporting events had been forbidden by the dictates of decency, made intercollegiate football an aspect of their emancipation. In 1885, for the first time apparently, they appeared in large numbers at the Yale-Princeton game in New Haven, and from that year dates the

[5] Enoch Albert Bryan: *Historical Sketch of the State College of Washington 1890-1925* (Spokane, 1928), pp. 282-3; Robert Sibley: *The Romance of the University of California* (San Francisco, 1928), opp. p. 31.

establishment of football on the social calendar. Until that
year the game had been played at the Polo Grounds in New
York. The change of location spelled a change of atmosphere,
one which a lady might enter without fear of compromising
her reputation.[6] Yet, there was more to it than that.
Intercollegiate baseball had not evoked a comparable enthusiasm among ladies of good name. But before long their
antics at football games, their cheering, their uncontrolled
admiration for the team would become a matter of almost as
much interest as the game itself. What was all the shouting
about? Perhaps no one ever put the matter as delicately and
as scientifically as G. Stanley Hall, the psychologist-president
of Clark University in 1900: "Glory, which is the reward of
victory and makes the brave deserve the fair, is . . . never
so great as when it is the result of conflict; and while the
human female does not as in the case of many animal species
look on complacently and reward the victor with her favor,
military prowess has a strange fascination for the weaker sex,
perhaps ultimately and biologically because it demonstrates
the power to protect and defend. Power . . . has played a
great role in sexual attraction." [7]

That being the case, the girls flocked to the arenas where
the gladiators fought—or became the instrument of playful
insults hurled by an alumnus of one college at an alumnus
of another. Such an incident occurred in Washington at a
cabinet meeting in 1907, when the Secretary of the Interior,
a Williams man, twitted the President of the United States, a
Harvard man, on Harvard's disastrous football season. "I
behaved with what dignity I could under such distressing
circumstances" was the way in which Theodore Roosevelt
met the suggestion of his Secretary of the Interior that
Harvard should call off its game with Yale and instead seek
a match with a team from Vassar.[8]

  [6] Stagg: *Touchdown!*, p. 191.
  [7] G. Stanley Hall: "Student Customs," *Proceedings of the American
Antiquarian Society*, XIV New Series (1900), 119.
  [8] Morison, ed.: *The Letters of Theodore Roosevelt*, V, 853.

19

❦

Academic Man

In the mythology of American education the old-time college professor, if nothing else, was a character. Beloved or unloved, tyrannical or permissive, stern or playful, tall or short, skinny or fat, young or old—he might be any of these things, but one thing for sure, he was a character. He was someone whom students played tricks on, and if he found a cow in his classroom one morning, somehow he would find some telling way of turning that disaster into a personal advantage. He was probably famous for college generations for that special lecture of his, the one that brought the Battle of Thermopylae right into the classroom. That hat, the one he wore twelve months of the year, too small, too old, too odd though it was—that made him a character, too.

Yet the old-time college professor as character was certainly less a product of his own times than of the imagination of later generations which were seeking some relief from their own times in a return to a carelessly constructed version of the good old days. In the presence of the complex organization institution which the American college and university became, in the face of the rise of the academician, the old-time college professor proved to be an absolute necessity. He humanized the past of institutions that were being dehumanized in the present; he symbolized the universal in the way that his successor symbolized the special; he was alive, old-fashioned, but all-around; he cared about you and the world at large, and of him it could not be said:

> *Here he sits droning*
> *On some forgotten truth;*
> *Heedless of Springtime,*
> *Intolerant of youth.*
>
> *Here he sits dryly*
> *Talking all day;*
> *Woodenly sober*
> *And slim as his pay.*[1]

In the ranks of the non-organization men of the past—among the mountain men, the yeoman farmers, the country store-keepers, the village blacksmiths—the American imagination placed the old-time college professor, that independent character whose only badge was an honest face and whose only uniform was a rumpled, baggy old suit of clothes.

But now the university was in the ascendancy and would insinuate its values into the lives of even the old colleges. The badge of the organization men who now replaced the old-time college professor was a degree of Doctor of Philosophy, the Ph.D.—the label of academic respectability, the mark of professional competence, the assurance of a certain standard sameness of training, experience, and exposure to the ideals, the rules, the habits of scientific Germanic scholarship. As late as 1884 on a faculty of 189, Harvard had but 19 professors with the degree of Ph.D.; Michigan, with a faculty of 88, had but 6.[2] This low proportion reflected

---

[1] Maurice Kelly, "Professeur," *American Mercury*, VIII (1926), quoted in Claude Charleton Bowman: *The College Professor in America: An Analysis of Articles Published in the General Magazines, 1890-1938* (Philadelphia, 1938), p. 20.

[2] W. H. Cowley: "European Influences upon American Higher Education," *Educational Record*, XX (1939), 183.

merely the short supply. By the 1890's Johns Hopkins and the newer graduate schools of arts and sciences were moving into high gear, and by then the men with Ph.D. degrees were beginning to overtake their less fully trained colleagues. Between 1888 and 1895 men with the doctorate moved into the majority at a place like Brown, which during those years drew for its appointments young men with the degree of Ph.D. from Hopkins, Clark, Yale, Chicago, Harvard, and Brown itself, as well as Freiburg, Strassburg, and Würzburg. At little Illinois College the entire faculty changed between 1900 and 1903 and when all the returns were in, the college was in the hands of university-trained doctors of philosophy. At City College in New York it was announced in 1904 that henceforth all professors must have the Ph.D. degree; eight years later the same demands were placed on instructors. The University of Illinois in 1905 looked to its reputation and declared that future appointments to the rank of professor would be drawn exclusively from men who had known the rigors of training for the Ph.D.[3]

The effort of the colleges and universities to gather within the fold an increasing number of instructors who wore the badge of scholarship was widespread. Obviously, of course, the better institutions—those with the prestige and the funds necessary to pay the higher price which the doctorate demanded—were the first to achieve what might be called doctoral domination, but in time the vast complex of American universities would be geared to producing all the doctors of philosophy that American education could consume. Until that day, however, some institutions of lesser resources and reputation covered their own embarrassment and that of others by trafficking in honorary Ph.D. degrees. Indeed, the custom was also indulged in by such greater institutions as

[3] Walter C. Bronson: The History of Brown University 1764-1914 (Providence, 1914), p. 431; Charles Henry Rammelkamp: Illinois College: A Centennial History 1829-1929 (New Haven, 1928), p. 432; S. Willis Rudy: The College of the City of New York: A History, 1847-1947 (New York, 1949), pp. 285-6; Allan Nevins: Illinois (New York, 1917), p. 241.

Princeton and Dartmouth. The rise of the honorary Ph.D. in
the 1870's and 1880's was of course striking evidence of the
need everywhere for being called "Doctor," the need for pos-
sessing some badge of identification that conveyed the impression that one was a fully enrolled, dues-paying member
of the organization. The decline of the honorary Ph.D., on the
other hand, was evidence that the real thing had carried
the day and, in fact, had summoned sufficient strength to put
the honorary version into disrepute. The United States Bureau
of Education, learned societies, and various professional organizations joined forces in deploring the sham Ph.D. The
peak year for the honorary doctorate was 1890, with a total
of thirty-nine. By 1910, surely benefiting from the temper
of Progressivism, the annual output had been reduced to
two.[4]

But if the sham degree could not withstand the new
strength of the academician, attacks on the real degree and
its portent for the academic community likewise went unheeded. In a notable challenge to the Ph.D. degree, the Harvard philosopher William James in 1903 called it an octopus,
"a mere advertising resource, a manner of throwing dust in
the Public's eye," "a grotesque tendency," "the Mandarin
disease," "a sham, a bauble, a dodge whereby to decorate
the catalogues of schools and colleges." He questioned
whether the degree was any assurance of effective teaching,
he deplored the tendency of Harvard in particular to keep
raising its standards for the degree as a means of carrying on
a kind of specious warfare with other universities, he re-
gretted the strength of this new form of academic snobbery
that enticed undistinguished students into failure, and he
feared for the consequences to the free spirit of the tendency toward excessive organization which he saw in the
Ph.D. requirement.[5]

    [4] Stephen Edward Epler: *Honorary Degrees: A Survey of Their
Use and Abuse* (Washington, 1943), pp. 59-67.
    [5] William James: "The Ph.D. Octopus," *Harvard Monthly*, XXXVI
(1903), 1-9.

In the 1880's and 1890's academic institutions occupied themselves with setting up their ladders of status achievement, thereby organizing, as had never been done before in the groves of academe, a competitive drive. The creation of a hierarchy of professors was not so much the function of the degree as it was a function, in the first place, of that awesome proliferation of knowledge which enlarged the scope of a particular area of human understanding and now required the labors of two or three men where one had once sufficed; and second, of that ever-increasing undergraduate and graduate enrollment which in some places now called for platoons of instructors where, also, one had once sufficed. There was nothing peculiar about this development in the colleges and universities. It was happening elsewhere in American life, particularly in business, where remarkable growth and expansion led quite naturally to new career patterns.

The organization of college faculties into ascending ranks of instructors and various levels of professors should not be construed as some villainous plot on the part of administrative officers to insinuate crass success motives into the placid, unreal world of learning. An academic hierarchy was a response to the expansion of the institutions themselves and to the growth of knowledge itself, and it was a conscious and clearly necessary effort to deal efficiently and effectively with problems that could not be met without order and organization. Perhaps, however, it was not necessary to go as far as President Harper did in 1891 when he set up what was probably the most elaborate chain of command and ladder of ambition open to a budding scholar.

His hierarchy at the University of Chicago began at the bottom with five different grades of one-year appointments. At the very bottom was the fellow who gave one sixth of his time to the university; above him, but clearly not very far, were the reader, the lecturer, the docent, and the assistant. Above these functionally differentiated young men at the bottom of the ladder were associates with two-year appoint-

ments, instructors with three-year appointments, and assistant
professors with four-year appointments; and above them
were three grades of permanent appointees: associate professors, professors, and head professors.[6] Surely no other
university hierarchy gave fuller play to all of the possibilities,
for good and for evil, that organization promised the American university.

To the apparatus of hierarchy was also added the concept of
departmentalization, a symbolic statement of the disunity of
knowledge which was never made by the old colleges. Then
a professor contained within himself the knowledge and the
interests necessary to sustain him as a teacher of several
subjects. Then an untrained professor like John Bascom at
Williams could teach rhetoric, write books on aesthetics and
political economy, and introduce courses in English literature
and sociology.[7] But now the old unity was gone, the avid
search for scientific truth was bringing forth great new contributions to knowledge, and specialization was leading to the
splintering of subject areas.

Size alone required departmentalization: a hierarchy of
biologists, for instance, had to be held together by some formal authority; their interests had to find expression in some
formally recognized locus of organization. But it was not
enough to have a department of biology, for such a department could not adequately reflect the splintering of knowledge and the rivalry for attention, for funds, for approval,
that now ensued. Departmentalization was not only a method

[6] Thomas Wakefield Goodspeed: *A History of the University of
Chicago Founded by John D. Rockefeller: The First Quarter Century*
(Chicago, 1916), p. 138; James E. Pollard: *History of the Ohio State
University: The Story of its First Seventy-Five Years 1873-1948* (Co-
lumbus, 1952), p. 102; Bronson: *Brown*, p. 428; Rudy: *C.C.N.Y.*, pp. 233
ff.; Daniel Walker Hollis: *University of South Carolina* (Columbia,
1951-6), II, 218; G. Wallace Chessman: *Denison: The Story of an Ohio
College* (Granville, 1957), pp. 271-2.

[7] Frederick Rudolph: *Mark Hopkins and the Log: Williams College,
1836-1872* (New Haven, 1956), p. 54.

of organizing an otherwise unwieldy number of academic specialists into the framework of university government; it was also a development that unleashed all of that competitiveness, that currying of favor, that attention to public relations, that scrambling for students, that pettiness and jealousy which in some of its manifestations made the university and college indistinguishable from other organizations.

Thus, in April 1893 the Department of Biology at the University of Chicago underwent an almost inevitable reorganization. Now instead of a Department of Biology there were five new departments: zoology, botany, anatomy, neurology, and physiology.[8] And that meant five new departmental chairmanships, five new little hierarchies, five new competing domains of knowledge and ambition and interest. Yet, in truth, scholarship could be served and the growth of knowledge assured in no other way. Such multiplication of departments took place everywhere. The method chosen might be addition or division. Departments of Modern Languages became Departments of German and Departments of Romance Languages. Departments of History and Political Economy became Departments of History and Departments of Political Economy. Departments of History became Departments of European History and Departments of American History. Departments of Political Economy became Departments of Political Science, Departments of Economics, and Departments of Sociology.[9]

With all the specialization which this departmentalization was intended to accommodate went a set of emphases, a set of values, that was foreign to the old-time college. For that catholicity of outlook and acquaintance with universal knowledge which had seemed so often to be a mark of the

[8] Goodspeed: *Chicago*, p. 322.
[9] See Burton Dorr Myers: *History of Indiana University 1902-1937* (Bloomington, 1952), pp. 486-7, 499; John Hugh Reynolds and David Yancey Thomas: *History of the University of Arkansas* (Fayetteville, 1910), p. 153; Nevins: *Illinois*, p. 145; Merle Curti and Vernon Carstensen: *The University of Wisconsin: A History, 1848-1925* (Madison, 1949), II, 328-34 ff.

best of the old-time professors there was now substituted a specialist's regard for the furthest refinements of his own interest. A critic of the new dispensation would lament: "One of the saddest, and at the same time, one of the most instructive sights imaginable, is a college professor digging up the upper skull and lower canine tooth of a Neanderthal man. It is a contrast between growth and petrifaction, the Neanderthal man representing growth. . . ." Others would conclude that there were no longer any great teachers in the colleges and universities, only specialists and young men learning how to be specialists. "Doctors of Dullness," one observer called them, pointing to "the tables of our university seminars . . . surrounded by monkish groups mulling lifelessly over stacks of hastily scribbled library cards and chanting, 'Professor Tweetzer and the recognized authorities say. . . .'" [1] For, as this particular observer implied, under the regime of specialization, narrowness of interest and inbreeding could lead to some of the greatest dangers of organization: dearth of originality, excess deference to authority, diffusion of responsibility. To the degree that specialization and organization achieved an upper hand, to that degree such perils became characteristic of academic life.

No one was more alarmed by these perils than was Dean Andrew Fleming West of Princeton, who, although charged with the direction of graduate studies, warned in 1905: "Many of our scholars seem to be subjects of some petty principality rather than freemen in the commonwealth of knowledge." Not hostile to specialization itself, West protested against the absorption in the trivial and against inflating the importance of those who were so absorbed. He referred to "the proof I read recently, showing minutely and beyond the shadow of a doubt . . . that unkindness or cruelty to an animal was from 30 to 50 per cent more shock-

---

[1] Simeon Strunsky: "The Shame of Health," *Harper's*, CXLV (1922), quoted in Bowman: *The College Professor in America*, p. 21; H. W. Whicker, "Doctors of Dullness," *North American Review*, CXV (1929), quoted in Bowman, p. 22.

ing to a girl than to a boy. Does one need to pursue higher university studies in order to know this?" Dean West was something of an old-timer, caught up in the scientific spirit but unwilling to surrender to it or to some of its absurdities. He spoke for the whole man, for values that could not be asserted except on faith, and in many ways he sought merely to remind the scholarly community that in certain important respects they were out of touch with the reality that mattered most. "The kind of scholar any man is to become, so far as the abiding value of his influence goes," said Dean West, "is determined in the last resort not so much by what he knows or says as by what he believes and loves." [2]

All this might be true, but the university was an organization that was building its own rationale, its own mores, its own set of peculiarities; it was achieving a size capable of camouflaging its own incompetencies and adept at elevating some of its gravest faults to the status of untouchable; in other words, it was developing some of the rights and privileges of organization. Where it all would end no one could be sure, but by 1923 Upton Sinclair could combine in one statement an attack on genteel culture, business, and academic specialization that would be difficult to surpass. Addressing himself at first to the employees of a Boston department store, Sinclair began: "Slaves in Boston's great department store, in which Harvard University owns twenty-five hundred shares of stock, be reconciled to your long hours and low wages and sentence to die of tuberculosis—because upon the wealth which you produce some learned person has prepared for mankind full data on 'The strong Verb in Chaucer.' . . . Men who slave twelve hours a day in front of blazing white furnaces of Bethlehem, Midvale and Illinois Steel, cheer up and take a fresh grip on your shovels—you are

[2] Andrew Fleming West: *The Changing Conception of "The Faculty" in American Universities* (San Francisco, 1906[?]), pp. 7, 9, 14.

making it possible for mankind to acquire exact knowledge concerning 'The Beginnings of the Epistolary Novel in the Romance Languages.' . . ." [3]

Publication, indeed, had become a guiding interest of the new academician. Each book, each article, was a notch pegged on the way to promotion. This embrace of Germanic scholarship was so great that by 1909 the Athletic Research Society was holding annual meetings at which coaches and athletic directors were reading research papers.[4] The transfer of emphasis from teaching to research was nowhere better revealed than in a conversation that was reported in 1909. "I took occasion not long ago," said one observer of the educational scene, "to ask a college dean who was the best teacher in his institution. He named a certain instructor." This conversation followed:

> What is his rank?
> Assistant Professor.
> When will his appointment expire?
> Shortly.
> Will he be promoted?
> No.
> Why not?
> He hasn't done anything! [5]

This de-emphasis of the teaching role of the American professor was introduced to American higher education at Johns Hopkins, and it was soon recognized as a necessary concomitant of the university idea. Scientific research—into the nature of molecules, moles, Molière, mollusks, and mollycoddles, into the nature of all the previously unexplored—required an outlet for all the productivity that was the consequence of university purpose. University rivalry required

[3] Upton Sinclair: *The Goose-Step, a Study of American Education* (Pasadena, 1923), pp. 90-1.

[4] Dudley Allen Sargent: *The History of the Administration of Intercollegiate Athletics in the United States* (New York, 1910), p. 1.

[5] Abraham Flexner, *Atlantic Monthly*, CIII (1909), quoted in Bowman: *The College Professor*, p. 122.

that each university be certain that its professors were better than its rivals, and one way of making that clear was by coming in ahead in the somewhat informal annual page count in which universities indulged.

This form of academic accounting not only had its public-relations purposes but it served as a prod to the slow performers. It shunted the teacher types off to limbo, to the country colleges or to exploitation and strangulation within the confines of the university. It made clear who was to be promoted, when, and why. The same relationship between production and rewards was also being established in the great organizations that now characterized American business life, not only in the giants like Standard Oil and U. S. Steel, but in the banks, the chain stores, the big department stores which were organizing on a complex impersonal scale functions once provided for by the neighborhood or the home. "Publish or Perish," the slogan became, and by the late nineteenth century at the University of Pennsylvania professors who insisted on pouring time and energy into teaching at the expense of research were told to go elsewhere.* For although one might be a most excellent teacher, and although effective teaching might lead untold students to self-discovery and self-mastery, the organization demanded something else: it fed on research, it regurgitated research, it promoted research. Without research, of course, there would be little or none of the exciting conquest of ignorance, the exciting advance on the frontiers of knowledge, which publication encouraged. But also, without research, there would be no departments, no departmental chairmen, no hierarchy—only teachers.

Like all circles, once the circle of publication had become an established routine, it was vicious. For it would lead a president of the University of North Dakota in 1909 to keep a running card file on his faculty. It would only with greatest reluctance make exceptions, break loose from the

*Richard H. Shryock: *The University of Pennsylvania Faculty: A Study in American Higher Education* (Philadelphia, 1959), pp. 34-5.

chains of organization. As President Harper explained with
great clarity and force in 1894: "The University . . . will
be patient, but it expects from every man honest and persistent effort in the direction of contribution to the world's
knowledge." At Harvard in 1892 Charles T. Copeland—
the famous "Copey"—was appointed an instructor in English,
and as a teacher of composition and as a friend who kept
open house for his students every Wednesday after ten, he
attracted the most devoted and apparently deserved undergraduate following in Harvard history. But he was a teacher,
and he had to wait eighteen years before his colleagues were
willing to promote him to assistant professor.[7]

The research emphasis of course created its own agencies:
learned journals, learned societies, university presses, and
sabbatical leaves. Johns Hopkins was "the cradle of the
scholarly journal in America." The founders of the university in Baltimore, conscious of their own research expectations, were equally conscious of the absence of those agencies that supported and diffused the results of research in
Europe. In France the government footed the bill, in England
the learned societies, and in Germany the universities. In
the absence of learned societies and in recognition of the
absence of any vital government tradition, Johns Hopkins
led the way for the universities with the founding in 1877 of
The American Journal of Mathematics. Soon chemistry,
biology, physiology, psychology, and philology belonged to
the battery of Hopkins journals. At the University of
Chicago provision was made for political economy, geology,
Hebrew, astrophysics, sociology, theology, and classics. By
1898 the number of copies of University of Chicago journals
printed in a year totaled 150,000. By 1904 Columbia profes-

[7] Louis G. Geiger: *University of the Northern Plains: A History of
the University of North Dakota 1883-1958* (Grand Forks, 1958), p. 200;
Goodspeed: *Chicago*, pp. 318-19; Samuel Eliot Morison: *Three Centuries of Harvard 1636-1936* (Cambridge, 1936), p. 402.

sors were churning out thirty-five serial publications.[8] The consequence of these massive journal performances was to lead many universities to the conclusion that respectability required its own set of journals; this conclusion led to a great deal of publication that was not exactly of high quality.

The journals of the learned societies provided another outlet for publication. The older learned societies which had served a more general purpose—the American Philosophical Society of 1743, the American Academy of Arts and Sciences of 1780, and the American Association for the Advancement of Science of 1848 which testified to the early attraction of science—were now joined by societies that represented the fragmentation of learning and that gave scholars a means of pooling their energies and their discoveries. Of the new wave of learned societies the American Philological Association was first in 1869. It was followed by the American Chemical Society in 1877, the Modern Language Association in 1883, the American Historical Association in 1884, the American Economic Association in 1885, the American Mathematical Society and the Geological Society of America, both in 1888.[9]

At their annual meetings these associations, as well as the numerous other groups that now required some means of personal communication to supplement the printed page, read and discussed learned papers, took measures to formalize and standardize their particular branch of learning, protected their interests from the claims of rival disciplines, enjoyed the temporary pleasures of life off the reservation, and institutionalized the annual meeting of the learned society as a kind of hiring hall for college and university presidents and departmental chairmen in search of new talent. Here the pro-

[8] Hugh Hawkins: *Pioneer: A History of the Johns Hopkins University, 1874-1889* (Ithaca, 1960), pp. 73-6; John C. French: *A History of the University Founded by Johns Hopkins* (Baltimore, 1946), pp. 50-6; Goodspeed: *Chicago*, pp. 319-20; John Howard Van Amringe, et al.: *A History of Columbia University 1754-1904* (New York, 1904), p. 254.

[9] Nicholas Murray Butler, ed.: *Monographs on Education in the United States* (Albany, 1900), II, 868-80.

fessors in the graduate schools paraded their most promising students (and others as well), and sent them out into the market which would in time propel them back into the college or university organization. The annual meeting, like the business convention, testified to the shrinking of distances, and it brought together groups of specialists who spoke in a language all their own, shared discoveries, and went back to their campuses with a renewed sense of belonging.

The larger, more affluent universities now added formally organized university presses to the apparatus designed to keep the wheels of research well oiled. An office at Johns Hopkins had been charged with publishing responsibilities as early as 1878, but with the requirement adopted in 1888 that all doctoral dissertations be published, the publication function of the university was notably increased. By 1891 this activity had clearly emerged as the Johns Hopkins University Press, the first clearly designated university press in the country. Chicago followed in 1892, and in the next year Columbia and the University of California. Early in the twentieth century, Princeton, Yale, and Harvard enlarged their own concept of university purpose to accommodate the university press. By 1916 the press at the University of Chicago had published 850 titles, 850 contributions to knowledge, 850 passports to fame and promotion.[1] To facilitate all this publication, and as if further to de-emphasize the teaching function, paid leaves of absence and sabbatical years began to become common in the 1890's.[2] In return for these months of relief from university duties, the professors knew what was expected and were indeed happy to oblige: a fresh batch of articles, a startling new laboratory discovery, a book in the university's series of scholarly studies. In such ways academic man fed and was fed.

[1] Hawkins: *Johns Hopkins*, pp. 111-12; French: *Johns Hopkins*, p. 226; Goodspeed: *Chicago*, p. 321.
[2] Lewis B. Cooper: *Sabbatical Leave for College Teachers* (Gainesville, 1932), pp. 9-10; Nevins: *Illinois*, p. 192; Reynolds and Thomas: *Arkansas*, p. 152; Van Amringe: *Columbia*, p. 156; Leon Burr Richardson: *History of Dartmouth College* (2 vols., Hanover, 1932), II, 710.

. . .

All this apparatus, all of these manifestations of organization, would be a tremendous boon to the academic itinerant, for whom a reputation in his profession was more important than any commitment to a particular institution. The tendencies of the new scholarship and of organization would make such a man loyal to professional standards and to the processes and attributes of organization but indifferent to the fate of the institution to which he might temporarily be attached. The towering authority of the president, the preference of the new academician not to become much involved in student affairs, and his honest and consuming commitment to learning often helped to establish an attitude of neutrality on his part toward the institution for which he worked—an attitude that was also reinforced by the growing authority of alumni in university and college affairs.

There were efforts to compensate for loss of the sense of unity, for the sense of commitment, for the sense almost bordering on brotherhood that had animated the old college governments. The perquisites were all a function of organization, and while in no sense could they replace what was now lost, they contributed immeasurably to the morale of academic man. The appearance on the campus of such peculiarities as faculty clubs and academic dress was a function of organization. These forms of psychic income enabled professors in some degree to establish their identity as a group before society as a whole.

The exhibition of professors displayed in academic robes not only tied the new academicians into an ancient tradition of learning, but it also paraded them like so many cadets in uniform; it underlined their oneness, their belonging. The commencement ritual which had well served the varied purposes of the American college now assumed a new purpose: the exhibition of the new professionals, drawn up in order of rank and wearing their badges of merit. If the faculty club was a conscious effort to stimulate an institutional cohesiveness that size made impossible, it was also what was required of any self-respecting group of organization men. The American faculty club was merely one more occupational variation of the gentleman's club—the manufacturer's club, the banker's club, the broker's club. There in an atmosphere of sociability the interests of organization could be advanced; there something of that old-time casual spirit and sheer good fun might be recaptured.

The rise of the academician, the organization of professors and learning in all the ways that have been suggested, was essential to the achievement of intellectual maturity by the United States. If there were losses in personal security and psychological certainty when the college professor underwent professionalization, there were also magnificent gains: the tremendous conquest of ignorance, the sheer increase in the number of Americans for whom intellectual pursuits brought pleasure, the harnessing of knowledge for the service of man.

The old-time professor would not have understood the demands that Frederick Jackson Turner made at the University of Wisconsin in 1900 as the price of his willingness to stay in Madison: "Enlargement of staff, fellowships, permanent funds for the purchase of books, a leave of absence, and provisions for publication of historical studies." [3] Nor would he have appreciated the technique of teaching developed by Elijah P. Harris, a Göttingen-trained chemist at Amherst, who made his lectures intentionally incomprehensible on the grounds that really interested students would stop after class for further instruction.[4] He might even have agreed with the old graduate who described the new professors as "self-deceiving dreamers who solace themselves with the idea that they are doing for the world a service by their books, while

[3] Curti and Carstensen: *Wisconsin*, I, 617.
[4] Claude M. Fuess: *Amherst: The Story of a New England College* (Boston, 1935), p. 178.

their class work goes unheeded." [5] But he would have been wrong. The new professors, it is true, had their own orientation, their own set of peculiarities, but life for them was no more a matter of solace and double-serving than it had been for the old-time professor. Intellect rather than piety was their touchstone, and ignorance was their particular challenge. If sometimes they were apparently oblivious to the world around them, if sometimes they seemed absorbed in study or caught up in organization, this was nothing more nor less than evidence of a deep-seated dedication to the advancement of learning. He who missed this did not know the new professor at all.

To these more apparent gains must also be added the establishment of highly regarded traditions of academic freedom and tenure. These new principles were hammered out during a time when academicians were acutely aware of the disjunction between society and its institutions, which John Dewey proposed to remedy on the level of the schools with a new concept of learning and teaching. In the universities correcting this disjunction often brought the academicians into conflict with important interests that had a stake in the status quo, perhaps in the very disjunction that the academicians sought to cure. Not always, but often, this meant conflict with representatives of the business community, men whose importance to the universities and colleges was made apparent every time a new building appeared on the expanding campuses. Out of these experiences there developed important and fundamental standards of freedom and tenure affecting the capacity of the American university to support effectively the life of the mind. [6]

This was not the first period when questions of freedom had arisen on the American college campus, for in the era

[5] Curti and Carstensen: *Wisconsin*, II, 99.
[6] This consideration of academic freedom relies heavily on Richard Hofstadter and Walter P. Metzger: *The Development of Academic Freedom in the United States* (New York, 1955).

of the colleges sectarianism had from time to time intruded
the charge of heresy into the academic community, but these
experiences had not shaped any broad principles to guide the
life of the colleges. A tendency on the part of the institutions to defend themselves from outside attack and to assert
their right to stand for unpopular causes, including the classical curriculum, stemmed in part from the colleges' function as preserver of ancient traditions. In this posture the
old-time colleges asserted a kind of freedom not to follow
the crowd.' But now under the impact of the scientific point
of view and of the traditions of the German university, the
idea of academic freedom in America would be invested with
strength and new purpose.

In a series of instances involving a conflict between
sectarian interests and the new science symbolized by Darwinism, science was not only victorious but it advanced a
"special conception of truth and a formula for tolerating error" that had the effect of investing academic freedom with
an ethic. In an environment of growing secularism and of
widespread acceptance of evolution among scientists, Vanderbilt University in 1878 forced Alexander Winchell, a biologist, from its faculty, only to see him warmly welcomed
at the University of Michigan. The Presbyterian Theological
Seminary at Columbia, South Carolina, dismissed Thomas
Woodrow in 1884 for similar reasons, but these were insufficient to keep Woodrow from the presidency of the
University of South Carolina in 1891. At the sectarian College of Wooster in Ohio in 1893, a professor of science,
subjected to close questioning by the board of trustees, was
defended by the president when he firmly told the board
that he had come to his views on evolution after much study
and thought and that he had no intention of changing
them. He kept his job. In the 1880's at Dartmouth a skeptical physics professor concluded a series of dramatic classroom experiments with the remark: "Behold the wonderful

' Ibid., pp. 209-74.

works of the Creator!" At the University of North Dakota a professor of biology taught advanced evolutionary theory without effective public protest.[8]

These and similar instances elsewhere revealed the professors in the process of discovering a common respect for the requirements of scholarship, in the process of defining academic freedom as a climate in which the scientific point of view itself was fundamental. This climate was shaped by a tolerance for error, by a preference for experiment and a respect for the unknown, by an indifference to tradition and inherited truth, by a need for continuous inquiry and continuous verification. Academic freedom, then, came to rest on the spirit of suspended judgment and changing truth that animated the laboratory or the scholar at work among his manuscripts. It would, among the academicians themselves, be reinforced by the principles that governed research and scholarship in the German universities, which in so many ways were the source of inspiration for the new American universities. The German university professor, in speaking of academic freedom, had in mind two words: *Lernfreiheit* and *Lehrfreiheit*. By *Lernfreiheit* he meant that absence of administrative coercion which freed the German student to roam from university to university, to take what course he chose, live where he would, and to be free from all those restrictions, characteristic of the English and American collegiate way, that were hostile to an atmosphere of dedicated study and research. By *Lehrfreiheit* the German professor meant the right of the university professor to freedom of inquiry and to freedom of teaching, the right to study and to report on his findings in an atmosphere of consent.[9]

[8] Ibid., pp. 320-66; Edwin Mims: *History of Vanderbilt University* (Nashville, 1946), pp. 100-5; Lucy Lilian Notestein: *Wooster of the Middle West* (New Haven, 1937), pp. 184-6; Cornelius Howard Patton and Walter Taylor Field: *Eight O'Clock Chapel: A Study of New England College Life* (Boston, 1927), p. 231; Geiger: *North Dakota*, p. 72.

[9] Hofstadter and Metzger: *The Development of Academic Freedom*, pp. 383-497.

The German experience in developing academic freedom
was an important factor in the achievement of freedom in
the American academic community, but the German conception applied only to life within the academic walls and
did not address itself to the privileges of the professor once
he chose to go beyond the university, to the outside where
actually no such freedom awaited him or any other servant
of the German state. In the American context, where freedom was a traditional right of all Americans, the American
academician was able to break down the distinction between
inner freedom and outer restraint which characterized the
German definition. In addition, *Lernfreiheit*, the freedom of
the student, assumed less importance in the American definition, in part perhaps because the elective curriculum was enlarging the domain of student freedom. The preoccupation
of the American professor with establishing *Lehrfreiheit* and
of investing it with a wider application unquestionably derived from the peculiar role that the American professor
played as both scientific researcher and as employee. What
finally happened was the assumption within the academic
walls of a posture of neutrality on controversial matters; in
the classroom the American professor used his professional
competence and his scientific knowledge of the facts to
present controversial questions in such a way that his own
neutrality protected the students from indoctrination. Outside the university the American professor took advantage
of the American commitment to the idea of freedom of
speech and thereby advanced the principle that the professor
might enjoy outside the classroom the same rights, the same
freedoms, as other Americans.

In this area, in this "attempt to assimilate the doctrine of
free speech into the doctrine of academic freedom . . . the
greatest amount of academic friction was generated." Here
the new academicians, particularly the social scientists, came
into conflict with important groups in the world outside the
academic community. For the professors, in seeking to apply
their economic and political and social discoveries to the real

world, often collided with the men who were serving the universities as benefactors and trustees. A distinguished roster of academicians learned that freedom, as they understood it, had not yet become a part of the understanding of benefactors and governing boards drawn from the business community, or even of farm and labor groups more closely associated with the people. Richard T. Ely, economist at the University of Wisconsin, spoke favorably of strikes and boycotts; for this economic heresy he was tried by a committee of the board of regents in 1894. Edward W. Bemis, economist at the University of Chicago, chose the period of the Pullman strike to make a public attack on the railroads; he was dismissed. James Allen Smith, political scientist at Marietta College, did not like monopolies, and he met the same fate as Bemis in 1897. President E. Benjamin Andrews of Brown revealed a preference for free trade and bimetallism that made his position at an old eastern college untenable. John R. Commons indulged in a range of economic views so disturbing that he ran into difficulty at both Indiana University and Syracuse. Edward A. Ross, sociologist at Stanford, disapproved of coolie labor, with the consequence that Mrs. Leland Stanford disapproved of him. In 1903 at Trinity College in North Carolina, John Spencer Bassett, a professor of history, asked the South to welcome the Negro into American life; the South arose in attack. At Kansas State during the 1890's the flow of professors in and out of the economics department depended on the election returns: Democrats and Populists were no friendlier to academic freedom than were Republicans. Economic nonconformity was the great and abiding sin of the professors who were involved in these key cases of academic freedom in the 1890's and early 1900's.[1]

[1] Ibid., pp. 405, 420-5; Curti and Carstensen: *Wisconsin*, I, 508-27; Arthur G. Beach: *A Pioneer College: The Story of Marietta* (Marietta, 1935), p. 226; Bronson: *Brown*, pp. 461-4; James Albert Woodburn: *History of Indiana University 1820-1902* (Bloomington, 1940), pp. 414-15, 440; Orrin Leslie Elliott: *Stanford University: The First Twenty-Five Years* (Stanford University, 1937), pp. 326-78.

Out of these cases, however, there emerged in strengthened
form the principles of American academic freedom, principles that could never be taken for granted and that would
often in the decades that followed be subjected to stress.
Each case became a discussion of the intellectual climate
necessary to the new American university; each case brought
the academic community to a profounder awareness of its
common goals and needs; each case became a course of instruction (which governing boards found themselves taking
whether they wished to or not) on the right of the professor
to the same freedom of expression enjoyed by businessmen,
farmers, and workers.

To these principles in the early decades of the twentieth
century were added principles of academic tenure, the terms
of professorial office, that would safeguard both the principles of academic freedom and the professor at his work.
In 1878 a Cornell trustee argued the right of the Cornell
board to dismiss professors as summarily as businessmen
might dismiss factory laborers. But the developing self-
consciousness of the academicians argued for greater job
security, for rank and seniority and salary schedules; it invited rules governing permanent and temporary appointments,
expectations of conditions conducive to scholarly work, and
collective commitment to the principles of academic freedom. The professor was being professionalized, and the consequence was to bring college and university presidents and
governing boards under increasing pressure to recognize
their obligations to the community of free scholars.[2]

In 1915 there was established the American Association of
University Professors, a professional society dedicated in
particular to the development and protection of standards
of freedom and tenure. Its establishment symbolized the arrival of academic man in America. Now the organization

[2] Hofstadter and Metzger: *The Development of Academic Freedom*,
pp. 413–67; Walter P. Rogers: *Andrew D. White and the Modern
University* (Ithaca, 1942), p. 153.

man, university model, had an organization to protect him from the organization itself, to sustain him in as noble an endeavor as man had ever assumed—the pursuit of truth, the conquest of ignorance.

20

❦

The
Organized Institution

The American colleges and universities, in their development from simple institutions to complex organizations, not only replaced the old-time professor with the academician, that trained specialist who knew the rights and privileges and responsibilities of a profession and who in so many of his experiences was indistinguishable from other organization men, but the colleges and universities also required a new kind of executive officer, new methods of financing, new areas of administration. Growth fed upon growth, and the answer to the problems of growth—unless it was to be chaos—was organization.

The extent to which university presidents themselves now adopted a kind of presidents' club psychology, the degree to which they recognized one another as being caught up in a web of problems and purposes that was characteristic of all of them, was revealed in the letters that Professor John H. Finley of Princton received in 1903 when he was elected to the presidency of the City College of New York. From President Nicholas Murray Butler of Columbia he heard: "You would be most heartily welcomed here by all of us who are already in the harness." From President Harper at Chicago came the assurance: "There are plenty of men to be professors; there are only a few to be presidents of colleges and universities. The profession will, I am sure, welcome you." [1]

Of course not every college or university president was yet prepared to think of himself as belonging to a society of self-conscious professionals. There were still many of the old type around, including Webster Merriefield at North Dakota who found time at the opening of the university each year to see that student baggage was properly delivered and who often used his own bank account as an interest-free student loan fund. [2] Others, too, were having their difficulties in making the transition. David Starr Jordan, by training an ichthyologist, as president of Indiana University had maintained some of the flavor of the old paternalism and had boasted of knowing every student by name. At Stanford he gave up trying when he discovered that every time he remembered the name of a student he forgot the name of a fish. [3] Actually the college and university president was on the way to being someone who would not remember the names of either, to being someone whose remoteness from the students would be paralleled by his remoteness from learning itself.

The office increasingly, in Veblen's phrase, called for a "captain of erudition," a manager who could perform for higher education those functions which elsewhere in American society were being performed by the captains of industry and the captains of finance. [4] What university governing boards were looking for in a president was described by

[1] S. Willis Rudy: *The College of the City of New York: A History, 1847-1947* (New York, 1949), p. 246.

[2] Louis G. Geiger: *University of the Northern Plains: A History of the University of North Dakota 1883-1958* (Grand Forks, 1958), pp. 128-9.

[3] Amos Alonzo Stagg: *Touchdown!* (New York, 1927), pp. 198-9.

[4] Thorstein Veblen: *The Higher Learning in America: A Memorandum on the Conduct of Universities by Business Men* (New York, 1918).

Rutherford B. Hayes, a member of the Ohio State board, in the early 1890's. Said Hayes: "We are looking for a man of fine appearance, of commanding presence, one who will impress the public; he must be a fine speaker at public assemblies; he must be a great scholar and a great teacher; he must be a preacher, also, as some think; he must be a man of winning manners; he must have tact so that he can get along with and govern the faculty; he must be popular with the students; he must also be a man of business training, a man of affairs; he must be a great administrator." Hayes had the wit to say to his colleagues on the Ohio State board, "Gentlemen, there is no such man," but many governing boards must have been possessed by some similar hope that they could find a man who combined the qualities of a Francis Wayland or a Mark Hopkins with those of a Rockefeller or a Morgan.[5]

Into discard went the clergyman, not so much because his godliness was an administrative encumbrance—indeed, a religious posture, whatever its sincerity, continued to be a desirable quality in a college president. The clergyman president went into discard because he lacked skill in the ways of the world, because his commitment to the classical curriculum stood in the way of the more practical and popular emphasis which commended itself to the trustees, and because the world in which the colleges and universities now moved was more secular, less subject to religious influences. One by one the colleges broke with tradition and elected their first nonclergyman to the presidency: Denison in 1889, Illinois College in 1892, Yale in 1899, Princeton in 1902, Marietta in 1913, Bowdoin in 1918, Wabash in 1926.[6] Ob-

[5] James E. Pollard: *History of the Ohio State University: The Story of its First Seventy-Five Years 1873-1948* (Columbus, 1952), p. 136.

[6] G. Wallace Chessman: *Denison: The Story of an Ohio College* (Granville, 1957), p. 234; Charles Henry Rammelkamp: *Illinois College: A Centennial History 1829-1929* (New Haven, 1928), p. 379; George Wilson Pierson: *Yale: College and University 1871-1937* (New Haven, 1952-5), I, 62; Thomas Jefferson Wertenbaker: *Princeton 1746-1896* (Princeton, 1946), pp. 388-9; Arthur G. Beach: *A Pioneer College: The Story of Marietta* (Marietta, 1935), p. 274; Louis C. Hatch: *The*

viously some did so sooner than others, but the trend was irresistible, and to the management of American colleges and universities there now came a strange mixture of scholars, former politicians, Civil War generals, businessmen, lawyers, men generally with some experience in dealing with people or with money, the two poles around which organization life necessarily revolved.[7]

The demands of growth, the tentacles of organization itself, the always certain uncertainty of a thousand loose ends —all this put the new university president into action on a broad front. No one was more typical than William Rainey Harper of Chicago, who would begin a conference with an administrative subordinate with the announcement, "I have forty points to be discussed this morning," and who, told by his doctors that he had cancer, turned out five books in the eighteen months left him and died in 1906 at the age of fifty, one of the great and memorable men in the history of American education.[8]

The new collegiate administrator, on the other hand, might be Alston Ellis of Ohio University, standing at his office window clocking professors as they arrived on the campus each morning, a man who wore so many emblems of various fraternal orders that he was once referred to on the floor of the Ohio legislature as "that man . . . who wears more medals than a stallion at a county fair." President Finley of C.C.N.Y. earned a reputation as "one of the greatest showmen in the American academic world" by perfecting great

History of Bowdoin College (Portland, 1927), p. 211; James I. Osborne and Theodore G. Gronert: *Wabash College; the first hundred years, 1832-1932* (Crawfordsville, 1932), p. 377.

[7]Leon Burr Richardson: *History of Dartmouth College* (Hanover, 1932), II, 762; Pollard: *Ohio State*, p. 283; John Hugh Reynolds and David Yancey Thomas: *History of the University of Arkansas* (Fayetteville, 1910), p. 111; George Matthew Dutcher: *An Historical and Critical Survey of the Curriculum of Wesleyan University and Related Subjects* (Middletown, 1948), p. 31.

[8]Thomas Wakefield Goodspeed: *A History of the University of Chicago Founded by John D. Rockefeller: The First Quarter Century* (Chicago, 1916), pp. 133, 410.

academic assemblies, introducing into commencement exercises an appropriately twentieth-century New York version of the Ephebic oath of ancient Athens, persuading national organizations to hold their conventions on the C.C.N.Y. campus, and by endeavoring to keep a flow of V.I.P.'s running through the campus. The new college president was someone like Langdon Stewardson who in his first report as president of Hobart remarked, "The President of Hobart, permit me to remind you, undertook his present duties with the express stipulation that he was not to be the financial drummer for the college, but its educational leader." By the time of his second annual report Stewardson had learned so much that he could confess: "Disagreeable as the job of money-raising actually is, the President clearly recognizes that it is for him a plain and imperative duty." [*]

The new university president was an off-campus celebrity: he was Andrew D. White absent from the campus between 1876 and 1881 for all but five months; he was James B. Angell on leave of absence as envoy extraordinary to China or as American minister to Constantinople. He might be Merrill Edwards Gates of Amherst, so impressed by the world beyond the campus that his students were required to bring him back to reality; they greeted a Gates remark ("When I was in Washington, I and the President. . . .") with scraping and catcalls so humiliating that Gates did not meet the class again. The new university president was Arthur Twining Hadley of Yale, reminding ambitious departmental chairmen of the chronic distaste of "the average millionaire" for wasteful duplication. He was the president of Ohio University who made a four-week tour of eastern universities in 1907, returned to Athens full of fresh ideas, one of which led to the appointment of a committee to procure some squirrels for the university green. He was John M.

[*] Thomas N. Hoover: *The History of Ohio University* (Athens, 1954), pp. 199-200; Rudy: *C.C.N.Y.*, pp. 302-8; Walter Schultz Stover: *Alumni Stimulation by the American College President* (New York, 1930), p. 73.

Thomas who, the morning after his election to the presidency of Middlebury, walked into the Columbia University library and began a year of study of college and university problems. He was Samuel C. Mitchell of the University of South Carolina, so conscious of his public-relations function that he delivered a lecture on "Mirabeau, the Foremost Figure of the French Revolution" before an audience of mill hands.[1]

It took time to develop anything like a perfect flowering of this new "captain of erudition," but by 1918 he could be found at the University of North Dakota in the person of Thomas F. Kane, a Johns Hopkins Ph.D. in classics, who took the occasion of his inauguration to remark: "I am inclined to think that if the faculty in any university in the country were submitted to as severe tests [as the football coach], it would lose probably one fourth of its members. . . . I may assure you, if you need assurance, that the men at the University are going to earn their salaries. We are going to drive them hard." A few decades later he would be joined by a North Dakota successor who issued a memorandum on faculty promotions and salaries which described a point system that, among other things, allotted thirty points for a professor's effectiveness in public relations; and by a president of Ohio State who clearly was a master at organizing everything: he introduced what was called "Prexy Hour," a monthly hour when he was available to students for questioning, a kind of open confessional *cum* press conference, where the cult of efficiency sustained the old paternal purposes.[2]

---

[1] Walter P. Rogers: *Andrew D. White and the Modern University* (Ithaca, 1942), p. 174; Burke A. Hinsdale: *History of the University of Michigan* (Ann Arbor, 1906), p. 75; Claude M. Fuess: *Amherst: The Story of a New England College* (Boston, 1935), p. 249; Pierson: *Yale*, I, 374; Hoover: *Ohio*, pp. 193-4; William Storrs Lee: *Father Went to College: The Story of Middlebury* (New York, 1936), p. 210; Daniel Walker Hollis: *University of South Carolina* (Columbia, 1951-6), II, 242.

[2] Geiger: *North Dakota*, pp. 293-4, 380-2; Pollard: *Ohio State*, p. 354.

Although there were laments for the passing of the old-time college president, on the broad front where the new university president was needed the old-timer was an inept anachronism. The capacity to lead now assumed a tremendous importance in college and university affairs. In contrast with the modern university, the old college was a place where nothing happened and where the president by a kind of indifference or remoteness or even superiority to mundane matters performed an effortless role in seeing to it that nothing did happen. The new era, however, demanded men who knew what they wanted and, better yet, what their various publics wanted, men who were prepared to try the impossible task of being the "reconciler of irreconcilabilities," the leader to students, faculty, alumni, and trustees—groups that too often did not find a common purpose to transcend their differences until the president found it for them. The collegiate or university organization was, at best, a delicate balance of interests, a polite tug of war, a blending of emphases, a disunity that found unity only through the refinements, the habits, the certainties of organization. Without a president the organization, depending on other factors as well, could for a time get along reasonably well, but on the president depended the degree to which the institution transcended the grip of organization and found expression in some vibrant, living purpose.

Upton Sinclair described the modern university president as "the most universal faker and the most variegated prevaricator that has yet appeared in the civilized world." [3] History must treat him more tenderly and attempt to understand the forces that shaped an office fraught with so many perils, shot through with so many ambiguities, an office that was many things to many men, but that at all times required remarkable resources of leadership, patience, and perseverance. "Don't overwork yourself," President Eliot wrote to

[3] Upton Sinclair: *The Goose-Step, a Study of American Education* (Pasadena, 1923), pp. 382-4.

Daniel Coit Gilman when he was elected to the presidency of Johns Hopkins in 1876.[4] No successful university president, including Eliot, ever followed this advice.

The financing of the American college and university was one of the problems that would keep many of the presidents overworked, for while the era of the university was the age of the big giver, it was also the age of the alumnus and the philanthropic foundation. If the president did nothing else, he could keep himself decently overworked merely by incorporating these agencies of financial support into the structure of his organization; and of course what happened was that the president often became both the symbolic and actual locus of this new formulation of university finance. The benefactor was no new phenomenon, but the size of his gifts and their regularity and number distinguished the university from the collegiate era. Without him the American college would have remained stagnant, the university movement lain dormant.

The continuing importance of the principle of the stewardship of wealth was neatly recorded during the dramatic concluding moments of the opening exercises at Vanderbilt University in 1875. The Reverend Charles F. Deems, Vanderbilt's minister in New York, arose and read a telegram: "New York, October 4. To Dr. Charles F. Deems: Peace and good-will to all men. C. Vanderbilt." Deems then gazed at a portrait of the benefactor hanging on the wall to his left and turned to the audience, quoting from Holy scripture, Acts, tenth chapter, thirty-first verse: "Cornelius, thy prayer is heard, and thine alms are had in remembrance in the sight of God."[5] By 1914 the South could turn to its own millionaires, but the stewardship principle was still powerful. In

[4] Willis Rudy: "Eliot and Gilman: The History of an Academic Friendship," *Teachers College Record*, LIV (1953), 309.
[5] Edwin Mims: *History of Vanderbilt University* (Nashville, 1946), pp. 13, 43, 67.

offering a million dollars for the support of university ambitions at Emory in Georgia, Asa Candler, the Coca Cola
millionaire, wrote: "God has blessed me far beyond my just
deserts by giving me such a measure of this world's goods as
to constitute a sacred trust that I must administer with conscientious fidelity with reference to his divine will." •

While stewardship as a religious duty in America was as
old as the first English settlements, it now also received a
secular definition, and benefaction became the obligation of
those who were the fittest in society, those whose special
aptitudes and talents had made them the winners in the
struggle of life. The application of Darwinian social analysis
to the meaning of his own life led Andrew Carnegie to devote a great fortune to the benefit of mankind. Unmoved by
religious principle he nonetheless found his way to a sense of
obligation that in the case of his fellow benefactor, John D.
Rockefeller, rested on the idea of religious stewardship. In
either case, the gospel of wealth stated the responsibility of
wealth to mankind, and it prompted much of the benefaction that underwrote the university era.

Also at work was the belief or hope of the benefactors that
in endowing colleges and universities they were preserving
American institutions. Henry Lee Higginson, who was himself a model Harvard benefactor, in a letter to a wealthy
kinsman and Harvard alumnus urged an immediate $100,000
contribution to Harvard as a fair share in the larger effort
to tame the masses. For, after all, did not all that really mattered in the world depend upon enlarging the influence of
Harvard before it was too late?[7]

A great deal of the new endowment went into institutes of
technology, into schools of applied science, and in the case
of the older foundations into science buildings and laboratories. These areas of academic interest appealed to practical

• Henry Morton Bullock: *A History of Emory University* (Nashville, 1936), p. 286.
7 Bliss Perry, ed.: *Life and Letters of Henry Lee Higginson* (Boston,
1921), p. 329.

men of affairs, and from these areas might be expected to come those material benefits, those opportunities for industrial growth and employment conducive to keeping the American workingman attached to the American system. Moreover, the benefactors, whether or not they had gone to college—and many of the biggest ones had not—realized that a college professor had made the analyses that indicated the commercial possibilities of petroleum and that the Carnegie Steel Company had been the first of the steel companies to employ a college-trained chemist.[8]

One by one the colleges and universities found their millionaires or hoped to find them. At Columbia between 1890 and 1901, under the presidency of Seth Low, in more than one year the annual gifts surpassed the total of all those before 1890. To the support of Columbia now came people with names like Morgan, Vanderbilt, Cutting, Havemeyer, Pulitzer, Schermerhorn, Schiff, Fish; President Low himself gave a million-dollar library. New York University was discovered by the family of Jay Gould; Brown continued in the favor of the family of Nicholas Brown but could now also call on John D. Rockefeller; Mrs. Cyrus McCormick took a kindly interest in little Tusculum College in Tennessee, which was soon celebrating her birthday; Kenyon received the favor of Marcus Alonzo Hanna and of William Nelson Cromwell; George Eastman began the benefactions that ultimately yielded plant and endowment of $24,000,000 for the University of Rochester; Mrs. Russell Sage gave the Rensselaer Polytechnic Institute a school of mechanical engineering, and Clarence Mackay, son of one of the most successful miners of the old Comstock lode, provided the University of Nevada with a school of mines one year, with an athletic plant the next.[9]

[8] Sarah K. Bolton: *Famous Givers and Their Gifts* (New York, 1896), pp. 297 ff.; Rogers: *Cornell*, p. 12.

[9] John Howard Van Amringe, *et al.*: *A History of Columbia University 1754-1904* (New York, 1904), pp. 157, 263; Theodore F. Jones, ed.: *New York University 1832:1932* (New York, 1933), pp. 169-70; Walter C. Bronson: *The History of Brown University 1764-1914*

The significance of these and similar benefactions was measurable in endowment, plant expansion, new departments, new professional schools. What was not measurable altogether was the extent to which the benefactors modified the life of the institutions themselves. Inevitably they found their way to college governing boards and there helped to insinuate many practices that they had learned in their roles as entrepreneurs or managers in the rough-and-tumble world of industry, business, and finance. The professionalization of the professors had not brought them any new authority in college and university affairs; actually it had only helped to widen the gap between them and the governing board, a gap which had existed even in the era of the colleges, when the professors were already on the road from being fellows charged with ultimate responsibility to being hirelings of those men of the world who increasingly dominated collegiate governing boards.

The structure of the colleges and universities in the end made room for an extremely professionalized faculty and for a governing board whose professional competence lay outside the main interests of the institution itself. This anomaly had historic roots. But it also reflected the process of organization going on in many other American institutions, including the press and the church, which were being caught up in all the efforts to deal with growth, numbers, expanded purposes, and enlarged responsibilities. It therefore did not seem an anomaly, especially to the governing boards, to have the pre-eminent organizers, the model managers, in control at the colleges and universities.[1]

(Providence, 1914), pp. 470 ff.; Albert E. Ragan: *A History of Tusculum College, 1794-1944* (Bristol, 1945), pp. 8, 82; George Franklin Smythe: *Kenyon College: Its First Century* (New Haven, 1924), pp. 258 ff.; Jesse Leonard Rosenberger: *Rochester, the Making of a University* (Rochester, 1927), p. 278; Palmer Chamberlain Ricketts: *History of Rensselaer Polytechnic Institute 1824-1914* (3d. ed.; New York, 1934), p. 139; Samuel Bradford Dolen: *An Illustrated History of the University of Nevada* (Reno, 1924), pp. 108 ff.

[1] An exaggerated but incisive study of this phenomenon is Veblen: *The Higher Learning in America.*

．　　．　　．

This development would be assisted by the rise of the alumnus to a position of power and to formal recognition in the structure of the organization itself. Building on the early nineteenth-century beginnings of alumni societies, capturing the kinds of loyalty that would actually lead an alumnus of the University of North Dakota to name his twin daughters Una and Versa, or that led Rufus Choate, then an "old grad" of Dartmouth, to remark, "My college life was so exquisitely happy that I should like to relive it in my son," the alumni movement now found expression in college and university governing boards, with duly elected representatives of the alumni body taking their place beside the self-perpetuating members.[2] The alumni-trustee movement began at Harvard with the legislative act of 1865 which completely separated the university from the Commonwealth and shifted the election of the board of overseers to the graduates; it was given a form more useful to the standard institution with a single governing body at Williams in 1868, which provided for the alumni election each year of one member of the board for a term of five years. This device for pumping new blood into old institutions was soon recognized by alumni groups everywhere as a means of freeing alma mater from clerical or conservative control.[3]

The rise of the alumni to power after the Civil War suggested not only that they had the will but that the colleges and universities were in no financial position to frustrate that will. The alumni were just beginning to arrive at a position of eminence and wealth which would enable them to join wealthy outsiders and the faculty in the support of American higher education. In exchange for their generosity

[2] Geiger: *North Dakota*, p. 271; Richardson: *Dartmouth*, I, 384.
[3] Samuel Eliot Morison: *Three Centuries of Harvard 1636-1936* (Cambridge, 1936), p. 309; Stover: *Alumni Stimulation by the American College President*, pp. 18-20.

the alumni expected also that their proprietary attitude toward the colleges and universities would be welcomed.
Whether welcomed or not, it was unquestionably true, as
President Porter of Yale admitted in 1870, that "Alumni
. . . retain and somewhat liberally exercise the traditional
privileges of all children, freely to criticise the ways of the
household." [4]

Their relationships to the colleges were embodied by the
alumni in a religion. If the college or university were the
church, they were its faithful communicants. They created
the supports and forms of an established church—the shrines
(the old fence, the monuments, the tables down at Mory's);
they wrote the inspired histories, the accounts of the past to
which alumni might turn for solace and for the undisputed
record. In regional alumni associations and city alumni clubs
they founded institutions for propagating and sustaining the
faith on the far-flung frontiers where alumni might be gathered. Before long the apparatus would be completed by
those traditional aids to conversion—the tracts and inspired
pamphlets which now took the form of alumni bulletins,
monthlies, and quarterlies; a permanent, resident high priest,
called an alumni secretary, became a necessity as the simple
alumni sect of the early days became a full-fledged church.
Refinements in almsgiving developed apace: bequest class
insurance plans, annual fund drives, twenty-fifth reunion
gifts; and, as with all aging churches, as the alumni movement grew older, the standards of admission were relaxed.
Toward the end of the nineteenth century nongraduates—
the baptized but unconfirmed—were welcomed into the fold;
for the first time they were included in the general catalogues of alumni. This elevation of the nongraduate gave
the unconfirmed a mantle of respectability that had been
lacking; it also gave the alumni societies men of wealth and

[4] Noah Porter: *The American Colleges and the American Public*
(New Haven, 1870), p. 244.

prominence whose position as outsiders had been something of an embarrassment.[5]

Although the alumni society in the college or university was a church to which a majority of the instructors did not belong and from which alumni were often in effect excommunicated by reason of their being instructors, yet the alumni movement was of tremendous importance. For it had its own rationale, its own purposes, its own life, and how remote these were from the purposes of the professors was revealed by a great celebration at the New York Yale Club honoring the crew that had defeated Harvard in 1922. Said the alumni speaker in what in a sense was the sermon of the evening: "I would rather see the color of the blue-tipped oars first across the finish line than gaze at the matchless splendor of a masterpiece of Titian. I would rather watch the hats go over the cross bar after a Yale victory than the finest dramatic performance the world has ever known. I would rather in the midst of a titanic gridiron struggle hear 'March, march on down the field' than listen to the music of a great opera. . . ."[6] Deeply imbedded in the structure of the American college and university were the values and the apparatus that made that speech possible and that henceforth could only confuse rather than clarify the nature and purpose of American higher education.

On the outside now there were growing up gigantic philanthropic foundations, complete organizations in themselves, which were evidence of the vitality of the stewardship idea, it is true, but also of the appeal of gigantism and the organization idea. For instead of, and in addition to, endowing colleges and universities, some millionaires translated their philanthropic interests into staffs of investigators and givers, and thereby erected within the academic world another power

[5] See Stover: *Alumni Stimulation by the American College President,* *passim.*
[6] Pierson: *Yale,* II, 568.

structure, another web of interest and of organization capable of leading a life of its own.[7]

The idea was not new. As early as 1803 the White-Williams foundation was chartered to aid "unhappy females who were desirous of returning to a life of rectitude," but the first of the important foundations oriented to the support of colleges and universities were the Peabody Education Fund of 1867 and the Carnegie Institute of Pittsburgh in 1896. The giants were creatures of the early twentieth century: Rockefeller's General Education Board of 1903, with resources of $46,000,000 and his Rockefeller Foundation of 1913, with resources of $154,000,000; the Carnegie Foundation of 1906 with $31,000,000 and the Carnegie Corporation with $151,000,000.[8] With these resources the philanthropic foundations became an apparent or a hidden presence on every American campus.

The foundations helped to shape the financial goals of the colleges. The great endowment drives between 1902 and 1924 were inspired by the necessity to raise $140,000,000 in order to receive $60,000,000 for endowment from the General Education Board. The addiction of the foundations to the matching-gifts principle was of course one of the reasons that college presidents got in the habit of spending so much time away from the campus, so much time raising money. For with their insistence on matching or even double gifts, the foundations sent the president out on the road, in poor times as well as good, forcing him to abandon teaching and sometimes almost his office as well.[9] Moreover, by establishing standards for institutions to be eligible for gifts, the foundations played a remarkably creative role. The

[7] See the General Education Board: *The General Education Board; an Account of its Activities, 1902-1914* (New York, 1915); Raymond B. Fosdick: *The Story of the Rockefeller Foundation* (New York, 1952); Howard J. Savage: *Fruit of an Impulse: Forty-Five Years of the Carnegie Foundation, 1905-1950* (New York, 1953).

[8] Frederick P. Keppel: *The Foundation: Its Place in American Life* (New York, 1930), p. 17; Ernest Victor Hollis: *Philanthropic Foundations and Higher Education* (New York, 1938), pp. 22, 39, 303-6.

[9] Hollis: *Philanthropic Foundations*, pp. 201-3, 274.

Carnegie Foundation, for instance, required that every department chairman have a Ph.D., and thus greatly accelerated the transformation of the old-time college. Both the Carnegie Foundation and the General Education Board tried to weaken further and kill off the weaker denominational colleges, underestimating the vitality of these institutions which for decades had simply defied all reason and now continued to refuse to die. The foundations surveyed the educational situation in various areas and states and held out the promise of attractive gifts if measures were taken to eliminate duplicate facilities, or to put state systems of financial support into better order, or to consolidate into a more efficient organization neighboring competitive institutions. They established uniform accounting systems. They supported in the South a network of university professors who were to function as counselors to the state high-school systems. They developed a preference for the experimental project in an already prestigious and wealthy institution and often supported experiments only to the point of success, thus throwing the colleges and universities back on their own limited resources.[1]

Nothing was more suggestive of their influence than the ambitious intention of the Carnegie people to provide every college and university professor with a pension. The ambition of the Carnegie staff to establish standards and to achieve what it called a "comprehensive system" of American higher education gave the impression that colleges and universities meeting certain standards needed only to apply. This impression was not changed by the official definition of a college to which the Carnegie people subscribed (among other things, six full-time professors, a four-year, liberal arts course, and a high-school course as a requirement for admission), nor by their announcement that denominational colleges need not apply. Bitter controversy developed over these proposals, which finally led to a pattern of joint institutional and professorial contributions. Before that day,

[1] Ibid., pp. 133-73.

the actuarial errors of the Carnegie planners threatened to
bankrupt even the mighty Carnegie Foundation. Foundation influence was strong, however, and more than one
denominational college threw off its denominational connections in the hope that its new-won freedom could be
exchanged with Mr. Carnegie's standardizers for a pension
program. Bowdoin, Wesleyan, Rochester, Drake, Coe,
Hanover, and Occidental were among the institutions that
found their denominational connections, obviously hitherto
tenuous, now dispensable. When the original Carnegie-
financed pension program collapsed from its own actuarial
errors, little Centre College in Kentucky decided to go back
to the church.[2]

The activities of the foundations bred a school of foundation critics, including President Jacob Gould Schurman of
Cornell who in 1909 declared that "the very ambition of
such corporations to reform educational abuses is itself a
source of danger. Men are not constituted educational reformers by having a million dollars to spend." The foundations thought otherwise, and in its 1914 report the General
Education Board advanced a justification for its standardizing
functions: "The states have not generally shown themselves
competent to deal with higher education on a nonpartisan,
impersonal, and comprehensive basis. . . . Rival religious
bodies have invaded fields fully—or more than fully—
occupied already; misguided individuals have founded a new
college instead of strengthening an old one." In the absence
of any pattern of state control over standards, as in the case
of France and Germany, or of tight university control
over the colleges, as in the case of England, the General

[2] Claude Charleton Bowman: *The College Professor in America*
(Philadelphia, 1938), pp. 57-63; Hollis: *Philanthropic Foundations*,
passim; Hatch: *Bowdoin*, p. 185; Dutcher: *Wesleyan*, p. 23; Rosen-
berger: *Rochester*, pp. 281-2; William Alfred M. Millis: *The History
of Hanover College from 1827 to 1927* (Hanover, 1927), pp. 47-51;
Robert Glass Cleland: *The History of Occidental College, 1887-1937*
(Los Angeles, 1937), pp. 45-6; W. S. Plummer Bryan: *The Church,
Her Colleges and the Carnegie Foundation* (Princeton, 1911); J.
McKeen Cattell: *Carnegie Pensions* (New York, 1919).

Education Board statement of 1914 sounded like unmitigated arrogance. But was it not true that the job needed being done? Was it not more than a whisper of approval mixed with awe that led one New York newspaper to comment in 1909 on the activities of the Carnegie Foundation: "Who anticipated that in less than five years it would effect profound changes in the constitution and management of our colleges, severing venerable denominational ties, tightening up requirements for admission, differentiating the college from the university, systematizing finances, raising salaries, and in more subtle ways modifying the life and work of thousands of educators"? The truth of the matter was that national growth and collegiate and university growth, both public and private, demanded something more than the chaos that had been traditional in American higher education. The foundations, using money as a lever, became one of many agencies for bringing order into American higher education, for standardizing, for organizing the academic community along chosen, rational lines.[3]

In responding to the problems of growth, the colleges and universities themselves were introducing new agencies of standardization. One of these was the whole apparatus that came to be known almost everywhere by the loose term "the administration." The growth of administration, the proliferation of administrators, was a response to enrollment increases and to demands for new services. It was a response also to the need to free research-minded scholars from the detailed but necessary work that went into the management of an organized institution.

Before the Civil War most institutions had managed with a president, a treasurer, and a part-time librarian. But now, with the enlargement of function and of scope, administrative responsibility was necessarily splintered: first a secretary of the faculty, then a registrar, and then in succession a vice-

[3] Hollis: *Philanthropic Foundations*, pp. 36, 39, 52, 312.

president, a dean, a dean of women, a chief business officer,
an assistant dean, a dean of men, a director of admissions,
and in time a corps of administrative assistants to the president
who were in charge of anything and everything—public
relations, church relations, civic relations, student relations,
faculty relations. In 1860 the median number of administrative officers in an American college was 4; in 1933 it was
30.5, with one institution admitting to 137 administrators.[4]
These administrators, who soon were joining clubs of
fellow administrators from other institutions, helped to establish patterns of standard procedure, and in many places
they became the very embodiment of the organization mind.

The one exception to this generalization was the dean. To
an extent, the deans were an effort to maintain collegiate
and human values in an atmosphere of increasing scholarship
and specialization. This was why so many of the early deans
resisted the full swing to intellectualism which their faculty
colleagues represented. Some of the old purpose remained
in Dean Jones of Yale who paid a $600 gambling debt of a
rich man's son, afraid to tell his father but required by the
good dean to repay the sum over a two-year period and then
tell his father. Dean Norton at Pomona, stern and warm,
Christian and learned, good-humored but insistent on honorable character and standards, kept from his mail two bundles
of letters, one labeled "When puffed up, read these" and
another, "When cast down, read these." Dean Briggs of
Harvard, a fine old-fashioned gentleman, knowledgeable in
the ways and manners of college students, represented to
them ideals, conscience, an utter sense of fairness and respect. Dean Keppel of Columbia in the single year 1911 had
3,500 visits from students in his office and entertained the
same year a third of the student body in his home. The
story was often told in New Haven of Dean Wright who was
called on at his home by a returning alumnus, whose greet-

[4] Earl James McGrath: *The Evolution of Administrative Offices in
Institutions of Higher Education in the United States from 1860 to
1933* (Chicago, 1938), pp. 190-3.

ing was: "You don't remember me." Leaning forward to
see him better in the dark, the Dean responded: "The name
escapes me but the breath is familiar." To resist many of
the dehumanizing consequences of organization was, of
course, a losing proposition, but these early deans were an
institutional expression of an unofficial longing to do so.[5]

All the impulse to organization, all the unquestionable need
for it, was most eloquently revealed in what happened to
college admissions. The sense of frustration which lay at
the basis of change was expressed best by the principal of
Phillips Academy at Andover who in 1885 complained: "Out
of over forty boys preparing for college next year we
have *over twenty senior classes.*" What he was asking for
were standards, sameness, a readiness on the part of the
colleges to decide what a college was, what college preparation was. No more of this variety, this not knowing who
would take Latin for what college, who could get by with
French. Tell us, said the Andover headmaster, or let us
tell you, but in any case let us substitute for the prevailing
chaos some order, some organization.[6]

In the last quarter of the century there developed sufficient distress among certain eastern schools and sufficient
leadership among the university presidents, especially Eliot
of Harvard and Butler of Columbia, to lead to the formation
of the College Entrance Examination Board. In its background were a pioneer conference of New England colleges
on uniform admission requirements in English which met at

[5] W. Storrs Lee: *God Bless Our Queer Old Dean* (New York, 1959),
pp. 48-86; Pierson: *Yale*, I, 156-7; Edith Parker Hinckley and Katharine
Norton Benner: *The Dean Speaks Again: Edwin Clarence Norton,
Pioneer Dean of Pomona College* (Claremont, 1955), p. 59; LeBaron
Russell Briggs: *Routine and Ideals* (Boston, 1904), *passim;* Dwight C.
Miner, ed.: *A History of Columbia College on Morningside* (New
York, 1954), p. 33.
[6] Edwin C. Broome: *A Historical and Critical Discussion of College
Admission Requirements* (New York, 1903), p. 127.

Hartford in 1879 and comparable conferences which continued through the 1880's. During the 1880's and 1890's in
New England and elsewhere colleges and secondary schools
created organizations that concerned themselves especially
with the question of admission standards. In this effort to
achieve order they were joined by the National Education
Association which at its 1892 meeting appointed the celebrated Committee of Ten on college and school relations, a
committee that set about achieving an approved standard
secondary-school curriculum. A later Committee of Twelve
addressed itself to the question of college entrance requirements; and by 1899, at a meeting of the Association of
Colleges and Secondary Schools of the Middle Atlantic States
and Maryland, the prospect of uniform college admission
requirements and a joint board of examiners was much
discussed.[7]

The stakes that were involved in such a prospect, the full
meaning for the colleges and for academic standards, were
made perfectly clear in a revealing exchange that took place
at the meeting between President Ethelbert D. Warfield of
Lafayette and President Eliot. "Lafayette College," said President Warfield, "does not intend to be told by any Board
whom to admit and whom not to admit. If we wish to admit
the son of a benefactor, or of a Trustee, or of a member
of the Faculty, and such action will benefit the institution
we are not going to be prevented from taking it." To
which the president of Harvard responded, in a way that must
have been infuriating to all who knew how right he was but
how much easier it was for Harvard to talk this way: "The
President of Lafayette College has misunderstood. . . . It will
be perfectly practicable under this plan [of a College Entrance Board] for Lafayette College to say, if it chooses,
that it will admit only such students as cannot pass these

[7] Claude M. Fuess: *The College Board: Its First Fifty Years* (New
York, 1950), pp. 9-27; Broome: *A Historical and Critical Discussion
of College Admission Requirements*, pp. 128-9.

examinations. No one proposes to deprive Lafayette College of that privilege." [8] Despite this clash, the idea was well launched, and the first College Board examinations were held in June 1901; by 1910, twenty-five leading eastern colleges and universities were making use of the standard examinations of the College Board.[9]

In the meantime in 1908 a conference on entrance requirements, sponsored by the Carnegie Foundation, put its mind to defining a unit of admission credit. It decided on a definition that described one unit as any one of four courses carried for five days a week during the secondary-school year, thereby creating the so-called Carnegie Unit, in some ways the ultimate in organization, the epitome of academic accountancy, the symbol of the search for standards.[1] To these agencies of standardization in admissions were added a host of national organizations that now recognized the existence of common problems and accepted the inevitability of choosing chaos or of achieving some common standards: the National Association of State Universities of 1896, the Association of American Universities, and the Association of Land-Grant Colleges, both of 1900. By 1906 these and other groups interested in establishing standards sought common ground at a meeting held at Williamstown, Massachusetts, and from their desires and efforts developed the whole fabric of collegiate and university accreditation.[2]

By the beginning of the First World War the apparatus of the organized institution was complete. On one assembly line the academicians, the scholars, were at work: from time to time they left *their* assembly line long enough to oil and grease the student assembly line. This was the least they could do, and it is probable that lectures could do little

[8] Fuess: *The College Board*, pp. 23-4.
[9] Ibid., p. 42.
[1] Hollis: *Philanthropic Foundations*, pp. 130-1.
[2] William K. Selden: *Accreditation: A Struggle over Standards in Higher Education* (New York, 1960), *passim.*

else. Above them, around them were the managers—the white-collared, chief executive officers and their assistants. The absentee stockholders, sometimes called alumni; the board of directors, at some places called the trustees or overseers; the untapped capital resources, known as benefactors and philanthropic foundations; the regulatory agencies and the commissions in charge of standards—by the First World War they were, on one level, what was meant by higher education in the United States. But not alone, for if the American college and university had become an organized institution, some attention would have to be given to the annual report. What did *it* show?

21

✦

Counterrevolution

Organization, with all of its characteristic paraphernalia—
committees, departments, hierarchies, codes, standards—
often manages to choke the last bit of life out of an enterprise, frustrate almost every tendency toward originality
and imagination, and militate against decision and responsibility. But it is a narrow and self-blinding look which only
sees the organization, its structure, its fascinating capacity
for process and technique. For any accounting of organization must get beyond process and consider some of the
concrete results. While it was true, therefore, that by the
First World War the American college and university had
become an organized institution, some attention must be
paid to the annual report, to the record that organization
itself helped to achieve. The history of American higher
education between the Civil War and the First World War,
while the history of organization, is also the history of a
tremendous number of changes, even improvements.

By 1900 a backward-glancing university president might
not think that every change was for the best, but who was
going to prefer the days of the common curriculum and all
the monotony, sterility, and superficiality which it meant
over the great variety, the libraries, the laboratories, the

museums which organization now accommodated? Was it
really a loss that in place of the old *in loco parentis* discipline
there now was an aura of laissez faire, which was unquestionably quite as friendly and considerably more respectful
of student freedom? If there were no longer any Hopkinses
or Waylands or Notts, no great moral guiding teachers, in
their stead was a body of trained professionals, with all the
self-consciousness and self-respect which that suggested, and
with an abiding devotion to the life of the mind.[1]

Colleges which had once, in a general way, prepared and
sent young men on to professional training were now great
universities providing that training themselves, for the old
professions and for dozens of new ones as well. Colleges
that had almost starved to death, in their dependence upon
a neighborhood of reluctant boys, had found new purpose
and new growth in the discovery that the American woman
was willing and able to learn. State legislatures, once hesitant
even to charter a college, were now pouring great sums of
money into giant systems of public higher education. Even
the great complex of intercollegiate athletics—was it not a
certain advantage to have worldly values so well established
in an environment quite capable of taking leave of reality?
To such minor blessings could be added, of course, the new
vitality of the relationship between the universities and the
public, the closing of that great yawning gap, so characteristic of the old era, between the college and all but a small
segment of society, and the increasing articulation between
the schools and the colleges and universities. All this, after
all, was made possible by organization.

Among the great consequences of university growth and
aspiration were the development of coherent systems of
public education, the legitimizing of new areas of subject
matter, and the mutual search of universities, colleges, and
schools for standards of excellence. Too often these fundamental achievements were overlooked in the welter of sta-

[1] James Burrill Angell: *Selected Addresses* (New York, 1912), pp.
129-53.

tistics that attested to sheer growth or in the certainly abundant absurdities and exaggerations which the university movement inspired. The physical growth was in itself impressive, with half of the total benefactions to higher education in the year 1910 given over to buildings and grounds. The spirit of this commitment to growth was caught by the slogan-makers at Pomona who in 1919 came up with the rallying call: "Every Goal a New Beginning," and by the trustees of Johns Hopkins who at the same time, despite a ten-million-dollar endowment, were busy accumulating an impressive indebtedness, at the rate of $65,000 a year.[2] It reached the epitome of curricular expression at the University of Nebraska where, by 1931, a student could take courses in early Irish, creative thinking, American English, first aid, advanced clothing, ice cream and ices, third-year Czechoslovakian, football, sewerage, and a man's problems in the modern home.[3]

Yet, hidden in the absurdity of such an offering and in all of the impulse to growth was the fact that between 1890 and 1925 enrollment in institutions of higher education grew 4.7 times as fast as the population.[4] The release from aristocratic ideals implicit in such a statistic was perhaps the most dramatic fact about the course of American higher education in the twentieth century. The road from the Yale Report of 1828 to the University of Nebraska course offering of 1931 was paved with the bodies of friends of the old-time colleges who tried to hold them true to intellectual and social ideals that could not adequately serve a democratic society. If in time the crowning glory and the glaring weakness of American higher education—indeed, of all American

[2] Frank P. Brackett: *Granite and Sagebrush: Reminiscences of the First Fifty Years of Pomona College* (Los Angeles, 1944), pp. 136-7; John C. French: *A History of the University Founded by Johns Hopkins* (Baltimore, 1946), p. 192.
[3] Norman Foerster: *The American State University* (Chapel Hill, 1937), p. 86.
[4] Lester William Bartlett: *State Control of Private Incorporated Institutions of Higher Education* (New York, 1926), p. 2.

education—should be one and the same thing, this would
be a paradox that would have surprised no one who understood the nature of democracy. As a young Cambridge graduate studying at Yale in the 1930's remarked, "The best
point about the American college is that it is popular. The
worst point about it is the same one." [5]

This era of great expansion, of changing goals, and of almost rootless flexibility would of course breed its own mis-
takes, its own disappointments, even a counterrevolution of
sorts. At the height of the university movement, however,
all the new emphases appeared to be invincible, and the confession of Professor Burgess of Columbia in 1884 that he could
see no future for the institutions that chose to adhere to the
old collegiate ideals was widely shared. President Harper
of Chicago, at the turn of the century, expected three out
of four existing colleges to be reduced to the status of
academies or modified into junior colleges.[6] President Butler
of Columbia was convinced that if the American college was
to be saved, it would have to reduce its course of study to
two or three years. David Starr Jordan of Stanford looked
into his crystal ball in 1903 and decided that "as time goes
on the college will disappear, in fact, if not in name. The
best will become universities, the others will return to their
place as academies." [7]

The notion that the high schools would extend themselves
upward and in time achieve levels of distinction and work
comparable to the German gymnasia lay at the basis of this
expectation that the colleges would be robbed of function.

[5] George Wilson Pierson: *Yale: College and University 1871-1937*
(New Haven, 1952-5), II, 296.
[6] John W. Burgess: *The American University: When Shall it Be?
Where Shall it Be? What Shall it Be?* (Boston, 1884), p. 5; William
Rainey Harper: *The Prospects of the Small College* (Chicago, 1900),
pp. 31-8.
[7] Quoted in Leon B. Richardson: *A Study of the Liberal College:
A Report to the President of Dartmouth College* (Hanover, 1924), p. 15.

THE AMERICAN COLLEGE AND UNIVERSITY

THE AMERICAN COLLEGE AND UNIVERSITY444

Of course what such a notion failed to reckon with were the diversity which was fundamental to the American educational experience, the failing efforts of some colleges to achieve university status and the consequent necessity to remain colleges, the duality of purpose and the cult of the average which would prevent the American high school from becoming a gymnasium. For a time it seemed as if any college that failed to regard itself as on the way to university status was lacking in ambition and self-respect.

As early as 1866 the trustees of the little College of Wooster in Ohio announced: "What we desire is to make Wooster the great educational center of Ohio as Oxford and Cambridge are in England and the Universities are in Germany and France." In 1887, Wabash College had as its complete offering in history, political science, and economics a one-term course on the United States Constitution, and ethics, logic, and psychology were represented by a general course in philosophy. Yet, in the context of this almost starvation diet of courses, Wabash College announced that it was now prepared to offer a Ph.D. program. In 1907 a refreshingly honest faculty pleaded with the trustees of Denison University to change the name to college, so as better to coincide with the purpose and performance of the institution. But a hopeful board refused, replying: "At no very distant day, it may become a University in fact." Six years later the United States Bureau of Education ranked Denison as a second-rate college and the Board of Education of the Northern Baptist Convention described it as third-rate.[8]

Often these university aspirations, whether achieved or frustrated, were mingled with the suspicion that what was

[8] Lucy Lilian Notestein: *Wooster of the Middle West* (New Haven, 1937), p. 24; James I. Osborne and Theodore G. Gronert: *Wabash College; the first hundred years, 1832-1932* (Crawfordsville, 1932), p. 152; James Henry Morgan: *Dickinson College: The History of One Hundred and Fifty Years 1783-1933* (Carlisle, 1933), pp. 358-9; George Matthew Dutcher: *An Historical and Critical Survey of the Curriculum of Wesleyan University and Related Subjects* (Middletown, 1948), p. 30; G. Wallace Chessman: *Denison: The Story of an Ohio College* (Granville, 1957), pp. 255-6.

required was some middle way. A professor at Brown remarked in 1908: "The problem that lies before all the stronger institutions is to mingle, in due proportion, the best from the old English-American college with the best from the modern German university." All this, however, was more easily said than done. Any happy middle ground at a place like Cornell had to cope with a hostility to the old colleges and most of their works, a hostility expressed by Andrew D. White in his description of the post-Civil War traditional college as "stagnant as a Spanish convent, and as self-satisfied as a Bourbon duchy." [9] At Cornell and many of the newer institutions there was such an emotional investment in novelty that the old, regardless of its proven value, was suspect. While the college as such might be retained, it might become only a shell where the student, freed from the old parental discipline, was also in danger of being freed from any vigorous intellectual experience as well. For in the university atmosphere, teaching might become, from the undergraduates' point of view, nothing more than the routine dissemination of knowledge no longer a vital personal experience. At Harvard certainly by 1900 everyone was aware that something disastrous had happened to Harvard College, however proud one felt about what President Eliot had done to make it Harvard University. At Yale for fifty years, from 1871 to 1921, the faculty struggled against surrendering the past to the ill-considered, indiscriminate appetite of university ambition.[1]

That some kind of compromise was necessary was almost everywhere acknowledged, and the decision of Johns Hopkins itself to support a full-blown undergraduate program was capped with the appointment in 1889 of Edward Herrick Griffin to serve as an undergraduate dean and to teach undergraduate philosophy. Griffin was called to Baltimore

[9] Walter C. Bronson: *The History of Brown University 1764-1914* (Providence, 1914), p. 489; Walter P. Rogers: *Andrew D. White and the Modern University* (Ithaca, 1942), p. 6.
[1] Pierson: *Yale*, I, 48, 266.

from Williams College from which he had been graduated and where he had succeeded Mark Hopkins as professor of moral and intellectual philosophy. At Johns Hopkins he represented "a type then already beginning to disappear, the clergyman-teacher who carried urbanely the best traditions of New England culture into other parts of the land." He was known as "the gentle Dean," and he symbolized at Hopkins the persistence of the collegiate way and the humanist tradition even in an environment aggressively dedicated to the purposes of scientific German scholarship.[2]

Within the universities the most forthright attack on the collegiate tradition was the acceleration movement of the late nineteenth century and early years of the twentieth century. What was at stake was the ancient tradition of four collegiate years—the "four-year fetish," William Rainey Harper called it.[3] Early in the nineteenth century many qualified students had been admitted directly from the better academies into the sophomore class at probably all colleges. These early experiences with acceleration, however, were in no sense philosophically hostile to the collegiate tradition; they simply recorded the absence of uniform standards in agencies of secondary schooling, as well as the intelligent decision of the colleges, committed as they were to a set course of study, not to require a young man to repeat in college what he had just studied in school.[4] In the years of university growth, however, the idea was also advanced that by covering in his undergraduate work subjects appropriate to his postgraduate professional training, a student might telescope his college years and arrive at the upper levels of university training earlier.

[2] French: *Johns Hopkins*, pp. 65-8, 354-5.
[3] William Rainey Harper: *The Trend in Higher Education* (Chicago, 1905), p. 89.
[4] See Dutcher: *Wesleyan*, p. 12. A rough study of Williams enrollment, 1845-54, suggests that as high as 33 per cent may have entered as sophomores (Michael A. Dively, course paper, Williams College, 1961).

At Johns Hopkins, for instance, the collegiate program took three years at the most; it could be taken in two years. At Columbia Nicholas Murray Butler developed what was called the "professional option" plan, whereby after two years of college a student might enter any of the professional schools other than law. As early as 1882 Harvard encouraged students with sufficient secondary-school credits to enter as sophomores. Chicago's contribution to acceleration was the four-quarter system which permitted a student to set a faster pace for himself than the traditional college calendar allowed; in addition, the university's own elementary school was reduced from eight to seven years and advanced credit was given for high-quality high-school work. The B.S. program at Yale's Sheffield Scientific School continued as a three-year course, and President Eliot at Harvard, to the dismay of most of his fellow university presidents, vigorously advanced the idea of a three-year B.A. for well-prepared and professionally motivated students—in other words, four years for the dawdlers and three for the young men who knew where they were going.[5]

Although this idea was bandied about among educators elsewhere and although as many as 36 per cent of the Class of 1906 at Harvard completed the course in three years, the idea did not sufficiently commend itself to the universities or their public to take hold. The tug of the collegiate way was too strong. Even Nicholas Murray Butler, friend of acceleration at Columbia, caught himself speaking wistfully in 1909 of the training that the colleges had once provided for "the simple profession of gentleman," for the "generous and reflective use of leisure."[6]

[5] French: *Johns Hopkins*, pp. 137-8, 148; Dwight C. Miner, ed.: *A History of Columbia College on Morningside* (New York, 1954), pp. 31-2; Samuel Eliot Morison: *Three Centuries of Harvard 1636-1936* (Cambridge, 1936), pp. 370-1; Thomas Wakefield Goodspeed: *A History of the University of Chicago Founded by John D. Rockefeller: The First Quarter Century* (Chicago, 1916), pp. 463-4; Pierson: *Yale*, I, 203-6, 210.
[6] Miner: *Columbia*, p. 32.

Moreover, all the apparatus of the collegiate way—the customs of undergraduate life, class loyalties, societies and fraternities, athletics, the various agencies of entertainment and character-building—had over the years won its own adherents who now were not prepared to allow a band of ambitious university presidents to discard what for many was the real essence of "bright college years." The acceleration movement was myopic; it overlooked the degree to which the idea of higher education rested on what happened outside the classroom. College was too much fun, too socially rewarding, too clearly effective as a means of getting ahead in the world, for people to be sure that a whole year could be surrendered. One who refused to take acceleration seriously was Franklin D. Roosevelt who earned his bachelor's degree at Harvard in three years and then stayed around a fourth year in order to edit the *Crimson*.[7]

Under these circumstances, the colleges that had no intention of becoming universities (or had the misfortune to try and to fail) committed themselves to the tradition of four leisurely college years, and the older universities assured their public that of course they had no intention of selling the Renaissance ideal short. They still believed in the whole man, in "the ideal of the gentleman, of the honorable and responsible citizen of enlightened and gracious mind."[8] The small liberal arts colleges, of course, had nowhere else to turn except to this tradition, but in adhering to it and by invigorating it with an elective curriculum and other attractions, they argued, perhaps without knowing it, that in a democracy every young man had the right to be a gentleman, the right to enjoy the leisure to reflect and master self-knowledge. And even the institutions of mixed allegiance, the universities trying so hard to be scientific, neutral, Germanic, found that they were expected to perform, in *one* of their functions, as a kind of finishing school for the

[7] Morison: Harvard: *Three Centuries*, p. 371.
[8] Lionel Trilling in Miner: *Columbia*, p. 19.

people. If the colleges and universities, in their extracurricular and collegiate capacities, did not really turn out
Renaissance gentlemen, at least they were doing what they
could to shape all-around organization men who surely were
in direct descent.

Collegiate ideals, therefore, were never entirely eclipsed by
the university movement, and by the 1920's the temper of
American higher education was really counterrevolutionary
as far as the university movement was concerned. The
university idea was no less secure, for growth in all of its
manifestations continued. The old collegiate values, however, were now asserted with more vigor; the critics of
university methods and emphases now spoke more openly.
Unquestionably the university idea, German import that it
was, suffered to some extent from the loss of intellectual
and emotional balance that many Americans experienced
during the First World War and the years just after. But
there was more to the counter movement than that.

  Among other things, the returns from the university way
of doing things were now more fully in. The Johns Hopkins
experiment was approaching its fiftieth year, and in the
United States that was a long time. The influence of the Baltimore experiment had been pervasive, and much of the
spirit and method that was university in inspiration had by
now become impressively widespread. Generations of students had found out what the university idea meant, and all
of it was not to their liking. By 1923, for example, a Yale
undergraduate, commenting on the lecture courses that had
become the standard university bill of fare, said: "Instead of
being a person . . . I am now merely a suit of clothes pinned
together by four or five seat numbers." [9]

  Surely this young man would not have preferred the old
recitations that had characterized the days of the college,

[9] Pierson: *Yale,* II, 61.

but he did know that he had a sense of being set adrift in an atmosphere which brought him to anchor but occasionally. In the graduate schools, the seminars, laboratories, source books, the study of documents, and the preparation of reports helped to establish a relationship between student and teacher that made the student central to the teaching-learning experience. It was difficult to know for sure *what* was central in the lecture experience, if it was an experience at all. For many undergraduates the lecture seemed to symbolize the cold impersonalization that had overtaken much of undergraduate life. The lecture was not alone responsible for a loss of any sense of individuality or even of self-importance. To this must be added the professional orientation of the professors, the posture of suspended judgment encouraged by the scientific spirit of the university, a spirit which saw truth as tentative and thus discouraged the kind of full-blooded commitment that was invigorating to self-identity. Moreover, while it was one of the arguments of the university emphasis that by being abandoned to the dictates of his own interests, his own passions, the student was being trained in the school of self-reliance, actually this did not always happen. Many young men and women knew the experience of being abandoned, but somehow the sensations of self-reliance never seemed to follow.

Of course even before the war there was serious concern about whether the intellectual orientation of the German-university idea was not excessive. For in combination with the amoral or neutral emphasis of the scientific outlook, the almost exclusive intellectual orientation of the university idea exposed young men and young women to the dangerous underdevelopment of the whole person. There was a warning at Harvard in 1909 when, after forty years of university-building under President Eliot, Abbott Lawrence Lowell was inaugurated and promptly voiced his growing impression that Harvard men were neither as intellectually nor as socially rounded as they ought to be.[1]

But nothing had been more instructive than the outburst of public criticism directed at collegiate debating which began as early as 1913 in the pages of such journals as *Outlook, The Nation,* and *The New Republic.* These keepers of the national conscience deplored the changes that had overtaken collegiate debating in recent years, the tendency of debate now to be centered on argument over evidence rather than over belief and opinion, and the requirement that a debater be prepared to take both sides of a question. The debates of the old literary societies had surely had their weaknesses, but one of them was not a blatant encouragement to relativism. In the old days, human beings debated on issues about which they felt deeply, and their appeals were to the whole nature of man, not only to his ability to recognize evidence when he saw it.[2]

In 1913 Theodore Roosevelt unleashed a vigorous attack on the notion that college debaters should be trained to debate both sides of an issue. "I know that under our system this is necessary for lawyers," he allowed, "but I emphatically disbelieve in it as regards general discussion of political, social, and industrial matters. What we need is to turn out of our colleges young men with ardent convictions on the side of right. . . . There is no effort to instill sincerity and intensity of conviction. . . . The net result is to make the contestants feel that their convictions have nothing to do with their arguments." An old college debater named William Jennings Bryan came to Roosevelt's support in this attack on scientific relativism, on the view that all matters were unsettled, open, free from conviction until thoroughly

[1] W. H. Cowley: "European Influences upon American Higher Education," *Educational Record,* XX (1939), 189.
[2] Egbert Ray Nichols: "A Historical Sketch of inter-collegiate debating: III," *Quarterly Journal of Speech,* XXIII (1937), 259-78. See also XXII (1936), 213-20, 591-602, for earlier history of debating.

and scientifically studied and argued.[3] This distinction between belief and fact, between persuasion and argumentation, was essentially the distinction between the old college and the new university. It was the distinction between a certain morality, a world of settled conviction, a regard for the whole man, between these and a moral neutrality, a world of unsettled and tentative conviction, a regard for man as mind.

This distinction lay at the basis of many of the curricular and administrative reforms that took firm root in the 1920's and which were given philosophic expression at Harvard and elsewhere by Irving Babbitt and a school of philosophers who were known as the New Humanists.[4] Babbitt and his colleagues were in revolt against the degree to which the university catered to the practical and to the individual. They saw the whole fabric of professional education as nothing but an expression of scientific materialism and a preoccupation with power. For them the optimistic commitment of the universities to service and to progress rested upon a naive and sentimental belief in the fundamental goodness of men. The full, free, unexpressed, undisciplined chaos of the elective curriculum, said Babbitt, was a consequence of the humanitarian substitution of service of man for the service of God. "The wisdom of all ages is to be naught," he wailed, "compared with the inclination of a sophomore."[5] Let us hear less about service and power, more about wisdom and character, he argued. Let us, indeed, assert the validity of intelligent control, the possibility of liberal education, an interest in what is human about a student rather than in what is merely individual about him.[6]

[3] *Quarterly Journal of Speech*, XXII (1936), 265-6.
[4] See especially Irving Babbitt: "President Eliot and American Education," *Forum*, LXXXI (1929), 1-10, and *Literature and the American College: Essays in Defense of the Humanities* (Boston, 1908).
[5] Babbitt: *Literature and the American College*, p. 47.
[6] Ibid., pp. 54-5, 247.

Babbitt essentially adhered to the Aristotelian ideal of leisure, proposing to capture higher education from the descendants of Bacon and Rousseau who had corrupted the humanist tradition with their commitment to science and the individual. He was fond of pointing out the contrast between Oxford where the able students were encouraged to remain for a fourth year and take honors, and the University of Chicago where able students were expected to hurry through in three years.[7] At Oxford a fourth year was an invitation to the leisurely contemplation of wisdom and growth of character; at Chicago a fourth year was evidence of some incapacity to serve, an unwillingness to grasp power. Babbitt and his fellow critics were quarrelling not only with the university but also with many of the consequences and perhaps even the essential meaning of a vigorous, even unbridled, democratic movement. For Babbitt was friendlier to the reflective values than was the service university, friendlier to the emphases that might be described as *Being* than he was to the emphases that might be described as *Doing*.[8]

This distinction was in many ways the distinction between a settled aristocratic society and a highly mobile democratic society. In a sense, what would be attempted in the 1920's was a clear return to aristocratic ideals—not for their exclusiveness, but for their suitability as standards of being for men and women in a modern democratic society. What would be attempted was a reconciliation between the aristocratic and democratic, between the English and Germanic, between the humanistic and scientific.

Whether the 1920's was a period when any such challenging undertaking could be expected to succeed was another matter. For the period would achieve a record difficult to

[7] Ibid., p. 79.
[8] See Charles McArthur: "Personalities of Public and Private School Boys," *Harvard Educational Review*, XXIV (1954), 256-62, for a perceptive study of the role of class values in shaping the life of the colleges.

interpret, and in education there were also those excesses as well as those flights of originality and imagination that make the 1920's so elusive: an age of disillusionment, irresponsibility, and moral decline, but also an age when a whole generation of creative writers came into fruitful evidence; an age of the flapper and bootlegger, but also an age of wholesome athletic heroes.

These were the years when state-university campuses and little colleges that wished to share the same mood set themselves to electing campus beauty queens, most popular men, and most athletic girls and awarding them suitable crowns; when a five-and-ten-cent-store millionaire would endow a chair of civil rights at Lafayette College and then complain that he was having difficulty hiring for the chair a professor prepared to sell the donor's political and social views. In the early twenties undergraduate behavior offered in evidence a young man at Yale, Lucius Beebe, who after breaking the stone treads of his dormitory stairs from top floor to bottom floor with a trunk trundler, then heaved the trundler through the dean's window. Yale promptly expelled him, whereupon he transferred to Harvard. In 1927 a new president of Iowa State College announced that the motto of his administration would be efficiency and that one of the matters that would command his immediate attention was "a better utilization of the rats used for experimental purposes." These and similar isolated incidents, however, argued no pattern and perhaps said no more than that colleges and universities naturally shared the peculiar madness of the time.[9]

[9] Louis G. Geiger: *University of the Northern Plains: A History of the University of North Dakota 1883-1958* (Grand Forks, 1958), p. 332; David Bishop Skillman: *The Biography of a College: Being the History of the First Century of the Life of Lafayette College* (Easton, 1932), II, 254-5; Pierson: *Yale*, II, 74-5; Earle D. Ross: *A History of the Iowa State College of Agriculture and Mechanic Arts* (Ames, 1942), pp. 341-2.

In the curriculum and in administrative practice, on the other hand, patterns did emerge. Of these, none was more important than the general education movement that was launched at Columbia University in 1919 as a peacetime adaptation of a "war issues" course which had proven successful. The Columbia course in contemporary civilization, which was heavily oriented toward history, advanced the proposition that "there is a certain minimum of . . . [the Western] intellectual and spiritual tradition that a man must experience and understand if he is to be called educated." [1] This pioneering thrust in the direction of general education at Columbia created its own texts, its own source books of reading materials, and profoundly influenced the shaping of college courses in Western European history, courses which under the Columbia influence emphasized the continuing intellectual traditions at the expense of some of the old stress on military and political events.

Where the general education or core-course program received its most dramatic treatment, there the forces of chaos had earlier made their most dramatic impact. Columbia, Chicago, Amherst, Wesleyan, and Harvard were especially vulnerable to the charge that they had lost touch with the ideal of learning as a body of thought and values by which an educated man was identified, for in all these institutions the elective principle had substituted an era of almost uncontrolled individualism for the older humanistic tradition. (Columbia had gone so far in subverting the older tradition that in 1904 it actually entertained the idea of giving the A.B. degree to any student with two years of work at another college and two years of work in a Columbia professional school.) [2] General education proposed to restore some balance, to revitalize the aristocratic ideal of the liberal arts as the passport to learning.

The general education movement, from its beginnings at

[1] Miner: *Columbia*, pp. 46-47, 53.
[2] Ibid., pp. 32 ff.

Columbia in 1919 to the celebrated Harvard report on the subject in 1945, was an attempt to capture some of the sense of a continuing intellectual and spiritual heritage that had fallen victim to the elective principle.[3] In the 1920's, together with the various devices of concentration and distribution by which most institutions were accommodating the elective principle, the movement marked a halt in the tendency toward specialization, as well as a new respect for the concept of education as the mark of a gentleman and a passport to human understanding.

An educational movement of the 1920's that also expressed an aspect of the new spirit was the honors program which was pioneered at Swarthmore College in 1922.[4] Even before World War I, the development of the preceptor system at Princeton under Woodrow Wilson and the growth of tutorials at Harvard under President Lowell had suggested that English methods of instruction might find a warm response in the American college. At Reed College in Oregon, opened in 1912, the preparation of a senior thesis was but one of many innovations that made the new institution on the West Coast a model liberal arts college. Before the Swarthmore experiment the most significant departure of the honors-course sort was the great-books course that John Erskine at Columbia in 1920 turned into a program known as General Honors.[5] Now, as president of Swarthmore, Frank Aydelotte, a former Rhodes Scholar, proposed to introduce into the

[3] See Patricia Beesley: *The Revival of the Humanities in American Education* (New York, 1940); Charles Tabor Fitts and Fletcher Harper Swift: *The Construction of Orientation Courses for College Freshmen* (Berkeley, 1928); *General Education in a Free Society: Report of the Harvard Committee* (Cambridge, 1945).

[4] See Frank Aydelotte: *Breaking the Academic Lock Step: The Development of Honors Work in American Colleges and Universities* (New York, 1944); Robert C. Brooks: *Reading for Honors at Swarthmore: A Record of the First Five Years 1922-1927* (New York, 1927).

[5] Miner: *Columbia*, pp. 43-4.

traditionally wary American foundations a device that would enable them to develop the most brilliant students to their fullest capacity.

The honors idea was not undemocratic, but it did reject the popular notion that the average man was superior to the most able man, a notion that had had a powerful history in the United States. In 1909 at Yale, for instance, President Hadley had admitted to his own readiness "to see the English system of separating honor men from pass men introduced at Yale," but he was firmly reminded by an Alumni Advisory Board that "the main purpose of Yale . . . is to fit the majority for useful work in the world." And when Yale finally came up with what it called an honors program in 1915 it was a compromise that revealed the university's devotion to the ordinary student and its unwillingness to stimulate intellectual ambition if that meant differentiating the intellectually ambitious and able from the "dull or frivolous or uninterested." [6]

Swarthmore established a pattern that not only separated the most able students from their fellows but also made much of such older collegiate values as close faculty-student relations, small classes, and attention to oral and written communication. The honors idea was not in revolt against specialization; indeed, it obviously encouraged it, for the seminar paper or the thesis which were its most characteristic products were clearly in the tradition of scientific scholarship. But the small class, the communion between professor and student which the small seminars encouraged, the self-directed quality of much thesis and seminar work, all this meant that the honors program was in revolt against the impersonalization, the machinelike quality of the university-oriented education. The spread of the honors idea to other colleges and universities in the 1920's and 1930's resulted in a bewildering number of variations of the idea, but wherever it appeared, the honors idea spoke for the recognition and

[6] Pierson: *Yale*, I, 319, 338.

encouragement of talent and for the return of intimacy and human considerations, even the return of the student, to the teaching-learning experience.

The most extreme expression of the return to Aristotle and the rejection of the German-university, scientific idea was the founding of Rollins College in Florida in 1926.[7] Rollins *was* extreme, and for that reason it may not generally have been recognized as being in the Aristotelian tradition. Moreover, whatever one expected to find in Florida in the 1920's, it was not Socrates. Yet, at the basis of the Rollins idea was the concept of leisure, the tendency to aristocratic emphases, which led President Hamilton Holt to declare that Rollins was on the road back to Socrates, to that relaxed atmosphere which recognized leisure as fundamental to the full discovery and development of self.

At Rollins there was no such thing as classroom preparation. The classroom was the locus of formal study, and at that, it was not very formal. Attendance was required, but the two-hour sessions at which a professor and ten students worked their way through the eternal problems and interests of man were in the very oldest tradition; here study and learning, scholarship and communication, character and intellect were firmly wedded. Unfriendly to the specialist, Rollins was the college of the complete man, the institution where a conference with a professor and a tennis match with one's roommate were of equal importance in the official scheme. Rollins symbolized, if it did not satisfy, all the sense of frustration, all the longing for recognition of human as opposed to scientific values, of liberal studies as the purpose of education, which in the 1920's were giving new emphasis to ancient purposes.

.   .   .

[7] See Hamilton Holt: "We Venture in New Paths," *Journal of Higher Education*, I (1930), 503-6.

On the administrative front the erosion of the collegiate way had for many years inspired efforts to find substitutes for the institutions and customs that were being undermined by university growth. The American college dean was a first response to the inevitable tendencies of the organization institution: he was the human touch. But he could not do the job alone. The old religious purpose, for instance, was no longer secure in an atmosphere of increasing secularism; the new presidents and the new professors could not be counted on to seize every opportunity to do battle for God and sect against the onslaughts of science, relativism, materialism. By 1880 the various religious denominations were beginning to feel uncomfortable in the new university atmosphere, and from this discomfort developed the university pastorate movement: the assignment of clergymen to work among college students, the growth of closer relationships between students and community churches, and the encouragement of denominational organizations in the colleges and universities. This movement was inspired in part by the loss of religious fervor in the universities, in part by the appearance in sufficient numbers of Catholics and Jews at institutions that were nominally Protestant in tradition. The first undergraduate Catholic Club apparently was founded at the University of Wisconsin in 1880, and before long it was recognized as the precursor of the Newman Club movement that attended to the religious needs of Catholic students in non-Catholic colleges and universities. The Episcopalians, Presbyterians, and Hebrews were soon equally involved in what had the appearance of a vast missionary movement among the state universities and the larger private universities. This early effort to compensate for the loss of religious vitality was essentially in support of the collegiate way, and it experienced new growth in the 1920's.[8]

[8] Henry Davidson Sheldon: *The History and Pedagogy of American Student Societies* (New York, 1901), p. 276; Robert Lincoln Kelly: *The American Colleges and the Social Order* (New York, 1940), p. 276; Clarence Prouty Shedd: *The Church Follows its Students* (New Haven, 1938), *passim*.

The whole apparatus of counseling was an effort to provide some equivalent for the *in loco parentis* tradition which suffered so severely as the university idea prevailed. The creation of a system of faculty advisers at Johns Hopkins in 1877 and the appointment of a board of freshman advisers at Harvard in 1889 were apparently the first formal recognition that size and the elective curriculum required some closer attention to undergraduate guidance than was possible with an increasingly professionally oriented faculty.[9] By the 1920's most colleges and universities were busy perfecting various systems of freshman counseling, freshman week, faculty advisers, and before long the campus psychologist as well as the college chaplain would join these many agencies in giving organized expression to a purpose that had once been served most simply by a dedicated faculty.[1] By 1938 this tendency had gone so far as to require of each Columbia sophomore a letter to the dean in which he revealed his worries, dreams, fears, likes, dislikes, successes, and failures.[2]

The great monuments to the return to Aristotle, the great monuments that symbolized the revolt against the university idea, were the benefactions of Edward S. Harkness which provided Harvard in 1928 with its house system and Yale in

[9] Hugh Hawkins: *Pioneer: A History of the John Hopkins University, 1874-1889* (Ithaca, 1960), pp. 248-9; Morison: Harvard: *Three Centuries*, p. 403.

[1] Carl F. Price: *Wesleyan's First Century* (Middletown, 1932), p. 190; James Gray: *The University of Minnesota 1851-1951* (Minneapolis, 1951), pp. 348-60; Henry D. Sheldon: *History of University of Oregon* (Portland, 1940), pp. 243-4; Ross: *Iowa State*, pp. 350-1; Miner: *Columbia*, p. 64; Henry Morton Bullock: *A History of Emory University* (Nashville, 1936), p. 313; Chessman: *Denison*, pp. 393-404; Walker Havighurst: *The Miami Years 1809-1959* (New York, 1958), p. 199; Orrin Leslie Elliott: *Stanford University: The First Twenty-Five Years* (Stanford University, 1937), pp. 449-50; James E. Pollard: *History of the Ohio State University: The Story of its First Seventy-Five Years 1873-1948* (Columbus, 1952), p. 285; Arthur G. Beach: *A Pioneer College: The Story of Marietta* (Marietta, 1935), p. 299.

[2] Miner: *Columbia*, p. 66.

1930 with its system of colleges.[3] The Harvard houses and
Yale colleges recognized the responsibility of the two great
old colonial institutions to inculcate patterns of social conduct and moral behavior and to provide in the crowded,
overgrown atmosphere of Cambridge and New Haven encouragement for those collegiate values that Harvard and Yale
had once so nobly sustained. What Harvard and Yale were
providing was an environment comparable to the one that
permitted a young spokesman for Pomona to remark in 1924:
"I have made more friends than I ever thought possible
in four years. It is a great opportunity for a man to round
out his personality, and to develop the ability to meet other
men and leave a good impression. I hate to think of saying
goodby [sic] to the old friends, but I have the consolation of
feeling that some day I am going to call a lot of congressmen
and college presidents names that don't sound like Doctor
and Honorable."[4] The same sentiments had often been expressed by young Elizabethan gentlemen at Oxford and
Cambridge. Now to encourage the life of the same old
values Mr. Harkness was putting up millions of dollars, and
here, there, and everywhere, gold medals and silver trophies
were being awarded each year at commencement to the
roundest all-around men and women, to the Renaissance
ladies and gentlemen in the Stutz Bear Cats.

[3] See Pierson: *Yale*, II, 207-52, 400-44.
[4] *As a College Man Thinks: Being Letters from a Senior at Pomona
College to a High School Senior* (Claremont, 1924), p. 19. Although
an obvious promotion piece, this book, probably by a synthetic senior,
reveals the institution's choice of values.

22

❧❦❧

An
American Consensus

The continuous search for purpose and definition on the American campus led to a revival of collegiate values in the 1920's, but university ideals were not in any serious way rejected because Harvard and Yale made dramatic efforts to deal with some of the problems of growth or because various new curricular proposals rested on English models. The innovations were expensive, so expensive that not even Harvard and Yale were able to afford the faculty, the tutors, in other words the intellectual equipment, which their new residential patterns encouraged. The Harvard and Yale residences never achieved the intellectual record of which they were capable, and although there were exceptions, the Harvard houses and Yale colleges were more successful in reviving the social and moral climate of the collegiate way than in sustaining any marked intellectual improvement.

In the meantime, naturally, the service ideal of the American university enjoyed continued support, and while the 1920's was not a period of agitation and reform such as evoked the Wisconsin Idea, schools of finance and business administration often addressed themselves to the needs of a society enjoying on the whole a remarkable period of growth and expansion. All of the tendencies with which the collegiate revival was intended to cope retained their vigor, for they were inherent in size and organization; those evils that were an outgrowth of the scholarly temper and the scientific spirit could, at best, be only neutralized. At the state universities and at the land-grant colleges there could be no significant rejection of the assumptions that made the American university something very much more than an agency for democratizing aristocratic values. Yet for a time at any rate the university idea had hit its high-water mark, and while the passage of time would mean more and bigger universities, higher and higher enrollments, the university idea, firmly planted, was now required to live with many of the ideas against which it had fought so long.

Growth would, indeed, feed on growth. Modern technology required a more highly educated population: the colleges and universities were called upon to provide the trained intelligence that would create, master, and find the terms on which man could live with that technology. American society itself was committed to education as an instrument of mobility, and since mobility was proof that the society worked, the demands placed upon formal agencies of higher education grew apace. Teachers colleges, outgrowth of onetime normal schools of high-school level, now moved toward full collegiate status. In local communities everywhere, but especially in the Midwest and Far West, junior colleges responded to the desire for education beyond the high school, less expensive and more convenient than that provided by the great universities.[1] The junior college became the agency for meeting the needs of "the non-academically minded high-school graduate."[2] The state universities began to grow toward such gigantic size that in

[1] See Leonard Vincent Koos: *The Junior College* (2 vols., Minneapolis, 1924); Walter Crosby Eells: *The Junior College* (New York, 1931).
[2] William H. Snyder: "The Real Function of the Junior College," *The Junior College Journal*, I (1930), 76.

a state like California only decentralization and emulation of the chain department store would in the end offer a way out of the problems created by an almost insatiable popular appetite for higher education. But henceforth growth would be tempered by a university rationale that would be philosophically characterized by consolidation, accommodation, by a certain regard for the whole man that an era of university-building had not permitted. Henceforth the long English tradition would stand beside the apparatus of growth and of German scholarship and would keep alive, even in the most hostile of territory, some respect for the idea of the liberally educated man.

During all the years of university growth, the extracurriculum played a major role in sustaining collegiate values. The athletic teams, fraternities and social clubs, theater groups, newspapers, and magazines, all of these various enterprises not only allowed young undergraduates to emulate and prepare for life, but also provided them with experiences that they knew to be profoundly human. Just as the extracurriculum in the collegiate era was a response to the sterility of the curriculum, in the university era it became a compensation for the one-sided intellectuality and the overwhelming impersonality of the official scheme of things. The great extracurricular growth of the 1920's, the remarkable advances made by intercollegiate athletics during these years, were only partially the conscious efforts of young men to learn organization values and to sharpen their other-directedness on the way to success. The extracurriculum was also an agency of the collegiate emphasis on fellowship, on character, on well-roundedness, and as such, it was a powerful instrument during the period of the 1920's in bringing the university ideal into accommodation with the collegiate ideal.

This accommodation was, or course, sustained by the society beyond the campus, which discovered in the athletic field, the fraternity, the college newspaper what could not

be found in the classroom: an earnest recognition and cultivation of those traits of personality most useful on the
road to success. The humanism of an Irving Babbitt, the moral
guidance of a great football coach, the honors program of a
Frank Aydelotte, the sense of a continuing tradition
fostered by Columbia's course in contemporary civilization,
a corps of deans and counselors, and work on the *Harvard
Crimson* clearly were derived from varied interests and
philosophies, but in combination they placed the university
spirit under control, and in the 1920's cemented that marriage
between collegiate and university ideals, that most striking
characteristic of American higher education.

The 1920's were followed by one of the most shattering
experiences the American people had ever known, over
fifteen years of economic collapse and war, a period when
all manner of values and institutions were subjected to the
shock of uncertainty, to the test of survival at a time when
everything that was old and tried seemed to be particularly
vulnerable to collapse or rejection. For higher education
the times were as perilous and as challenging as for other
institutions, and it was therefore probably something of an
advantage that during the 1920's, before the long years of
economic drought and then of enrollment drought during
the war, the colleges and universities had already achieved
some kind of equilibrium. In the 1930's and 1940's change
and uncertainty were the order of the day.

In 1925 the regents of the University of Wisconsin, apparently making a public display of their self-reliance, adopted
a resolution forbidding the future solicitation or acceptance
of foundation benefactions, but by 1930 Frederick Keppel
of the Carnegie Foundation was in a position to say: "I may
add that this action [of the Wisconsin regents] has been
rescinded since the beginning of the present year." The
prevailing uncertainty, both personal and institutional, was
revealed by one thousand students at the University of Michi-

gan who withdrew at the end of the spring term, 1930. For professors, salaries which never had kept up with increasing costs of living now began to slide downward. In 1932 professors at the University of South Carolina were being partially paid in paper promises. When the budget balancers at Marietta ordered a 50 per cent salary reduction in 1933, the student newspaper came to the happy conclusion that the faculty had "come a lot nearer to a common feeling with the students. Now everyone on the campus can admit quite freely that he is broke." [3]

Within the colleges and universities there was just as lively a quarrel with old gods as there was outside, for if the gold standard was gone, if businessmen themselves were so unsure of their own infallibility as to commit suicide wholesale or to rush to Washington and beg for the nationalizing of the bituminous coal fields, if Wall Street was begging for the diplomatic recognition of Soviet Russia and sending forth open suggestions that what America needed most was an effective but genial dictator, if all this was true, the climate on the campuses was not likely to be altogether friendly to old idols and to received ideas. At Yale undergraduate social conscience took the form of biting social criticism. William Lyon Phelps, a venerable Yale tradition, the very embodiment of the teacher-friend, a popular if not brilliant entertainer in the classroom, was now criticized in undergraduate publications for violating professional decorum by bringing Gene Tunney and Queen Marie of Rumania to the platform of his Yale classroom. The university itself was criticized for the phoniness of the architecture of the new collegiate quadrangles. [4]

[3] Frederick P. Keppel: *The Foundation: Its Place in American Life* (New York, 1930), p. 29; Kent Sagendorph: *Michigan: The Story of the University* (New York, 1948), p. 310; Daniel Walker Hollis: *University of South Carolina* (Columbia, 1951-6), II, 332-3; Arthur G. Beach: *A Pioneer College: The Story of Marietta* (Marietta, 1935), p. 293.

[4] George Wilson Pierson: *Yale: College and University 1871-1937* (New Haven, 1952-5), II, 286-314.

Everywhere most students were in revolt over something or thought that they were: perhaps only compulsory chapel or compulsory military training. Disillusioned by the nature of the post-Versailles world, they registered their disgust in peace demonstrations and in solemn pledges never to go to war. They joined picket lines, they helped to organize labor unions. In the great urban centers a small number even signed up with the Communist party. "The depression . . . broke the spell of Wall Street and big business. It recalled many an innocent from the worship of social success. . . . Lack of jobs kept many young people in school, and sent others back to graduate or professional study. . . . A more serious tone soon became manifest." [5]

While the young man or woman who normally would have spent most of the time playing now was absorbed by courses in economics and political science, there were also the under-graduate editor at Columbia who was dismissed for his leftist leanings, the students at Williams who ceremoniously burned a copy of *Mein Kampf*, the Oberlin students who charged that faculty and students alike were guilty of living off the slave wages paid by the Aluminum Company of America, in which over four million dollars of the Oberlin endowment were held.[6] At C.C.N.Y. there was that dramatic moment when President Frederick B. Robinson wielded his umbrella on a group of student antimilitarists during a Communist-inspired demonstration in the spring of 1933. On the other hand there was the calm, good sense of Dean Hawkes of Columbia who remarked to a group of alumni alarmed by the radical tenor of the student newspaper: "You fellows are, I think, color-blind. What you mistake for red is simply green." [7]

Very few students, it is true, were red, and many certainly were green, but most in any case were party to that

[5] Ibid., 265.
[6] James Wechsler: *Revolt on the Campus* (New York, 1935), *passim*.
[7] S. Willis Rudy: *The College of the City of New York: A History, 1847-1947* (New York, 1949), p. 418; Dwight C. Miner, ed.: *A History of Columbia College on Morningside* (New York, 1954), p. 140.

spirit of change, social protest, and repudiation of the past that was one of the most significant characteristics of the American campus in the 1930's. The colleges and universities did not make many socialists, nor were they responsible for making many Democrats out of Republicans, but on the campus and in the classroom the American past, present, and future were subjected to a critical scrutiny that helped to shape a social awareness and a social outlook that the United States had never known before.

In this unsettled era the educational outlook of John Dewey made headway in the colleges for the first time. Dewey's insistence that education and experience were one and the same thing, his concern over the disjunction between education and society, found new acceptance in a period when the failings of organized society pressed in upon individual experience. The period witnessed the growth and founding of experimental colleges in the Dewey tradition as well as a new interest in the social sciences, which experienced a remarkable popularity. Clearly what was happening in the economics, government, and sociology classrooms was a closing of that gap between education and society which Dewey found so injurious to both.

In the classic statement of his educational philosophy, *Democracy and Education,* in 1916, Dewey had defined what for him were the requirements of thought and learning.[8] First, said Dewey, there must be an experience that interests the student, and then a problem developing out of that experience. For effective handling of the problem, the student needed the information and observation on which he might base possible solutions and then, ideally, test those solutions, making their full meaning clear, discovering their validity. Many Americans had become familiar with this philosophy in the elementary and secondary schools, and even

[8] John Dewey: *Democracy and Education: An Introduction to the Philosophy of Education* (New York, 1916), p. 192.

in the 1930's it was a target for why Johnny could not spell and why Dottie spent what seemed like the better part of a year reconstructing a Pharaoh's tomb.

History itself delivered the American colleges and universities over to this Dewey-like point of view during the 1930's. Young men and women who had expected to pay and play their way through college were now working or being paid by federal funds, $93,000,000 of which went to the support of college and university students in the form of emergency assistance between 1935 and 1943.[9] Perhaps for the first time since the Civil War an entire college generation had known an experience that vitally interested it and that brought within student comprehension a wide range of vital social, economic, and political problems. Had one's father lost his job because of a fundamental dislocation in the distribution of wealth? Would the man next door have been relieved of the despair that led him to suicide if there had been more effective regulation of the securities exchanges? Was it right that the last men hired should be the first men fired, particularly when patterns of race and religion were involved? What was wrong with a society that could find no way to transfer crop surpluses to the urban starving? Was the problem overproduction (as it seemed on the farms and in the factory warehouses), or was it underconsumption (as it seemed when one looked into the urban slums from the window of a passing railroad car)? Who ran the country anyway? Political bosses? Big businessmen? The people? The cynical, monopolistic press? Would the men be striking at the factory back home if they really had a living wage? What was to become of the good things in life—resort homes darkened, yachts held in permanent unreadiness, servants dismissed? How had all this happened anyway? Was everyone in this fix, or just the democracies? Was it true that there was no unemployment in Germany, that the trains ran on time in Italy, and that Russia was making gigantic strides?

[9] Richard G. Axt: *The Federal Government and Financing Higher Education* (New York, 1952), pp. 79-81.

Obviously the climate was congenial to Dewey's insistence that education required an atmosphere free from "the grip of the authority of custom and traditions as standards of belief," and this element of flux and of distrust of the past greatly encouraged in the colleges and universities the penetration of an attitude so strikingly congenial to the Dewey orientation.[1] Yet Dewey himself was not hostile to an understanding of the past and, again in his classic statement of 1916, he pointed out: "We live not in a settled and finished world, but in one which is going on, and where our main task is prospective, and where retrospect . . . is of value in the solidity, security, and fertility it affords our dealings with the future." [2]

Almost as if licensed by this 1916 statement of Dewey's, the colleges and universities now created programs of study in what was called American Civilization, American Studies, or American Culture. These new programs which often brought together such disciplines as history, government, literature, sociology, and the history of art focused the past on the present and gave a new dimension to what for many had been the sterile disciplines of history and literature.[3] Who are we and why? these new programs asked, often addressing themselves through time to the problems that the social scientist treated with more of a sense of immediacy.

The world lay in chaos perhaps exactly because there had been too many specialists, too many scientists, too many engineers, and not enough men prepared to think widely and wisely, prepared to consider subtleties, connections, the whole fabric of emotions, institutions, decisions, values, and traditions that defined modern man. The colleges and universities were not at this perilous moment in the history of Western man prepared to jettison the humanities and the concept of a liberal education because of the scholarly findings being brought to their attention by some of the

[1] Dewey: *Democracy and Education,* p. 356.
[2] Ibid., p. 177.
[3] Tremaine McDowell: *American Studies* (Minneapolis, 1948).

disciples of progressive education at Teachers College in New York.

Should they have been? In a study entitled *Students' Use in Leisure Time of Activities Learned in Physical Education in State Teachers Colleges*, they would have discovered that of such activities most students reported that basketball was of least use as a leisure-time activity, but they would have discovered nothing more earth-shattering than that. In a doctoral dissertation entitled *A Study of the Achievement of College Students in Beginning Courses in Food Preparation and Serving and Related Factors*, there were probably some rewards for the reader, most of them of the gratuitously humorous variety. But what was one to say to the very last paragraph in this study: "There are numbers of high school graduates whose interests and mental ability do not make academic work attractive to them, but who want to have some of the benefits that college study of food preparation affords. For such students the approach [should be] . . . that of developing abilities and skills in food preparation rather than that of trying to build up a large store of exact and abstract knowledge. Such work would offer opportunity for students of lesser general ability to succeed, also, along with their more capable fellow [college] students." [4]

Was it for this—to construct tantalizing and undemanding courses so that even the slowest, most disinterested student could know the delights of success—was it to this end that Harvard College had been founded, that the belief in enlightened leadership had blanketed the American countryside, even the wilderness, with a multitude of colleges? Was it to this end that the new subjects had crept into the colonial curriculum, slowly achieved a tenuous status in the years after the Revolution, and arrived at respectability in the decades after the Civil War? Was it to this end that dedicated

[4] Ethel Julia Saxman: *Students' Use in Leisure Time of Activities Learned in Physical Education in State Teachers Colleges* (New York, 1926), pp. 71-3; Mary K. Wilson: *A Study of the Achievement of College Students in Beginning Courses in Food Preparation and Serving and Related Factors* (New York, 1949), p. 75.

denominations had fought to sustain the ancient traditions?
Was this to be the final outcome of those first efforts in
the Jacksonian period to harness the ancient institutions to
more popular purposes? Was this where schools of applied
science led? Was this the final pay-off of Ezra Cornell's
equality of studies and of the Johns Hopkins discovery of
German scholarship, the offspring of the marriage between
equality and science: *A Study of the Achievement of College Students in Beginning Courses in Food Preparation and
Serving and Related Factors?* Was this where the land-
grant college idea led? Was this what President Eliot unleashed? For this had higher education been opened up to
women? For this had William Rainey Harper labored, the
General Education Board been founded, alumni fought for
control of the colleges and universities? Was this the ultimate
right, the ultimate privilege, that academic freedom was
called upon to sustain?

The last chapter in the history of American education, of
course, had not yet been written. It was true that a bachelor's
degree no longer meant as much intellectually or socially as
it once had. It was true that all manner of subjects and
interests had become mixed up with the old medieval purposes and were now deeply embedded in the traditions, in
the course of study, even in the physical organization of
the American college and university. But college courses in
food preparation for young men and women of limited
academic interest and ability did not yet define American
higher education—only a part of it, and not the best
part.

American colleges and universities were flexible enough
in many ways to bring the liberal tradition into closer
conjunction with the society that was now for most undergraduates synonymous with education and experience. This
unconscious progressivism was about as far as most of them
went, with the result that the Progressive Education Associa-

tion found itself loudly complaining of the whole structure of American education. The secondary schools, it charged, lacked any clear-cut central purpose. They provided inadequate citizen training and understanding and failed to develop in their students any strong and significant sense of social responsibility. Teachers were failing to challenge students to the level of their ability, failing to understand and guide them effectively. The secondary schools were frozen by tradition. They were not creating the conditions most conducive to learning; they were not succeeding in releasing and developing creative energies; they were perpetuating the old, harmful divorce between studies and activities. Foreign languages, history, and science had lost all vitality and significance for most students; the English language had become a major area of student incompetence. The ordinary high-school program lacked unity and continuity, but everywhere complacency reigned. Teachers were inadequate, and articulation between schools and colleges hardly existed.[5]

All this the Progressive Education Association proposed to change and in 1932 it set up an experiment between thirty co-operating private and public secondary schools and the colleges and universities, which were asked to ignore the traditional entrance requirements for classes entering between 1936 and 1943. Freeing the schools from the need to provide the traditional college-preparatory course enabled them to operate, in varying degrees and with varying success, according to the emphases of progressive education. When the first experimental groups passed through college with better records than the groups prepared and tested by traditional methods, progressive educators and others as well were ready to recognize the experiment as a victory for progressive education; however, the reports of the experiment made a more lasting impression on experimental colleges with a progressive orientation than on the

[5] William M. Aikin: *The Story of the Eight-Year Study* (New York, 1942), pp. 1-12.

more traditional institutions. The widely publicized and widely influential report of the Harvard Committee on General Education in a Free Society, published in 1945, addressed itself not so much to the problems raised by the progressives as it did to that most ancient question: what *ought* an educated man to know?[*]

Perhaps the earliest of the progressive experiments in the colleges was launched by President Arthur E. Morgan at Antioch College in Ohio in 1921. Under Morgan's leadership Antioch achieved a new mixture of liberal education, work experience, and social training. A five-year, so-called work-study plan required the student to divide his time between the campus, where he took such courses as mathematics, personal finance, English composition and literature, chemistry, physics, history, philosophy, and other traditional subjects, and the outside world, where every five or ten weeks he was employed in work that, to use Morgan's phrasing, brought him face to face with "practical realities in all their stubborn complexity." On the campus there were few class meetings; attendance was not required; for each student there was an individual, self-directed plan of study. A democratic community government, composed of students and faculty, made and carried out decisions normally left to governing boards and administrators in the traditional colleges. Morgan rested his case for the Antioch scheme on his belief in life-preparation as the controlling purpose of a college and on his deep commitment to the idea that the distinction made in the traditional colleges between "culture" and "professional preparation" was invidious, dangerous, and false. A "quest for democracy," the Antioch experiment was called, but it was a quest that found few, if any, real disciples. Antioch itself made a success of its experiment, but no other college found itself so moribund as to require a similar rejuvenation, or so free or disposed to

[*] Ibid., *passim; General Education in a Free Society: Report of the Harvard Committee* (Cambridge, 1945).

shake itself loose from the traditional distinction between liberal and practical studies.[7]

At Hiram College, also in Ohio, there was adopted in 1934, after several years of experiment, what was called the intensive course system, essentially another effort to apply new understanding of the learning process to the collegiate experience. The notion of studying intensively one subject at a time was not new in the history of American education: it had been used at Rensselaer as a matter of principle in the 1820's, at Indiana University as a matter of novelty in the 1830's, and after the Civil War at little impoverished Tusculum College as a matter of necessity. But as a solution to the distracting variety and discontinuity of study of the usual college program, it was an achievement of the Hiram faculty and a new president, Kenneth I. Brown, who when offered the presidency in 1930 was given the almost unprecedented orders from his board of trustees to make a unique and worthwhile contribution to the conduct of higher education in the United States. Hiram at first made a success of the scheme, but as in the case with the Antioch experiment, the idea did not prove to be contagious.[8]

What was clear to most friends of the progressive persuasion was the almost immovable nature of the traditional institutions, for which flexibility in subject matter was proving to be more significant than flexibility in method as a means of sustaining student interest or of breaking down the disjunction between education and society. The solution of the progressives, therefore, lay in the founding of new colleges such as coeducational Black Mountain in North Carolina and the experimental women's colleges of Sarah Lawrence and Bennington, or in the thorough overhauling of

---

[7] Algo D. Henderson and Dorothy Hall: *Antioch College: Its Design for Liberal Education* (New York, 1946), pp. viii, 1-63; Arthur E. Morgan: "The Antioch Plan," *Journal of Higher Education*, I (1930), 497-502.

[8] Kenneth Irving Brown: *A Campus Decade: the Hiram Study Plan of Intensive Courses* (Chicago, 1940), *passim.*

old institutions such as Goddard College in Vermont in 1937 and St. Stephen's College, which fell into the hands of professors from Teachers College and by 1935, with its name changed to Bard, was known as Columbia's Hudson River experimental college.[9]

In all these institutions, and in many of the junior colleges for women, there was a basic attachment to the emphases associated with John Dewey: individual programs to fit each student's needs, abilities, and interests; an insistence that each student, with the help of a competent adviser, take charge of his own education; an orientation toward contemporary society, the elevation of the theory and practice of fine arts to full curricular status, interdisciplinary courses, winter field periods somewhat reminiscent of the Antioch extramural work program, wide student option; effective student responsibility in student government and social affairs; a de-emphasis of such traditional practices as grades, examinations, degree criteria, and entrance requirements.

Bennington College, which opened in 1932, was, according to its first president, a response to the need for a college where such values of progressive education as initiative, self-expression, creative work, independence, and self-dependence could be accommodated; a response to the dilemma of progressive secondary schools inhibited by the admissions procedures of the standard college. The progressive orientation of Bennington was further revealed in its refusal to honor the distinction between the curriculum and extracurriculum which sustained in the traditional college a false distinction between life and learning; at Bennington the professors were charged with the responsibility of closing the gap, of making work and play, classroom and theater, classroom and poetry journal, one undifferentiated experi-

[9] See Lawrence A. Cremin: *The Transformation of the School: Progressivism in American Education 1876-1957* (New York, 1961), pp. 308-18.

ence. To this emphasis was added Bennington's bias against the university-trained specialist with a Ph.D. and its preference for professors whose recommendation was not a degree but a full life of significant experience, preferably outside academic life, perhaps as an artist, or a musician, or a government bureaucrat.[1]

Here and there, the Bennington and Sarah Lawrence examples encouraged an occasional women's college to depart from traditional practices, but these brave excursions into progressive education did not undermine any of the older foundations. The Bard, Bennington, Black Mountain, and Sarah Lawrence experiments were not for the run-of-the-mill student; they proposed to take only the well-motivated and able and to cater to their interests. These were not really peoples' colleges; in one sense they were simply variations on the old elite institutions now operating according to new principles.[2]

It took the Experimental College of Alexander Meiklejohn at the University of Wisconsin and the General College of the University of Minnesota to reveal how some of the progressive emphases might be generalized. At Wisconsin Professor Meiklejohn was given authority to create a two-year experimental college that would come to grips with the old problem of student motivation. In 1928 the college opened with Meiklejohn's announcement that what he hoped to create was a community of liberal learning by accepting a cross section of applicants. In a sense, he proposed to discover whether a climate of learning could be created that would enable the ordinary American boy to make some vital connection with the great tradition of the liberal arts. Teachers' offices and students' bedrooms were placed in the same building, subject courses as such were avoided, emphasis was

[1] Barbara Jones: *Bennington College: The Development of an Educational Idea* (New York, 1946); Robert L. Leigh: "The Bennington College Program," *Journal of Higher Education*, I (1930), 520-4.
[2] For Sarah Lawrence, see Constance Warren: *A New Design for Women's Education* (New York, 1940).

placed on student initiative. Yet, while the cult of informality (which was a fixture of the progressive persuasion) entered into the Wisconsin experiment, Meiklejohn was too warm a friend of the ancient learning to permit progressive psychology to lead him to indulge individual interests and abilities: the experiment at Wisconsin turned out to be a return to the idea of a prescribed course of study: for the first year, of the Athens of Pericles and Plato; for the second year, of modern America. The Wisconsin college was a brave, but failing, effort to bring Jeremiah Day and John Dewey into happy union.[3]

In 1930 Dean J. B. Johnston of the University of Minnesota was quoted as saying that "One of the functions of the freshman and sophomore years is to bring to a graceful end the habit of going to school on the part of those who can learn lessons fairly well but can never do anything more." Something of this notion that a democratic college should provide for graceful failure went into the planning of Minnesota's General College which opened in 1932 with the announced purpose of catering to poorly motivated, low-quality students not likely to complete a four-year course. The course of study consisted of a two-year program in general education, combining an emphasis on life adjustment with a nod to the richness-of-living or culture theme. Some of the courses offered by the college were Current Reading, How to Study, Foods and Nutrition, House Furnishing, Earth and Man. By 1939 the program was enrolling over 1,100 students a year, young men and women of doubtful academic potential, a fifth of whom had failed elsewhere.

The General College at Minnesota was a significant commentary on developments in American education in the three hundred years since the founding of Harvard College. It represented the state university's obligation to society at large; it underwrote the American commitment to the idea that in democratic America there are no failures. It used

[3] Alexander Meiklejohn: *The Experimental College* (Madison, 1928); *The Experimental College* (New York, 1932).

life-adjustment progressive education to support a diluted verson of general education.[4]

The Minnesota example did not lead to any significant adaptations in other universities for several reasons. Minnesota's motive, in the first place, had obviously been mixed, for by siphoning off poor students the General College permitted a strengthening of the four-year degree programs, as well as the creation of a University College for superior students. Thus, a desire to tighten standards as well as to abandon them was a requirement for conducting such an experiment. Many institutions, however, were satisfied with things as they were, and unquestionably in every state university and every land-grant college there were by now programs, courses, fields of concentration that had been quietly developed for the benefit of great numbers of young men and women for whom college was anything but an intellectual experience. Private and public junior colleges were also performing, although not exclusively, a similar function. All this was not properly progressive education but it was an exaggeration of one of its emphases—its social orientation, its preference for what was useful and life-preparing and wholesomely democratic.

The tendencies of these progressive and popular movements in higher education brought into the arena Robert Maynard Hutchins, young chancellor of the University of Chicago, a trenchant critic of modern society, a kind of strange and wonderful throwback to Jeremiah Day and the Yale Report of 1828. In a series of lectures published in 1936, lectures that were sarcastic, bitter, and sometimes funny, he looked at American higher education and found it characterized by disorder, by surrender to an acquisitive society, defined by

[4] Ivol Spafford, *et al.: Building a Curriculum for General Education; a description of the General College Program* (Minneapolis, 1943), pp. 1-9, 15, 24; James Gray: *The University of Minnesota 1851-1951* (Minneapolis, 1951), pp. 308-22.

its trade-school, finishing-school qualities.[5] Hutchins was at war with the insidious combination of progress, evolution, and empiricism in jettisoning the past, in promoting adjustment as an ideal, and in substituting vocationalism for thought as the focus of the university. Down with vocationalism, cried Hutchins. Down with empiricism. Down with the whole fabric of anti-intellectualism masquerading as experience, adjustment, and preparation for life.

What did he propose instead? A forthright return to the old scholastic curriculum, to the certainties of what he called "the single-minded pursuit of the intellectual virtues," to a general education in the classics, grammar, rhetoric, logic, and mathematics, all to be ordered through the guiding influence of Aristotelian metaphysics. And as if several thousand years of human experience had not proved otherwise, he rested his case on the assertion: "The heart of any course of study designed for the whole people will be . . . the same at any time, in any place, under any political, social, or economic conditions." [6]

The great-books and general education programs which Hutchins developed at Chicago and which Stringfellow Barr and Scott Buchanan used as an instrument of rejuvenation at St. John's College, Maryland, were evidence of a search for order in a society and world torn by chaos. Their belief that the world had gone astray was widely shared, but that it could be straightened out by a return to ancient Rome and Greece was not an idea that recommended itself to most educators and observers. No one was more incisive in his criticism of Hutchins's position than was a member of his own faculty, Professor Harry Gideonse, who recognized in Hutchins a fundamental hostility to the scientific spirit, an effort to revive a discarded metaphysics, a rejection of the climate of freedom which, while capable of creating great

[5] Robert Maynard Hutchins: *The Higher Learning in America* (New Haven, 1936).
[6] Ibid., pp. 32, 66.

chaos, had also built the University of Chicago.[7] Gideonse himself gladly accepted the contributions and results of the scientific method; he insisted that truth was in the process of constant redefinition and that experience and fact were not to be considered inferior to thought—that indeed they were essential to thought. Thus another entered the battle between the past and the present in American higher education, a battle between certainty and uncertainty, between absolutism and relativism, between revealed truth and science. It was not the first time that the battle had had to be fought, for the principles of American academic freedom rested not on the fixed truth that President Hutchins enshrined in books but on the spirit that ironically was enshrined in the motto of the University of Chicago: "Let knowledge grow from more to more, and thus be human life enriched."

By mid-twentieth century this motto had actually become the motto of all American higher education, symbolic of a consensus to which even Hutchins in his more reflective moods might subscribe. Under the elms of Harvard, under the eucalypti of Pomona, far above Cayuga's waters or on the shore of Lake Michigan, the commitment to the growth of knowledge and to the expansion of educational opportunity was the same. "Knowledge" itself was an elusive concept, and while in one place it might appear as a laboratory discovery in chemistry or engineering, in another it might be the moment at which some depth of inner wisdom was touched by an almost, but not quite, unsuspecting student. The "enrichment of life" was also open to a variety of understandings, and whether life was to be enriched by the grasp of power and the devotion to service, which the American university in some of its moods supported, or by the growth of human wisdom and character, which the American university also supported—this was a question that was not going to be

[7] Harry D. Gideonse: *The Higher Learning in a Democracy: A Reply to President Hutchins' Critique of the American University* (New York, 1937).

resolved at all. Every American was free to write his own definition of both knowledge and enrichment, but no definition would avoid a fundamental attachment to the American consensus: "Let knowledge grow from more to more, and thus be human life enriched."

꧁꧂

Epilogue

"When Adam walked with Eve in the Garden of Eden he was overheard to say (presumably by the angel just arrived with the flaming sword): 'You must understand, my dear, that we are living through a period of transition.'"[1] This story, from the repertoire of President Lotus D. Coffman of the University of Minnesota, after World War II assumed a peculiar appropriateness for the history of higher education in the United States. One era was over—the era of university growth and rationalization, and another awaited definition and recognition.

The years after the war unquestionably one day would be distinguished by some phrase more revealing than "The Age of the Report." Yet, these were busy years for men prepared to address themselves to the questions that a period of transition naturally raised, and a growing series of reports of diverse origin provided the academic community with distinguished, if sometimes conflicting, advice.[2] The Harvard fac-

---

[1] James Gray: *The University of Minnesota 1851-1951* (Minneapolis, 1951), p. 263.
[2] *General Education in a Free Society: Report of the Harvard Committee* (Cambridge, 1945); *Higher Education for Democracy: A Report of the President's Commission on Higher Education* (6 vols., New York, 1957); John D. Millett: *Financing Higher Education in the United States* (New York, 1952); Robert M. MacIver: *Academic Freedom in Our Time* (New York, 1955); Educational Policies Commission:

ulty, shocked at the distance that it had traveled in the direction of election, belatedly discovered the idea of general education. A committee appointed by President Truman took a six-volume look at the present and future of higher education in 1947. John D. Millet probed the mysteries of collegiate and university finance. Robert M. MacIver looked in upon the academic community at a time when it was wrestling with serious challenges to its traditions of freedom. The Educational Policies Commission of the National Education Association assessed the needs and predicted the problems of the 1960's. The academicians issued a study of their own, a glimpse of *The Academic Mind*. A college trustee and provost joined forces to write a *Memo to a College Trustee*, a plea for the kind of efficiency in the groves of academe that would permit a solution to the faculty salary problem. The Carnegie Foundation, in turn, sent a memo to the country's graduate schools. Up the Hudson the American Assembly pondered the role of *The Federal Government and Higher Education*. And there were others. The woods, indeed, were full of task forces, but there were few generals.

The air was also full of questions. Should the federal government support higher education? Should the American college and university be reformed? Should higher education in the United States sacrifice quality to quantity? These were, of course, futile questions, for history had already given the answers. While men debated, the government increased its annual investment in higher education. While governing boards and faculties went about their business as usual, students quietly and unknowingly reformed the American

Higher Education in a Decade of Decision (Washington, 1957); Paul F. Lazarsfeld and Wagner Thielens, Jr.: *The Academic Mind: Social Scientists in a Time of Crisis* (Glencoe, 1958); Beardsley Ruml and Donald H. Morrison: *Memo to a College Trustee: A Report on Financial and Structural Problems of the Liberal College* (New York, 1959); Bernard Berelson: *Graduate Education in the United States* (New York, 1960); Douglas M. Knight, ed.: *The Federal Government and Higher Education* (Englewood Cliffs, 1960); Nevitt Sanford, ed.: *The American College: A Psychological and Social Interpretation of the Higher Learning* (New York, 1962).

college and university. And the choice between quality and quantity was not made because American tradition and the national purpose allowed no such choice. The spectre of numbers, nonetheless, was real. For the first time in history, American institutions of higher learning experienced prosperity and called it a problem. All the colleges that were not needed and that the Carnegie people early in the century hoped to assist to a decent burial were now, by virtue of the pressure of numbers, earning a new lease on life. The successful were more successful, and in an atmosphere of concern about the burgeoning applications for college admission, an element of self-satisfaction developed where there might better have been the most fundamental inquiry and self-analysis. For the problem of numbers was not a problem of numbers alone; it was also a matter of purpose.

The college was early recognized as an agency of social and economic mobility; by 1897 one observer remarked that "if it is at all noteworthy that many of the very rich men of the United States, who have made their riches by their own energy and foresight, are not college-bred, it is certainly most significant that the sons of these men are receiving a college education." [3] Educational opportunity, however, was also in the process of being greatly enlarged for the sons and daughters of men who were not rich. The technological revolution in American life, combined with an almost obsessive trust in education, reduced at an accelerating pace the need for hands and bodies and conversely increased the number of young men and women who went to school and then to college because society had nothing else for them to do. [4] Late in the nineteenth century G. Stanley Hall could

[3] Charles Franklin Thwing: *The American College in American Life* (New York, 1897), p. 273.
[4] See Crane Brinton: "Whither Higher Education," *Journal of Higher Education*, XXVII (1957), 409-13.

define a college as a place "where picked youth and maidens are protected from the necessities of self-support, exempted from competition, business and to some extent from social restraint, and within the largest practicable limits left free to follow their own will." [5] All this was essentially still true, except that technology now demanded and the economy allowed that this indugence be widely spread and no longer the privilege of "picked youth and maidens." This was the meaning of the question of numbers for higher education in the United States.

What other country after World War II would have—or could have—undertaken a vast program of government-financed education for veterans, a program that after 1945 postponed the working-and-earning careers of eleven million veterans, of whom a third entered colleges and universities? [6] Where else was the generalization of educational opportunity so dramatically portrayed as in the statistics of college and university enrollment? In 1870 American institutions of higher learning enrolled somewhat over 50,000 young men and women; a hundred years later the City University of New York alone would be enrolling almost four times that number. In 1870 but 1.7 per cent of the young people aged 18-21 were enrolled in colleges and universities; by 1970 half of the age group 18-21 would be at college. In 1960 approximately 3,500,000 young men and women attended institutions of higher learning; by 1970 that figure would be doubled.[7] In 1876 there were 311 colleges and universities; in 1960 there were 2,026.[8]

[5] G. Stanley Hall: "Student Customs," *Proceedings of the American Antiquarian Society*, New Series XIV (1900), 83.

[6] Bradford Morse: "The Veteran and His Education," *Higher Education*, XVI (1960), No. 3-6, 7, 16-19. See also Charles A. Quattlebaum: *Federal Aid to Students for Higher Education* (Washington, 1956).

[7] Educational Policies Commission: *Higher Education in a Decade of Decision*, pp. 22, 31.

[8] Charles F. Thwing: *American Colleges: Their Students and Work* (New York, 1878), p. 144; United States Office of Education: *Education Directory 1960-1961, Part 3: Higher Education* (Washington, 1960).

The institutions represented in these statistics revealed fundamental changes in the nature of the college and university population. The independent liberal arts college, traditionally "the nucleus and backbone of American higher education," was now challenged on the one side by the great university complexes and on the other by the new community colleges which everywhere were answering an insistent demand for the collegiate experience. In 40 states 160 community colleges developed out of onetime normal schools. In California more than half of the upperclassmen in colleges and universities spent their first two collegiate years in community junior colleges.[9] Only madness seemed to account for the projection of a community college at Rutherford, New Jersey, in 1941; fifteen years later, the college, now Fairleigh Dickinson University, was enrolling 7,821 students on two campuses. In 1948 in New York the state board of regents created the State University of New York out of its varied educational enterprises, and to forty-two campuses carried the motto: "Let Each Become All He is Capable of Being." The question of numbers was no question at all, except perhaps in the little quality colleges and Ivy League universities of the East, where the belief existed that a choice could be made between quantity or quality: here the admission standards would go up faster and higher than the dormitories. Elsewhere in characteristic American fashion the pursuit of quality *and* quantity would, in the tradition of Philip Lindsley attempting to create a university on the Tennessee frontier, be accepted as an inevitable challenge and as a public responsibility. Of course there would be problems. A Harvard psychiatrist reported that "teen-age anxiety over college admission" was "becoming a mental health problem."[1] And even Philip Lindsley had been prepared to admit that "though the ass may make a pilgrimage to Mecca,

---

[9] M. M. Chambers: "Diversify the Colleges," *Journal of Higher Education*, XXXI (1960), 10-13.
[1] *The New York Times*, June 28, 1961.

yet an ass he will come back." [2] The truth of the matter was, however, that the American college and university were about to share their traditions and purposes with over half of the young men and women of the country.

To all these factors contributing to the problem of numbers was added the hopeful probability in the 1960's that the Negro in the United States would gain a meaningful freedom. An occasional Negro had been graduated from an American college before the Civil War (the first two, in 1828, from Bowdoin and Ohio University), but free Negroes had overwhelmingly resisted the blandishments of white leaders of the colonization movement who hoped, through higher education, to create a body of dissatisfied Negroes who would lead an emigration to Liberia. [3] After the war the activities of the Freedmen's Bureau and the Christian impulse of the stronger caste led to the founding of a great number of institutions which, while collegiate in name, did not remotely resemble a college in standards or facilities. [4] By 1917 two institutions alone, Howard in Washington and Fisk at Nashville, approximated what was coming to be understood as an American college. [5]

Thereafter foundation philanthropy and state legislatures strengthened the Negro colleges of the South, but as late as the 1930's Negro leaders were deploring the evidence that Negro colleges were graduating students who were unable to read and write. [6]

[2] Leroy J. Halsey, ed.: The Works of Philip Lindsley, D.D. (Philadelphia, 1866), I, 558.
[3] Carter G. Woodson: The Education of the Negro Prior to 1861 (New York, 1915), pp. 256-82; Thomas N. Hoover: The History of Ohio University (Athens, 1954), p. 50.
[4] Dwight Oliver Wendell Holmes: The Evolution of the Negro College (New York, 1934), pp. 4-15, 46, 69 ff.
[5] Ibid., pp. 158-62; Walter Dyson: Howard University: The Capstone of Negro Education (Washington, 1941).
[6] John W. Davis: Problems in the Collegiate Education of Negroes (West Virginia, 1937), p. 19; and Land-Grant Colleges for Negroes (West Virginia, 1934).

Despite all the problems normally experienced by American institutions of higher learning, as well as the problems created by caste and the history of the Negro in America, a strong group of Negro colleges nonetheless developed. From them in the 1960's came the young men and women who provided leadership in the new movement for freedom. Thirty-three of these institutions banded together to form the United Negro College Fund, but the higher education of the Negro in America was more likely henceforth to be identified with the whole spectrum of institutions, including the southern state university, the quality college of the North, and the onetime Negro college in the process of desegregation. The potential of this movement for the statistics of college-going in the United States would have to be measured against the fact that it promised to bring into full participation in American life 10 per cent of the population hitherto largely denied access to the American experience.

How all this education was to be paid for became a matter of some concern for a number of groups: for parents to whom it had not occurred that society would prefer to postpone the earning years of their children until the early 20's; for young men and women whose talents were uncovered and whose expectations were thereby enlarged; for foundations and corporations and alumni groups all of which significantly, indeed dramatically, enlarged their giving; for administrators who recognized the gargantuan appetites of educational institutions; for professors who enjoyed the rare experience of being very much more in demand than in supply; and for government. The concern of government on the state and community level arose most simply from the fundamental patterns of college-going. Sixty per cent of American college and university students attended public institutions in 1960. More susceptible to public pressure, these institutions expected to increase their share of the college population. Clearly they were concerned about the financing of higher education, but for the first time in American history in any far-reaching way so also was the federal government.

The question, moreover, was no longer *whether* the federal government should support higher education but *how*. Homer D. Babbidge, Jr., assistant commissioner for higher education in the United States Office of Education, estimated that between 1.5 and 2 billion dollars of federal funds flowed to the colleges and universities annually. During the years after 1957 25 per cent of the cost of construction on the American campus was paid for with funds borrowed from Washington.[7] By 1960 20 per cent of the operating income of the colleges and universities was being provided by federal funds (at a place like Harvard, 25 per cent). Indeed, university research became a major enterprise of the federal government, which now bought (and therefore paid for) 70 per cent of all university research.[8] In 1960 approximately 100,000 students borrowed 53 million dollars from the federal government in order to go to college.[9] The government was already very much in the business of supporting higher education, and its commitment would grow. It would grow because the accelerating scientific revolution would not permit it to do otherwise; it would grow because the shrinking of time and distance had destroyed the parochialism which once sustained the tradition of local support; and it would grow because there was no other agency able or willing to underwrite the financing of higher education for over half the young people in the country.

In the meantime the task of providing a meaningful edu-

[7] Homer D. Babbidge, Jr.: "Higher Education and the Federal Government," *Higher Education*, XVII (1960), No. 1, 3-6. See also James Russell: *Federal Activities in Higher Education after the Second World War* (New York, 1951); and Seymour E. Harris, ed.: *Higher Education in the United States: The Economic Problems* (Cambridge, 1960).

[8] *Harvard and the Federal Government: A Report to the Faculties and Governing Boards of Harvard University* (Cambridge, 1961), pp. 1, 4; Charles V. Kidd: "New Government-University Relationships in Research," *Higher Education*, XVI (1960), No. 3-6, 8, 18-19.

[9] *Higher Education*, XVI (1960), No. 9, 8.

cational experience for this accelerating portion of the nation's youth brought forth imaginative responses to the gnawing question: How can all this be done? Electronics fascinated and promised some assistance to the beleaguered universities. The New York Institute of Technology set up an electronic classroom where, contrary to what might be expected, "the emphasis is on individual instruction."[1] The University of Detroit announced that it was prepared to provide two thirds of a college course by television channeled into students' homes, and it intended to discover whether tuition might be "adjusted to offset the price of a TV set."[2] But mechanical innovation would neither define nor save the educational era that began after World War II. The reforms that would define the college and university were likely to be more far-reaching than those made possible by television sets, teaching machines, language laboratories, and testing machines. For none of these touched upon purpose; they were but instruments, as useful and as neutral in their way as the ancient human practices that they copied: the lecture, recitation by rote, classroom drill, and the daily quiz.

Resistance to fundamental reform was ingrained in the American collegiate and university tradition, as over three hundred years of history demonstrated. A historian of the University of Rochester described the traditional policy of his institution as one of "wise conservatism modified by a spirit of liberal progressivism when warranted by circumstances."[3] This was also, except on rare occasions, the historic policy of the American college and university: drift, reluctant accommodation, belated recognition that while no one was looking, change had in fact taken place. The determination to hold on to what was good and true about the past inspired the notable report of the Yale faculty in 1828,

[1] *The New York Times,* January 9, 1961.
[2] Ibid., February 18, 1957.
[3] Jesse Leonard Rosenberger: *Rochester, the Making of a University* (Rochester, 1927), p. 303.

and a similar determination in the 1950's inspired President Pusey of Harvard in his effort to return Harvard to God, President Griswold of Yale in his eloquent briefs for humane learning, and President Goheen in his insistence that Princeton would not be rushed into accelerating its collegiate program. If the history of American higher education could serve as a guide, these men were not likely to be remembered as shapers of the age. The creators in American educational history—Thomas Jefferson, Francis Wayland, Andrew D. White, Charles W. Eliot, Daniel Coit Gilman, William Rainey Harper—were not defenders, and the memorable inheritors—John Leverett, Jeremiah Day, Mark Hopkins—were privileged to establish their reputations in an age less caught up in change.

The reforms that in the end would define the new era would be the work of administrators and faculties at some of the older institutions that were particularly prepared to grasp the meaning of their times and to take hold of the future. At the University of California, Stanford, Duke, and the University of Wisconsin such men were making an effective attack on some of the problems posed by quality *and* quantity, liberal learning *and* professional training. Some small colleges, unwilling or unable to cope with the challenge of numbers, abandoned a commitment to the all-around boy which their genteel traditions encouraged and organized new programs and inaugurated new practices designed to facilitate the training of an intellectual elite. Amherst was consciously developing into a preprofessional honors college, Wesleyan was moving toward a new integration of collegiate and university purpose, and Swarthmore was discovering that its long experience with the honors-program idea made it a model for venturesome colleges of the 1960's.

Not yet, however, was there any widespread innovation that might be called a break-through, no experiment that clarified the needs and the opportunities that confronted the inheritors of the American collegiate and university tradition. Experimentation, which was the life of the university, and innovation, which was its gift to society, were seldom tried upon the colleges and universities themselves. There timidity prevailed. "The University must accommodate itself promptly to significant changes in the character of the people for whom it exists," President Eliot told the audience gathered to hear his inaugural address at Harvard in 1869, but creative accommodation became more difficult as the university became too eclectic to be understood, too much propelled by what happened to it rather than by what it caused to happen.[4] In the 1950's curricular movements responsive to the new catchword *excellence* crept into the life of institutions that had expected to pursue forever a comfortable mediocrity. Everywhere independent study made headway, honors programs and efforts to provide greater flexibility gained entry. The sophomore- or junior-year abroad was no longer a peculiarity of the experimental college; calendar revision became a necessity of public relations; and enriched high-school courses permitted advanced placement as well as credit toward early graduation from the colleges.[5]

Montieth College of Wayne State University in Detroit and the University of South Florida at Tampa were opened— laboratories in the search for a definition of direction and purpose. In the Connecticut River Valley of Massachusetts four old institutions turned loose the creative imagination of their faculties, who dared to ask: What would be the ideal college? And they dared to answer: Few lectures and much reading, no departments, no college rank or faculty hierarchy, a president drawn from faculty ranks for a five-year term, no fraternities or sororities, no intercollegiate athletics, a vast reduction in the number of courses offered, and costs low enough to permit operation on tuition fees alone.[6] The

[4] *Addresses at the Inauguration of Charles William Eliot as President of Harvard College, Tuesday, October 19, 1869* (Cambridge, 1869), p. 62.
[5] See the series of United States Office of Education pamphlets, *New Dimensions in Higher Education* (1960-   ).
[6] C. L. Barber, *et al.*: *The New College Plan: A Proposal for a Major Departure in Higher Education: Prepared at the Request of the Presi-*

"New College" these faculty dreamers called their unborn child, which might one day be remembered, as Harvard was by Cotton Mather, as a "brave and happy thought." For the need existed for a college that would define an age of educational maturity, that would end spoon-feeding as a norm, substitute sport for entertainment, reject all the inherited fetishes—the four-year college, the five-course program, the ancient practices of measurement and accounting —in other words, for a college that would free itself from the entire straitjacket which argued that nothing had happened since the founding of Oxford and Cambridge.

The chances were large that the United States could now support an institution that was honest (as a college with an intercollegiate athletic program could be only with tremendous difficulty), and solvent (as no institution would be until it paid salaries that required no apology), and unafraid of a commitment to the intellectual and moral purposes that could be served more effectively by a college or university than by any other social institution.

In the meantime, where governing boards and faculties debated the unreal questions: Should the federal government support higher education? Should we make some changes? Should we choose quantity or quality?—the students themselves took charge of change. The very number of them was creative, destructive, potential, dangerous, enigmatic, exciting. They turned the colleges into way stations on the road to graduate and professional schools. They spoke and understood the language of psychology without quite knowing that they did so, while their teachers labored under the ignorance which even yet the force of tradition and the Yale Report established as an acceptable psychology of learning. They rejected the "old college try," and they left their elders bewildered.

The problems facing any bold effort to define the new era

dents of Amherst College, Mount Holyoke College, Smith College, and the University of Massachusetts with the Assistance of a Grant from the Fund for the Advancement of Education (Amherst, 1958).

were large. They transcended financing, numbers, the recruitment of faculty, the role of government. A student at the University of Texas, for instance, gave expression to a distressingly widespread definition of education: "If a professor can make an evaluation of how much education he thinks the students received, then the student is also in a position to make an evaluation of how much education he thinks the professor gave him." [7] At the University of Chicago, after several decades of reform and of brave educational leadership, a spokesman announced a return to once-abandoned values: "We . . . have asked ourselves if beauty and brawn do not deserve a place on our campus as well as brains. . . . The ordinary American boy who will only make a million in later life, the ordinary girl, who wants a husband as well as a diploma, are as welcome here as the Quiz Kid." [8] In 1958 Oberlin celebrated 125 years of educational leadership with a three-day convocation on the theme "Education —Safeguard of a Dynamic Democracy," and then awarded twenty honorary degrees to an assortment of businessmen, academic administrators, and government officials, but did not give one to a teacher. [9] At the State University of Iowa a student leader announced with enthusiasm: "I feel that I can become a really good organization man—bright, eager, personable. . . . You've always got to be in there pitching and smiling and happy and keeping the shining personality turned on." [1] And even at Harvard, basking in the success of a fund drive for $82,500,000, library services and expansion were curtailed because of a failure of alumni to earmark enough of that sum for the heart of the university.

The problem was large, but no larger than it was in 1826, when James Marsh at the University of Vermont cautioned his friends: "We cannot be too often reminded, that we are making an experiment . . . as yet untried in the progress

[7] *The New York Times,* August 24, 1960.
[8] Ibid., May 21, 1959.
[9] Ibid., October 12, 1958.
[1] *Washington Post and Times Herald,* November 30, 1958, "Parade," p. 13.

of human society." The experiment was not only still worth continuing; it had already given men everywhere reason to believe with Manasseh Cutler, one of the earliest college founders, that "Institutions for the liberal education of Youth [are] essential to the progress of Arts and Sciences, important to morals and religion, friendly to the peace, order, and prosperity of Society, and honorable to the Government which patronizes them." [2]

[2] James Marsh: *An Address Delivered in Burlington, upon the Inauguration of the Author to the Office of President of the University of Vermont, Nov. 28, 1826* (Burlington, 1826), p. 5; Hoover: *Ohio University*, p. 15.

BIBLIOGRAPHY

Historiography of Higher Education in the United States

INTRODUCTION

Because the footnotes and index provide a guide to studies on specific subjects and to published documentary material most useful in the present study, I have chosen not to prepare a conventional bibliography. It has seemed to me that the best service to historical scholarship would be to supplement a consideration of standard titles with some general observations on the development of the historiography of higher education in the United States and with some suggestions on needs and opportunities in the field.

THE BEGINNINGS: HISTORY BY HISTORIANS

There is a notion current among historians that educational history is a recent interest among them and that this interest promises to save the subject from professional educators and old grads, to whose care they have heretofore been content to leave it. This view of the matter is approaching the level of myth, even though the first significant volumes on the history of higher education in the United States were the work of professional historians under the guidance of that early master of the research seminar, Herbert Baxter Adams of Johns Hopkins.

Published between 1887 and 1903 by the United States Bureau of Education as *Circulars of Information*, these volumes attempted a state-by-state survey of the educational history of the American people.

The early volumes in the series bore the subheading, *Contributions to American Educational History*. While most of the volumes were state studies, some of the more notable were not, including the first two written by Adams himself, *The College of William and Mary* (1887), and *Thomas Jefferson and the University of Virginia* (1888). (In 1887 the Bureau of Education also published another volume by Adams: *The Study of History in American Colleges and Universities*.) Still useful are Frank W. Blackmar: *The History of Federal and State Aid to Higher Education* (1890); J. P. Gordy: *Rise and Growth of the Normal-School Idea in the United States* (1891); and Francis Newton Thorpe, ed.: *Benjamin Franklin and the University of Pennsylvania* (1893).

Among the authors in the series were John R. Commons, Charles Homer Haskins, George W. Knight, Andrew C. McLaughlin, Bernard C. Steiner, and William Howe Tolman, whose work outside the series, in political and economic history, has found a place in the standard bibliographical work: Oscar Handlin, *et al.*: *Harvard Guide to American History* (1954). Of the almost forty volumes in the series, however, only the volume by Gordy is included in the Harvard bibliography.

These writings have been forgotten, and so also to a considerable extent has a significant work in intellectual history that appeared in 1900 and which deals at great length with the beginnings of American education, Edward Eggleston: *The Transit of Civilization to America in the Seventeenth Century*. This pioneer study has recently received the benefit of a new edition (1959) with an introduction by Arthur M. Schlesinger and has been warmly praised in an important new guide to research opportunities in early American education: Bernard Bailyn: *Education in the Forming of American Society* (1960).

The suggestion sometimes made that this early work has been forgotten because educational history fell into the hands of the teachers colleges and the old grads overlooks the degree to which such a development was a consequence of default by the professional historians. It seems to me that Herbert Baxter Adams and his co-workers were essentially occupied with an aspect of their larger interest, institutional history, and that they soon ran out of the questions necessary to sustain a developing historical inquiry. Eggleston's little book might have suggested to them unlimited possibilities, but it did not. The historians were engaged in establishing themselves as a profession, and Eggleston was himself not a professional. He was one of the last of a dying race—the self-taught, free-lance historian, a writer who was willing to take a large subject and to ask large questions of it, and one of the first of a breed of historians who would seek an understanding of American society beyond the traditional bounds of political activity. In 1900 the future of historical study belonged to German-oriented scientific historians who were asking many small questions often of small subjects. Eggleston's work was unwelcome; it came before the professionals were prepared to honor the insights of what has come to be known as social, intellectual, and cultural history.

HISTORY BY EDUCATORS

The wells of historical inquiry, as far as educational history was concerned, were all but dried up by the professionals. The task of writing educational history was henceforth left to the alumni, who had been making their often saccharine and pietistic contributions since before the middle of the century, and to another group of developing professionals—the educators, for whom educational history became a source of inspiration and a guide to action. Under these auspices significant historical study languished. An occasional volume in the long series, *Teachers College, Columbia University, Contributions to Education* (1905-51), was of a historical nature, but it was often marred by the necessity to recommend action and by the absence of any sure sense of historical inquiry.

Yet out of Teachers College have come fundamentally useful studies to which the historian must turn, often in the absence of any better study but always in the rightful expectation that he will find some rewards: Lester William Bartlett: *State Control of Private Incorporated Institutions of Higher Education* (1926); Louis Tomlinson Benezet: *General Education in the Progressive College* (1943); Philip R. V. Curoe: *Educational Attitudes and Policies of Organized Labor in the United States* (1926); Sylvanus M. Duvall: *The Methodist Episcopal Church and Education up to 1869* (1928); Frances E. Falvey: *Student Participation in College Administration* (1952); Benjamin Fine: *College Publicity in the United States* (1941); Edna Hays: *College Entrance Requirements in English: Their Effects on the High Schools* (1936); Joseph Lindsey Henderson: *Admission to College by Certificate* (1912); Dwight Oliver Wendell Holmes: *The Evolution of the Negro College* (1934); Edgar W. Knight: *The Influence of Reconstruction on Education in the South* (1913); Jesse M. Pangburn: *The Evolution of the American Teachers College* (1932); Domis E. Plugge: *History of Greek Play Production in American Colleges and Universities from 1881 to 1936* (1938); David Potter: *Debating in the Colonial Chartered Colleges: An Historical Survey, 1642 to 1900* (1944); Ora Edgar Reynolds: *The Social and Economic Status of College Students* (1927); Daniel Sammis Sanford, Jr.: *Inter-Institutional Agreements in Higher Education* (1934); Walter Schultz Stover: *Alumni Stimulation by the American College President* (1930); Donald G. Tewksbury: *The*

Founding of American Colleges and Universities Before the Civil War: With Particular Reference to the Religious Influences Bearing Upon the College Movement (1932).

Of these studies the most durable is the one by Tewksbury, and while the subject would benefit from a redoing, particularly with reference to the hundreds of colleges that did not survive, it stands as the most useful historical study to come out of the nearly one thousand titles in the *Teachers College, Columbia University, Contributions to Education* (1905-51). Many of these titles, of course, will have a documentary value to the historian of education, who will find the series among those listed in the always useful work by Eleanora A. Baer: *Titles in Series* (1953-60), 3 vols.

Professional education elsewhere has also been responsible for a small body of historical literature of which the American historian should be aware. While some of these studies possess much the same orientation as the Teachers College series, in general they are somewhat more free of the prescriptive and inspirational elements.

The most useful of these studies are Sadie Bell: *The Church, the State, and Education in Virginia* (1930); Viva Boothe: *Salaries and the Cost of Living in Twenty-Seven State Universities and Colleges 1913-1932* (1932); Claude Charleton Bowman: *The College Professor in America: An Analysis of Articles Published in the General Magazines, 1890-1938* (1938); Edwin C. Broome: *A Historical and Critical Discussion of College Admission Requirements* (1903); Elsie W. Clews: *Educational Legislation and Administration of the Colonial Governments* (1899); Lewis B. Cooper: *Sabbatical Leave for College Teachers* (1932); John W. Davis: *Land-Grant Colleges for Negroes* (1934); Watson Dickerman: *The Historical Development of the Summer Session in Higher Institutions in the United States* (1948); Charles Tabor Fitts and Fletcher Harper Swift: *The Construction of Orientation Courses for College Freshmen* (1928); Luther L. Gobbel: *Church-State Relationships in Education in North Carolina Since 1776* (1938); Allen Oscar Hansen: *Liberalism and American Education in the Eighteenth Century* (1926); Elsie Garland Hobson: *Educational Legislation and Administration in the State of New York 1777-1850* (1918); Ernest Victor Hollis: *Philanthropic Foundations and Higher Education* (1938); Roy J. Honeywell: *The Educational Work of Thomas Jefferson* (1931).

Also, Edward Safford Jones: *Comprehensive Examinations in American Colleges* (1933); Park R. Kolbe: *Urban Influences on Higher Education in England and the United States* (1928); Fred Eugene Leonard: *A Guide to the History of Physical Education,* 3d. ed. (1947), and *Pioneers of Modern Physical Training,* 2d. ed. (1918); Earl James McGrath: *The Evolution of Administrative Offices in Institutions of Higher Education in the United States from 1860 to 1933* (1938); Henry

501   *Bibliography*

Davidson Sheldon: *The History and Pedagogy of American Student Societies* (1901); Louis Shores: *Origins of the American College Library 1638-1800* (1934); Mary Lovett Smallwood: *An Historical Study of Examinations and Grading Systems in Early American Universities* (1935); Louis Franklin Snow: *The College Curriculum in the United States* (1907); James J. Walsh: *Education of the Founding Fathers of the Republic* (1935).

The authors of most of these studies were more interested in some current problem or development in higher education than they were in finding out what the past might tell them about the past. Statistics frequently serve as a substitute for analysis, and despite the title, an author seldom conceives of his study as an exercise in American history; first of all, it is an exercise in American education.

Snow's 1907 study on the curriculum, and a later study with a progressive orientation, R. Freeman Butts: *The College Charts Its Course* (1939), have become standard references in the historiography of the curriculum, but neither is as satisfactory a model of curricular history as is the little study by George Matthew Dutcher: *An Historical and Critical Survey of the Curriculum of Wesleyan University and Relevant Subjects* (1948) or the more ambitious history of Yale by George Wilson Pierson: *Yale: College and University 1871-1937* (1952-5), 2 vols. A history of the elective principle and the curriculum could be a revealing study in nineteenth-century intellectual and social history, but no such history exists. Nor is there any study that has viewed curricular developments sectionally, assessing the influence of the East on South and West, weighing the importance of local factors in shaping curricular commitments.

While some of the studies previously listed move into the area of church and state relations, there is still a need for a history that will clarify this relationship and the process by which church and state became separated, with emphasis on the meaning for higher education. And nowhere is there a study that reveals with clarity and depth the development in the nineteenth century of the concept of private, as opposed to public, higher education in the United States.

Sheldon's study of undergraduate extracurricular life, an early Ph.D. dissertation at Clark University, is almost unique in the literature of the history of American higher education, so little has been done to explore the manner in which education has been shaped by the undergraduates. There is no responsible history of American college fraternities; a history of undergraduate literary societies remains buried in microfilm; the discovery and exploitation of muscle, otherwise known as the rise of athletics, awaits a historian—indeed, a score of historians—for who has yet studied the rise and fall of the gymnasium, the purification movement in football, the brave but unsuccessful intramural movement, the history of athletics as public relations, and athletics and the nurture of the perennial graduate sophomore? Clarence P. Shedd has contributed two useful histories of undergraduate religious life, *Two Centuries of Student Christian Movements: Their Origin and Intercollegiate Life* (1934) and *The Church Follows its Students* (1938), but who has written the book that tells the story of religion in the American college in the eighteenth and nineteenth centuries? What would a study of the revival of 1858 reveal?

Broome's account of the history of collegiate and university admissions is of course no longer the definitive study it was in 1903. Today the best available work on admissions is Claude M. Fuess: *The College Board: Its First Fifty Years* (1950). Yet, an understandable preoccupation with the changing standards of admission by those who have thus far worked in the area means that a whole range of subjects is as yet unexplored: the role of the college as a secondary school and the history of the integral preparatory department in institutions of higher learning, admission with advanced standing as a collegiate practice in the academy era, the role of the American state university and the certification movement in the rise of the high school. No one has ever tackled the obviously trying job of making a full-scale historical study of collegiate and university enrollment, and thus far we have little more than educated guesses as to what a history of college preparation in the United States might tell. The vast, if ephemeral, why-go-to-college literature could be the subject of a revealing study, and in any era it should tell much about the relationship between the institutions of higher learning and society. Patterns of undergraduate drop-out unquestionably exist, but no one has discovered them.

HISTORY BY GOVERNMENT

The *Circulars of Information* issued by the Bureau of Education between 1887 and 1903 established the United States Government as a fundamental sponsoring agency of studies in the history of higher education. The tradition of the volumes edited by Herbert Baxter Adams has been sustained in such useful studies of the Office of Education as Bird T. Baldwin: *Present Status of the Honor System in Colleges and Universities* (1915); Bailey B. Burritt: *Professional Distribution of College and University Graduates* (1912); Florian Cajori: *The Teaching and History of Mathematics in the United States* (1890); Sheldon Emmor Davis: *Educational Periodicals During the Nineteenth Century* (1919); Roscoe H. Eckelberry: *The History of the Municipal University in the United States* (1932); Charles Hart Handschin: *The Teaching of Modern Languages in the United States* (1913); Walton C. John: *Graduate Study in Universities and Colleges in the United States* (1935); W. J. Osburn: *Foreign Criticism of American Education* (1922); Louis E. Reber: *University Extension in the United States*

(1914); Jesse B. Sears: *Philanthropy in the History of American Higher Education* (1922); Alfred C. True: *A History of Agricultural Education in the United States, 1785-1925* (1929).

Intended to be useful in meeting some current interest or problem, government bulletins are often satisfied to dismiss the historical aspect of the subject with a brief introductory survey. Yet, Sears's bulletin on philanthropy remains the standard work in the field. His study and Blackmar's in the Herbert Baxter Adams series are landmarks in the history of private and public assistance to higher education. Both are very much outdated, and a look into either of them suggests many possibilities for further study. Certainly the 1913 Congressional investigation of the Rockefeller and Carnegie foundations should be a rewarding subject for revealing the Progressive temper. The process whereby the American college alumnus developed a philanthropic and proprietary role has not been thoroughly studied or understood. The significance of state aid in the life of the nineteenth-century college has been neglected both by present-day spokesmen for the colleges and by historians. Margery Foster, however, has written an economic history of Harvard College during the Puritan period (to be published shortly), and Seymour E. Harris is at work on a forthcoming economic history of Harvard since its founding. These promise to be valuable additions to the literature.

Cajori's history of the teaching of mathematics and Handschin's history of the teaching of foreign languages, although standard studies, have long been out of date. Histories of particular academic disciplines require a peculiar combination of expertness in the subject of investigation as well as an aptness for historical research. This combination has seldom been achieved, but two published Ph.D. dissertations reveal the possibilities in this area of investigation: Anna Haddow: *Political Science in American Colleges and Universities, 1636-1900* (1939), and Michael J. L. O'Connor: *Origins of Academic Economics in the United States* (1952).

HISTORY BY FOUNDATION

The great foundations turned historians when the idea of encouraging a particular reform took their fancy. The Carnegie Foundation for the Advancement of Teaching has published a number of bulletins of a historical nature: *The Financial Status of the Professor in America and in Germany* (1908); Howard J. Savage, *et al.: American College Athletics* (1929), and its bibliographical companion piece, W. Carson Ryan: *The Literature of American School and College Athletics* (1929); Edward C. Elliott and Merritt M. Chambers: *The Colleges and the Courts: Judicial Decisions regarding Institutions of Higher Education in the United States* (1936); W. Carson Ryan: *Studies in Early Gradu-*

ate Education: The Johns Hopkins, Clark University, The University of Chicago (1939); Fred J. Kelly and John H. McNeely: *The State and Higher Education: Phases of Their Relationship* (1933). These foundation-sponsored studies have become standard works on their subjects, and while each makes an important contribution, an imaginative reading of any one of them should suggest topics for investigation.

A recent foundation excursion into an area neglected by historians is a product of the Fund for the Advancement of Education: Beardsley Ruml and Sidney G. Tickton: *Teaching Salaries Then and Now: A 50-Year Comparison With Other Occupations and Industries* (1955). Logan Wilson: *The Academic Man: A Study in the Sociology of a Profession* (1942) and Theodore Caplow and Reece J. McGee: *The Academic Marketplace* (1958) make a contribution to the understanding of contemporary academic life, but the history of the American college professor is waiting for the perceptive and sensitive student, someone who is prepared to search out the changing nature of his recruitment and social origins, his social and economic status, and his social function—and, as well, prepared to tell that story without losing sight of the professional life and the human record that it has built. Faculty-student relations in themselves offer unlimited possibilities to explore changing institutional purposes and theories of learning, as well as that most neglected of subjects—the history of teaching.

THE RETURN OF THE HISTORIANS

George P. Schmidt: *The Old Time College President* (1930), a systematic and sympathetic treatment of the pre-university era college president, signaled the return of the historians to the neglected subject of educational history. Developing from a seminar paper under Dixon Ryan Fox at Columbia, it earned the author his doctorate and a reputation as an expert on the old-time college. The same year at Harvard, Samuel Eliot Morison brought forth the first of a number of volumes on the history of Harvard, a collection of chapters written by others on the Eliot era but edited by Morison: *The Development of Harvard University since the Inauguration of President Eliot 1869-1929* (1930). *The Founding of Harvard College* (1935), *Harvard College in the Seventeenth Century* (1936), 2 vols., and *Three Centuries of Harvard 1636-1936* (1936), Morison's later volumes, lent a new respectability to college and university history, demonstrating as they did that a first-rate historian could turn himself toward such a subject without damaging his reputation and, as well, that university history could make significant contributions to an understanding of American social and intellectual development.

Although college and university history thereafter attracted professional historians in greater number, a few competent studies attempted synthesis and interpretation on a broader level: Albea Godbold: *The Church College of the Old South* (1944); Richard Hofstadter and C. Dewitt Hardy: *The Development and Scope of Higher Education in the United States* (1952); Richard J. Storr: *The Beginnings of Graduate Education in America* (1953); Richard Hofstadter and Walter P. Metzger: *The Development of Academic Freedom in the United States* (1955); Wilson Smith: *Professors and Public Ethics: Studies of Northern Moral Philosophers before the Civil War* (1956).

These are all models of their kind, and the Hofstadter and Metzger, in its effort to put the development of academic freedom into a historical context, deals extensively with the history of higher education in the United States. It provides a detailed study of the rise of the profession of college and university teachers, with special attention to the creation of professional standards and conditions of work, and it also effectively explains the factors that have shaped collegiate and university government in the United States. Yet this work and Schmidt's on the old-time president still leave much opportunity for those who would explore aspects of the administration of higher education in the United States, including public relations, institutional rivalry, the new-style college and university president, architectural planning and campus design, social and economic attitudes of governing boards.

Godbold's study is excellent in what it does, but there is opportunity for comparable investigations into the denominational colleges—southern, northern, western—since the Civil War. The strength of religion in the colleges and the strength of the ties between the colleges and universities and the denominations are questions that may be difficult to tackle, but in the absence of sound study, a great deal of nonsense is purveyed on the general subject.

Storr's study of the background years of graduate education, begun as a doctoral dissertation under Arthur M. Schlesinger at Harvard, has been extended (see below) by Rogers on Cornell, Hawkins on Johns Hopkins, Barzun and Hoxie on Columbia, and Pierson on Yale. Storr is himself at work on a history of the early years of the University of Chicago. Smith's study on the moral philosophers is a pioneering work in the whole area to which a committee of historians, under the sponsorship of the Fund for the Advancement of Education, addressed themselves in a report issued in 1957 as *The Role of Education in American History*. Smith's monograph and the historians' report of 1957 stress the role of educators and education in shaping society and suggest limitless possibilities in aspects of American history heretofore almost totally neglected. Smith's essay, "The New Historian of American Education," appearing in a number of the *Harvard Educational Review* (XXXI, 1961), 136-43, devoted to the history of education in America is a consideration of tendencies in the contemporary study of the history of American education.

In recent years there have been several studies that have incorporated sound historical narrative and analysis with a focus on some educational question of contemporary interest, particularly the relationship between government and higher education: Frank C. Abbott: *Government Policy and Higher Education: A Study of the Regents of the University of the State of New York, 1784-1949* (1958); Richard G. Axt: *The Federal Government and Financing Higher Education* (1952); A. Hunter Dupree: *Science in the Federal Government: A History of Policies and Activities to 1940* (1957); William K. Selden: *Accreditation: A Struggle over Standards in Higher Education* (1960).

College and university history was probably headed for some kind of revival even before the Morison volumes which were intended to help Harvard celebrate its three hundredth birthday, for many of the American institutions founded before the Civil War were also approaching important birthdays, and on college and university faculties there were professionally trained historians prepared to do a more responsible job than an earlier band of devoted alumni. And in the graduate schools the growth of interest in intellectual and social history invited attention to the history of colleges and universities. In the list below of the institutional histories that have been particularly useful in this study, Fletcher on Oberlin began as a doctoral dissertation under Frederick Merk at Harvard, and Le Duc on Amherst and Rudolph on Williams are the products of doctoral study with Ralph H. Gabriel at Yale. The following historians were brought into the ranks of college and university historians during these years: Carl L. Becker, Edward P. Cheyney, Arthur C. Cole, E. Merton Coulter, Merle Curti, Wayland F. Dunaway, George M. Dutcher, John Tracy Ellis, Walter L. Fleming, Dixon Ryan Fox, Claude M. Fuess, Ralph H. Gabriel, George W. Pierson, William Warren Sweet, and Thomas Jefferson Wertenbaker. They have contributed richly to the literature of the American college and university.

The following list includes college and university histories, new and old, good and bad, but all useful in my search for a sense of the collegiate and university experience in the United States. Unquestionably other histories might have been included without changing the essential directions that this study has taken. An effort was made to select for particular study a number of institutions that would reflect geographical and denominational variety.

Patrick Henry Ahern: *The Catholic University of America 1887-1896: The Rectorship of John J. Keane* (1948).

Charles Elmer Allison: *A Historical Sketch of Hamilton College, Clinton, New York* (1889).

507 Bibliography

Alfred Williams Anthony: *Bates College and its Background: A Review of Origins and Causes* (1936).
Wallace W. Atwood: *The First Fifty Years* [of Clark University]: An *Administrative Report* (1937).
W. Charles Barber: *Elmira College: The First Hundred Years* (1955).
Colman J. Barry: *The Catholic University of America 1903-1909: The Rectorship of Denis J. O'Connell* (1950).
Jacques Barzun, ed.: *A History of the Faculty of Philosophy Columbia University* (1957).
Kemp Plummer Battle: *History of the University of North Carolina* (1907-12), 2 vols.
Arthur G. Beach: *A Pioneer College: The Story of Marietta* (1935).
Carl L. Becker: *Cornell University: Founders and the Founding* (1943).
Winstead Paine Bone: *A History of Cumberland University 1842-1935* (1935).
Catherine Drinker Bowen: *A History of Lehigh University* (1924).
Frank P. Brackett: *Granite and Sagebrush: Reminiscences of the First Fifty Years of Pomona College* (1944).
Marion Luther Brittain: *The Story of Georgia Tech* (1948).
Walter C. Bronson: *The History of Brown University 1764-1914* (1914).
Robert Preston Brooks: *The University of Georgia Under Sixteen Administrations 1785-1955* (1956).
Philip Alexander Bruce: *History of the University of Virginia, 1819-1919* (1920-2), 5 vols.
Enoch Albert Bryan: *Historical Sketch of the State College of Washington 1890-1925* (1928).
Henry Morton Bullock: *A History of Emory University* (1936).
Ernest Elmo Calkins: *They Broke the Prairie* [Knox College] (1937).
Malcolm Carron: *The Contract Colleges of Cornell University: A Cooperative Educational Enterprise* (1958).
Nora Campbell Chaffin: *Trinity College, 1839-1892: The Beginnings of Duke University* (1950).
G. Wallace Chessman: *Denison: The Story of an Ohio College* (1957).
Edward Potts Cheyney: *History of the University of Pennsylvania 1740-1940* (1940).
Russell H. Chittenden: *History of the Sheffield Scientific School of Yale University 1846-1922* (1928), 2 vols.
Robert Glass Cleland: *The History of Occidental College, 1887-1937* (1937).
Wilson O. Clough: *A History of the University of Wyoming, 1887-1937* (1937).
Arthur C. Cole: *A Hundred Years of Mount Holyoke College: The Evolution of An Educational Ideal* (1940).

Varnum Lansing Collins: *Princeton* (1914).

Florence Converse: *Wellesley College: A Chronicle of the Years 1875-1939* (1939).

Roberta D. Cornelius: *The History of Randolph-Macon Woman's College: From the Founding in 1891 Through the Year of 1949-1950* (1951).

E. Merton Coulter: *College Life in the Old South* [University of Georgia] (1951), 2d. ed.

Thomas Evans Coulton: *A City College in Action: Struggle and Achievement at Brooklyn College 1930-1955* (1955).

Merle Curti and Vernon Carstensen: *The University of Wisconsin: A History, 1848-1925* (1949), 2 vols.

George R. Cutting: *Student Life at Amherst College* (1871).

John M. Daley: *Georgetown University: Origin and Early Years* (1957).

William H. S. Demarest: *A History of Rutgers College 1766-1924* (1924).

Samuel Bradford Doten: *An Illustrated History of the University of Nevada* (1924).

Joseph H. Dubbs: *History of Franklin and Marshall College* (1903).

Wayland Fuller Dunaway: *History of the Pennsylvania State College* (1946).

David R. Dunigan: *A History of Boston College* (1947).

George Matthew Dutcher: *An Historical and Critical Survey of the Curriculum of Wesleyan University and Related Subjects* (1948).

Walter Dyson: *Howard University: The Capstone of Negro Education* (1941).

James Harold Easterby: *A History of the College of Charleston Founded 1770* (1935).

Edward Dwight Eaton: *Historical Sketches of Beloit College* (1928).

Orrin Leslie Elliott: *Stanford University: The First Twenty-Five Years* (1937).

John Tracy Ellis: *The Formative Years of the Catholic University of America* (1946).

Elizabeth M. Farrand: *History of the University of Michigan* (1885).

Merritt Caldwell Fernald: *History of the Maine State College and the University of Maine* (1916).

William Warren Ferrier: *Origin and Development of the University of California* (1930).

Donald Fleming: *Science and Technology in Providence 1760-1914: An Essay on the History of Brown University in the Metropolitan Community* (1952).

Walter L. Fleming: *Louisiana State University 1860-1896* (1936).

Robert Samuel Fletcher: *A History of Oberlin College from its Foundation through the Civil War* (1943), 2 vols.

Sidney Forman: *West Point: A History of the United States Military Academy* (1950).

Dixon Ryan Fox: *Union College: An Unfinished History* (1945).

John C. French: *A History of the University Founded by Johns Hopkins* (1946).

Claude Moore Fuess: *Amherst: The Story of a New England College* (1935).

Ralph Henry Gabriel: *Religion and Learning at Yale: The Church of Christ in the College and University, 1757-1957* (1958).

William Freeman Galpin: *Syracuse University: The Pioneer Days* (1952).

Louis G. Geiger: *University of the Northern Plains: A History of the University of North Dakota 1883-1958* (1958).

Roy Gittinger: *The University of Oklahoma 1892-1942* (1942).

Wilbur H. Glover: *Farm and College: The College of Agriculture of the University of Wisconsin: A History* (1952).

Thomas Wakefield Goodspeed: *A History of the University of Chicago Founded by John D. Rockefeller: The First Quarter-Century* (1916).

James Gray: *The University of Minnesota 1851-1951* (1951).

Alice Payne Hackett: *Wellesley: Part of the American Story* (1949).

Raphael N. Hamilton: *The Story of Marquette University: An Object Lesson in the Development of Catholic Higher Education* (1953).

Alfred J. Hanna: *The Founding of Rollins College* (1935).

Louis C. Hatch: *The History of Bowdoin College* (1927).

Walter Havighurst: *The Miami Years 1809-1959* (1958).

Hugh Hawkins: *Pioneer: A History of the Johns Hopkins University, 1874-1889* (1960).

Algo D. Henderson and Dorothy Hall: *Antioch College: Its Design for Liberal Education* (1946).

William Murray Hepburn and Louis Martin Sears: *Purdue University: Fifty Years of Progress* (1943).

Waterman Thomas Hewett: *Cornell University: A History* (1905), 5 vols.

Edith Parker Hinckley and Katharine Norton Benner: *The Dean Speaks Again: Edwin Clarence Norton, Pioneer Dean of Pomona College* (1955).

Burke A. Hinsdale: *History of the University of Michigan* (1906).

Peter E. Hogan: *The Catholic University of America, 1896-1903: The Rectorship of Thomas J. Conaty* (1949).

Daniel Walker Hollis: *University of South Carolina* (1951-6), 2 vols.

Thomas N. Hoover: *The History of Ohio University* (1954).

Arthur J. Hope: *Notre Dame: One Hundred Years* (1943).

James F. Hopkins: *The University of Kentucky: Origins and Early Years* (1951).

R. Gordon Hoxie, *et al.*: *A History of the Faculty of Political Science Columbia University* (1955).

Joseph D. Ibbotson and S. N. D. North: *Documentary History of Hamilton College* (1922).

Barbara Jones: *Bennington College: The Development of an Educational Idea* (1946).

Rufus M. Jones: *Haverford College: A History and an Interpretation* (1933).

Theodore F. Jones, ed.: *New York University 1832:1932* (1933).

Frederick Paul Keppel: *Columbia* (1914).

William Lathrop Kingsley, ed.: *Yale College: A Sketch of its History* (1879), 2 vols.

Anna Heubeck Knipp and Thaddeus P. Thomas: *The History of Goucher College* (1938).

Madison Kuhn: *Michigan State: The First Hundred Years* (1955).

Thomas Le Duc: *Piety and Intellect at Amherst College 1865-1912* (1946).

William Storrs Lee: *Father Went to College: The Story of Middlebury* (1936).

Delavan L. Leonard: *The History of Carleton College* (1904).

Edwin S. Leonard, Jr.: *As the Sowing: The First Fifty Years of Principia* (1951).

Julian Ira Lindsay: *Tradition Looks Forward: The University of Vermont: A History 1791-1904* (1954).

David A. Lockmiller: *History of the North Carolina State College of Agriculture and Engineering of the University of North Carolina, 1889-1939* (1939).

Henry M. MacCracken, *et al.*: *New York University* (1901).

Edward D. McDonald and Edward M. Hinton: *Drexel Institute of Technology, 1891-1941* (1942).

Philip M. Marston, ed.: *History of the University of New Hampshire 1866-1941* (1941).

Cornelia Lynde Meigs: *What Makes a College? A History of Bryn Mawr* (1956).

Gilbert Meltzer: *The Beginnings of Elmira College, 1851-1868* (1941).

Annie Nathan Meyer: *Barnard Beginnings* (1935).

William Alfred Millis: *The History of Hanover College from 1827 to 1927* (1927).

Edwin Mims: *History of Vanderbilt University* (1946).

Dwight C. Miner, ed.: *A History of Columbia College on Morningside* (1954), one of the volumes in *The Bicentennial History of Columbia University* (1954-7), 15 vols.

James Henry Morgan: *Dickinson College: The History of One Hundred and Fifty Years 1783-1933* (1933).

Samuel Eliot Morison, ed.: *The Development of Harvard University since the Inauguration of President Eliot 1869-1929* (1930).

Samuel Eliot Morison: *The Founding of Harvard College* (1935).

———: *Harvard College in the Seventeenth Century* (1936), 2 vols.

———: *Three Centuries of Harvard 1636-1936* (1936).

Alfred J. Morrison, ed.: *The College of Hampden-Sidney: Calendar of Board Minutes 1776-1876* (1912).

Burton Dorr Myers: *History of Indiana University: 1902-1937* (1952).

Allan Nevins: *Illinois* (1917).

John Scholte Nollen: *Grinnell College* (1953).

Lucy Lilian Notestein: *Wooster of the Middle West* (1937).

James I. Osborne and Theodore G. Gronert: *Wabash College; the first hundred years, 1832-1932* (1932).

Edwin Oviatt: *The Beginnings of Yale (1701-1726),* (1916).

George Sessions Perry: *The Story of Texas A & M* (1951).

George Wilson Pierson: *Yale: College and University 1871-1937* (1952-5), 2 vols.

James E. Pollard: *History of the Ohio State University: The Story of its First Seventy-Five Years 1873-1948* (1952).

William H. Powers, ed.: *A History of South Dakota State College* (1931).

Samuel C. Prescott: *When M.I.T. was 'Boston Tech' 1861-1916* (1954).

Carl F. Price: *Wesleyan's First Century* (1932).

Allen E. Ragan: *A History of Tusculum College, 1794-1944* (1945).

Charles Henry Rammelkamp: *Illinois College: A Centennial History 1829-1929* (1928).

Andrew Van Vranken Raymond, ed.: *Union University: Its History, Influence, Characteristics and Equipment* (1907), 3 vols.

John Hugh Reynolds and David Yancey Thomas: *History of the University of Arkansas* (1910).

Leon Burr Richardson: *History of Dartmouth College* (1932), 2 vols.

Palmer Chamberlain Ricketts: *History of Rensselaer Polytechnic Institute 1824-1914* (1934), 3d. ed.

Walter P. Rogers: *Andrew D. White and the Modern University* (1942).

Jesse Leonard Rosenberger: *Rochester, the Making of a University* (1927).

Earle D. Ross: *A History of the Iowa State College of Agriculture and Mechanic Arts* (1942).

Frederick Rudolph: *Mark Hopkins and the Log: Williams College, 1836-1872* (1956).

S. Willis Rudy: *The College of the City of New York: A History, 1847-1947* (1949).

Kent Sagendorph: *Michigan: The Story of the University* (1948).

Edmund C. Sanford: *A Sketch of the History of Clark University* (1923).

James B. Sellers: *History of the University of Alabama 1818-1902* (1953).

Henry D. Sheldon: *History of University of Oregon* (1940).

Robert Sibley: *The Romance of the University of California* (1928).

David Bishop Skillman: *The Biography of a College: Being the History of the First Century of the Life of Lafayette College* (1932), 2 vols.

George Franklin Smythe: *Kenyon College: Its First Century* (1924).

Leverett Wilson Spring: *A History of Williams College* (1917).

Walter Stemmons: *Connecticut Agricultural College—A History* (1931).

Charles Burt Sumner: *The Story of Pomona College* (1914).

William Warren Sweet: *Indiana Asbury-DePauw University, 1837-1937: A Hundred Years of Higher Education in the Middle West* (1937).

Thomas Gaffney Taaffe: *A History of St. John's College, Fordham, N. Y.* (1891).

Allen P. Tankersley: *College Life at Old Oglethorpe* (1951).

James Monroe Taylor and Elizabeth Hazelton Haight: *Vassar* (1915).

John Howard Van Amringe, et al.: *A History of Columbia University 1754-1904* (1904).

Jonas Viles, et al.: *The University of Missouri: A Centennial History* (1939).

Frederick Clayton Waite: *Western Reserve University: The Hudson Era* (1943).

David Duncan Wallace: *History of Wofford College* (1951).

Estelle Frances Ward: *The Story of Northwestern University* (1924).

Thomas Jefferson Wertenbaker: *Princeton 1746-1896* (1946).

Marian Churchill White: *A History of Barnard College* (1954).

Julius Terrass Willard: *History of the Kansas State College of Agriculture and Applied Science* (1940).

Samuel H. Willey: *A History of the College of California* (1887).

Louis R. Wilson: *The University of North Carolina, 1900-1930: The Making of a Modern University* (1957).

James Albert Woodburn: *History of Indiana University 1820-1902* (1940).

GENERAL HISTORIES

The first attempt to take a comprehensive view of a major aspect of the history of higher education in the United States was by Andrew Ten Brook: *American State Universities, their Origin and Progress* (1875). It has had no successor, although the great flowering of the state university has come since 1875. The attitudes of state legislatures

toward state universities constitute a changing record of social and
intellectual importance. A history of the state universities of the South
during Reconstruction would provide at least one clear answer to the
question, what was Reconstruction really like? The great role of public
service assumed by the state universities, in the tradition of such colonial
establishments as Harvard and Yale, has been understood by most
friends of the state universities, but just what that role has meant for
American society and life in general has not been properly studied.

Charles F. Thwing: *A History of Higher Education in America*
(1906) was the first comprehensive one-volume effort to provide a general history. It has long been out of print and out of date. Ernest Earnest: *Academic Procession: An Informal History of the American College, 1636-1953* (1953) is entertaining but also unreliable. George P.
Schmidt: *The Liberal Arts College* (1957) is an uneven but often lively
survey of the liberal-arts college. John S. Brubacher and Willis Rudy:
Higher Education in Transition: An American History: 1636-1956
(1958) is marred by uncertain organization and by an effort to be more
inclusive than a one-volume study can successfully be.

The land-grant colleges have fared better than the state universities.
Earle D. Ross: *Democracy's College: The Land-Grant Movement in
the Formative Stage* (1942) and Edward Danforth Eddy, Jr.: *Colleges
for Our Land and Time: The Land-Grant Idea in American Education*
(1957) are useful surveys, although there are aspects of the history of
the land-grant college movement that need to be treated in more depth
and with more imagination, especially the great public indifference to
the Morrill Act of 1862, the deep-seated hostility of the Grange and
Populists to the early colleges, the opposition of the private colleges
to the extension of federal aid to the land-grant colleges, the peculiar
career of the land-grant idea in New England, the history of military
training in connection with the colleges, and the land-grant college as a
function of the agrarian myth in the United States.

The junior college is too recent a major phenomenon to have built
a body of historical literature, but a vast amount of published material
of a documentary nature awaits study. Leonard Vincent Koos: *The
Junior College* (1924), 2 vols., and Walter Crosby Eells: *The Junior
College* (1931) are really documents of the junior-college movement
rather than histories.

The higher education of women is treated in Thomas Woody: *A
History of Women's Education in the United States* (1929), 2 vols.,
and in Mabel Newcomer: *A Century of Higher Education for Women*
(1959). Neither is the full-bodied study the subject deserves. We need
to know more about the pre-emption of the liberal arts by women
students in coeducational institutions. So much that has been written
about the higher education of women has been tinted by apologia or
zeal that it is often forgotten that for perhaps three quarters of a cen-

tury the higher education of most men in the United States has taken place in institutions open to women. The meaning of this phenomenon either for the education of men or for American life in general has been little understood or explored.

A small but disappointing body of general historical writing on Catholic higher education has developed: Sister Mary Mariella Bowler: *A History of Catholic Colleges for Women in the United States of America* (1933); Francis Patrick Cassidy: *Catholic College Foundations and Development in the United States (1677-1850)* (1924); Sebastian A. Erbacher: *Catholic Higher Education for Men in the United States 1850-1866* (1931); Edward J. Power: *A History of Catholic Higher Education in the United States* (1958). These studies are best in their efforts to establish the record of collegiate beginnings and growth, but only inadequately do they tell to what a remarkable degree the Catholic institutions were like any other denominational colleges. As for the ways in which the Catholic institutions were different, particularly in matters of discipline and standards, the historical record remains hazy. One subject awaiting a careful history is the struggle developing in the late nineteenth century within the Church in America over Catholic attendance at non-Catholic colleges.

General studies of professional education are either out of date or too professionally oriented to satisfy many of the demands of historical scholarship. The appropriate chapters in Richard Hofstadter and C. DeWitt Hardy: *The Development and Scope of Higher Education in the United States* (1952) are useful and suggestive. The whole territory of professional education remains essentially unexplored by trained historians except as an aspect of particular institutions. The education of clergymen, lawyers, doctors, engineers, and members of the other newer professions offers a field of tremendous opportunity for research. A recent model is Daniel Hovey Calhoun: *The American Civil Engineer: Origins and Conflict* (1960).

Edgar Bruce Wesley: *Proposed: The University of the United States* (1936) is a brief survey of the career of the idea of a national university in the United States. The subject deserves a thorough study, for it has been debated often enough to have left an intriguing record of public sentiment toward federal sponsorship of higher education. Congressional consideration of a national university during the period of decision on the Smithson will after 1835, the revival of the national university idea in the 1870's, and the launching and support of Howard University in Washington as a Negro institution (but as a national university nonetheless) are aspects of the subject worthy of fuller study.

PERIODICALS

Probably no more than a half dozen articles on the history of higher education have appeared in the leading professional historical journals— the *American Historical Review* (1895-   ) and the *Mississippi Valley Historical Review* (1914-   ). The *American Quarterly* (1949-   ), representing the search for a sense of discipline in the area of American studies, has been friendlier to educational history than have the more traditional journals, but the most rewarding journals for the student of American higher education are those that have enjoyed the sponsorship and support of professional educators: *American Association of University Professors Bulletin* (1915-   ); *American Journal of Education* (1855-82); *American Quarterly Register and Journal of the American Education Society* (1827-46); *Educational Record* (1920-   ); *Educational Review* (1891-1928); *Harvard Educational Review* (1931-   ); *Journal of Higher Education* (1930-   ); *School and Society* (1915-   ); *Teachers College Record* (1900-   ). The recently reorganized History of Education Society has launched the *History of Education Quarterly* (1961-   ) in the hope of creating a new outlet for the growing interest in educational history. The annual proceedings and publications of the various professional organizations catering to the needs and interests of higher education also constitute a profitable source of study.

BIBLIOGRAPHICAL AND DOCUMENTARY

Oscar Handlin, *et al.*: *Harvard Guide to American History* (1954) is the standard bibliographical aid for research in American history. It may be supplemented by *Writings on American History* (1902-   ), a series of volumes prepared by the American Historical Association. William W. Brickman: *Guide to Research in Educational History* (1949) provides a general orientation in the field of educational history, but for higher education it is not as useful for recent years as the annual volumes of the *Journal of Higher Education*.

Among the bibliographical bulletins published by the United States Office of Education, particularly helpful are the following: *Analytical Index to Barnard's American Journal of Education* (1892); *List of Publications of the United States Bureau of Education, 1867-1910* (1910); *List of Publications of the Office of Education, 1910-1936* (1937); *Publications of the Office of Education, 1937-1959* (1960); Sheldon Emmor Davis: *Educational Periodicals During the Nineteenth Century* (1919); Walter Crosby Eells and Ernest V. Hollis: *Administration of Higher Education: An Annotated Bibliography* (1960); and Walter Crosby

Eells and Ernest V. Hollis: *The College Presidency 1900-1960: An Annotated Bibliography* (1961).

Many of the specialized studies listed above contain quite excellent bibliographies, but just as there is need for a reliable compendium of historical statistics, there exists no general guide to such published documentary material as diaries, letters and speeches, no guide to the historical material in general periodicals or the specialized journals, and no listing or critical evaluation of the available biographical and autobiographical literature. Nor is there any inventory of the published historical material of more than parochial interest and importance that has accumulated at almost every institution. These bibliographical opportunities deserve the attention of the friends of the history of higher education in the United States.

Anthologies of documentary material until recently have been lacking. Edward C. Elliott and M. M. Chambers: *Charters and Basic Laws of Selected American Universities and Colleges* (1934) is useful, and there is appropriate material on higher education in Edgar W. Knight, ed.: *Documentary History of Education in the South* (1949-53), 5 vols. Richard Hofstadter and Wilson Smith: *American Higher Education: A Documentary History* (1961), 2 vols., provides an excellent anthology of important documents in the development of American higher education. While it was not available during the preparation of the present study, it contains large selections from many of the writings to which I turned during my researches. The Hofstadter and Smith selections, however, do not preclude the need for further comparable work, especially in areas that they have neglected or minimized in their successful effort to produce a representative, but not a comprehensive, collection.

SUPPLEMENTAL
BIBLIOGRAPHY
Prepared by John R. Thelin

Frederick Rudolph's original bibliographic essay endures as an insightful analysis of the state of the art of historical writing on higher education in 1962. As such it deserves to stand intact for reading by subsequent generations of scholars and researchers. This supplemental bibliography attempts to update the original bibliography, with fidelity to Rudolph's original organizing scheme and categories. In discussing books and articles published over the past three decades, I have sought only to track major research trends. This bibliographic essay is selective and illustrative and does not claim to be exhaustive in citing all related works. This essay charts two distinct yet related dimensions to the scholarship: first, an end point that indicates the extent of historical writing about higher education between 1962 and 1990; and, second, a high point that indicates the stature achieved by historians of higher education. These will serve as points of reference from which to flesh out discussion of key themes and significant works.

As suggested in my introductory essay, publication of Rudolph's book coincided with an impressive ground swell of scholarship in the history of American higher education. As an end point, the work that best illustrates the breadth and bulk of the cumulative research effort over the subsequent three decades is the 673-page anthology, *ASHE Reader on the History of Higher Education* (1989). Edited by historians Lester F. Goodchild and Harold Wechsler, and sponsored by the Association for the Study of Higher Education (ASHE), this impressive volume suggests the substantial amount of historical writing about higher education and reveals the substantive quality of the work, characterized by diverse methods and topics. Its bibliographies and recommendations for additional readings make the *ASHE*

Reader an indispensable reference volume. Above all, it provides tangible evidence that Rudolph was correct in noting that the history of higher education had indeed been rediscovered by the historians. Scholarly success extracts a price. The impressive quantity of research on the history of higher education published over the past thirty years has become increasingly difficult for scholars to review or manage as a coherent whole. Fortunately, a number of excellent bibliographies provide useful guides. Joe Park's *The Rise of American Education: An Annotated Bibliography* (1965) includes specific attention to the histories of colleges and universities as part of the broader sphere of American education. Two references from the 1970s endure as fruitful sources: Jurgen Herbst's *American Education* (1973) and Mark Beach's *A Bibliographic Guide to American Colleges and Universities: From Colonial Times to the Present* (1974). Institutional histories within the United States receive thorough coverage in the reference work, *Institutions of Higher Education: An International Bibliography* (1990), compiled by Linda Sparks. For researchers who seek to look beyond books and journal articles, Arthur P. Young's compilation, *Higher Education in American Life, 1636–1986: A Bibliography of Dissertations and Theses* (1988), exhaustively surveys nascent scholarship that has emerged from master's and doctoral degree programs in university graduate schools. Thomas Diener's *Growth of an American Invention* (1986) brings together key excerpts and references on a historically understudied and relatively young institution, the American junior and community college.

In addition to such specific bibliographies, historians of higher education are well served by landmark works in the broader sphere of the history of American education. Lawrence Cremin's three-volume study, *American Education*, begun in 1967, is organized according to the themes of the colonial experience, the national experience, and the metropolitan experience, with higher education treated as part of the complex social and educational fabric. The 1976 edition of John S. Brubacher and Willis Rudy's *Higher Education in Transition: A History of the American Colleges and Universities* represents an expanded, revised version of their 1958 study, which has persisted as an invaluable classic.

Whereas the *ASHE Reader* illustrates the broad extent of scholarship over time, other works examine the stature of scholarship in the history of higher education in the years since publication of Rudolph's *The American College and University: A History*. If one seeks a high point for the history of higher education, 1971 stands as a likely candidate. Two memorable artifacts support this claim: the *History of Education Quarterly*'s special Winter 1971 issue; and Lawrence Stone's lead article, "The Ninnyversity?" in the January 28 issue of the *New York Review of Books*. In the *History of Education Quarterly* editor Paul Mattingly used the theme of "the liberal college in the age of the university" to enlist four stellar historians—Hugh Hawkins, David F. Allmendinger, David Potts, and James Axtell—to write original essays in response to the scholarship about the founding of the new universities and the heroic era of "university building" that had dominated the field during the preceding decade. The articles, each a classic in its own right, were lively, substantive, and provocative. The issue demonstrated good health for the study of colleges and universities within the field of the history of education.

The January 28 issue of the *New York Review of Books* signaled that the history of higher education was "news" among the American intelligentsia. The lead article, Lawrence Stone's essay review "The Ninnyversity?," was the tip of an academic iceberg: Professor Stone (well known for his concept of "total history" in probing the seemingly interminable debates over the rise and fall of England's seventeenth- and eighteenth-century gentry) was to lead Princeton University's Shelby Cullom Davis Center in its historical study of "The University in Society." The history of higher education was a topic that had, at least for the moment, acquired prestige and publicity—and now, funding. Such real and symbolic gains in research fulfilled the prospect Rudolph had outlined a decade earlier. Indeed, Princeton University Press's subsequent publication of Lawrence Stone's two-volume anthology, *The University in Society* (1974), showed that the history of higher education was a topic that had enduring attraction and appeal. I cite these notable selected works to introduce, rather than to conclude, analysis of the historiography of higher education over the past three decades. On closer inspection, however, the context of both 1971 documents and the 1989 *ASHE Reader* indicate some weaknesses and uncertainties as well as strengths in the research of the history of higher education.

INSTITUTIONAL CHRONICLES:
VERTICAL HISTORIES

One disappointing trend in the history of higher education is that the genre of "house histories" has improved little since 1962. Most commissioned works continue to be written by old grads, with only incidental connection to social history. Such works tend to be "vertical histories," that is, works preoccupied with the insular events and historical records of a single, specific campus. Even those works that celebrate undergraduate life seldom provide any analytic framework that truly analyzes a particular campus's distinctive student cultures. Writing an institutional history has even sometimes been a career liability; for example, in 1983 Louise Blecher Rose faced administrative censorship and reprimand at Sarah Lawrence College when, in the course of her commissioned research for the college's official institutional history, she inadvertently discovered (and analyzed) confidential files dealing with admissions quotas in the 1930s. There have been some important exceptions: namely, Thomas Dyer's *The University of Georgia: A Bicentennial History, 1785–1985* (1985) and Paul Conkin's *Gone with the Ivy*

(1985), a history of Vanderbilt University. These studies provide models for fusing a campus chronicle with American social history, which have not been sufficiently heeded elsewhere. In 1990 it is interesting that many institutions have not recently published "official" histories. Stephen R. Graubard, professor of history at Brown University and editor of the journal *Daedalus*, argued in the December 1989 issue of the *Brown Alumni Monthly*: "We need a modern history of Brown" to supplement its last official institutional chronicle in 1914. The problem for Brown and other universities is that the institutional history genre is crystallized and cannot offer much peer recognition for a legitimate scholar. The fear of censorship coexists with the sense that such projects are time-consuming and not especially interesting either to fellow scholars or to external funding agencies. In sum, the primary commitment of serious scholars is to the study of issues not to a single institution.

One possible explanation for this lack of critical analysis in the histories of individual institutions is the virtual absence of linkage with some academic disciplines. Even though colleges and universities are perennially concerned with raising money and balancing budgets, there is little sign that economic historians have been invited to join the institutional history projects. For example, in his bibliographic essay, Rudolph brings attention to a new book, Margery Somers Foster's *"Out of Smalle Beginings . . .": An Economic History of Harvard College in the Puritan Period* (1962). This meticulous study relied on such archival materials as ledger sheets, annual reports, and student diaries to provide a reconstruction and interpretation of collegiate "getting and spending." Here was a fascinating analysis of institutional life that moved economics from the category of a "dismal science" and suggested at the same time a strategy for rescuing institutional chronicles from superficiality. One searches in vain for comparable researches and publications by and about other American colleges and universities—even though Foster's intensive case study tied to economic concepts was well suited to the institutional history genre.

INSTITUTIONAL HISTORIES WITH A DIFFERENCE: HORIZONTAL HISTORIES

Historians, in opting to shy away from institutional chronicles, have tended to identify substantive themes that cut across administrations. This analysis is horizontal, focusing on a significant question where research is not confined to the specific experience of a single campus. Here is the framework for connecting institutional history to issues. Rudolph believed that social history and intellectual history would be the umbrella under which histories of higher education might flourish. The latter variant—intellectual history—has been markedly underdeveloped. Certainly it is so-

cial history's connection of the campus to trends in demography, regional
history, and urban history and to questions of class, race, and gender that
has been the source of scholarly energy.

Even though the report card for house histories is not favorable, there
have been promising innovations in our conception of institutional history.
George Peterson's *The New England College in the Age of the University*
(1963), originally an undergraduate honors thesis at Amherst College,
showed how institutional history might move beyond preoccupation with a
single campus to probe more interesting questions of institutional heritage
and collective identity. An exciting new wrinkle in institutional history has
come from sociologist Burton Clark, who has developed the notion of "organizational saga." His work, *The Distinctive College* (1970), used historical
case studies of three liberal arts colleges—Antioch, Reed, and Swarthmore—
to show how "organizational memory" and the legends and lore associated
with an embellished past coexist with a college's official chronicle and administrative records. His overarching theme of saga helped to salvage historical analysis from the insularity of a single campus. The salient feature of
such analysts as George Peterson and Burton Clark has been their tendency
to shift institutional research from what I have termed here vertical history
to horizontal history. Significant themes across time and place provide social and educational historians an intriguing perspective on colleges and
universities.

Nowhere was the rigor and complexity of this new direction in institutional history more evident than in Laurence Veysey's *The Emergence of the
American University* (1965). Cited by *Change* magazine as one of the most
influential books in higher education since World War II, *The Emergence of
the American University* is a study of organizational behavior between 1870
and 1910. The interplay of ideas and institutions and the tensions among
rival conceptions of learning led Veysey to describe and probe a period of
heroic campus-building that culminated with what came to be known by
World War I as the "standard American university." Veysey's monumental
work also has elicited healthy revision, namely, the aforementioned 1971
special issue of *History of Education Quarterly* and, more recently, Paul Mattingly's essay, "Structures Over Time: Institutional History," published in
John Hardin Best's anthology for the American Educational Research Association, *Historical Inquiry in Education: A Research Agenda* (1983). Important
to note is the sense of debate over the conceptualization of historical research, a dimension often missing in the institutional chronicles. This sense
of scholarly maturity is illustrated by Richard Angelo's seminal article, "The
Students at the University of Pennsylvania and the Temple College of Philadelphia, 1873–1906" (*History of Education Quarterly* 19, no. 2 [Summer 1979]:
179–205), in which he complicates rather than simplifies questions about institutional mission and who went to what college.

SOCIAL HISTORY AND INSTITUTIONS: THEMES OF
ACCESS AND EXCLUSION

If social history has been the organizing lens for institutional history, its related themes of access, opportunity, and exclusion have been the major instruments for critical analysis in the history of higher education. Oscar and Mary Handlin's *The American College and American Culture: Socialization as a Function of Higher Education* (1970), Marcia Synott's *The Half-Opened Door: Discrimination and Admissions at Harvard, Yale, and Princeton, 1900–1970* (1979), and Harold Wechsler's *The Qualified Student: A History of Selective College Admissions in America* (1977) are exemplary works in which the particulars of selected campuses are introduced into discussions of "going to college" as part of the American experience.

The subjects of access and exclusion have provided good analytic concepts with which historians can probe the rhetoric of college and university public relations. An interesting finding by several historians is that discrimination and snobbery within the student life of campus match or surpass the exclusionary policies and practices of, say, the admissions office. Such research perspectives have been fruitful for historians who examine consequences and trade-offs associated with educational policies of coeducation or integration. Charlotte Conable's *Women at Cornell* (1977) effectively pierced the rhetoric of coeducation to reconstruct a critical profile of women students that indicated systemic gender discrimination and tracking within the coeducational structure. The nuances and intricacies of coeducation policies and institutional ethos were elevated to a new level of comparative analysis in Lynn D. Gordon's "Co-Education on Two Campuses: Berkeley and Chicago, 1890–1912," published in Mary Kelly's anthology, *Women's Being, Women's Place: Female Identity and Vocation in American History* (1979). Following Frederick Rudolph's emphasis on students as the major characters in the higher education drama, historian Helen Lefkowitz Horowitz's *Campus Life* (1987) developed the scheme of student subcultures ("insiders," "outsiders," and "rebels") for an interpretative survey of undergraduate life from the end of the eighteenth century to the 1980s. In an earlier work, *Alma Mater* (1984), Horowitz had used campus architecture as a crucial element for tracking attempts to foster distinctive educational missions and curricular innovations at various women's colleges from the late nineteenth century to the 1930s.

Campus culture has been an important bridge to the study of regional culture. Indeed, as David Potts has effectively shown, a recurrent limitation of works published before 1960 was their tendency to confine themselves to the Northeast. Promising scholarship that counters that bias comes from the 1985 anthology, *The Web of Southern Social Relations: Women, Family and Education*, edited by Walter Fraser, R. Franklin Saunders, and Jon L. Wakelyn. Especially pertinent for the study of collegiate cultures is Wakelyn's chapter, "Antebellum College Life and the Relations Between Fathers and Sons," in which the analysis of letters provides an estimation of what socialization was occurring on the Southern campus. At the same time, Wakelyn's essay provides a rare glimpse at parental expectations of the college experience.

BIOGRAPHY OF INSTITUTIONS

One fruitful research synthesis has been to connect biographical profile with organizational history to create a good case study. Hugh Hawkins of Amherst College, author of the exemplary institutional history of The Johns Hopkins University, *Pioneer* (1960), eventually focused on the biography of President Eliot in *Between Harvard and America* (1971), his study of Harvard in its university-building decades. Maresi Nerad has used the biography of Professor Elizabeth Morgan as a vehicle to examine treatment of women both as individual scholars and as administrators in her forthcoming book, *Gender in Higher Education: The History of the Home Economics Department at the University of California, Berkeley*. In a similar vein Joyce Antler's *Lucy Sprague Mitchell: The Making of a Modern Woman* (1987) goes beyond insular biography to provide good historical description and interpretation of "academic women" and the institutional cultures of such universities as Columbia and Berkeley. Academic biography has demonstrated the power to counter familiar institutional stereotypes. The portrayal of the 1862 Morrill Act and its resultant land grant colleges as a success story of educational practicality and opportunity takes on a markedly different hue in light of Roger Lea Williams's award-winning doctoral dissertation, *George W. Atherton and the Beginnings of Federal Support for Higher Education* (1989). Contrary to earlier accounts, Williams shows that federal support for extension programs and other activities of the land grant colleges suffered neglect until political economist Atherton started an organized lobbying effort and ultimately became president of Pennsylvania State College.

HIGHER EDUCATION AND PUBLIC POLICY

Williams's study of Atherton and the land grant effort provides a useful transition from biography and institutional history to the study of higher education and public policy. Public policy has proven to be an area where historians of higher education have made excellent contributions, once again showing skill in moving beyond the parochial concerns of institutional chronicle to more enduring questions that link institutional case studies to general concerns about the context of higher education. John Whitehead's *The Separation of College and State* (1973) uses profiles of five selected colleges founded in the colonial period to present an intriguing interpretation of the changing notions of "public" and "private" institutions in American higher education. Jurgen Herbst's *From Crisis to Crisis: American College Government, 1636–1819* (1982) draws from primary sources at numerous colleges and universities to look at the distinctive hybrid arrangements between college and host governments. Perhaps the best sign of life within the historians of higher education is that these two memorable works ultimately led to a lively forum in which Herbst and Whitehead sparred in companion essays, "How To Think About the Dartmouth College Case," published in the Fall 1986 issue of the *History of Education Quarterly*.

Public policy is hardly confined to colleges' governmental relations. Ellen Condliffe Lageman's *Private Power for the Public Good* (1983) makes a significant contribution to thinking about higher education by shifting attention from the campus to the policies and programs of the Carnegie Foundation for the Advancement of Teaching. More recently, Hugh Hawkins's work-in-progress on the federal grant universities of the post–World War II period promises to be a relatively new perspective. Roger Geiger's book, *To Advance Knowledge: The Growth of American Research Universities, 1900–1940* (1986), fuses both campus and external foundations and government agencies as actors and architects in what Clark Kerr called "the Knowledge Industry."

PUBLISHING THE RESEARCH RESULTS:
PERIODICALS AND JOURNALS

In contrast to the stagnation associated with publication of institutional histories, historians of higher education have acquired access during the past three decades to quality journals. Outstanding journals that have encouraged research in the history of higher education include the *History of Education Quarterly*, the *History of Higher Education Annual*, the *Review of Higher Education*, and the annual publication, *Higher Education: Handbook of Theory and Research*. Since 1960 a generation of newer and younger historians of higher education have found that it is the refereed journal article or monograph, not the commissioned institutional history, that is the primary vehicle whereby one contributes to the scholarly debate.

A good example of this pioneering shift in form and content is the 1961 article in the *History of Education Quarterly* by Merle Borrowman, "The False Dawn of the State University." Borrowman relied on concise profiles of three understudied nineteenth-century institutions (Transylvania University, University of South Carolina, and University of Nashville) to break through the isolation of the house history. In so doing he spared readers the boring trivia of an extended descriptive chronicle; in a more positive light, his study advanced a significant historical thesis about the character and composition of American colleges in the early nineteenth century. He also prompted readers to think about the public-private dichotomy and to consider an alternative to Whig history—namely, to include study of forgotten episodes and "lost" institutions. All this was accomplished in about twenty-five pages. This was the kind of article that transformed the *History of Education Quarterly* into a highly respected forum for research and debate. The editorial excellence originated by Henry Perkinson was developed admirably by Paul Mattingly at New York University, and later continued at Indiana University by Edward McClellan and William Reese. The result is that the history of higher education as an integral part of American social and educational history found a publication hospitable to scholarly presentation and debates.

The troubling, uncertain dimension is that the combination of cumulative scholarship and peak achievements over the past three decades has not left the history of higher education with a secure place. Although both the quality and quantity of scholarship have been very good since publication of Rudolph's 1962 book, historians of higher education find themselves and their works scattered. Their influence on policy and their contributions to interdisciplinary debates, although appreciated, have in the main not been accompanied by substantial resources or even institutional positions. Perhaps it is an irony that today's historians of higher education are heirs to the legacy of a group they have studied: the wandering medieval university scholars whose dedication and good works are not guaranteed a secure academic home.

INDEX

Index

Chicago, University of (*cont.*) 405; sponsors learned journals, 405; and publishing activities, 407; Edward W. Bemis academic freedom case, 414; four-quarter system, 447; contrasted with Oxford, 453; general education, 455-6; R. M. Hutchins, 479-81; motto of, 481; retreats to collegiate values, 495

Choate, Rufus, 142, 428

Christian Church, 55

church-state relations: *see* state-church relations

City College of New York: personnel counselors' report, 86-7; rebellion at, 98; and aristocratic opposition, 207; old curriculum, 236; night school, 344; college color, 386; and Ph.D. of professors, 396; Pres. J. H. Finley, 417, 420-1; Communist demonstration, 467

City University of New York, 486

civil engineering, 229, 231-2

Civil War, 241-3

Clark University, 332, 335, 350, 396

classes, college: *see* college classes

classical course of study: standard subjects, 126; and compulsion, 129; at New York University, 129; and extracurriculum, 156; low salaries and low tuition, 197-8; and aristocracy, 205-6; Francis Wayland on, 218, 220, 238; support for, 239-40; and Pres. Eliot, 244; and Civil War, 244-5; Justin Morrill, 249; new subjects in land-grant colleges, 255-6; Cornell, 268; state universities, 279-80; high school movement, 284; at Boston College, 296; defense of James McCosh, 299; evils of prescribed nature, 304-5; *see also* curriculum; motiva-

classical course of study (*cont.*) tion problem; Yale Report of 1828

classics: and Benjamin Rush, 43; and infidelity, 81; and founding fathers, 111; at Lafayette, 113; and James Marsh, 115; new subjects, 115-16; at Harvard, 120; and idea of progress, 122-3; at Amherst, 122-4; at University of Virginia, 125; in psychology of Yale Report, 132-3; Francis Wayland, 238; at Johns Hopkins, 270; and Pres. Eliot, 292, 295; and elective principle, 306; "culture course" epithet, 324-5; journal founded at Chicago, 405; and R. M. Hutchins, 480; *see also* Latin; Greek; Yale Report of 1828

Clay, Henry, 111

clergymen, 170, 173-4, 428; *see also* religion; theological education

Clifford, John H., 292-3

Clinton, Dewitt, 51

Cliosophic Society, 137

coaches (athletic), 391-2, 422, 465

Coe College, 433

coeducation, 307, 311, 314-16, 321-6, 339

Coffman, Lotus D., 483

Colby College, 53

Coleridge, Samuel Taylor, 121

college classes, 26, 121, 162, 325, 369

College Entrance Examination Board, 436-8

college founding, 7-8, 11, 35-6, 51-3, 72, 84, 197-9, 211, 219

college laws, 105-6; *see also* discipline

college movement, 44-67, 110, 330; *see also* college founding; purposes of colleges and universities; university movement

college preparation, 281-2, 284, 325; *see also* academies; high schools; secondary education

college settlement house movement: *see* settlement house movement
college spirit: *see* collegiate way; dormitories
college-state relations: *see* state-college relations
Collegiate School: *see* Yale University
collegiate way: and English patterns, 26-7; manifestations of, 86-7; English origins, 87, 124; American environment, 87-8; and Pres. Eliot, 88; paternalism, 88-9, 104-8; discipline, 88-9, 104-8; anti-intellectual character of, 88-9, 140; critics, 90-1; rural setting, 91-5; and agrarian myth, 95-6; dormitories, 96-7, 99-101; and rebellion, 97-8; commons, 101-2; restrains university development, 108; and transfer and itinerant students, 108; Pres. Porter on, 108-9; and faculty authority, 157; at Johns Hopkins, 271-2; James McCosh on, 299-300; and women's colleges, 325; and *Lernfreiheit*, 412; and Pres. Merriefield at North Dakota, 418; "Prexy Hour" at Ohio State, 422; and deans in university era, 435-6; and paternalism, 441; and acceleration movement, 446-9; revival in 1920's, 449-61; extracurriculum, 464-5
colonial colleges, 3, 6-13, 19-20, 23-43, 185-6
Colorado College, 53
Columbia University: early purposes, 12-13; governing board, 16; denominational orientation, 18; prospectus of 1754, 31-2; William Smith's proposal of 1753, 32; during American Revolution, 33-4; relations with state, 36, 186, 278; name changed, 41; new professorships, 41; Dewitt Clinton en-

Columbia University (*cont.*)
ters, 51; chapel, 77; and collegiate way, 88, 91; urban setting deplored, 93; and dormitories, 99, 100; adopts parallel course, 115; and Yale Report, 131-2; fraternities, 144; nonclergy presidents, 170; scholarships, 191; botany introduced, 222; and graduate education, 235, 335; agricultural chemistry, 247; and high school growth, 284; elective principle, 302; Barnard College, 320; liberal arts, 324-5; John W. Burgess quoted, 330; fellowships for foreign study, 337; and New York theological seminaries, 344; Pres. Barnard and Pres. Low as university builders, 348-9; extension courses, 363; and football, 376, 379; sponsors learned journals, 405-7; Dean Keppel, 435; "professional option" plan, 447; general education, 455-6; General Honors program, 456; and the dean, 460; Dean Hawkes, 467; Teachers College, 470-1
commencement exercises, 30, 64, 127, 142, 180, 262-3, 408, 420-1
commerce, schools of, 126
Committee of Ten, 437
Committee of Twelve, 437
common schools: New York, 212; Missouri, 212; 1837 Treasury surplus, 213; Jacksonian support, 215; as agencies of mobility, 216; preparation of teachers for, 217; college students as teachers, 222; R.P.I., 230; and Tappan at Michigan, 233-4; land-grant colleges, 265; state universities seek link between, 281-2; accept girls, 309-10; and state universities, 314; Pres. Angell on, 359
commons, 26-7, 101-2, 205-6
Commons, John R., 414

Rhode Island College: see Brown University
Rhode Island School of Design, 344
Rhode Island, University of, 252
Rice, Luther, 72
Rich, Isaac, 179
Robinson, Frederick B., 467
Rochester, University of, 100, 169, 232, 426, 433, 491
Rochester Theological Seminary, 349
Rockefeller, John D., 245, 349-52, 380, 382, 419, 425-6; see also General Education Board; Rockefeller Foundation
Rockne, Knute, 287
Rogers, Henry D., 195
Rogers, William Bartram, 225, 245
Rollins College, 458
Roosevelt, Franklin D., 448
Roosevelt, Theodore, 65, 357, 365-6, 368, 376-7, 390, 393, 451
Roosevelt, Theodore, Jr., 390
Rose Bowl, 388
Ross, Edward A., 414
Rousseau, Jean Jacques, 306, 453
Royce, Josiah, 338
Rugby, 373, 380-1
Rush, Benjamin, 37, 40, 42-3, 65, 90, 308-9
Russell, William C., 327
Russian studies, 343
Rutgers, Henry, 181
Rutgers University, 11, 15-16, 181, 253, 255, 302, 325, 373

sabbatical leaves, 405, 407
Sage, Mrs. Russell, 426
St. Ignatius, 94
St. John's College (Md.), 480
St. Louis University, 297
St. Mary's College (Texas), 184
St. Stephen's College, 476
salaries in higher education, 193-200, 203, 353, 391-2, 466, 484
Sandemanian, 69

Sanders, Daniel Clarke, 44-5
Santayana, George, 91
Sarah Lawrence College, 475, 477
Schermerhorn, William C., 426
Schiff, Jacob H., 426
scholarly journals: see learned journals
scholarly societies: see learned societies
scholarship and learning: H. P. Tappan at Michigan on, 233-4; at Cornell, 266-8; Johns Hopkins, 269-75; and certification movement, 283, 285-6; in collegiate era, 287-8; in university era, 288-9; university emphasis and students, 290; and elective principle, 293-4, 300-1, 304-5; and university movement, 344-5, and faculty, 434-5; see also German university influence; graduate schools of arts and sciences; piety and intellect
scholarships, 178, 190-2, 198-9, 203; see also federal support; fellowships
scholasticism, 30-1, 479-81
Schurman, Jacob Gould, 433
Schuyler, Philip, 35
science: in colonial curriculum, 28; at College of Philadelphia, 32; and partial course idea, 113; and ancient course, 115-16, 221-33; at Amherst, 123-4; and student interest, 124; and elective principle, 127-8, 293-4; and extracurriculum, 144; early popularization, 223-8; early museums, 226-7; student scientific societies, 227-8; at West Point and R.P.I., 228-31; at Yale and Harvard, 231-2; growth of scientific school idea, 232-3; in Wayland's program at Brown, 238-9; after Civil War, 244, 247-8; M.I.T., 246; Cornell, 265-8; at Johns Hopkins, 270-5; skepticism toward, 274; in high schools, 285; and James Mc-